D1246582

THE
Prayers *and* Tears
OF
JACQUES
DERRIDA

Since you're already
'incurably corrupted by the
influence of lycée-inspired
affectation, this book can't
possibly harm you

Best

Jerry

THE INDIANA SERIES IN THE PHILOSOPHY OF RELIGION
MEROLD WESTPHAL, GENERAL EDITOR

THE
Prayers *and* Tears
OF
JACQUES DERRIDA
Religion without Religion

JOHN D. CAPUTO

INDIANA UNIVERSITY PRESS   BLOOMINGTON & INDIANAPOLIS

The paper used in this publication meets the minimum requirements of American
National Standard for Information Sciences—Permanence of Paper for Printed Library
Materials, ANSI Z39.48–1984.

Manufactured in the United States of America

Library of Congress Cataloging-in-Publication Data

Caputo, John D.
The prayers and tears of Jacques Derrida : religion
without religion / John D. Caputo.
p.   c. — (The Indiana Series in the philosophy of religion)
Includes bibliographical references and index.
ISBN 0-253-33268-0 (cl.) — ISBN 0-253-21112-3 (pbk.)
1. Deconstruction. 2. Derrida, Jacques—Religion. 3. Religion.
4. Irreligion. I. Title. II. Series.
B809.6.P37   1997
194—dc21   96-47839

2 3 4 5 02 01 00 99 98 97

To Katie,
for songs and laughter,
for Parisian phantoms and Italian jumping ropes

CONTENTS

I. The Apophatic   1

II. The Apocalyptic   69

VI. Confession   281

Acknowledgments

An earlier version of Part IV, §§13–14 appeared in "Instants, Secrets, Singularities: Dealing Death in Kierkegaard and Derrida," in *Kierkegaard in Post/Modernity*, eds. Martin Matustik and Merold Westphal (Bloomington: Indiana University Press, 1995), pp. 216–38. Excerpted sections of Part V appeared in "A Community of the Impossible," in *Research in Phenomenology*, Vol. 26 (1996). With the permission of the editors, a few passages in Part I have been excerpted from "The Good News About Alterity: Derrida and Theology," *Faith and Philosophy*, 10 (1993): 453–70; and "Mysticism and Transgression: Derrida and Meister Eckhart," *Continental Philosophy*, II (1989): 24–39. A few paragraphs of §10 appeared in German translation in "Soll die Philosophie das letzte Wort haben?," in *Annäherungen an Martin Heidegger: Festschrift für Hugo Ott*. Ed. Hermann Schäfer (Bonn: Haus der Geschichte, 1996), pp. 209–31.

I wish to thank Janet Rabinowitch, my editor at Indiana University Press, and Merold Westphal, the Series Editor at Indiana, for their extremely helpful advice in improving the final shape of this manuscript. The reader will notice throughout the improvements that have been made on this manuscript as a result of the astute comments of Edith Wyschogrod whose kindness in reading this manuscript for Indiana I am pleased and honored to acknowledge. Finally, I am deeply indebted to my copy editor at Indiana, Nan Miller, who has saved me from myself more times than I can count.

The time to undertake and complete this project was provided by a sabbatical leave and a subsequent reduced load that was kindly granted to me by Villanova University whose support of my work, both now and in the past, has been strong and constant. I am indebted to the students in my "Honors Program" seminar at Villanova who had the good will (well, it was required!) to work through this manuscript in a course on "Derrida and Religion" that it was my great pleasure to conduct. Keith Putt, of Southwestern Baptist Theological Seminary, who spent a sabbatical semester with me at Villanova, was a constant source of encouragement and perceptive advice. Barbara Romano deserves many thanks for help in preparing the index.

I am grateful to Jacques Derrida for his work, for his inspiration, and for the kind encouragement he gave to this project, although he can hardly be held accountable for the risks I have taken in this reading of his work.

Above all, I thank my wife, Kathy, my best friend and favorite artist, who put up with the hours this work demanded and who, as she has in the past, did the art work for the cover of this book.

Abbreviations

Note: References to Derrida's work will be made to the French, followed by the English translation, separated by a slash. The French and English editions will bear their own abbreviations, with the exception of *Glas*, where the titles are the same, and *Cinders*, which is a bilingual edition.

AC   *L'autre cap*. Paris: Éditions de Minuit, 1991. Eng. trans. OH.

AF   "Archive Fever: A Freudian Impression." Trans. Eric Prenowitz, *Diacritics*, 25 (1995): 9–63.

AL   *Jacques Derrida: Acts of Literature*. Ed. Derek Attridge. New York: Routledge, 1992.

Aporias   *Aporias*. Trans. Thomas Dutoit. Stanford: Stanford University Press, 1993.

Apories   *Apories: Mourir—s'attendre aux limites de la vérité*. In *Le Passage des frontières: Autour du travail de Jacques Derrida*. Colloque de Cérisy. Paris: Galilée, 1994. Pp. 309–38. Eng. trans. *Aporias*.

Archive   *Mal d'archive: Une impression freudienne*. Paris: Galilée, 1995. Eng. trans. AF.

Cinders   *Cinders*. Trans. Ned Lukacher. Lincoln: University of Nebraska Press, 1991. A bilingual edition containing the text of *Feu la cendre* (Paris: Des femmes, 1987) in facing columns.

Circon.   *Circonfession: cinquante-neuf périodes et périphrases*. In Geoffrey Bennington and Jacques Derrida, *Jacques Derrida*. Paris: Éditions du Seuil, 1991. Eng. trans. *Circum.*

Circum.   *Circumfession: Fifty-nine Periods and Periphrases*. In Geoffrey Bennington and Jacques Derrida, *Jacques Derrida*. Chicago: University of Chicago Press, 1993.

DCR   *Derrida: A Critical Reader*. Ed. David Wood. Oxford: Blackwell, 1992.

DDP   *Du Droit à la Philosophie*. Paris: Galilée, 1990. Eng. trans. of pp. 461–98: PR.

DiT   *Difference in Translation*. Ed. Joseph F. Graham. Ithaca: Cornell University Press, 1985.

DLE   *De l'esprit: Heidegger et la question.* Paris: Galilée, 1987. Eng. trans. OS.

DLG   *De la grammatologie.* Paris: Éditions de Minuit, 1967. Eng. trans. OG.

DM   *"Donner la mort."* In *L'Éthique du don: Jacques Derrida et la pensée du don.* Paris: Métailié-Transition, 1992. Eng. trans. GD.

DNT   *Derrida and Negative Theology.* Eds. Howard Coward and Toby Foshay. Albany: SUNY Press, 1992.

DPJ   *Deconstruction and the Possibility of Justice.* Ed. Drucilla Cornell et al. New York: Routledge, 1992.

DT   *Donner le temps, I. La fausse monnaie.* Paris: Galilée, 1991. Eng. trans. GT.

ED   *Écriture et la différence.* Paris: Éditions de Seuil, 1967. Eng. trans. WD.

FL   *Force de loi: Le 'Fondement mystique de l'autorité.'* Paris: Galilée, 1994. Eng. trans. "The Force of Law: 'The Mystical Foundation of Authority.'" Trans. Mary Quaintance. In DPJ, pp. 68–91.

Foi   "Foi et Savoir: Les deux sources de la 'religion' aux limites de la simple raison." In *La Religion.* Ed. Jacques Derrida and Gianni Vattimo. Paris: Seuil, 1996. Pp. 9–86.

GD   *The Gift of Death.* Trans. David Wills. Chicago: University of Chicago Press, 1995.

Glas   *Glas.* Paris: Galilée, 1974. Eng. trans. *Glas.* Trans. Richard Rand and John Leavey, Jr. Lincoln: University of Nebraska Press, 1986.

GT   *Given Time, I: Counterfeit Money.* Trans. Peggy Kamuf. Chicago: University of Chicago Press, 1991.

HOdG   *Husserl: L'origine de la géométrie.* 2nd. ed. Paris: PUF, 1974. Eng. trans. HOG.

HOG   *Edmund Husserl's* Origin of Geometry. Trans. John Leavey, Jr. Boulder: John Hays Co., 1978.

Khôra   *Khôra.* Paris: Galilée, 1993. Eng. trans. *Khôra.* Trans. Ian McLeod. In ON, pp. 87–127.

LO   "Living On/Border Lines." Trans. James Hulbert, in Harold Bloom et al., *Deconstruction and Criticism.* New York: Continuum, 1979. Pp. 75–176.

MB   *Memoirs of the Blind: The Self-Portrait and Other Ruins.* Trans. Pascale-Anne Brault and Michael Naas. Chicago: University of Chicago Press, 1993.

MdA   *Mémoires d'aveugle: L'autobiographie et autres ruines.* Paris: Éditions de la Réunion des musées nationaux, 1990. Eng. trans. MB.

MdP   *Marges de philosophie.* Paris: Éditions de Minuit, 1967. Eng. trans. MoP.

MfPdM *Memoires: For Paul de Man.* Trans. Cecile Lindsay, Jonathan Culler, and Eduardo Cadava. New York: Columbia University Press, 1986.

MoP *Margins of Philosophy.* Trans. Alan Bass. Chicago: University of Chicago Press, 1982.

Moscou *Moscou aller-retour.* La Tour d'Aigues: Editions de l'Aube, 1995. Eng. trans. pp. 11–98: "Back from Moscow, in the USSR," trans. Mary Quaintance, in PTC, pp. 197–235.

MpPdM *Mémoires: Pour Paul de Man.* Paris: Galilée, 1988. Eng. trans. MfPdM.

Number "A Number of Yes." Trans. Brian Holmes. *Qui Parle,* 2 (1988): 120–33.

OG *Of Grammatology.* Trans. Gayatri Spivak. Baltimore: Johns Hopkins University Press, 1974.

OH *The Other Heading: Reflections on Today's Europe.* Trans. Pascale-Anne Brault and Michael Naas. Bloomington: Indiana University Press, 1992.

ON *On the Name.* Ed. Thomas Dutoit. Stanford: Stanford University Press, 1995.

OS *Of Spirit: Heidegger and the Question.* Trans. Geoffrey Bennington and Rachel Bowlby. Chicago: University of Chicago Press, 1989.

Parages *Parages.* Paris: Galilée, 1986. Eng. trans. pp. 118–218: LO. Pp. 250–87: "The Law of Genre," trans. Avital Ronell, in AL, pp. 221–52.

Pass. *Passions.* Paris: Galilée, 1993. Eng. trans. "Passions: 'An Oblique Offering.'" Trans. David Wood. In ON, pp. 3–31.

PdS *Points de suspension: Entretiens.* Ed. Elisabeth Weber. Paris: Galilée, 1992. Eng. trans. *Points.*

Points *Points . . . Interviews, 1974–94.* Ed. Elisabeth Weber. Trans. Peggy Kamuf et al. Stanford: Stanford University Press, 1995.

Pol. *Politiques de l'amitié.* Paris: Galilée, 1994.

PR "The Principle of Reason: The University in the Eyes of its Pupils." Trans. Catherine Porter and Edward Morris. *Diacritics,* 13 (1983): 3–20.

Psy. *Psyché: Inventions de l'autre.* Paris: Galilée, 1987. Eng. trans. pp. 11–62: "Psyche: Inventions of the Other," trans. Catherine Porter, in RDR, pp. 25–65.
Pp. 159–202: "At this very moment in this work here I am," trans. Ruben Berezdivin, in RRL, pp. 11–48.
Pp. 203–35: "Des Tour de Babel," Eng. trans. DiT, pp. 165–207.
Pp. 535–96: "How to Avoid Speaking: Denials," trans. Ken Frieden, in DNT, pp. 73–142.
Pp. 639–50: Number.

PTC   *Politics, Theory, and Contemporary Culture.* Ed. Mark Poster. New York: Columbia University Press, 1993.

RDR   *Reading de Man Reading.* Ed. Lindsay Waters and Wlad Godzich. Minneapolis: University of Minnesota Press, 1989.

RRL   *Re-Reading Levinas.* Ed. Robert Bernasconi and Simon Critchley. Bloomington: Indiana University Press, 1991.

RTP   *Raising the Tone of Philosophy: Late Essays by Immanuel Kant, Transformative Critique by Jacques Derrida.* Ed. Peter Fenves. Baltimore: Johns Hopkins University Press, 1993.

Sauf   *Sauf le nom.* Paris: Galilée, 1993. Eng. trans. *"Sauf le nom* (Post-Scriptum)." Trans. John Leavey, Jr. In ON, pp. 33–85.

Schib.   *Schibboleth: pour Paul Celan.* Paris: Galilée, 1986. Eng. trans. "Shibboleth: For Paul Celan." Trans. Joshua Wilner. In WT, pp. 3–72.

SdM   *Spectres de Marx: État de la dette, le travail du deuil, et la nouvelle Internationale.* Paris: Galilée, 1993. Eng. trans. SoM.

SoM   *Specters of Marx: The State of the Debt, the Work of Mourning, and the New International.* Trans. Peggy Kamuf. New York: Routledge, 1994.

SP   *Speech and Phenomena and Other Essays on Husserl's Theory of Signs.* Trans. David Allison. Evanston: Northwestern University Press, 1973.

Ton   *D'un ton apocalyptique adopté naguère en philosophie.* Paris: Galilée, 1983. Eng. trans. "On a Newly Arisen Apocalyptic Tone in Philosophy." Trans. John Leavey, Jr. In RTP, pp. 117–71.

UG   *Ulysse gramophone: Deux Mots pour Joyce.* Paris: Galilée, 1987. Eng. trans. pp. 15–53: "Two Words for Joyce," trans. Geoff Bennington, in *Post-Structuralist Joyce: Essays from the French,* ed. Derek Attridge and Daniel Ferrer. New York: Cambridge University Press, 1984. Pp. 145–59.
Pp. 57–143: "Ulysses Gramophone: Hear Say Yes in Joyce," trans. Tina Kendall and Shari Benstock, in AL, pp. 256–309.

VP   *La voix et le phénomène.* Paris: PUF, 1967. Eng. trans. SP.

WD   *Writing and Difference.* Trans. Alan Bass. Chicago: University of Chicago Press, 1978.

WT   *Word Traces: Readings of Paul Celan.* Ed. Aris Fioretos. Baltimore: Johns Hopkins University Press, 1994.

Introduction: A Passion for the Impossible

In his notebooks of 1976, Jacques Derrida proposes to himself the task of describing his broken covenant with Judaism in a work that would "leave nothing, if possible, in the dark of what related me to Judaism, alliance [*alliance*, covenant; Hebrew: *Berit*] broken in every respect" (*Circon.*, 145/ *Circum.*, 154). For Derrida is Jewish without being Jewish, Jewish *sans* Judaism, married outside Judaism, his sons uncircumcised, he an atheist. Of this broken covenant, this breach of an *alliance* that stretches "throughout thousands of years of Judaism," he says—now the time has changed to 1989 and this note has been stitched into *Circumfession*—"that's what my readers won't have known about me," with the result that he has been "read less and less well over almost twenty years, like my religion about which nobody understands anything" (*Circon.*, 145–46/*Circum.*, 154).

Personne ne comprend rien! No one, not even his mother, who was afraid to ask him whether he still believed in God, understands his religion or his broken alliance. His mother, Georgette Safar Derrida, like St. Monica, worried herself half to death over her son, *quotiens abs te deviare cernebat*, "each time she saw him wandering away from thee" (Augustine, *Conf.*, IX,ix,22), praying all the while that the son of these tears, *filius istarum lacrymarum* (III,xii,12), Jacques/Augustine, would not be lost. Still, Derrida says, his mother must have known that "the constancy of God in my life is called by other names," and that even though he does indeed "quite rightly pass for an atheist" with respect to the God of the orthodox faiths, still he has an "absolved, absolutely private language" in which he speaks of God all the time (*Circon.*, 146–47 / *Circum.*, 155–56).

To understand the "religion" of Jacques Derrida, about which no one understands anything, not even his mother; to understand the covenant cut in his flesh at circumcision, the broken alliance and ring (*alliance*) that manages still to bind him (*se lier*) to Judaism—"without continuity but without rupture"—while also seeing to it that he is read (*se lire*) less and less well; to understand Jacques Derrida as "the son of these tears," even as a man of prayers and tears,[1] like a Jewish Augustine from El-Biar; to understand the (cir)confessions of Jacques de la rue Saint-Augustin—all that is the point of the present study, its daunting—impossible—task.[2]

It is an amazing scene, as if, to our surprise and embarrassment—or even to his: has he not surprised himself?—we have stumbled upon Jacques Derrida at his *prie-Dieu, coram deo,* alone before God, his head bowed, his eyes swollen with tears, unaware that we are observing him! Too late have I loved thee, he seems to sigh (*Circon.*, 290 / *Circum.*, 324). An improbable, unlikely, impossible hypothesis: Jacques Derrida has religion, a certain religion, his religion, and he speaks of God all the time. The point of view of Derrida's work as an author is religious—but without religion and without religion's God—and no one understands a thing about this alliance. Little wonder. What is this link that does not quite hold yet does not quite break, between "my religion" and this leftist, secularist, sometimes scandalous, post-Marxist Parisian intellectual?

He has his whole life long been "hoping sighing dreaming" over the arrival of something "wholly other," *tout autre,* praying and weeping over, waiting and longing for, calling upon and being called by something to come. Day and night Derrida has been dreaming,[3] expecting, not the possible, not the eternal, but *the* impossible.[4] All his life long he has been setting a place for Elijah, his namesake, making notes for a "book of Elie." As Jacques says to Derrida, as "Jackie"[5] says to Jacques, and I will not presume to intervene in this dialogue, to interrupt this self-affection, which evidently gives him considerable pleasure, except to graph it a little:

> . . . you have spent your whole life
> inviting calling promising,
> hoping sighing dreaming,
> convoking invoking provoking,
> constituting engendering producing,
> naming assigning demanding,
> prescribing commanding sacrificing
> (*Circon.*, 290–91 / *Circum.*, 314)

Six times three, eighteen ways to pray and weep, to dream of the innumerable, to desire the promise of something unimaginable, to be impassioned by the impossible.[6] Eighteen ways to begin *by* the impossible, to be set in motion by the prospect of the unforeseeable, by the call of something that calls us before we open our mouths, to be sought by something, I know not what, that seeks me out before I seek it. Eighteen chapters of a work that could be called variously "Derrida" or "Deconstruction," the "Book of Circumcision" or the "Book of Elijah," "Dreaming" or "Desiring." Or perhaps, simply, "Passion."

Six times three ways to think and write, eighteen prayers or performatives, eighteen openings and reopenings, eighteen ways to make or keep a promise, to be promised in advance, like a newborn who cannot yet speak for himself; eighteen ways to act or suffer or expect, to read literature or do architecture, to practice law and do justice, to *do* the truth (*facere veritatem*), which means to put justice before truth, passion before representation; eighteen ways to teach and to learn—in short: to do whatever you need, whatever you are needed to do. Six times three instructions in the religion without religion of Jacques Derrida, in a new *alliance*.

What we will not have understood about deconstruction, and this causes us to read it less and less well, is that deconstruction is set in motion by an overarching aspiration, which on a certain analysis can be called a religious or prophetic[7] aspiration, what would have been called, in the plodding language of the tradition (which deconstruction has rightly made questionable), a movement of "transcendence." Vis-à-vis such transcendence, the immanent is the sphere not only of the actual and the present, but also of the possible and the plannable, of the foreseeable and the representable, so that deconstruction, as a movement of transcendence, means excess, the exceeding of the stable borders of the presently possible. Deconstruction is a passion for transgression, a passion for trespassing the horizons of possibility, which is what Derrida calls, following Blanchot, the *passion* of the *pas*, the *pas* of *passion* (*Parages*, 53). What we will not have understood is that deconstruction stirs with a passion for the impossible, *passion du lieu*, a passion for an impossible place, a passion to go precisely where you cannot go (*Sauf*, 62–63/ON, 59). Deconstruction is called forth in response to the unrepresentable, is large with expectation, astir with excess, provoked by the promise, impregnated by the impossible, hoping in a certain messianic promise of the impossible.[8] This is the stuff of what can be called, not ignoring certain precautions (for he rightly passes for an atheist), Derrida's religion, "my religion," his new alliance—his, Jacques's, Jackie's. Deconstruction begins, its gears are engaged, by the promptings of the spirit/specter of something unimaginable and unforeseeable. It is moved—it has always been moving, it gives words to a movement that has always been at work—by the provocation of something calling from afar that calls it beyond itself, outside itself. Settling into the crevices and interstices of the present, deconstruction works the provocation of what is to come, *à venir*, against the complacency of the present, against the pleasure the present takes in itself, in order to prevent it from closing in on itself, from collapsing into self-identity. For in deconstruction such closure would be the height of injustice, constituting the simple impossibility of *the* impossible, the prevention of the invention of the *tout autre*.

Deconstruction is a passion and a prayer for the impossible, a defense of the impossible against its critics, a plea for/to the experience of the impossible,[9] which is the only real experience, stirring with religious passion. By religion I mean a pact with the impossible, a covenant with the unrepresentable, a promise made by the *tout autre* with its people, where we are all the people of the *tout autre*, the people of the promise, promised over to the promise. Hear, O Israel (Deut. 6:4), you are the people of a call, constituted from the start by a call, a solicitation.[10] Deconstruction is a child of the promise, of the covenant, of the *alliance* with the *tout autre*, of the deal cut between the *tout autre* and its faithless, inconstant, self-seeking followers who are in regular need of prophets to keep them on the straight and narrow and to remind them of the cut in their flesh, to recall them to the call that they no longer heed. Derrida's religion meets the most rigorous requirements of Johannes de Silentio's delineation of the traits of the religious, where to make a pact with the possible is mere aestheticism, and with the eternal, mere rationalism, while expecting the impossible, making a deal with the impossible, being impassioned by the impossible, is the religious, is religious passion. The ultimate passion of thought, Johannes Climacus says, is to discover something that thought cannot think, something impossible, something at the frontier of thought and desire, something paradoxical. That is what gives it passion—otherwise it is a "mediocre fellow."[11]

Will deconstruction then have been a Jewish discourse, marked by the mohel's blade, on an analogy with the question posed by Yosef Hayim Yerushalmi to Freud about whether psychoanalysis is a Jewish science, which Derrida follows in *Mal d'archive*? If psychoanalysis is Jewish without Judaism, even without God, it is not Freud's atheism that proves an obstacle to this hypothesis, Yerushalmi says, but rather his "closure of the future," his "hopelessness," his "nonfuture." "Jewishness here," Derrida comments, "comes down, in its minimal essence . . . to the openness of the future" (*Archive*, 79/AF, 34). If so, then is not deconstruction very Jewish, albeit without God?

Derrida's religion is what we will not have known about Derrida and deconstruction, and our ignorance of it, he says, has led us to read him less and less well. For he has broken one deal to make another, broken one pact to form another, been a Jew *sans* Judaism "*sans continuité mais sans rupture*," in order to enter into a new *alliance*, a new covenant (*con-*

venire) with the incoming (*invenire*), which "repeats" (DM, 53/GD, 49) the movements of the first covenant in a religion without religion. Deconstruction repeats the structure of religious experience (SdM, 266/SoM, 168), i.e., of a specifically biblical, covenantal, Abrahamic experience, according to the strange logic of Blanchot's *sans*, which is no simple negation.

Deconstruction regularly, rhythmically repeats this religiousness, *sans* the concrete, historical religions; it repeats nondogmatically the religious structure of experience, the category of the religious. It repeats the passion for the messianic promise and messianic expectation,[12] *sans* the concrete messianisms of the positive religions that wage endless war and spill the blood of the other, and that, anointing themselves God's chosen people, are consummately dangerous to everyone else who is not so chosen; it ceaselessly repeats the *viens*, the apocalyptic call for the impossible, but without calling for the apocalypse that would consume its enemies in fire and damnation; it repeats the work of circumcision as the cut that opens the same to the other *sans* sectarian closure; it repeats Abraham's trek up to Moriah and makes a gift without return of Isaac, *sans* the economy of blood sacrifice, repeating the madness of giving without return; it repeats the movements of faith, of expecting what we cannot know but only believe—*je ne sais pas, il faut croire* (MdA, 130/MB, 129)—of the blindness of faith *sans savoir, sans avoir, sans voir* (*Parages*, 25) in the impossible, but without the dogmas of the positive religious faiths.

What we will not have understood about deconstruction, unless Derrida tells us, unless he gives it to us as a gift and springs it on us as a surprise, is that deconstruction repeats the prayers and tears of "Jackie," "a little black and very Arab Jew" (*Circon.*, 57/*Circum.*, 58), who played truant from Hebrew school in order to dream of the impossible. (While rightly passing for an atheist.)

What we will not have understood about Derrida, which causes us to read him less and less well, is precisely his tormented *alliance*, his broken pact and covenant with "thousands of years of Judaism." For deconstruction arises from "a certain experience of the promise" *sans* the dogmatics of any particular faith (SdM, 146–47/SoM, 89), where "experience" is taken not in Husserlian terms as the presence of the given but in Abrahamic and messianic terms as the expectation of something unrepresentable, running up against the unforeseeable, a certain absolute experience. The passion of this promise is the very heart of deconstruction, the heart it has in a heartless world. This promise is the passion of deconstruction, provoking the prayers and tears of Jacques Derrida, the "hoping sighing dreaming," the religion, the religious aspiration of deconstruction. Deconstruction transpires in the ambiance of an aspiration and expectation, in the time of a promise; it is driven mad by a passion for the promise, by an impossible deal, by a covenant cut with the *tout autre*.

What we will not have understood about deconstruction is its passion for God, for "my God," his, Jackie's. The question is not whether there is a *désir de Dieu*, a passion for God, in Jacques Derrida. Who could ever doubt that? Where would we find someone so hard of heart, so parsimonious and pusillanimous, so slow to tears, so unfeeling and insensitive, as ever to imagine that? The question is, rather, the one put by his North African "compatriot" (*Circon.*, 19/*Circum.*, 18) Saint Augustine: "What do I love when I love my God?" Upon the groundless ground of this beautiful and bottomless question, which is as much a sigh and a hope and a prayer as a question, *quid ergo amo, cum deum meum amo?*, Derrida's life and work is an extended commentary. "Can I do anything other than translate this sentence by SA [Saint Augustine] into my language," he writes, "the change of meaning and of reference turning on the *meum*?" (*Circon.*, 117/*Circum.*, 122).[13] To what do I pray, over what do I weep, when, in *my* language, I pray and weep to *my* God? For what am I "hoping sighing dreaming" when I hope and sigh and dream of my God? For what am I "inviting calling promising" when I invoke my God? For what do I call when I call, in my language, *viens*? By what am I impassioned in my passion for God? To what am I promised, to what do I consent, in this pact with the impossible? What do I expect when I expect the impossible?

Has Derrida ever been able to do anything his whole life long other than try to translate this question? Did not this question first sweep down upon him many years ago, on the rue Saint-Augustin in Algiers, and has it not rolled over his works ever since, for more than thirty years now? Is this question not a powerful wind that blows from thousands of years of Judaism? Is it not as old as the streets of Algiers, as old as Augustine, as old as Amos, as old as old father Abraham himself? Does it not belong to a past that was never present? Does not the power of this question, like a question put by Qoheleth, disturb everything, overturn every idol of presence, every graven image, making every constituted effect tremble in insecurity? Does not the passion of this question make everything questionable, opening the doors and the barriers of everything that wants to keep itself closed, opening even the graves of the dead to let their specters soar, disturbing everything that wants to rest in peace, stalking the world with ghosts? And does not the abyss of this question make utter nonsense of the Heideggerian dogma, to which all the epigones and acolytes in the Church of Freiburg bow their heads in thought-less assent, in un-thinking intolerance of biblical texts, that faith in God puts questioning to sleep? Does not the thought beyond thought of God, *quid ergo amo?*, come over us like a distant thunder that grows louder and louder until at last, holding our hands over our ears, we no longer know who we are or what we love, *cum deum meum amo?*, until everything wavers in insecurity and we tremble before I know not what?

Who am I? Who are you? What is coming?

Viens, oui, oui.

We will have read Derrida less and less well, understood less and less of the provocation of Derrida, of the events that the name "Derrida" provokes, if we have not heard the promise of this question and the question of this promise. For the promise sweeps over "Jackie," a weepy little child whom the adults teased because it was easy to make him cry, even as it sweeps over "Derrida," a philosopher of international stature, a leftist Parisian intellectual, a secularist and an atheist, who is even known to have penned a sometimes slightly lewd and scandalous passage or two, even when he is writing about Saint Augustine, which seems simply sinful. Then, sweeping over Derrida, the promise comes to us, so long as we let it come. The passion of the promise resonates in every sentence he writes, yes, and in every fragment of a sentence, yes, every word and shard of a word, every play and, yes, every argument. We will read him less and less well unless we hear the yes that punctuates and accents the text, the yes to the promise that resonates throughout all his works, a yes first, a yes last, a constant yes. *Oui, oui.* The yes comes from him to us, to "you" (he means us), and to him from a distant time and place, from who knows where. He is "convoking invoking provoking," we are responding, yes, language is happening, *il y a la langue*, the impossible is happening, yes, the *tout autre* is breaking out (UG, 124/AL, 296–97).

Yes, yes. *Oui, oui.*

Amen. That is Derrida's prayer, yes, *amen*, a very old and ancient Hebrew word. Amen to the God of amen (Isaiah 65:16), the God of yes, *"Jah"-weh*, yes first and last, yes, yes, according to an Irish/German, Catholic/Jewish/Islamic, slightly atheistic prophetic tradition.

Viens, he prays, "hoping sighing dreaming," as if he were waiting for Elijah, who has promised to come, "inviting calling promising," calling upon Elijah to come again (UG, 104–05/AL, 284). Even like the early Christians who were waiting for the kingdom to come. Come, *Adôn Yéshoua*. And this "come" came to Derrida before he knew what had come over him; it overtook him before he knew what had happened (*Ton*, 87/RTP, 162). It took him by surprise, before he even knew that, as he was saying *viens* as he may have thought for the first time, he was in fact citing the last verses of the *Apocalypse* to John, re-citing an ancient Christian prayer, the closing prayer of an old book. He was reciting, "repeating," all the ancient prayers that have breathed over Judaism ever since Abraham packed his bags and headed out for who knows where, solicited by the *tout autre*.

The sails of deconstruction strain toward what is coming, are bent by the winds of *l'avenir*, by the promise of the in-coming, of the *in-venire*, of the wholly other, *tout autre*, *l'invention de l'autre*. The prophetic, messianic bent of deconstruction, its posture of expectancy, its passion for *the* impossible, which is always and structurally to come, runs deep. So deep that if the messiah ever showed up, in the flesh, if, as Blanchot recounts, someone were to recognize him living incognito among the poor and the wretched on the outskirts of the city (or in the bowels of the inner city), the one question we would have for him is "when will you come?"

For the passion for the impossible is precisely not to be quenched. The one who is coming, the just one, the *tout autre*, can never be present. He must always function as a breach of the present, opening up the present to something new, to something impossible. Were the horizon of possibility to close over, it would erase the trace of justice, for justice is the trace of what is to come beyond the possible. The law of the impossible, the "impossible-rule," is never to confuse his coming (*venue*) with being present (*Pol.*, 55n), never to collapse the coming of the just one into the order of what is present or absent.

By focusing this study on Derrida's Jewish *alliance*, the covenant without continuity but without rupture that he has been working out in his more recent writings, we are also able to *re*situate Derrida's confrontation with negative theology, something that was visited upon him early on in his career and has continued on even into the 1990s. For as long as we center everything on Derrida and "negative theology"—a "European, Greek, and Christian term" (*Sauf*, 39/ON, 47)—important as this issue is, the question of Derrida's religion, of the heart of "my religion," of his prayers and tears, remains somewhat out of focus. For it is important to see that Derrida's religion is more prophetic than apophatic, more in touch with Jewish prophets than with Christian Neoplatonists, more messianic and more eschatological than mystical. His writing is more inscribed by the promise, by circumcision, and by the mark of father Abraham than by mystical transports, more like Amos and Isaiah than Pseudo-Dionysius, moved more by prophetico-ethico-political aspiration than by aspiring to be one with the One. The non-knowing, the "without knowing" (*sans savoir*, what he calls in *Cinders* "the passion of non-knowing" (*Cinders*, 75), *la passion du non-savoir*, of deconstruction has more to do with bearing an ethico-political witness to justice than with the *docta ignorantia*. As he himself says, the most important thing of which he is *not* speaking in "How Not to Speak" is his own Jewish Arab provenance; he is the most apophatic of all when he speaks of Greeks and Christians instead of Jews and Arabs (*Psy.*, 584/DNT, 122). Still, that does not excuse us from carefully following the confrontation with negative theology, which represents deconstruction's first brush with theology. For this classical discourse on the name of God, this desire to efface the trace of this very name, praying God to rid it of "God," is close to Derrida's desire for the impossible, and it will be of no small import to follow the path that is traced in Derrida's works from an apophatic to a prophetic passion.

By rooting the present study in passion, in prayers and tears, in "hoping sighing dreaming," in lingering over Derrida's later, more autobiographical pieces, I have, I confess, blurred the borders between "Derrida" and "deconstruction," between "Jacques" and "Derrida," between "Jackie" and "Jacques." For such confusion I accept full responsibility, if there is one, although I would also pass the buck to him, too, for he is always speaking of himself without speaking of himself (*Pass.*, 91n12/*ON*, 144n14). For the undecidability between these two is the condition of a decision that each of us, one by one, must make. We must, on our own, sort out how much of this is buried in the streets of El Biar, embedded in the prayers and passions of a little black and very Arab Jew, and how much of this is "everybody's autobiography" (*Circon.*, 288/*Circum.*, 311). To what extent am I too, or you, "hoping sighing dreaming," impassioned by the impossible, caught up in a deal with the *tout autre*? I will always be a little lost, betwixt and between the appropriating proper name of Jacques and the circumcised signature that opens to the other. For the one cannot be insulated from the other, not if we are going to speak of the prayers and tears of Jacques Derrida, of the passion of Jacques Derrida, seeing that "deconstruction," "*la*" *déconstruction*, if there is any such thing, cannot sigh or pray or weep or bend a knee or ever feel a thing.

I will move unsteadily and unstably, circumspectly, between the shibboleth of the singular circumcision of Jackie, which happened only once, in 1930, in El Biar, and something of more general interest, something iterable and repeatable. But this more general structure, which is borne on the wings of repetition[14]—and here is all the difficulty—cannot take the form of an essence or a universal. It cannot be the effect of an *epoche* (which means a cutting off) of his circumcision. It is too Jewish to be catholic (*katholou*), even though it proceeds *sans* Judaism. It is not as if we are seeking some sort of invariant transcendental, some uncircumcised, Hellenistic *eidos*, some *essentia sans* circumcision. Even if it is borne on the wings of repetition, this "religion" cannot circle high above us in an essentialistic, Hellenistic sky, like the *aigle* of *savoir absolue*, some bloodless *transcendens* soaring beyond us bloodied mortals below. For then this Jewish bird would be cooked (*cuit*).[15]

We cannot excise or cover over deconstruction's circumcision when Derrida's whole idea is to expose it. Deconstruction feels with a bleeding, circumcised heart in the midst of a heartless world, hears with a bleeding, circumcised ear, writes with a heart and an ear for the other, speaks with circumcised words. Indeed, at the risk of giving endless scandal, of sending my secular academic colleagues into a dead swoon, I will say that for Derrida deconstruction *is* circumcision, where circumcision cuts open the same to the event of the other, thus constituting the breach that opens the way to the *tout autre*:

> . . . the breach necessary for the coming of the other (*à la venue de l'autre*), of an other whom one can always call Elijah, if Elijah is the name of the

unforeseeable other for whom a place must be kept. (UG, 120–21/AL, 294–95)

The circumcision of deconstruction cuts it off from the absolute, cuts off its word from the final word, from the totalizing truth or *logos* that engulfs the other. Deconstruction proceeds not by knowledge but by faith and by passion, by the passion of faith, impassioned by the unbelievable, by the secret that there is no secret. It is called forth by a promise, by an aboriginal being-promised over to language and the future, to wander *destinerrant*, like Abraham, underway to who knows where. Deconstruction proceeds in the dark, like a blind man feeling his way with a stick, devoid of sight and savvy, of vision and verity, *sans savoir, sans avoir, sans voir* (*Parages*, 25), where it is necessary to believe, where the passion of faith, *la passion du non-savoir* (*Cinders*, 75), is all you have to go on. *Je ne sais pas. Il faut croire*: that is how the *Memoirs of the Blind* concludes, if that is a conclusion (MdA, 130/MB, 129).

I myself will conclude this introduction with a prayer and a plea, by begging the pardon of my academic colleagues, imploring the forgiveness of my secularizing friends, for whom the only blasphemy is infidelity to Nietzsche,[16] whom I will have shocked and traumatized by this provocative scene of Derrida weeping at his *prie-Dieu*, by all the events that this scene provokes. Forgive me, one and all, forgive me everything, as I forgive you, but also, I beg you, *je vous prie*, lend me your ear for this other. To which I add an argument from authority, purely in the interests of reading: Derrida himself has said, these are *ipsissima verba*, that by forgetting the promise and the *alliance* we have read him less and less well.[17]

Derrida at prayer (all the while rightly passing for an atheist)? Derrida weeping? Derrida's *désir de Dieu*, his passion for God, for the *tout autre*? Derrida bowing his head and saying *amen, oui, oui*? A circumcised Derrida? A messianic deconstruction? An apocalyptic, prophetic deconstruction? A deconstruction that has not lost faith? Derrida, the follower of father Abraham and namesake of the prophet Elijah? Derrida reading *écriture (sainte)*, glossing the stories of Babel and Abraham, of the *shibboleth* and Tobias? And not by chance or incidentally, but regularly, rhythmically, repeatedly, irresistibly, as if in response to something calling to him from afar, as if returning to and repeating something deeply provocative at work in his writing that he does not know how to avoid? A Derrida who has perhaps surprised not only Geoffrey Bennington but himself?

Is that not a little *too* other, too *tout*, too *autre*?

How *could* I?

How could *he*?

Je ne sais pas. Il faut croire.

A Map for the Perplexed

For a philosopher like Derrida, who is so much taken with aporias and impasses, who thinks that you are really getting somewhere only when you are paralyzed and it is impossible to advance, only when there is no plannable, programmable way to proceed, there is a fitting irony in supplying a map, a little "Michelin's Guide to Jacques Derrida," which is something like giving the Cartesian coordinates of the Promised Land (*Foi*, 15). Still, a map gives the tourist and casual visitor to the country, who only has a few days to take in everything, a chance to see the major sights. What follows is an altogether excellent map, a bit of flawless cartography, I assure the reader, but for a few minor faults: I am not sure, for example, that all of these roads have been finished (they have all been promised) or that many of the places mentioned here actually exist.

That being understood between us, I give you a map which passes through six major cities, monuments, or tourist attractions that you simply cannot miss.

The story of Derrida's religion without religion begins with Derrida's first encounter of a close kind with theology, with the claim (charge/congratulation) made early on that deconstruction is a negative theology. The *apophatic*, the unnameable, unknowable secret, is a subject Derrida does not know how to avoid and has not been able to drop, recurring as it does even in a recent triptych on the "name." The apophatic constitutes a crucial moment in this story, and it also helps us understand his relationship to Levinas. But the story is, on my telling, always slightly out of focus if you do not move on.

For it is necessary to get past his dialogues with Christian Neoplatonism to his more biblical, prophetic, Jewish side, past the apophatic to the messianic that shows up in his most recent work. That is where the focus sharpens and you find his "religion," if it is one. That transition I effect by way of the *apocalyptic*, when Derrida begins to call "come!", to pray and call *"viens, oui, oui."* Which sounds a little apocalyptic, like a prayer at the end a famous book of *Revelation*. But with this exception: that this is an apocalypse without apocalypse, announcing a messianic-apocalyptic secret—which makes the *Aufklärers* nervous—that there is no secret and no apocalypse, which thus constitutes a neo- or more enlightened Enlightenment, inflaming our hearts with messianic longing for something to come, something absolutely secret to come.

The discussion of the *messianic* that follows is the pivot of this text, the point at which the path of deconstruction swings off in an unmistakably prophetico-messianic direction. That direction emerges sharply in the desert-like messianic discussed in the Marx book and the seminar at Capri. Here we touch upon the heart of Derrida's religion, of the call for a justice, a democracy, a just one to come, a call for peace among the concrete messianisms, issuing from a neo-*Aufklärer* looking for a (post-secular) religion within the limits of (a certain) reason alone (almost). This messianicity means to bring, if not eternal peace, at least a lull in the fighting in the wars among the concrete messianisms.

The apophatico-apocalyptico-quasi-atheistic messianic in turn allows us to pose the question of giving without reserve, of the *gift*, which, like justice and the secret, also does not quite exist. I follow in particular Derrida's analysis of Abraham's terrifying gift without reserve in a much awaited (by me, at least) gloss on *Fear and Trembling*, which also re-poses (restlessly) the question of the war between the Christian and the Jew that has mined the field of the history of the West and of quite a few Arab fields too. That war is an important part of the stakes of having something to say about religion for Derrida, and this discussion allows us to refine the distinction between the messianic and Abrahamic messianism.

The elaboration of the messianic makes it possible to take up the figure and the flesh of *circumcision*, of the Jew, of the cut in the flesh of the Jew. Odd as it may seem, circumcision has been in one way or another the theme of Derrida's work all along, the subject of a secret autobiography for his eyes only. (Circumcision is a very private matter.) Indeed, it would have been possible to begin this study here (you can follow the course of this map in different ways). Here I move from Derrida's gloss on Hegel's hateful portrait of the Jew vis-à-vis the religion of love in *Glas* (1974) up to a recent essay (1995) which wonders whether psychoanalysis (read deconstruction) is really a Jewish science.

All along I will have been clutching *Circonfession* close to my breast. All along I will have been reading and leading up to a reading of Jacques's *confession*, his Jewish Augustinian circum-confessing book of prayers and tears, which fills our eyes with tears over a little black and very Arab Jew. At last Jacques fesses up that he has all along had religion, his own religion, without religion, and that the failure to understand his religion has resulted in reading him less and less well over twenty years. That book, which has a beautiful sibling rival in *Memoirs of the Blind*, opens our eyes about Derrida, if only to blur them over with tears and to force us to proceed *sans voir, sans savoir*.

Along the way I insert a series of edifying divertissements, little road-side chapels to refresh the weary traveler's spirit, or audio-taped sermons meant to "up-build" the faithful (as the new Hong translations of Kierke-gaard put it so maladroitly) as you drive from site to site. The reader might treat these freelance pieces as occasional, quasi-theological musings and amusements that have hitchhiked a ride with Derrida. In them I, who have never meant to get as far as theology, have from time to time gotten up the nerve to speak in tongues, as it were, feeling inspired to point out some possible import of deconstruction for religious and theological re-flection.

Treat these rash outbursts as so many little sermons in between the readings, or as a bit of organ music while we take up a collection, passing the hat in order to maintain the pastor in the manner to which he has grown accustomed, on the sound theological principle that nothing is too good for God's poor. For his reverence is an honorable man, a defender of the Good and the True, sworn to keep the world safe from Evil (within which he might very well include deconstruction), and we wish him well.

As to the "Conclusion," which I must not forget, I cannot say whether it is an edifying discourse or not, a gloss on Jacques or not, whether it has to do with his religion or mine. I do not know where to draw the line in this game of Jacks.

THE

Prayers *and* Tears

OF

JACQUES
DERRIDA

I. The Apophatic

§1. God Is Not différance

An Impossible Situation

The messianic tone of deconstruction was not at all evident at the start. Instead, in the midst of what looked more like a certain Nietzschean tone recently adopted in French philosophy in the 1960s, Derrida was visited with a suggestive "objection" that occasioned his first encounter with theology. "[V]ery early on," he says, "I was accused of—rather than being congratulated for—resifting the procedures of negative theology" (Psy., 537/DNT, 74), of putting these procedures to work, it would seem, in the service of some *magnum mysterium* called *différance*.

As usual, his accusers/congratulators were only half right. For impossible things have on the whole always exercised a greater fascination over Derrida than the garden variety possibilities whose conditions philosophy is traditionally content to supply. So it makes perfect sense that Derrida would "have always been fascinated" (Psy., 545/DNT, 82) by the impossible situation in which negative or apophatic[1] theology finds itself, of denying that it is possible to speak of God even while, as theology, it keeps on speaking. As a good friend of mine once said, "Of God I do not believe we can say a thing, but, on the other hand, as a theologian, I have to make a buck." That is "the impossible."

Derrida was understandably fascinated with the syntactical strategies and discursive resources of negative theology, with a deployment of signs intent on the "rarefaction of signs," with a play of traces aimed at effacing the trace, with a language that is "more or less than a language," that "casts suspicion on the very essence or possibility of language" (Sauf, 41/ON, 48), with a "wounded" language, where the "scar" of the "impossible" has left its mark (*Sauf*, 63/ON, 59–60), with "the most economical and most powerful formalization, the greatest reserve of language possible in so few words" (*Sauf*, 113/DNT, 321). He has long been fascinated by the "experience of the impossible," the possibility of this impossibility, by the absolute heterogeneity that the *hyper* introduces into the order of the same, interrupting the complacent regime of the possible. Derrida has always been interested in hyperbolic movements, in the whole family of *hyper, über, epekeina, au-delà,* and in movements of denegation, like *pas* and *sans*, which try to speak of not speaking.

Nonetheless, negative theology is worlds removed from deconstruction; the *mise en abîme* of deconstruction is separated by an abyss from the abyss of the Godhead beyond God. The paradox of negative theology— how to speak of the unspeakable transcendence of God—is at best provocatively analogous to the difficulty in which deconstruction finds itself —how to name *différance*, that word or concept that is neither word nor concept. So it is for substantively different albeit strategically analogous reasons that deconstruction, like negative theology, finds itself constantly writing under erasure, saying something without saying it, even deforming and misspelling it (*différance* being the most famous misspelling in contemporary philosophy).

That is why when, one day "early on," in the discussion following the original 1968 presentation of the famous paper "*Différance*" (which, for the most loyal deconstructionists, has a status something like the Sermon on the Mount), an interlocutor who had heard enough exclaimed with some exasperation, "it [*différance*] is the source of everything and one cannot know it: it is the God of negative theology,"[2] Derrida responded with the most exquisite precision and deconstructionist decisiveness, "It is and it is not." Yes and no.

As we will see, Derrida easily made the "no" stick. He dispatched this accusation, or deferred this congratulation, effectively and efficiently, persuasively arguing that whatever their "syntactical" similarities there is a deep "semantic" divide between God and *différance*, that "it," *différance*, is not the God of negative theology. (We cannot fail to notice that "God" here is not exactly Yahweh, not the God of prophets like Amos or Isaiah, a God who wants justice, but the God of Christian Neoplatonism.) However highly it is esteemed, *différance* is not God. Negative theology is always on the track of a "hyperessentiality," of something hyper-present, hyper-real or sur-real, so really real that we are never satisfied simply to say that it is merely real. *Différance*, on the other hand, is less than real, not quite real, never gets as far as being or entity or presence, which is why it is emblematized by insubstantial quasi-beings like ashes and ghosts which flutter between existence and nonexistence, or with humble *khôra*, say, rather than with the prestigious

Platonic sun. *Différance* is but a quasi-transcendental anteriority, not a supereminent, transcendent ulteriority.

I will insist throughout that establishing that negation, getting that denial on the table, is only the beginning and not the end of the story of Derrida's encounter with theology. What Derrida has done is thoroughly misunderstood, I submit, if it is thought that deconstruction has somehow or other "dispatched" negative theology, simply sent it packing, or shown it to be a transcendental illusion that has been done in by the metaphysics of (hyper)presence, so that our time would now be better passed reading Nietzsche on the death of God. Deconstruction is never merely negative; its desire is never satisfied with "no, no." Deconstruction is thoroughly mistrustful of discourses that prohibit this and prohibit that, that weigh us down with debts and "don'ts." Deconstruction is so deeply and abidingly affirmative—of something new, of something coming—that it finally breaks out in a vast and sweeping amen, a great *oui, oui—à l'impossible*, in a great burst of passion for the impossible. So over and beyond, this first, preparatory and merely negative point, deconstruction says yes, affirming what negative theology affirms whenever it says no. Deconstruction desires what negative theology desires and it shares the passion of negative theology—for the impossible.

Oui, oui. Sic et non.

What has become increasingly clear about deconstruction over the years is that, like negative theology, deconstruction has been taken by surprise, overtaken by the *tout autre*, the wholly other, about which it does not know how not to speak. Like negative theology, deconstruction turns on its desire for the *tout autre*. Derrida analyzes that desire, not like Doctor Derrida, his patient spread out on the couch before his clinical gaze, but with fascination and respect, with a little dose of *docta ignorantia*. For we do not know what we desire. Derrida has not been sent—who would have sent him?—to police negative theology and to tell it what it may desire. For he recognizes this desire for the *tout autre* as his own—yes, yes—indeed as a desire by which—if he is right—we are all inhabited. We are all dreaming of an absolute surprise, pondering an absolute secret, all waiting for the *tout autre* to arrive. So Derrida finds in negative theology a unique and irreducible idiom for answering the call by which we are all addressed, whether our discursive inclinations are theological, antitheological, or a/theological (or something else). For we are all—this is Derrida's wager—dreaming of the wholly other that will come knocking on our door (like Elijah), and, taking language by surprise, will tie our tongue and strike us dumb (almost), filling us with passion. That is why, with the passage of the years, Derrida's relationship with negative theology became more and more affirmative, more and more linked by the impossible. The difference is that in negative theology the *tout autre* always goes under the name of God, and that which calls forth speech is called "God," whereas for Derrida every other is wholly other (*tout autre est tout autre*). But the name of God is not a bad name and we can love (and save) this name (DLG, 62/OG, 42).

It is a serious misunderstanding, a little perverse, I would say, to think that there is something inherently atheistic about deconstruction, as if, lodged deep down inside *différance* or "the trace" there were, à la Jean-Paul Sartre, some sort of negative ontological argument against God, against God's good name, as if what Derrida calls "the trace" knocks out the name of God. On the contrary, Derrida, who "rightly passes for an atheist," is an atheist who has his own God, and who loves the name of God, loves that "event" and what "takes place" or eventuates in that good name. He has no desire, it goes against *everything* that deconstruction is and desires, to prevent the event of that "invention." Indeed, getting ready for the "invention" of the other, covenanting (*con-venire*) with its in-coming (*in-venire*), initialing a pact with the impossible, sticking to the promise of inalterable alterity, *tout autre*—that, says Derrida, "is what I call deconstruction" (*Psy.*, 53/RDR, 56). That is his passion.

So Derrida follows with fascination the movements of what theology calls God, observing how theology speaks, and how it finds it necessary not to speak under the solicitation of the wholly other. When Meister Eckhart says, "I pray God to rid me of God," he formulates with the most astonishing economy a double bind by which we are all bound: how to speak and not speak, how to pray and not pray, to and for the *tout autre*. But in theology the *tout autre* goes (and comes) under the name of God.

Derrida is all along formulating a way to read negative theology, a way to hear it, be addressed by it, to be claimed and taken by surprise by it, which involves all along a way to "translate" it. His reading makes negative theology of the utmost importance even to those who thank God daily in their temples that they do not believe in God, to those who have closed themselves off to the name of God (and this, often enough, in the name of resisting closure). But in "translating" negative theology deconstruction has no part in the familiar, nineteenth-century ruse in which a clearheaded master hermeneut, striding to the podium, explains to misty-eyed theologians, their eyes cocked heavenward like that painting of Monica and Augustine in *Circumfession* (*Circon.*, 21/*Circum.*, 17), what they are talking about. Deconstruction is no Dupin deciphering theological self-mystification and showing theology plainly, scientifically, that if theologians could somehow, *per impossibile*, clear their heads ever so briefly they would realize that what they really meant all along by God was Man (Feuerbach), that what they really desired all along was their mommy (Freud), or even, *mirabile dictu, différance* itself, *sainte écriture* (the remarkable Mark Taylor, whose work I deeply admire, but who errantly missed the mark, "early on," in his first major brush with Derrida in *Erring*).

"Translating" in deconstruction is nothing reductionistic, and that is because *différance* opens things up rather than barring the door closed. Of itself, if it had an itself, *différance* does not tell for or against, does not say or gainsay, monotheism or atheism, even as it loves the name of God. It is no part of the business, or the competency, or the responsibility of deconstruction to decide *what* or *who* is calling in what theology calls God, in what calls theology to order. Theology and faith, all the theologies and their determinable faiths (*Sauf*, 86/ON, 71)—Christian, Jewish, Islamic, whatever—are the responsibility of whoever decides to venture out upon those stormy seas, a responsibility with laws and motivations of its own. The business of deconstruction is not to police theologians or anybody else, to maintain an unbroken Neokantian surveillance over the business of science or everyday life, but to keep things open. Its business is a certain quasi-analysis and affirmation of the trace, of the claims and exclamations that take shape in that place, there (*là*), where things are happening, language and everything else, *il y a du langue* (UG, 124/AL, 296). Its business is the trace, what the trace demands of us, what it inscribes upon us, and what we inscribe within it, whether that is theological or atheological—or perhaps something else, something we can only dream of, something of an absolute surprise.

Deconstruction is not out to undo God or deny faith, or to mock science or make nonsense out of literature, or to break the law or, generally, to ruin any of those hoary things at whose very mention all your muscles constrict. Deconstruction is not in the business of defaming good names but of saving them. *Sauf le nom.* Where would it get the authority? Who would have given it the power to wipe away the horizon, to dry up the sea, or to fill up the abyss with such a decisive, definitive result, such an unbelievable, unbelieving, atheistic closure? Would it mount a public campaign? Where would it get the funds? Would it expect support from the National Endowment for the Humanities? (Dream on!) Why would deconstruction want to associate itself with the *prevention* of the wholly other? What kind of madness would that be for something that arises from a pact with the *tout autre*?

Deconstruction is rather the thought, if it is a thought, of an absolute heterogeneity that unsettles all the assurances of the same within which we comfortably ensconce ourselves. That is the desire by which it is moved, which moves and impassions it, which sets it into motion, toward which it extends itself.

But let there be no mistake: "early on" deconstruction *does* delimit the *metaphysical* side of theology. Still, is that not an honorable and hoary religious project? Does it not have an honorable name, the name of "dehellenizing Christianity," more generally of "dehellenizing biblical faith"?[3] Is it not an idea as old as Luther, and older still, tracing its origins back to the first chapter of First Corinthians, and older than that, given that the prophets never heard of the science that investigates *to on he on*? Is it not in step with Abraham Heschel's remarkable extrication of the prophets from the grips of metaphysical theology?[4] By inscribing theology within the trace, by describing faith as always and already marked by the trace, by *différance* and undecidability, deconstruction demonstrates that faith is always *faith*, and this in virtue of one of the best descriptions of faith we possess, which is that faith is always through a *glas* darkly.

Even early on, the effect of deconstruction on theology—by which I mean the attempt to bring faith to discursive form—and in particular on negative theology, is not to defame theology but to reinscribe it within the trace and, by putting "hyperessentialism" in its place, to resituate negative theology *within faith*. For the "hyperessentialism" of negative theology, which Derrida delimits, would shatter faith and turn it into union, into oneness with the One, "but then face to face," which is to get impatient with *glas* and jump the gun. That hyperousiological high for Derrida has always been so much hype. But on the view that I take, a deconstructive theology would find it necessary to deny hyperessentialism in order to make room for faith. *Il faut croire* (MdA, 130/MB, 129).

Deconstruction saves apophatic theology from telling a bad story about itself, about how it speaks from the Heart of Truth, and how the rest of us had better get in line with it. Or else! That kind of Truth always implies a threat, a dangerous triumphalism. Deconstruction saves the name of negative theology by subjecting it to the same necessity that besets us all, the same *il faut* (*Psy.*, 561/DNT, 99), which is to pull on our textual pants one leg at a time, to forge slowly and from below certain unities of meaning in which we put our trust, understanding all along the mistrust that co-constitutes that trust, the undecidability that inhabits and makes possible that decision. Deconstruction saves negative theology from closure. Closure spells trouble, which is why *différance* cloaks itself in a misspelling. Closure spells exclusion, exclusiveness; closure spills blood, doctrinal, confessional, theological, political, institutional blood, and eventually, it never fails, real blood. *Salus in sanguine. Pro deo et patria* spells big trouble, with big words, master words, that need deconstructing.

I pray God to rid me of God, said a master of *Lesen und Leben*.

The course I will pursue in Part I is to follow Derrida's early differentiations of *différance* from the *hyperousios* of negative theology (§1), which in turn will cast an interesting light on Derrida's relation to Levinas in "Violence and Metaphysics" (§2). Then I will turn to the later essays, "How Not to Speak: Denegations" (§3) and *Sauf le nom* (§4), which will allow me to offer a little edifying discourse on what deconstruction does for and to "faith."

The Hype in Hyperousiology

Let us establish this simple negation, a first principle (almost), which, because of its simplicity and its self-assured authority, we will be obliged in various and diverse ways to take back (to denegate): God is not *différance*.[5] *Différance* is especially not a hidden God, the innermost concealed Godhead of negative theology. *Différance*, "this almost nothing of the unpresentable" (PdS, 89/*Points*, 83), is not an entity, nothing present or manifest, makes no appearance, is not a *phainomenon*, and has no truth. Still, for all that, *différance* is not to be taken lightly, for while it has no truth or manifestness itself (indeed, it has no "itself"), *différance* enables what is manifest to make a show (MdP, 6/MoP, 6). But what can that be if not the God who withdraws behind the veil of creation, whose disappearance makes the appearance of the created world possible, that ultimate unknowable the un-knowing of which constitutes the most learned wisdom of all (*docta ignorantia*)? As Derrida says in a text whose significance justifies a lengthy citation, all this bears an unmistakable resemblance to negative theology:

> So much so that the detours, locutions, and syntax in which I will often have to take recourse will resemble those of negative theology, occasionally even to the point of being indistinguishable from negative theology. Already we have had to delineate *that différance is not*, does not exist, is not a present-being (*on*) in any form; and we will be led to delineate everything *that* it *is not*, that is, everything; and consequently that it has neither existence nor essence. It derives from no category of being, whether present or absent. And yet those aspects of *différance* which are thereby delineated are not theological, not even in the order of the most negative of negative theologies, which are always concerned with disengaging a superessentiality beyond the finite categories of essence and existence, that is, of presence, and always hastening to recall that God is refused the predicate of existence, only in order to acknowledge his superior, inconceivable, and ineffable mode of being. . . . *Différance* is not only irreducible to any ontological or theological—ontotheological—reappropriation, but as the very opening of the space in which ontotheology—philosophy—produces its system and its history, it includes ontotheology, inscribing it and exceeding it without return. (MdP, 6/MoP, 6)

So even though the "detours, locutions, and syntax" in which Derrida strives to mark off *différance* will resemble, almost to the point of indistinguishability, the twists and turns of negative theology, still deconstruction is no negative theology. That is because negative theology is always a higher, more refined way of affirming that God exists, or hyperexists, or exists-by-not-existing, that God is really real or hyper-real or sur-real. God exists so purely, so perfectly that as soon as we make this affirmation we have to take it back, taking back not only the "is" but even the name of "God." God is, but God is more than that; God is beyond (*au-delà, über*) being, without (*sans*) being, Being beyond being, God beyond God. Negative theology is caught up in a higher modalization of onto-theo-logy, an ontotheology *eminentiore modo,* a variation on the philosophy of presence which takes the form of a theology of super- or hyper-presence, delivering a surge of presence of which the metaphysics of presence can only dream. That differentiates the *différance* of deconstruction from the God of negative theology. Derrida has consistently maintained this view, and I think has been consistently right, although he has by no means thereby cut out the heart of negative theology (nor does this lay a glove on what he calls "my religion"). Hyperousiology is, as he says later on, but *one* of negative theology's several voices, albeit its loudest, most booming, most vociferous, and most self-deceptive voice.

Hence, if we find Derrida saying that *différance* is neither a word nor a concept, that there is no name for what he means to say, that is not because Derrida has been breathlessly overtaken by a being of such supereminence that, his heart afire, words fail him and he finds himself lost for words (dream on!). Rather, it is because Derrida is coolly addressing the conditions under which words and concepts are formed in the first place, which means that *différance,* as the "word" for that, is a kind of non-word, anterior to words, the general, de-formed condition for the formation for words, a bit of a forgery for indicating how words are forged. Hence if *différance* is a certain *nomen innominabile,* it is not a mystical but a grammatological one. If Derrida is right, *différance* is older than the name of being, older than any name, is not itself a name, in the French language or any other, which is why he deformed the word. But this, Derrida says, is to be understood not in all its mystical depth but in all of its grammatological platitude:

> The unnameable is not an ineffable Being which no name could approach: God, for example.[6] This unnameable is the play which makes possible nominal effects, the relatively unitary and atomic structures that are called names, the chains of or substitutions of names in which, for example, the nominal effect *différance* is itself enmeshed. (MdP, 28/MoP, 26–27)

The namelessness of *différance* does not consist in being an unnameable being but in pointing to the differential matrix that generates names and concepts, in which they are produced as effects. Of course, as Richard Rorty points out, and as Derrida would concede, that is only true the first few times Derrida uses this non-word.[7] As soon as it was coined, uttered, and repeated often enough, as soon as hoards of poststructuralist assistant professors who desire tenure and who knows what else swarmed all over it, it began to catch on, to link up, and it became itself another more or less stable nominal unity, one more effect of the differential matrix of which it means to be no more than an indicator, a mute finger pointing to the moon, which too soon assumed a place of honor in the lexicon of deconstruction as one of Derrida's most famous words.

§1. *God Is Not* différance

So it would be a serious misunderstanding to think that *différance* is a master name, the secret, hidden name of Being beyond Being, the hidden name of a presence so pure that it cannot itself appear and be present except by means of the imperfect traces of itself that it leaves behind as it withdraws from the world seated on a cloud of unknowing. Lacking all ontological profundity, all mystical depth, all royal dignity, all principial honor, forever uncapitalized, *différance* stretches out laterally over the surface of our beliefs and practices as the chain of substitutability. *Différance* is not the trace left behind by the *deus absconditus* but the coded tracing within which are generated all names and concepts, all the relatively stable nominal unities, including the name of the unknown God, or G-d, or *Gottheit*, including even itself, the name *différance*. *Différance* does not have the wherewithal to lay down its uncapitalized head:

> It governs nothing, reigns over nothing, and nowhere exercises any authority. It is not announced by any capital letter. Not only is there no kingdom of *différance*, but *différance* instigates the subversion of every kingdom. Which makes it obviously threatening and infallibly dreaded by everything within us that desires a kingdom, the past or future presence of a kingdom. (MdP, 22/MoP, 22)

That is well said, for now, early on. But, as with everything else, one has to speak *sous rature*, with a measure of *sic et non*. I have not given up on every kingdom, on the coming, or the incoming, *l'invention*, of every kingdom, and Derrida has not given up on the messianic. I pray you, *je vous prie*, be patient.

Derrida's delimitation of negative theology is made perfectly clear by an adroitly chosen text of Meister Eckhart. Eckhart was from time to time brought before the Law, called on the carpet by the Vatican to answer those coldhearted, tough-minded bureaucrats (Franciscans, if you can believe it) for the extremes to which he was wont to go in his sermons in order to encourage his hearers tenderly to love God with all their heart and to let go of their overgrown egos. The Meister is one of the best examples—"and what an example!" (*Psy.*, 576/DNT, 113)—of the trouble you can buy yourself by speaking of the impossible. That is why, when he was accused of—instead of being congratulated for—denying Being to God, Meister Eckhart said:[8]

> When I said that God was not a Being and was above Being, I did not thereby contest his Being, but on the contrary attributed to him a *more elevated Being*.

Eckhart tried to explain to the Vatican apparatchiks that all these negations at bottom serve a positive point, that even his most extreme formulations redound to the greater honor and glory of God, and that he is a loyal Dominican friar who agrees with (fellow Dominican) brother Thomas (Aquinas). Everything Eckhart says is held safely in check within what Derrida would call, following Bataille, a "restricted economy," serving always to redound, to give back, *ad majorem dei gloriam*, whatever it takes away, in a classic economy of sacrifice.[9]

Negative theology, always going about its Father's business, always engaged in the business of establishing "the ineffable transcendence of an infinite existent" (ED, 217/WD, 146), concludes that the best way to say that God exists is to un-say it, and this in order not to contract God's being to something familiar and finite, to the logic of the same. That is why Eckhart was able to write, to the puzzlement of his commentators and to the consternation of the Inquisitors, both that God is *esse* while creatures are a pure nothing (not even a little bit), *and* that God is an absolute nothing, a naked desert, while being is the first of all creatures. The affirmation of God's being has to be continually purified by a denial of Being of God. In the Latin works, Eckhart spoke of the *puritas essendi*: both the purity *of* being and purity *from* being, like the fruitful French conflation *plus d'être*, (no) more being (*Psy.*, 552/DNT, 90).

Given the similarities between the syntactical and rhetorical resources of deconstruction and negative theology, John Dominic Crossan rightly asks, "Why, then, are the syntactics so similar if the semantics are so different?"[10] To which Kevin Hart quite precisely responds:

> [W]e may answer Crossan's question by distinguishing between ineffability as a consequence of the subject being *transcendent* and because of the subject being *transcendental*. If God is understood as transcending the phenomenal world, one cannot hope to describe Him because language is restricted in its scope to the realm of the phenomenal. Similarly, if *différance* enables concepts to emerge it cannot be described adequately by concepts.[11]

Amen. Although I think that Derrida would say not transcendental but "*quasi*-transcendental." God does not *merely* exist; *différance* does not *quite* exist. God is ineffable the way Plato's *agathon* is ineffable, beyond being, whereas *différance* is like the atheological ineffability of Plato's *khôra*, beneath being (*Khôra*, 30/ON, 96).

If Derrida admires the discursive resources of negative theology, he begs to differ with it insofar as negative theology turns out, upon analysis, to be actually a higher way to trump language and representation, to jump out of the skin of *différance* and the trace, by means of a hyper-being which exceeds our powers to speak or name it. So when the negative theologian, falling upon our breast and looking up to heaven, sighs that she cannot name or say a thing about God, she also knows, in secret, even if she knows by unknowing, that if we call the Vatican guards on her, she has an answer. Way down deep, negative theologians know what they are talking about; they have not entirely lost their way or their balance; they are not *destinerrant*.[12] Their experience is so deep and powerful that it overwhelms the frailty of language, of the "faculties," i.e., of representations, i.e., of the chain of differential marks. Thus conceived, the God of negative theology is a transcendental signified, the dream of being without *différance*, of being outside the text, outside the general text, outside the play of traces.

As a hyperousiology, negative theology drops anchor, hits bottom, lodges itself securely in pure presence and the transcendental signified, every bit as much as any positive onto-theo-logy, and in a certain sense more so. Its difference from kataphatic or onto-theology, from "metaphysics," lies in claiming to touch bottom not by means of representational thinking, of concepts and discursive reasoning, but by leaving all such representational paraphernalia and parerga in the vestibule and entering into a wordless, imageless, timeless inner sanctum of the temple, into a still point of unity in the very heart of God, a point where God's ground and the soul's ground are one. Far from providing a deconstruction of the metaphysics of presence, negative theology crowns the representations of metaphysics with the jewel of pure presence, and effects in a still higher way, *eminentiore modo*, the triumph of presence over representation. In one of its voices, its most authoritative, negative theology is a still more effective way that presence has found to trump representation. To that extent, deconstruction is its nemesis. But that does not have the effect of leveling or razing negative theology, but rather of liberating negative theology from the Greek metaphysics of presence in which it is enmeshed and forcing it to come up with a better story about itself than the hyperousiological one that it has inherited not from the Bible but from Neoplatonism.

The deconstruction of theology (positive or negative) consists in allowing *différance* its say or sway, allowing *différance* to inscribe and exceed negative theology without return (MdP, 6/MoP, 6). The deconstruction of theology re-commits theology to the grammatological flux from whence negative theology would take its leave. The last thing that could be claimed in deconstruction is that one has reached the point of ineffability, of silent union, beyond words and concepts, with the One. (It would always be too late to say that.) If Derrida is fascinated by the syntactics, pragmatics, and rhetoric of this discourse that is driven, sparked, and solicited by *the impossible*, it is because it arises from a certain shattering, a breakdown of conventional discursive resources, but one that cannot, in virtue of *différance*, be understood as something utterly nonlinguistic. For Derrida, negative theology is an event *within* language, something happening *to* language, a certain trembling or fluctuation *of* language. That is why the effect of negative theology is always so verbal and verbose—so grammatological—and why these lovers of wordlessness are so excessively wordy, why Meister Eckhart, for example, was one of the greatest preachers of the day and one of the founders of the German language, there at the creation, *l'invention*, of modern *Deutsch*.

Derrida wants to hold the hand of negative theology to the fire of its word (to the word): that it does not know what is happening, that it is exposed to something elusive, amorphous, undeterminable, *sans savoir, sans avoir, sans voir* (*Parages*, 25), so that one is not sure whether this is God, or *il y a*, or a bit of indigestion. Then, instead of having a hyperousio-logical answer up her sleeve, the negative theologian would find herself asking with Augustine, "what do I love when I love my God?" To lend a Derridean ear to negative theology is, in my view, to be led to the doors of *faith*, which negative theology tends to leave at the door. Faith is a certain resolve to hold on by one's teeth, to put one's hand to the plow, to push on in the midst of the grammatological flux, to repeat forward, to say *oui* today knowing that this must be repeated later on tonight, and then again tomorrow morning, again and again, *oui, oui*, which is why monastic prayers were hourly. Reread in the light of deconstruction, neg-ative theology has next to nothing to do with a supercharged, hyper-ousiological experience, which is I think not an *invention de l'autre* but a flat-out invention of Neoplatonism.[13]

Armed Neutrality

In order to see how deconstruction is deeply affirmative, how it loves the name of God, we must first clarify that there is thus something im-portantly, if provisionally, "neutral" about *différance*.[14] The quasi-transcen-dental work of *différance* is to establish the conditions which make possible our beliefs and our practices, our traditions and our institutions, *and* no less to make them impossible, which means to see to it that they do not effect closure, to keep them open so that something new or different may happen.

A transcendental condition is a sufficient and enabling condition; a quasi-transcendental condition is insufficient and equi-disabling, seeing that the effect that it makes possible is also made unstable. *Différance* supplies a condition under which something is constituted or construct-ible and at the same time through and through deconstructible. *Différance* is a groundless ground that founds and unfounds languages, vocabula-ries, institutions, systems, theories, laws, artworks, theologies, religions, practices—whatever you need—showing how they are both possible and impossible, useful up to a point but chastened by a sense of their insuffi-ciency.

Transcendental conditions nail things down, pin them in place, inscribe them firmly within rigorously demarcated horizons; quasi-transcendental conditions allow them to slip loose, to twist free from their surrounding horizons, to leak and run off, to exceed or overflow their margins. The problem in a transcendental philosophy is how to establish communication across the borders; the problem in a quasi-transcendental philosophy is how to keep things from running into each other and contaminating everything. But a quasi-transcendental condition is a condition of or for entities, not an entity itself; a condition under which things appear, but too poor and impoverished, too unkingly, to dictate what there is or what there is not, lacking the power to bring what is not into being, lacking the authority to prohibit something from being.

So *différance* describes the possibility and the impossibility of a language that addresses God, of positive, onto-theo-logical languages, like that of Thomas Aquinas, and the extraordinary languages of mystical theologians like John of the Cross, of mystical poets like Angelus Silesius, with all their paradoxes and paralogisms, detours and dissonances. *Différance* describes the languages of faith and prayer which, as Derrida's work evolves, prove to be not just particular examples of language, but exemplary uses that exceed linguistic categorization and tend to coincide with language itself, to become the very yes, or *amen*, of language to what is happening. That is why deconstruction is not ultimately neutral. Even so, *différance* describes the possibility and impossibility of the language in which God is coldheartedly denied by Hume or Bertrand Russell, excoriated by Nietzsche for all of His failings, or brushed off with a shrug by Rorty, who does not see why we need bother to talk like that.

Différance is altogether too meager and poor a thing to settle the question of God, as if there were only one question instead of a *mise en abîme* of questions spreading out in every direction. God has not been waiting from all eternity for *différance* to come into the world to settle His affairs (or Hers). *Différance* does not settle the God question one way or the other; in fact, the point is to un-settle it,[15] to make it more difficult, by showing that, even as we love the name of God, we must still ask what it is we love. One of the smarter things Nietzsche said about God is that atheism too represents the ascetic ideal, which is the desire to pin things down, to put them firmly in their place. *Différance* will lead us up to a point, to be discussed below, of endless translatability and substitutability, to the point of what Derrida calls "exemplarism," where we do not know what is an example of what, where things become unnervingly open-ended.

The effect of allowing *différance* its two cents is disturbing and subversive, for monotheists, atheists, and pantheists, for believers as well as unbelievers, for scientists as well as philologists, for *Seinsdenkers* as well as psychoanalysts. For *différance* makes—or should make; this is part of the ethics of deconstruction—the theist worry about what we affirm when we affirm our God, even as it makes the atheist worry about what is denied when God is being denied. For there are idols of belief and of unbelief, graven images being affirmed and denied every day. If the affirmation of God is liable to the surgings of resentment or fear, the denial of God is liable to denial pure and simple, the denial of something that is not God and that is well denied.

But do not expect *différance* to settle these disputes; *différance* has not come to bring peace but the two-edged sword of undecidability.

That is why I am unhappy with Mark Taylor's first, interesting and innovative adaptation of Derrida, early on, in *Erring*, in which he too closely assimilated Derrida to the theology of the "death of God."[16] Taylor starts off on the right foot by saying that he wants to write an "a/theology," to stay on the slash, to write in the difference between theism and atheism, if these are stable, firm, upright positions. He situates himself within the crucial Derridean gesture of undecidability, inasmuch as it is not the business of *différance* to show either that there is or is not a God, but only how much trouble we have bought for ourselves once we venture out into the troubled waters of judgment and decision—about God or anything else. The problem with *Erring* is that it is insufficiently aporetic, that it allows itself to be led straight down the path (*poreia*) inerrantly I would say, of the death of God, fully equipped with a *grand récit* in terms of which the *Gottestod* is announced. According to this tall tale, the transcendent God of Christianity pitches his tent under the immanent Spirit of Hegel, which becomes in turn the divine Man of Feuerbach, which releases the First Age of the death-of-God. Then *différance*—or sacred *écriture*—is sent into the world to release an even more radically non-humanistic atheism by stamping out the last remnants of the old God, Man himself, leaving no trace of God or Man behind. In the final scene, God has become *écriture* with nothing left over. The sacred scripture has become all there is of the sacred itself: God as glyph, hier-glyph. *Erring* does not stay on the slash of undecidability but makes a reductionist decision *against* God, thereby reducing the ambiguity of a genuine a/theology and turning *différance* against God. But that version of deconstruction is undone by deconstruction itself, which refuses such closure, such exclusions and such clean sweeps.

The provisional neutrality of *différance* is not a neutral neutrality but, to take up Kierkegaard's wonderful expression, an *armed* neutrality, which means that it is even-handedly antagonistic to all claims of existence or nonexistence, that it views them all with a certain alarm and suspicion. It plays no favorites when existence claims are afoot, but gives all parties to the dispute an equally hard time. Deconstruction shows the limits under which discourse labors when "someone says something to someone about something" (*hermeneia*). *Différance* is neutral by being uniformly nasty about letting vocabularies establish their credentials and get set in place, as if they really were making good in some strong sense on their claims. Its neutrality lies in its unremitting and unbiased antagonism, which does not single out theologians for particular abuse but which is equally hostile to all ontological claims, across the board. Deconstruction is, for example, just as inhospitable to empiricists and phenomenologists who talk about the "perceptual" world as it is to theologians, for there never really was "perception," no pure, prelinguistic experience. "Perception," too, like the old God, is the dream of presence without *différance* (VP, 116/SP, 103).

Such armed neutrality is not, however, aimed at locking us inside a chain of signifiers but at making us think twice about claiming that our discourse has accomplished what it set out to do. This is rather like the trouble that God, who is clearly on the side of the deconstructor and the disseminator, gave the Shemites who wanted to build a famous tower in Babel (*Psy.*, 218/DiT, 184), and rather like Qoheleth who warned us about the vanity of vanities (Eccl. 1:2), i.e., of our constituted effects. Deconstruction throws a scare into our discourse, questions the too tall prestige of the towers of reference, of the self-importance of "meaning," but without simply destroying meaning and reference themselves. Deconstruction creates a salutary distrust in the power of language to do what it says it is doing, along with providing an account of how language accomplishes what it does manage to do. But all of this, it cannot be repeated too often, takes place with the idea of keeping things open to something new.

The notion that deconstruction denies reference and locks us inside a prison house of signifiers, in a kind of linguistic-subjective idealism that leaves us unable to do anything but play vainly with linguistic strings, is a particularly perverse one, given the dynamics and motivations of deconstruction. For deconstruction sees itself as a pact with the *tout autre*, with the promise of the different, an *alliance* with the advent, the event, of the invention of alterity. What an odd result for a philosophy intent on the invention of the other, what an unkind fate to visit upon a philosophy whose every effort is bent upon welcoming the other, like Elijah knocking at the door! Were this absurd charge true, Derrida's work would surely be of no use for understanding biblical faith and tradition—or any faith or tradition, or science or law or architecture or literature or anything else (PdS, 227–28/*Points*, 213–15)—since it would make nonsense out of the interpretation of classical texts and the articulation of shared beliefs. In fact, what is interesting about deconstruction lies in exactly the opposite tendency of this misunderstanding, in the special skills it has cultivated in awakening us to the demands made by the other. This has interesting and provocative implications for theological reflection, a point largely lost in the midst of the ill-conceived and panicky reactions the name of Derrida provokes among the Good and the Just.

This misunderstanding of deconstruction, which even supposes that the very idea of "misunderstanding deconstruction" is undermined by deconstruction, is often the result of too hastily construing the texts of a difficult, elusive and playful author. But this distortion of Derrida is not without political significance, for it is frequently attached to a reactionary political agenda which vigorously opposes the efforts of women, homo-sexuals, and ethnic minorities to have their voices heard, in the academy and in the church. In the world of Anglo-American philosophy, it arises from the hegemonic agenda of the "analytic" establishment, which has succeeded in making philosophy tedious and culturally irrelevant, and which feels threatened by a style of thinking which, to say the least, analytic philosophers have denounced but simply have not read.[17]

Allow me here to make a point that by now should be superfluous. Derrida's justly famous, but unjustly notorious, declaration, "There is nothing outside the text" (*il n'y a pas de hors texte*) (DLG, 227–28/OG, 158), has been widely interpreted as a denial of reference, as if Derrida thinks there *is* nothing other than words and texts. That, were it construed as a metaphysical claim, would constitute a sort of linguistic Berkeleyianism, which is incoherent on its face. Texts are, after all, material objects in whose materiality—graphic spacing, copyrights, the power of publishers, etc.—Derrida takes great interest. Alternatively, and somewhat less ab-surdly, Derrida is taken to advocate a vague subjectivistic skepticism, according to which signifiers are seen as leading only to other signifiers, leaving in doubt the character of anything outside of signifiers, anything real or really other, and leaving us in a cloud of confusion, a paralysis of undecidability and inaction. One way to see the error here—a "serious, stupifying, and apparently indestructible misunderstanding" (*Moscou*, 108)—he may be excused, I think, for his impatience with this stupidity—is to see that it conflates the "*hors*" of "*hors texte*" with the "other of language," with the referent or *ens significatum*. For while there is nothing which, for Derrida, would escape the constraints of textuality, it is no less true that everything that Derrida has written has been directed toward the other of language, toward the alterity by which language is claimed:[18]

> It is totally false to suggest that deconstruction is a suspension of refer-ence. Deconstruction is always deeply concerned with the 'other' of lan-guage. I never cease to be surprised by critics who see my work as a declaration that there is nothing beyond language, that we are im-prisoned in language; it is, in fact, saying the exact opposite. The critique of logocentrism is above all else the search for the 'other' and the 'other of language'. Every week I receive critical commentaries and studies on deconstruction which operate on the assumption that what they call 'post-structuralism' amounts to saying that there is nothing beyond lan-guage, that we are submerged in words—and *other stupidities* [my em-phasis] of that sort. Certainly, deconstruction tries to show that the question of reference is much more complex and problematic than tradi-tional theories supposed. It even asks whether our term 'reference' is entirely adequate for designating the 'other'. The other, which is beyond language and which summons language, is perhaps not a 'referent' in the normal sense which linguists have attached to this term. But to distance

oneself thus from the habitual structure, to challenge or complicate our common assumptions about it, does not amount to saying that there is *nothing* beyond language.

This "primitive misunderstanding" is "motivated by political and ideological reasons" (*Moscou*, 109). So again a political coefficient:

> This misinterpretation . . . is symptomatic of certain political and institutional interests. . . . I totally refuse the label of nihilism. . . . Deconstruction is not an enclosure in nothingness, but an openness towards the other.

Deconstruction means to complicate reference, not to deny it; it insists that there is no reference without difference, no reference (*il n'y a pas*) outside of a textual chain (*hors-texte*). It argues that the range of reference of a term is set by its place within a systemic code, that its reference is both made possible and delimited by the space that it occupies within qausi-systems of difference (linguistic, social, political, economic, etc.). Deconstruction wants to trouble the expression "reference" as an excessively subjectivistic term which overestimates the *ego cogito* of the speaking subject while underestimating the power of the systems within which the speaker operates.[19] This delimitation of reference is motivated not by subjectivism or skepticism but by a kind of hypersensitivity to otherness, by a profound vigilance about the other of language and of the possibility of something different, something "impossible." Derrida is constantly alerting us to the constructedness of what we call the "reality" of the "extra-linguistic," and he is relentlessly, let us say, Socratically suspicious of the prestige of the ruling discourse, of the system of exclusions that is put in place when a language claims to be the language of reality itself, when a language is taken to be what being itself would say were it given a tongue.

Every claim to the "things themselves" is a claim made within and by means of the resources of certain semi-systems, linguistic and otherwise, situated within the framework of a complex set of contextual presuppositions which can never be saturated. There are no things themselves outside these textual and contextual limits, no naked contact with being which somehow shakes loose of the coded system which makes notions like the "things themselves" possible to begin with and which enables speakers to refer to them and indeed to get themselves in heat about their access to them. But all this is said not in order to lock the speaker up in a linguistic prison, but out of a hypersensitivity to the other of language. This "other" is not reducible to language nor is it something which can shake loose from language as if it fell full blown and wholly constituted from the sky.

As a work of delimitation, of understanding the limits under which we labor, deconstruction is a "new Enlightenment" (DDP, 496/PR, 19; *Points*, 400) which raises our level of vigilance about what calls itself meaning or reference, subjectivity or objectivity—or "truth," "tradition," or "ethics." The impetus and the point of all such work is never destructive, never aimed at simply leveling or razing these structures. The point of deconstruction is to loosen and unlock structures, to let the shock of alterity set them in motion, to allow them to function more freely and inventively, to produce new forms, and above all to say yes, *oui, oui,* to something whose coming eye hath not seen nor ear heard. Deconstruction gives old texts new readings, old traditions new twists. It urges that regularizing structures and normalizing institutions—everything from literature to democracy—function more freely, more open-endedly. Deconstruction exposes them to the trauma of something unexpected, something to come, of the *tout autre* which remains ever on the margins of texts and traditions, which eludes and elicits our discourse, which shakes and solicits our institutions. Deconstruction warns against letting a discursive tradition close over or shut down, silence or exclude. I do not mean to suggest that deconstruction is the doing of a cunning and powerful subjective deconstructive agent, some secret agent or detective Derrida. Rather, in a deconstructive analysis, one lets it be seen that the discourse in question is a whitened sepulcher which thanks God that it is not like the rest of discourse, that it lacks the very cohesiveness and closure to which it lays claim, that it is not what it says it is. But by letting this out, one points to something there, in these systems, which struggles to twist free of the system. The watchword of deconstruction, one of them at least, is the open-ended call *viens!* Come, let something new come.

Seen thus, deconstruction is not the sworn enemy of faith or religious institutions, but it can cause a lot of well-deserved trouble to a faith or an institution that has frozen over into immobility. Deconstruction is a way to let faith function more ad-ventfully, with an enhanced sense of advent and event, gladdened by the good news of alterity by which we are always and already summoned. Beyond that, deconstruction is *itself* a form of faith, a faith in the *viens,* a hope in what is coming, one which says we are always a little blind and it is necessary to believe. *Il faut croire.*

The armed neutrality of *différance* makes it plain that there is no built-in brief against religion, faith, or God in deconstruction, a point about which I think Kevin Hart is especially helpful. The tendency among Derrida's commentators, Hart rightly argues, has been to make deconstruction safe for secularism by stationing a ring of formidable secularist hermeneutic guards around the text—such as Freud and, above all, Nietzsche. They would saturate Derrida's horizons with secularism and insist that deconstruction's rejection of the transcendental signified means the death of God, as if the little *a* in *différance* spells the end of religion, God, and faith.

In fact, however, all that deconstruction tells against are the totalizing tendencies of theological discourse, theology's tendency to think that it has hit upon pure presence without representation, which is the same complaint that deconstruction would have about secularism or naturalism, about any totalizing tendency. Theology has hardly cornered the market on totalization. If there is any totalizing going on here, Hart points out, it is among the secularist commentators on Derrida who would forbid the contamination or "infestation"[20] of good secular academic goods such as deconstruction with God. As Hart so nicely quips, such academics would be scandalized to see the little letter of *différance* end up being delivered at the door of the Chicago Divinity School.[21]

Secularizing deconstructionists, Hart says, want to still the oscillation in *écriture* between "writing" and "scripture," to sanitize deconstruction, to draw a rigid border around Derrida, in order to keep deconstruction decidedly safe from religious infiltration and subversion. But, as Hart says, "the 'atheistic' reading of deconstruction is itself open to deconstruction." The point is, Hart says, that whatever Derrida's authorial intentions, even if Derrida himself has a heart of stone when it comes to religion, even if Jacques Derrida is "rightly taken to be an atheist," *écriture* cannot help signifying both 'writing' and 'scripture'. Hence, even if Derrida were personally *antagonistic* to religion—which he is not: he is a man of prayers and tears, and he has his own religion!—the conversation between religion and deconstruction, as Hart points out, would belong to that relationship in Derrida's texts between what he commands and cannot command (DLG, 227/OG, 158).[22] Indeed, as we shall show below, over and beyond its armed neutrality, the point of *différance*, far from destroying faith, is to lead us up to faith, even to the "blindness" of faith, *sans savoir, sans voir*, which is the argument of *Memoirs of the Blind*, to what is called in *Cinders* "the passion of non-knowing," that is, of faith (*Cinders*, 75).

Deconstruction shows what God and a perceptual object have in common, that they are each effects of a certain faith, and that they differ from each other as different forms of faith, with different protocols, discursive resources, and motivations. In deconstruction God and a perceptual object do *not* differ from each other as the uncertain from the certain, or the fictitious from the verifiable (empiricism), or the really real from the apparent (Platonism), etc. The undecidability that befalls our beliefs and practices in virtue of *différance* is not the last word, but the first. For *différance* is a certain sort of quasi-condition of all our choices and judgments, which must thereby take the form of a *faith*, a bit of a leap, with the proviso that leaps of faith differ in terms of their motivations and legitimations, that we are better off making some leaps than others. Clearly, it is not to the disadvantage of religion and theology to show that faith is an omnivalent, ubiquitous condition.

§2. Dreaming the Impossible Dream:
Derrida and Levinas on the Impossible

If Derrida thinks that the surcharge of surreal, hyperousiological being dreams the dream of pure presence without *différance*, does that imply that something that would be plainly and simply "absolutely other" is plainly impossible? Now this is a delicate point about which we must be clear because, as we have seen, Derrida is not against dreams, is not against the impossible, and is not against the *tout autre*. Far from it. Everything in deconstruction, we are contending, turns on a passion for the impossible, on setting a place at the table for the *tout autre*, which is the impossible. So some distinctions are in order and we have to get straight this talk of the impossible or we risk missing everything deconstruction desires.

The problem of the impossible also goes to the heart of Derrida's relationship to Levinas, and it would be helpful at this point to examine Derrida's early negotiations with negative theology in tandem with Derrida's first encounter, over thirty years ago, with Levinas (cf. PdS, 278–79/*Points*, 263–64). For like the negative theologian, Levinas too advances the idea of the absolutely wholly other, *l'infini*, which is utterly exterior to and shatters the limits of our horizons. Indeed, Derrida's earliest delimitation of negative theology occurs in the context of his first and justly famous essay on Levinas, "Violence and Metaphysics." If we pause over this subtle essay, we will get a surer sense of what Derrida makes of negative theology and, more importantly, of the impossible.

Derrida felt called upon to "respond" in the name of "the two Greeks named Husserl and Heidegger" to the provocation made by the messianic eschatology of Levinas (ED, 123/WD, 83). Levinas charged them with the "violence" of submitting the "other" (*autrui*) to anticipatory horizons that confined the other within the same, that alter and compromise the other's alterity, submitting the other in advance to the violence of a horizon of expectation. But what Levinas calls the positive infinity of the infinitely other is, according to Derrida, "unthinkable, impossible, unutterable." "Perhaps," Derrida adds, "Levinas calls us toward this unthinkable-impossible-unutterable beyond (tradition's) Being and Logos" (ED, 168 /WD, 114). That may be, Derrida responds at once—in italics, which the English translation suppresses—but if so, that is not something one would be able either to say or think, as we have just done. This difficulty—saying something it cannot say—is the one in which both Levinas and negative theology find themselves. But Levinas cannot avail himself of the classical recourse of which negative theology avails itself in this situation, which is to renounce language as a foreign medium. "[H]e has already given up the best weapon, disdain of discourse" (ED, 170/WD, 116). This would not be a problem for "a classical infinitism of the Cartesian type" (ED,

169/WD, 115), but it is so for Levinas, who holds that language is the very point of encounter—"*Bonjour!*"—with infinity, with the wholly other. Like Derrida, Levinas is committed in advance to the trace, and the attempt to efface the trace is for both a mistake (and impossible). (Cf. ED, 219/WD, 147–48.)

So we have two parallel but instructively different impossibilities and aporias. (1) Absolute Heterology: As long as Levinas affirms language and commits himself to the trace, he cannot affirm a positive, infinite alterity, for that would wipe language out without a trace, would efface the trace without remainder. (2) Hyperousiology: As long as negative theology affirms intuitive unity with a positive, infinite alterity, it cannot avail itself of language, for language would compromise its intuition; but it is already too late, and negative theology does not know how not to speak.

Now there is an interesting chiasmic effect in Derrida's "debate," if it is one, with Levinas. Derrida's "objections," if he has any (ED, 125/WD, 84), against Levinas, as Robert Bernasconi and Simon Critchley have shown, appear to have forced Levinas to refine his views and to develop the distinction *within* language between *le dit* and *le dire* in *Autrement qu'être, ou au-delà de l'essence*. Beginning with *Totality and Infinity* itself, Levinas had along conceded the necessity to "betray" whatever he might say, which was to concede from the start that he was in a certain impossible situation. By the same token, Derrida repeatedly warns us in this essay that, all appearances to the contrary, he is not objecting to Levinas's views and that the "legitimacy" of Levinas's provocation of Greek philosophy "does not seem to us any less radical" (ED, 195/WD, 133). The upshot of this is that the delimitation of Levinas recoils on Derrida, who can agree that, once Levinas's position is properly delimited, once one has faced up, if I may say so, to the necessity of an *archi*-violence, of the play of *différance*, then *the* impossible is just what deconstruction is all about, so that, properly delimited, Derrida can never find anything to disagree with in Levinas.[23] Over and beyond any debate about the proper exegesis of Husserl's "literal ambitions" in the Fifth Meditation, this "interpellation of the Greek by the non-Greek," this opening that is opened up in Greek philosophy, this questioning of philosophy on the part of philosophy's other, which by "hypothesis" (ED, 226/WD, 152) we may call Judaism, could not be more necessary (ED, 195–96/WD, 133).

Just what this "proper delimitation" amounts to becomes clear in Derrida's defense of Husserl and Heidegger, which consists in showing that if you remove the anteriorities that Husserl and Heidegger put in place, the *tout autre* will no longer be *tout autre*, that it will reduce to a simple logical contradiction, which is an outcome that Levinas himself would very much regret. That means that the *tout autre, per impossibile*, requires a lot of preparation in advance, that a long and difficult advent is needed to prepare for this *invention*—and deconstruction *is* the preparation for the *tout autre*. The complex transcendental intermediation elaborated by Husserl in the Fifth Meditation, which is all very Greek, the tortured argument about the reduction to the sphere of ownness, the work of transcendental pairing and analogical apperception, is an elaborate gesture of respect for the other, without which ethical respect would be impossible. Husserl's notion of "*ap*-perception," far from compromising the *tout autre*, positively preserves the other ego from direct perception, shelters the alterity of the other by putting the other off limits to intuition. The transcendence of the other positively demands that the *Erlebnisse* of the other be inaccessible to my perception, otherwise the other's experience would be mine and her otherness undermined (ED, 182/WD, 124). Furthermore, in order to save the alterity of the other it is necessary to insist that the other be the same, so that if the other were different, not an ego, it would not be *tout autre*. Whatever ethical dissymmetry between the self and the other Levinas has uncovered can only be protected by a prior transcendental symmetry (ED, 185/WD, 126). According to the paradoxical grammar and logic of an *alter ego*, which has to do with the alterity of a fellow human being, the otherness of something different, a mere thing or object, would not be nearly so other. So the other is "absolutely other" only if the other is the same (ED, 187/WD, 127). Otherwise the other will be *less* transcendent, not more, an animal or a thing, for example, the *tout autre* will make no sense, and "no ethics would be possible" (ED, 202/WD, 138). If we have not adequately prepared ourselves in advance for the shock of alterity, the alter, instead of shocking us, will just pass us by without a ripple.

What Derrida shows then is that the *tout autre* comes but it comes relative to a horizon of expectation which it shocks and sets back on its heels, instead of confirming and reinforcing this horizon in its complacency. The *alter ego* comes with a certain optimal alterity, neither too great (positively infinite) nor too small (more of the same); the *tout autre* is *tout autre* only up to a point; there are limits! The incoming of the other occurs within a field of perception which it resists, which resistance, forcing as it does a merely approximating ap-perception, constitutes its transcendence. Its transcendence is the transcendence of the other person, different *from* me, let us say, but not different *than* me, a field of novelty and surprise within a pregiven horizon of perception. That would constitute what might be called, given certain constraints, an absolute surprise, so long as that means an absolute surprise *relative to* what we were expecting. In order to be overtaken by something we were not ready for, Elijah, for example, we have to be ready.

That notion is what Derrida will later on adopt under the name of *the impossible*, of the incoming of the *tout autre*, the excess or breach that exceeds and shocks our expectation, which thereby depends upon anticipatory expectations and pregiven horizons that had been set too low or within too narrow a tolerance.[24] The impossible is opposed to something that is impossible, *simpliciter*, the non-sense of something absolutely absolute or some absolutely plenitudinous and positive infinity that is infinitely other, which is senseless and incoherent, inasmuch as "infinite" and "other" are *already* traces (ED, 168 / WD, 114). So let us give up the dream of pure nonviolence, of an alterity that is not somehow or other inscribed within the trace, but precisely in order to keep the dream of the alterity of the *tout autre* alive. So there are dreams and there are dreams, and Derrida would never dream of doing away with all dreams, would never dream of doing away with a passion for the impossible. On the contrary, he has found it necessary to deny the dream of pure nonviolence, which is an impossible dream, in order to make room for the dream of the *tout autre*, which is the dream of *the* impossible, the dream of the emergence of something different, something that disturbs the sleep of the rule of the same, something shocking, provocative, evocative, *tout autre*. For the trace makes the other possible and impossible, allowing a shock to the system of the same that forces the same (possible) open and opens it to a difference it did not expect or see coming (*the* impossible). The dream of pure nonviolence is too violent; it would be a breach of speech, history, and phenomenality that would, moreover, put the rest of us at risk (ED, 218/WD 146–47). But dispelling that dream opens the way to a new dream, to dreaming otherwise, with a passion for the impossible.

At the end of this brilliant study, Derrida makes a remark that virtually forecasts the future and chiasmic course of his own work and that of Levinas by suggesting this rehabilitation, or delimitation, of the impossible, in the direction of the later notion of *the* impossible. Levinas, he says, has foreseen this whole line of argument against *Totality and Infinity* (he was ready, he was not taken by surprise); he is "resigned to *betraying* his own intentions in his philosophical discourse" (ED, 224/WD, 151), which is of course the tact that Levinas took up in *Otherwise than Being*, having first announced it at the end of the Preface to *Totality and Infinity*. Now what Levinas is clearly *not* resigned to is having his views shown to be false on their face, or even incoherent. He is not resigned to a notion of the other which does not protect its alterity, which exposes the other to being taken and treated as a thing or an animal or an *Unsinn*. But he is resigned to a higher-order "betrayal," a certain hyper-betrayal, to saying something that comes unstuck as soon as it said, because of the objectification and thematization to which it is subjected by—that old nemesis—"philosophy," *Greek* philosophy (a redundancy, according to Heidegger).

Levinas has a passion and a dream. He is "dreaming" of something that only barely peeks through the crevices of philosophy, dreaming the impossible dream of "a purely heterological thought," "a *pure* thought of *pure* difference," a thought that negates itself, a trace that effaces itself, in order to let the other be. That is a dream that would go under the name of a pure "empiricism," or pure experience-of-the-other, which is non-philosophy, philosophy's dream of what the world is like before philosophy arrives on the scene or after philosophy would take its leave, would close up its shop, and let the things themselves speak for themselves. Now since a pure experience of the other must be *my* experience or it is no experience at all, neither of the same nor of the other, that is purely impossible, and the "dream must vanish at daybreak, as soon as language awakens" (ED, 224/WD, 151).

But again the rejoinder: Levinas is "resigned" to this! There is nothing you can say to which he is not resigned! But that is not quite true. Levinas's resignation has its limits; he is resigned, *not* to denying the experience of alterity or rendering it incoherent, but to betraying it by saying it, as in negative theology, with the difference that he cannot opt for silent commerce with the other but has to find a solution to his aporia *within* language.

What this comes down to for Derrida, I think, is this. Levinas shows that "nothing can so profoundly *solicit* the Greek *logos*—philosophy—than this irruption of the *tout autre*" (ED, 226/WD, 152). What we are to learn from Levinas is "*solicitation*," which means a shocking of the horizons, a passage to the limits, a jarring loose of the same, an opening up of enclosing surroundings. That means the *tout autre* is not some sort of being-in-itself on the "other side" of the horizon, the being-there (*être-là*) of some absolute outside, some absolute exteriority, something absolutely other in the *là-là* land of absolute alterity, a sort of subsistent alterity or exteriority. The *tout autre* is a shock to the system in place, an inside/outside transgressive alteration that modifies the same, that alters it instead of confirming it in its complacency. But if that event is to take place, then the horizons to be shocked, the limits to be trespassed, the frontiers to be crossed, the same to be jarred loose, the enclosure to be opened, along with a readiness to be surprised—all of that must be in place, must antedate, must anticipate and prepare for the incoming arrival.

Now *that* arrival, that incoming *invention* is an arrival of which we may dream, and *that* dream does not vanish at daybreak when language awakens, because that is a dream *within* language, a dream which language itself dreams, a dream dreamed by the trace, by the *viens* and the *oui, oui* which are traces, which dreams that something different may take place, may eventuate, the dream of the event of an *invention* to come. The trace makes this taking-place im/possible, prepares the way for *the* impossible. The passion for the impossible takes place within the trace.

Shall we call this *tout autre* that stuns philosophy's complacent conceptuality "Judaism" while calling philosophy "Greek"? Ironically, Levinas's own views in this matter, as I will argue elsewhere, surrender too much to philosophy's conceptual appetite. Levinas thinks, in the most amazing Eurocentrism of the same, that Greek *logos* is, as he says in *Difficult Liberty*, "the medium of all comprehension and of all understanding in which all truth is reflected" (cf. ED, 226/WD, 152). In emphasizing this Greek side of the equation, in emphasizing what Levinas is resigned to, Derrida says that Greece is prepared for any surprise, however Jewish, that in Plato's *epekeina tes ousias,* and in the notion of *heteros* in Plato's *Sophist,* Greek philosophy "has protected itself forever [*sic!*] against every [*sic!*] absolutely *surprising* convocation," *à jamais! toute!* (ED, 227/WD, 153). That would mean we all end up Greek after all, that you can't take philosophy absolutely by surprise. We would all come hurtling back to Philo Judaeus translating the God of the prophets into Greek, and everything in Judaism will have been translated into Greek, even when we shock Greece with the trauma of Jahweh. About that, I think, Levinas is fundamentally mistaken, surprisingly far too philosophical, far too Greek, and—he will hate this—far too Heideggerian. Levinas seems to me to swing wildly between extremes. After protesting too much on behalf of the *tout autre,* Levinas concedes too much to philosophy, as if Plato's *epekeina tes ousias* or the form of *heteros* in the *Sophist* had *anything—sic!*—to do with the widows and orphans and strangers of prophetic faith, with the compassionate Lord of Amos who wanted nothing more than to let justice flow like water over the widow, the orphan, and the stranger; as if the blind and mute *agathon,* the unfeeling and faceless Platonic progenitor of entity and knowledge, an unseeing sun not an eye or a heart, had *anything—sic!*—anything at all to do with Yahweh, whom any good Jew would call *abba.* But about that, more later (I promise).

"Are we Jews? Are we Greeks?" Derrida asks. "We live in the difference between the two," he acutely responds, "which is perhaps the unity of what is called history" (ED, 227/WD, 153). But for Derrida, history is not the *reconciliation* of this difference, as in Hegel, or the *translation* of the Hebrew into Greek, which is the surprise Levinas has in store for us. For Derrida, history is a field of transgression, of the *solicitation* of boundaries, the crossing of borders, the parergonality of bounded works, the possibility of something different, all of which loosens the soil for something *tout autre,* which is coming, which is the substance of our passion, of the passion of history.

Shall we call the *tout autre* "God"? To be sure, but that is not an answer, it is the stuff of another question. For if we say, as one does in theology, that the *tout autre* is God, we then must ask, with Augustine, "what do I love when I love my God?" It is not within deconstruction's jurisdiction to determine the *tout autre* further, because deconstruction has no jurisdiction, is not a Neokantian court. Everything about deconstruction requires that we let the *tout autre* tremble in undecidability, in an endless, open-ended, indeterminable, undecidable *translatability,* or *substitutability,* or *exemplarity,* where we are at a loss to say what is an example of what, what is a translation of what. That open-ended, disseminative undecidability is the space of "history," which a good Jew like Levinas should not be so quick to write off as an Hegelianism (ED, 220/WD, 148), no more than it is very Jewish of him to privilege speech over writing (ED, 151–52/WD, 102).

But once again, I hasten to add, the point of deconstruction is not to let us all hang out to dry, twisting slowly in the winds of indecision while Rome or, more pertinently, Jerusalem burns, but to mark off the place of the trace within which each of us must decide for herself what is what, what is going on, and what is coming down. The point of undecidability is not apathy and impassivity, like a Hellenistic unmoved mover, but the prick of passion, which is a little more Jewish. What interests Derrida about both Levinas and negative theology is that both are discourses on the limit, on the *passage des frontières*, on the transgressiveness of *tout autre, le pas au-delà*, on the extremes to which discourse is driven when it is addressed by that which comes as other than anything of which discourse can dream, as impossible, as *the* impossible, as a dream, as more than a dream.

What does this dream desire? What desires so to dream? What is the *tout autre*? Is it Greek? Is it Jewish? What is coming?

Je ne sais pas. Il faut croire. (MdA, 130/MB, 129.)

Viens! Oui, oui.

§3. Affirmation at the Limits: How Not to Speak

"Jah"-weh

"*Jahweh spricht nur immer 'Ja,'*" Angelus Silesius quipped (multilingual-ly).[25] "Jahweh always says only 'yes.'" "Jah"-weh means, *pace* Nietzsche (God love him), something affirmative, and beyond that, affirmation itself: I am (*jah*, Hebrew) "yes" (*Ja*, German). I am affirmation at the limits, a limitless affirmation of *the* impossible, *tout autre*. What shall he say if the people ask for the name of God, Moses asks the Lord God:

> God said to Moses "I am *yes*." He said further: "Thus shall you say to the Israelites, 'I am *yes* has sent me to you. The Impossible, the Incoming'." (Exodus 3:14, NRquasi-SV)

The voice of "negative theology"—one of them, for it has several—is deeply, resoundingly affirmative. *Oui, oui.*

That is why, some twenty years later, Derrida finds himself revisiting, revisited by, negative theology, asked to take it up again, really for the first time, since the very first time, early on, was for the most part a promissory note to take it up again, later on. The first time was too negative, too "brief, elliptical, and dilatory" (*Psy.*, 539/DNT, 77): no, no, *différance* is not God and deconstruction is not negative theology. That is a merely provisional way of taking up the question, too cautious and dispassionate, too concerned with dissociating deconstruction from hyperousiology. That misses the sharp tip of deconstruction's desire, of its passion, and hence of deconstruction's abiding, affirmative interest in negative theology. For negative theology is nothing negative, no more than deconstruction itself, but rather, just like deconstruction itself, is a deeply affirmative irruption, "from the depths," *de profundis*, as the Jewish psalmist sings (in Latin?), a passion for the impossible, for trespassing and transgression. Deconstruction is driven by a movement of *"hyper, ultra, au-delà, über,* which will precipitate discourse or, first of all, existence. This precipitation is their passion" (*Sauf,* 73/ON, 64).

So the next time, in two provocative pieces, in Jerusalem (1986), "How Not to Speak: Denials," and then again in *Sauf le nom* (1993), Derrida takes up another voice of negative theology, outside its hyperousiological voice. In its other tone, negative theology gives voice to a desire, and responds to an address, that is visited upon us all, even those who rightly pass for atheists, thus constituting a generalized apophatics that is of general interest. That is why he cannot avoid speaking of negative theology.[26]

Next time (next year!) in Jerusalem! Then we will talk of Jahweh, of *"Jah"*-weh, of how not to speak of the Most High, how to avoid naming the Unnameable. Not quite. For a lecture held in Jerusalem about the unnameability of God, this address is singularly silent about the great negative theological traditions of Judaism and Islam and about Derrida's own Jewish-Arab provenance. "How Not to Speak" is a massive act of not-speaking, of evading the topic, *la chose même,* in which Derrida avoids speaking of Jews and Arabs and, in so doing, of himself (*Psy.,* 562–63/DNT, 100; *Psy.,* 585/DNT, 122). Derrida has too frequently allowed the question of the *tout autre* to be co-pted by Christian Neoplatonism. For the question of what *Jah-weh spricht* has a more deeply Jewish and hence a more personal sense, with roots that go all the way back to the streets of El-Biar, his childhood home, evoking a more Jewish scene, and a certain Jewish Augustine who speaks of "my God" and "my religion."

"Despite this silence, or in fact because of it," he writes, this is the most autobiographical piece he has ever risked. That it is hardly autobiographical at all is just what is so autobiographical about it, however "obliquely," so that what is being avoided is just what is being said. For whenever he turns to the question of the *tout autre,* he speaks of "others," of Christian Neoplatonists, and he does so "in *all* of my foreign languages: French [*sic!*], English, German, Greek, Latin, the philosophic, metaphilosophic, Christian, etc." Whenever he opens his mouth, he speaks the language of the colonizers of Algeria, "Christian Latin French" (*Circon.,* 57/*Circum.,* 58). Were he to try to speak of himself, that should take place in his mother tongue, which would have to be Hebrew or Arabic, which he never learned, which means that Derrida would be lost for words, *mirabile dictu,* having always already lost his native language, *sans voix*, in a past that was never present:

> But if one day I had to tell my story, nothing in this narrative would start to speak of the thing itself (*la chose même*), if I did not come up against this fact; for lack of capacity, competence, or self-authorization, I have never yet been able to speak of what my birth, as one says, should have made closest to me: the Jew, the Arab. (*Psy.*, 562n1/DNT, 135n13)

Suffice it to say, this story is to come, *à venir*, and it is to this story that I wish in particular to turn in this study.

The question of Derrida and theology, which is really a question of Derrida's religion, remains oddly out of focus until Derrida comes back to what he is, a circumcised Arab Jew, which is also—how could it be otherwise?—what he is not. As he says, it is difficult not to speak of oneself, but then again, how *is* one to do it "without allowing oneself to be invented by the other? or without inventing the other?" (*Psy.*, 562n1/DNT, 135–36n13). The question of Derrida and "negative theology"—the very expression is an *appellation contrôllée* of Christian vineyards, whatever equivalents there may be in Jewish and Islamic thought (*Sauf*, 70/ON, 63)—and of his dialogue with Greco-Christian texts, does not get us to the heart of the matter, does not "start to speak of the thing itself." For Derrida's heart is Hebraic and prophetic, and we will not get far until we see that the entire question needs to be recast and resituated, away from negative theology to the prophets, away from Greco-Christian texts to Jewish and biblical ones, and more generally away from "theology" to "religion."

To follow that more Jewish and religious turn will be the work of the subsequent sections and the main work of the present study. My present purpose is to pursue the other voice of negative theology to which Derrida attends in these later writings, in "How to Avoid Speaking: Denials" (1986), §3, and in *Sauf le nom* (1993), §4. Throughout I will argue for what I will call here a "generalized apophatics," by which I mean that negative theology is everybody's business, that it has a general translatability, that we cannot trust any discourse that is not contaminated by negative theology (*Psy.*, 560–61/DNT, 98). A deeply affirmative desire for something that is always essentially other than the prevailing regime of presence, something *tout autre*—too, too other, *oui, oui*—is of general interest. A passion for the impossible is a matter of general concern.

The Promise

What is taking place (*avoir lieu*) in negative theology? Over and beyond whatever hyperousiology negative theology may harbor and protect, over and beyond its understandable desire to draw itself into the safety of a hyperessential circle, what is happening there? What takes place if negative theology is left exposed, out in an open and unprotected place, divested of its hyperousiological assurances? What is left of a discourse in which everything determinate and determinable, every positive, predicative, entitative content, is burnt to a cinder? What remains if, divested of its hyperessential voice, negative theology is driven naked into the desert? What takes place except the place itself, except taking place itself, the event itself?

Those are the formidable questions Derrida poses to himself in order to separate the several voices of negative theology, in 1986, in Jerusalem, in the promised land, in the place of the promise. Now at last he will fulfill, or at least approach the "threshold" (*Psy.*, 559/DNT, 96) of fulfilling, a promise to speak of negative theology, a promise he has never quite managed either wholly to avoid or to fulfill.

Almost at once, the promised lecture in the place of the promise becomes a lecture on the promise and the place. One must cultivate a taste for the *mise en abîme*, or at least to tolerate such gestures, in order to read Derrida, an irksome task for philosophers, who have been carefully trained to cut straightaway, like a good surgeon, to the logocentric guts. But I pray you, be patient.[27]

> I will speak of a promise, then, but also within the promise.
> (*Psy.*, 547/DNT, 84)

The lecture tries to speak *about* (*de*) a promise, which is a particular, determinate "act,"[28] and more radically still to speak "within" (*dans*) a promise, within *the* promise, within the place of the promise. Thus the lecture becomes a lecture *of* the promise, springing from, in response to, a promise that is somehow older than him or us, than Derrida or negative theology, that takes place before us all, a promise that prompts speech.

> Why can't I avoid speaking, unless it is because a promise has committed me even before I begin the briefest speech? . . . Discourse on the promise is already a promise: in (*dans*) the promise. (*Psy.*, 547/DNT, 84)

Unable to be contained within a determinate promissory act that Jacques Derrida has made, the lecture rapidly spreads out into a promise within which we all are inscribed:

> I will thus not speak of this or that promise, but of that which, as necessary as it is impossible, inscribes us by its trace in language—before language. From the moment I open my mouth, I have already promised; or rather, and sooner, the promise has seized the *I* which promises to speak to the other, to say something, at the extreme limit to affirm or to

confirm by speech at least this: that it is necessary to keep silent. . . . This
promise is older than I am. (*Psy.*, 547/DNT, 84)

The "I"—yours, mine, Jacques's—is committed, pro-mitted, sent forth in
advance, into language, into the trace, always and already. The subject is
committed by an archi-promise (MpPdM, 119/MfPdM, 119) that is prior
to any conscious speech act (PdS, 397–98/*Points*, 383–84), older than the
monitoring presence of an intentional agent who knows what he promises
and promises what he knows:

> The promise of which I shall speak will have always escaped this
> demand of presence. It is older than I am or than we are. In fact, it renders
> possible every present discourse on presence. Even if I decide to be silent
> . . . this silence remains a modality of speech. (*Psy.*, 547/DNT, 84–85)

Derrida sounds highly Heideggerian here, evoking some sort of quasi-
Heideggerian saying, *die Sprache spricht*, language speaking us, speaking
before human speech. Or better, to adapt Paul de Man's variation, *die
Sprache verspricht*, language *promises* us; we are promised over in advance
by language to language (MpPdM, 99–103/MfPdM, 94–98). But if language is a promise to speak to one another of the things themselves, to
give one another meaning and truth, that is a promise that cannot be kept.
Thus speaking is a mis-speaking (*ver-sprechen*), a *Sprache* that is unable to
deliver the things themselves. Still, this failure or default is an opening,
one that opens up the errant space of history, of destinerrance. A promise
is an excess, a necessary but impossible opening to the future, *structurally*
open to the future, the very structure of openness to the future, a word
given in advance, to the other, to the future, to what is coming. By dis-
rupting the (Heideggerian) gathering together of Being in the present, in
presence, the promise takes on a "messianic" look, prying the present
open, "[t]he condition of the possibility and impossibility of eschatology,
the ironic allegory of messianism" (MpPdM, 139–40/MfPdM, 145).

By thus situating human speech within the *Ver-sprechen* of the "trace,"
Derrida describes a more barren, desertlike site than Heideggerian
Sprache, which is too *Schwarzwald*ian, too lush and too overgrown with
Greco-Germanic saplings sprouting up everywhere, with words unctuous
with Being's voice, awash with everything pure and uncontaminated and
aboriginary. Derrida's is at most a quasi-Heideggerian place, structurally
akin to *Sprache*, perhaps, *sans* the *Heimat*, *Ursprünglichkeit* and the all-gathering centrality of aboriginary Greco-Eurocentrism (see MpPdM, 134–
36/MfPdM, 139–42).

Remember what Derrida says is being avoided, the Jew and the Arab.
For the pedigree of the "promise" of which he speaks is more Hebraic
than Heideggerian, more messianic than Hellenic, and has to do with the
pact that has been made with the *tout autre*, the covenant with the im-

possible, and the promise that the *tout autre* has made to its people. The promise has to do with Derrida's broken *alliance*, for he has broken one alliance, that of a determinable biblical faith, in order to keep faith with another one, which he is here discussing. For the promise involves an "act" in the sense of an archi-act that one might also call "an act of faith" (MpPdM, 142/MfPdM, 150).

Every time we open our mouth we act upon an aboriginal promise made for us in advance, placed as we are in the space of this promise, under an inescapable, "undeniable necessity" to speak (*Psy.*, 561/DNT, 99). Even if we *said* we are going to keep silent, even if we sealed our lips, even then, it would already be too late and we would be enacting the promise. *Il faut*: it is necessary to speak, even in keeping silent, and this *il faut* arises from of old. "Language has started without us, in us and before us" (*Psy.*, 561/DNT, 99). The trace has always and already taken place.

We are always saying "yes" to this promise. Yes is not just one more word, but the beginning, the *Urwort* behind all words, the "Amen" which gives every word the right to exist, which silently accompanies every word. That is what Heidegger calls the *Zusage*, which means the acceptance, the pledge, the promise, the affirmation and assent, and faith. Yes, "faith": how could Heidegger ever be so foolish as to think that faith could be excluded from thinking? (*Foi*, 79–80). The *Zusage* is the very pre-engagement of thinking in a primordial language, even and before any question.[29] So we must be alert to the plurivocity of "yes," which, over and beyond its presence in the vocabulary of any natural language, is older than any language. As Derrida argues in "A Number of Yes," this archi- and quasi-transcendental yes is older than any determinate affirmation or negation (*Psy.*, 644–45/Number, 125–26). Resembling an "absolute performative," the performative that performs (and pre-forms) us before we perform it, that sets all determinate performatives in action, the archi-originary yes is an archi-engagement in language (*"engage dans une sorte d'archi-engagement"*), a certain *alliance* (MpPdM, 42/MfPdM, 19) or covenant, a consent or promise into which we are entered. This yes opens up and clears the way for the eventiveness of any event, even as it is never present as such. Older than any ontological or transcendental inquiry, "yes" is neither an object/entity studied in ontology nor a condition of the possibility of objects studied in a transcendental inquiry (*Psy.*, 648/Number, 130–31).

The Secret Place of Negative Theology

Negative theology belongs to the promise precisely insofar as it protests that it cannot say a thing. That is apophaticism's particular twist, its most particular trait (*trait*), its special way of being drawn into the trace—by retreating and withdrawing (*retrait*) what it has to say. Over a long and powerful tradition, negative theology responds to language by promising silence and gives its word not to say a word. It is at its most eloquent just when it says it is lost for words. By promising to efface the trace, negative theology traces out its place within the archi-promise, within the trace (MpPdM, 119/MfPdM, 119). But in Derrida's view, what happens in negative theology happens to us all, is of "general" import. We are all dreaming of the *tout autre,* about which we do not know how not to speak, under many names, so we will all have to learn negative theology, if not in the "original," if such a thing exists, at least in translation, in a generalized apophatics.

In apophatic theology, that which renders speech necessary and impossible, that which makes it necessary to speak and necessary to efface that speech, goes under the name of God:

> This is what God's name always names, before or beyond other names: the trace of the singular event that will have rendered speech possible even before it turns itself back toward—in order to respond to—this first or last reference. (*Psy.*, 560/DNT, 98)

Negative theology is both from God and to God; it is determinate, destined, "destinate" discourse:

> That is why apophatic discourse must also open with a prayer that recognizes, assigns, or ensures its destination . . . (*Psy.*, 560/DNT, 98)

As long as it keeps praying, it is not lost, does not lose its place and destinal assurance, does not end up adrift and *destinerrant.* Negative theology is not only a predicative discourse *about* God, a "theology," what Levinas calls *le dit,* but also a discourse sent *to* God, *à Dieu,* addressed to God, a prayer ("Oh, God"), what Levinas calls *dire* ("*Bonjour,*" or better, "*adieu*").

Negative theology takes place because something older and prior has already taken place, has already solicited theology's word, opened its mouth, loosened its tongue, elicited its response. That is what it calls God, a name that it wants to "sacrifice," to efface, in order to save what it names:

> A trace has taken place. Even if the idiomatic quality must necessarily lose itself or allow itself to be contaminated by the repetition that confers on it a code and an intelligibility, even if it *occurs only to efface itself,* if it arises only in effacing itself, the effacement will have taken place, even if its place is only in the ashes. *Il y a là cendre.* (*Psy.*, 560–61/DNT, 98)

The play of traces has always already taken place, even and especially where a discourse tries to deprive itself of meaning and reference, when it tries to empty and immolate itself, to turn itself into ashes, *il y a là cendre*,[30] to make itself a burnt offering, to head out into the barrenness of the desert, to make itself pure enough to pass through the vestibule into the inner sanctum, into the holy place of the godhead. The idiom of apophatic discourse is to be called, solicited, beckoned by a *tout autre* that awakens a desire for a self-effacing trace. But that always comes too late (*Psy.*, 561/DNT, 99), since the discourse has by then already taken place, called up by the other.

> This call of the other, having always already preceded the speech to which it has never been present a first time, announces itself as a *recall*. Such a reference to the other will always have taken place. (*Psy.*, 560/DNT, 97)

By what is this tortured discourse so inwardly disturbed? By what experience of otherness and alterity—"negative theology holds to a promise, that of the other" (*Psy.*, 547/DNT, 84)—is it solicited? What is its provocation, its provenance, its *prévenance*? That is what apophatic theology calls by and with the name of God, which is enfolded within a "secret" where it is guarded and kept safe. To be sure, this is a secret that negative theology cannot quite keep, whose safety it cannot quite ensure, about which it does not know how to avoid speaking. The secret is divulged as soon as it is kept; it is divulged by being kept; the promise to keep the secret is broken as soon as it made, is broken in being made. For the secret is structurally constituted by its being divulged as a secret. As soon as I say "I have a secret," the secret of the secret has been divulged. There is no secret until I constitute it as such, until I announce that I am protecting something, that I have something that I will not share with you. What does apophatic theology have that it will not give when it says by un-saying "God"? What does it give us when it gives the name of God? Does it give us something it does not have?

That brings us back to the subtitle of the lecture, "*dénégations*," which is misleadingly translated as "denials." A secret is a negation (a nondisclosure) that is itself de-negated—i.e., un-negated or divulged—as soon as it is constituted as a secret. But it does not become, in Hegelian fashion, the negation of a negation and hence a disclosure or manifestation; rather, it becomes a secret. The secret is constituted by saying and thinking it *as* a secret, so that it is both divulged and negated, and hence divided against itself. This is a structural feature of the secret, occurring in virtue of its very constitution, not by an external circumstance by which it is accidentally "spilled." If it were utterly secret, if the secret were purely secret, there would be no secret to keep safe. A pure secret, like a pure gift, makes no appearance and has no phenomenality. "There is no secret *as such*; I deny it" (*Psy.*, 558/DNT, 95). The pure secret would be lost.

This has an important political significance. The secret must be kept alive—"the secret of the secret—as such—[must] not remain secret" (*Psy.*, 557/DNT, 95). For as long as it is kept alive, as long as it is well known that there is a secret which some have and others do not, then it has the power to divide esoteric from exoteric knowledge, insiders from outsiders, and thus create a "*politique de lieux*," a politics of assigning places (*Khôra*, 49/ON, 104), of speaking from an authorized site, *ex sede, ex cathedra*, distributing speakers across a hierarchized space. As long as secrets and gifts are well known and acknowledged, there is power: authorities to acknowledge, debts to be paid.

A secret requires the self-presence of an interior monological consciousness that knows what it knows and will not share it with others. The secret in negative theology—the inwardly possessed intuitive vision, union, knowledge, or experience—clearly converges with its hyperousiology and it is this hyperousiological deep secret that deconstruction deconstructs. But for Derrida the secret is there is no secret, i.e., no hidden semantic content, no privileged access, no transcendental signified, no hyperessential intuition, no *Ding an sich* to which we have extratextual (extra-terrestrial) access (*Pass.*, 67/ON, 29). There is no escape from the surface of the text, and hence no way to put to rest our interpretative controversies. If our hearts are restless until they rest in the secret, then, in this Jewish Augustinianism, they will never rest. Indeed, that is just what is *productive* about the secret and why it impassions. There is no privileged access to a *hyperousios*, beyond the name of God, to some deep truth that arrests the play of traces in the text. There is nothing beneath the surface of the text—*scriptura et traditio*—or the trace that is left in a text that is tormented and disturbed by the desire to efface itself before the wholly other. That secretless secret is a matter of permanent provocation, and it is necessary to talk about it. How can we avoid it? It drives us mad and fills us with passion.

Three Ways to Avoid Speaking

In the second half of "How Not to Speak: Denials," Derrida locates negative theology along a line of three stages or paradigms of trying not to speak, of self-effacing traces: the Greek (Plato), the Christian (Pseudo-Dionysius and Meister Eckhart), and the Heideggerian (neither Greek nor Christian, or both), the Jewish and Islamic being noticeably absent. Here the privilege that he accords to the experience of place acquires its particular force (*Psy.*, 559/DNT, 96): what is taking place, he asks, in the self-effacing trace? What is the place such a trace takes?

(1) *Plato*. Of the Platonic paradigm Derrida says, there are "*two* movements or *two* tropics of negativity" (*Psy.*, 563/DNT, 101). The first move-

ment presses toward the most prestigious, the most reputable, the highest and most honorable place in philosophy, the idea of the Good (*agathon*), at whose name every philosophical knee must bend, that which Plato says is *epekeina tes ousias*, the place beyond being and essence. That famous expression, philosophy's first and most famous attempt to say what cannot be said, ignited the whole Neoplatonic tradition and has been revisited upon us in our so-called postmodern day, first, in Levinas's provocative title *Autrement qu'être, ou au-delà l'essence*, and then in Jean Luc Marion's "magnificent title" (*Psy.*, 540n1/DNT, 133n3) "*Dieu sans l'être.*"[31] It is here that negative theologians from Pseudo-Dionysius to Marion think that the biblical God left his trace in Greek philosophy. In the honorable company of Thomas Aquinas, Derrida holds that, however upwardly mobile this "hyperbolism"—this logic of the *hyper* or the *sur*, of eminence and sur-reality—may be, the Good nonetheless maintains at least an analogical community and continuity with Being and knowledge. For these are said to be its offspring, as the Good itself is said to be, unnameable though it be, their higher cause (*Psy.*, 564–65/DNT, 102). If the Good is neither Being nor knowledge, it is as their progenitor and the medium of their commerce a "third thing" (*triton genos*).

But there is another way to be *sans l'être*, beyond the border of being, one that "eludes all anthropo-theological schemes, all history, all revelation, all truth" (*Khôra*, 92/ON, 124), in which one is likewise forced to unsay what one says. This is the place called *khôra*.[32] *Khôra* is neither form (*idea*) nor sensible thing, but the place (*lieu*) in which the demiurge impresses or cuts images of the intelligible paradigms, the place which was already there, which, while radically heterogenous with the forms, seems to be as old as the forms. Plato has two different languages for relating the forms and *khôra*. When *khôra* is reappropriated by ontology and treated "analogically," in various and famous figures, likely stories meant to illustrate a philosophical point, "didactic metaphors" (*Khôra*, 21–22/ON, 92), then it is described as receptacle (*hypodokhe*), space, or matrix/mother. By being said to participate in *both* the sensible and the supersensible without quite being either, *khôra* is given a role interior to philosophy, assigned a proper place inside philosophy, and engenders a long history of philosophemes, as the matrix and mother of offspring like Aristotle's *hyle* and Descartes's *extensio*.

But in the other language, the one that is of greater interest to Derrida, *khôra* is an outsider, with no place to lay her/its head, in philosophy or in mythology, for it is the proper object of neither *logos* nor *mythos*. In this more negative trope, in this second tropic of negativity, there is there (*il y a là*) something that is said, very apophatically, to be *neither* being nor non-being, neither sensible nor intelligible, that is not analogous to either, and is unable to be hinted at by metaphors. *Khôra* is neither present nor absent, active nor passive, the Good nor evil, living nor nonliving (*Timaeus* 50c). Neither theomorphic nor anthropomorphic—but rather atheological and nonhuman—*khôra* is not even a receptacle, which would also be something that is itself inscribed within it. Nor is this discourse metaphoric, for it does not have to do with a sensible likeness of something supersensible, a relationship that is itself within *khôra* (*Psy.*, 567–68/DNT, 105–06). *Khôra* has no meaning or essence, no identity to fall back upon. She/it receives all without becoming anything, which is why she/it can become the subject of neither a philosopheme nor a mytheme (*Khôra*, 42–43/ON, 102). In short, the *khôra* is *tout autre*, very.

That is why, above all, we must avoid speaking well of *khôra*, avoid praising (and praying) to her/it as the giver of all good gifts, as the generous mother who engenders all. We must even avoid saying of her/it that *es gibt*, that she/it gives, that *khôra gives*. For that Heideggerianism sounds too beneficent and theological, like God giving. Unlike God, *khôra* cannot rise to the level of a command or promise or of a determinate giver; and unlike *Ereignis* there is nothing proper or properly giving about *khôra*. That is why Derrida refers to *khôra* as "this 'thing' that is nothing of that to which this 'thing' nonetheless seems to 'give place' (*donner lieu*)—without, however, this 'thing' ever *giving* anything" (*Khôra: Prière d'insérer*, 3/ON, xv; cf. *Psy.*, 568/DNT, 106). Even if, "perhaps, *khôra* gives place (*donner lieu*)," it does so "without the least generosity, either divine or human" (*Foi*, 86). *Khôra* is not even *ça* or *es* giving before all subjectivity. By letting take place (*avoir lieu*), she/it does not give or produce or create anything. If in giving place *khôra* gives at all, she/it gives without giving and so without producing debt, even as she/it receives without incurring debt. Of *khôra* we cannot say either that she/it "exists" or that "*es gibt*" *khôra*. *Il y a khôra*, but what there is (*il y a*) there (*là*) does not exist. *Il y a khôra* but this *il y a*

> . . . gives nothing in giving place or in giving to think, whereby it will be risky to see in it the equivalent of an *es gibt*, of the *es gibt* which remains without a doubt implicated in every negative theology, unless it is the *es gibt* which always summons negative theology in its Christian history. (*Khôra*, 30/ON, 96)

Without essence, nature, or identity, she/it is radically atheological, a-donational—and hence the only gift, if there were one, which is given without debt and exchange—and about her/it "there is neither negative theology nor thought of the Good, of the One, or of God beyond Being" (*Prière d'insérer*, 4/ON, xvi). *Khôra* is not even a third kind, because it is not a kind, a *genos*, at all but is radically singular, as if she/it were a singular individual with a proper name—"Who are you, *Khôra*?" (*Khôra*, 63/ON, 111). (*Bonjour!*)

§3. Affirmation at the Limits

How to speak of *khôra*? How not to? Derrida writes:

> In this context, the singularity that interests me is that the impossibility
> of speaking of it and giving it a proper name, far from reducing it to
> silence, dictates an obligation by its very impossibility: it is necessary (*il
> faut*) to speak of it and there is a rule for that. (*Psy.*, 569/DNT, 107)

We look for something that, "beyond all given philosophemes, has nevertheless left its trace in language" (*Psy.*, 569/DNT, 107), a word (*khôra*)
that already existed in the Greek language, the only recourse Plato had.
The resources of the Greek language were marked by the unheard trace
that promises nothing, that is inscribed in Greek and other languages
(*Psy.*, 568–69/DNT, 106–08). So *khôra* is a good word, a good *atheological*
word, as opposed to the theological name, the name of God, whose singularity comes of being marked by the unheard trace which calls us into
language.

If Levinas thinks to find a Greek echo of a very theological *tout autre* in
the *epekeina tes ousias*, Derrida seeks out an alternate, outlying, atheological, desert site in *khôra*. The otherness of the *khôra*—the "barren, radically
nonhuman, and atheological character of this 'place'"—is something "irreducibly other," and in "a certain manner" it is "wholly other." But this
tout autre does not go under the name of God, is not an event or promise
or gift, and has nothing to do with negative theology—although its very
barrenness obliges us to speak of it as if it were *the* Wholly Other that
theology calls God, the very same.

Il y a là, there is there something that is nearly nothing, so void and
devoid of content as not even to be a container, something, which is not
a thing, that is just there, *là*, already there, only there, *a* there, *the* there,
Khôra, capitalized and like a proper name; something, which is not a thing,
of which we cannot say a thing, so that the discourse about it must turn
itself into a barren desert, into ash. *Il y a là cendre.*

There is an interesting fluctuation or undecidability between the two
tropics of negativity, between the discourse about *khôra* and the kenotic,
self-emptying desertification of apophatic theology. What takes place in
this discourse about a desert, about a barren and naked place, a pure
taking place, an empty place? God or *khôra*? What is the wholly other (if
we may, *quia absurdum est*, ask such a question): God or *khôra*? What do I
love when I love my God, God or *khôra*? How are we to decide? Do we
have to choose? What takes place in this barren place, this desert, this
no-place in which nothing positive, predicative, or entitative takes place,
this withering, radically dis-placing place? Deprived of its ousiological
assurances, speaking in its other, less assured voice, apophatic theology
records the traces of a certain taking place of the trace, of a response to
the wholly other, which bears testimony, witness, like a martyr, to the

inescapable trace, to the solicitation of and by the wholly other that the I cannot have invented (*Psy.*, 570/DNT, 108), which is inscribed in the trace, even if, especially if, only to efface its very inscription, to turn itself into ashes, into a bare taking place, a desert place. Ashes and ashes, abyss and abyss, God and *Khôra* (like a proper name).

(2) *Pseudo-Dionysius.* Derrida wants to know about the commerce, the path, the "passage," what passes between (*que se passe-t-il*) *khôra* and the God of negative theology (*Psy.*, 569–70/DNT, 108). But surely that is an impassible passage, a path without passage, an *aporia*. The obvious, well-known, classical passage, the high road that has always been taken, is between *agathon* and the God beyond or without being. That high road is the link between the most honorable fathers the West has (un)known, between Plato and Christian patrology. But that is the high road of a high ousiology, the assured path provided by the *hyperousios*, the well-rounded circular path of *aletheia*, whereas Derrida wants to know about the desert, about those disreputable desert fathers with a lean and hungry look.

(*Saint Jacques*, Derrida the Desert Father! An anchorite, an an-khora-ite! [*Foi*, 11.] When you went out into the desert, what did you expect to find there?)

The *khôra* has none of the generosity and goodness of the God whom Dionysius praises, the God to whom he prays; *khôra* does not give or promise. So what dominates Dionysius's works, despite their apophatic "rigor," is not *khôra* but *agathon*, the "affirmative theologemes [that] celebrate God as the Good, the intelligible Light, even the Good 'beyond all light'" (*Psy.*, 571/DNT, 109), the object of a *hyper-eros* beyond amorous *eros*. What keeps Dionysius's discourse safe, what guides it through the aporia of the desert, is *prayer*, the prayer and praise he steadily directs toward the hyperousios. Prayer is not an adornment, a separable preamble, an accessory, but the very thing that allows Dionysius to keep his head, that allows his apophatic, kenotic, self-emptying discourse to reach its destination and not to end up *destinerrant*. Dionysius does not get lost in the desert.

Of prayer, (Saint) Jacques has two things to say—he will have a good deal more to say in *Circumfession*—both perhaps slightly sinful. (a) Every prayer is addressed to the other as other, any other, no matter who—"*for example*—I will say, at the risk of shocking—*God*" (*Psy.*, 572/DNT, 110), the shock being that I could pray to others, to you, for example, to be patient; or, an even greater shock, when we pray to God, for example, it might be that we are praying to someone else, and I say this without even succumbing to the temptation to say "preying on" someone else. Prayer is sent to the other and supplicates the other to give his presence; it is purely performative, a *dire* not a *dit*, to God (*à Dieu*) not about God.

(b) But prayer contains another element, of encomium or praise, which not only speaks *to* God, but *of* God, so that prayer preserves a relationship with a predicative content, a constative. Dionysius opens *The Mystical Theology* by saying (writing, praying) "Oh Trinity beyond being" (*Trias hyperousie*).[33] That is not an accessory but an essential operation, directing the discourse to a You, to the Other, as Hyperousios, in a supplication of God, closely akin to praise. The encomium predicatively determines the prayer, making it Christian prayer, directed to a Trinity and hyperousios (which clearly would not be ingredient in the prayers and tears of Jacques Derrida). Pseudo-Dionysius is trying to speak well (*eulegein*) of God even as he understands that this is a "gift" *from* God. God is the Cause who provokes or orders speech, who gives the gift of speech, even as God is also what is promised to this speech, the "gift of the gift." After opening *The Mystical Theology* with a prayer, Dionysius then cites or mentions the prayer he has just prayed, and then makes an aside or apostrophe to Timothy.[34] This little aside to Timothy is also quite essential, and what is actually behind the text, since it would not be necessary to write to God, to put one's prayer in the mail to God, even if we knew his address, since God already knows whatever Pseudo-Dionysius has on his mind. An analogous structure is also found in Augustine's *Confessions* (cf. *Sauf* 21– 24/*ON*, 38–39), *cur confitemur Deo scienti*: why do we confess to God who knows everything already?, a conundrum which also draws Derrida's attention in *Circumfession*. This prayer is thus thoroughly inscribed and textualized, woven together of a prayer, a mention, and an apostrophe. Dionysius is not only writing but praying as he writes, not only praying but writing as he prays. *The Mystical Theology* is both text and prayer, *ratio et oratio*.

Dionysius's apophaticism has not lost its way or its destination, is not *destinerrant*, but is more or less safely inscribed in a circle originating from and returning to "God," the saving name, the giver of all good gifts, the grammatical mark of which is *prayer*. Even when apophatic theology seems to gravitate close to saying *khôra*, when it speaks of formlessness, it means the hyperbolic giver of forms "beyond" all forms. That keeps it safe from the abyss of *khôra*, from getting lost in the desert. It must go into this desert place to find God, that is its *invention de tout autre*, but it goes forth and comes back guided by prayer; prayer is its desert guide. Even its darkest nights are black with the light beyond light. Even if it seems lost, even if it seems abandoned by God, still it is by God that it is abandoned. "My God, My God, why have You abandoned me?" is still a prayer to God who, thus far, has not abandoned us. "Lord, I do believe, help thou my unbelief" is still prayer, still belief.

But the question posed by deconstruction is this: to what extent does negative theology succeed in making itself safe from *khôra*, within which it, negative theology—any theology, any discourse—would be inscribed? For what is emerging (*donner lieu*) or taking place (*avoir lieu*) in *khôra* is the "spacing" or the "interval" within which things find their place (*Khôra*,

92/ON, 125), "the very spacing of de-construction" (*Sauf*, 103/ON, 80), which makes *khôra* sound like an apophatic name, a surname, for *différance*. What else is the desert *khôra* for Derrida than a nameless name for the desert of *différance*, of the trace, which is the constant companion of apophaticism? Does not the "ankhoral religion" (cf. *infra*, §17) of *khôra* haunt negative theology like a specter, hover over it like a desert mirage? Does not the aporia of the desert inhabit apophaticism from within, structurally, disturbing it from within?

(3) *Heidegger*. The third phase of trying not to speak discussed by Derrida is Heidegger's attempt to avoid saying Being by crossing it out as soon as he said it. All that we need point out here is that Heidegger, too, is not lost or *destinerrant*, but has the strongest sense of destiny and how it can be fulfilled, and the strongest sense of a giving that gives with a certain generosity. Derrida is content to point out that Heidegger's texts too, like Plato's, differentiate themselves from genuine "theology" (as opposed to metaphysical "theiology") because they remove themselves from "the movement of faith" (*Psy.*, 593–94/DNT, 130). "If faith summoned me in this manner," Heidegger wrote, "I would close down shop."[35] Like Plato, Heidegger is not praying.

But should we not say, Derrida suggests, that there is a certain reverence for prayer in the fact that Heidegger and Plato do not pray in their philosophical treatises? Does not Matthew have Jesus tell the disciples that when they pray they should pray in secret, not like hypocrites whose public prayer lets everyone see how holy they are? But can a prayer really escape all publicity? Can it escape writing and inscription, the structural possibility of being written and repeated? Is prayer distorted or constituted as prayer by being written? Would Derrida himself ever be able to avoid going public with his prayers? Would that be pharisaical? Derrida concludes:

> Perhaps there would be no prayer, no pure possibility of prayer, without what we glimpse as a menace or as a contamination: writing, the code, repetition. . . . If there were a purely pure experience of prayer, would one need religion and affirmative or negative theologies? Would one need a supplement of prayer? But if there were no supplement, if quotation did not bend prayer, if prayer did not bend, if it did not submit to writing, would a theiology be possible? Would a theology be possible? (*Psy.*, 594–95/DNT, 131)

A purely pure prayer would not be prayer but union and it would have nothing to supplicate, no promise of presence to fulfill; it would replace prayer with presence, for after the prayer for presence is answered, as St. Thomas saw, there would be nothing left to do but die. Pure life is pure death. A purely pure prayer would be deadly, and would not need or even tolerate religion or its scriptures, institutions, theology kataphatic or apophatic, or even, "at the limit" any determinable faith (*Sauf*, 86/ON, 71). Short of death, while we are still living on, there is always already the trace, the play of the trace, within which prayer inscribes its figure. Once inscribed, prayer exposes itself to repetition, to empty rote or enthusiastic reenactment, to ritualistic ceremony or to a daily rhythm of prayerful life. Those are structurally ingredient possibilities within prayer, within the play of the trace, without which we would be left without a prayer.

I TRUST NO TEXT THAT IS NOT IN SOME WAY
CONTAMINATED WITH NEGATIVE THEOLOGY, AND EVEN
AMONG THOSE TEXTS THAT APPARENTLY DO NOT HAVE,
WANT, OR BELIEVE THEY HAVE ANY
RELATION WITH THEOLOGY IN GENERAL.
(PSY., 81/DNT, 309–10)

GO THERE WHERE YOU CANNOT GO,
TO THE IMPOSSIBLE,
IT IS INDEED THE ONLY WAY OF GOING OR COMING.
(SAUF, 94/ON, 75)

§4. Save the Name, Wholly Other: Toward a General Apophatics

Saving the Name of God

The *tout autre*, on Derrida's telling, is everybody's business, a matter of general interest which belongs to a generalized apophatics. That is why, however dutifully we have been instructed in the *odium theologiae*, which in many quarters goes hand in hand, nose in nose, with an *odium decon-structionis*, we must learn to read apophatic theologians. Negative theology is an old and venerable form of heterogeneity, an ancient and complex tradition—"a memory, an institution, a history, a discipline. It is a culture, with its archives and its tradition" (*Sauf*, 53/ON, 54). We must learn to "translate" negative theology (*Sauf*, 38–40/ON, 46–48), even if we are not Christian, even if we do not belong to the tradition or "community" (a word Derrida "never much liked") of any of the great monotheistic filiations that owe everything to Abraham, the father of us all. Even if the constancy that the name of God supplies goes under other names for us, even then, especially then, we must learn to translate negative theology. For the very thing that localizes negative theology and assigns it to its

proper place also dislocates it from that place and "*engages* it in a movement of universalizing translation" (*Sauf*, 71/ON, 63). Who would trust a
discourse whose steel has not been tempered by negative theology, that
has not learned a thing or two about the *tout autre*?

That work of saving the name of God and of negative theology itself for
everybody is the task of *Sauf le nom* (1993). Nobody is to be left out or
excommunicated from this saving name or told it is a secret they are not
entitled to share. Everybody, not just Jacques, can and should be both accused
of and/or congratulated for being a negative theologian, so that nothing can
be trusted that tries to get along without (*sans*) negative theology, that is not
at least "contaminated by negative theology" (*Sauf*, 81/ON, 69). *Sauf le nom*
turns on the paradoxes of universality and community, trying at once to lift
the idiom of negative theology up beyond the private interests of a closed
circle, but without turning it into a hegemonic universal, an *Aufhebung*, a
universal community and metalanguage. Perhaps we should say in the spirit
of a certain circumcision, he wants to find the cut in negative theology that
opens it to others, the wound that will not let it close over.

Sauf le nom, first published in a shorter English translation entitled
"Post-Scriptum: Aporias, Ways and Voices" (DNT, 283ff.) as a response
made to a 1991 colloquium on "Derrida and Negative Theology" at which
he was not personally present, is a dialogue or polylogue of several un-
identified voices. The expanded French text (1993) was supplemented by
a series of insertions, sometimes whole pages, sometimes a phrase in the
middle of a sentence, each one of which adds something, true to its name,
about *saving the name* (cf. *Sauf*, 61–62/ON, 58 and DCR, 302; *Sauf*, 111–
13/ON, 84–85 and DNT, 321). A four-page insert that accompanies the
book—"please (I pray you) insert": *prière d'insérer* (is that a command? a
law? an invitation? a prayer?)—links *Sauf le nom* with *Passions* and *Khôra*
as a triptych on "the *question of the name*" (*Sauf*, Prière d'insérer, 1/ON,
xiv), three texts that were subsequently gathered together in one volume
only in the English translation *On the Name* (ON).

In *Sauf le nom*, Derrida returns to the thematic of *sauf* that first drew his
attention in "*Pas*" (1976), a study to be examined below (§6), which pursued the dynamics of *sauf, pas, sans,* and *viens* in Blanchot:

> —What does *sauf* mean?
> —It is a powerful and elusive word, more or less than a word, neither
> adjective nor preposition, both the one and the other, at times almost a
> name. (*Parages*, 85)

And again:

> I follow—elsewhere—the internal rhythm of *sauf*, the law of its multipli-
> cation and its contamination, always undamaged and always altered, its
> pulse resonating across an immense corpus: attribute without subject,

preposition with no one in charge (*prépose*), word making an exception, word without word, without language. (*Parages*, 104)

In accordance with this law of multiplying the voices of *sauf*,[36] I offer here a sampler of its dissemination into prepositional (save/except), adjectival (safe), and verbal (to save) operations: Saving (*sauver*) the name of God by keeping it safe (*sauf*); sacrificing the name of God precisely in order to save it. Sacrifice everything, save or except (*sauf*) the name of God. Save everything about God (keep God safe) save (except) the name of God, lest it become an idol that blocks our way. The thing itself slips away leaving nothing behind, save the name. Save the name of God for everybody, not just the faithful in the determinable faiths (cf. *Sauf*, 61–62/ON, 58; ON, xii–xiii). *Sauf* plays a saving game, a game of salvation, of the "hope of salvation, of the economy of 'being saved'" (DM, 83–84/GD, 87).

Derrida begins with the first and dominant sense of saving, which is also the leading voice of negative theology, where saving is inscribed in the classical economy of salvation, the circle of losing-in-order-to-save. Everything that happens in negative theology—this "sweet rage against language," this "jealous anger of language within itself and against itself," this "passion that leaves the mark of a scar in that place where the impossible takes place" (*Sauf*, 63–64/ON, 59–60), this wounded, breached, auto-deconstructing writing—all this has an affirmative end. This rigorous kenosis, this language that attempts to empty itself of content, to deprive itself of the very name of God around which it is organized, to turn itself into a kind of *théologie blanche*,[37] is undertaken just in order to respect the otherness of God and to save the name it crosses out. That is the double bind of apophaticism, its effort both to negate the name of God and to negate everything except (save, *sauf*) the name of God, the double bind of a discourse that has been wounded by the logic of the impossible:

> As if it was necessary both to save (*sauver*) the name and to save everything except (*fors*) the name, *save the name* (*sauf le nom*), as if it was necessary to lose the name in order to save what bears the name or that towards which one is borne across the name. (*Sauf*, 61/ON, 58)

As an economy of sacrifice, a logic of the most classical asceticism, negative theology dies in order to live (live on, *survie*, hyper-live), lives without altogether avoiding dying, deprives itself of what it most desires, empties itself of its richest treasure, losing, striking out, the name of God, but all this precisely in order to save it. By giving God a name we give the gift of what we do not have. For by naming we risk binding what is named, enslaving it, prescribing to it "an assigned passion" (*Sauf*, 112/ON, 84–85), which is why God himself "slips away" (*dérobe*) from every name we give to Him—like the "thing itself" in the final page of *Le voix et le phénomène* (VP, 117/SP, 104).

To pursue a Husserlian analogy, the name of God in negative theology is like an arrow—like Husserl's intentional arrow—aimed at God, pointed toward God but never reaching its intentional object, never reaching fulfillment. The arrow is "everything save (*sauf*) what it is aimed at" and fails to reach, so that the target remains safe (*sauf*) (*Sauf*, 67–68/ON, 62). The name "God" is an empty intention, a merely indicative arrow, an arrow that points, like a Buddhist finger pointed toward the moon, not an arrow that wounds, not a weapon. Indeed, we find it necessary to lay down our arms (*Sauf*, 91–92/ON, 74) in order to keep God safe, in order to love (PdS, 176–77/*Points*, 166). The whole multifarious tradition of negative theologies is like a sky filled with arrows aimed at a target they cannot reach but toward which they all silently, lovingly fly. The real wound would be inflicted if the name of God were actually to hit its mark and so to wrench God into manifestation, thus putting a violent end to God's absolute heterogeneity and holy height. The only way to keep God's alterity safe is to save Him from the cutting tips and incisions of the accusing *kategoriai* of kataphatic theology, from ensnarement by some name. *Sauf le nom de Dieu*: safe the name of God is when it names everything save God. Safe God is when we know nothing of God, save the name.

That is why negative theology has recourse to the Platonic, Neoplatonic, and Plotinian movement of the *epekeina tes ousias* which carries God safely off, in a hyperbolic movement, well beyond the reach of the arrows of "reference" that are aimed His way (*Sauf*, 73–74/ON, 65). That gives us another way to read the beautiful cross that Jean-Luc Marion[38] puts over the name of God, by means of which he would strike it out. This cross keeps God safe, like crossed swords or arrows that defy anyone who would dare trespass. Only a god can save us, but only a god whom negative theology keeps safe. Outside the saving gestures of negative theology there is no salvation.

Hence, this failure of knowledge, the knowing which un-knows the un-known God is a sweeping success that keeps God safe. That is why Angelus Silesius sings of the "The Unknowable God" (*Der unerkandte Gott*), upon which Derrida comments:

> —[O]f him there is nothing said that might hold
> —Save his name (*Sauf son nom*)
> —Save the name (*Sauf le nom*) which names nothing that holds, not even a *Gottheit*, nothing whose withdrawal (*dérobement*) does not carry away every phase that tries to measure itself against him. "God" "is" the name of this bottomless collapse, of this endless desertification of language. (*Sauf*, 56/ON, 56)

In naming the desert of the Godhead, negative theology becomes itself a desert, a desertification, a kenosis, or self-emptying, which empties itself of every predicate or attribute of God, every accusative category, and this because God is *not* whatever we say God "is." Praying God to rid us of God, apophatic theology empties itself of God, because God is the *Gottheit* beyond God, and then of the Godhead, because God is an *Über-Gottheit.* Yet all this is one great saving ascetic gesture. For God is safe in the bottomless abyss of nothingness, this desert place, leaving but His trace on language, burning and scarring language as He leaves the world, which is the event of language named negative theology. *Il y a là cendres.* "God" "is" the name of this abyss. While wanting to become nothing, it is necessary, *il faut,* that the name of God remain something, an imprint left on the scarred body of language. The name of God is a trace of "an internal onto-logico-semantic auto-destruction" (*Sauf,* 55/ON, 55), i.e., of a certain desert.

This "paradoxical hyperbole" is under a "double bind": it cannot name what it must and most desires to name. But, in the "economy" of negative theology, the double bind—it cannot win—also means it cannot lose; its failure spells success. The double bind is a double save. That is why Derrida says there are two voices (at least!) in these aphorisms of Angelus Silesius (and the same is true of Meister Eckhart and Pseudo-Dionysius), which constitute a certain "uprooting rooting," giving it Christian roots even as it pulls its roots up (*Sauf,* 76/ON, 66). The several voices of negative theology are brought back into monological unison, encircling the expenditure of negations in a higher affirmation. Derrida settles himself inside this plurivocity and from there offers this gloss.

There is, on the one hand, a voice of *hypercritique,* in which nothing seems assured, neither philosophy nor theology, neither science nor common sense, neither the church nor tradition, a voice of nothing but the emptiest, most desert-like intentions. Yet, at the same time, there is the most assured *authority* which speaks from out of the element of the secret and the paradox, from out of the heart of truth, as Eckhart would say, with a surplus and surcharge, a plenitude of intentional fulfillment, which "saturates intention with intuition," as Marion so powerfully puts it.[39] (Too powerfully, I would say.) Two voices (at least): one of desertification, the other of plenitude; one of the most arid empty intention, the other of the most lush overflowing hyperfulfillment; one a virgin, the other a mother; one of desiccated, desert aridity, the other of an intuitive flood; one of meontic and meontological desolation, the other of hyperousiological saturation.

In one voice—back to Husserl; is Husserl one of these anonymous voices in the dialogue? (cf. *Sauf,* 78/ON, 67)—a negativity and suspension of theses which ruins its philosophemes and theologemes, engaging in parricide and self-uprooting, a reduction that reduces everything to ruins, a de-position of the every ontical assurance and positional certitude. But, on the other hand, this hyperbole is meta-metaphysical, hyper-thetic beyond all theses, super-positional, loyal to ontotheology, countersigning theology, rendering the truth of the name, giving the name back to its truth.

In the long run, the identifiable traditions and discourses of Christian apophatic theology are loyal to the thing itself and its Truth. Apophatic theology in the long run is not mad. Its self-emptying kenosis is a witness and a martyr (*témoigner: Sauf*, 80/ON, 68) which gives itself to "referential transcendence," to *die Sache Selbst*, to the truth at any price:

> . . . to the thing itself (*la chose même*) such as it ought to be named by the name, *that is to say, beyond the name*. It saves the name (*sauf le nom*). (*Sauf*, 80/ON, 68)

So the double bind of negative theology is a double save. When negative theology says that God is beyond every name we give to Him, that is a way of saying and saving "God such as he is," beyond all idols and images, a way of "respond[ing] to the true name of God, to the name to which God responds and corresponds." Every time negative theology engages in negation, "it does so in the name of a way of truth," of a goddess whose name is *aletheia*, under the protective auspices of a truthful and authoritative name (*Sauf*, 82/ON, 69).

But that is only one of negative theology's voices, for *Sauf le nom* is not intended by Derrida as an *epoche* of negative theology, as a way of reducing it to silence, of stilling its voice, as if it were a nemesis with which he has lost his patience over the years, but rather as a way of saving negative theology. Derrida means to let himself be addressed by the name of God and to that end to see whether and how negative theology can be translated, whether and how it overflows its boundaries so that it is something more than Greco-Christian Neoplatonism, something more universal— but without becoming a hegemonic universal, a community of fusion (*Sauf*, 38/ON, 46). Traditional studies of great Christian neoplatonic mystics, most famously Meister Eckhart, grappling with a similar duality, have noticed an important tension between the Christian element in these works and another element, more transcultural, that tends to uproot itself from Christianity. For example, if, as Eckhart says, the Father bears his Son in the soul in a purely inner process, why would it have been necessary for the Son/*logos* to have become flesh in historical time, in Jesus of Nazareth? Why would there be any need for an Incarnation or a Resurrection or—the Vatican did not fail to take note of this point—for the Vatican?[40] However Christian their formulations, writers such as Eckhart and Angelus Silesius seem eager, as Derrida says, to assert their independence of the contingencies of the history of Christianity—as if there were only *one*—of its doctrines and dogmas, of the historicality of the New Testament, in order to effect a kenosis that would free them from dogma and doctrine "and at the limit from every *determinable* faith" ("*de toute foi déterminable"*) (*Sauf*, 86/ON, 71 and DNT, 311). Interestingly, Derrida added *déterminable* in italics in the Galilée edition—although the English translator, John Leavey, missed it, leaving the original "from all faith" unrevised—because Derrida does not want to be free from faith itself, from *all* faith: *il faut croire*.

That is a telling point. Suppose negative theology were to fulfill its promise—*per impossibile*, for it belongs to the very possibility of this promise to be impossible (MpPdM, 104–05/MfPdM, 101). Suppose its intentions were to be "saturated" with intuition. Suppose it were to become what it says it is, at least in the more assured and self-rooting voice that Derrida describes, the authoritative one which speaks out of the heart of truth, that is carried along by the plenitudinous rush, the self-fulfilling flood of intuition. Were that to happen there would no longer be faith, no longer be anything through a *glas* darkly, *sans savoir, sans avoir, sans voir* (*Parages*, 25), but knowledge, face to face *now* (not then). Negative theology would have managed to lift itself up into a pure presence above time and history, above language and the play of the trace, above the mediation of the trace and *différance*. Now apart from the fact that such an excessively hyperlogocentric hyperessentialism is incoherent, since it will have already begun to speak in language and in time, it is also something that lends itself to a consummately dangerous political and ecclesiastical absolutism, to a politics of negative theology that is a threat to everyone, from which Marion does not seem to me immune.[41] Then negative theology would not save the name of God, or its own name, but would endanger everybody with a dangerous absolutism, for which, alas, history, both past and present, supplies too many examples. Were apophatic theology ever to fulfill its promise, it would have no need of faith or the scriptures, of time or history; it would run on its own and be neither Christian nor Jewish nor faith, having run itself off the road of language and history.

So, by returning apophatic theology to the trace, i.e., to the fold of language and history, deconstruction returns negative theology to the fold of faith, the effect of which is to diminish the danger of what Derrida is calling here the *"determinable"* faiths. For determinable faiths—as the history of all the fundamentalisms, Jewish, Islamic, and Christian, instruct us—are uncommonly dangerous to everybody's health, that of their own members as of everyone else, a threat to everyone's safety, not just Palestinians, or Salmon Rushdie, or a woman's right to choose, and this precisely because they forget that they are faith and not intuitive knowledge. That is why the "political" dimension of theology, negative or positive, is never an addendum, never a little afterthought, but goes to the heart of Derrida's concern with theology or with any powerful discourse. Theology is political all the way down. What is not? (MpPdM, 137/MfPdM, 142–43.) Derrida differentiates the "determinable" faiths, which are always dangerous, in order to differentiate their triumphalism from faith "itself," the *indeterminate* faith and open-ended hope in what is coming, in the incoming of the *tout autre*, the passion for which is what deconstruction is all about, what deconstruction "is."

Deconstruction provides the condition for any determinable faith (and the same is true of art, or architecture, or law, or whatever you need), but only a quasi-condition, not a full-fledged condition like a classical *a priori*. For the condition it provides is so shifting that instead of steadying faith (or the law or whatever, *n'importe*), deconstruction exposes faith to indefinite recontextualization, substitution, and translation. It does not so much surround faith with a horizon, or protect it with a shield and crossed arrows, as it leaves it vulnerable and exposed to multiple interpretation, to a multiplicity with which it is the business of faith to cope. That means the believer must keep the faith, fight the good fight, and that faith must be its own shield, fend for itself, and save the name of God. In that sense, deconstruction cannot quite save it. Deconstruction is not the business as usual of philosophy providing foundations and making things safe, of saving the name of Art, Truth, Being, the Good, and God, of the "philosophy of this" or the "philosophy of that," of God, for example.

Translating the Name of God

Accordingly, there is something inscribed within the mysticism of Eckhart and the mystical poetry of Silesius that translates them, carries them beyond their Greco-Christian site, in order to say something of general interest, even if one is not a believer, a Christian, say, or even a theist. What interests Derrida himself, Jacques Derrida, and also deconstruction, is that the name of God is the name of the "wholly other" (*tout autre*) and that the *tout autre* is nobody's proper name, not exclusively saved for Christian Neoplatonism, or for Judaism, or for any "*determinable* faith." Indeed to a great extent it must be saved from them, for they are dangerous. *Tout autre* is not an *appellation contrôllée*.

The *tout autre* is not the private property of the determinable faiths, not a proper name over which they alone, or they in particular, have any proprietary rights. Inasmuch as the *tout autre* is *tout autre*, it is certainly wholly other than anything that the determinable faiths determine it to be, anything they say about its being, or nonbeing or hyperbeing. They do not own a copyright on this name. The name belongs in the public domain; it is not theirs. Indeed, it is absolutely necessary, *il faut*, to save the indeterminacy of the *tout autre* in order to keep it safe, so that it remains, as Heidegger said of death, which is certainly *tout autre*, "certain but indefinite" (we will return to this in §6).

That is because—and everything turns on this—"every other is wholly other" (*tout autre est tout autre*) (*Sauf*, 92/ON, 74).[42] What negative theology says of God can be said with a certain "serene indifference," a kind of *Gelassenheit*, about anything or anybody whatsoever, no matter who or what (*n'importe*, *Sauf*, 90/ON, 73). In the French edition Derrida inserts the following crucial remark about this *Gelassenheit*. If we speak of *Gelassenheit* here, he says, why not speak of love, so that saying *tout autre est tout autre* would be a way of loving and letting others be, the "hospitality" of a "passage to the other"? After all, Meister Eckhart said that in its highest reaches *Gelassenheit* is love, that love is "without why" and love is "letting the other be."[43] Derrida expands upon the theme of love in the longest insert to the Galilée edition:

> But why not recognize there love itself, that is, this infinite renunciation which in a certain way *surrenders to the impossible*? (*Sauf*, 91/ON, 74)

"*Se rend à*," "to give oneself back," to surrender, to the impossible, "to the other, this is the impossible" (*Sauf*, 91/ON, 74). To surrender to the other, to love the other, means to go over to the other without passing the threshold of the other, without trespassing on the other's threshold. To love is to respect the invisibility of the other, to keep the other *safe*, to surrender one's arms to the other but without defeat, to put the crossed swords or arrows over the name of the other. To love is to give oneself to the other in such a way that this would really be giving and not taking, a gift, a way of letting the other remain other, that is, be loved, rather than a stratagem, a ruse of jealousy, a way of winning, *eine vergiftete Gift*. Then it would turn out that the passion for the impossible would be love.

The other is *any* other, God or someone or something else. So love means love the other as other, any other, any wholly other, *n'importe*, going under any name whatsoever.

That would start to bring Derrida's secret in line with my favorite line from St. Augustine (contributing still further to a certain Jewish Augustinianism that is slowly being forged/faked in these pages), love and do what you will, *dilige et quod vis fac*, whatever (*quod*), any other, *n'importe*, even the impossible, a line which is so powerful that we can readily forgive Augustine for having invented original sin, which is an other we did not need invented. (Go and invent sin no more; invent no more sin; come and invent something other than sin, wholly other.)

When Angelus Silesius says "Go, where you cannot go," that for Derrida is a discourse on loving the other, on *the* impossible, on the impossible place, like a desert or a *khôra*. In the Galilée edition Derrida inserted this remark:

> Go (*Rends-toi*) there where you cannot go, to the impossible, that is at bottom the only way of going or coming. To go there where it is possible, that is not to surrender (*se rendre*), rather, it is to be there already and to be paralyzed in the in-decision of the non-event. (*Sauf*, 94/ON, 75)

It is only when you give yourself to, surrender to, and set out for the wholly other, for the impossible, only when you go where you cannot go, that you are really on the move. Anything less is staying stuck in place, with the same. Going where you cannot go, going somewhere impossible, constitutes true movement, genuine coming and going, since going where it is *possible* to go is only a pseudo-motion, the "paralysis" of a "non-event" (*Sauf*, 94/ON, 75). When you go to the possible nothing much happens. The only event, the only e-venting, or in-venting, is to go to the impossible. If the possible spells paralysis, the impossible is an impassioning impetus. If the possible means the paralysis of the programmable, the impossible is the passion of decision.[44]

One is strongly reminded of Kierkegaard's interpretation of *metanoia* in the "Interlude" in the *Philosophical Fragments*, where this utter change of heart is the only real *kinesis* or motion under the sun (or beyond it for that matter), for *metanoia* is a motion from nothing to being, from sin to grace.[45] That movement *ex nihilo* was of course just what the Greeks thought was impossible, which it is, which is why it is our passion, what we really desire, what we affirm, why it is so necessary. It is *the* impossible, for with God, with any *tout autre*, *the impossible*, the *tout autre*, is just what happens (*événement*), otherwise nothing happens (*inavènement*). For an event occurs when something happens (*événement*), something new, something different, a real motion, not the paralysis of standing always in the same place. Kierkegaard and Derrida in Kierkegaard's wake are invoking a biblical model of the "new," the psalmist's song *renovabimus faciem terrae*. To this Kierkegaard opposed philosophy's un-motions: Platonic recollection, which is a movement backwards, and hence a movement only in the sense that an army in full retreat may be said to be "on the move"; and the sham movement of the Hegelian *Aufhebung*, which is a movement that never takes a step forward, a purely logical and circular movement of appropriation, reminding us of a mime who gives us a remarkable impression of motion while never moving a single step forward. With Plato and Hegel, nothing happens, nothing radically new, just the paralyzing circulation of recollection and *Aufhebung*, of an *in-avènement*; and if time means the eventuation of something new, then the Greeks, as Kierkegaard said, lacked the idea of time. The one exception that Kierkegaard makes to this is Aristotle, where Kierkegaard thought to detect certain signs of life and movement, because Aristotle did the best he could to make time and motion respectable to the Greeks. Kierkegaard thus has in mind, as does Derrida, a movement that does not remain confined within an economy of the same, that overcomes the "paralysis" of the possible. Kierkegaard and Derrida describe the movements of the repetition that repeats forward, into something new, the movement of an unrestricted giving without reserve, of the gift, the *qualitative* leap, the leap into something *tout autre*, the leap into the impossible, the transformation, the motion of the event, of a new time, of time *simpliciter*, of *l'invention de l'autre*, the on-coming, the in-coming of something *tout autre*.[46]

Like deconstruction itself, this voice of negative theology has to do with an affirmation, a desire, a passion for the possibility of this impossibility:

> This "more," this beyond, this *hyper* (*über*) obviously introduces an abso-lute heterogeneity in the order and in the modality of the possible. The possibility of the impossible, of the "more impossible" that as such is also possible ("more impossible than the impossible"), marks an absolute interruption in the regime of the possible that nonetheless remains, if this can be said, in place. (*Sauf*, 32–33/ON, 43)

The *hyper* of God's hyper-nym introduces an absolute heterogeneity that interrupts the regime of the possible. *Das Überunmöglichste ist möglich*, Angelus Silesius says. To confine oneself to the possible is to remain within an economy of the "same" (*Psy.*, 60–62/RDR, 60–62). By the im-possible Derrida clearly does not mean impossible *stricto sensu*, the simple modal opposite of the possible, but the more-than-possible, the transgres-sion, the chance, the aleatory, the breach, the rupture, the passage to the limits, the *ébranler* and the *solicitation* of the same. The possible is not other, not other enough, not enough at all. The desire of deconstruction for the more-than-possible impossible is a passion that it shares with apophatic theology. Theology and deconstruction share a common passion and de-sire, a common *désir de Dieu* and *désir de l'impossible* and *amor dei* (a famous double genitive). The impossible is what gets both underway, impelling and impassioning them, setting them in motion, sparking Silesius's an-gelic peregrinations, even as deconstruction begins "by (*par*) the impossi-ble." Everything comes down to what is called the impossible, or *tout autre*, under whatever name it goes or comes, God, for example.

So the *via negativa* of Pseudo-Dionysius, Eckhart, and Angelus Silesius runs beyond the borders of Christian Neoplatonism, widened by a for-mula that is not a secret code but the opening of a cut that unlocks its general interest.

> The other, that is, God or no matter who, precisely, any singularity what-soever, as soon as every other is wholly other. For the most difficult, indeed the impossible, dwells there: there where the other loses his name or is able to change it in order to become no matter what other. (*Sauf*, 92/ON, 74)

The *tout autre*, the wholly other: God, for example, or any singularity whatever, no matter what. Like the singularity of an event whose unique-ness makes of each occurrence both an unprecedented first time and an unrepeatable last time: "Each time it is the event itself, a first time is a last time. Wholly other" (SdM, 31/SoM, 10). The wholly other is any singu-larity whatever, whoever, whose this-ness we cannot lift up, cannot generalize, cannot universalize, cannot formalize, any singularity which fixes us in this place so that we cannot look away, cannot look up to the *eidos* of which it would be "but an example," which would allow us to get on top of it, dominate it, enable us to envisage it instead of finding ourselves fixed by its gaze. Derrida here takes up a uniquely biblical sense of singularity, as opposed to a Greek sense of subsuming the less real particular under the truer universal. *Tout autre*—it does not matter what or who—*est tout autre.*

Derrida's formula, which is no hermeneutic key or a semantic secret, goes like this: wherever you read the name of God in negative theology, remember, whatever you believe, that is the name of the wholly other, and remember as you read that every other is wholly other. That is Derrida's way of saving the name of God, the way he proposes to translate negative theology. "[O]ne should say of no matter what or no matter whom what one says of God or some other thing" (*Sauf*, 90/ON, 73). Every singularity is a wholly other whose alterity should be respected, not assimilated to the same, not subsumed under the universal.

But this formula, *tout autre est tout autre*, the very tip of Derrida's stylus, the point of his interest in negative theology, goes hand in hand with what he calls "exemplarism" (*Sauf*, 95–96/ON, 76), which has to do with his taste for literature. For literature sets the problem of exemplarism in motion:

> Something of literature will have begun when it is not possible to decide whether, when I speak of something, I am indeed speaking of something (of the thing itself, this, for itself) or if I am giving an example, an example of something or an example of the fact that I can speak of something. . . . (*Pass.*, 89n12/ON, 142–43n14)

Something of literature will have begun when it is not possible to decide, *pace* Kant, whether Jesus is an example of the Moral Law, or whether the Moral Law is an example we learn from Jesus; when we cannot tell which way the mimesis goes, whether empirical actions imitate the Idea or whether Ideas imitate factical life (*Pass.*, 85–87n10/ON, 140–41n9). Something of literature will have begun when we cannot decide with assurance what is an example of what, whether justice is an example of God, for example, or whether God is an example of justice, for example. One can always make one name, even the name of God, an example of some other name, or even of the name in general. There is an endless substitutability and translatability among these names that neither Derrida nor deconstruction is authorized to stop. Neither Derrida nor deconstruction can save the name from this substitutability. The "other" is an example of what is named with the name of God; the name of God is an example of what is named by the "other." God is the exemplar of every "other," the other is the exemplar of God. When John says "God is love," "love" exemplifies what "God" means, but it is also true that "God" exemplifies what "love" means. Is God an example of justice, or justice of God? Does it matter?

It is in any case none of Jacques's business, nor of deconstruction's, to settle this one way or the other. That's your business. It is enough, more than enough, to incite the passion for the *tout autre*, which is to save the name of God.

That is why Derrida's quasi-principle of translatability is no definitive hermeneutic key. For keys turn locks in both directions, and this powerful little key, *tout autre est tout autre*, can lock theology up inside the walls of atheology as well as unlocking its doors to untheological readers. The last thing we want is to make this little shibboleth into a hermeneutic secret, which would put Derrida in the position of the Most High Hermeneut who holds the master key that unlocks the conundrums of negative theology and deconstructs its passion down into the death of God or Feuerbach or your mommy or whatever. God forbid. The idea behind deconstruction is to break all such locks, to unlock texts and institutions, beliefs and practices, not in such a way as to say that you cannot have such things, but only to say that you cannot have a lock on them. The idea behind deconstruction is to let the *tout autre* shimmer in all its a/theological undecidability, to let the translations run in both directions, in theological and atheological directions, without trying decisively to call a halt to the play. Translatability should be, *per impossibile*, like a river running in both directions at once, a flux of which even snooty old Heraclitus never dreamed. In the end, Derrida concludes, there is no end.

The translation of negative theology that interests him is the one whereby we are ourselves translated, carried over, into the desert by negative theology. The movement beyond the Greco-Christian site of negative theology oscillates between a pure formalism, an empty techno-scientific formalization of the language common to several traditions—a (badly done) comparative religion, e.g.—and a "hive of inviolable secrets" and untranslatable idioms. But Derrida's concern is with "something" which is neither the one nor the other, which is anterior to both, something which is not a thing, "something like an indeconstructible *khôra*," not because it is invulnerable to deconstruction but because it is "the very spacing of de-construction" (*Sauf*, 103/ON, 80). In the end we are translated to something that Derrida consistently shelters from translation, *khôra* (*Khôra*, 23–24/ON, 93). The desert *khôra* is the site where "negative theology" and its "analogates" happen, so that Derrida is more interested in the communication of negative theology with the Platonic *khôra* rather than with the *epekeina tes ousias* (cf. *Psy.*, 567–69/DNT, 105–07). That desert site is older than or prior to the local sites of Christian, Jewish, or Islamic apophaticism. There, there are cinders, the desert of a desire, the desire of a desert—"*desert* is the other name, if not the proper place, of desire" (*Sauf*, 103/ON, 80)—that is older even than the desert fathers. It is into that desert site that Derrida is carried by negative theology, over and beyond negative theology and its "analogues." In that desert we are all a little lost, straying beyond the reassuring economy of sacrifice, outside the circle of losing in order to save, wandering a little *destinerrant*, no less lost than safe.

The Politics of Translatability

The thesis of translatability in deconstruction does not say that everything can be translated but that translation cannot be stopped, that it is both necessary and impossible, necessary because impossible, and something we deeply love just because it is impossible (*Moscou*, 118–21). How could it be stopped, and why should we even want to stop it? Translatability is the slippage that is built right into things, but this slippage is productive, not a punishment, or at least it is a productive punishment. We are both summoned and consigned to continual translation, like the Shemites. To translate is to come to grips with untranslatability, with a singular idiom that you just have to learn to use and that you want to share. Deconstruction is a thesis about un/translatability, about the conditions of possibility of translation and about the impossibility of translation reaching closure, about what you gain and lose, when you translate. Whether or not deconstruction is on the side of God, it is clear that God is on the side of deconstruction, who intervened at a crucial moment in the construction of a famous tower, calling construction to a halt, disseminating Shemite tongues, and making translation necessary and impossible (*Psy.*, 203ff./DiT, 165ff.).

The saving gesture that deconstruction can extend to theology is tied up with Derrida's insistence that there can be no politics or law "without" (*sans*) negative theology, which also means without translatability (*Sauf*, 106/ON, 81).[47] Again it is a question of the two voices, two desires of negative theology (*Sauf*, 110/ON, 83–84). In one voice, negative theology gives comfort to an elitist law and politics of the esoteric secret from which everyone else is excluded—the "politics of sites (*lieux*)" (*Khôra*, 49/ON, 104), of authoritative and authorizing places—which is perhaps what happens historically in various mystical sects. But in its other voice, the one that deconstruction sets loose, there is an apophatic politics of the *tout autre*, of the "wholly other," where every other is wholly other. That releases a politics of the singularity of the other, of the "democracy to come," of the promise of a more radical democracy (*Sauf*, 108–09/ON, 83), a politics which keeps on saying that the other is not this or that, not I or we, not like us or anything that is privileged by the I or we, by my place. That is why one of the senses of *sauf le nom* is to save the name of the victim. The "absolute victim" is "a victim who cannot even protest," who is erased as a victim, his memory reduced to dust or "cinders," which is "a trope that comes to take the place of everything that disappears without leaving an identifiable trace," a trope for absolute disappearance. "The name is *necessary* (*Il faut le nom*), love consists perhaps in *sur-nommer*," in naming to excess, in lovingly nicknaming, in order to save the victim from the flames, even if we fail (PdS, 403–05 / *Points*, 389–91).

Derrida aims particularly at delimiting the hegemonic rule of a Christian Europe, of the privileged site of Greco-Euro-Christianity, of which the Pope is dreaming (*Sauf,* 99 / ON, 78),[48] which led the Pope, in his recent best-seller, to oppose Christianity to Buddhism as an "atheistic system."[49] The Pope's complaint about Buddhism means that Buddhists do not agree with the Pope about how to use the word God, which is their business; but it also means that the Pope does not admit that the name of God is translatable, and that in general the meaning of the name of God should be fixed by popes who are in charge of authorized translations, which is serious business.

Derrida's politics of translation aims at delimiting the hegemonic rule of a Christo-Euro-centric world, of a whole world translated into Europe's language, like the NATO world dreamt of by Rorty, who, whatever his views about the contingency of our vocabularies, thinks that everything should be translated into NATOese (minus the Christianity).[50] Deconstruction wants to find the way to a universal, international law (*Sauf,* 105–06 / ON, 81) that would not be co-opted by the special interests of the "super"-powers whose superiority carries them beyond, *super, hyper, au-delà*, the impoverished *ousia* of the third world. A democracy to come, a democracy without its current limitations, practical and conceptual, must pass through such aporias, so that we cannot define the politics and ethics to come any more than apophatic theology can define God. The paradox of passing through the aporias of negative theology—there is no going *without* the apophatic impasse—is just what makes clearing the way to a democracy to come interesting, since doing what is possible soon becomes tiresome.

Toward a Generalized Apophatics

I wish to conclude this discussion of Derrida and negative theology by suggesting what I will call a "generalized apophaticism" as the generalized truth or wider translatability of negative theology. This is what the learned unknowing called negative theology has always known, what it has to say, or un-say, in a generalized way, and why the passion that drives negative theology is a matter of general concern.

In my favorite book on Foucault, James Bernauer suggests the strategy of interpreting Foucault on the model of a negative theology, the result being that one would find in Foucault a certain apophatic anthropology.[51] Foucault does not advocate some positive, normative notion of the human in the "name" of which we can desire and should strive to effect "emancipation." But instead of seeing here the name of dark despair, Bernauer sees in Foucault the desire of the singular individual to twist free of normalizing standards in the name of something different. On Bernauer's accounting, Foucault says of human beings what Eckhart says of the divine being: whatever you say God is, that is what God is not; you cannot say what human beings *are* but only what they are not. They are not necessarily this or that, especially what is presently in place, heterosexuality being Foucault's favorite example of being the same while Foucault finds a heterology in homosexuality.

So to the *theologia negativa*, one could add a *anthropologia negativa*, an *ethica negativa, politica negativa*, where of the humanity, or the ethics, or the politics, or the democracy to come we cannot say a thing, except that they want to twist free from the regimes of presence, from the historically restricted concepts of humanity, ethics, and democracy under which we presently labor. Humanity, ethics, politics—or whatever, *n'importe*— would belong to a general apophatics. Such an apophatics would turn on a generalized nominalism, where the best way to save the name would be to treat each name as a *nomen negativum*. The aim of this nominalism is not to shut knowledge down in simple ignorance but to open it up to the affirmation of the *docta ignorantia* taught by the late medieval mystical masters, *sans voir et sans savoir*, but in a general form. The effect of this *ignorantia* is to keep the possibility of the impossible open, to keep the future open, to have a future, which means something to come, lest like Thomas Aquinas the only decent thing left to do is to die.[52]

The *à-venir*, the "dream" of a democracy to come, is not the vision of a democracy in the future present, not the gradual realization of an already envisaged ideal. The *à-venir* is not foreseen but "blind," and does not have a positive content but remains "absolutely undetermined" (SdM, 111 / SoM, 65), the object of a faith, not a plan. The future is not a positive, regulative ideal which admits of gradual empirical approximation; deconstruction is not a form of essentialism or idealism turning on an Idea in the Kantian sense or Husserlian infinite ideal. The *à-venir* of which deconstruction "dreams" is rather a completely open-ended, negative, undetermined structure—the heart of what I am calling here a generalized apophaticism—that goes along with a non-essentialism, a nominalism, and a generalized *ignorantia* about what is coming, that cultivates the possible not *as possible*, but as *the* im-possible. For the future present, insofar as it is already pre-envisioned, belongs to the regime of the same, as a "future modality of the living present" (SdM, 110 / SoM, 64–65), which is not the absolutely undetermined surprise that Derrida calls the "messianic hope" (see §§ 9–10 below).

Of this future to come we can only say "come." To say or to pray. For "come!" is a prayer, a famous one at the end of the book of Revelation.

When someone says "Come!" the conventions that convene to make this event possible allow someone else to link on with "Amen!" And "amen" can be translated *"oui, oui."*

So, then, Derrida is praying, and when we read *viens* we have stumbled upon him as his *prie-Dieu*, and there are others there with him, all bowing furiously before the wall. Now we are coming to his more Jewish, circumcised side.

Viens! oui, oui!

♦ *Edifying Divertissement No. 1.*
Bedeviling Faith

In "How Not to Speak," Derrida refers to critics of deconstruction who want to see in it "a symptom of modern or postmodern nihilism" and who could, "if they wished, recognize in it the last testimony—not to say the martyrdom—of faith in the present *fin de siècle*. This reading would always be possible." (*Psy.*, 539/DNT, 77). I wish to show here, in a kind of quasi-theological addendum to this treatment of negative theology, that deconstruction is something like a *fin de siècle* faith, but without the martyrdom and without the nihilism. The effect of deconstruction is not to undo a specifically religious faith but to resituate it within the trace and thereby to let faith be faith, not knowledge or triumphalism. Deconstruction can have no brief against faith, because deconstruction is *itself* faith, miming and repeating the structure of faith in a faith without dogma.

Faith (with)in the Trace

For Derrida, the trace is the element of undecidability, the formlessness in which determinate forms are inscribed, a desert place within which determinate decisions—theological or atheological—are made, each checked and confused by the other, each movement disturbed by a countermovement, so that we do not know what is taking place; in the desert one never knows whether what is coming is an oasis or a mirage. Prayers, laws, constitutions, works of art, all of our theologies and atheologies, are so many markings, configurations inscribed in the flux, so many figures carved in the shifting sands of the desert, so many ways of making our way through an aporia.

In the midst of this abyss, theology and faith keep their heads by bowing their heads in prayer, by calling upon the name of God, "Oh, God!" That is how they respond to the provocation, the solicitation, the disturbance. God is how they name the whirlwind. Other discourses

have other idioms and atheological names, like Being or world or perhaps even Capital (in capitals) or Will. For Jacques Derrida himself, and
I would say for deconstruction, this provocation or *prévenance*, which
has always taken place, cannot be said to come decidably and univo-
cally from either Being or what the determinable faiths call God. I say
this not because Derrida knows that it comes from something still
higher (*hyper*), but because, for Derrida, the call lacks an assured origin
and destination, because it is adrift and casts us adrift, in a desert
place, because it is not guided and held steady by its prayer. I do not
want to say that there are no prayers in deconstruction—far from it—
but that in deconstruction prayers are adrift, because the name of God
is subject to the un-law of exemplarity (*Sauf*, 95–96/ON, 76), so that we
do not know whether God is an example of something else, or everything is an example of God, an *imago dei*. For Derrida, it is enough that
apophatic theology takes place, that is has a place given to it, enough
that, struck by the thunder of the *tout autre*, it takes the place of saying
something, no matter what, that it has something to say—God, for example. For the taking place itself, the place itself that it takes, is the matter at issue here.[53]

For Derrida, the trace of the place ought not to be conceived as a surrounding transcendental condition that makes safe, but as a quasi-transcendental open-endedness that leaves us at a loss. The theological or
the atheological, the ontological or the economic, are *determinations*, "*determinable* faiths" (*Sauf*, 86/ON, 71), ways to give the promise determination and destination (*Bestimmung*), for which each one must take the
responsibility, attempts to close the circle and complete the rounds of
the *kula*. For Derrida the trace leaves us all a little lost, and so Derrida
himself can speak only of the asymmetrical "*prévenance*"[54] of the trace,
the language before language, without knowing or being able to say
what solicits us, what has promised us in advance to the trace and what
is promised to us. This lack of origin or destination is the an-economy or
a-logic of the gift, a certain drift—as opposed to the heaving and sighing
of creation for God, the Father of all gifts, the diastole and systole of *exitus* and *reditus* in theology, especially in Christian Neoplatonism.

But Derrida is not, here or anywhere else, ruling out religious faith,
or negative theology; rather, he re-situates them, relocates them, finds
their site (*lieu*) within the trace. If deconstruction were a topology,
which it is not, if it were centered around a privileged place, instead of
being lost and exiled, in diaspora, then that place would be not the
lush growths of a Greco-Germanic *Schwarzwald* but the desert.
Deconstruction would have an ankhôral topicality. *Khôra* names the
site, the interval, the spare spacing, within which both theology and
atheology, both faith and faithlessness, theism and antitheism, faith in
this or faith in that, would take place, would have a place (*avoir lieu*).

♦ *Edifying Divertissement No. 1.*

How could Derrida—for whom everything depends upon faith—rule out religious faith? Why would Derrida want to ban the name of God, a name he dearly loves? That would imply the excessively foolish notion, already sufficiently rebutted, that there is some sort of negative ontological argument embedded in *différance* which shows the non-existence of God, as if the spacing or interval of *différance* has the effect of elbowing certain entities off the chessboard. Far from knocking out discourses on the *tout autre*, or putting out the fires of such discourses, the whole idea of deconstruction is to *incite* them, to inflame our passion for the impossible, for the incoming of something absolutely surprising. Deconstruction is trying to inflame the passion of faith, to incite a riot, to drive us mad with passion, not to neutralize exciting and inflaming discourses.

By inscribing, or reinscribing, faith and theology (or atheism and atheology, if that is your desire) within the movements of the trace, by making the movements of faith and theology further, determinable moves within the general field of the trace, Derrida sends them back to the desert whence they sprang like desert flowers. If faith and theology understand themselves well, if they learn to speak of themselves and of God well, if they recall they are desert discourses, then they understand that they cannot, that they are structurally unable to, in virtue of the trace, close the circle, finally and effectively to assure their own destination, truth, and validity. *Homo viator*, yes, but without knowing the destination, a little lost in the desert, caught in an aporia so that the path is given just where the way is blocked (MpPdM, 129–30/MfPdM, 132), *homo a-viator*, which is what allows a decision to be absolutely responsible. Derrida does no more than follow Johannes de Silentio, Abraham's poet, from whose fear and trembling we learn that faith "must never be a certainty" but passion, "the highest passion" that, locked as it is in the secret of non-knowledge, still has the heart to push ahead (DM, 78/GD, 80), which is the repetition forward and the marvel.

Deconstruction does not adopt the absurd position of giving instruction to theology, as if it were appointed a Neokantian judge of theology, for deconstruction always comes *after* theology, lately on the scene, *post-posé*, after the fact (*Sauf*, 42–43/ON, 48–49). At most it whispers in theology's ear, gives it a little gift purely gratuitously, putting a little contribution in theology's collection plate. The gift is to insist that it is in virtue of the trace that faith is always *faith*, a decision made in the midst of undecidability, a way to make one's way in the midst of an aporia, something forged (formed/faked) in *khôra*, which is, I would say, a *general* condition of any "belief," of any positing or positional attitude. A determinable religious faith, say in one of the great monotheisms, takes the form of a "yes, yes" "*oui, oui*," *within* the general affirmation, the *oui, oui* by which we all respond to the language before language, which must be repeated from moment to moment.

In other words, Derrida does not discredit negative theology but gives us an alternative, non-metaphysical, non-ousiological, or non-hyper-ousiological way to read or hear it, *sans* the pure "experience" or naked contact with a secret presence from which standpoint the negative theologian looks back, with a certain serene *Gelassenheit* (that is a little *too* assured) on the play of signifiers in which the rest of us poor mortals are trapped, which thereafter appear as mere straw, *sicut palea*. That, were it to "take place," would actually spell the end of faith and replace it with union—"but then face to face"—after which there would be no further need to sur-vive, to live on. But by reattaching negative theology to faith, to the hard work of seeing through a glass darkly, *différance* gives us a reason for living-on.

I have now twice alluded to the famous story of Thomas Aquinas, which, praying your patience, I will tell (again). After saying mass on December 6, 1274, Saint Thomas Aquinas is said or reported (by his Dominican brethren, there being nothing outside the text), to have been blessed with just such a mystical, unitive experience. After this, the Dominicans said (he himself was silent), he stopped writing, saying nothing except to say "all that I have written is as straw compared to what I have seen." Then he fell silent and died. That made perfect sense, for at that point he had no need for a future. There was for him nothing more to come, *à-venir*, the secret having already been disclosed, the gift of presence having already been given, his passion for the impossible having been sated. That was a very consistent tale for the Dominicans to tell the Curia, and it evidently made a persuasive case for sainthood, which was handed down in 1325. Now, however difficult it is to keep this story safe against the suggestion that he actually had a cerebral hemorrhage,[55] a suggestion that is so heartless and cerebral that I will not even mention it—Is it necessary to choose between them? Might not a visitation by the *tout autre* bring on a cerebral hemorrhage?—it confirms in an oblique way that the deadness of the trace is, after all, a condition of life and a reason for living. Were the gift of full presence actually granted, were the secret ever actually fully revealed, were anyone actually to *know* the secret (who could we trust with it?), life would be revoked, there being no reason for living-on (*sur-vie*). This would confirm something that the masters of spirituality have long known, that it is by having our prayers answered that we are often done in, so that you should take care what you pray for lest it be granted. No person can actually know the secret, see presence and live! Who would want to? Why bother? What would you be living *for* if you had no future? If the promise of your future, the future that comes of having a promise, the passion of the promise, had actually been fulfilled, why would you live on? In dying, Thomas did the only decent thing. He always did; that is why they called him the "angelic" doctor, and there was nothing left to do but canonize him. This angel of a man was a saint.

Now, Jacques Derrida, who is not an angelic doctor but a more devil-ish deconstructor, although he is very interested in ghosts and spirits, is not out to undo faith and theology, negative or positive. Derrida is not a Neokantian policeman but a ragpicker and reader of lost mail who saves theology from itself, from its worst, hyperousiological side, by re-minding it that it is inscribed in the trace, and hence in faith. Deconstruction constitutes a lovely little bit of documentation—and this is the humble little offering it puts in theology's collection plate, its widowy two cents—that faith and its theology grow like desert flowers in a desert place, blooming when all the elements conspire against it.

Like an absolute surprise. *Oui, oui.*

Like an experience of something that will, in a manner of speaking, knock us dead.

Sancte Thomas, ora pro nobis.

A Devilish Hypothesis: Faith without Faith

Let us put this devilish doctrine of faith under the bubble.

By saving the name—of God, of the *tout autre, n'importe*—Derrida is not trying to make everything safe. The trip Derrida takes through the desert of negative theology is risky business, without recourse to the safety of a desert guide, of a prayer that knows its destination, nor to the propriety of a lush Greco-Germanic destination, where we will be bathed by words of elemental, *ursprünglich* power. Derrida's trip ends up in a *khôra*/place, a desert place disturbed by demons of every sort.

Let us here, by way of a devilish hypothesis, posit an asymptotic point of contact toward which religious faith and the thought of the trace tend to touch, a desert meeting place at which they would tend to make contact. That point pricks, but it pricks both ways: for theology suffers an inscription in the trace, even as the trace suffers a "becoming theological" (*Psy.*, 538/DNT, 76). I have in mind a point at which theol-ogy, opening itself to translatability, opens the wound of its own keno-sis and suffers from its passion for the impossible.

The hypothesis goes like this. What if theology were to confess itself no longer able to save the name of God? What if, beyond the economy of sacrifice, it were to give up the name of God to translatability without return? What if it were to pray without (*sans*) knowing where to direct its prayers, without its sense of destinal assurance, without trusting that its prayers up to heaven rise? What if it were it to have faith without faith, *foi sans foi* (maybe even *foi à sang froid*), the *sans* serving to save faith from dogmatism, to believe without quite knowing in what it be-lieved, so that it had to ask, "what do I love when I love my God?"

What if theology, negative or no, were so to subscribe to the trace, to be subscribed and inscribed by the trace, that it would begin to drift in deconstruction's direction, start to head out into the desert, adrift with deconstruction's ankhôral *destinerrance*, so that it drifted in the direction of a God without God?

Suppose, God forbid, that the desire for God fluctuated undecidably with atheism? In a discussion of the *désir de Dieu* (*Sauf*, 18–20/ON, 36–37), Derrida remarks upon the possibility of a desire in the "other voice," foreign to anthopo-theo-morphism, a desire going toward the "absolute other," that renounces the momentum of appropriation. This other desire is not driven by the passion of a subject for possession—it is *sans avoir*—for something determinable, but by the passion for the impossible, the affirmation of the *tout autre*. When this desire takes shape in the most radical forms of religious discourse, it looks like atheism to the orthodox, as Eckhart and Silesius testify. That is why Derrida also writes that "[t]he desire of God, God as the other name of desire, deals in the desert with radical atheism" (*Sauf*, 103/ON, 80).

These questions lead us back to the logic of the *sans* in which Derrida is so much interested in *"Pas"* and *Sauf le nom*: the *sans* in *Dieu sans l'être* (God without being, God without being God), the *ohne* in *Die Ros' ist ohn' warum* (the rose without why), the *sine* in Augustine's wise without wisdom, good without goodness. This is the logic of a "quasi-negative predication" (*Sauf*, 27/ON, 40–41) in which whatever is said must subject itself to the discipline of the *sans*, must stand up under, must survive, a self-effacing, auto-deconstructing *sans*. Following this logic, to save the name of God negative theology says we must do without God, pray God to rid us of God, seek God without God. So, by an analogous but admittedly devilish gesture, I would say that to save the name of faith, faith must be faith without faith, without the assurances of faith.

A faith without faith can easily cross over into a faithless despair (which is also, let us not forget, inscribed within the trace), and if that is what becomes of it, so be it. Save what we may, nothing is safe and there is no economizing on anxiety. But despair is not what I have in mind with my hypothesis. I mean a faith that is inhabited by the thought that the "name of God" gives way to translation, that it disseminates itself, that it multiplies itself into other forms and figures, that the patent faith holds on this name does not give it exclusive rights, remembering, on no less an authority than God himself, that when the Shemites wanted to make themselves a master name, God was on the side of dissemination. Is not the story of Babel God's way of urging that there are no master names, not even the name of God? Is that not even God's own word?

Removed from the reassuring circle of an economy of sacrifice, what is the classic "dark night of the soul," the moment of spiritual aridity, of a spiritual desert, if not the dark advent of *différance* or *khôra*? Faith without faith is not faithlessness *simpliciter*, not the simple modal opposite of faith, not the simple negation or undoing of faith, but an ankhôral faith inscribed in the trace, a trace of *sans* inscribed in faith, inscribing an atheistic trait in every faith. A faith without faith is a decision inscribed in undecidability where undecidability is structurally ingredient in faith, not the opposite of faith but the element of faith. The undecidability is first, last, and constant, the element, the space in which faith makes its leap, the horizon in terms of which faith understands its limits, understands that it is faith, through a trace darkly.

Faith is a path that must pass through the aporia of the *sans*:

—How can a path pass through aporias?
—What would a path be without aporia? Would there be a way (*voie*) without what clears the way there where the way is not opened . . . ? Would there be a way without the necessity of deciding there where the decision seems impossible? Would there be a decision there where the decision is possible and programmable? (*Sauf*, 109/ON, 83)

Faith without faith is precisely such *an* impossible, a translation of the impossible and impassable, forced to make its way in the midst of an aporia; faith without faith is precisely—faith. Otherwise it is not a battle, not through a glass darkly, but a high road assured of success. The deconstruction of faith, which has *nothing* to do with its simple destruction—*au contraire!*—saves faith from closing around itself by opening this wounded discourse to the wound of translatability or substitutability. Undecidability and substitutability do not form a bottomless pit down which every decision is dropped never to be heard from again. They constitute rather the haze of indefiniteness with which decision must daily cope, the gluey, glassy *glas* which conditions even very ordinary decisions, in which the urgency and passion of decision are nourished. The quasi-theses of translatability, substitutability, undecidability, open up the space in which faith fights its good fight and tries to save its good name.

The Number of Faith

But over and beyond opening up a certain space for faith, for the determinable faiths, while saving them from their worst, most dogmatic side, deconstruction is *itself* a form of faith—something that becomes unmistakably clear in *Memoirs of the Blind* (*infra.*, §19). The passion for the impossible is the passion of faith. Not only does deconstruction reinscribe the determinable faiths within undecidability, which is a very salutary reminder, but deconstruction's undecidability goes hand in hand with a certain faith, *sans savoir, sans avoir, sans voir* and a certain

64

passion of non-knowing (*Cinders*, 75). Deconstruction takes the form of a general or non-determinable faith in the impossible, of what Derrida calls in the Marx book "the essence of faith *par excellence*, which can only ever believe in the unbelievable" (SdM, 227/SoM, 143). Deconstruction comes down to an affirmation or hope or invocation which is a certain *faith* in *the* impossible, in something that pushes us beyond the sphere of the same, of the believable, into the unbelievable, that which exceeds the horizon of our pedestrian beliefs and probabilities, driving us with the passion of *the* impossible, *the* unbelievable, producing another amazing North African mix, a certain devilish Derridean version of Tertulian, *credo quia impossibile est*.

Deconstruction describes "the very condition of fidelity" (*Psy.*, 649/Number, 131), the fidelity of faith, the very way faith is engaged, the very engagement of faith, which is, for Derrida, the structure of repetition, of repeated affirmation, the structure of the *oui, oui*. Repetition is an affirmation made in the very condition of multiplicity, the promise to remember and the memory of a promise, over and against "the menace of forgetting." Far from ruling out faith, deconstruction *is* itself faith, which is why the archi-act of promising can be described as "an act of faith" (MpPdM, 142/MfPdM, 150). Given its wariness about the self-assurance of *voir et savoir*, what else can deconstruction be but faith, faith in something unforeseeable, in what is coming? Faith must be affirmed again and again, must first say yes and then, putting its hand to the plow without looking back, says yes again. And again. *Oui, oui*. Faith is a certain loyalty to itself which presupposes its own lack of identity, its own divided, undecidable un-essence. If there ever were a plenitudinous now, there would be no faith, since everything would have come, and, as we have learned from Thomas Aquinas, the only decent thing left to do would be to die.

But it is no business of deconstruction—indeed it goes against the grain of deconstruction—to specify some *determinable* faith, to specify what faith is faith in, to calm the storm or arrest the play in which faith takes shape by proposing a determinate object of faith, some common faith. Deconstruction has no business in identifying the *tout autre*. That is your business, your faith—if you are smart, you will not "identify" it too precisely unless you are prepared to suffer a loss—your business or mine, your faith or mine, where "I" and "you" are but "formal indicators" of certain singularities, singularly responsible respondents. In deconstruction faith says yes to the stranger to come, "*Oui, à l'étranger*" (*Psy.*, 639/Number, 120), yes to the stranger to whose shores deconstruction points without attempting to land, to explore or, God forbid, to conquer. It says yes with an affirmation that is "unconditional, imperative, and immediate" (PdS, 299/*Points*, 286).

♦ *Edifying Divertissement No. 1.*

This is all explained very powerfully and beautifully in the closing pages of *"Nombre de oui"* (*Psy.*, 648–50/Number, 130–32), in which Derrida comments on the work of Michel de Certeau.[56] There can never be an "analytic" of the yes, he says, but at best a quasi-analytic, because an analytic is supposed to resolve into simples, to come back to simple conditions, but to come back to the yes is to come back to something that is already doubled within itself, structurally and not by some accident that befalls it from without. That is so, fittingly, for two reasons. (1) The archi-yes by which we are promised and engaged, is already, as soon as it starts, a *response* to what calls upon and engages us; the first yes comes second, in response to a demand that precedes it. (2) Furthermore, to say yes is to bind oneself to the future, to a further confirmation in a second yes, which promises to keep the memory of the first yes and confirm it, to repeat it. When we say yes, we do not know as yet if we have said yes. When we inaugurate something we do not know if we have inaugurated anything yet; inaugural days come after the fact, years later, *a posteriori*. We are just beginning and we are not sure if this beginning is a beginning or if it will fail, if we will fail to remain faithful to it. This is what Derrida calls "repetition," close to Kierkegaard's, the repetition that repeats *forward*, that *produces* what it repeats, the repetition that comes *first*. The first yes will not have taken place without the second, without the promise of the second, even as the second is the memory of the first, the yes itself being internally divided into yes, yes. But the necessity of the second yes also *menaces* the yes, exposing it to the possibility of becoming something mechanical and rote, a semblance of itself, a simulacrum, a fable, fictitious, which no longer believes in itself, which would be a "bad" repetition, unloyal and untrue. What is so dear, so close to our heart, that we learn it by heart is menaced by the automaton, the automatic repetition (PdS, 306/*Points*, 294–95). This menace is older than and prior to the question of "subjective intention"; there are subjectively good and bad intentions, good and bad faiths, well-intended and ill-intended subjects, only within the structural framework of repetition, the structure that requires repetition.

The second yes is a promise to remember, a memory of a promise, which takes place in a place of *événementialité*, of the very coming to pass of the event, the very structure of the event, prior to the psychology of memory, of the psyche and morality. But in order to fulfill its mission to repeat, memory must also be able to forget. The second yes must be an absolute renewal, a new inauguration all over again, acting as if the first yes were entirely forgotten, as if it were forced to begin all over again. This forgetting is not psychological omission, something we forgot to remember, but a structural condition, "the very condition of fidelity," which, to be faithful to the first yes, must forget it, i.e, have all the *ab initio* freshness of a first start. That is what Derrida calls the possibility and impossibility of the signature, the possibility that can never reach the closure of absolute assurance. Faith, fidelity, for Derrida, has the structure of the signature, of the second yes that must put its signature on the first. The second yes must countersign the first, in the face of the divisibility, the extension from moment to moment, against which a signature strains and stresses and stretches itself (*se tend*) (*Psy.*, 649/Number, 131). The second is a first yes, once again, a second one, a doubled yes, a second one cut off from the first in order to be itself first. Each day, every day, each time, it is the first time. "Thanks to the menace of forgetting," *felix culpa*, memory can each time take the first step, so that the *cut* (*coupure*) between the first and the second yes is also what provides the *opening*, in which, as Michel de Certeau says, upon whom this writing is a graft, "the same phoneme (*Ja*) makes the cut and the opening coincide" (*Psy.*, 650/Number, 132), which is itself a graft upon Angelus Silesius who said "*Gott spricht nur immer Ja.*" Jahweh, the Cut, the Separate One, who is what He is and who separates himself from every name, is the Opening of the yes, which also cuts a way through to reading circumcision as a yes, just as the circumcised heart and ear cut the other a break, a point we will pursue below.

Faith is this incalculable number, *oui, oui.* "Already [the first yes] but always [the second first] a faithful countersignature, a *yes* can never be counted" (*Psy.*, 650/Number, 132). Faith is not calculable in advance, cannot be counted on to coast on its own, cannot be taken for granted, but must be given again and again, without calculation, *sine ratione*, in a faith without faith, a faith which is reinvented from moment to moment, *oui, oui.*

A Holy Dissemination

That is why there is something a bit perverse in thinking of *différance* or the trace as Jean-Luc Marion does, as some kind of anterior authority, some sort of overseeing secular power that asserts its primacy over God, that sets itself above God, and hence as a higher order and more sophisticated "idol." If it is a "screen," as Marion argues,[57] it is nothing other than the glass screen of *glas* through which faith sees darkly so that we do not now see face to face, the quasi-transcendental glass spoken of by Paul, who knew a thing or two about faith, who also told us to put our hands to the plow, not look back, repeating forward in the *oui, oui.* Deconstruction does not set itself "over" the name of God but below God, so that God is always *tout autre*, ahead of it, before it, too much for it, more than it, of itself, is capable, while deconstruction itself comes limping along lamely "after" the name of God, *post-posé*, after the fact, like a little post-script (*Sauf*, 42–43/ON, 48–49).

Deconstruction affirms, says yes to, gives its assent and consent (*Zusage*), has a faith in what is to come, prays and weeps for what is coming, for "my God." Since we know, on Derrida's own word, that Jacques rightly passes for an atheist and that this is something that worried his mother, what he means by "my God" is in the end his business. That is why the distinction is so crucial between Derrida and deconstruction, or between Jacques and "Derrida," where the name of the thinker is the name of texts to read, of a "signature" that can be countersigned by the other. This is the distinction between the aleatorical contingencies of Jacques's history and the resources of deconstruction after the death of the father, which is an easier distinction to make with "Plato" or "Aristotle," who have been dead long enough that we do not know them personally. But deconstruction in itself, if there is such a thing, *sans* Jacques Derrida, keeps the space of undecidability open, letting "God" and "justice," *tout autre "et" tout autre*, tremble in the winds of undecidability, which is the space within which any decision, the passion of any determinable faith, is inscribed.

Deconstruction does not sit like a judge judging the name of God (let alone, God forbid, judging God) but wonders all the while whether the name of God can be translated into something else, is an example of something else. Of justice or love or death or the other or singularity or the gift, for example. If negative theology seeks "God without being," as Marion says, deconstruction asks whether we might have God without God, God without being God (*l'être*, being Him, God), which is one of the ways Derrida suggests we translate Jean-Luc Marion's remarkable title that Marion may or may not intend. In that sense, deconstruction comes not "before" or "over" the name of God, like a screen, "before" or "over" faith, but after God, after faith, in order to ask, with interest and admiration, "what is happening?"

Deconstruction does not think that "God" is a bad name, even though its most assured secularist admirers would have it so. On the contrary, some of the most profound things are said under the name of God. That is why Derrida cannot avoid speaking of God, cannot get along without (*sans*) it. Here, for example, is a *sans* Derrida very much admires:

> God himself, if He wants to live for you, must die:
> How do you think, without (*ohne, sans*) death, to inherit His life?

"Has anything more profound ever been written on inheritance? I understand that as a thesis on what *inherit* means to say" (*Sauf*, 106–07/ON, 82). Now, when Angelus Silesius writes this, he has St. Paul in mind, and he adds a little Pauline *post-scriptum* to his verse, about our living now, not I but Christ in me. All *ohne*'s in Silesius, including "*Die Ros' ist ohn' warum*," come attached with Christian postscripts. If Heidegger does not like this, "it will be necessary for him to write another *post-scriptum*, which is always possible" (*Sauf*, 108/ON, 82), and that would institute another "inheritance" and another "syllabification," i.e., another translation, tradition, substitution, or contextualization. Silesius's Pauline postscript is his business; the verse can be translated *without* it.

By translation Derrida does not mean translation without remainder, absorption into a *mathesis universalis* or a *lingua franca* that assimilates everything. He means recontextualization: it can be repeated and re-newed, repeated with a difference, so that it keeps on giving off sparks, living on otherwise. When the prophets, for example, use the name of God, they—like Derrida—seem to mean "justice"; and when they speak of justice, they seem to mean God. This translatability, this substitutabil-ity, this disseminative slippage that slips back and forth between the name of God and the name of justice, that is what deconstruction em-phasizes—and celebrates.

Can we say what "God" means to say in some other way? Do we dare? Or conversely, and this is what we must bear in mind, here, where faith and theology are at stake, are the other things we say—jus-tice, death, the other, for example—ways of saying God, of saying the name of God? Without (*sans, ohne*) God? God without God? (I pray God to rid me of God: Is not that Jacques's prayer, too?) Are there ways of praying without praying "God," praying to God where I do not know what I am praying to, of loving God without knowing what I love when I love my God?

The believer is someone who privileges the name of God, who for reasons of her or his own is committed, is pro-mitted, or given over in advance, to the name of God, who has a sense of destinal assurance. That is not a bad thing. Everyone privileges something; no one speaks pure chaos; we are all always and already factically situated in some *de-terminable* (*Sauf*, 86/ON, 71) faith or another, some *determinable* socio-historico-linguistic world or matrix or another. How could it be otherwise? The danger is only to think that your privileged name can-not be translated, that if someone does not use it, they are against you, like the Pope and his Buddhists, so that when the Pope says, from his balcony, *urbi et orbi*, "my God," he wants the whole city and the whole world to fall in line with him.

Deconstruction pries open the prayer "My God," so we pray and weep to God while remaining all the while a little lost, not knowing to whom we pray. God or Justice? Is it a matter of choosing between these two? Do they not pass back and forth in a kind of holy dissemination?

II. The Apocalyptic

§5. Viens!

Something coming . . .
Viens.
Something unforeseeable and incomprehensible . . .
Viens.
Tout autre . . .
Viens.
Let every one say,
Viens
To every gift,
Viens, oui, oui.
Amen.
(Fragment from *The Book of Elie*)[1]

The transition from the apophatic to the messianic, from Derrida's several confrontations with the negative theology of Christian Neoplatonism to the more Jewish and prophetic strains of the later works, is best made by following his analysis of *venir* and *à venir*, of something "coming," something, I know not what, that comes over us like an absolute surprise. If Derrida's apophaticism is deeply messianic, as I hope to show, that is because it is not a little apocalyptic. Over the years, deconstruction has become, with increasing insistence and urgency, more and more a discourse and a meditation, and no less a politics of and even a prayer for what is coming. Everything in deconstruction turns on the constellation of *venir* and *à venir*, *viens* and *invention*, *l'avenir* and *événement*.

Viens sounds a little apocalyptic, like a line lifted from John of Patmos. *Viens* has the ring of an invocation or a prayer for what is coming,[2] like the closing recitative of "come" (*erkhou*, *veni*) in the last chapter of The Apocalypse to John (22:17). Derrida had struck up this tone in all innocence, while reading Blanchot, not the Bible. He first started saying and praying *viens* before he was "aware of the citational resonance of this 'Come,' or at least that its citation . . . was also a reference to John's Apocalypse" (*Ton*, 87/RTP, 162). He had been repeating and mimicking an apocalyptic tone, *à insu*, without even knowing it, blindsided, we might say, by an apocalyptic (non)vision. But when Jacques of El-Biar realized that he sounded a little like John of Patmos, he did not hold it back but let it come.[3]

The apocalyptic tone of *viens* is not an accident, not another little brush with religious discourse—like the apophatic and messianic—that we can, with a wipe of our brow, safely push aside. There are too many such "accidents" in deconstruction, too many chance occurrences that recur with a rhythmic regularity.[4] Derrida is continually "repeating the possibility of religion *sans* religion," miming and mimicking a "non-dogmatic doublet of dogma" (DT, 53/GT, 49). He is continually producing deconstruction as a certain deconstructed religion (perhaps a religiousness "D," to outdo Johannes Climacus).

The call of "come," the apocalyptic tone of *viens*, belongs to another time, other than philosophy's time, to a more Jewish and biblical time, a time organized around the promise not the present. The Bible does not think of time in terms of the enduring permanence of *ousia* but in terms of fidelity to the promise of something that is to come, even something a little impossible. What lies behind the "come" and the "apocalyptic tone" —John's or Jacques's—is another, more Jewish "messianic" time where time is focused on the *à-venir*. The axioms of ousiological time, of the more familiar Greco-philosophical time, on the other hand, are all variously organized around enduring presence, even and especially those that are planning for the future, which means for them the future-present.

Viens, oui, oui are not just two or three more words for deconstruction, but words of event and advent, supplying the very opening within which words take place, opening messianic time. *Viens* is not an a-lethic opening, a clearing made by Truth and old Greeks, but an opening of and for justice, where justice precedes truth. *Viens* precipitates a more Jewish or at least a more Jewgreek opening than a Greco-German *Lichtung*, more a prophetic breach than a phainaesthetic clearing. *Viens* opens the messianic space and time of justice, for truth always walks a step or two behind justice in deconstruction. In this more Abrahamic opening, *voir* and *savoir* give way to *croire*, so that rather than basking in a hoary Hellenic light, we are all struck a little blind.[5] This is the opening of the "*l'ouvre où ne pas voir*" (MdA, 37–38/MB, 32–33): the open, where not to see; the place of not-seeing (the Louvre!), the place not of seeing but of faith in the impossible. Here one wends one's way with weeping eyes and seeing tears.

To be sure, Derrida is not a rabbi. He is repeating religion with a difference, miming religious time nondogmatically, for this is a messianic

§5. Viens!

time *sans* a Messiah, an apocalypse *sans* apocalypse, a religion *sans* religion. Unlike John of Patmos, Jacques of El-Biar is not threatening anybody with a plague (Apoc. 22:18) if they add or subtract something from deconstruction, or even if they write a critical review of his books. This *viens* is directed to *the* impossible—*sans* the blood that gets spilled every time someone assures us that they speak for God Who has assured them that He will back them up with a plague or two if their enemies give them trouble.[6] This is "an apocalypse without vision, without truth, without revelation" (*Ton*, 95/RTP, 167). This is the secret that there is no secret, at once "as secret and superficial as the postcard apocalypse" (*Ton*, 42/RTP, 136), the unveiling of the bad news that nobody has a revelation, that we are all in this together and that nobody has won the high ground of the *grand seigneur*. The visionaries of the *viens* are all blind, *sans vision, sans vérité, sans révélation* (*Ton*, 95/RTP, 167). They live in a kind of community of the blind, are granted only an apocalypse of the *sans*, where everything turns on learning to live with this without. But this *sans* is not the scene of a loss but of an opening that lets something new come. Derrida certainly wants to dislocate the apocalyptic tone of John's Apocalypse, to cut it down a notch or two. For the apocalyptic notion of a privileged access, the high-handed politics of a special message from on high granted to a few from which the rest of us are excluded ("cryptopolitics": *Ton*, 42/RTP, 136; a *"politique de lieux," Khôra*, 49/ON, 104), the epistemics of a secret access to the revelation of a mystery, which goes to the heart of historical apocalyptic literature—that is everything that Derrida resists.

Beyond all that, he had come upon this "come" and this other, more messianic time, in all innocence, not in John of Patmos but in Blanchot. When the symptoms of an apocalyptic disorder first began to surface, he was in good faith; he did not know he was citing the Apocalypse of John.

I will begin Part II with "Psyché: The Invention of the Other," one of Derrida's most direct and helpful presentations of *viens* (§5). Then I will take up his initial encounter with Blanchot's *viens* (§6). In §7, I will pursue his confrontation with the apocalyptic tone that deconstruction had (by then) recently adapted when Derrida addressed the eschatologists who had come together at Cerisy in 1980 to hear the apocalyptic call of/for "the ends of man." I conclude with a presentation of "the secret" which impassions, for the secret is the condition of the "come!" (§8). Then a little organ music, an edifying discourse in between Parts II and III—while we await the messianic.

The In-coming of the Wholly Other

The powerful thematic of *venir* and *à venir* in Derrida's works can be clearly identified in the 1980 essay *"Psyché: Inventions de l'autre,"* the lead essay of a volume that bears its name and a pivotal essay for the present study. "Deconstruction is inventive, or it does not exist," he says (*Psy.*, 35/RDR, 43).[7] Deconstruction is engaged in and by the *in-venire*, the incoming, the arrival (*venue*), of what is coming, what is to come (*à-venir*), in and by the future (*l'avenir*) and the adventure (*aventure*) of the future (cf. PdS, 136/*Points*, 127). Deconstruction is "eventive" (*événement, é-venir*) or it is nothing, the event emerging from the abyss that lurks beneath conventions (*con-venir*) (DM, 81/GD, 84).

In plain English, if there is such a thing, *l'invention de l'autre* means the "advent of the other." In plainer English still, *invention* means "incoming!" as an interjection, like "fore!," where "incoming" means that something is coming at us, at our head. When someone shouts "incoming!" the right response is to duck. *L'invention de l'autre*: heads up! Deconstruction is a way of staying heads up, of shouting heads up—or it does not exist.

Derrida differentiates this invention and its politics from the "modern politics of invention," which he calls an invention of the same, which means a managed invention. Then invention is monitored by existing institutions, by universities, foundations, and governmental programs, for example, that support and authorize, that authorize by supporting, only certain lines of research, only certain works of art, only certain discourses. In this conventional invention, invention is domesticated, kept in check within the economics of the "same," and "inventive" human subjects are given limited rein or latitude within a fixed horizon. The "invention of the same" is a discovery—*invention* also means "discovery," to "come upon"—of something lying already embedded in the system. In this invention, the assemblage of existing institutions is strengthened and confirmed by reabsorbing every novelty. The existing order lies "ready and waiting to reduce it [invention] to the same" (*Psy.*, 36/RDR, 43), to give it status and a patent within the current configuration, tending thus "to integrate the aleatory into its programmatic calculations" (*Psy.*, 51/RDR, 54). "No absolute surprise. (*Pas de surprise absolue.*) That is what I will call the order of the same" (*Psy.*, 53/RDR, 55).

The invention of the other is the deconstruction of the prevailing concept and practice of invention:

> [W]e dream of reinventing invention on the far side of the programmed matrices. For is a programmed invention still an invention? Is it an event through which the future (*l'avenir*) comes to us? (*Psy.*, 40/RDR, 46)

There is no question of "opposing" the invention of the same to the invention of the other, since even opposition belongs to the logic of the same, as in Hegel's dialectics, for example. The invention of the other is different differently:

> [I]ts difference beckons toward another coming about, toward this other invention of which we dream, the invention of the wholly other (*tout*

§5. Viens!

autre), the one that allows the coming of a still unanticipatable alterity and for which no horizon of waiting as yet seems ready, in place, available. (*Psy.*, 53/RDR, 55)

Divested of a "horizon of waiting,"[8] one must still prepare for it. Even if we cannot, like heroic subjective agents, invent the wholly other, even if the invention of the other is the wholly other's own in-coming, still we must allow the wholly other to come, which is not a simple impassivity or inertia. For however incalculable and unprogrammable, however aleatory and heterogeneous to calculation the incoming of the wholly other may be, one must get ready, one must be prepared, in order to let the other in.[9]

To prepare oneself for this coming (*venue*) of the other is what can be called deconstruction.

Deconstruction: that means to say "come!" (*viens!*):

To invent would then be to "know" how to say "come" and to answer the "come" of the other. Does that ever come about? Of this event one is never sure. (*Psy.*, 53–54/RDR, 56)

Deconstruction says come to the "step of the other" (*pas de l'autre*), to the step of Elijah at our door, to the step of the absolute surprise (*pas de surprise absolue*), so that the other will not be my doing, the mirror image of my "psyche," which is one of the things this word means in French (*Psy.*, 58–59/DNT, 59–60). If anything, it is I who will be invented by the other.[10]

That is Derrida's desire, the passion of Derrida or of deconstruction for the impossible, the unbelievable. For dreams and desires, prayers and passions, belong together in the overreaching, messianic and slightly Jewish expectant trespassing that deconstruction "is," if it is. Derrida is dreaming of what is not and never will be present, what is structurally to come (*à-venir*). He is dreaming and praying over an "absolute" future, a future sheltered by an absolute secret and absolved from whatever is presentable, programmable, or foreseeable. The prayers and tears of Jacques Derrida are not a matter of wishing, willing, or wanting some determinable, foreseeable object, a future present at which one can take conscious aim. Every determinable telos is still "present," has already been anticipated within the horizon of what presently prevails, of what is merely "possible." The future present has already happened, save actually bringing it about with a little effort, or even a lot. That is what he means by the "same," something we can imagine and foresee that we could bring about with a certain amount of luck and work. Dreaming and desiring, praying and weeping, on the other hand, are a passion for the beyond, *au-delà*, the *tout autre*, *the* impossible, the unimaginable, un-foreseeable, un-believable ab-solute surprise, which is ab-solved from the same.

Derrida's distinction between the invention of the same and the invention of the other invites a certain comparison, which is instructive up to a point, with a Kuhnian distinction between "normal" and "revolutionary" scientific change. The normal progress of science, the day-to-day discoveries of science, occur within a predelineated horizon of anticipation. In normal science the apprentices of the prevailing paradigm confirm the expectations of the dominant practice and conceptuality, verifying and strengthening the rule of the same. But from time to time the rule of that conceptuality is disturbed from within by the anomaly—*tout autre*—a singularity that precipitates the moment of crisis by resisting assimilation into the same. The anomaly throws the whole into undecidability, and, by mobilizing the younger practitioners in the discipline, brings about a holistic, revolutionary reconfiguration, one that the present paradigm, the prevailing regime of presence (the "same") can neither foresee nor absorb.[11]

Still, the differences that divide Derrida from Kuhn are even more instructive. Derrida's *tout autre* is not satisfied with the formation of new horizons, the establishment of new paradigms, although it does explain how that happens. The figure of the future is an absolute surprise, and as such, Derrida says, something "monstrous." To prepare for the future, were that possible, would be to prepare for a coming species of monster, "to welcome the monstrous *arrivant*, to welcome it, that is, to accord hospitality to that which is absolutely foreign or strange." Whatever arrives as an "event," as an absolute surprise, first takes "the form of the unacceptable, or even of the intolerable, of the incomprehensible, that is of a certain monstrosity." But with this addendum: we always try to domesticate this monster, to make the surprise part of our familiar habits, which means that we transform our habits and assume new habits, that we "transform the nature of the field of reception" (PdS, 400–401/*Points*, 386–87). But beyond this settling in and acculturating of the event, the *tout autre* for Derrida is always, more importantly, structurally outside, out of place, out of power, im-possible, to-come. If the *tout autre* ever won the revolution, if the Messiah ever actually showed up, if you ever thought that justice has come—that would ruin everything.

Furthermore, Derrida's distinction is not restricted to or even chiefly concerned with science or even knowledge (PdS, 370–71/*Points*, 359). Derrida is not thinking in Greco-ontological terms of a paradigm shift *in* understanding, but of a more Jewish, more Levinasian ethico-political alterity that *shatters* understanding, that underlines the saliency of the incomprehensible, something we confess we do not understand—*Je ne sais pas. Il faut croire*—before which we can only say *viens, oui, oui*. The *tout autre* is not a new way of seeing things, a new way to envision, but a blindness, a confession that we are up against something, *sans savoir, sans avoir, sans voir* (*Parages*, 25), to which we can only bear witness. "*L'invention de l'autre*" is a more messianic than Kuhnian crisis, more attuned to the anomaly of Abraham on Moriah than the scientific anomaly, more a prophetic call for a justice to come than a theory of scientific change, even a revolutionary one (*Foi*, 27).[12]

The advent of the other, its incoming, adventful invention, is to be distinguished, Derrida says, from a "theological" order—(pray be patient; he is not ruling out religion)—where theology means onto-theo-logy, where invention *ex nihilo* is mine, sayeth the Lord, where the theological means the God-given, pre-given order of what is already there. For such an invention there is little left to do save "supplement" God's work, to fill in the divine sketch, to fill up what is lacking in what is divinely pre-delineated. That is to remain safely within the invention of the same. Schelling, trying to make the most of such a finite situation, treated the "productive imagination" as a supplement of God's creation, as adding what is missing in the totality of revelation, making a finite addition to an infinite program, completing, inventing God in that supplementary sense (*Psy.*, 56–58/RDR, 58–59).

That gives invention its "patent," a legitimate status and standing within the present politics, within a restricted, albeit divine economy, a role to play within the same, as a supplement of the same. Invention thus is "possible" and, as the invention of the possible, it does not break the law. However, it is just this very logic of a supplementary invention that creates the space for an unanticipated opening. For by operating *within* a frame of presupposed conventions, within a certain respect for the rules and conventions of the prevailing economy—and where else *can* one operate? Where else can we begin other than where we are? (DLG, 233/OG, 162)—it is possible to bend the rules and improvise inventions on these conventions, to repeat and mime them, to repeat them with a difference. Deconstruction comes down to

> bending these rules with respect for the rules themselves in order to allow the other to come or to announce its coming in the opening of this dehiscence. That is perhaps what we call deconstruction. (*Psy.*, 59/RDR, 59–60)

By respectfully inventing, inventively respecting, respecting with a little bending or mimicking, we can twist free of the same, altering it just enough to let a little alterity loose. That is different from straightforward opposition, confrontational countering, which succumbs to dialectical assimilation. The invention of the permissible and possible, the inventiveness of "a human subject in an ontotheological horizon" (*Psy.*, 59/RDR, 60), invention within the limits of possibility alone, invention in conformity with institutional horizons, that all adds up to a confirmation of the same, the mirror image (*psyche*) that is sent back to the same. Then, in that invention, the other does not come and invention invents nothing (new), and this because nothing comes to the other or from the other. For the other is not the possible. So it would be necessary to say that the only possible invention is the invention of the impossible. . . . [A]n invention has to declare itself to be the invention of that which did not appear to be possible; otherwise it only makes explicit a program of possibilities within the economy of the same. (*Psy.*, 59/RDR, 60; cf. AC, 43/OH, 41–42)

It is the paradox of this impossible, of *the* impossible, that engages (*engager*) deconstruction, that gets its gears in motion, by means of which deconstruction can let the other come:

I am careful to say "let it come" because if the other is precisely what is not invented, the initiative or deconstructive inventiveness can consist only in opening, in uncloseting, destabilizing foreclusionary structures so as to allow for the passage toward the other. But one does not make the other come, one lets it come by preparing for its coming. (*Psy.*, 60/RDR, 60)

We can only prepare for the incoming of the other, but we cannot invent it, cannot effect it, bring it about, by a cunning deconstructive agency. We are called upon, paradoxically, to prepare for the incalculable, to prepare without calculating in advance. "Is this possible? Of course it is not; that is why it is the only possible invention" (*Psy.*, 60/RDR, 60).

Deconstruction is a discourse and a politics that works at not letting itself be enclosed by the same, at not being encompassed within "the economic circle of invention," which amounts to a method for reappropriating the different. Deconstruction dreams of the "absolute surprise," "*au-delà du possible*," of a writing, a *différance*, "without status, without law, without a horizon of reappropriation, programmation, institutional legitimation" (*Psy.*, 61/RDR, 61). Thus is it turned to the future, to the time to come:

For the time to come is its only concern: allowing the adventure or the event of the *tout autre* to come. Of a *tout autre* that cannot be confused with the God or Man of onto-theo-logy or with any of the figures of the configuration (the subject, consciousness, the unconscious, the self, man or woman, and so on). (*Psy.*, 61/RDR, 61)

That is deconstruction's passion, its only concern (*seul souci*): to make way for a *tout autre* that is not the God of onto-theo-logic, or the (Hu)Man of metaphysical Humanism. The *tout autre* cannot be programmed in advance by a "theological order," where everything has been providentially settled in advance, or by an anthropological order, where everything is our doing, which would doubly prevent this advent, issuing a *non, non* to the "coming of the other." Deconstruction means to bend this *non, non* into a *oui, oui*.

§6. Messianic Time: Derrida and Blanchot

Messianic Time

It was in the work of Maurice Blanchot that Derrida had first come upon the thematic of the "come!" Hence, without presuming to excavate fully the relationship between Derrida and Blanchot,[13] to map out the labyrinthine corridors of a relationship that, it is obvious, is also deeply implicated with Levinas, it is important to say a word or two about Blanchot's *viens*, at least about certain fragments of Blanchot that have worked their way into Derrida's *viens, oui, oui* and contributed to its apocalyptico-messianic tone. Blanchot is a crucial source, particularly inasmuch as he is a secular and not a biblical source, of Derrida's *viens* (as also of the logic of the *sans* and of the *pas*). For Derrida's *viens* belongs in greater proximity to Blanchot than to John of Patmos. I take *Le pas au-delà*—gamefully translated as *The Step Not Beyond*—as my point of departure.

Blanchot distinguishes ordinary, lived time (*temps ordinaire*) from an "other" time—and the "other language" that it requires—a time without the present, an exceedingly un-Husserlian time, to be sure, without retention or protention, which for Husserl would be a time *sans* time. The familiar notion of time, phenomenology's "lived time," is synthetically formed out of the present, past-present, and future-present, a schema which, as Heidegger points out, stretches all the way from the Greeks to Husserl. In this "other" time—which would be un-phenomenal, un-lived, non-experiential, extraordinary—the past is always already past, a past that was never present, never lived through, a *tout autre* past that did not pass through conscious life and experience only then to assume its irrevocable place in the flowing off of past nows. By the same token, the future, no less *tout autre*, is not a future present, a not-yet-present toward which consciousness can stretch out, protend, foresee, anticipate living through, as it gradually comes about, but rather a future that will never be present, that is prohibited in principle from ever being actualized at some future point in time. Such a future constitutes a certain event (*événement*) or non-event that is shot through with "nonoccurrence" (*inavènement*), what Derrida calls in "Pas" the "other event" (*l'autre événement*), or "*pas de événement*" (passage to and negation of the event) (*Parages*, 73). It is around such a future that the step/not beyond is organized, as the passage that is always made but always blocked.

The interruption of the living present is also the disruption of the living, conscious self, the self-presence of the self. This disruption is described variously by Blanchot as the anonymous, the neuter, the "he/it" (*le "il"*), the "disaster." Under any name, Blanchot means an erosion and hollowing out of the conscious subject, the master of the living present, the knight who confronts death's ominous possibility head on (or flees from it like a slave). Against this active, conscious subject living in the present while protending the future (Husserl), as also against authentic Dasein resolutely projected upon its being-possible (Heidegger), Blanchot thinks in terms of a radical passivity that he calls "dying" (*le mourir*).

There are indications in Blanchot that the "other" time can be given a *messianic* twist, that his notion of a future that will never be present has a messianic side, albeit a messianic *sans* any particular messianism. This messianic side, which draws Derrida's attention, is what I want to draw out in the present discussion. In *Le pas au-delà*, Blanchot writes that murder—in addition to its ethical horror—is a futile attempt to assume mastery over dying, to bring dying into the (living!) present, to actualize dying in an instant in which it is brought to stand as a finished fact, an actualized event, accomplished and achieved. So for Blanchot "thou shalt not kill" means:

> [D]o not infringe on dying, do not decide the indecisive, do not say: this is done, claiming for yourself a right over this "not yet"; do not pretend that the last word is spoken, time completed, the Messiah come at last. (SNB, 108)[14]

What is coming—here death—never actually arrives, is prohibited or blocked from passing over into actuality, from collapsing into the order of presence. Indeed, that is the source of a peculiar horror, not anxiety over the possibility of death, but horror before its impossibility, the horror that death does not come, like the insomniac to whom sleep does not "come." But this non-arrival of what is to come is also, and this is what interests me here, a way of safeguarding the indeterminacy, chance, and lightness of what is to-come—which is its messianic side. That can be expressed by saying that the Messiah never comes, that the very idea of the Messiah would be destroyed were the Messiah, to everyone's embarrassment and consternation, to have the indiscretion to show up and actually become present. The very idea of the Messiah is that he is *to* come, *à venir*, someone coming, not that he would ever actually arrive. The very function of the messianic idea is to evoke or provoke the come, *viens* or *venez*, in the singular or the plural (SNB, 137). The messianic idea turns on a certain structural openness, undecidability, unaccomplishment, non-occurrence, noneventuality, which sees to it that, in contrast to the way things transpire in ordinary time, things are never finished, that the last word is never spoken. Were the Messiah ever to show up, that indiscretion would ruin the whole idea of the messianic.

That messianic sentiment can be found in a wonderful little story about the Messiah that Blanchot tells in *The Writing of the Disaster*, a story that Derrida cites in a footnote to *Politiques de l'amitié* (Pol., 55n), in connection with the philosophers of the future of whom Nietzsche speaks in *Beyond Good and Evil*. Such philosophers are able to think the future, Derrida says, to "bear and sustain the future, that is to say, for the metaphysician who is allergic to the *perhaps*, to endure the intolerable, the undecidable, and the terrifying" (*Pol.*, 55). Then Derrida cites this text from the end of *The Writing of the Disaster*, which Blanchot introduces as follows:

♦ Jewish messianic thought (according to certain commentators) suggests the relation between the event (*événement*) and its nonoccurrence (*inavènement*).[15]

Jewish messianic thought gives us a way to think about time, about events, about the way they eventuate precisely inasmuch as they do not occur. Let us suppose, the story goes, that the Messiah shows up one day, at the gates of Rome, but in disguise, dressed as a beggar or a leper, an incognito meant to "protect or prevent his coming (*venue*)." The *venue* of the Messiah, his coming or arrival, is something to shelter or protect from ordinary time and the present. The whole order of *venir* and *à-venir* belongs to an other, messianic time and an other language, so that nothing coming (*venue*) could ever actually occur or come about, or have occurred or have come about, in ordinary time. The Messiah's "coming" can never actually correspond to an actual-historical appearance in ordinary time. Whatever appearance the Messiah does make must be carefully protected or sheltered by the discretion of a disguise, lest the infinite provocation, the discreet delicacy and lightness, of what is coming be destroyed by its exposure to ordinary time, by its absorption into the grossness of the order of presence. That is why when someone "obsessed with questioning"[16] indiscreetly penetrates the beggarly disguise and recognizes the Messiah, he asks, "When will you come (*viendras-tu*)?" For the Messiah's being-there is not his coming: "*Le fait d'être là n'est pas la venue*." Even if the Messiah is there, *là*, in the flesh, present in ordinary time, such a presence can never amount to a coming, for coming—*venue, venir, l'avenir*—does not belong to the order of presence, "*sa venue ne correspond pas à une présence*," but to a messianic order. Even if the Messiah stands before us, even if we poke him in the ribs, it will still be necessary to say, to call and invoke, "*viens, viens*," for the coming of the Messiah is not a gross event, heavy and thick with presence. Blanchot's "come" comes along with a "don't come!" if coming is reduced to becoming present.[17]

It is interesting that even in Christian messianism, when the historical Jesus of Nazareth is proclaimed the Christ—too little patience and discretion? too much haste?[18]—it is necessary for Jesus to die so that we may wait for him to come *again*. Then the Christian community may continue to recite and repeat *viens*, to hope in what is to come, and to organize itself around the "Come, Lord Jesus," memorably inscribed in the last chapter of The Apocalypse to John. For Blanchot, the Christian dogma of the Incarnation turns on a confusion of messianic time with historical time, on a certain contraction of the lightness of messianic time to the grossness of the order of presence.

Now suppose, Blanchot continues, the Messiah, in answer to the question as to the time of his coming, were to respond by saying "Today." That is an answer likely to make an impression. There is no waiting for the Messiah; he is here, today, now—"although to wait is an obligation," since we are always waiting for what is coming and "something coming" is always something to await. Then Blanchot says the question is *when is this now?*" Raising a question which he answers in the same breath, he writes, "When is this now—a now which does not belong to ordinary time, which necessarily overturns it, which does not maintain it but destabilizes it?"[19] *This* now, the Messiah's now, belongs to messianic time and is not the now of ordinary time; the messianic now does not maintain the *maintenant* of *temps ordinaire* but breaks it up, breaks it open, and opens it to what is coming, which is the very structure of messianic time. So when the Messiah says "today," now, he means "Now, if only you heed me, or if you are willing to listen to my voice." The messianic "today" means: if you will begin, now, to respond to the call that the Messiah himself addresses to you, begin to answer the demands he places upon you, if, in order words, you are willing now to say *viens* as a response to the Messiah's call, and to call for the Messiah not with hollow words but with virtue. There is a way of waiting for the future that is going on right now, that begins here and now, and places an urgent demand upon us at this moment. That is why Blanchot says that merely calling *viens* would not be enough, if the call were hollow, full of sounding brass but unaccompanied by virtue and repentance. That call for doing justice is also signaled by the setting of the Messiah's appearance—among beggars, among the poor, the widow, the orphan, and the stranger, those who demand justice now, for justice deferred is justice denied. The messianic "today" means: if you are willing to respond—by your passivity and your patience—to the coming of the Messiah, for the Messiah's kingdom is always to come, the very meaning of the Messiah is of a kingdom to come, of what is structurally coming, even as it makes an urgent demand upon us now.

That is why Blanchot attaches a little Levinasian, slightly non-Christian conclusion to his story. The Messiah could never be a God-man, or anything divine, nor some gigantic Hegelian event which would signify "the end of history, the suppression of time." The Messiah might simply be a just man, one who tends to God's poor. Perhaps not even that, perhaps not even some *determinable, identifiable* person, who would of course become such only by stepping into the gross event of ordinary, lived time.

The Messiah might simply be each one of us just insofar as we wait for the coming, because

> justice won't wait; it is to be done at every instant, to be realized all the time. . . . Every just act (are there any?) makes of its day the last day or—as Kafka said—the very last: a day no longer situated in the ordinary succession of days but one that makes of the most commonplace ordinary, the extraordinary.[20]

This passage is very close to Derrida's notion of justice, which we have also insisted is deeply resonant with the prophetic notion of justice, of being faithful to the coming of justice, making justice happen, now, for justice, which is to come, cannot wait (FL, 57–58/DPJ, 26). Justice means doing justice, doing the truth, *facere veritatem*, in order that he might come, in order to bring about "the messianic time," the *epoche* of the Messiah. *That future*, that messianic future to come, is more futural than any future-present, even as it cannot wait. Blanchot concludes the tale with a citation of Levinas and Scholem, who have written:

> All prophets—there is no exception—have prophesied only for the messianic time [*epoche*]. As for future time, what eye has seen it except Yours, Lord, who will act for him who is faithful to you and keeps waiting.[21]

Messianic time is prophetic time; the time to come is the time of the justice to come, that disturbs the present with the call for justice, which calls the present beyond (*au-delà*) itself. For the most unjust thing of all would be to close off the future by saying that justice is present, that the present time is just, "to pretend that the last word is spoken, time completed, the Messiah come at last" (SNB, 108) (like the right-wing extremists on the American Supreme Court who overturn affirmative action policies as if egalitarian justice has already come, here, now, right in the middle of American apartheid!).

Dying

The messianic notion of time is inextricably linked with Blanchot's notion of "dying." The arrival of what is to come (the coming of the Messiah) is nothing we can control or master, nothing over which the self has any authority or powers of disposition, nothing the self can actively bring about but something summoning our deepest passivity. The step beyond, *le pas au-delà*, the *pas-sage*, the transcendence, or the "transgression," is not a step the self takes; transgression is not aggression. The step beyond is not an action and not an ordinary passion but, in Levinasian fashion, a passivity more passive than passivity. *Le pas* is not a work but a non-work or worklessness (*désoeuvrement*) of patience, not the doing of an *agens* but the suffering of a *patiens*:

> Transgression transgresses by passion, patience, and passivity, trans-gressing always the most passive of ourselves in the "dying in the light-ness of dying." . . . (SNB, 119; cf. *Parages*, 53)

The *pas* in *le pas au-delà* is the *pas* of *passage, passion, passivité, patience, faux-pas*, which, along with *il ne faut pas, plus de pas*, and *pas de plus*, constitute a string that Derrida continually explores in "Pas." "Dying" is what precisely bears the structure of *le pas au-delà*. Dying (*le mourir*) is to be distinguished from death (*la mort*), where death has "the crushing solidity" and weight of presence, the irrevocable being or non-being of something finished or accomplished, the obscene visibility of a determi-nate, definite, decided fact, of "a gross or inert event" (SNB, 93–94). Death is an event in ordinary time, while dying, on the other hand, is "the non-arrival of what comes about," "the prohibited mocking the prohibi-tion, there where it would be, in some way, forbidden to die" (SNB, 95; cf. *Parages*, 62–63). Dying is *le pas au-delà* in the double sense of *pas* that interests Blanchot and Derrida: (1) the *step* beyond, the transgression or transcendence, exposing the present to what is coming; (2) the *not* beyond, no beyond, the prohibition of transgression: *no* going beyond, *pas au-delà*, for dying can never mean being actually, decidedly dead. We are "ar-rested" in life, our "death sentence" is, as it was for "J." in *L'arrêt de la mort* (the point of departure of Derrida's "Living-On: Border Lines"), "arrested," "stayed," deferred, impossible. Dying cannot come about, can-not be realized; dying is a step beyond (transgression) but a step that cannot be taken (prohibition). Death, even if it is slow, is always sudden, always visible, vulgar, obscene, exposed, public, and it takes place only once. But dying happens discreetly, invisibly, with an unbearable light-ness, in an innumerable repetition, like a beating heart or a recitative, again and again, which is why Derrida's interest from beginning to end in "Pas" is with citation ("the drama of its citationality was what mattered to me at the outset," *Ton*, 87/RTP, 162). "*Viens*" is always a citation, a re-citation, a repetition, that must be continually repeated, *oui, oui*, in a double affirmation:

> [T]he yes, which says nothing, describes nothing but itself, the perfor-mance of its own event of affirmation, repeats itself, *quotes, cites* itself, says *yes-to* itself as (to an-)other in accordance with the ring. . . . (*Parages*, 149/LO, 104)

"It is forbidden to die" is not a law of God or man or nature announcing the obligation to live, but a pronouncement by time that death is a being-finished with life that life cannot know. There is no present, no living present, for death, no moment on the stage of living time upon which death could make its entrance; there is no time to die. Dying is an *inavènement* that belongs to the order of *viens* and *venir*, not of presence.

That makes dying sound like *Sein-zum-Tode* in *Being and Time*, not the definite actuality of death in a future-present, the death of "actuarial" studies, but the "certain but indefinite possibility," the futural possibility of an impossibility, that haunts and, by haunting, awakens Dasein's freedom and *Seinkönnen*, that gives Dasein the gift of an authentic *Zu-kunft*. Indeed, Heidegger's notion of a certain but indefinite possibility arose, to the chagrin of Heidegger's secularizing admirers, on the occasion of a lecture course Heidegger gave on Paul's Letters to the Thessalonians in which Heidegger formulated his notion of authentic temporality in a reflection precisely dedicated to messianic time. The impatient Thessalonians demanded to know of Paul *when* Jesus would come again, to which Paul responded, as Heidegger construes it, do not worry about calendar time, about *temps ordinaire;* the coming of the Lord is not a matter of marking your calendars in anticipation of a future-present, but of existential transformation. This *when* is a matter of *how*, of being ready, of holding fast, of saying constantly *viens*, come, Lord Jesus, no matter what is happening now.[22]

But, as Derrida says in *Aporias*, while Blanchot "constantly repeats . . . the impossible dying, the impossibility, alas, of dying, he says at once the same thing and something completely different from Heidegger" (*Apories*, 337 / *Aporias*, 77). For everything in Blanchot moves in the opposite direction (a Levinasian direction), along an opposed trajectory—not the "possibility of an impossibility," but the "impossibility of possibility." Dying is not a possibility, not a power or *potens*, a *Seinkönnen*, an active, resolute projection of authentic Dasein that has gathered itself together in order to effect a macho, phallic face-off with the fell reaper, out there all alone in its *Eigentlichkeit* without its mommy, facing up to death's certain but indefinite spectrality. On the contrary, dying is *im-potens*, the ruin of the self, *désastre* not *Selbstsein*, not a resolute possibility the self assumes and that indeed constitutes and organizes the self as a self, but the breaking out of the neuter or anonymous in the self.[23] Dying is not something I do, actively and resolutely, as a work of life. Dying comes about in an order different from the living present, *sans* life and *sans* death, neither (*ne uter*) life nor death. Not I die, but it dies, *le "il"* in me is dying. Dying (like writing, like the language no one speaks) has no author, no personal authority; it is not the personal deed of a prestigious knight of death or hero of authenticity (SNB, 109) but the im-personal, in-finitive "to die," *mourir* (like *"dire"*). Dying is the fragility, the patience and passivity, of responding in the neuter, in a passion more passive than all passivity, of dying *before* any consent (any active assumption of a possibility):

> In the neuter—the name *sans* name—nothing responds, except the re-
> sponse that fails, that has always just missed responding and missed the
> response, never patient enough to "go/beyond," without this "step/be-
> yond" being accomplished. (SNB, 118)

The neutrality of dying, the passion beyond passivity, is an ur-passivity
that lies deeper than any determinate yes or no, affirmation or negation,
action or passion, directed at a determinate entity.

As the anonymous rumbling of the neuter within me, dying is not *my*
possibility. "Not 'I die,' that does not concern me, but 'dying that does not
concern me' puts me in play in all dying" (SNB, 123). My concern is not
that I die but rather that I be unconcerned with my dying. Dying is not a
matter of my *Selbstsorge* but of my concern with the other, a concern that
puts me in relation with, in play with, the other's dying. So the step
beyond, *le pas au-delà*, is not a step I take to the other but the step of the
other at my door, the knock that solicits my welcoming response (I think
it is Elijah, or at least Levinas knocking). But again that is not a relation
that I bring about or even assume; it lies deeper than ordinary responsibility in *temps ordinaire*. Even when I die deliberately for the other: that is
like this passivity wanting to act in its very passivity, to make an appearance in historical time; that is what practical generosity is, which is to try
to make real the unrealizable (SNB, 123).

By "dying," Blanchot appears to be drifting in the direction of Levinas, of
what Levinas means by substitution, being-for-the-other, transcendence as
the absolute passivity of being-already-delivered over to the other before any
conscious act or choice. In Blanchot, dying does not mean getting sick or
growing old, which are visible events in ordinary time, but a kind of ontological erosion of the self, a hollowing out of self-ishness, I-hood, which
begins to take on the look of Levinasian substitution, of turning the self inside
out—not my death but the death of the other—of a deep responsiveness
before all responsible action to the approach, to the step of the other at my
door. Seen thus "the step not beyond" is what Blanchot calls "*éloignement*,"
which Derrida translates with the Heideggerian term "*Ent-fernung*" (*Being
and Time*, §23) de-distancing, an approach to the other that does not, that
cannot, remove the alterity of the other. As Derrida says in "Shibboleth," "the
step not beyond" is a step toward the other, toward "you":

> you toward whom I must take a step which, without bringing me nearer
> to you, without exchanging myself with you, without being assured
> passage, lets the word pass and assigns us, if not to the one, at least to
> the same. (*Schib.*, 92/WT, 55)

The step not beyond is the necessity and impossibility of approaching the
other; it means to approach the inappropriable, to approach without appropriating.

§6. Messianic Time

"Dying" thus means, on the one hand, the "neutral" process in virtue of which the anonymous, the neuter, le "il" hollows out the *moi* and strips it of its authority, power, and positive possibilities, the horror, not of being headed for the grave but of being arrested in life, unable to die, like an insomniac in a night without end. But, on the other hand, and beyond (*au-delà*) this anonymity, dying also tends to take on an *ethical* sense, clearly deriving—if anything is clear in Maurice the Obscure—from Levinas, which turns the being-for-itself of the self inside out and makes of it a being-for-the-other.

Simon Critchley raises the question of the extent to which there is a genuinely ethical movement in Blanchot, whether beyond or within "the space of literature" there is also a space for ethics, whether the ethical is not swallowed by the disaster. Critchley asks to what extent the religious and theological "tone" of what Levinas calls "ethics" puts a definitive distance between him and Blanchot. However this question of Blanchot vis-à-vis Levinas is resolved, it is clear that, like Blanchot, Derrida has no theological or sectarian agenda to pursue, but, like Levinas, Derrida clearly takes the *viens* to be a call for justice to come, as a prophetic call.[24]

To the extent that dying has an ethical dimension in Blanchot, it is an emblem for the corruption of the *conatus essendi*, the congenital rot or erosion of the *conatus vivendi*, the depletion or ruination of my *Seinkönnen*, the scattering of my possibility to be or not to be (SNB, 131). With the word "dying," Blanchot means to point a silent finger at the weakness, the fragility of the self, the inertia, the *désœuvrement* (the worklessness or being out of work), being cut off from the busy flow of the world, "outside," the disaster, the impotent, impoverished weakness from which, on his view, any *oeuvre*, any work of art, would issue. While that deep ontological ruin is lighter than, prior to, older than anything transpiring in ordinary time, it appears, from the texts from *Le pas au-delà* that we have examined, that it also can translate into altruistic action (just saying *viens* will get you nowhere without justice). For Blanchot, a generous, heroic, active dying for the other is a grave, heavy, responsible deed that transpires in all the visible light of living time, paying the "ultimate sacrifice" in *temps ordinaire*. But such action seems to me to be a visible correlate to dying, which is something "light," invisible, and discreet, a deep ontological structure that is prior to, or lighter than, a responsible decision, lighter than the actuality of a deed or an event, of actually being dead, killing oneself, or giving oneself up for the other, a surrendering to the lightness of chance prior to the gravity of choice (SNB, 123).

Viewed thus, the step not beyond, *le pas au-delà*, is the necessary but impossible demand laid upon us by the other who has stepped up to our door. It heeds the call from afar to set out for, to book pas-sage for, that "other shore"[25] (both death and the other), to ar-rive at that distant shore (*rive*) of the other—which stirs in a Levinasian image with the recurrent image of the sea and water (*l'eau*, "0") in Blanchot, which interests Derrida throughout "Pas" (*Parages*, 63). *Le pas* is a *faux-pas*, a pas-sage to what could never be completed, an attempt to cross the uncrossable, to a *tout autre* whose utter alterity would be destroyed were it ever reached. The other could never actually come.

At the end of *Le pas au-delà* Blanchot writes:[26]

> Come, come, come (*viens, viens, venez*), you whom the injunction, the prayer, the wait could not suit. (SNB, 135)

As a structure of messianic time, the *viens* (s.) or *venez* (pl.) is not to be taken as a determinate word in ordinary time, like a specific prayer or injunction directed toward a determinate future-present person or thing, toward a determinable Messiah, for example, or a determinable End of History, Hegelian or Marxist. Outside all human mastery and control, *viens* hopes for a break within the interstices of the laws of regularity, an outbreak of chance within the crevices of the continuous flow of presence. Everything turns, Derrida comments, on "the chance, the risk: that the other of language comes to pass (*se passe*) in the step not beyond of language (*le pas au-delà de la langue*)" (*Parages*, 74). *Viens* is "a wild word" (*un mot sauvage*), something that it shares with *sauf* and *pas*; it does not take its place inside language, settling itself within a familiar "part of speech," but has a certain "non-linguistic wildness" (*Parages*, 84–85). It is not an isolatable part of language, an imperative, in the present tense, second person singular (or plural); it is not a determinable prayer, demand, or desire. It does not describe or show some subject or object; it does not call up a definite something that was not there before (*Parages*, 26–27). *Viens* is rather a certain *Ur*-affirmation, older and lighter than any determinate word or deed, that silently and invisibly tears open lived time and ordinary language, that renders them always already structurally open to what is coming, that prohibits (*pas!*) closure while soliciting transcendence (*le pas*). The *viens* is the order, or disorder, of messianic time, of *venir* and *avenir*, that disturbs the order of presence, that hollows it out, so that what is coming does not, never did, never can, correspond to presence and presence cannot close over. That, I think, goes to the heart of what Derrida means by the messianic as opposed to any historical messianisms, all of which transpire in ordinary time.

It should not go unnoticed that, for Blanchot, as for Derrida, *viens* is not God-less. *Viens* has nothing to do, in principle, with garden variety theism or atheism, which would concern themselves with the gross presence or absence of an entity. Blanchot, like Derrida, is deeply fascinated by the name of God, a name that stretches language toward the "other," constituting a language of the other. The flow of ordinary time and language are interrupted and disturbed by certain supercharged words—like "madness" and "fear"—among which is also to be numbered the name of God. These are names "too charged with themselves, as charged with all the surcharge of language," words which function like "a messenger of another language," which tend to tear themselves loose from ordinary language, to fall outside language but precisely in such a way as to constitute another language. "God is thus a name, pure materiality, naming nothing, not even himself," a name whose tendency to disappear or withdraw from ordinary language is an indication not of its nullity or illusoriness, but of its significance *sans* significance, an indication of something extra-ordinary that never was or will be present but is also coming:

> The "death of God" is perhaps only the help that historical language vainly brings to allow a word to fall outside of language without another announcing itself there: absolute slip. (SNB, 60; cf. 48, 71, 121)

That is very close to Derrida's interest in the name of God. The name of God tends to disappear, to efface itself, to make itself meaningless, to void and avoid itself, a name *sans* name. But it does so precisely in order to point to the possibility of something wholly other, *tout autre*, the advent of *the* impossible, of what is never present, what never collapses into presence, never falls into the gross idolatry of the present. God's name obeys the strange syntax of the *sans*—almost exemplarily I am tempted to say:

> The same word and the same thing appear removed from themselves, subtracted from their reference and from their identity, fully continuous with letting themselves be traversed, in their old body, towards a *tout autre* dissimulated in them. But no more than in *pas* does this consist in a simple privation or negation, far from it (*il s'en faut*). It forms the trace or the step (*pas*) of the *tout autre* that is at issue in it, the re-treat of the *pas*, and of the *pas sans pas*. (*Parages*, 90; cf. *Parages* 151/LO, 105–06)

It is in virtue of the agrammatical syntax of the *viens* that, were the Messiah actually to come, say, among the wretched living under the bridges in any American city, dressed in rags, among the beggars and the lepers and the HIV-positive, the only sensible thing to ask him, if we felt obliged to ask anything at all, would be, "When will you come?" But it would be better if we could get past the indiscretion, the scorching aggression, and the delaying tactics of questioning to a simpler, more elemental word or two, doubly affirmed with a passivity more passive than all passivity.

Viens.

Oui, oui.

I WARN EVERYONE WHO HEARS THE WORDS
OF THE PROPHECY OF THIS BOOK:
IF ANYONE SUPPLEMENTS THEM,
GOD WILL SUPPLEMENT THAT PERSON
WITH THE PLAGUES DESCRIBED IN THIS BOOK.
(REV. 22:18)

§7. An Apocalypse sans Apocalypse
to Jacques of El Biar

By 1980, Derrida realized that all this talk of *viens* and *oui, oui* had begun to sound a little revivalist and Bible-thumping, like the last chapter of John's Apocalypse. Hence he found it necessary to address head-on the question of the apocalyptic tone that had recently been adopted in French philosophy, including and especially his own. The time had come to explain the peculiar passion of his particular apocalyptic secret, which he called his apocalypse *sans* apocalypse.

To its critics deconstruction seems to threaten the university and intellectual life generally with a kind of antimodernism that jettisons all that the Enlightenment had achieved.[27] Indeed, it looks like the *Schwärmerei* worked over the coals by Kant in "On a Newly Arisen Superior Tone in Philosophy." In this essay Kant adopted a very sarcastic—shall we say, superior?—tone toward religious and mystical enthusiasts who put feelings and private communications with the supersensible world in the place of pure passionless practical reason. Derrida's gloss on Kant, and on all the twentieth-century Kants who want to declare deconstruction unreconstructed *Schwärmerei*, is to say that there are *Aufklärers* and there are *Aufklärers*, and there are apocalyptics and there are apocalyptics. Just as we regularly require an *Aufklärung* to put out the fires of religious fanaticism which threatens everyone who is *extra ecclesiam*, it is no less true that we require an apocalyptic tone or two to raise holy hell whenever the *Aufklärers* try to shut the door and throw away the key on anything that departs from what they call reason. Whenever the *Aufklärers* try to saturate the horizon of the possible, to set forth definitively the defining conditions of possibility for everything in sight, to put off limits what Derrida calls *the* impossible, then an apocalyptic tone is required to shout, to cry, to pray, even very loudly, "*viens*," let the impossible come! (That is not to say that deconstruction is all shouting and no hard work.) Then it is time to shift into messianic time.

Derrida's "On a Newly Arisen Apocalyptic Tone in Philosophy"[28] is a provocative delimitation of his relationship to the Enlightenment, an unsettling settling of accounts with modernity, a kind of Derridean counterpart to the Foucauldian tract on Kant's "What is Enlightenment?" This is an essay on what could have been called "postmodernism," that is, of how to work one's way *through* modernity (not around it), how to work with it (not jettison it), had not this word suffered the ill-fortune of being ground into senselessness by overuse, by a wild circulation that is "postmodern" in the very worst sense.

Deconstruction inhabits the space that separates the light of Kant's pure reason from the visions of the spirit-seers. Derrida, who distrusts both visions, does not advocate either light, but a little blindness; he does not take either side but explores the space that separates the two, looking there for the chance of an opening, for the opening of the *viens*, which is much more a Jewish or Jewgreek opening for justice than are the lights of the *Lumières* or the spirit-seers.

Kant is doing combat with "mystagogues," purveyors of secret, supernatural visions who dispense with the necessity for public argumentation and use their private visions to establish their "gogic," "ductive," seductive power over others. The mystagogues are upstarts (*parvenus*) who give themselves airs, a lordly (*vornehm*, *grand seigneur*) and undemocratic tone that would ring in the death of philosophy. To these spirit-seers Kant opposes not only the unforced force of reason but also a powerful counterforce, the counter-tone of sarcasm and satire, which he otherwise claims has no place in philosophical argumentation (*Ton*, 20/RTP, 124). These *Führers* claim to possess a secret (*Geheimnis*) that authorizes them to lead the rest of us around (*Ton*, 27–29/RTP, 127–28). But the mystagogues are "cracked," *verstimmt*, deranged, delirious, derailed, and out of tune. They march to the tune of their own private voices, which they alone are authorized to interpret, instead of heeding the voice of reason, which speaks in publicly adjudicable and democratic tones (*Ton*, 33–34/RTP, 131–32). They lay claim to secret intuitions that are denied to the rest of us who do not wander beyond the limits of possible experience. These mystagogues have mystified philosophy, turning it into a kind of cryptopoetics, in which metaphors are substituted for arguments, and philosophy is confused with literature. The plaintive tones of Kant's complaint, Derrida complains, have a familiar ring (*Ton*, 45/RTP, 138). At the end, Kant, ever and perpetually a man of peace, proposes a concordat, a peace treaty, to which everybody should sign on, mystagogue and *Aufklärers* alike, to the effect that everybody should fall in line behind the Moral Law, which is the *unum necessarium*, without making pretensions to identifying this Law any further (*Ton*, 54/RTP, 143), for example, as a privileged communication from a goddess made in private to a few. The spirit-seers would cease their voyeurism, no longer trying to lift up the goddess's skirt and reveal her secrets. *Apokalupto*.

The mystagogues, however, do not have a monopoly on apocalyptic eschatology, and with this point Derrida tries to shed some light on the scene at Cerisy, 1980, where the "ends of man" are under the bubble. Ever since the time of Kant, philosophy has been visited by one eschatology after another, beginning with the Hegelian and Marxist ends of history (the latter of which, he says, anticipating *Specters of Marx* and Fukuyama, we today too quickly want to forget) (*Ton*, 59/RTP, 145). Nowadays philosophers try to outdo one another by announcing the end of one thing after another—of history, philosophy, metaphysics, Christianity, Oedipus, the university, literature, God, and God knows what else. Even the "end of the book," we might add, as Jacques of El Biar revealed to us in a special apocalypse called *Of Grammatology*. Those who declare the end of this or that have their own ends in view, and we must stay alert as to where they are trying to lead us, pedagogically, demagogically, mystagogically, synagogically, or whatever.

We must vigilantly keep the *Lumières* burning. "We cannot and we must not—this is a law and a destiny—forgo the *Aufklärung*," the desire for critique and truth; we must keep alive a healthy desire to demystify that discourse which speculates on vision, theophany, and parousia (*Ton*, 64/RTP, 148). That vigilance is a defining feature of Enlightenment, modernity, and emancipation with which Derrida does not mean to break (cf. DDP, 497/PR, 19). On this point at least, on the denial of what Kant would call an intellectual intuition, an *intuitus originarius*, a direct and intuitive insight into some sort of *mundus intelligibile* or other, which would be a transcendental signified *par excellence*, a supersensible secret, Derrida is a Kantian all the way down. But the post-Kantian, post-critical point he makes is that all along we must also be vigilant about these Enlightenment vigilantes, and watch where these demystifying pedagogues are leading us. For we must beware just as much those who claim they have seen the lights of the *Lumières*, for the well-hidden (eu-kalyptic) flower of apocalypticism can conceal itself under the rock of all these demystifications. Now he is closing in on his vision.

If we imagine, by a kind of provisional fiction, that there were but one apocalyptic tone, instead of a generalized derangement (*Verstimmung*) and unmasterable polytonality of apocalypticisms (which is what Derrida really thinks), it would sound something like this: I have come to unveil the truth for you about the end of the world. The end is near and I can see it; we are going to die, the faithful and the goyim alike. I alone can reveal the truth, the destination. We must form a closed community of those who stay awake while the others sleep (*Ton*, 69–71/RTP, 151–52). The Apocalypse of John embodies this scene. I, John (John who? Which John? Last name, please?), have come to tell you that the Lord, who is and was, who is first, last, and always, is one who "will be" but who comes, *ho erkhomenos, venturus est* (Rev. 1:4, 1:8). I am coming, I am going to come—now the "I" has switched from John to Yeshoua (watch out)—I am right on the verge of coming. That at least is what John says that Jesus says, at least that is what is written in the best manuscripts we have. John is in the wind, *in spiritu*, and he writes as if Jesus were whispering in his ear, dictating to him to write what he sees and send it to the seven churches (Rev. 1:9–12). One imagines the postcard Derrida found in the Bodleian Library in Oxford, a frontispiece of a fortune-telling book, with John seated, writing, while Jesus dictates in his ear; and then, by a catastrophic reversal, Jesus, who never published a word, seated, writing, while John dictates in his ear, which is just about the scene that *New Testament* scholarship today describes, which a good many of the faithful take to be a catastrophe, pure and simple.

The scene described in the opening paragraph is still more complicated, depicting a system of messages (*envois*) sent out over a complex apocalyptic postal system. This is the apocalypse of Yeshoua the Messiah, but it was given to Yeshoua by Elohim, and from Yeshoua it was delivered to an angel, who passed it on to John, who is writing it down and mailing it to the seven churches in Asia (of which we have manuscripts in varying conditions). There are a lot of people on the line. In the days long before fiber optics, this was called a "party line," a line shared by numerous customers, which was not only very inconvenient if you needed to use the phone, but could eventuate in a very confusing babble/Babel of voices when other parties broke in on the conversation. If we add to this the confusion over who "John" is to begin with—in the early centuries of the Church he was identified with the author of the fourth gospel, whereas nowadays that idea is out of favor—we start to get an idea about the Babelian confusion of voices here (nowadays even John the Evangelist, like the other evangelists, is a community, a John Incorporated). In this multiplicity of divided voices, beyond a calculable plurality, the *envoi* leaps from one sender to another, each messenger making reference (*renvoi*) back to another, forming a relay system of *envoyés, apostoli, angeli,* envoys or messengers. If we press this issue hard—which really is what happens in the debates in which New Testament scholarship is enmeshed, about what is Jesus, what is Matthew, what is "Q," etc.—we can see where Derrida is trying to lead us. He is trying, devilishly, to lead us astray, to make us more and more unsure of who addresses what to whom, more and more caught up in a scrambling or *Verstimmung* of the hermeneutico-apocalyptic lines (*Ton,* 74–77/RTP, 154–56).

Of course, the Church will only allow this scrambled situation to get so far before it calls the police. The Church can always establish a biblical commission to settle these disputes and to keep the identity of everybody on the line clear, and generally to keep everybody in line, or else. The Church will tolerate the anarchy or energy of *écriture* only so long before it puts its institutional, foundationalist foot down.[29] Institutional powers are very good at settling hermeneutic debates one way or another (usually by putting their foot down—on somebody's neck; *silentium laus*). But since Derrida is adrift among the powerlessness of *écriture*, devoid and divested of institutional support, things are prone to be a little more Babelian and slippery, and this profusion of voices is a symptom of a quasi-transcendental slip. So, by what Derrida's calls a "catastrophic reversal," we can venture a much more Babelian hypothesis: "as soon as one no longer knows who speaks or who writes, the text becomes apocalyptic" (*Ton*, 77/RTP, 156). That would make for an unbelievable apocalyptic structure (or maybe the only one we can believe, however much apoplexy this may cause believers): a text is apocalyptic just when the confusion and profusion run wild. Catastrophes and cataclysmic ends-of-the-world, of course, are what apocalyptic writings are all about, what they are always prognosticating, but without thinking that they too would *themselves* be swept up in their very own winds, in their very textuality, in the confusion of *écriture*. On the contrary, these revealed texts take themselves to be above the fury and the fray, to speak from a safe and elevated site, to be getting it right and seeing clearly, to be building their towers straight into the clouds. Otherwise it would be a catastrophe.

By a catastrophe Derrida has in mind a certain textualist turning around. *Strephein* means to move; a *strophe* is what the chorus sings as it moves from right to left across the stage; hence, a *kata-strophe* means a reversal of movement, to get the chorus moving in the opposite direction, to sing a new song and strike up a change of tone. By this Derrida means reversing the strong sense of *destination* in the apocalyptic tone, which is the note that biblical commissions and institutional authoritarians strike. Deconstruction would disturb this scene of assured destination, un-veiling or exposing the structure of a system of relays in which we do not know who is saying what to whom, thereby stirring up *la passion du non-savoir*. The result would be an apocalypse without destination, lost letters in the sacred mail, the revelation of the fact that when it comes to revelation we are a little lost and devoid of uncontrovertible visions. (Call it an apocalytic, apoplectic apophatics.)

That catastrophe is the very scene of "literature," the secret that there is no secret, the very situation in which we all more or less find ourselves, if we renounce the voyeuristic claim to have seen beneath the goddess's skirt. Thus it belongs to the very structure of the *viens* to pray without knowing the destination of one's prayers, to weep without quite knowing why or over whom or whence one weeps, to expect what one cannot possibly envision, to look forward, through blinding tears, to the unforeseeable. Messianic time is through and through a time of hope and faith and blindness, of the passion of a blind faith. It does not engage, does not get in gear, until one is lost, destinerrant, having been divested of the guiding light of a future present. The secret, *sans vision, sans vérité*, impassions.

For Derrida, the catastrophic scene of every writing is one in which messages (*envois*) refer (*renvoient*) to other messages without decidable destination. When he says this is a "completely angelic" structure he is being a little devilish, since he really means that things have gone to the devil and we are in a hell of a mess. On the slightly diabolical twist of this catastrophic reversal, the apocalyptic takes on an *a*-destinal sense, a sense of *destinerrance*, which would be, he says, "a transcendental condition of all discourse, of all experience even, of every mark or every trace" (*Ton*, 77–78/RTP, 156–57). On the catastrophic reading of the Apocalypse, "apocalyptic" discourses in the narrow sense, like John's, "would be only an example, an *exemplary* revelation of this transcendental structure" (*Ton*, 78/RTP, 157). In that case, apocalypse here would mean not the revelation of a secret truth, but, quite the reverse, letting the secret out of the bag that there is no secret, no *Geheimnis* that anybody knows or can get straight, no high ground above the *goyim*, but only "the divisible *envois* for which there is no self-presentation nor assured destination" (*Ton*, 78/RTP, 157). That would be a catastrophe, part of the difficulty of life if you believe, as I do, that believing is seeing through a *glas* darkly. That would not undermine belief but, on the contrary, reinforce the idea that belief—blindness, not vision—is all you have to go on. *Je ne sais pas—je ne vois pas—il faut croire* (MdA, 130/MB, 129).

But this is no doomsday forecast. For this *je ne sais pas* is also what impassions, what drives the passion of deconstruction for the impossible, what drives poetry, or literature, as we learn in "Shibboleth":

> "I don't know," *je ne sais pas*, signals a situation. In what I have elsewhere called its *restance*, remnance, the poem always speaks beyond knowledge, *au-delà du savoir*. It writes, and what it writes is, first of all, this very fact, that it is addressed and destined beyond knowledge, inscribing dates and signatures which one may encounter and bless, without knowing every-thing of what they date or sign. Blessing beyond knowledge, commem-orating through forgetting or the unimparted secret, partaking yet in the unimpartable. (*Schib.*, 63–64/WT, 37)

When "we" today—"we, *Aufklärers* of modern times"—when "we con-tinue to denounce the impostor apostles, the 'so-called envoys' not sent [*envoyés*] by anyone . . . all those charged with a historic mission of whom nothing has been requested and who have been charged with nothing," we find that we still stand in the shoes of John of Patmos, in "the best apocalyptic tradition," which has always denounced false apocalypses (*Ton*, 80–81/RTP, 158–59). The question is where do we draw the line, what are the limits of this denunciation and demystification of apocalyp-tics? To begin with, which is the Kantian move, the movement through Kant: "this demystification must be led as far as possible." Like Kant, Derrida will have nothing to do with secret knowledge—with intellectual intuition, privileged access, *schwärmerische Vision*, divine mysteries or rev-elations—which are apocalyptic stratagems in which one purports to shed one's textual skin or, if you will pardon the catachresis, to peek beneath the goddess's skirt. Apart from the suspect epistemology of this cryptology, this cryptopolitics supports the most dangerous conservative politics. But one should no less mercilessly expose the so-called dispassionate *Aufklärers* who expose such *Schwärmerei*. For Derrida, the only secret is, there is no secret.

But, and there is always a but, deconstruction is a matter of buts, it is also true that "nothing is less conservative than the apocalyptic genre," nothing more useful than the shrill voice of apocalyptic outcries when the killing curtain of censorship is about to close, nothing more powerful, say, than a recitative at the foot of the Lincoln Memorial, than a black American eschatological apocalyptic who claims to have a dream, to be dreaming of the impossible. I have a dream. *Viens.* The historical apocalypticisms grew more frequent just in proportion as the power of Rome over the Jews grew more complete; apocalypticism is what is required wherever "Caesar" is too strong. Of course, censorship need not be always Caesarian and state-sponsored; it can be practiced just as well by the "moral majority," the (anything but) "silent majority," by straight, white, family-value advocates, which harbor the enormous power to exclude everything that is not considered "legitimate" political discourse. Then we need apocalyptics to dislocate destinations, derail them, drive them *verstimmt*, break up concordats, challenge the established receivability of messages, defy the postal police, be the outspoken advocate of what is taken to be inadmissible, *(irrecevable)*, in general collocution (*Ton*, 82–83 / RTP, 159–60). "Saints and postmoderns," to invoke Edith Wyschogrod's magnificent convocation and synogogic convergence of seeming opposites, have this in common, that they tend to be irrepressible, "impossible" advocates of everything that differs from established codes.[30] Saints and deconstructionists alike will always be made out to be mystagogic, obscurantist, apocalyptics who need to be demystified and who certainly should not be crowned with garlands, *honoris causa*, by Cambridge University. That is one limit to demystifying apocalypticism.

But there is another, "more essential" limit, that goes to the heart of differentiating "deconstruction" from a straightforward Enlightenment project of demystification (*Ton*, 83–84 / RTP, 160). It is more or less obvious, not much of a secret, that when Derrida talks about apocalypticism in this address to a conference at Cerisy convened to discuss "*le travail de Jacques Derrida*," he has also been talking about deconstruction, and about the apocalyptic tone of which he has been "suspected," especially in the United States, whose liberal, analytic establishment, Limited Inc., he has offended, rather the way he has been accused of / congratulated for being a negative theologian. Now while I think that deconstruction has never been in any historically precise sense comparable to a negative theology, the claim (charge / acclamation) of an apocalyptic tone is closer to the mark. That is because it touches upon the prophetic and messianic dimension of Derrida's "religion," its pact with the impossible, its shift into messianic time. Indeed, as Derrida points out, all sorts of "bastard apocalyptic filiation[s]" from John's Apocalypse have worked their way into *La Carte Postale* and *Glas* (*Ton*, 86/RTP, 162; cf. *Parages*, 175–81/LO, 123–37). This issue is not laid to rest merely by pointing out that Derrida is not predicting the chronological end of the "book" or "metaphysics," not predicting anything at all, that he is setting forth or delimiting a structural closure, not forecasting a diachronic, historical end.

The second, more essential limit to demystification comes down to "Come," to *viens*, the elaboration of which is the most important moment of this text, the *viens* that invokes the moment of messianic time. Derrida draws the line of demystification at *viens*, which is for him an apocalyptic word, the apocalyptic word *par excellence*, if it is a word at all, the Blanchotian word Derrida started using before he even knew he was citing the closing hymn and prayer of John's Apocalypse. For inasmuch as apocalypticism is the call of this "come," a hymn and recitative of *viens*, then deconstruction is apocalyptic through and through, *grace à Dieu*, and Derrida would never think of shedding his apocalyptic tone. But this is, we must never forget, an apocalypse *sans* apocalypse, an apocalypse of the *sans*, of the secret *sans vérité*, so that when we call and cry, weep and pray *viens*, we are still a little lost and do not know who or what is coming.

Derrida writes:

> The event of this "Come" precedes and calls the event. It would be that starting from which there is (*il y a*) any event, the *venir*, the *à-venir* of the event that cannot be thought under the given category of event. (*Ton*, 91/RTP, 164)

The event (*événement*) is not merely something that happens in the order of presence, in the most usual and commonplace taking place of the familiar and ordinary time, but the *é-venir*, the coming out, that breaks out in messianic time. *Viens* calls for a break, for breaking out into the open, for something new or different, something that shatters the horizon of the same, *l'événement de l'autre*; or, seen from without, the *in-venir*, the in-coming, *l'invention de l'autre*, the breaking in of something new into the circle of the same. *Viens* and *événement* belong to messianic time. The *viens* is correlated to the *événement*, as that which precedes and calls for the event, calls it up, prays and weeps and sighs for it, "inviting calling promising, hoping sighing dreaming, convoking invoking provoking," events. The blind eye of *viens* is set on what is coming in all of its indeterminable "a-venticity," and "e-venticity," "e-ventiveness," "event-uality," which are the elemental categories of messianic time. But *viens* is not a true Husserlian "cor-relate" because it is no con-temporary of the event, not simultaneous or co-equal, like noesis and noema. Rather the *viens* is earlier than the event, "precedes" it and "calls" for it, messianically, prophetically. The *viens* is like still *another* John, the precursor John whose Baptist voice cries out in the desert of the same for the other who is to come. *Viens* precedes the event structurally; it *always* precedes and calls for the event because, in messianic time, the event is always *yet* to come, struck through with non-occurrence, no matter what is presently in place. The very structure of the *viens* is to disturb the horizon of the present with the call of the impossible, to disturb the flow of ousiological time with promise and expectation. *Viens* is not the last word but the first, the call that proclaims that the last word is never spoken and the Messiah has not at last come, so that, even if the Messiah actually showed up, we have to ask, "When will you come?" The *viens* calls ahead, calls beyond, calls for a step beyond that it is structurally impossible to complete. In messianic time, the future is always, structurally, to come (the step beyond), even as the present is always structurally open to transgression (do not tres-pass). The step beyond is not beyond; the step beyond is never complete; the step that is completed is never beyond. As the dialogue partner in "Pas" asks, speaking of Levinas's *Autrui*, the "other shore" (*autre rive*):

> But is one able, is one obliged, *is it necessary* to approach that other shore (*cette autre rive*)? Would it not cease at once to be other? Would the event have arrived yet? Would it not be struck by interdiction (*ne pas*) by its very arrival . . . ? (*Parages*, 66)

This apocalypticism, this apocalyptic tone that Derrida has adapted, cannot be "contained simply by philosophy, metaphysics, onto-eschato-theology and by all the readings they have proposed of the apocalyptic" (*Ton*, 91/RTP, 165), all of which move within the horizons of ordinary, presential time. There is no *logos*, no rule or formula—be it metaphysical and teleological, be it theological and eschatological—that could render an account of what is to come, that could determine or foresee its outlines, that could predict its coming or protend its content. *Viens* does not let itself be brought before the court of reason (*arraisonner*) by any "onto-theo-es-chatology" or by any "logic of events" (*Ton*, 92–93/RTP, 165). Both teleology and eschatology, however much they may differ, are guided by a logic: the *logos* of the *telos* toward which each moment strains in a rational process of ongoing development; the *logos* of the *eschaton*, of the extreme end point which things reach in which death and judgment rain down on us.[31] But the *à-venir* will come like a thief in the night, beyond all account-ing. *Viens* is not a matter of counting, but of watching, staying awake in messianic time. *Viens* is a certain structural wakefulness or openness to an impossible breach of the present, shattering the conditions of possibility, by which we are presently circumscribed. I do not know "what" *viens* is, or "what" is *à-venir*:

. . . not because I yield to obscurantism, but because the question "what is" belongs to a space (ontology, and from it the knowledge of grammar, linguistics, semantics, and so on) opened by a "come" come from the other. (*Ton*, 93/RTP, 166)

"Come, opening the scene, could not become an object, a theme, a representation . . . " (*Ton*, 92/RTP, 165). *Viens* is not a determinable object inside the opening, but the invocation of the opening, the call that precedes and opens up the "scene," the field or space of the event, opening messianic time. That is why *viens* is not just one more word and cannot be fitted into a determinate category of words, like a "jussive" or a "performative." It is not reducible to a citation (of the Apocalypse, for example), subsumable under a determinate category, not even under the categories of "coming" or "event," because *viens* is the "affirmation" of language that is deeper than or prior to any determinate word or sentence or linguistic category, even that of affirmation if that is opposed to negation. So everything that Derrida is doing in the present essay risks deforming "*viens*" in order to "ex-tract" its *trait*, which he calls here "the demonstrative function in terms of philosophical discourse."

It is in this sense that he says, "[i]n this *affirmative* tone, *viens* marks in itself, in oneself, neither a desire nor an order, neither a prayer nor a request" (*Ton*, 93/RTP, 165), inasmuch as these are determinate grammatical and linguistic categories (PdS, 158–59/*Points*, 149–50). *Viens* is the *Ur*-affirmation of our relationship to the language and the world itself, the "wild" or uncultivated (*sauvage*), a-grammatical (Baptist) "cry" in the wilderness, a cry of passion, older than language, not a domesticated, law-abiding part of speech, with its own proper, legitimate name (*Parages*, 60, 75 et passim). As Derrida says in "Pas," because *viens* does not know what it is calling for, cannot describe what it wants, it cannot be subsumed by the usual categories of desire, imperative, order, cannot be fixed metalinguistically in one linguistic category or another, including that of prayer. It is better to say that *viens* runs the "chance, the risk: that the other of language happens in the step/not beyond language," that the *tout autre* happens (*se passe*) when *viens* happens (*Parages*, 74); the risk that in the language of the same, the other can come (*Psy.*, 160–61). When Derrida speaks of his prayers and tears in *Circumfession*, he means not the determinate prayer of a determinable faith (*Sauf*, 86/ON, 71), not a particular grammatical category, but the deeply affirmative invocation, the *oui, oui*. Such a prayer would be, according to "the strange syntax of the *sans*" (*Parages*, 83), a prayer without prayer, the prayer of the *sans*, in a religion without religion, a religion of the *sans*. This *sans* separates Derrida's prayers and tears from, even as it joins them to, the determinable faiths. Derrida's *viens* occupies the unstable space of something that cannot be a pure ahistorical a priori even as it must not sound too Jewish.

Viens, oui, oui is an upbeat and affirmative tone of passionate affirmation, maybe even a slightly Jewish tone, by which we open ourselves to the event and shift into messianic time. The passion of Derrida's apocalyptic tone is not dire fire and brimstone, not a wild-eyed declamation of imminent doom, nor is he trying to terrorize his critics with a forecast of eternal damnation. He does not think the world is about to go up in smoke once and for all, although he does think, *feu le cendre*, that we in our time, now, are capable of the most terrifying holocausts, the most appalling apocalypses now, from Auschwitz to Sarajevo. The apocalyptic tone recently adapted in deconstruction is upbeat and affirmative, expectant and hopeful, positively dreamy, dreaming of the impossible. "[L]et's say it one more time"—deconstruction is affirmative, not a destruction or demolition (PdS, 224/*Points*, 211).

Viens has an absolute singularity (as a primal affirmation) that is also absolutely divisible, requiring regular recitation, repetition, and redeployment like a *récit* and a *récitative* and a song, again and again, *oui, oui, mutatis mutandis*, shifting with the shifty circumstances of events. The differences among the "come"s are tonal. To hear its tone, try it out, try hard, alter it, say *viens*, and then you will hear the tone, or the other will hear first. For if the *viens* is a kind of first, an *Ur*-affirmation, *oui*, it is a second first, *oui, oui*, coming first in response to the call of what is other. *Viens* calls for the other, for the *à-venir*, but it calls in response to the solicitation of the other, it calls *for* the other because it is called *by* the other. The step beyond is the step of the other, of Elijah knocking at my door.

Viens is *"au-delà de l'être,"* beyond being, where by "being" Derrida means the same, the regular, the possible, the horizon of the present. *Viens* both comes *from* beyond-being, that is, it is a response solicited and called upon by the other who is coming, and it calls *for* and solicits the other, the movement beyond being, the possible, the same. On this point, it is like Heidegger's *Ereignis* which, out beyond Being (*hinausüber*), gives or grants Being, but its disanalogy with Heideggerian *Ereignis* is, I would say, even more important. First, *viens* is not governed by any logic of propriation and disappropriation, any logic of the proper. Secondly, *viens* is a call for justice not truth, a more Jewish and prophetic call for justice, not for a Greco-Germanic a-lethic opening. "Heidegger would not have liked this apparently personal conjugation or declension of coming" (*Ton*, 94/RTP, 166).

Viens is "an-agogic"; it "does not try to lead" (*Ton*, 94/RTP, 166); it is not an over-lordly, aristocratic, high-flying tone, not ductive, seductive, gogic, but anagogically open to the (im)possibility of what is to come. But it is not, of course, foolproof and absolutely safe. There is nothing to protect it, absolutely, from ductive violence, nothing to say that *viens* cannot be co-opted into the rallying call of the worst violence, nothing to stop *viens* from being used to lead the charge in which innocents are slaughtered, as the name in whose name the most extreme dogmatic and doctrinal, apocalyptical and eschatological violence, is perpetrated. (D. H. Lawrence thought the Apocalypse Christianity's most violent book.)

That is a risk, a possibility, a danger that is built into *viens*, a risk that Derrida would avert by preserving *viens* in its indeterminability, its indefiniteness, *Unbestimmtheit*. *Viens* for Derrida is not the call for a fixed and identifiable other, foreseeable and foregraspable, for that would release the manic aggression of a program, the mania of an all-out rush for a future-present. *Viens* is not governed by a destiny; it is *destinerrant* (*Ton*, 86/RTP, 162) not a *Geschick*; it does not give voice (*Stimme*) to a determinate vocation (*Bestimmung*), an identifiable destined *telos*. *Viens* is "a drift" (*une dérive*), "adrift" (*à la dérive*), headed for the other shore (*rive*) of the *tout autre*, but "underivable from the identity of a determination" (*Ton*, 95/RTP, 166–67). It is just this indefinite indeterminacy that would keep safe. For *"Come"* comes from the *tout autre*, the wholly other, what is structurally other, from which it de-rives:

> *Viens* is *only* derivable, absolutely derivable, but only from the other, from nothing that may be an origin or a verifiable, decidable, presentable, appropriable identity, from nothing not already derivable and arrivable *sans rive* [without bank or shore]. (*Ton*, 95/RTP, 166–67)

The only way to keep *viens* safe is for it to proceed by way of the *sans*, *sans savoir, sans avoir, sans voir*, without seeing, knowing, or having in advance an idea of what is coming or of what coming means (*Parages*, 25).

Yet, rather than keeping us safe, such a *viens* seems to portend a disaster, a catastrophe; rather than a promise, *viens* sounds more like a threat, for *viens* is the summons of

> an apocalypse without apocalypse, an apocalypse without vision, without truth, without revelation, *envois* (for the "Come" is plural in itself, in oneself), addresses without message and without destination, without sender or decidable addressee, without last judgment, without any other eschatology than the tone of the *"Viens."* (*Ton*, 95/RTP, 167)

This apocalypse without any vision, verity or un-veiling, this apocalypse *sans* apocalypse, is not John's, which calls determinately and identifiably for Adon Yeshoua. It is not Heidegger's, which calls for an identifiably Greco-Germanic *Anfang*, another one, come, now, *a-letheia*, in the end-time of the *Gestell*. It is not a Hegelian teleology according to which the *Begriff* heaves and groans to know itself in itself. It is nothing eschatological, theological, metaphysico-teleological, and if it is messianic, as it is, it is a messianic without messianism. *Viens* has the tone of the apocalypse that there is no apocalypse, no apocalyptic unveiling of what the goddess of truth is hiding under her skirt, no a-lethic unveiling in Ur-Greek (too bad for the French who cannot think in their language), no Word of God whispering the words of revelation in Hebrew in the prophet's ear (too bad for Egyptians and the *goyim*) or in Greek in the evangelist's ear (too bad for the Jews). This is an apocalyptic without, the secret that there is no secret, a scrambled message, many of them, calling for something to come. This apocalypse without apocalypse belongs to and opens up a messianic time without any messianisms, without Yeshoua or any other identifiable Messiah, Jewish, Christian, Islamic, without any Hegelian, Marxist, Nietzschean, or Heideggerian messianic coming. So if John sings and dreams, prays and weeps, at the end of the Apocalypse, "Amen. Come, Adon Yeshoua" (22:20), Derrida can only—but this is already quite a lot—sing, pray, and weep, at the end of "Pas," "*Viens, oui, oui*" (*Parages*, 116).

This apocalypse without apocalypse, the secret without secret, this a-destinal, destinerrant apocalypse is not kept straight by any *Geschick* of Being or Divine Providence or Absolute *telos*, but is loosened by the aleatory alogic of messianic time, by a certain chance. It moves by chance, not by a logic, not even a Heideggerian eschato-logic, whose *Spiel* is that the *Geschick*, gathering itself together in the unity of a *legein*, drives itself into an end-time, and then flips into another beginning. *Plus de chance*: no more chance, not the chance of a Heideggerian gift; *plus de chance*: more chance, only the chance, of a gift, of an opening for a gift, that may break loose, if things break our way and we keep the *viens* coming and something *tout autre* comes.

This apocalypse follows the strange syntax of the *sans*, Blanchot's syntax, according to which "X *sans* X," is not a simple negation, nullification, or destruction, but a certain reinscription of X, a certain reversal of the movement of X that still communicates with X. Hence the apocalypse without apocalypse, in the most precise cata-strophic sense of *sans*, is one in which a certain apocalyptic tone is struck up even as a certain tone is struck out, an apocalyptic tone *without* being caught up in the cataclysmic tones of the determinable apocalyptic revelations.

Of course, who or what is to say, Derrida asks in closing, as if to add a dangerous little supplement to the book, that this "aleatory errance," is not already inscribed in the text of John of Patmos, which would give the apocalypse to Jacques of El Biar a little opening? That is to say, what can stop the aleatory errance of *viens*, Derrida's *viens*—which of course is not the personal property of Jacques's—from working its way into John's *viens*, from showing up here or there? Can John keep his Apocalypse absolutely safe and sealed tight from deconstruction? What could keep the *viens* of deconstruction out—other than a Biblical Commission? What could "seal" John's message off? *There, là*, is the opening for which Derrida, on cat-soft paws, was searching. The Lord told John expressly *not* to seal it up (Rev. 22:10), to keep it open! Enter Derrida, with the Apocalypse in his hands (the devil!). Is the Apocalypse not structurally open to this catastrophic reversal?

Would that mean that, when John of Patmos calls for Yeshoua the Messiah to come, something else and more than that is calling John and is called for by John, something John cannot master? Would that mean that something else and something more, *plus de* Yeshoua, is making itself heard, is getting called, something of which "Adon Yeshoua" would perhaps be an example, perhaps *the* exemplification or the exemplary case?

That would be a very dangerous supplement to make to the Apocalypse and Derrida might be buying himself more trouble than all the police in Prague could ever give him. Were we not warned, in the most violent apocalyptic tones, not to add any supplements to or make any subtractions—no *sans* allowed, *sans sans*—from this text (in almost the same breath that we were told to keep things open)? If anyone adds a dangerous supplement to this book, John says, God himself will add to that person a dangerous supplement of His own: all the plagues described in this book! (22:18–19)

John is sure he can speak for God, and that God will back him up on this.

Such apocalyptics know how to make things hot for deconstructors, for anybody who plies at sacred texts with supplements and *sans* and secrets without secret, for anyone who dares to tinker with *their version* of the *tout autre*.

Viens.

Oui, oui.

[O]NE MUST NOT THINK ILL OF THE PARADOX,
FOR THE PARADOX IS THE PASSION OF THOUGHT,
AND THE THINKER WITHOUT A PARADOX
IS LIKE THE LOVER WITHOUT A PASSION: A MEDIOCRE FELLOW. . . .
THIS, THEN, IS THE ULTIMATE PARADOX OF THOUGHT:
TO WANT TO DISCOVER SOMETHING
THAT THOUGHT ITSELF CANNOT THINK.

JOHANNES CLIMACUS[32]

§8. The Secret

The Passion of Non-Knowing

The secret is the condition of the "come!", the quasi-transcendental condition of its possibility and impossibility. For it belongs to the very essence of *venir* and *à venir* that what is coming be unknown, not merely factually unknown but structurally unknowable, which is what Derrida calls the "secret" or the "absolute secret." Otherwise nothing is really coming, nothing *tout autre*. This structural secrecy is what keeps the future open, letting *l'avenir* be truly *à venir*. So the apocalypse *sans* apocalypse is also the revelation of the "secret," the secret *sans verité* that nobody has or knows the secret.[33] That is good news, indeed, the good news that what is coming is always *to* come. For just as the revelation that nobody has the Apocalyptic Word from On High means that no one can lord it over the rest of us and keep us all in line, so letting the secret out, the absolute secret that no one knows the secret, keeps the future open.

In deconstruction, the "apophatic secret" has a "messianic" point. The "messianic secret" is, there is no secret and the Messiah is never going to show up. Derrida's secret is not some hyperousiological high he has had and that he now whispers in our ear. Far from it. To be "in on the secret" does not mean you know anything, that you are "in the know"—but rather in the "no," *non-savoir* (*Pass.*, 74n1/ON, 131–32n1). It is only when the "come!" calls for something it cannot know or foresee that the come really has passion. Jacques's secret, if there is one, lies on a textual surface, inconspicuous by its superficiality, without a martyr to bear it witness, without a revelation to unveil it, without a second coming or even a first. It is always to come.

So the secret is good news and no cause for alarm. For the secret without secret impassions, drives us mad with desire, provoking incessant prayers and tears. The secret that impassions is what is called in *Cinders* "writing in the passion of non-knowing (*la passion du non-savoir*) rather than of the secret" (*Cinders*, 75)—but here by secret he means the determinate secret hidden under some hermeneutic rock or other. There is no secret hidden at the bottom of the phrase *"il y a là cendre,"* he says in *Cinders*, no secret code or coded Truth, but only the "non-knowing (*non-savoir*)" toward which writing and confession are precipitated (*Cinders*, 51–53), by which they are impassioned, which is what he calls the "absolute secret" (*Sauf*, 62/ON, 59; *Pass.*, "Prière d'insérer," 2/ON, xiv). "The secret of secrecy," he says in *Donner la mort*, is "that it is not a matter of knowing and that it is there for no-one" (DM, 88/GD, 92).

By un-knowing or non-knowledge, Derrida explains elsewhere, he does not mean some sort of despair which just gives up trying to know, or an obscurantism which takes delight and prefers non-knowledge. "I am all for knowledge!" he protests.[34] He has in mind a structural non-knowing, something irreducibly foreign and heterogeneous to knowledge, which constitutes a "more ancient, more originary experience, if you will, of the secret," setting writing in motion, moved by the impossible of non-knowing (PdS, 214–15/*Points*, 201).[35] "Where we are going" is not a question for knowledge, as if history has a single mission which we must target like the "smart missiles" of the Gulf War, but a matter of responsibility that passes through the aporetic of non-knowledge (PdS, 370–

71 / *Points*, 359). Non-knowing puts faith and passion to the test, stretching them beyond the too limited expectations that knowledge tolerates. Derrida does not propose a learned unknowing, which is but a more oblique and negative way to know something still higher. The "come!" does not arise from a knower's unknowing, a *"docta" ignorantia*, but a lover's unknowing, an *ignorantia amans*, not a learned but a loving, expectant unknowing, which keeps the future open by the passion of its love, its messianic yearning for what is "to come."

In contradistinction to the oldest and most Platonic of traditions, fire for Derrida is not a figure of light for seeing but of heat for burning. Fire for Derrida belongs with ash, *feu la cendre*, as opposed to Platonic fire, *feu la lumière*, fire / cinders as opposed to fire / light.[36] Light for Derrida is concentrated by a lens and burns the paper we are trying to read, so that seeing is converted into non-seeing:

> . . . a concentration of light as a result of seeing in order not to see, writing in the passion of non-knowledge rather than of the secret. I would say, for the protection and illustration of its own sentence, "I" the cinder would say that his writing is not interested in knowledge. The raw cinder, that is more to his taste. (*Cinders*, 75)

Feu sans voir, sans avoir, sans savoir. Fire for Derrida is an Hebraic rather than a Platonic figure, the fire of *ne pas voir, la passion de non-savoir*. Spirit is fire not only in Trakl, he reminds Heidegger, but also for the Jews (*ruah*)—"Without being able to invoke here the vast corpus of prophetic texts . . . a whole tradition of Jewish thought as an inextinguishable thinking about fire," a tradition which Heidegger systematically "forgets" in an act of "brutal foreclosure" (DLE, 164–66 / OS, 100–101).[37]

Fire is the heat of passion, the passion of faith and non-knowing, of the secret which severs us from truth, which leaves us with ashes rather than *die Sache selbst*. Derrida has found it necessary to delimit knowledge in order to make room for faith in what is to come. For knowledge always means a prescient programming of the future, predelineating the foreseeable range and foreclosing the possible scope of the future. That closure within the possible is what Derrida means to cut open by speaking of the impossible surprise, the absolute secret. The passion of non-knowledge protects the future and keeps it open by keeping it secret—indeterminate, unforeseeable, unprogrammable—as opposed to confining it within the parameters of the possible.

That is why I conclude Part II with Derrida's account of the secret, of the *"exemplary* secret of literature" (*Pass.*, 67 / ON, 29) in *Passions*, which is the condition of the "come!", which gives it passion. After that, a little organ music, an edifying divertissement, on the God of the prophets— while we all await the Messiah (Part III).

The Secret Impassions

Passions (1993), Derrida's best account of the secret—and of passion— first appeared in a slightly shorter form in English under the title "Passions: 'An Oblique Offering.'" In its expanded French edition, *Passions* is the first part of the triptych on the "name," which includes *Sauf le nom*, examined above (§4), and *Khôra*, which is the third part, which I am always discussing in one way or another.[38]

Derrida had been invited to respond to a collection of essays on his work entitled *Derrida: A Critical Reader*, part of a series of critical studies from Blackwell, all following the same rubric: *X: A Critical Reader*. Derrida wonders, farcically, whether editor David Wood is setting the scene (*scène*) for a ritual Last Supper (*Cène*) (*Pass.*, 45–46/ON, 19) in which the contributors are gathering to consume his body, the corpus "Derrida." After all, there are—count them!—twelve contributors to this volume, twelve "followers" gathered around the table—the very number of the apostles gathered around the table. When Wood suggests the title "An Oblique Offering" Derrida suspects some sort of religious ritual with guess who as the sacrificial lamb (*Pass.*, 19/ON, 6). When Wood says that such an "oblique entry" into the discussion might constitute "a stimulus, the germ of a passion" (*Pass.*, 84n8/ON, 139n8), Derrida gets downright nervous. Is Wood making an oblique reference to the passion of Jacques Derrida? How can Derrida be part of this almost blasphemous situation into which, intentionally or not, David Wood is trying to draw him? So to protect himself from this blasphemy, to avoid this occasion of sin, Derrida twists and twits Wood's words and refashions them into his own title, "Passions," in the plural, set over "An Oblique Offering," which becomes the subtitle. That allows Derrida to play off a passion of a somewhat different sort than the sacred passion of Jesus, a messianic passion of his own, one that drives deconstruction (mad).

Once again, *je vous prie*, I pray your patience; something serious is astir in all this devilish play on "passion." Derrida's scandalous, not to say sinful scenario in *Passions* is this: How is he to escape the double bind of this invitation which has so effectively nailed both his hands in place (*Pass.*, 53/ON, 22)? How is he supposed to answer a kind invitation, an act of friendship, for which he is grateful, without being drawn into some sort of eucharistic sacrifice, in which his *corpus* is consumed by an assembly of academic critical readers? This is a fictive, farcical way of getting to the issue. Still, we ought not to dismiss this religious scenario too hastily, for such scenarios are serious and recur in Derrida with an unsettling, rhythmic regularity that leaves his secularist admirers in fear and trembling.

The issue is twofold: (1) the double bind embedded in "how to respond"; (2) the secret that impassions, the secret that he has no secret word up his sleeve for these friends and critics, which is what lets his texts give off sparks. That is what is finally at stake in this piece, as we will see, so long as we are patient:

> [T]hat is why we must *tell* (*dire*) the secret, not reveal it, and, with the example of this secret, pass judgment on the secret in general. What is a secret? (*Pass.*, 20/ON, 7)

We put this question, Derrida adds, even if it may turn out that the secret is a "secret which is a secret for no one," like a *"secret de Polichinelle."* "Polichinelle" is "Punchinello," an Italian puppet, an absurd figure, the prototype of Punch in the "Punch and Judy" show. Punch's secret is an Italian joke, an open secret: a secret to no one (but that may be no joke).

First, the double bind: how is Derrida to respond to the twelve, these friends and followers? How can he best show his gratitude for the attention the twelve pay his work? An invitation, if it is polite, should be neither coercive, so that we are forced to respond, nor indifferent, so that it does not matter whether or not we respond. Politeness is the paradox of a rule without rule (*Pass.*, "Prière d'insérer," 2/ON, xiv–xv; *Pass.*, 24/ON, 9). It would hardly be an act of friendship and courtesy to respond to one's friends out of duty. Is there any such thing as an obligation without the debt of duty, a duty without debt? (*Pass.*, 75–76n3/ON, 133n3)

Were he to take on the twelve frontally, head on, or be more oblique and indirect (a merely strategic difference) he would be equally unfriendly—linear, violent, and aggressive. (*Pass.*, 34–35/ON, 13–14) Would it not be more responsible, more "responsive" (in English), more friendly and respectful of their alterity, to concede that he is not up to responding to the difficult questions posed by the twelve?

Suppose he responds: would that not be very "irresponsible" (*Pass.*, 43/ON, 18)? Would he not then make himself complicitous with the "odious attitude of treating all these thinkers as disciples" (*Pass.*, 44–45/ON, 18)? Furthermore, would that not constitute an act of supreme hubris that would assume itself capable of answering any question? Would he not run the risk of making it appear that "Derrida" is a powerful name that can put every critical reader of "Derrida" in his or her place, that the name "Derrida" coheres as a transcendental unity, that everything in his corpus can be gathered under the protective unity of that name which accompanies all his representations, stamped with the seal of that unifying name, no matter what question you put to it (cf. *Pass.*, 44–50/ON, 18–21)? "Derrida": that is a name nobody is going to knock! Or circumcise! A circumcised signature—this will be the reading of Celan—is one that exposes itself to the other, that makes itself vulnerable to the other's gloss, to the glint of the other's blade.[39]

Suppose he does not respond: would he not take an even bigger risk? Would he not appear to brush off the others' offerings, to fail to take them seriously? Indeed, is not a selective non-response, a calculated silence, part of the rhetoric of war, academic or otherwise, with rules of its own, an insolent weapon that can humiliate the other who addresses you even more incisively than a sharp rejoinder? Would it not be a well-known ruse, transparent bad faith, to say he cannot answer these questions, that they are too difficult, when everybody knows he could knock his critics dead if he took them seriously? Would it not be better, more honest and more forthcoming, just to take the trouble to give the best response that time and space permit and cut the theatrics of not being able to respond (*Pass.*, 50–52/ON, 21–22)?

So what is he to do in this aporia, in which it is impossible either to respond or not to respond? Either way, he is sacrificed; this is a double bind in which his two hands are tied or nailed down (*Pass.*, 53/ON, 22). And how is it that he can keep on talking? What sort of language is this that keeps on running in the midst of such an aporia, a language that lacks all traction? What, if anything, can escape this economy of sacrifice?

That brings us to the secret. His most responsive and responsible non-response (he does not comment on the critics' papers) is to whisper a little secret in their ear:

> Let us say that there is a secret here. Let us testify: <u>*There is* something secret</u> (*Il y a là du secret*). We will leave the matter here for today, but not without an exercise on the essence and existence of such a secret, an exercise that will have an apophatic aspect. The apophatic is not here necessarily dependent on negative theology, even if it makes it possible too. (*Pass.*, 56/ON, 23–24)

The secret has an apophatic quality, *not* in the sense of negative theology, which is a hyperousiological high to which certain select initiates may be introduced, and, more generally, *not* in the sense of some secret knowledge testified to by someone, a mystic or poet, say, some martyr who has been sacrificed to the secret. Rather the "absolute secret" is apophaticism itself, the stuff of what I called in Part I a "general apophatics," which is the condition of all these other relative and determinate secrets. Apophatic theology in the strict sense then is but a particular "example" of this general apophaticism (but remember the law of exemplarism: how are we supposed to know what is an example of what?), one that turns on a determinate, ontico-semantic secret, a secret about something (even it is not a thing) particular (even if it is not limited), God, for example. Apophatic theology does not trade in the absolute secret itself, if it has an itself. The absolute secret makes possible the particular secrets that are kept safe in particular places.

So the "traits" of this absolute secret will always be apophatic, negative re-traits; to characterize it we will always find ourselves saying, it's not this, not that. But this radical, absolute secret is not hiding a positive content, which can be revealed under the right circumstances to initiates or to those who are qualified to hear it, who have been given a certain security clearance. This secret—which is *sans savoir* and *non-savoir*—has no semantic content. This secret has nothing to hide. This is an odd sort of a secret, something of a non-secret, the secret that *there is no secret* in the sense of some sort of secret knowledge, some secret knowing, some positive content. Still, such *non-savoir* is "a more ancient, more originary experience" of the secret (PdS, 215/*Points*, 201)—and it has a messianic twist.

That is why Derrida writes, "We testify to"—changed from "we speak of" in the earlier English version—"a secret without content, without content separable from its performative experience . . . " (*Pass.*, 56/ON, 24). Then there follows a series of apophaticisms, of denials—it's not this and it's not that—which obey a protocol, like a ritual, sacrificial offering, like a litany or a recitation: first the invocation of a (more ancient) secret, followed by the apophatic denial or sacrifice (of determinate, revealable secrets).

> Let us say then: There is there something secret (*il y a là du secret*). It would not be a question of . . .

Six such denials ensue (*Pass.*, 56–63/ON, 24–27).

(1) The secret would *not* be a question of the incommunicable skill of a gifted artist, or of the art of imagination hidden in the depths of the human soul of which Kant spoke.

(2) The secret would *not* be a hidden representation in a conscious subject, or even hidden in the unconscious; nor even the Kierkegaardian secret of subjectivity, which hides itself from the eagle of Hegel's absolute knowledge.[40] Although Derrida does not mention it, Kierkegaard's secret is like the "secret" which is lost in the gabbiness of everyday Dasein, where nobody can keep a secret, where having a secret of one's own is the secret of Ownness (*Eigentlichkeit*). In everydayness, "[e]very secret loses its force" (*Jedes Geheimnis verliert seine Kraft*), Heidegger complains.[41]

(3) The secret would *not* be something private that, under special circumstances, could be made public, like military secrets, secrets revealed in the confessional, lawyer/client privileges. Those are only conditional secrets that in principle could be revealed when certain conditions require disclosure.

(4) The secret would *not* be some secret harbored by a revealed religion, the "learned ignorance" of a Christian brotherhood which practices negative theology, or some esoteric Pythagorean mystery. Despite the hype, mystics and negative theologians do not *know* something to which the rest of us are denied access. They have not broken through the surface of things to speak to us from out of the depths of Being or Otherwise than or Beyond Being, out of the heart of the Godhead beyond God.

(5) The secret would *not* be something that belongs to the order of truth at all, that "conceals itself" and could become un-hidden; it exceeds the play of veiling and unveiling, forgetting and recalling. It is not the *lethe* in alethic truth; it does not give rise to Germanic profundities about the *Geheimnis* or the *Unheimliche*. Even when one "does the truth," bears testimony or witness to it, witnessing does not make it true. The secret is that one calls it secret, which is a homonym for all other secrets. The secret does not have one name, a proper name, a name for its proper essence, having neither essence nor propriety.

(6) The secret is *not* something that is disrupted by speaking of it. It will remain secret even with all the stories it unleashes, with all the apophatic discourses it sets into motion. Silently subtending all these discourses, all these histories and epistemes, the secret will remain passive and mute as a *khôra*—in the French edition Derrida adds, "like *Khôra*," as if that were its proper name. The secret is foreign to speech, but not because it is withheld from speech. It cannot be called to account. You cannot bring it out by a process, however many proceedings are brought against it. The secret is intractable (*intraitable*): it has no traits (its apophaticism), it cannot be treated of in a treatise from which it would be in retreat, its traits being re-traits. No discussion starts or continues without it; you have to respect it whether you want to or not.

The apophatic recitation concludes:

> There is there no longer time nor place. (*Là il n'y a plus le temps, ni la place.*) (*Pass.*, 63/ON, 27)

A little like the *khôra*, like *Khôra*, the secret passively tolerates everything without becoming anything.

Finally Derrida comes clean—he always repays our patience—and "confides" a little secret to the twelve and to us, who are flies on the wall of the upper room, so that suddenly we notice the letter hanging plainly from the fireplace mantle, in plain view all along:

> A confidence to end with today. Perhaps all I wanted to do was confide or confirm my taste (probably unconditional) for literature, more precisely for literary writing. (*Pass.*, 63/ON, 22)

That spills it all. The secret is out. The secret is the "absolute secret" of literature discussed also in *Given Time, I: Counterfeit Money*. Literature is a textual surface without semantic or intentionalist depth, "the readability of the text . . . structured by the unreadability of the secret, that is, by the inaccessibility of a certain intentional meaning or of a wanting-to-say (*vouloir dire*) in the consciousness of these characters and *a fortiori* in that of the author . . . " (DT, 193/GT, 152). There can be no "hermeneutic" key to this crypt, and this because of the structural "unreadability," the absolute indecipherability, of a literary secret. There is no hidden reality behind the tissue of texts, behind the "essential superficiality of their [the fictional characters'] phenomenality" (DT, 194/GT, 153). The *"exemplary* secret of literature" means "something of literature will have begun" (*Pass.*, 89n12/ON, 142n12) whenever we try to sort out what is an example of what. The absolute secret is not some sort of conditional secret that could be revealed, but the secret that there is no secret, that there never was one, not even one.

What Derrida likes about literature is not some formal aesthetic quality but rather something "in the place (*au lieu*) of the secret." The "call of this secret" is not a negative result, but one that gives off sparks, that impassions:

> There is in literature, in the *exemplary* secret of literature, a chance of saying everything without touching upon the secret. When all hypotheses are permitted, groundless and *ad infinitum*, about the meaning of a text, or the final intention of an author whose person is no more represented than non-represented by a character or by a narrator, by a poetic or fictional sentence, when these are detached from their presumed source and thus remain in secret (*au secret*), when there is no longer any sense in making decisions about some secret beneath the surface of a textual manifestation (and it is this situation which I would call text or trace), when it is the call (*appel*) of this secret, however, which points back to the other or to something else, when it is this itself which keeps our passion aroused, and holds to the other, then the secret impassions us. Even if there is none, even if it does not exist, hidden behind anything whatever. Even if the secret is no secret, even if there has never been a secret, a single secret. Not one. (*Pass.*, 67–68/ON, 29–30)

We suffer no loss from this secret but are in fact impassioned to multiply readings. There is no loss in our loss of the *Sache selbst* beneath the textual surface, in the inability to consult Hamlet to ask him what he is brooding about, or to ask Shakespeare what is going through Hamlet's mind. Shakespeare does not know any more than we do (DT, 193/GT, 152) and Hamlet does not have a mind. *Hamlet* is all we have. There is no Hamlet outside the text, no mind of Hamlet outside *Hamlet*, to whom we may have recourse. And even if we could, *per impossibile*, exhume and resuscitate Shakespeare, like Lazarus, or track down the "historical Hamlet," if there was one—or the historical Jesus, or the twelve, or his later bio-hagio-graphers who called him by the name of Lord—they could not give us the secret, not in principle.

So when "the twelve" send *Derrida: A Critical Reader* to Jacques, they should not expect to hear a secret, to have something beyond the text obliquely slipped into their pocket, or whispered in their ear, perhaps to reward their loyalty, to unravel all the aporias and conundrums, a secret that is denied to everyone else who "only" have the texts to read and have never met Jacques in the flesh. "Derrida"—the name of the thinker is the name of a text to be read, of a signature that invites incision and circumcision—that sets off sparks (or fails to), that stands or falls on its own, whether or not we can get Jacques to show up and, sticking a microphone in his face, get him to comment upon the studies that "Derrida" impassions. Even if we can get him to appear in person and even if we then transcribe his *ipsissima verba*, even if all the sayings get red beads, that will just create another text to interpret. He can't be everywhere at once and live forever, and he is not coming again. We are all going to have to assume a little responsibility for our readings.

That is why the absolute secret is not a negative result but a secret that impassions. What other response is possible to *Derrida: A Critical Reader*? His texts are on their own. The worth and the value of his texts—of any text, of any X who will henceforth be read in a *Critical Reader*—lies in the "stimulus" they provide, "the germ of a passion" (*Pass.*, 84n8/ON, 139n8) they plant, the "passions" they arouse, the controversies and contested readings they impassion and provoke, the sparks that fly up in the clash of contesting interpretations. "Derrida" is the name of a chain of interpretations of "Derrida," of Derrida on "Heidegger," on "Kant," or "Plato," of apostolic letters that are sent out by those who are historically close to the author, of a long string of readings that are made of these readings, *ad infinitum*, until a "tradition," as if there were only one, forges itself out of such readings—or fails to, depending on the "passions" they stir; it is too soon to tell. But do not expect Jacques to give the contributors, or the readers of the volume, the "Answer," the "Response," the "Secret." There is nothing he can say, no secret to reveal.

Far from paralyzing us, the secret without secret drives reading and interpretation, translation and transgression, impelling us to go precisely where we cannot go. The self-negating language of the secret "*necessitates* doing the impossible, necessitates going (*Geh*, Go!) there where one cannot go. Passion of, for, the place, again" (*Sauf*, 62–63/ON, 59).

Democracy, Testimony—and Blackmail

By denying knowledge—or "intuition"—in order to make room for faith, the secret without secret has a political payoff:

> The secret, if there is one, is not hidden at the corner of any angle, it does lay itself open to a double view or to a squinting gaze. It cannot be seen, quite simply. No more than a word. As soon as there are words—and this can be said of the trace in general, and of the chance that it is—direct intuition no longer has any chance. One can reject, as I have done, the

word 'oblique'; one cannot deny the destinerrant destination as soon as
there is a trace. Or, if you prefer, one can only deny it. (*Pass.*, 68/ON, 30)

Everything that Derrida has been doing under the name of deconstruction strains against allowing such a secret knowledge from gaining a
footing, from dropping anchor. There are a lot of seamy, unseemly
things you can do with secret knowledge—lie and cheat, for example,—
and also use it "to secure oneself a phantasmatic power over others"
(*Pass.*, 69/ON, 30). That is why, to go back to negative theology, when
deconstruction knocks negative theology down a peg it backs it off a
dangerous precipice and saves its good name. For the texts of the negative theologians are to be treasured, not because they have been given
privileged access to the Secret Godhead, but because they elicit passion,
set off sparks, invoke holy names, tell marvelous stories, draw us down
labyrinthine corridors, always and in wondrous ways pushing language
to its apophatic limits, to the limits of the wholly other. But it must be
conceded that what theology calls God has other names, that the secret
generates endless names, that it cannot be secreted behind just one
name, God, for example, that every other is wholly other, that the music
plays on and on, that we have always to do with readings and con-
struals which are contestable in the very act of being proposed, deconstructible in the very act of being constructed, revisable and recallable
in the very act of being instituted, retractable in the very act of being
traced, that *la chose même se dérobe toujours* (VP, 117/SP, 104): the secret
in itself always slips away.

While the passion for an impossible place is, as far as it goes, a salutary
desire, while it pushes up to the limits of language, evokes something
heterogeneous, it ought not to be confused with being actually trans-
ported into some secret, extra-textual location, some extra-terrestrial place
to which the rest of us have been forbidden access. We are all stuck in the
same place, in the text, pulling on the pants of textuality one leg at a time.
We are all "in the secret" (*au secret*), "which does not mean that we know
anything" (*Pass.*, 74n1/ON, 131–32n1); on the contrary, the secret catches
us up in un-knowing (*non-savoir*), all equally blind in an abocular egalitarian polity, in a democracy to come.

There are no eyewitnesses to a secret knowledge—whether it poses as
theology, metaphysics, or economics—about which the rest of us are just
going to have take its word and accept its testimony. Testimony is testimony to good faith, to good *faith*, not to a privileged *knowledge*. Testimony
is what we do vis-à-vis something to which we can only testify because
we do not know, not because we have given up or do not want to know,
but because of a structural unknowing (PdS, 214–15/*Points*, 201). Testimony is always made to some *je ne "sais" quoi*, something of which there
could never be any question of knowing. Martyrs die for their faith—be

it Christian, Islamic, or Marxist—but their dying does not turn it into knowledge—not for us, and as for what it does for them, that remains an unknown secret.

The secret without secret protects us from terror and blackmail, from letting anyone secure phantasmic power over others, faithful or infidel, letting them terrorize others by their fearsome asceticism. That is why there is a constant and irrepressible political theme in the question of the "absolute secret" that puts an end to secret authorities and authoritative secrets. "Literature" and democracy are coextensive, where literature is the name of the letter, not of the genre of "literary genres," of the institution of literature, of the profession that grants tenure and secure academic livings. Literature is the name of the trace and the text, which for Derrida implies "the unlimited right to ask questions" (*Pass.*, 65/ON, 28), a new Enlightenment *sans eine Aufklärung*. No authoritative authorial voice, no authoritative institution, no authoritative tradition or traditional authority is authorized to "respond," to answer the question and put the text to rest. The text plays on and on, generating open-ended debate.

That is why, in the French text of *Passions*, Derrida has inserted a series of passages on the question of testimony or witness that consistently demarcate it from knowledge. For otherwise witnessing would be blackmail. Testimony "would never be reducible, precisely, to verification, to proof or to demonstration, in a word to knowledge" (*Pass.*, 54/ON, 23). When we say "let us testify" that does not somehow give us any firm assurance about our testimony (*Pass.*, 56/ON, 23–24). The secret sees to it that no witness nor, as the name suggests, the "history of any martyr (*martyria*)" can settle the destinerrance in which we are unsettled by the trace. Then he adds in the Galilée edition:

> For one will never, it is impossible and it must not be done, reconcile the value of a testimony with that of knowledge or of certitude. One will never, it is impossible and it must not be done, reduce the one to the other. (*Pass.*, 70–71/ON, 31)

Every text—*The Mystical Theology* of Pseudo-Dionysius no less than *Hamlet*, *Of Grammatology* no less than the Constitution of the United States—is inhabited by the "absolute solitude of a passion without martyr" (*Pass.*, 71/ON, 31), that is, without a credentializing witness. There is no outside-text to which we may steal away without leaving a trace behind, without a "remainder." This remainder (*reste*) gives us no rest. And if the secret ever were revealed, all that would remain is to rest in peace. *Requiescat in pace*. R.I.P.

For then there would be nothing coming and, there being nothing to pry open the present with expectation, messianic space would collapse upon itself in instant, endless, passionless death.

♦ *Edifying Divertissement No. 2.*
From Elea to Elohim:
The God of the Same, the God of the Other

The philosophically inclined reader will, I trust, excuse me if I inter-rupt this exposition to drop a coin in theology's collection plate, a coin minted from Derrida's apocalypticism, from his *viens!* and the "in-com-ing of the other." Seen from the point of view of Derrida's apocalyptic tone, the God about which deconstruction is rightly a-theistic, the God to whom we can all say good riddance, the God whose death is good news and no cause for grief or mourning, the God well lost, is the God of onto-theo-logic. That is the God who divinely, eternally precontains all things in a mind so immense that all creation is but a supplemental *imago dei*, a simulacrum of the Infinite and the Eternal, which means In-finitely and Eternally the Same. Deconstruction can be of service to the-ology in breaking the grip of this excessively Eleatic idea of God which has overrun the biblical traditions ever since Philo Judaeus decided that Yahweh needed to square accounts with Greek ontology, the result being that Greek ontology settled the hash of Yahweh and Elohim. But if you give theology a deconstructive bent, if you read the name of God in close coordination with the deconstruction of the metaphysics of the Same, then the name of God is not the name of some sort of divine sen-sorium (censorium? preventorium?), not some infinitely preemptive pre-container or all-encompassing necessity, but rather the name of *the* impossible, of novelty, of the coming of the Other, of the *tout autre*, of what is coming with the shock of an absolute surprise, with the trauma of absolute heterogeneity. Cast in a deconstructive slant, God is not the possible but the impossible, not the eternal but the futural. To call upon God, to call God's name, to pray and weep and have a passion for God, is to call for the *tout autre*, for something that breaks up the ho-hum homogeneity of the same and all but knocks us dead. The name of God is a name that calls for the other, that calls from the other, the name that the other calls, that calls upon us like Elijah at the door, and that calls for something new.

That desire for an absolute surprise, for a justice to come that will count our every tear, is, according to the (slightly unbelievable) premise of the present study, an old prophetic passion, a dream dreamt in pro-phetic expectation, a call shouted by a long line of prophets. Is not the name of God hurled by the prophets like a sling against the same, flung in the face of the foreclusionary structures that convene around the different? Do the prophets not seek to reinvent invention, to shatter convention—have they not been known to walk around nude, which is pretty unconventional?—in order to let the other come? Is not

114

II. THE APOCALYPTIC

l'invention de l'autre just what the prophets call for? Do they not call *viens*, in Franco-Hebraic, for something they know not what? Do they not give passionate voice, I will even risk saying an *exemplary* voice, do they not exhibit an exemplary passion for a justice to come? The prophets dream of letting justice flow like water over the land, of letting justice come "for all of God's children," as a very biblical, prophetic, and passionate voice put it at the foot of the Lincoln Memorial.[42] They lend their voice—and their hides—to calling for a justice to come. They call upon, they call for, the *tout autre*, something unimaginable, impossible, for with God all things are possible, above all *the* impossible.

So, if theology is given a deconstructive bent, is it not bent *back* to prophetic expectation and prophetic passion? But this bending produces a disturbing chiasmic effect. For if, in deconstruction, one has no assurance about what is an example of what, then how are we to decide whether biblical faith and prophetic passion are examples of a deconstructive bent, or whether deconstruction here acquires a biblical bent? How is one to tell the difference between what impassions the prophets and what impassions deconstruction? Does the invention of the other in deconstruction turn out to be upon analysis a little variation on Isaiah or Amos? Did Derrida not get his ears bent with all this passion, years ago, in El Biar, so that now, in his later years, all this incoming of the other and this messianic passion, this passion for a justice to come, is coming back on him? Is that not his confession in *Cir-confession*?

Oui, oui: yes, yes to two comings, two passions: the prophetic passion to let justice flow like water over the land; the deconstructive passion for the coming of the other, for a justice to come. Which comes first? If they are both first, as in any *repetitio* worthy of its name, which is the second first? Which is the repetition of which?

Who cares? Does it matter, so long we say *viens*, and then, once more, yes, yes, with passion?

There really is no way to decide this undecidable, to tell if all of this passion, if deconstruction itself—"To prepare oneself for this coming (*venue*) of the other is what can be called deconstruction" (*Psy.*, 53–54/RDR, 56)—is not itself but a determinate case of the passion for God, which is an older and more general condition. Jacques has already circumfessed that what we will not have understood is that his passion for invention and reinvention is his passion for "my God." What if—at the risk of seeing my secularizing academic friends faint dead away (it must have been something they had read)—giving religion a deconstructive bent turns itself around and deconstruction turns out to have a religious, a biblical, and prophetic bent, so that deconstruction is driven by a prophetic passion, having entered into an *alliance* with the impossible?

♦ *Edifying Divertissement No. 2.*

The incoming of deconstruction upon religion and theology, the advent of deconstruction in theology, turns theology around to the future, to what is coming, which returns theology to what it was meant to be all along, *quid quod erat esse*, before the wilderness camp of the prophets was overrun by Eleatic ontotheologicians, before their prophetic, desert voices were drowned out by an excessively Hellenistic logos. But what if, in a remarkable turn of events, theology returns the favor and reinvents deconstruction so that deconstruction turns out to be just a way of translating the prophets, of giving prophetic passion a new turn? Would that be a surprise? An absolute surprise? Maybe not. Maybe we have been making ready the way for the coming of something like this.

But, is this possible? Of course it is not; that is why it is the only possible invention of deconstruction. Remember the impossible-rule: "Only write what is impossible" (*Circon.*, 181/*Circum.*, 194). This impossible, unbelievable deconstruction would be *the* impossible, which pushes us beyond the tiresomeness of the possible, beyond all the possible academic deconstructions, especially literary deconstruction, which have enjoyed a too considerable status. What if this impossibility is just what we need, just what is required to push us beyond, *au-delà*, the prevailing deconstructions and let something new come, letting the nose of biblical novelty under the desert tents of deconstruction?

Who could disentangle this chiasmic intertwining, prevent this event, prevent the eventuation of this invention? Who would want to undertake a *prévention de l'autre*? Why bother? Why would one want to?

Who has been authorized to speak for the *tout autre*? Who has the status and standing to decide its undecidability? Who has the authority to rule out what is coming in the formless form of an absolute surprise, to suppress this vote (*voix*), to cut off this different voice, to disallow this translation?

Indeed, after saying "the other: that is what is never inventable and will never have waited for your invention," does Derrida not say—are these not *ipsissima verba*, do they not get red beads?—"The other calls to come and that happens only in several voices" (*Psy.*, 61/RDR, 62)?[43] Is not the prophetic voice, the dream of prophetic religion, a biblical theology of the future, is that not a good voice? Might not the invention of the other turn out to be, in the final accounting, beyond all ontotheology, the invention of God, the God of the invention, the expectation of the incoming of the kingdom? Watch (out).

I am not saying that Derrida is a crypto-theologian of the *tout autre*. I have never been to the crypt and I cannot decipher cryptic writing. I do not know and cannot reveal to you the absolute secret. I confess, I am, like Jacques, *sans voir et sans savoir* and the absolute secret is lost on me. I am, like Jacques, a ragpicker, picking up the fragments of the System that have fallen to the floor.

I am not coming back full circle and saying that, in the final account, Derrida is a negative theologian after all and *différance* is divine. I am not eating my words, not taking anything back. Nor am I saying that, in the final analysis, deconstruction is a crypto-form of prophetic theology and that Jacques de la rue Saint-Augustin is a prophet after all.

No, no, I am saying that, in the final account, there is no final account, no "after all" after all. According to the alogic of exemplarism and endless translatability, I do not know what is an example of what or how to disentwine a chiasmic mess. I do not know how to disentangle the passion of Jacques Derrida and the passion of the prophets.

To be in the secret does not mean you know anything. As for me, I do not know who I am or whether I believe in God. That is not wrong, but it is a very parsimonious way to put the secret, not very passionate.[44] I do not know whether what I believe in is God or not. That is a little more upbeat, a little more grateful. Best of all (I am always looking for a way to say this in such a way as not to lose all my old friends): I do not know what I love when I love my God—*Quid ergo amo, cum Deum meum amo?*— when I pray and weep over my God, when I am driven mad by a passion for God. To be in the secret does not mean you know anything, but the secret impassions and multiplies formulations.[45]

Can I, can you, like Jacques, do anything other than pass our days trying to translate "my God," my passion for God? I do not know whether the passion for God is an example of the passion for justice and the absolute surprise—which is, I would guess, what Jacques guesses, but that is his business—or whether the passion for justice and for the absolute surprise are examples of the passion for God—which is, I would guess, what theology and the faithful in the determinable faiths (*Sauf*, 86/ON, 71) would guess, but that is their business. Nor do I know what other examples and translations are possible, are still to come or are lost in the mail of the immemorial past, which is after all, in the final account, not a totally surprising thing to say about an absolute surprise. It's a secret, after all, which is what deconstruction is, or it does not exist.

I am saying, too, and this is also my only concern, one of many of my only concerns, that as long as one's only concern is with what is coming, as long as one's passion is for the impossible, for a justice to come, for the incoming of the *tout autre*, where *tout autre est tout autre*, then what translation you take up, what translation has taken you over, is your business, your only concern, your passion, your religion. According to *différance*, it does not make much difference.

Who (or what) is calling? Who (or what) is coming?

It's a secret. God only knows!

Come!

Heads up!

III. The Messianic

By 1993, Derrida himself, like Levinas before him, had begun to associate himself with the word "messianic"—almost always by way of a reference to Walter Benjamin[1]—and to feel around for a general "messianic" structure or "messianicity" that he could live with, one that is cut to fit the hand of deconstruction.

In the 1989 text of "The Force of Law,"[2] delivered in New York, Derrida said:

> I would hesitate to assimilate too quickly this "idea of justice" to a regulative idea (in the Kantian sense), to a messianic promise or to other horizons *of the same type*. (FL, 56/DPJ, 25)

Of this type there are many competing versions, viz., the "messianism of the Jewish, Christian, or Islamic type," as also of the "neo-Hegelian, Marxist, or post-Marxist type." The reason for his hesitation, he says, lies in his resistance to the very idea of a "horizon," for any horizon, be it that of a regulative idea or of a "messianic advent," sets limits and defines expectations in advance (FL, 57/DPJ, 26). He hesitates to assimilate justice to any horizon of this type because the very type of a "horizon," its very idea, is to anticipate the other, to head it off in advance.

But, in the 1994 Galilée edition of this lecture, he amends his remarks as follows:

> I would hesitate to assimilate too quickly this "idea of justice" to a regulative idea in the Kantian sense, to any content whatsoever of a messianic promise (I say *content* and not form, for every messianic form, every messianicity, is never absent from a promise, whatever it may be) or to other horizons of the same *type*. (FL, 56)

Thus he distinguishes in 1994 between the determinate content of particular messianic promises and the messianic form of the promise itself, messianicity itself, which goes to the heart of a promise, which is the form of any promise of something to come. Once the messianic is given determinate content, it is restricted within a determinable and determining horizon, but the very idea of the messianic, of messianicity, is to shatter horizons, to let the promise of something *tout autre* shock the horizon of the same and the foreseeable. Messianicity is not a horizon but the disruption or opening up of the horizon.

What has intervened in between these two editions of "Force of Law" is the deconstructive reading of Marx in *Specters of Marx* (1993), in which Derrida had discovered an irreducible messianic (I do not find the word *messianicité* in *Spectres de Marx*) structure that is at work in Marx, on Marx, behind Marx's back.[3] In the Marx book Derrida gropes for a certain "atheological" and desert-like messianic, as opposed to the concrete biblical or philosophical messianisms. He distinguishes an "undetermined, empty, abstract, and dry form" of the messianic in general, a "quasi-atheistic messianic" as opposed to a biblical or Abrahamic messianism (SdM, 266–68/SoM, 167–69).

It will be the particular point of Part III to formulate this distinction more precisely, to sharpen the tip of the "messianic" bent in deconstruction. For, as I have all along been insisting, it is this messianic or prophetic passion that impassions deconstruction, and it is in messianic or prophetic religion—beyond classical negative theology—that the central point of convergence and interaction between deconstruction and religion and theology is to be found. Like prophetic religion, deconstruction awaits the coming of the just one and burns with messianic passion. We will follow the messianic first in Derrida's Marx book (§9, §10) and then in his recent delineation of the messianic as a contribution to a "religion within the limits alone" (*Foi*, 16, 18, 70) (§11).

§9. Of Marx and the Messiah

Hauntology: The Schema of the Ghost

In *Specters of Marx*, the notion of the messianic is developed in the context of what Derrida calls a pure (or impure) "hauntology," that is, the schema of the ghost. For the "messianic" is the ghost or specter of a religion with which Marx—and I will add, here, Derrida—with which neither Marx nor Derrida can dispense, of an irreducible religious structure of which both make use, however much the specter of that thought may spook deconstruction's (not to mention Marx's) most loyal acolytes. I will go so far as to say, for the sake of provocation (DM, 53/GD,49), this messianic structure goes to the heart of deconstruction, that is, to the heart of Derrida's religion, to the heart of the religion of Saint Jacques, to

Derrida's heart, which means to have a heart in a heartless world. For Derrida has all his life been praying and weeping over some coming messiah, over something coming, something or other, I know not what, that is coming.

Along with Freud and Nietzsche, Marx is the author of one of modernity's most powerful critiques of religion, of a searching criticism of the tendency of the human spirit, driven by fear or resentment or world-weariness, to turn the misty fabrications of its own imaginings into a realm of invisible beings. But of Marx and of his exorcism of these religious ghosts Derrida says that "[h]owever alive, healthy, critical, and still necessary his burst of laughter," Marx

> perhaps should not have chased away so many ghosts too quickly. Not all of them at once or not so simply on the pretext that they did not exist (of course they do not exist, so what?)—or that all this was or ought to remain past. . . . (SdM, 277/SoM, 174)

However potent and important Marx's sometimes satiric critique of religion's ghosts, and of religion's cooperation with the oppressiveness of capital, and even of the spell that religion continued to cast over young Hegelians like Feuerbach and Stirner, still, Marx acted a little too hastily.

Very few things illustrate more nicely the movement from a modernist critique to a postcritical "deconstruction"—here is a point where the word "postmodern" would have made perfect sense had it not been ground into senselessness by opportunistic overuse—than Derrida's relationship to Marx in *Specters of Marx*, a book which clearly continues the discussion of the two genders/genres of *la/le capitale* in *The Other Heading* (1991) and in *Moscou aller-retour*, written after his 1990 trip to Moscow.[4] For Derrida's purpose to is move beyond critique, beyond reductionism, beyond the simple opposition of faith and reason (*Foi*, 13), and beyond the "modern," which he associates with an "imperative for totalitarianism" (AC, 44/OH, 42). But he does all this precisely in the name of that for which critique is designed, viz., "emancipation"—a word which, *pace* Lyotard (SdM, 125–26/SoM, 75; cf. FL, 62–63/DPJ, 28), Derrida does not want to write off, no more than he wants to write off religion. Derrida is not trying to remove the revolutionary scare that the specter of Marx's name throws into our hearts. Indeed, contrary to popular presentations of "poststructuralism" or "postmodernism," Derrida takes deconstruction as a way to continue the project of emancipation and Enlightenment (SdM, 145/SoM, 88), and even of a "'rational' and universal discourse on the subject of 'religion'" (*Foi*, 28)—but always by another means.[5] If deconstruction moves beyond critique, it does so only by first moving through it (AC, 76/OH, 77; PdS, 368/*Points*, 357). It proceeds by way of shaking the assured distinctions of the ontology upon which Marxist critique rests: between the real and the unreal; between the effective actuality of economico-material forces and the unreal or fantastic; between full presence and absence; and, above all, in this book, between life and death, the fullness of a living present and the void of death. Of the philosophy of living presence, Derrida says, "[w]e are attempting something else"; "we are directing our attention to the effects or the petitions of a survival or of a return of the dead," which precede and make possible the living subject and which allow the living subject to leave traces of itself behind, beyond the living presence of its own life, not to mention the spirit of all those who are not yet born, the specter of those to come:

> For all these questions, and such is the hypothesis of the present reading, the work of the specter here weaves, in the shadow of a labyrinth covered with mirrors, a tenuous but indispensable guiding thread. (SdM, 179n1/SoM, 187–88n7)

The guiding thread of the "specter" (*spectre, Gespenst*), the "schema of the ghost," however strange it may seem at first, belongs among the most recurrent Derridean schemas. The specter is an undecidable which, like any undecidable worthy of the name, like ashes or the supplement or the parergon, is neither present nor absent, is not real—"so what?"—but is real enough to inhabit and disturb our dreams of presence. Indeed Derrida's belief in ghosts—he is the author of books on soul (*Psyché*) and spirit (*De l'esprit*) and ghosts (*Spectres*)—is linked with the oldest Derridean haunt of all. For deconstruction opened shop by disturbing the assurances of the phenomenology of the living present. The schema of the phantom haunts the self-giving presence of phenomenality and *phainaesthai*, the phenomenal appearance or apparition, with a specter that is neither present nor absent, for there is something ghostly about the "irreality" of the noema, which makes Husserl's phenomenology a certain spectral inquiry (SdM, 215–16n2/SoM,189n6).

With typical flare, Derrida describes his reading as a movement from Marxist "ontology" to a postcritical "hauntology" (in French, these are homonyms; in English, they are close) (SdM, 10/SoM, 31–32), to a logic of haunting in which the assured distinctions between being and non-being have been disturbed; a specter has an *unheimlich* way of being-there while not being there, a weird way of being *epekeina tes ousias* (SdM, 165/SoM, 100). Having to wrestle with such undecidables is, of course, the cursed fate of Hamlet whose famous tryst with ghosts was the scene of one of English literature's greatest ghost stories. In *Hamlet*, the assured logic of to be or not to be had broken down, and both the time and the being of Hamlet's Denmark were out of joint. That is why, in order to work out this "hauntology," Derrida has chosen to interweave the text of *Hamlet* with Marx's *Kapital, The German Ideology*, and *The Eighteenth Brumaire*.

§9. Of Marx and the Messiah

The schema of the specter is a postcritical, postsecular, post-Enlightenment, postphenomenological paradigm of life/death, of sur-vivance, which means, at one and the same time, of a life that is haunted by death: bygone spirits and spirits yet to come; as also of a death that continues to live: of the power of the non-living to live on, which frames the question of tradition and heritage—and all this precisely in the name of justice. For it belongs to the hypothesis of Derrida's reading that, while justice can and must be delivered to the living, justice is not just a matter of and for the living. Rather, if there is any hope of justice, justice is due to the dead and the not yet born. For justice means responsibility and we are responsible to the dead, to their dying and the heritage they have handed down through their death, as well as to the not yet born. The spirits of the dead constitute a flood of *revenants*, a revisitation of the so-called living present by the spirits of the past. But the present is disturbed no less by *arrivants*, by all those who are to come, and indeed by the *revenant* as *arrivant*, by what is to come as what is coming to us from the past, as repeatable.

If the cause of justice is not served by chasing away so many ghosts so quickly, as Marx has done, then, by implication—and this is a specter from which Derrida does not flee—it follows that it is not served by chasing away the religious. In Derrida's view, the religious plays a double role in Marx, one over which he has control, the other one which works behind his back:

> The religious [for Marx] is thus not just one ideological phenomenon or phantomatic production among others. On the one hand, it gives to the production of the ghost or of the ideological phantasm its originary form or its paradigm of reference, its first "analogy." (SdM, 264/SoM, 166)

The commodity is explained by Marx as having taken on a magical life of its own which only the "misty realm of religion" helps us understand, because the relation between commodities is a "phantasmagoric" form of social relations of which religion provides the "only possible analogy." In religion, the products of the human head are given autonomous form and take on a life of their own. That, by an analogous process, is what happens in the production of a commodity, which is what Marx calls fetishism. As soon as a product is taken to the market it is overtaken by idealization, autonomization, and spectral incorporation. In "The Fetishism of the Commodity and its Secret" in *Kapital*, Marx descries the famous magical, mystical wooden table, which, upon becoming a commodity, takes on a life of its own, stands upright on its feet, then on its head, and spins about more marvelously than any spinning seance table. But according to Derrida, Marx is trying, unsuccessfully, to *limit* spectralization to commodities, to contain the spectral effect and not to let it contaminate the effective reality of use-value, to which Marx attributes ontological status, a natural, uncorrupted, originary, self-identity (SdM, 253–54/SoM, 159). That for Derrida is Marx's attempt to "exorcise" the ghost from use-value—even while he is being haunted by another ghost which is operating on him from behind:

> On the other hand (and first of all, no doubt for the same reason), the religious also informs, along with the messianic and the eschatological, be it in the necessarily undetermined, empty, abstract, and dry form that we are privileging here, that "spirit" of emancipatory Marxism, whose injunction we are reaffirming here, however secret and contradictory it appears. (SdM, 264/SoM, 166–67)

Marxism is inspired by one of religion's ghosts, by an irreducible and powerful "messianic" spirit, by an irreducible religious aspiration and respiration, by the specter of a justice to come that breaks the spell of the living present and haunts our present projects. The comment echoes Derrida's reference in 1980, in "Of an Apocalyptic Tone," to "that Marxist eschatology that people have too quickly (*trop vite*) wanted to forget these last years in France" (*Ton*, 59/RTP, 145). This communist spirit also haunts "old Europe," which is scared half to death by the specter of a coming communist justice.

In a certain sense, Derrida is here, quite independently and for motives of his own and inspired by Benjamin, reinventing the wheel of liberation theology, at least in a postcritical form, and taking us back to authors like Roger Garaudy, where the intersection of "the 'spirit' of emancipatory Marxism" and the prophetic spirit, the spirit of *the* Jewish prophets, Amos and Isaiah and the like, has long been recognized.[6] Instead of a purely modernist-Marxist reduction of religion to economic forces, one sees Marxism as itself invoking a certain religious passion, a certain religio-messianic structure. Derrida sees that, like the prophets themselves upbraiding the Jews for idolatry, Marx denounced capitalism as "theological fetishization," as gold-become-God. How else is one to describe Marx's opposition to the spectral ghost of money than "prophetic"? We know, Derrida says, that Marx loved Shakespeare's *Timon of Athens* and that Timon, using the very words of Ezekiel, cursed corruption like a Jewish prophet. How much Marx loves the "prophetic imprecation" that Shakespeare cast against this "yellow slave," which can make withered widows look good (SdM, 75–78/SoM, 41–44)!

Messianic Time Is Out of Joint

This discourse on the ghost, which is also a discourse *with* ghosts, a communing with spirits, is undertaken "in the name of *justice*," that is, from a "respect for those others who are no longer or for those others who

§9. Of Marx and the Messiah

are not yet *there*, presently living, whether they are already dead or not yet born" (SdM, 15/SoM, xix). There is no justice without this respect and responsibility which divide the present, which knock it out of joint and unhinge it, no justice "[w]ithout this *non-contemporaneity with itself of the living present*" (SdM, 16/SoM, xix). The time that is out of joint is a messianic time, a time that does not close in upon itself, that is structurally ex-posed to an out-side that prevents closure. Injustice is closure, juncture even as messianic justice lies in disjuncture and being out of joint.

Derrida's take on "out of joint" is out of step with the common meaning of this expression as also with Heidegger's account of *dike* in "The Anaximander Fragment." Countering Heidegger's gloss of this famous fragment, Derrida takes the *Fug* as *droit* and the *Un-fug* as justice. On Derrida's telling, it is only if (the) time is out of joint, if time is an un-gathering *Un-fug*, unhinged from the gathering unity of the living present, disjointed and opened up to the specter of what is not there, that justice is possible (SdM, 44/SoM, 19–20; 49–57/23–29; cf. AC 17/OH, 11; DT, 201–04n1/GT, 159–61n28; DT, 205/GT, 162). The movement of justice is a movement beyond the hinges and fixed junctures of the law to the ghost of the other, who unhinges me from my fixity in the present, whose coming before me (*prévenance*) comes over and dispossesses me of my self-possession, drawing me out into the excess of the dis-juncture. In *Specters of Marx* the "other" has the specific sense of the non-living, who intervene upon and interrupt the identity of the living present. The other is the bygone generations (*revenants*) whose death and labors and heritage we need actively to take up, interiorize, and "mourn," which is *stricto sensu* impossible,[7] the "dearly departed," the "community of saints," where the loss of memory, the effacement of their trace causes the greatest suffering (PdS, 153/*Points*, 143–44). Mourning is an interiorization of the other, which is impossible, which cannot be completed, a fidelity to the other that always retains a trace of infidelity, because the other always retains an irreducible, inappropriable alterity (PdS, 161/*Points*, 152). The impossibility of true mourning comes close to what Johannes Baptist Metz calls preserving "the dangerous memory of suffering."[8] The other is also the generations to come, the most literal *à-venir*, *les arrivants*, in which is lodged the specific weight of messianic hope.

Hence the gift of undeconstructible justice, beyond the law, before the law, is located in the *Un-fug*, which keeps things sufficiently dis-lodged and open-ended as to give an opening to the singularity of the other.[9] Otherwise deconstruction would come back to the good conscience of rules kept and duty done that would close off the chance of the future:

> [The chance of] this desert-like messianism (without content and without identifiable messiah), of this also *abyssal* desert, "desert in the desert," that we will talk about later (p. 167), one desert signaling toward the other

. . . —in the waiting or calling for what we have nicknamed here without knowing *le messianique*: the coming of the other, the absolute and unpredictable singularity of the *arrivant as justice*. We believe this messianic remains an ineffaceable mark . . . of Marx's legacy, and doubtless of inheriting, of the experience of inheritance in general. Otherwise one would reduce the event-ness of the event, the singularity and the alterity of the other. (SdM, 56/SoM, 28)

This "messianic" is not Christian or Jewish, Marxist or Hegelian "messianism" but a universal, formal structure upon which the very movement of justice, and hence of deconstruction, turns. It turns out that deconstruction—to the surprise of both its friends and its foes—believes in the ghost of a chance-event, in the chance of a ghost-event, in the "misty realm" of a religious figure, a veritably, literally, haunting messianic figure. Would it be too much to say that this messianic figure constitutes "the only possible analogy" for this Derrida/Marx, for this postcritical, postsecular deconstruction that is inspired by a Marxian specter, scared by a religious ghost? That formidable question is matched by another: How can deconstruction sit down to table with a "universal, formal structure"? How is that not simply a straightforward transcendental, or even, as Critchley muses, a "foundationalist" structure, as opposed to a quasi-transcendental structure? Are we to believe that Derrida is in his dotage and is becoming foundationalist and religious? We defer these formidable difficulties for the moment.[10]

This dis-jointed, messianic time which provides the opening for the invention of the event of the other, is an effect of *différance*—no thanks to *différance*—which opens the space between a memory and a promise. So *différance* does not mean only deferral, delay, and procrastination, but the spacing out, the extension between memory and promise or *à-venir*, which opens up the here-now in all of its urgency and absolute singularity, in the imminence of the instant. The call of what is coming calls for action now. There is the *gage*: engagement, promise, injunction and response to injunction, the pledge that is given in and for us before any concrete decision, the time of the promise, the response to the demands of justice, which is impatient, uncompromising, and unconditional (cf. FL, 57–63/DPJ, 26–29). But by the here-now Derrida does not mean the fullness of the living present but the passion of the appeal that is made upon us, here and now, the appeal for what is to come, for *the* impossible (SdM, 60–62/SoM, 31–33). If, upon meeting up with him, we still ask the Messiah when he will come, he will say "today" (*Pol.*, 55n1). Indeed *Specters of Marx*, as Critchley emphasizes, is itself an enactment of this engagement, a piece written in the midst of politics *today*, an urgent response to a pressing and present situation, in the age of the "new world order."[11] "Faith and Knowledge," the contribution to the Capri seminar, addresses the return of religion *today*, above all in the midst of fundamentalist violence that is sweeping over us. Deconstruction is not meant to be a soft sighing for the future, but a way of deciding now and being impassioned in the moment.

Virtual Reality

The scene or stage of justice today is haunted by another ghost, by another spectral "medium," viz., the media and the rapid advances of the teletechnologies. Spectral space is the space of "virtual reality" and "virtual events" (SdM, 268/SoM, 169): the odd being, time, and space of instant presence, worldwide dissemination, on-the-spot reporting; of a sea of images and simulacra, of sound bites and electronic messages sailing through cyberspace, in which the simulacrum runs the show. This is a being and a time that is neither real nor unreal but is constituted by the power of the media to produce images, simulacra, ghostly specters. Future televisions, it is reported, will even dispense with the "screen," and project images directly upon the eye, the way sound is lodged directly in the ear. Advancing techniques in animation aim at animating the recorded images of "real" people. We could then have a sequel to *Gone With the Wind* that actually would (or actually would not) star Clark Gable and Vivian Leigh, a festival of films haunted by the ghosts of the most beloved dead actors and actresses of the past; historical films in which the dead would be brought back to life in the most *unheimlich* way. A *JFK* that would be positively spooky. Elvis lives. Unlike a poor, lame ontology of presence and absence, hauntology soars through the para-ontological world of virtual reality, where the *phainaesthai* of phenomena runs wild, shaking the "assured distinction" between being and non-being to its root.

In virtual reality, injustice runs rampant and the time is out of joint in the more conventional sense of that expression. Today, in the United States, right-wing demagogues stampede public opinion, fan popular resentment against minorities, women, homosexuals, and immigrants, appeal to greed and nationalist hatred of the other, to the most base popular instincts—all under the mask of "fiscal responsibility" and "reform." They shout simplistic solutions into the ears of an undiscerning public, degrade the character of pubic discourse and dialogue, hurl inflammatory and searing sound bites at politicians who dare to take their stand with children and the homeless, with the poor and the defenseless, they scream invectives into the microphones of right-wing talk shows against those who would impose limits on carrying concealed firearms—and all this to the delight and profit of the wealthiest, most powerful national and international interests. Responsible and deliberative politicians are reduced to media images of themselves, hounded to the right, cowed into silence, demoralized, or simply defeated at the next election by right-wing extremists who will market an image of their opponents that will poison their chance for reelection and their capacity to raise campaign funds. The media "manufacture consent" to everything from the Gulf War to poisoning the air and seas and the lungs of children with carcinogens in the name of economic freedom. In this virtual world, the ghosts of fundamentalist religion fly about with powerful abandon; right-wing "televangelists" enlist the name of Jesus in support of all the forces that crucified Jesus and killed the prophets. Christian fundamentalism today, which is fundamentally a frenzied media event, produces appalling violence, the final madness of which is murder in the name of the right to life (cf. *SdM*, 77–80 /SoM, 129–34).[12]

Derrida wants to interrupt the frenzy of this free-market euphoria with what he calls a ten-word telegram on some of the most important things that are out of joint in this tele-techno-world, whose praises Fukuyama sings. These are, in turn, unemployment, homelessness, economic wars within the European Community, economic protectionism, the foreign debt of the poorest nations, the arms industry, the spread of nuclear weapons, interethnic wars, the mafia and drug cartels, and the present state of international law (SdM, 134–39/SoM, 81–84). Beyond that, the furious wars that rage on in the Middle East between fundamentalist extremists on both sides, holy wars, if you can stomach that expression, blood spilled in the name of God, all depend upon their ability to hitch their cause to the visibility that the media provide. They do not merely spill blood; they spill blood before the cameras of CNN International. That is what Derrida analyzes in "Faith and Knowledge" (§14).

Better than anyone in his own times Marx understood all this, at least in principle. But he could never have imagined the contemporary scope of what Derrida calls "technicity," the teletechnical and technoscientific constellation that Heidegger called the *Gestell*, which in Heidegger himself served reactionary and fascist purposes. The spirit of such a Marx must never be forgotten or assimilated, never left on the shelf of the great dead white European male. This spirit of Marx must sur-vive, live on, and be a ghost by which we must never cease to be haunted.

Today Marx himself is the object of just such a media blitz, which is why Derrida and deconstruction, always loving the *contretemps* and *contra-pied*, rise to his defense. Deconstruction itself arose in the generation that witnessed the end of another Marxism: Stalinism. Deconstruction is political all the way down and its politics arise from the end of totalitarianism, of Stalinism, and of the Third Reich, to the ascendancy of international capital and the hegemonic rule of the superpowers. Deconstruction means to be the delimitation of totalization in all its forms. Today, the spirit of Marx has become a specter to be exorcised with increasing intensity.[13] At the beginning of *The Communist Manifesto* Marx said that old Europe, the wealthy aristocracy, the vested interests, the hierarchy of the old church, were haunted by the specter of an approaching communism

§9. Of Marx and the Messiah

(*das Gespenst des Kommunismus*) and that all these ancient powers conspired against that looming specter. Today, Derrida says the ghost of Marx continues to haunt Europe, not the specter of a communism to come but the spectre of communism past, the fear that this specter will come back again, *revenant*, to haunt us if we do not take care. The return of Marx is the one specter to menace the "new world order," the one threat to establishing and maintaining the kingdom of God on earth, to the neo-evangelical "good news" of God's coming in the form of the Christian State or Superstate, which, according to both the Pope and a good Protestant like Hegel, *mirabile dictu*, is the very *Wesen* of Europe. The Polish Pope, John Paul II, boasts of having helped bury communism so that from now on Europe "will be what it should always have been according to him, a Christian Europe" (SdM, 164/SoM, 100). Of course, as with every *Wesen*, this leaves very little room for the inessential, for Arabs, Jews, *Gastarbeiter*, and other infidels and remnants (SdM, 104–05/SoM, 60–61). The specter of a Christian Europe, of Christo-centrism, is one that continually haunts Derrida, and he worries constantly over proposals—like Jan Patõcka's Christian politics examined below (§13)—that argue that Europe gets to be really free and responsible, and the West gets to be the West, indeed humankind gets to be really human, only when they all become Christian. Amen. (Watch!)

To describe this ghost, Derrida would be served just as well by *Macbeth*, which was Levinas's favorite Shakespearean play, where the ghost of Banquo keeps coming back to torment the murderer. Today Marx is dead and buried, over and done with, *vorbei*; the ancient battle between the western Euro-American Good and the Evil Empire, between Locke and Rousseau, Adam Smith and Marx, has been settled in favor of the West. After long deliberation, God has taken sides with the Free Market and with Trickle Down Economics. The West has won; the cold war is won; the end of history is at hand; God's rule on earth begins; Marx (not God) is dead. Of that good news the new world order keeps trying to assure itself, again and again, to the point that it is obsessed and haunted by the prospect that the ghost of the dead man will return to disturb the euphoria of "liberal democracy" and the celebrations of the triumph of the "market economy" (cf. *Moscou*, 35/PTC, 206).[14]

Derrida then offers a delicious gloss—a careful reading of which I commend to the reader's spirit—on Fukuyama's *The End of History and the Last Man*.[15] Fukuyama is a right-wing Johnny-come-lately (by about three decades) to the end-of-history discourse, a ghost from the past whose book has enjoyed enviable media success considering that it defends a thesis taken from Hegel's metaphysics. Fukuyama's success is a spectral phenomenon in the sense both of a work of exorcism of Marx's ghost and of a media event fanned by teletechnologies, something like an exorcism broadcast on CNN International. The heart of Derrida's deconstruction of

Fukuyama is to point out the way in which Fukuyama trades on the assured, metaphysical distinction between the ideal and the real, the Idea in the Kantian (and Husserlian) sense and the empirical fact, a distinction that Derrida and others have been troubling for decades now. Whenever the hideous injustices of the Free Market are pointed out, so that it looks as though, perhaps, the End has not yet quite arrived, these are treated as empirical shortcomings, contingent blights on the Idea's relentless progress. The End has arrived; it is here; it has already come about. Well, ideally, in principle, almost. It is almost here, and the final results, as Johannes Climacus said of the Hegelian System, are due in a matter of weeks. The end has not arrived, millions of people are starving, homeless, persecuted, not only under the Stars and Stripes, but all over the globe, but that is but a contingent blip on the Idea's relentless realization of its infinite task. Fukuyama follows an unfalsifiable logic which, in the best Hegelian spirit, assimilates and consumes every counter-evidence.

But if Derrida wants to resist this Holy (unholy!) Alliance of Hegel, Kojève, the Pope, Adam Smith, and the Federal Reserve Board, this Christian-Hegelian messianic eschatology, it is not by opposing every messianic structure or every thinking turned toward the future, but by way of a certain adaptation of a hope for a messianic future that alters it while repeating it, that bends it up a little in the best style of deconstruction. The *determinable* messianisms, the specific biblical and philosophical messianic eschatologies, are consummately dangerous. They describe a scene of violence and war, among which is to be included not only the wars that are waged over the holy city of Jerusalmen (SdM, 100–01/SoM, 58) but Marxism itself. For Marxism, too, has a determinable messianic content, an onto-eschatology that tells us how the wheels of historical materialism are inevitably turning, and how everything that resists this progress is to be crushed, presuming of course that one could explain how anything can resist what is inevitable and irresistible.

To deal with the complexities of this situation, Derrida proposes a certain *epoche* of the content of any particular messianism, a "desertification" and "abstraction," in order to think "the messianic in general, as a thinking of the other and of the event to come," where the "formal structure of promise exceeds" or "precedes" the particular promises made in the particular, concrete covenants. The messianic in general has to do with something irreducible and undeconstructible, which Derrida describes as

> a certain experience of the emancipatory promise; it is perhaps even the formality of a structural messianism, a messianism without religion, even a messianic without messianism, an idea of justice—which we distinguish from law or right or even human rights—and an idea of democracy—which we distinguish from its current concept and from its determined predicates today. (SdM, 102/SoM, 59)

So it is not by deconstructing every passion for a promise to be kept in the future, by exorcising every messianic spirit, that Derrida deconstructs Fukuyama's double dealing from both sides of the ideal/empirical deck. Rather, deconstruction proceeds by rethinking the very notion of an "event," of something that is to come, that slips beyond the limits of the ideal/real duality. For the *à-venir* of a justice or a democracy to come is not a future-present, not a present-able, re-presentable, utopian or Kantian ideal, not a horizon of expectation of this type; it is "the unforeseeable, the *unanticipatable*, the non-masterable, non-identifiable" (AC, 23/OH, 18), so that one cannot gauge the extent to which it is being approximated or realized, even while conceding that it is consistently deferred. For that allows us to tolerate, to be patient with the most massive injustice. Because the *à-venir* of the "messianic in general" is completely open-ended, negative or apophatic, a dry and desert-like structure that goes along with Derrida's inveterate and persistent desert-like non-essentialism, it is profoundly *urgent* and unable to be placidly complacent with the present. It is not—and the importance of this cannot be overestimated—a positive, presentable, regulative ideal. For that admits of gradual empirical approximation and constitutes the very essence of essentialism or idealism, of an idea in the Kantian sense, or of a Husserlian infinite task. That is what permits Fukuyama to double deal so serenely with present injustice. Justice is not a heavenly form which we are assigned the infinite task of copying on earth—but the Messiah, dressed in rags, saying "today."

"The idea, if that is still what it is, of democracy to come," is the pledge (*gage*) that engages the gears of deconstruction to "summon the very thing that will never present itself in the form of full presence." So there is always a gap between, on the one hand, an infinite promise—infinite respect for singularity and for the infinite alterity of the other but also for the countable and calculable—and, on the other hand, what is measured against this promise. But this gap is something otherwise than an empirical or contingent shortfall. Rather, it is structurally unforeseeable and as such urgently summons us to the possibility—the im/possibility—of the un-presentable, of an "absolute surprise" whose coming will shatter our horizon of expectation. For the *tout autre* is just what we do not expect. Setting a place at the table of expectation for Elijah does not mean his knock on the door will not come as an absolute surprise. Both the democratic promise and the communist promise must preserve

> this absolutely undetermined messianic hope at its heart, this eschatological relation to the to-come of an event *and* of a singularity, of an alterity that cannot be anticipated. Awaiting without horizon of the wait, awaiting what one does not expect yet or any longer, hospitality without reserve, welcoming salutation accorded in advance to the absolute surprise of the *arrivant*. (SdM, 111/SoM, 65)

When the *tout autre* knocks, when the *arrivant* is *tout autre*, we will not ungraciously and inhospitably insist on making him or her or it meet certain preconditions in order to gain admittance. The spirit of hospitality, the spectrality of welcoming power, is a "messianic opening to what is coming," to what cannot be awaited or recognized in advance, for whom one leaves a completely open, empty place. The spectral *arrivant* does not confirm the horizon of the same. Welcoming the event of this coming specter is the condition of the possibility of a deconstructive account of history—beyond any idealist or materialist history, beyond Hegel's, Marx's, or Fukuyama's history, beyond any metaphysical conception of history (SdM, 120/SoM, 70). A deconstructive history, transpiring in a messianic time, turns on the coming of an event, the arrival of something new, in short, on the passion for the impossible itself:

> like this strange concept of messianism without content, of the messianic without messianism, that guides us here like the blind. But it would be just as easy to show that without this experience of the impossible, one might as well give up on both justice and the event. (SdM, 112/SoM, 65)

It is precisely in order to screen out (*cribler*) the possibility of something absolutely new that ethics and the several concrete messianisms establish multiple checkpoints and scrupulously patrol their borders in order to prevent the occurrence of just such an event, of such an *arrivant*. Indeed Kojève himself, whose misleading quip that the United States (even California—how concrete can messianism be!) is the final end of history has helped lure Fukuyama down this triumphalistic path,[16] suggests something of this messianic promise when he insists on a future beyond the end of history, an end beyond the end, an open-endness beyond the teleology of history. History in a certain sense is closed; it has run a certain course to its end, but only in such a way as to remain open to something post-historical, something indeterminate beyond history's horizons, a pure form of the future beyond any specific content. "It is," Derrida glosses, "what we are nicknaming the messianic without messianism" (SdM, 124/SoM, 73). Deconstruction is the thought of an other, messianic historicity, beyond the archeo-teleo-logical concepts of history in Hegel, Marx, and even Heidegger's epochal eschatology, a historicity that represents, as Derrida says,

> another opening of event-ness as historicity that permitted one not to renounce, but on the contrary to open up access to an affirmative thinking of the messianic and emancipatory promise as promise: as promise and not as onto-theological or teleo-eschatological program or design. (SdM, 125–26/SoM, 75)

That is why deconstruction, while it has never been Marxist, has always "remained faithful (*fidèle*) to a certain spirit of Marxism, to at least one of its spirits" (SdM, 127/SoM, 75; cf. *Moscou*, 45–47/PTC, 210–11). Deconstruction keeps faith with the spirit of messianic promise, a spirit that is also religious, which is why it is a spirit that is likely to spook even deconstruction's most loyal deconstructors.

The New International

Deconstruction is to be understood as having always been loyal to a certain spirit of Marx, and to a certain spirit of the Enlightenment:

> Now, if there is a spirit of Marxism which I will never be ready to renounce, it is not only the critical idea or the questioning stance (a consistent deconstruction must insist on them even as it also learns that this is not the last or first word). It is even more a certain emancipatory and *messianic* affirmation, a certain experience of the promise that one can try to liberate from any dogmatics and even from any metaphysico-religious determination, from any *messianism*. (SdM, 146–47/SoM, 89)

It must take the form of a promise "to produce events, new effective forms of action, practice, organization, and so forth" (SdM, 147/SoM, 89). As against certain Althusserians, who resist a Marxist messianic eschatology, and against anti-Marxist eschatologies with an onto-theo-logical content, deconstruction turns on the irreducibility of affirmation and the promise, on the unconditionality of justice. Deconstruction is a movement toward the future:

> the movement of an experience open to the absolute future of what is coming, that is to say, a necessarily indeterminate, abstract, desert-like experience that is confided, exposed, given up to its waiting for the other and for the event. In its pure formality, in the indetermination that it requires, one may find yet another essential affinity between it and a certain messianic spirit. (SdM, 148/SoM, 90)

It is around this messianic promise that a "new International" takes shape, a community without community, which barely deserves the name of community, a community of all those who have stood against Marxist dogma and at the same time against reactionary and conservative impulses, who stand for a "new Enlightenment for the century to come," who want to think democracy otherwise (SdM, 148/SoM, 90; cf. AC, 77/OH, 79), for what has sometimes been called a non-Marxist, or post-Marxist left. The new International represents the heirs of Marx, those who owe Marx a debt, but selectively, by a reaffirmation of Marx that filters out and selects among his several spirits. That is the only responsible way to be responsible to a tradition, to be in debt to the dead, to allow oneself to be haunted by the past. Lacking an international organization, a permanent headquarters, and an executive council and secretary—perhaps it should get a home page on the Internet—the new International Derrida is describing looks to me like something of a mystical body or a community of saints for the spirit of a resurrected Marx. Still, a new International is nothing ephemeral, but rather a spiritual coalition of intellectuals and activists across national borders who take the "state of the debt" not only as a spiritual debt to Marx but also as a massive, material reality that oppresses millions of people in the nations of the Third World and central and east Europe, and that looks forward to the open-ended possibility of something otherwise than nationalism, to living in a nation differently than in the current scene of nationalist strife.

Saint Ma(r)x

Derrida then offers a fascinating gloss on *The Eighteenth Brumaire of Louis Bonaparte* and the discussion of Max Stirner in *The German Ideology*, a gloss which views Marx as engaged in a competition with the young Hegelians over who has done the best job of exorcising all the ghosts of German Idealism. All the young Hegelians, left or right, want to be rid of the ghosts that ultimately emanate from the paternal spirit of Hegel himself. Neither Feuerbach nor Stirner nor Marx wants to be "possessed" by spirits, but they disagree over the means and the strategy. They battle over who is the best exorcist, in the course of which Marx produces a scathing satire of Stirner which shows that Stirner was thoroughly spooked. According to "Saint Max" (Stirner), the world is teeming with spirits: *"Ja, es spukt in der ganzen Welt,"* Stirner wrote. Millions of man-made spooks roam the earth and speak through the mouths of men, turning the whole world into a phantom, a process that can ultimately be traced back to the Hegelian *Geist* (SdM, 216–18/SoM, 136). When he was innocent (like a child, Marx comments), Saint Max reports, God and the Emperor, the Pope, and the fatherland hovered over him like ghosts (*Gespenster*), but when he came of age intellectually he learned how to dispel these spirits, to make them disappear, to undo their spectral power, and to reappropriate them into his own body. But Marx thinks Saint Max's body is but an interiorizing gathering of repatriated specters, the resubjectification of an objectification. These are only thought-products to begin with and Max misses the actual, real removal of these specters for which actual work is necessary. Saint Max manages to dispel not the actual emperor but only his ghost, whereas the point is to get rid of the real emperor, not a mental representation (SdM, 207–09/SoM, 131–32). Both Max and Marx say they are against ghosts and that they love life. But both are spooked enough by death to deny that death is part of life, something eating away inside life. They wage a war over who is better at conjuring away ghosts. For Marx, it is a matter of knocking down oppressive practical structures and of not being content to expel mere phantasms. But that exposes Marx to the risk that he is himself chasing after phantasms from which he keeps trying compulsively, obsessively, like Lady Macbeth, to cleanse himself.

Marx ticks off ten ghosts that Stirner chooses to combat—instead of doing battle with the real forces of production, over the first of which we will pause just a moment:

Gespenst No. 1 (ghost No. 1): the supreme being (*das höchste Wesen*), God. Speaking now of Marx on Stirner, Derrida comments:

> Not a minute is wasted on this "incredible belief," Marx notes. Neither Stirner nor Marx, moreover, stops to consider the essence of believing, here the essence of faith *par excellence*, which can only ever believe in the unbelievable, and would not be what it is without that, beyond any "proof of the existence of God." (SdM, 227/SoM, 143)

In shocking contrast with a modernist critique, a contrast that is just plain spooky, deconstruction is not out to belittle believing, the "essence of believing (*croire*)" or of faith (*foi*). What would ever possess it to do such a thing? For deconstruction comes down to an affirmation, an invocation, a hope in the future, and what is that if not a certain *faith*, indeed the passion of an extreme faith in the unbelievable, in *the* impossible, for to the extent that something is believable it does not require that much faith. What else is deconstruction if not a faith in something that pushes us beyond the sphere of the same (cf. AC, 77/OH, 78)? What is faith if not a certain deconstruction that breaks the spell of the credible, that opens us up to the incredible, to the possibility of the impossible, since, with God everything is possible even *the* impossible? What else is deconstruction than faith, deconstruction which, proceeding *sans savoir, sans avoir, sans voir* (*Parages*, 25), finds it necessary to believe. "*Je ne sais pas. Il faut croire*" (MdA, 130/MB, 129).

So unlike Stirner and Marx, deconstruction does not stand in a simple, critical opposition to religion that attempts simply to reduce belief in ghosts, but rather it takes up, repeats, alters, and bends into different shape a fundamentally religious figure—the messianic promise—and a fundamentally religious posture, faith in the impossible, structures which are for Derrida irreducible and irreducibly ingredient in deconstruction itself. Marx, on the other hand, even if he outwits Feuerbach and Saint Max in a conjuring contest, shows himself all the more massively and obsessively preoccupied with ghosts and exorcisms, all the more compulsively washing away the stains of religions. Meanwhile, all the world knows that whenever Saint *Marx* opens his mouth generations of Jewish ghosts come streaming out, haunting the whole house of Europe, filling it with the spirits of Ezekiel and Habakkuk, Amos and Isaiah. "*Ja, es spukt in der ganzen Welt.*" The Jewish prophet Karl, not Saint, perhaps, but Rabbi Marx, denounces the hand-made gods, the golden calves, of Israel (the money-fetish), lamenting the falsity of the chosen people (Europe) to their truest, deepest promise, which is to make space for what is coming, for a justice to come, and to remain faithful to the revolutionary, messianic promise. Such a revolution, Marx says, is not to be draped in the costumes of the past (for Derrida, invention of the same) but is to be allowed to be truly revolutionary, as the coming of the future to come, forming a kind of Marxist *invention de l'autre* (SdM, 187–88 / SoM, 115).

§10. *Messianic Passion and the Religion of Saint Jacques*

Two Messianic Spaces

Derrida elaborates the distinction between two messianic spaces, in the final pages of *Specters*, in the context of a discussion of what is at stake in the "singular configuration" that "*today* links Religion and Techniks" (SdM, 265 / SoM, 167; cf. 56 / 28). There are, he says, two things at stake here, the first of which he describes as

> the return of the religious, whether fundamentalist or not, and which overdetermines all questions of nation, State, international law, human rights, Bill of Rights. . . . (SdM, 265 / SoM, 167)

Such a *retour* would represent of course a certain revisitation of the present by a ghost from the past, a religious specter that a reductionist Enlightenment critique took to be dead and buried. Today, however, religion is alive and well, resurrected in its ugliest form in the resurgence of the fundamentalisms that spill the blood and destroy the civil liberties of people around the world, for which the struggle over Jerusalem may do emblematic or symptomatic service. We will come back to the second point, the violent return of religion, of fundamentalist religion, and its link to technoscience or teletechnology in the next section, when we take up Derrida's contribution to the 1994 seminar at Capri (§11).

Derrida puts the question of this distinction as follows:

> If the messianic appeal belongs properly to a universal structure, that irreducible movement of the historical opening to the future, therefore to experience itself and to its language (expectation, promise, commitment to the event of what is coming, imminence, urgency, demand for salvation and for justice beyond law, pledge given to the other inasmuch as he or she is not present, presently present or living, and so forth), how is one to *think* it *with* the figures of Abrahamic messianism? (SdM, 266 / SoM, 167)

Inasmuch as Abraham is the father of us all, that is of all the religions of the Book, "Abrahamic messianism" here does service for all the concrete messianisms of the historical religions of Judaism, Christianity, and Islam. What of Marxism itself? Marxism is *not* the messianic structure itself, as Critchley suggests,[17] but still another concrete messianism, since the Marxist messianic promise gives a determinable, economic content to the pure, desert-like messianic form. So Derrida appears to be posing the question of the relationship between a "universal" structure and the concrete realization or embodiment of that structure, between, as he says, "a structure of experience" and a "religion." But that is a very imperfect formulation of this question on Derrida's own terms, turning as it does on the classical distinctions between form and content (FL, 56/DPJ, 25), the ideal and the real, universal and particular, essential and empirical which Derrida vigorously deconstructs in the discussion of Fukuyama (and elsewhere). Furthermore, this formulation also seems to embrace the distinction between a universal structure and its exemplifications, which is undone by the Derridean notion of exemplarism, according to which we do not know what is an example of what.

Given this formulation, Derrida poses two possibilities: is the messianic merely an abstraction ("abstract desertification") *derived* from the concrete messianisms or is it their *origin* ("originary condition")? Does the abstract messianic come before or after the concrete messianisms? Does Abrahamic messianism serve as the source or origin from which we derive an abstract concept of the messianic? Or is the messianic a condition of possibility that antedates the concrete messianisms which are but exemplifications of it?

These questions lead to another formulation: Can there be an "atheological heritage" of the biblical messianisms? Can one strip the biblical messianisms down to an atheological core? Can one, by a work of "desertification" and denuding, by a deconstructive ascesis, remove a biblical surface from a messianic structure? The idea is to remove the "determinable" content from the messianic, so that we are not waiting for the liberator of Israel, since Egypt too deserves liberation, or for the second coming of Jesus, or for a classless society in which the state withers away. That is because deconstruction means to be an absolute (as opposed to determinable) responsibility, absolute hospitality, "the 'yes' to the *arrivant(e)*, the 'come' to the future that cannot be anticipated . . . " (SdM, 266/SoM, 168):

> Open, waiting for the event *as* justice, this hospitality is absolute only if it keeps watch over its own universality. (SdM, 267/SoM, 168).

The messianic is a waiting without a horizon of determinate expectation, so that we do not know who or what we are waiting for; an "absolute" hospitality, ab-solved of determinable expectations, that is open to, that welcomes I-know-not-what.

So the question is whether the atheological messianic, the "quasi-atheistic dryness of the messianic," is the condition of the biblical messianisms.

If so, it would then be, paradoxically, an arid desert in which the living figures of the historical messianisms would grow (so that the historical messiahs would be like desert flowers, a cactus flower, say, which is quite beautiful). Or should we say that the messianic in general is a distillate, an aftereffect, an empty structure about which we do not have the least knowledge, about which, without the historical messianisms, we would neither know nor suspect anything. The historical messianisms would be "the only events on the basis of which we approach and first of all name the messianic in general, that other ghost which we cannot and ought not do without." The messianic in general would be a conceptual ghost, a specter of philosophy, a poor abstraction, whose sole cash value is drawn from the accounts of the religions of the Book. While millions of people over the centuries have found a home in the historical religions, no one would be able to live in the rare air, the ether or the desert, of the messianic in general. The figure of "absolute hospitality" would then be as inhospitable and unlivable as a desert, *unheimlich*, ghostly, impossible, unsure. The messianic in general—this "quasi 'messianism,'" this "quasi-transcendental 'messianism,'" this desert-like *khôra*, this "despairing 'messianism'"— would then seem quite fragile and impoverished. On the other hand messianic hope has to mix with despair, otherwise it is the program for a calculated future, something we can count on, and then it would be neither absolute hope nor an absolute future, but a matter of waiting for a future-present to make its more or less scheduled arrival. Such a despairing messianism would have the curious taste of death, no doubt—but then life for Derrida is life/death, not the purity of the living present.

In a 1994 roundtable discussion of this point, Derrida put the question he is posing in *Specters of Marx* in a particularly perspicacious manner, where, speaking in English, he speaks of "messianicity" rather than "messianic":[18]

> The problem remains—and this is really a problem for me, an enigma— whether the religions, say, for instance, the religions of the Book, are but specific examples of this general structure, of messianicity. There is the general structure of messianicity, as a structure of experience, and on this groundless ground there have been revelations, a history which one calls Judaism or Christianity and so on. That is one possibility, and then you would have a Heideggerian gesture, in style. You would have to go back from these religions to the fundamental ontological conditions of possibilities of religions, to describe the structure of messianicity on the ground of groundless ground on which religions have been made possible.
>
> That is one hypothesis. The other hypothesis—and I confess that I hesitate between these two possibilities—is that the events of revelation, the biblical traditions, the Jewish, Christian, and Islamic traditions, have been absolute events, irreducible events which have unveiled this messianicity. We would not know what messianicity is without messian-

ism, without these events which were Abraham, Moses, and Jesus Christ, and so on. In that case singular events would have unveiled or revealed these universal possibilities and it is only on that condition that we can describe messianicity.

Between the two possibilities I must confess I oscillate and I think some other scheme has to be constructed to understand the two at the same time, to do justice to the two possibilities. That is why—and perhaps this is not a good reason, perhaps one day I will give up this—for the time being I keep the word "messianic." Even if it is different from messianism, messianic refers to the word Messiah; it does not simply belong to a certain culture, a Jewish or Christian culture. I think that for the time being I need this word, not to teach, but to let people understand what I am trying to say when I speak of messianicity. But in doing so I still keep the singularity of a single revelation, that is Jewish, Christian revelation, with its reference to Messiah. It is a reinterpretation of this tradition of the Messiah.

Either: the messianic fits into a Heideggerian-Bultmannian schema of a demythologizing fundamental ontology in which one would strip away the existentiell particularities of the particular historical religions in order to unearth the universal, existential structures, the existentialia that represent the condition of possibility of ontico-existentiell messianisms. *Or*: the historical messianisms have a kind of absolute anteriority without which the messianic would be completely unknown.

In fact, the two possibilities are entirely compatible and complementary approaches that arise from alternately taking two different but compatible points of view. To invoke the most venerable language of the tradition, the messianic in general is the ontological ground or basis (the *ratio essendi*) of any historical messianism. But in the order of learning or knowing, one would never have had the least idea or suspicion of the structure of the messianic without the help of these historical revelations, which are the *ratio cognoscendi* of the messianic. The two standpoints complement rather than compete with each other and it is not a matter of choosing between them.

Viewed thus, Derrida would have been drawn into the old debates concerning the possibility of a "Christian philosophy"—debates, I think, that are being replayed today with respect to the "Jewish philosophy" of Levinas. The upshot of these debates is to say that there are certain things that are philosophically coherent in themselves, *idealiter*, that we would not have come upon, *de facto*, without the aid of revelation—the creation of the world, say, or, in Levinas, the notion of ethical substitution, of the *me voici*. Were one to add the "messianic" or "messianicity" to this list, the curious—very spooky and *unheimlich*—result would be to bring deconstruction within the orbit of some sort of Jewish or even Judeo-Christian philosophy, which might be proving a little too much about Derrida and theology.

The problem with all this, and I include here the way that Derrida himself tends to put the question, is that the whole discussion is framed within an assured set of distinctions—between fact and essence, example and exemplar, real and ideal, particular and universal—which it is the whole point of deconstruction to disturb. For deconstruction, I have been maintaining, constitutes a certain anti-essentialism or nominalism, which ought not to be drawn into any debates about whether facts precede essences or essences precede facts, or whether each precedes the other but in different orders and in different ways.

The issue gets a sharper tip if we pay closer attention to Derrida's mention of "absolute events, irreducible events which have unveiled this messianicity," since by an absolute event he means something that is not a case of something more general, not a particular x subsumable under a universal F, as in Fx, but an irreducible singularity. In the messianic time of singularities, historical happenings are idiosyncratic "events" and not "moments" in a larger, teleological or eschatological movement. An event is not a moment that can be taken under a more sweeping process, included as an instance or phase that is subordinate to and serves the ends of some deeper purpose. Furthermore, given the Babelianism of deconstruction and its delimitation of the traditional idea of translation, of "the neutrality of a translating medium that would claim to be transparent, metalinguistic, and universal" (AC, 58/OH, 58), Derrida can hardly put himself in the position of saying that the "messianic" represents the overarching, universal metalanguage into which the various concrete messianisms can be translated. In just the way a religious sensibility resists the translation of the God of Abraham into the God of philosophy, one ought to resist the translation of Abrahamic messianism into a universal messianic, which would in the end be just more philosophy. Among other things, there would be nothing, or hardly anything *quasi* about this *quasi-transcendental*, which would then have become indistinguishable from a straightforward transcendental. The matter is complicated in the Capri seminar when Derrida says he is in search of "a universal culture of singularities" (*Foi*, 28), the universalizability of the non-universalizable, where every other is wholly other. But what sort of universality can that possibily mean?

Were it the case, and I think it must be, that the historical messianisms are to be treated as irreducible singularities, and were that point adhered to in a sufficiently steadfast way, then it would be impossible to say that the messianic in general is a universal, essential structure under which the historical messianisms may be subsumed, for that is exactly what is excluded by treating an event as a singularity as opposed to a particular subsumable under a universal. So, the first option, of treating the concrete messianisms as instances of an abstract form, would be cut off, and the way would likewise be blocked to saying that together the two possibilities are complementary approaches, since they would not be related to each other as particular and universal, fact and essence.

The difficulty is not so much that we do not know what the messianic *means*, since Derrida is clear enough, even quite eloquent, about "the 'yes' to the *arrivant(e)*, the 'come' to the future that cannot be anticipated" (SdM, 266/SoM, 168). The difficulty is that we are at a loss to describe the *status* of this undeterminability, this indeterminable messianic, without specific content, which cannot be a true or conventional or garden variety universal.

A Number of Messianisms

I think that help in this matter is forthcoming from the young Heidegger's notion of a "formal indication," an idea forged in the midst of Heidegger's own attempt to extract existential structures from the experience of "factical life" in the early Christian communities. Unlike the traditional concept or category that purports to seize or comprehend its object, the "formal indication" is but a projective sketch that traces out in advance certain salient formal features of an entity or region of entities. Instead of a conceptual mastery of its material that reduces the individual to an instance of the general, the formal indication is related to the factical region as the imperfect to the perfect, as a schema or anticipatory sketch to the idiomatic fullness of concrete life. The formal indication is not a universal that "contains" "particulars" "underneath" it, but a sign—and we recall that in *Specters* Derrida asks which "signals" (*fait signe*) to the other (SdM, 266/SoM, 168)—pointing at a region where it itself cannot enter. Fully to "understand" the factical would require a certain act or engagement (*gage, engagement*) or *praxis*, giving oneself over to the factical matter at hand, which would no longer be the business of philosophy. That is where philosophy excuses itself and politely takes its leave, leaving life to face the worst.

Heidegger identified two such *pre*philosophical sources as particularly important to his project: the early Christian experience of time and the ethical experience of the Greek *polis*. To be sure, access to these "revolutionary" experiences could be gained only by means of the most traditional texts, the New Testament and the *Nicomachean Ethics*. Accordingly, such texts could not be approached by conventional academic reconstructions but required a new, more radical method Heidegger called "*Destruktion*." A "destruction" does not destroy but breaks through to the originary factical experiences from which the text arises, the term having been suggested to him by Luther's notion of a *destructio* through the crust of scholasticism to the life of the New Testament. Lecturing on the "phenomenology of religion," Heidegger analyzes the temporality of the *parousia* in Paul's letters to the Thessalonians. The "second coming of Christ" is not a "when" to be calculated but a "how" to be lived, not a matter of reckoning a definite time in the future, but of being ready, existentially transformed and radically open to an indefinite possibility that must be preserved in its indefiniteness. Recast in terms of a relationship to one's own death, this analysis became a centerpiece of *Being and Time*.

Heidegger thinks that philosophy is nourished, enriched, and renewed by its *pre*philosophical sources and, at least in the first Freiburg period, he numbers the biblical experiences inscribed in the Scriptures as central prephilosophical experiences. But Heidegger shows a distrust of the university and of the universality of its discourse and he insists on questioning and rethinking the traditional conceptuality. That is why Heidegger does not propose a project of "translating" the categories of the New Testament into philosophical terms, for that seems unduly to trust philosophy and the discourse to which factical life will be handed over, unduly to trust the Greeks, who on the young Heidegger's view reduced being and time to static presence. Rather, Heidegger wants to forge a new, let us say, a quasi-conceptuality, formed of "formal indications" which are related to the singularity of existence, to factical life, as imperfect sketches or anticipatory foreshadowings of a prior and irreducible excess, an excess that can only be "engaged" or entered into existentially, not grasped conceptually. For this, there are no formal rules but only formal schemata or indexes of a kingdom of complexities, ambiguities, and undecidabilities that are resolved only in the doing.

The central move that Heidegger makes that can help Derrida out is this. In a formal indication, the individual, the singularity, is not taken as an *instance* or example of the universal, does not become a subsumable case or a *casus* that falls off the pedestal of Greek universality, a temporal specimen of an unchanging species. Rather, the singular is affirmed in all of its singularity, respected in all of the richness of its idiosyncratic *haecceitas*, this-ness. The singular is thought not as a particular under a universal but as an unrepeatable, irreplaceable individual. What better embodiment of such a "kingdom of singularities" than the biblical kingdom itself, where God has counted every tear, and numbered every hair on our heads, where God knows every secret nestled in someone's heart, where every least little nobody in the kingdom is precious beyond measure? In short, where every other is wholly other? A formal indication provides as much as it is possible, or desirable, to "conceptualize" of such a world. A concept on Heidegger's accounting is not a "universal" but a sketch, not a universal *con-capere* or *be-greifen* that comprehends the particular round about, not an essence that turns the individual into a contingent fact, but a finger (*index*) pointing at the moon. By the same token, the singular is not a *fall* (*casus*) from universality whose feet are soaked by the particularity of matter or potency, but an *excess* that cannot be contained. A concept, on that account, is but a certain precursive indicator or "pre-cept," a light sketch of a region that can only be entered, engaged, existed, leaving philosophy and its conceptuality back home in the security of its academic chairs.

The hermeneutics of facticity is not a project of "translation," for the latter is exposed to a naive conception of language as some kind of relatively neutral or noncorrosive container, and assumes the possibility of shipping or transporting the contents of one discourse into another without suffering any major losses to one's cargo. A formal indication does not translate from one self-contained discourse to another, from a concrete discourse into an overarching metadiscourse, but rather moves from factical life—but always *through* texts, like the Letters to the Thessalonians—to a delimited, desert-like discursive structure. It tries to bring the factical life embedded in excessively rich texts, like biblical texts, for example, to a certain pale formal structure which remains beholden to life, which remains but a handmaiden to life, which at most, at best, issues an invitation to live life and to keep thinking in its place. Heidegger thinks that for the most part philosophers have merely rearranged the furniture on their academic deck without returning to sources. They keep operating with a more or less finished conceptuality, first handed down by the Greeks, which has taken on a life of its own, which has acquired an unquestioned authority, and which they at most reconfigure, modify, or from time to time touch up, but which they never radically question and expose to trembling. Philosophy requires the trauma of revisiting its sources, and a new humility about its own conceptuality, which needs both to be reforged on the basis of its exposure to factical existence and to be distrusted in terms of the extent of its reach, a reach which is never transcendental but at best "quasi-transcendental."

On such a reading, the messianic in general would be a formal indication of the concrete messianisms that are to be found in the religions of the Book. But a formal indication, on Heidegger's accounting, has the status of an empty schema which lacks existential *engagement* whereas Derrida's "messianic" is the very structure of urgency and engagement. The messianic goes to the heart of deconstruction and of deconstruction's passion and deconstruction's religion, its affirmation of and engagement in the world, in events, in what is happening, in traditions and what is to come, in "life/death," *survivance*, surviving *today*. The messianic, I am arguing all along, is deconstruction's passion and deconstruction is impassioned by this impossible. That is why I think, in accord with a fundamental gesture of deconstruction, that there cannot be a clean-cut and well-maintained border between the two messianic spaces. Derrida has always insisted that the borders between our most important distinctions are porous, and that applies as well to the distinction between the messianic and the messianisms. Derrida's desert-like and arid, an-khôral, atheological messianic enjoys a great deal of the life of the historical messianisms, of their historical hope, of their religious affirmation of something freeing that is to come, a great deal of the energy of *engagement*. The *whole idea* of "abstracting" from the concrete messiahs is to intensify the urgency of the messianic.

So rather than taking Derrida's messianic as in anyway overarching the three historical messianisms of the religions of the Book, or the three plus one, if you include Marx's messianism, I would say that Derrida's is a fifth (or if you include Benjamin's a sixth, or even a certain later Heidegger's, a seventh), that is to say, *one more* messianism, but one with a deconstructive twist, one that deconstruction has bent to its own purposes so that the idea of a *true* messianic in general, or a true universal, is a mistake, even if you take it as a formal indication, for that implies *some kind* of general validity. Messianisms multiply across the surface of the earth in disseminative plurality and they never quite succumb to a general messianic. The issue is not to feel about for their general essence or invariant structure but to invent something new, to repeat and alter all hitherto existing messianisms, to bend them up until a fourth is wrung from the first three, and a fifth from that, in a number of messianisms.

Indeed, I would say that a true messianic in general, if there is one, would have the form of absolute *inhospitality*, of uninhabitability. We live where we are, in the concrete, in a historico-political world, so that every messianic structure takes the form of some sort of messianism. After all, the Derridean messianic does have *certain* determinable features, some of which—e.g., its being turned to the *à-venir*—it has borrowed from the prophetic tradition, and some of which are Derrida's own invention. For Derrida's messianic is through and through an ethico-political idea, having to do all the way down with justice and a democracy to come, and organized under the idea of the "new International." Having begun, like everyone else, and just as he himself predicts, where one is (DLG, 233/OG, 162), Derrida's messianic has emerged under determinate historical conditions and takes a determinate form. Deconstruction first arose at the end of the totalitarianisms of the left and the right, of fascism and Stalinism, which was when deconstruction was first being forged. Deconstruction has assumed its most recent form as a witness to the surprising collapse of the Soviet Union—now that it has happened Sovietologists will descend on the scene and explain that it was "inevitable"—and its East European bloc in the last decade, by the consequent resurgence of nationalism and neoconservativism, and by the alarming rise of fundamentalism. So Derrida's empty, desert-like messianic is determinately situated at the end of this century and is turned toward an "absolute surprise" and the possibility of the impossible that *does* after all—what would not?—reflect certain determinate circumstances even as it conceives itself as a "radicalization . . . in the tradition of a certain Marxism" (SdM, 151/SoM, 92). The "new International," Derrida's passion for the impossible, is Derrida's dream, his quasi-Marxist messianism, his passion for a postcritical Marx and a post-capitalist democracy, of a posttriumphalistic new world order where our discourses have been sensitized to his ten grievances with the new world order, what he calls "these plagues of the 'new world order.'" All the grievances ticked off in this ten-word telegram on the disasters of post-modernity turn on "suffering itself, a suffering that suffers still more, and more obscurely, for having lost its habitual models and language once it no longer recognizes itself" in "old word[s]" like unemployment or class conflicts (SdM, 134–35/SoM, 81).[19]

The scene of deconstruction, the present scene, the time that is out of joint, *today*, is a scene that is utterly transfixed by the spectral phenomenon of technicity, by a world in which "doubtless everything which *today* links Religion and Technics in a singular configuration"—captured quite well in the neologism "televangelists"—is "at stake" (SdM, 265/SoM, 167). The second part of this *unheimlich* link, the teletechnical part, Derrida describes as "the differantial deployment of *tekhne*, of techno-science or teletechno-logy." The "virtualization" of space and time that is produced by the teletechnologies has effected a "dis-location" of space that, for better or worse, constitutes "another space for democracy. For democracy-to-come and thus for justice." The question is, as it always is for Derrida, how to make this place habitable without closing off the future. The messianic "trembles on the edge of this event" but this trembling, this "messianic hesitation," is not an experience of paralysis but rather constitutes the very condition of decision and affirmation and responsibility (SdM, 268–69/SoM, 167). I will return to this point in §14.

Derrida's Seance: "Es spukt"

Marx is both for and against ghosts. He both exorcises them and be-lieves in them—since an exorcist is someone who believes in ghosts, who takes them seriously—but without quite being able to monitor these op-erations. Marx is in a double bind. On the one hand, he exorcises the ghost of the commodity, the spectral table that stands up on its feet and dis-courses with other commodities. He reduces that specter back to the artifactual, technical body that is constituted by labor. But, on the other hand, he founds this exorcism of the ghost on a pre-deconstructive "cri-tique," on an "ontology" of the presence of what is really real that aims at dissipating this phantom into thin air, conjuring it away inasmuch as the real forces of production have no more to do with these fantastic beings than does a railway with Hegelian philosophy. A deconstruction of this critique does not jettison it but opens it up to questions that the critique itself tends to close off, questions that are actually "more radical" than critique or ontology. Indeed, Derrida adds, these questions are prac-tical events, "seismic events":

> These seismic events come from the future; they are given from out of the unstable, chaotic, and dis-located ground of the times. A disjointed or dis-adjusted time without which there would be neither history, nor event, nor promise of justice. (SdM, 270/SoM, 170)

The essence of religion for Marx is to take a mental representation (*Vorstellung*) and turn it into an alien world, that is, to attribute external reality to it by forgetting its real genealogy. But it will not do to trace the genealogy of these spectral objects back to our own thoughts and imaginings, as Feuerbach and Stirner have done, but to see their genesis in the "existing modes of production." Things ought not to be too heady, Marx says; it is not enough to stuff these heady imaginings back into the head, we need to see that there is something more to life than the head.

Now what Marx knows and does not know, what he knows but acts as if he does not want to know it, is that everything depends upon the "survival" of these ghosts outside the head, and the irreducibility of the religio-messianic structure—everything, including Marx's own critique. Stirner—a pseudonym suggesting it's all in your head (*Stirn*)—said to the folks who are taken in by religious phantasies, "*Mensch, es spukt in deinem Kopfe!*" "O, humankind, it's all in your head!" Marx thought it enough to revisit this same critique upon Saint Max, reminding him that his remedies are all in his head, and that *Stirner* has done nothing until he has unseated the real emperor, not the simulacrum of the emperor in his head. But for Derrida nothing can stop this critique of Saint Max from recoiling upon itself, from generating a Saint Marx (and so how far can we be from Saint Jacques?), that is, from revisiting the ghost of this *revenant* upon Marx himself, from saying, "*Marx, es spukt in deinem Kopfe!*"

But what is this *es spukt* that is going on behind Marx's back (or outside his head), this invisible ghost that is not in his line of vision? As an impersonal verb, the expression reminds us of Heidegger's *es gibt*, which Heidegger deployed to find a way to name or signal something that is neither an entity nor the Being of an entity, a more or less middle-voice operation that avoids supposing some subject that gives; and also of Nietzsche's *es blitz*, which describes the discharging of the forces without succumbing to the trick of grammar which makes us posit some doer separable from the deed. The expression does not mean "a ghost exists" or "there is a ghost," as if it were identifying an entity, but that something ghostly is happening. The most literal way to translate it, which is also closest to its spirit, is "it ghosts" (*ça spectre, ça apparitionne*).

Where is this all happening? Where does "it ghost"? In the head. But "head" here means for Derrida—at this point Derrida's reading is very strong, very deconstructive, and he is writing heavily in Marx's margins—not a subject or consciousness but a "passive movement of an apprehension, of an apprehensive movement ready to welcome," "the possibility of such an experience," the very "indefiniteness" of the *es spukt* (SdM, 272–73 / SoM, 172). So the "head" becomes for Derrida an air of weirdness, an indefinite air, an ambient sphere of apprehensiveness about something strange going on, a realm of apprehensive welcoming, a welcoming that is a little uneasy about what is to come, a little spooked. For welcoming is unnerving. Welcoming is really welcoming when it welcomes the "stranger," when it does so truly, without falling back into a "domestic hospitality" which tries to force the stranger to conform to domestic standards and remain within the closed communal circle of the same. Welcoming must practice an "absolute hospitality," welcoming the stranger without preconditions. That is a movement fraught with anxiety, since it involves the operation of taking into one's home the *unheimlich*, the one who is not part of the home, the stranger, and that is the source of considerable apprehension and anxiety, involving a very uncanny (*unheimlich*) operation.[20]

The messianic figure is a little terrifying and unnerving. For it belongs to the very structure of the messianic event that the Messiah is always coming, so that even if we meet him at the gates of Rome we will want to know when he is coming, for the arrival of the Messiah is *le pas au-delà*, the step *not* beyond, the step that can never be taken. "[D]o not pretend that the last word has been spoken, time completed, the Messiah come at last" (Blanchot, SNB, 108). But the messianic event, the coming of the Other, also fills us with dread. We do not want what we want. We hope for his coming but then again we are also hoping that he never shows up. We prefer to keep talking, to keep saying *"viens!"*, which is preferable to his actual arrival, which would mean that we would then have to stop talking and deal with him. That is why the welcome extended to the other is so spooky, and why we are liable to fall back into assimilating the *tout autre* into the same, into not accepting his arrival.[21]

The *es spukt* is the ghosting, the scene of spectral apparitioning, the appearing without quite appearing of the stranger, the trace or specter of the stranger, the uncertain, indefinite, undecidable outline of someone or something coming, something I-know-not-what. The *es spukt* announces the coming of the *tout autre*. Enter the ghost. "*Specter*" then ought to be understood as part of a long line of Derridean marks or graphemes—like supplement, pharmakon, hymen, margin, cinder—meant to signal the intervention upon or contravention of simple presence / absence schemas which opens up the invention of something *tout autre*. About "*this*" (*ça, cela*)—this coming spectral figure, this messianic figure—we can hardly say a thing. We are reduced to apophatic utterances, for the *tout autre* slams against our thought and language, shatters our horizons of expectations, as a being that leaves us groping for words and puts whatever we mean to say to rout. *This* is not of the order of *savoir, vouloir,* or *vouloir dire; this* returns, in urgency:

> [W]ell, *this* comes back, *this* returns, *this* insists in urgency, and *this* gives
> one to think, but *this*, which is each time irresistible enough, singular
> enough to engender as much anguish as do the future and death. . . .
> (SdM, 273/SoM, 172–73)

But *this* "revenance," this ghost that keeps coming back to haunt us, is not a blind repetition compulsion, not the blind automatism of compulsive repetition described by Freud (or Shakespeare, whose Lady Macbeth keeps trying compulsively to wash out the damned spot). Rather *this* "gives us to think all this (*tout cela*), the wholly other (*tout autre*) from which the repetition compulsion itself arises, viz., that every other is wholly other (*tout autre est autre*)" (SdM, 273/SoM, 173).

The ghost, the *revenant*, is the ever recurrent specter, the messianic prospect of the *tout autre* who haunts our self-presence, our self-sufficiency, who disturbs the order of the same, who comes to us as the voice of the dead to whom we bear a responsibility, and as the voice of the ones still to come, as those others, other-than-the-living present who lay claim to us. That coming, that *à-venir*, that coming messianic figure, is the religious automatism that Marx knew but did not know, that he would not let himself know, the specter with a life and operation all its own. Marx too prays and weeps, citing and reciting the *viens* at the end of the book of Revelation. That is the spectral recurrence that haunts all of Marx's work, the specter of Marx by which his work is animated, the desire, the dream of something to come, praying and weeping over something other, something *tout autre*.

The *tout autre* is the specter of Marx in which Derrida fully believes, and *tout autre est tout autre* is the first un-principle of this Marxist-Derridean an-economics.

Freud said in "Das Unheimliche" that he should have made his point of departure the *"es spukt,"* which is the best example of uncanniness he can imagine, the question being whether it is just a good example or whether it is the thing itself, *la chose même*. Freud really should have begun there, and Marx should have, too. Perhaps they did not, Derrida says, because it is so scary, and it would disturb the serenity of a scientific study, and both Freud and Marx took themselves to be men of science. For after all, the most *unheimlich* thing imaginable is a dead body come back to life, although no respectable man of science would be caught dead entertaining the ideas of spooks and haunted houses (*ein Haus in dem es spukt*) (cf. SdM, 274–75n1/SoM, 195n38).

Marx should have started with the uncanny (*unheimlich*) power of *es spukt*, with the spooky power of *das Un-heimliche*, of the one who does not make his or her home (*Heimat*) here, the stranger, the Other, the *tout autre*. Even as Marx remains a stranger to us: *Marx—das Unheimliche*, the stranger whom we wish to domesticate, to assimilate to our existing borders, within the horizon of the same, so as to stop being frightened half to death by him.

So Marx chased away one ghost too many. It was hardly an objection that these ghosts do not exist "(of course they do not exist, so what?)" (SdM, 277/SoM, 174). We cannot, must not, should not chase away the ghost of what is to come, the specter of the stranger, nor can we let the dead bury the dead. "Only mortals, only the living who are not living gods can bury the dead." And apart from ghosts, "[o]nly mortals can watch over them, and can watch, period" (SdM, 277/SoM, 174–75). The dead cannot bury the dead. That is impossible, but it is an impossible that can nevertheless take place, that is "alas, always possible." Here is another Derridean *impossible*, not one of which we dream but an impossible of which we live in dread: that we will forget the dead, that the dead will have died in vain. The most terrifying death of all is to die forgotten and to disappear without a trace—without a ghost, without a *revenance*, a recurrence which comes back to the living to disturb the self-complacency of their self-presence. Indeed that self-presence and self-enclosure constitutes, for Derrida, the very definition of "absolute evil"—"which is, is it not, absolute life, fully present life, the one that does not know death and does not want to hear about it" (SdM, 278/SoM, 175):

> One must always remember that it is on the terrible possibility of this impossible that justice is desirable: *through* but also *beyond* right and law. (SdM, 278/SoM, 175)

So it is in the interests of avoiding evil and "out of a concern for *justice,*" that Derrida recommends "exorcism," the sort that is bent not on chasing the spirits of the past away but on conjuring them up—so it is more a mediumistic *seance* than an exorcism—to let them come back alive, as *revenants*, and more, beyond that, "as other *arrivants* to whom a hospitable memory or promise must offer welcome" (SdM, 277/SoM, 175). So we must learn to live with the ghost of the *tout autre*, learn to live by learning how to talk with the ghost, like Hamlet in the castle at Elsinore:

> [learn] how to talk with him, with her, how to let them speak or how to give them back speech, even if it is in oneself, in the other, in the other in oneself; they are always *there*, specters, even if they do not exist, even if they are no longer, even if they are not yet. They give us to rethink the "there" as soon as we open our mouths. . . . (SdM, 279/SoM, 176)

The Religion of Saint Jacques

The same spectralization effect that Marx applies to Saint Max, and that Derrida applies to Marx, applies no less to Derrida himself. That is said not as a criticism of Derrida, nor as an attempt to outsmart and out-deconstruct Derrida, but by way of indicating the obvious point of *Specters of Marx*. The difference between a postcritical deconstruction and a pre-deconstructive and reductionist critique is that deconstruction does not undertake rigorously (religiously) to reduce, exclude, and emancipate itself from every religious spirit, does not take religion to be the devil itself, does not think there is a clean break between the sigh of the oppressed masses[22] and messianic longing. Deconstruction does not try, in critical fashion, to police the borders between political economy and religion, and by a rigorous epoche to reduce the fantastic to the real, the spectral to the actual, the religious to the rational. It does no good in deconstruction to say that something does not exist, that it is no more than a phantom or a ghost. On the contrary, deconstruction defines itself as a certain spirit-seeing, as a dream, as a passion for the impossible, as a certain faith in the possibility of this impossible and unbelievable, as an apocalypse without apocalypse, and even as a certain messianic hope. Unlike reductionistic critique, or transformational criticism,[23] deconstruction first identifies the way in which Marx himself unwittingly borrows the irreducible resources of religion and depends upon them and then makes it plain that such borrowing is self-consciously true of deconstruction itself—whose kinship with negative theology was spotted "early on."

Derrida's idea of a democracy to come, of an *à-venir*, the very idea of "dreaming" itself, dreaming of the future, or of the "wholly other," the very idea of the wholly other, sounds and is, by a certain analogy, religious, turning as it does on a quasi-religious, negative messianic hope, constituting the prayers and tears of Jacques Derrida. While it goes too far to say what Marx says of the commodity fetish, that religion supplies "the only possible analogy" for understanding deconstruction, the temptation to say just that is a good measure of the extent to which Derrida opens up deconstruction to religious infiltration and contamination, the extent to which he allows deconstruction to be haunted by religion, by a *certain* religion, by a prophetic religion, a khôral, an-khôral-ite and desertifying religion. As a non-essentialist, he would never say that theology or religion always and essentially means bad news, the *ancien regime*, a reactionary, world-negating, and fear-driven pathology, a disguised way of longing for one's mommy. That is the way religion is portrayed by a certain Enlightenment which exercises critical vigilance lest religion return (*Foi*, 40–41), by religion's dogmatic academic critics, including many pre-deconstructive deconstructionists, who—although they would otherwise number themselves among the non-essentialists—on this account practice a reductionistic, nineteenth-century, pre-deconstructive critique. They are not a little haunted themselves, not a little afraid of ghosts, not a little spooked. They keep washing their hands of the damned spot of religion, while Derrida says he does not trust anything that is not contaminated by negative theology.[24]

§10. *Messianic Passion and the Religion of Saint Jacques*

Deconstruction talks with (*s'entretenir avec*) ghosts, with a spectral messianic figure, a figure of the impossible, of a *tout autre* whose comings we can only invoke but cannot foresee. This spectral figure is "uncanny," which is an excellent Anglo-Saxon word which we do not need to treat only as a poor translation of *unheimlich*, which is also an excellent word. Uncanny means something of which we have no "ken," no *kennen, connaître*, or *savoir*, something unnerving that does not conform to the horizons of present knowledge. Eye has not seen nor has ear heard what is coming. The uncanny coming of the *tout autre* is beyond our ken.

This is what Derrida means by "messianic." This postcritical deconstructive messianic, what he is perfectly willing to call "religion within the limits of reason alone" (see §11), is oriented by the hope of what has no present substance, and is itself the substance, the stuff and the testimony, of things that appear not, of what is utterly heterogeneous with the present or current state of things. The famous Pauline formulae for faith— seeing enigmatically in a mirror image (I Cor. 13:12), through a *glas* darkly, and in Hebrews 11:1, as the *hypostasis*, the real stuff of what is not real yet but only hoped for, as the substance of things that have no substance yet, and as the *elenchos*, the proof positive of what cannot be calculatively proven—strike a deep chord in deconstruction. What better way to describe the *tout autre* than as the spectral image of something that cannot be seen or calculated, that is beyond the horizons of appearance and calculation, beyond proof and perception (*Foi*, 49), and what better way to describe Derrida's *viens!* than as a certain faith, as the substance and the testimony of what does not appear?

Je ne sais pas. Il faut croire.

Deconstruction is a certain faith. Indeed, what is not? When I speak to you that exchange transpires in the "magical," "miraculous" (*Foi*, 83–84) medium of our mutual faith—that I am trying to tell the truth as I see it, believe me, and you are trying to understand me—a faith that of course is never self-identical, that is always already disturbed from within by bad faith. The stock market crashes when investors—widely taken to be a tough-minded lot who are not given to religious fantasies or betting on miracles—get spooked and lose their faith: in the American dollar, in the ability of the Congress to limit deficits, in the Federal Reserve Board, in a thousand other, sometimes intangible and ghostly things. Novices preparing for the holy orders of science train religiously around the faith they put in certain paradigms and scientific practices. What is not faith or does not turn on faith? What is language, money, commerce, science, institutional structure, the rule of law, society itself, if not a certain faith that we trade in a currency that will be accepted?

Deconstruction takes the form of a certain re-ligious re-sponsibility to what is coming, to what does not exist. Deconstruction turns on a certain pledging of itself to the future, on a certain *religio* that religiously observes its covenant with the *revenant* and *arrivant*, to what is coming back from the past, and to what is arriving from the past as the future. Deconstruction is, in that sense, a messianic religion within the limits of reason alone, that is, it is inhabited and structured in a messianic-religious way.

But deconstruction is as critical as it is possible to be—viz., with a postcritical deconstruction—of fundamentalist religions, of the fundamentalist versions of the religions of the Book, of the way they spill the blood of those who dissent from their "faith," put out contracts like common gangsters on the life of novelists, and crush the civil liberties of the other wherever they take root. By the same token deconstruction keeps a safe distance from any "*determinable* faith," even if it is not fundamentalist or even religious in the conventional form, for example, orthodox Marxism. It keeps a safe distance from ever letting its faith be a faith in a determinate thing or person, from ever contracting the *tout autre* within the horizons of the same.

Deconstruction conducts its business in the desert—and Saint Jacques, if there is one, is a desert father, an anchorite, an "an-khôra-ite"—in an atmosphere of apophatic renunciation, in a purely apophatic ankhôral void or *khôra* of the *tout autre*, of a negative messianic, an atheological messianic, which is not and cannot be, which must offer absolute resistance to becoming, Christian or Jewish or Islamic or Marxist. That is not because it represents the overarching, transhistorical, transcendental, universal essence of these concrete historical messianisms but because, beginning where he is, Derrida has bent and altered, repeated with a difference, certain religious and messianic resources which have been handed down to him by the books he has read and the life he has led, bent it all into the service of justice, into a passion for justice.

The question of Derrida and religion, the question of the religion of Saint Jacques, turns on the spectralization of deconstruction, which involves the twin questions, the two ghosts, both of the deconstructive resources of religion (above all, I am arguing, of prophetic religion) and of the religious resources of deconstruction (above all, I am arguing, of its messianic makeup). Cornel West's expression "prophetic postmodernism" is a good spectral image for this convergence. It may be that life/death in such an absolute desert is unlivable and that the messianic hope cannot live apart from the "determinable faiths"—or even that deconstruction, which is marked by the *gage* or *engagement* of a determinable faith, is something like a certain messianism.

For the believer in the conventional sense, the believing Jew or Christian, for example, deconstruction provides a saving apophatics, a certain salutary purgation of the positivity of belief, which reminds us all that we do not know what is coming, what is *tout autre*. Although deconstruction is not far removed from a certain religious faith, although it is constituted through and through by a believing affirmation of the impossible, it reminds us that we do not know what God is, or whether we believe in God or not, or whether what we believe in is God or not, or what we love when we love our God. For deconstruction, it would be enough, rather a lot really, to be impassioned by the impossible, to pray and weep over a spectral figure of a justice to come, of which we must learn how not to speak.

The prayers and tears of Jacques Derrida are trying—to cite a man who knows a thing or two about spectral space and messianic aspiration—to "keep hope alive."

Viens!

§11. *Religion within the Limits of Reason Alone (Almost)*

"One of the questions I will not avoid," to cite the text of Genet which Derrida appends in 1995 to his presentation at a seminar on the isle of Capri, "is that of religion" (*Foi*, 86). The question keeps returning. When first asked to suggest a topic for the 1994 seminar he responded, almost without a moment's hesitation, almost automatically, as if the words were dictated to him by who knows what, this ancient name coming back to him from afar, resonating across "thousands of years of Judaism"—"La Religion" (*Foi*, 52). He cannot avoid it, he does not know how to avoid it, how not to speak of it. It remains one of his most elemental resources, religion, *the* religion that keeps returning on him. *La religion. Ma religion* (*Circon.*, 146 / *Circum.*, 154).

The Capri lecture was entitled "Faith and Knowledge: The Two Sources of Religion within the Limits of Reason Alone," a slightly whimsical stitching together of three famous essays on religion by Hegel, Bergson and Kant. Here Derrida raises the question of the "return of religion" and its link with the world of cyberspace first mentioned in *Specters* (SdM, 265 ff./SoM, 167). He addresses the question of religion itself, *elle-même*, but no less of religion *today*, of the massive and worldwide resurgence of fundamentalism today. But he also used the occasion to address again the commencing and re-commencing of his desert-like, an-khôral, messianic religion without religion, the return of another religion, after a certain Enlightenment. This messianic religion he says, in a startling formulation, "alone permits a rational and universal discourse on the subject of 'religion'" (*Foi*, 28).

How are we to believe that?

Faith and Knowledge

Just when the *Aufklärers* thought the old God was dead and buried, demythologized, psychoanalyzed, and transformationally criticized into the grave by the light of what they called pure reason alone, the old God returned with a fury, in a veritable resurrection, making a surprising counterattack that flattened the forces of rationalization and scattered the troops of secularization. Even the *Seinsdenkers*, no friends of the *Aufklärers*, gathered (*legein*) together in solemn assembly, gathered unto *Seyn selbst*, if it has a self, their heads cowled, reverently chanting (a cappella, of course) "*das Ereignis ereignet*," have long been mourning the flight of god and the gods. Meanwhile, the rest of world, which has electricity, turns on its TV or links up with the worldwide web to behold the most massive overrunning of the globe by—(gasp!)—religion! While Heidegger thinks that the globe-engulfing *Gestell* has driven off *das Heilige*, maybe for good, Derrida points out that, to the contrary, religion has hitched its wagon to the *Gestell* and has returned—with a vengeance—more massively than ever. Of course, to speak of return is already to presuppose a previous absence, as if religion were ever absent from any place other than the godless groves and tenured tracks of academia. It is that return, today, all over the world, of "religion," even and especially fundamentalist religion, for better or worse, especially for worse, that Derrida proposed as a topic for reflection for some white European males—no women, no Muslims invited (*Foi*, 13)—speaking in Western European tongues. Of course, even by agreeing on the very word "religion" they—like the rest of the world— all agreed to speak Latin, before anyone opened his mouth (*Foi*, 39).

Dr. Derrida here gives us his "analysis" of fundamentalist religion, of the resurgence of fundamentalism; he admits to being a little psychoanalytic, to stretching fundamentalism out on his couch (*Foi*, 71–72). He offers a certain hermeneutics of fundamentalism, which deciphers what is "encrypted" within its shell, so that the fundamentalist resurgence, the explosion of these shells (literally), the minefield it makes of certain sites around the world, represents the return of the repressed (*Foi*, 36). The strings of religion today have been drawn tight by an explosive tension: a traditional faith finds itself locked in an embrace with the uprooting, delocalizing, decorporealizing, detraditionalizing forces of teletechnological science. Religion is in the simultaneous condition both of "reactive antagonism"— it hates this new technology and the modern world it brings along with it—and of "reaffirming outbidding"—it also loves it, and tries to outdo everyone else in making use of it (*Foi*, 10). To employ a category of Dr. Vigilius Haufniensis, another acute psychological observer of the "present age," religion today generally, and fundamentalist religion particularly, is in a state of "sympathetic antipathy," of a dizzying repulsion/attraction, which Vigilius called "anxiety." Religion today is very ill at ease and it has developed a symptomatic twitch or two that demands immediate attention.

The anxiety is no surprise. People who have let it get into their heads that the world is 6,000 years old make use of powerful and sophisticated telecommunicational technologies whose scientific presuppositions flatly contradict the mythological cosmologies in which they (literally) believe. Bible-thumping televangelists make use of a satellite technology that reduces to absurdity their geocentric, flat-earth fundamentalism. People who actually believe that the human race goes back to Adam and Eve use advanced digital systems to address a world in which the completion of the human genome project can be foreseen. Closed religious cultures are assaulted daily by images of the modern world that dart across cyberspace into television sets in little villages. That has to cause a reaction, a bit of a pathological tic, a spasmodic jerk, in fundamentalist religion which cannot easily digest what it has managed somehow to swallow, or, to use the trope that Derrida uses, which is having trouble suppressing its defenses against the technoscientific transplant.

Think of the biblical believer as endowed with a certain "immunity" to the modern world. Like Father Damien at Molokai he spends his life working in the leper colony of modernity without ever contracting the disease. The believer *ad literam* watches jet planes fly high overhead and disappear from the horizon, reads about carbon dating, watches men walk on the moon, is treated by modern medicines, and yet *never* contracts the disease of techno-moderno-rationalization, never falls ill with the fever of secularization. That is faith's natural immunity to modernity (it's a miracle!).

But religion today is more complicated than that, more involuted than the simple antagonism between urban modernity and rural faith in which a certain Enlightenment has always believed. For today is the day of the "televangelist" and "Christian" television networks, of right-wing extremist Christian radio talk shows, of a charismatic and photogenic Pope who travels around the world by jet and knows how to charm journalists and the media, of fundamentalists who know how to magnify the effects of their terror worldwide on CNN International. So religion today has received an artificial organ: it has been given a transplant of teletechnology into its mystical body. Hence its immune system, which naturally rejects technoscience, must be suppressed (repressed), so that it can tolerate this foreign substance. Religion must embrace the "terrifying but fatal logic" of "autoimmunity." If the immune system protects the organism by producing antibodies that combat foreign antigens, autoimmunity consists in protecting the body against its own protective powers, in suppressing/repressing the natural immune system that would otherwise reject the transplant, so that the body may tolerate the graft (*Foi*, 58–59, 59n23).

That is dangerous and it produces explosive, pathological, spasmodic side effects, the return of the repressed, of which we today are the horrified witness. The fanaticism, terrorism, and oppression of women in fundamentalism today, the denial of the most elemental civil liberties, all represent a "brutal immunary and indemnifying reactivity" (Foi, 60n29), like a raging fever in a patient having a bad reaction to an immunity-suppressant drug. Religion returns—with a vengeance; it rages in its most violent virulent form. For religion is nurtured on historical tradition, on home and people and nation, on the bodily cycle of birth and marriage and death, on native language and idiom. In short, religion is nourished by its "place" (lieu). So it reacts all the more violently, indeed it "declares war on that which confers on it this new power only by dislodging it from all its proper places, in truth from place itself, from the taking place of its truth" (Foi, 62). It is not only time that is out of joint, he said in Specters, in these religio-ethnic archaisms and the wars that stem from the primal phantasm of native land, but also space and place (SdM, 137/SoM, 82–83). That is why, Derrida thinks, fundamentalist violence assumes such particularly brutal forms, particularly in Islam, which witnesses the world-historical process of the Latinization and Romanization of the globe, a "world-Latinization" (mondialatinisation) in which everybody, philosopher or Christian, speaks Christian Latin (Foi, 20). The "slaughters" and "atrocities"—the mutilations, sexual brutalities, decapitations, for example, in Algeria today, between combatants, both of whom speak in the name of Islam—represent "the vengeance of the corps propre against technoscience, which delocalizes and expropriates" in the midst of militaro-capitalistic "world-Latinization" (Foi, 70).

Ankhôral Religion (Within the Limits of Reason Alone)

But this is not to say that there is no place for religion, that religion is in every sense out of place, today. On the contrary, in the spirit of a new, postmodern modernity, of a new Enlightenment, Derrida means to mime and mimic the Enlightenment's desire for a universal, transnational, neo-international, purely rational religion, by proposing a certain desertification of religion, but without entirely deserting it and without excluding faith. Rather than a local place, the sort of place over which blood is spilled, the place that displaces and makes the stranger out of place, Derrida, as we have seen, has set out for a desert place, a little like a left-bank anchorite (Foi, 11), or "an-khôra-ite," a postmodern desert father. The desert is more an "anarchic" and "anarchival" place (Foi, 26), more an austere, abstract, barren place than a lovely isle (Capri) or the milk and honey of the "promised land" (or a Schwarzwald peak). His desert is a kind of placeless, displacing place—or a place for the displaced—that gets us past the politics of place and the wars over place, not a Heimat but an open place, without borders or immigration laws, a kind of "postgeographical meta-country."[25] The desertifying abstraction upon which he is intent is the stuff of what he does not hesitate to call a "universal" religion (*Foi*, 23), a religion that can be thought within reason alone, not a local or a national religion but a religion for all and everywhere, a place for the displaced. But that requires that we do not imagine that reason stands alone, without faith—like a garden variety *Aufklärer* trying to cut "religion"—"*la*" *religion*, as if there were only one—down to the one-size-fits-all of what a certain Enlightenment called "reason."

Relative to the desert *Gottheit* of negative theology, this desert is the desert in the desert, an extreme of abstraction, where there grows the desert flower of a religion which is "older" than any known religion. This desert religion is older than any religious bond: than *re-ligare*, the suspect etymology of the bond (*ligare*) that ties men to God; or than *re-legere*, the bond which gathers us back together; or than the bond that holds back (*Verhaltenheit*) as a discreet reserve before the mystery. Because this desert gives place to (conditions and opens up) what it withdraws from, its trait is *retrait*, retreat, abstraction, and subtraction (*Foi*, 26–27). Although it is not historical, Derrida says, we press upon it two historical names, which are like the traces of invisible tracks left in the desert: the *messianic* and *khôra*.

Its first name is the messianic, or messianicity without messianism, which means opening to the future, "the coming of the other as the advent of justice, but without the horizon of waiting and prophetic prefiguration," exposure to the absolute surprise, "under the phenomenal form of peace or justice," none of which can be confined within Abrahamic religion, even though it bears an Abrahamic name (*Foi*, 27–28). But such an "invincible desire for justice" is shot through from the start with an experience of faith which permits us to hope in a "universal culture of singularities." That universalization of singularity, of what cannot be treated as a universal—this "kingdom of singularities," let us say—is the stuff of a new Enlightenment, the key to what Derrida is willing to describe as deconstruction's version of "religion within the limits of reason alone." "The universalizable culture of this faith . . . alone permits a rational and universal discourse on the subject of 'religion'" (*Foi*, 28), one which, in the spirit of this neo-*Aukflärung*, means to defuse the murderous wars among the historical religions. Religion as a universal messianicity despoiled of all messianism, as a faith without dogma advancing in the risk of absolute night, is the foundation of the law, the law of the law, the origin of institution and constitution, the performative event which does not belong to the whole that it founds or inaugurates, which Derrida elsewhere called the "mystical force" of law (FL):

> There where this foundation founds by collapsing (*s'effrondrant*), there where it slips away under the earth of what it founds, in the instant where, losing itself in the desert, it loses the trace of itself and the memory

of a secret, "religion" is only able to commence and re-commence: quasi-automatically, mechanically, mechanismically, spontaneously. (*Foi*, 29)

Sponte sua, by its own accord, unaided and automatic, for better or worse, without anthopo-theological assurance or horizon. Without this desert in the desert, there would be no act of faith or promise or future:

> The chance of this desert in the desert . . . is to uproot the tradition which bears it, to atheologize it; without denying faith, this abstraction frees a universal rationality and a political democracy which is indissociable from it. (*Foi*, 29)

As the most barren, desert-like atheologization of the concrete messianisms, with no ties (*ligare*) to the determinable faiths, as their most extreme abstraction, this religion returns, again and again, as postmodern faith and hope, as postmodern reason and universality, the heart of a justice and a democracy to come in a heartless world.

Its second name is *khôra*, the placeless place of absolute spacing, which is more "without being" than any Platonic or Christian Neoplatonic *epekeina tes ousias*, older than any "Greco-Abrahamic" synthesis of Yahweh with the *ousia* of the unmoved mover. *Khôra* is neither Being nor Nothing, God nor Man, Nature nor History, Matter nor Spirit, but a "place of an infinite resistance, of an infinitely impassible remainder: a *tout autre* without face" (*Foi*, 31). More desert-like than of the more familiar deserts—than the Nothing that gives Dasein anxiety, the mystical *Gottheit*, or the death of God—*khôra* is the desert in the desert, inappropriable, immemorial. *Khôra* is the stuff of a new tolerance, not of familiar Christian or Enlightenment tolerance, which are disguised ways of keeping the "same" in place, but of a tolerance that "would respect the distance of the infinite alterity of singularity," would respect justice as the dis-juncture (SdM, 49/SoM, 23) of the differend. Such respect would be *religio* as a respectful reserve before the *tout autre*, the religion of an an-khôra-ite, that would perhaps relieve the violence by which the concrete messianisms are consumed. The return of this religion would spell the end of religion's everrecurring wars, of religion's return with a vengeance, of religion as a recurrent cycle of revenge.

The Two Sources of Religion

Such a desertifying, messianic, an-khôral "religion" is very closely bound up with testifying and testimony. "Religion is *response*" (*Foi*, 39); the return of religion takes the form of religion's return response to the address of the other. When I am addressed by the other, I respond, I swear, I an/swear, I pledge my troth, I give the other my word: I am speaking the truth, believe me, have faith and trust in my good faith, "I promise you the truth." That structure is in place even—and especially—when I am lying through my teeth. For then above all I am counting on, relying upon, the trust and faith that sustains and supports the address to the other. If no one ever believed a word I say, I would never be able to lie at all. Historically, testifying has been paradigmatically conducted "before God." I swear to you before God, in front of God, who is my witness; *testis* is *terstis*, the third one. Testimony functions within a mathematical formula, within deconstruction's "well-formed formula": n + One. Deconstruction is never monism, never One-ism, but n + One-ism, at least two, and then more; it always raises the stakes and outbids monism (*Archive*, 142–43/AF, 57). When n = the respondent, the I who answers to the One, n + One is two, *à deux*, the response always implicated in pairs. But two leads to the third, for I address myself to you before the One, God, for example. For this desert, khôral religion does not necessarily involve God, and while it certainly involves faith, faith is not necessarily faith in the God of the great monotheisms.

To give testimony is to promise to speak the truth, *oui*, to keep on speaking it, to stick with one's word, again and again, to repeat, to reiterate, to confirm that I am speaking the truth, *oui, oui*. No faith without repetition, and no repetition without the risk of technical, wooden, automatic, rote repetition, which ruins the faith and sinks down into a mere repetition mechanism. So testimonial faith runs the risk of "radical evil," which is a topic Kant too took up in his famous essay, which for Derrida is false testimony, bad faith (*Foi*, 63).

Testimony is a good example, maybe the exemplary one, of how what Derrida is calling, in this paper, miming Bergson, the "two sources" of religion run together. Religion, be it that of the concrete messianisms or of abstract messianicity, arises from two sources, two separable traits or chains: (1) faith: the family of fidelity, the fiduciary, credence, credibility, and credit; (2) the sacro-sanct: the hale and whole and holy, the intact (*in-demne*, not being damned or damaged), the safe and sound (*sain et sauf*), the saintly (*saint*), in a sense which includes both *saint* and *sacré*, the holiness of the other and the sacredness of the earth. In virtue of the second structure, religion is often given over to a problematics of respect for the sanctity of life, as in John Paul II's *Evangelium vitae*, with its wholesale condemnation of abortion, birth control, and artificial insemination. This respect can be very violent. It has never been extended to all life, since it is very carnovoracious, nor even to all human life, having once included human sacrifice and never excluded just wars, and it can take a very ugly turn, when abortion doctors are murdered by right-to-life supporters. The great monotheisms have valued life only by valuing something more than life (*Foi*, 67–68).

In Derrida's more desertifying khôral religion, the experience of testimony is an exemplary case of the confluence of these two sources, of faith and the holy. I promise you the truth, beyond any proof or perceptual intuition. Believe me, believe in my good faith. "Believe what I am saying the way one believes in a miracle" (*Foi*, 83). Believe me the way you would believe that Lazarus was raised from the dead or the loaves and the fish were multiplied, if you believe that—leaving no chance for disenchantment. Testimony is a marvel, a miracle, which walks on the water or the air of interpersonal space, in which I promise and you believe. Without this miracle of faith, everything, the most quotidian and ordinary transactions of daily life would come crashing down (*Foi*, 84). That is why Heidegger is so wrongheaded in so rigorously, so scrupulously, so religiously excluding faith from thinking, and above all from the *Zusage*, in which I pledge my word to and put my faith in the *Sprechen* of *Sprache* (*Foi*, 77–82). Not only ordinary life, or Heideggerian *Denken*, but science and philosophy too draw upon this faith, and society, and monetary systems. Where would we be without faith, without this elemental "believe me"?

But it is just insofar as "faith (*croyance*) is the ether of the address and of the relation to the *tout autre*"—the air they breathe, their respiration— that we can, following Levinas and Blanchot, have also "the experience of non-relation or of absolute *interruption*" (*Foi*, 84–85), of distance, alterity, of the secret removal of the other to whom I must pledge my word or whose word I take. The relation to the other is a relation without relation, punctuated by distance and respect. Such "hypersanctification" would pass through desacralization, through a certain "atheism," through a negative theology and beyond, toward what can be called in Hebrew *kidouch*, Levinas's notion of holiness (*sainteté*). In testimony, good faith is required and elicited by the distance, the holiness, which opens up the space of faith, even as the distance, the interruption, the untimeliness is affirmed and sustained by the faith. Disenchantment, the risk of disenchantment, is the very resource of the religious, the first and last resource of the two sources. So the *Aufklärers* should be very careful in speaking of our times as an era of secularization or disenchantment, for that will only precipitate more faith!

This desert, khôral, ankhôral religion stands or falls with radical evil, which Derrida characterizes as "perjury, lying, telecommanded murder, commanded at a distance even when it violates and kills with the naked hand" (*Foi*, 86). Violence always crosses the distance of the other who commands a halt, violates the space of the other, whether it is carried out with smart missiles or hand-made tools. The messianic is destroyed, violated, by radical evil, even as it is instituted, called into being by the other who calls for respect.

§11. Religion within the Limits of Reason Alone (Almost)

Of the khôral, desert place of this religion without religion, of this desertified, atheistic messiancity without messianism, of this ground without ground, Derrida writes in conclusion:

> This place is unique. It is the One without name. It *gives rise to* (*donne lieu*), *perhaps*, but without the least generosity, neither divine nor human. Not even the dispersion of cinders is promised there, nor given death. (*Foi*, 86)

What did you expect to find when you went out to the desert?

IV. The Gift

The gift, one might say, is *how* things "come," how *the* impossible happens.

The gift is an event, *é-venir*, something that really happens, something we deeply desire, just because it escapes the closed circle of checks and balances, the calculus which accounts for everything, in which every equation is balanced. The circle prevents the event, blocks the incoming of the new, tethers the *tout autre* to the horizon of the same. The tighter the circle is drawn, the less there is of gift. For when a gift produces a debt of gratitude—and when does it not?—it puts the beneficiary in the debt of the benefactor, who thus, by giving, takes and so gains credit. Hence, there is no gift and what gifts there are, if there are any, turn to poison (*Gift*).

Of the pure gift we may say what we say of justice and the absolute secret: it is nowhere to be found. The gift is of a kind, of an un-kind, with the secret. The gift pure and simple does not make an appearance, never presents itself in the order of presence, like a Messiah who is never going to show up. The gift, if there is any, does not give itself to be seen, even as the absolute secret is that there is no secret to be learned.

But that is why the gift impassions, like justice and the secret and the absolute future, igniting a passionate desire for the impossible. The secret and the gift are equally un-phenomenalizable, equally desirable, co-equally *the* impossible. That is why they arouse so much passion.

The aporia of the gift goes to the heart of Derrida's "religion without religion," as well as to his "hyper-ethics" (DM, 70/GD, 71) or "ultra-ethics."[1] For there can be no question of simply voiding or avoiding the circle, no question of occupying a site that is simply exterior to the circle, but only of learning, *pace* Heidegger, how to *leave* the circle in the right way. There is no question of wiping away narcissism without a trace, but only of degrees or economies of narcissism, so that "[w]hat is called non-narcissism is in general but the economy of a much more welcoming, hospitable narcissism, one that is open to the experience of the other as other" (PdS, 212–13/*Points*, 199). Even the relation to the other, which affirms and welcomes and loves the *tout autre*, preserves a trace of reappropriation. To welcome the other, to be as hospitable as possible, still involves remaining master of one's house.[2] When I love the good of the other, I am doing what I love—and I will not brook interference. It is never a question of simply stepping outside the circle, but of keeping the circle as loose as possible so as to let the impossible come. Giving means giving the other some slack, with more and more hospitality. Uninterrupted narcissism, on the other hand, draws the circle of the self ever tighter, turning the gift to poison.

In Part IV, I begin with *Given Time* (*Donner le temps*), an earlier work that goes back to the 1970s, in which the aporia of the gift is developed in some detail (§12). Then I turn to *The Gift of Death* (*Donner la mort*, 1992), a more recent work in which Derrida discusses Kierkegaard's *Fear and Trembling* and the fearsome gift that Abraham makes of Isaac on Moriah (§13) followed by the Christian account of the counterfeit coin of pharisaical giving in Matthew (§14). Along the way, there will be an edifying interlude or two, little religious intermissions with a word from the sponsor of us all, or, if you will, a hymn or two and a bit of organ music in between the readings.

§12. *The Time of Giving and Forgiving*

The Time of the Gift

"*Commençons par l'impossible*": Let us begin *by* the impossible, not *with* the impossible, as with some initial object of inquiry or interrogation judged to be impossible, but *by* the impossible, jolted or shocked by it into action. Let us allow ourselves to be engaged, impassioned by the impossible, set in motion by something that shatters the assured horizons of possibility and jars us off dead center.

To that end, we must ask: What is the time of giving, the time that befits the gift? How does it relate to what we called above "messianic time"? Certain times are gift times; on birthdays and Christmas, for example, "presents" are "exchanged," mutually presented, among circles of friends, on the spot, right away. If you exchange presents on birthdays with someone, with people in certain circles, and it is the other's birthday, then you are willing to wait for your birthday to roll around, for the year is a circle or a cycle and your time will come, and so will your present. Whether immediately or with a little deferral, presents move in a circle of time, forming a circulation, a circular economy of exchange, like the *kula* described by Marcel Mauss in which gifts make their way around a circle of islands. Indeed, the subtitle of Mauss's *The Gift*, which gets this whole discussion going in French letters, into which Derrida too is now putting his two cents, is *The Form and Reason for Exchange in Archaic Societies*.[3] Presents always come home, right away or after some time, like Ulysses, circling back economically to the *oikos*, as opposed to father Abraham who left the land of his fathers, never to return again.

But would not the gift, if there is any (*le don, s'il y en a*), be something that breaks this circle of time and interrupts this schedule of departing and arriving presents? Would it not defy the symmetry of reciprocity or return so that it would be in the end an-economic (DT, 18/GT, 7)? "It is perhaps in this sense that the gift is the impossible. Not impossible but *the* impossible. The very figure of the impossible" (DT, 19/GT, 7). But how can we escape this circle? Why would we even want to? Who wants to give up Christmas or birthday presents? (Is Derrida the Grinch?) Does not Heidegger say that the issue is not to escape the circle but to learn how to enter it in the right way? But who are we to believe, in whom are we to put our trust, Abraham or Heidegger? Is it a question of choosing between these two patriarchs?

If time is a circle, if it always has been a circle from time immemorial, from Aristotle to Hegel, Husserl, and Heidegger, then the gift, if there is any, must belong to an eccentric time, an exorbitant, aneconomic moment in which the circle is torn up. It would take place in a moment of madness, like a paradoxical *Augenblick* in which Abraham, for example, visited by the law of the *tout autre*, tore time up. When Abraham raised the dagger and resolved to plunge ahead, to give (death) without return, without knowing where this mad leap would land him in the next moment, then, in that very moment when the angel stayed his dagger from Isaac's breast, Abraham severed the circle of time and left it gaping open:

> There would be a gift only at the instant when the *paradoxical* instant (in the sense in which Kierkegaard says of the paradoxical instant of decision that it is madness) tears time apart. In this sense one would never have the time of a gift. In any case, time, the "present" (*présent*) of the gift, is no longer thinkable as a now, that is, as a present bound up in the temporal synthesis. (DT, 21/GT, 9)

A gift does not belong to the circle of presents (*présents*) or among the presents exchanged within certain circles of friends. You can never get a *gift* (*don*) on your birthday or Christmas. Presents (*cadeaux, présents*) are exchanged within certain circles of friends (and of time), within the horizon of now-time, the time of the present, the rounded circle of the give and take of time. The *cadeau* is a little link, from *catena*, which enchains you. But the gift (*don*), if there is one, eventuates in the excess of the moment, the *Augenblick* and, breaking loose from the closed circle of friends, heads out for the *tout autre*.

Over and beyond the circulation of presents, of the time of the present, the horizon of the presentable and representable, Derrida dreams and desires, prays and weeps over the unrepresentable gift, if there is any. To "think"—in a sense a little like Kant and a little like Heidegger—the gift is, accordingly, to direct oneself at something disproportionate, at the disproportion of the impossible, while leaving the possible—the proportionate, properly graspable objects—to other determinate operations, like perception, science, or intuition. That is a distinction that parallels, up to a point, Heidegger's distinction between thinking and philosophy (grasping), and Kant's distinction between thinking and conceiving (determining).

What then is the gift, the thought of the gift, of "this impossible thing, this impossible itself"? (DT, 22/GT, 10) An avowed anti-essentialist to the end, Derrida maintains that the "essence" of the gift is that it not answer to its own essence, that it must not be what it ought to be (DT, 94n1/GT, 69n23). For a gift, "according to our common language and logic," means that someone "intends-to-give" (*vouloir donner*, as in *vouloir dire*) (DT, 43/GT, 27) something to someone, that A intends to give B to C (DT, 23/GT, 11), an idea which trades in the coin of intentional consciousness and self-identical elements. As soon as there is an identifiable donor and an identifiable donee, as soon as there are intentional, conscious subjects who know what they are doing, and an identifiable object/gift, as soon as there is an identifiable transaction between subjects about an object, then the "gift-event" (*événement, il y a*) which has just taken place is annulled and presents have been exchanged instead.

The conditions that make the gift possible simultaneously make it impossible. For in the act in which A gives B to C, C comes to be indebted to A, if only by gratitude, which means that C has not been given something but has been put in debt. A, on the other hand, has not given anything away, but has been taking under the guise of giving, having acquired credit, whether material or symbolic, even if only silently in A's own mind, just in case A chose to remain an anonymous donor. "For there to be a gift, there must be no reciprocity, return, exchange, countergift, or debt" (DT, 24/GT, 12), no chain of creditors and debtors. Otherwise the gift is undone in the very giving, which can be seen most easily in the extreme case that C would immediately return B to A, on the spot, just give it back. The more tactful thing is to defer the return until a later time and even then to return not the same thing but something different of a comparable price or value.

The impossible gift then is one in which no one acquires credit and no one contracts a debt. That in turn requires that neither the donor nor the donee would be able to perceive or recognize the gift as a gift, that the gift not appear as a gift. The gift must "happen" below the plane of phenomenality, too low for the radar of conscious intentionality (DT, 25–26/GT, 13). The mere consciousness of giving sends the gift hurtling back to the donor, "sends itself back to the gratifying image of goodness or generosity, of the giving-being who, knowing itself to be such, recognized itself in a circular, specular fashion, in a sort of auto-recognition, self-approval, and narcissistic gratitude" (DT, 38/GT, 23).

Nothing is gained by having recourse to the unconscious, since a subject can certainly contract a debt unconsciously, unconsciously feel and be indebted. As a deep stratum within consciousness, a layer thicker and darker than the flow of conscious time, the unconscious is still a structure of the subject. Indeed, in the unconscious the roots of subjective debt and credit are sunk even deeper. Because what is repressed is still kept in memory, if only in a more secret place, "unconscious repression" is by no means the "absolute forgetting" required by a "pure" gift, by no means the absolving, forgetting, forgiving that does not leave a trace behind, or which leaves only a trace, an ash, a cinder, which is the "destruction of memory" (DT, 28–30/GT, 15–17; PdS, 221–23/Points, 208–209), which burns the trace of gift-giving behind it and makes a holocaust of its holocaust (Glas, 270–71/243).

Es Gibt

That is why Derrida's search for an absolutely presubjective stratum of giving leads him to Heidegger, to the es gibt of the 1962 lecture "Time and Being" (TB), the "gift" (Gabe) of time and Being by the It, which gives. There he finds a Vergessenheit that is structurally deeper than any conscious or unconscious forgetting.[4] What is given in the es gibt is no thing, but Being, which is not an entity but a mark of entities, and time, which is nothing temporal but a mark of temporal things. Here, too, what gives is "forgotten" not by slipping the mind of someone's psyche, but by a structural withdrawal from the phenomenal field, withdrawing in and through the giving, and this withdrawal is the very condition of the appearance of beings in their Being. What Heidegger's remarkable, formidably difficult lecture addresses is the givenness of things, the sheer happening of things, in virtue of which things happen as they happen, and that is all, "without why." "Only the 'that'—that the history of Being is in such a way—can be said" (SD, 56/TB, 52). Only the "because" (weil) endures. Things happen because and for the while (dieweil) that they happen and then sink away into the concealment from which they emerge, fleeting, fragile triumphs over all-consuming lethe. Of entities we may say that they "are," and of Being that "there is/it gives" (es gibt) Being. But of the giving or the granting of Being, of the "event" (Ereignis) which gives, "[w]hat remains to be said? Only this: the event events (das Ereignis ereignet)" (SD, 24/TB, 24). The event happens, and it happens because it happens.

But then what about this "It"? The mistake would be, Heidegger warns, following the admonition of Nietzsche about the seductiveness of grammar, to hypostasize or reify the Es (the avoidance of which is not promoted by Heidegger's decision to capitalize "It" and to speak of *"das Es"*). For *das Es* is not some entity, nor the Being of entities, no more than there is a separable subject doing something when we say, in Latin, *pluit* ("it's raining"). By *"das Es"* we mean nothing more than the very event or happening of entities, the epochal process of the granting and withdrawal of presence, the coming to presence and passing out of presence of entities, which is the "sending" (*schicken*) of the epochs and the "reaching over" (*reichen*) of the dimensionalities of time. We can bring the "It" in "It gives" into view only by thinking "It" in terms of the "giving" (SD, 19–20/TB, 19), the extending of time and the sending of the epochs, allowing the "It" to sink back into giving, to collapse into giving, the way the "it" which "rains" sinks into the rain that falls.

So then we are faced with something faceless, an "anonymous" process, a "sheer" eventiveness, hollow and heartless, without depth or "distance," in which there is no doer separable from the deed, no "one"—but "It"—"doing" anything. Instead, things are happening because they are happening and for the while that they are happening; it plays because it plays, without why. But that is not without a danger of its own and Heidegger is not about to leave things happening so starkly:

> There is a growing danger that when we speak of "It," we arbitrarily posit an indeterminate power which is supposed to bring about all giving of Being and time. However, we shall escape indeterminacy and avoid arbitrariness as long as we hold fast to the determinations of giving which we attempted to show. . . . (SD, 17/TB, 16–17)

We escape the danger of a faceless, indeterminate anonymity as long as we think in harmony with the tune of giving, of a certain beneficence, which gives Being and time (rather like a eulogy that says that so and so was "given" to us, without saying by whom). It is at this point that Heidegger strikes up the tune of propriety, of the *"eigen"* in *Er-eignis*, which keeps a kindly eye over what is given. The "It" sends Being into its "own" (*eigen*), and extends time into its own, and, owning Being and time to each other, owns both to "humans," to whom both are given, and so brings humans into their own, in a multiply appropriate act of appropriation. The arbitrary, indeterminate anonymity of *"es gibt"* is expunged by the generosity of a process that gives things their *Wesen*, truth, and ownness.

That is what Derrida flags (DT, 36/GT, 21–22), for the thematics of propriety, the "desire of the proper"—as opposed to desiring, dreaming, of the *tout autre*—is a thematics of identity, which draws the withdrawal of the "It" away from the ominous indeterminacy that Heidegger sought to avoid, but in so doing draws it back into the circle of a proper or identifiable Giver which gives us a proper or identifiable Gift. That is why Derrida says:

It is in this direction that we would have a few reservations to indicate
regarding the most essential Heideggerian motifs, whether it is a matter
there of determining what is originarily proper to Being, time, the gift,
or of acceding to the most "originary" gift. (DT 205/GT, 162)

These Heideggerian motifs serve to reactivate the circle of credit and debt,
and puts "us"—first "us Germans," and then, after the war, "us Westerners" (which is only slightly better, but we should be thankful even for
little things, little gifts)—all back in the debt of father Parmenides and
other Greek fathers and creditors, of the entire line of a distinctly Heideggerian *patrologia graeca* upon whom Abbé Migne never made a profit. For
back there in *Greichenland*, which is the true spiritual *Heimat* and *Vaterland*
of the *Abendland*, Being was spoken in its proper tongue (Greek), nestled
and nurtured in the native land of Being and thinking, given a good and
proper name, a holy and a hale name, *aletheia*, at the sound of which every
Greco-German knee is obliged to bend, at the mention of which Greco-
Germans everywhere should fall on one another's breasts, sighing and
heaving for the first beginning, back in the homeland of Being and
thought. The effect of Heidegger's "history of Being," which traces everything back to the Greek opening, is massively to indebt us all, to put us
all back in the debt of the Great Fathers who spoke Greek, sending us back
on a pilgrimage to the old country of Being, seated at the feet of Greek
temples with the pages of "The Origin of the Work of Art" spread out like
Sacred Scripture before us. Then, in that blessed time, the Proper Event
gives Proper Gifts and so ap-propriates us to what is Proper to us, drawing us back into a Proper Debt to the Proper Father of us all, to Proper
Greeks and their Proper sons and heirs, which is rather a "calculating"
way to deal with what is *grundlos* and *sine ratione*. Against all that Derrida
invokes the motif of the "superabundant" "from Nietzsche to Bataille"
(DT, 205/GT, 162).

Thinking now means thankfully-thinking-back on (Greek) Being,
bound over in memorializing thinking-thanking (*denkendes Danken*, or
dankendes Denken) which thinks on (*an-denken*) and never forgets that to
which thinking is bound in endless debt. On Being, which is a Greek Gift,
on Greece, which is Being's Gift. Watch out for Greeks bearing gifts! *Das
Ereignis ereignet. Die Gift vergiftet.*[5]

All of which would be "wildly funny," as Derrida says, were it not so
"horribly dangerous" (DLE, 109/OS, 68). For such gratitude is exceedingly
ungrateful to and unthoughtful about whatever is not Greek or Greco-German, whatever is Hebrew or Christian, Latin or Romance, which are dis-
dainfully brushed off as "derivatives" or "fallings," not to mention
whatever is African or Third World.[6] So if there is a danger in the indeterminate, ominous, anonymous "it" in the "*es gibt,*" the danger of all this
propriety, all these proper tongues and proper homelands, is greater still.

By taking the turn toward propriety, by identifying the it (*Es*) as propriety's own happening (*Ereignis*), Heidegger turns out to be a part of "the great transcendentalist tradition" (DT, 74/GT, 53), which would station a hermeneutic guard around the disseminative excess of *es gibt*. For otherwise, without the monitoring properties of Propriety, *es gibt* would just give because it gives, in a certain "dissemination without return" (DT, 130/GT, 100). Of itself, *es gibt* is a little wild, a little excessive and overflowing, a bit out of order, out of control, out of joint, an excessive *Un-fug* for which Heidegger is not prepared and which seems dangerous to him, threatening to let everything go up in smoke (or turn to ash), its fumes dissipating into the air, leaving traces here, there, and everywhere (cf. DT, 129–32/GT, 99–101).

To guard against *this* "danger," in which Heidegger finds nothing saving, Heidegger inscribes the gift of Being in something Originary, which puts him in the transcendental tradition of inscribing things in "the originary given of a gift which comes down to and comes back to Nature, Being, God, the Father—or the Mother—as well as in the phallus in general (transcendental signifier sealing a symbolic order that guards the gift against its dissemination, which is perhaps to say, against itself)" (DT, 74–75/GT, 53). *Ereignis* too then operates as a kind of seal that holds dissemination in check, sealing the leaks in *es gibt*, not unlike Levinas's seal, which seals the cracks in ethics. *Ereignis* is likewise made to function in a way analogous to the Good in the *Republic*, which is a Father that engenders children from a place beyond Being, the proper father of legitimate children.

If Heidegger's *es gibt* serves Derrida's purposes as a subjectless process, a wholly non-psychological event, prior even to the unconscious, it does not escape deep *identitarian* tendencies which want to own the giving process, to hold it in check, under the sway of the rule of the proper and the proprietary, of the originary granting of the Origin of all of us, all of "us" (Germans, Europeans, Euro-Americans, Westerners, NATO types). However grateful Derrida may be to Heidegger for the *es gibt*, he is driven to look in a different direction for the "gift," if there is one.

No Thanks to *différance*

That is why Derrida said in *Khôra* that it is risky business to see in *il y a là khôra* "the equivalent of an *es gibt*, of the *es gibt* which remains without a doubt implicated in every negative theology, unless it is the *es gibt* which always summons negative theology in its Christian history" (*Khôra*, 30/ON, 96). The way around this risk is to stick with *il y a*, or *khôra*, or *différance*, since *khôra* is the interval or spacing of *différance*, and *différance* demands no thanks.

Différance is a subjectless process, an anonymous field in which "effects" are produced below the level of conscious subjects, and below the unconscious as well, in which events happen below the level on which conscious subjects intend to do anything. Hence *différance* resists the lure of propriety, the dream of the Proper and the Originary, the prestige of the Father of us all, of Greek fathers and creditors, the lure of the Good. For the Good too is a father, of life and knowledge, beyond *ousia* because it is the progenitor of all *ousia*, whereas *différance*, in an almost perfect anti-Platonism, is something like a *khôra*, a more maternal simulacrum, a non-originary origin (cf. DT, 204–05/GT, 161).

Différance is an anonymous, quasi-transcendental, pre-subjective field in which effects are produced without control. Events happen in *différance* not *from* (*par*) a spirit of generosity, but *with* generosity (DT, 205/GT, 162), that is to say, with a profusion and abundance that is the issue not of a subject's generosity but of a certain disseminative excess. Events happen with a kind of aleatory gratuitousness and anarchic abandon which lets something different come, with a grace or graciousness which unbinds events, which lets them loose, lets them eventuate. Events happen in *différance*, no thanks to *différance*. We should not think, Derrida writes, that *écriture* is a generous fellow, a giving subject, because it is not a subject at all. Indeed, "[w]e will venture to say that this is the very definition of the *subject as such*." The "very idea" of a subject is, as something conscious, that which *never* does anything, never gives anything "without calculating, consciously or unconsciously, its reappropriation, its exchange, or its circular return—and by definition this means reappropriation with surplus-value, a certain capitalization" (DT, 131–32/GT, 101). A subject is a capital fellow, a capitalist and an old boy, bent on making a profit.

One could say of this quasi-transcendental, *pre*-subjective something-I-know-not-what, something like what the medieval masters said of the transcendental *bonum*, that it is *disseminativum sui*, that it disseminates itself, not diffusing itself, however, like the God of Christian Platonism with boundless generosity, but in the middle voice, profusely, without the police of propriety to keep it in check. When the Neoplatonists said that the bonum is *diffusivum sui* they had in mind a more orderly, circular process, of *exitus* and *reditus*, of going out and coming back, a veritable hyperousiological *kula*, a good exchange of credit and debit (a *reditus* is also income, "revenue"), a very perfect circle in which everything is returned to its proper place, without loss. *Dissemination,* on the other hand, is almost the perfect opposite of that kind of giving, profuse and non-returning, although nothing is perfect.

Indeed, when one looks for a classical correlate to this sort of non-generous dissemination, Derrida points us in the direction, as we have insisted, not of the *agathon* which is *epekeina tes ousias*, but of *khôra*. If the *khôra* gives place this "does not come to the same thing as to make a present of a place." *Il y a khôra*, but she/it does not generously "give" anything and this "does not refer to the gesture of a donor subject" (*Khôra*, 37–38/ON, 100). Rather she/it is the spacing within which an unlimited number of events take place, in her/its place.

In dissemination, events come, and there is a powerful "donative eventiveness" (*événementialité donatrice*), but without the benefit or the encumbrances of anybody's good intentions, no thanks to anybody. A gift is an event (DT, 152–53/GT, 119–20), not an intentional act but something that happens, and always as a bit of a surprise, a fortuitousness, a fortunate break, something aleatory, beyond the horizon of anticipation, something irruptive, tearing up time, an instant (*Augenblick*), the effect of nothing foreseen (DT, 156–57/GT, 122–23), an unforeseeable sequence, neither the deep longing of the *Seinsgeschick* heaving and sighing toward its long-concealed eschatological issue (*Austrag*), nor the tidy circle of Neoplatonic *exitus* and *reditus*.

But *différance* could care less. *Différance* gives, no thanks to *différance*. *Différance* gives without being generous, the way *khôra* gives, which is the "interval or the spacing" of *différance*, a strange mother who gives without engendering (*Khôra*, 92/ON, 124–25). So do not start falling all over *différance* with gratitude. *Différance* does not love you or even know you are there. *Différance* gives, but *différance* could care less.

(When you pray, do not say thanks.)

By the Impossible

But what about the subject, since there *are* subjects, indeed subjects are given all over the globe, the very idea of the subject being that the subject never gives without expecting a return? *Différance* opens the space—and keeps it open—within which the self-seeking subject moves about. But how can the subject make a move? That brings us back to the beginning that Derrida deferred (DT, 19/GT, 7), to beginning *par l'impossible*:

> For finally, if the gift is another name of the impossible, we still think it, we name it, we desire it. We intend it. And this *even if* or *because* or *to the extent that* we *never* encounter it, we never know it, we never verify it, we never experience it in its present existence or its phenomenon. (DT, 45/GT, 29)

As something we never come upon, the gift pure and simple—*le don lui-même, le don en soi*, which never presents itself in the order of presence—drives us on, drives us mad, like the secret, which engenders endless interpretations. The gift belongs to a thought beyond knowledge, a desire beyond mere wishes, a naming beyond ordinary nomination. Indeed, there are names and thoughts and desires *only* to the extent that we name and think and desire the gift, *the* impossible. There is passion only to the extent that we are impassioned by the impossible. Anything else, anything less, would be too parochial and presentable, too pedestrian and too possible, to be worthy of "thinking" or "desire" or "passion." Anything less would remain within the horizon of the same, as inventions of the same, as merely new moves within old games. So, "[o]ne can desire, name, think, in the proper sense of these words, if there is one, *only*" to the extent that we seek, we desire, we name the gift, which is the measure without measure, *modum sine modo*, which is *the* impossible, which is not and cannot be present (DT, 45–46/GT, 29).

Deconstruction inhabits the distance between *le présent* and *le don*: between the empirical objects of determinate concepts and wishes, the empirical passions and particular *présents*, which remain within the subject's circle of the same, and the gift, *le don*, which never presents itself. But does that mean, when one desires the gift, that one is grasping at a specter or a ghost? Does one succumb to a "transcendental illusion," in which a concept (which determines something *présent*) loses its empirical traction and is allowed to spin freely on its own in the empty air of ideality (*l'aire de temps de don*)? Would not everything in deconstruction then go up in smoke or turn to ash? The secret, the gift, justice, the democracy to come, *à-venir*— would they not all become a transcendental illusion? Almost, sort of (*sorte de*). There would indeed be a certain "analogy" to a transcendental illusion, and the analogy might help us out, since there is in deconstruction something analogous to Kant's transcendental desire and thought. There would be a certain *quasi*-transcendental illusion, which would not simply reproduce a Kantian illusion (DT, 46/GT, 29–30). For after all, we do not make the mistake of thinking *the* impossible is real, nor do we make the Kantian move of treating it as a foreseeable regulative ideal. The gift of which deconstruction dreams and by which it is impassioned will not be the object of a simple Kantian faith in a non-empirical ideal which exceeds the limits of experience and science, no future-present which establishes an ideal horizon of expectation that we simply seek after.

Accordingly, the gift implies a double risk, of illusion and of hypocrisy: on the one end, the risk of entertaining a transcendental illusion; on the other end, the risk of "entering the destructive circle," of getting ground up in the wheels of giving-in-order-to-get-back, the hypocrisy of taking under the guise of giving.

The way to negotiate this double risk is with the delicacy of a double gesture. Everything comes down to seeing that the gift is a *quasi*-transcendental, slightly messianic engagement (*gage*) which both plays the economic game and outplays it:

> On the contrary, it is a matter—desire beyond desire—of responding faithfully but also as rigorously as possible both to the injunction or the order of the gift ("give" [*donne*]) as well as to the injunction or order of

> meaning (presence, science, knowledge): *Know still what giving wants to say, know how to give*, know what you want and want to say when you give, know what you intend to give, know how the gift annuls itself, commit yourself [*engage-toi*] even if commitment is the destruction of the gift by the gift, give economy its chance. (DT, 46–47/GT, 30)

Derrida enjoins a double injunctive, both to move within the grooves of the existing circles of knowledge and economy and also to outmaneuver them, both to give beyond economy and to give economy its chance. There are always circles of exchange, contractual ties and duties, marriage contracts and financial contracts; the law we will always have with us. The idea is not utterly to demolish them—we are all for the law and knowledge—but to interrupt them, to loosen them long enough to let something new happen, to let the gift be given. *Le désir au-delà du désir*, the desire for the *don* beyond the commerce and transactions of daily life, both is and is not outside every economy and circle of exchange. It is impossible, in the straightforward sense of the simple modal opposite of the possible, to do without subjects of knowledge and action who retain a certain measure of self-interest, who know what they are doing and do what they know. Where would we be, you and I and Jacques, if that were not true? Still, give, *donne* (*la donna bella*), give beautiful gifts, give without reserve. The way Abraham gives. Now, as we shall see, we do not know what is going on in secret, in Abraham's heart. (Nor does he.) How would we ever be able to get back past Genesis to find that out? Even if, *per impossible*, we were able to invite Abraham himself to give a seminar at the College International—perhaps with an eye to giving him tenure and a reduced teaching load, as Johannes Climacus quipped about the god[7]—how would Abraham himself know why he gave his *me voici* to this unknowable voice? God says "*donne*" and that is what he meant to do.

In order to give, we need to know everything that undermines giving and draws it back into the circle of exchange, but still be engaged in and by giving. We need to appreciate what is going on with gifts, but still give. We plunge ahead, knowing full well that knowing and wanting work constantly to undermine and annul the gift, the idea being that, if we know the trap that giving sets, at least we will not walk into it straightaway:

> For finally, the overrunning of the circle by the gift, if there is any, does not lead to a simple exteriority that would be transcendent and without relation. It is this exteriority that sets the circle going, it is this exteriority that puts the economy in motion. It is this exteriority that *engages* in the circle and makes it turn. (DT, 47/GT, 30)

The dream and the desire for the gift, the passion that the gift impassions, are the passion and the desire to exceed the circle *even while not remaining entirely outside the circle*. That is what Derrida means by the *mover* of the circle, by the impossible impulse that engages the circle and sets it in motion, so that it will not be a perfect circle but just a little skewed and will not stay on dead center. That is why he speaks of beginning, getting underway, *by* the impossible, being impassioned by the impossible. We know in the instant in which the gift tears up the circle, in the instant of madness that ruptures the circle of time, at the same time, in that same instant, alas, the gift is inevitably drawn back into the circle. That is because the very idea of the conscious subject is to be a *vouloir* and not a pure *désir* or a pure *passion*; the subject is a wanting to give, to say, to have for oneself, a *Sorge* and a *conatus essendi*, an economic being. *There is no simply stepping outside that.*

But it is no less true that the aneconomic gift keeps the circle turning, so that *the circle depends upon the very thing it excludes, the gift.* The circle needs the gift no less than the gift cannot avoid the circle. For Derrida's point is not to find a spot of simple exteriority to the circle, but to loosen the circle and to create an opening for the *tout autre*. The point is not to escape the circle nor even to enter it in the right way but, to turn Heidegger on his head, to know how to breach it in the right way. That is why Derrida says that there are many narcissisms, various degrees of narcissism, the best of which are hospitable and welcome the other. There is always a movement of narcissism in any gift and, indeed, "without a movement of narcissistic reappropriation, the relation to the other would be absolutely destroyed." Even love, the affirmation of the other, would be impossible without the trace of narcissism (PdS, 212–13/*Points*, 199).[8] When I love the good of the other, that is the good I love. In the most hospitable, open-ended narcissism, the good I seek for my self is the good of the other. If you don't believe that, try getting in the way of someone who is intent on doing good for the other. They will chew you up if you try to stop them from getting what they want—which is to give to the other. That is what they want, and don't try to take it away from them.

"Beginning *by* (*par*) the impossible" means that the circle turns on a gift even as the gift is turned into a circle. When workers decide that they are just going to "work the contract," that means they are angry and they will do only what they are obliged to do. That means that not a lot is going to get done and the circle is not going to move very much at all. A pure contract will stop dead in its tracks. To do the work well requires "more" of us than is spelled out in the contract; the contract requires a little supplement by the gift. Doing the work well requires a gift, but without contractually obliging it. The work must be done with passion and love, beyond duty. The circle turns on a gift. The gift works, not like a regulative ideal, but like a kind of efficient cause that sets a circle in motion, gets it going and keeps it open, makes something happen, a little like a Kantian noumenal freedom.

§12. The Time of Giving and Forgiving

The circle cannot turn without the gift, and the gift has nothing to exceed without the circle. The gift will be inevitably drawn back into the circle, but the circle will not spin without gifts. Pure gifts without circles are empty; pure circles without gifts are blind. It is not a question of one or the other, of the gift pure and simple, if there were one, or of pure economy, if there were one, but of inhabiting the distance between the two with as much grace and ambiance and hospitality as possible.

Literary Gifts

Up to now we have ignored the inscription of *Given Time* within the texts of Marcel Mauss, Claude Lévi-Strauss, and Baudelaire. To Mauss's *The Gift*, the text first published in 1950 that has provided the context for a steady stream of French discourses on the gift ever since,[9] Derrida pays the gratitude of ingratitude. He upbraids Mauss for speaking always of the circle (*kula*) of exchange in archaic societies, that is, for speaking of everything *except* the gift, and, then, forgives him. For Mauss never really meant to say (*vouloir dire*) anything else to begin with, and there is no fault in that (DT, 145–46n1/GT, 113n4). In the end, Mauss wanted to put us all in the debt of this archaic, eternal, natural, bedrock morality, that kinder, gentler Rousseau-istic world of reciprocal giving (DT, 88–89/GT, 65), as opposed to the crassness and artifactuality of modern commercial transactions, even to one of the spirits of a certain Marx (DT, 61–66/GT, 42–45).[10]

So Mauss's title *The Gift* is a counterfeit, which provides Derrida with the transition to Baudelaire's story "Counterfeit Money" (*La fausse monaie*), within whose context Derrida inserts his most important commentary. In this story, the narrator's friend gives a two-franc silver piece to a beggar, eliciting first surprise from the narrator and then, upon hearing the friend's confession that it was a counterfeit, a series of speculations on the narrator's part as to the friend's intentions and the consequences of the deed, culminating finally in a condemnation of the stupidity of a man who could think to win heaven economically. Derrida, who is exploring the link between "money" and "literature," proceeds by way of nibbling at the margins of the text, first at its title and then at its dedication.

Because "Counterfeit Money" is fiction about a fiction, its title is an autonym that proclaims, "I am a counterfeit." Of course it does not say this outright, partly because it does not want to discredit itself from the start, and partly because it has no "I," no *cogito*, with which to tell the truth or to lie (DT, 127–28/GT, 98). The story is a fiction about a counterfeit coin, about a fictive thing, a sign, a simulacrum, but a false sign, or rather a true sign with a false value (DT, 121/GT, 93). It is thus a story about story-telling, about all stories. A "real" author invents a "fictional" narrator who tells a "true" story about "false" money. Literature is (like) a counterfeit, a fiction we "credit" with being true, that we "believe" in the sense of suspending disbelief. The difference is that the reader's trust is not being abused; the reader is not being duped or deceived by literature, whereas a "true" counterfeit's success depends upon deception.

But suppose the friend were being deceptive about his deception and in fact gave the beggar a real coin while passing it off to the narrator, for whatever reason, as a counterfeit, so that he was only making a simulacrum of a confession to the narrator? What, then, Derrida asks? (DT, 125/GT, 96). In a sense, Derrida will devote the rest of the text of *Donner le temps* to this question.

We must be wary of a trap at this point. For a text is not a solid piece of *ousia*, like a piece of personal property, a *datum* lying before our eyes, around which an awake and conscientious Husserlian could, with steady pace, take in its perspectival perceptual variations, slowly accumulating more and more presumptive force for the intuition of this given. A text is but a misty, ephemeral, spectral thing, an event (*événement*) with a kind of merely mystical force that seems to sustain it above an abyss. That is to say, a text is a matter of faith, of credit, and of the credence we give to traces and to the conventions that surround, sustain, and constitute them, that keep their play in play, which thereby links economics, religion, and literature, all of which are kept from dissipating into thin air by some sort of religio-mystical force, like Marx's magical, mystical table (DT, 126/GT, 97). If you believe in economics or literature—and who does not?—you believe in ghosts. If with your right hand you denounce religious superstition, you had better find a way not to let it know that with your left hand you participate in literary and economic practices.

That leads Derrida into the question of the dedication, of the one(s) to whom the text is given. A text is given, not like a datum for a *gebende Anschauung*, but given to be read by a reader. For while Baudelaire dedicated "Counterfeit Coin" to Arsène Housaye, it is also true that "from the moment he let it constitute itself in a system of traces, he destined it, gave it . . . above and beyond any determined addressee, donee, or legatee" (DT, 130/GT, 100), he let it be handed over to a long and endless line of readers over whom he could exercise no control or maintain no authorial authority. He delivered it up to a "dissemination without return" and he cannot have it back. The structure of the trace overflows the phantasm of return which goes to the heart of a "gift." "That is why there is a problematic of the gift only on the basis of a consistent problematic of the trace and the text." The text or trace is just the sort of thing, or non-thing, the sort of ghostly apparatus, in which things are happening, events are given, beneath or beyond the control of intentional consciousness. Texts give, but no thanks to *différance*. Texts give, but not like generous, giving subjects with whose narcissism we all have to cope, who are always calculating a return, if only unconsciously:

> [T]here where there is trace and dissemination, if only there is any, a gift can take place, along with the excessive forgetting or the forgetful excess that, as we insisted earlier, is radically implicated in the gift. (DT, 132/GT, 101–102)

Texts forget their authors much more deeply than subjects forget those whom they should remember, more deeply than the neurotic has forgotten his desire for his mommy.

So the gift depends upon the death of the donor, who leaves us something in her will, over and beyond and even against her will. For no matter how rigorously an author writes her will, we can always break it, her fatal mistake being that she left it in writing (instead of living on forever), and writing can always be read otherwise. Whatever the *vouloir dire* or *vouloir donner* of their authors, texts are a little legacy, a perpetual gift that keeps on giving and (quasi-)living, long after the death of their authors, even if the latter are, biologically speaking, alive and well, in the next room autographing copies of their books. This is not to say that only the dead can give but rather that giving is a matter of life and death, life/death, *survivance*, neither pure death nor immortal life. Literary gifts require a living author who by committing herself to words and texts agrees to death, agrees to deal herself death, *donner la mort*, to give a gift without return and let her text go up in smoke, or turn to ash, that is to say, to disseminate without return, however fit she may feel when she signs her contract and checks the royalty clause.

Beggars and the Duty to Give

The mute subject in Baudelaire's story who never gets to say a thing is the beggar. Beggars are of course the most jewgreek, biblical, Levinasian figures of all, figures of paradigmatic disfigurement, figures of flesh laid low that come to us from on high,[11] the most literal marginalia, scandals to Fukuyama and the new world order, the last stand of Marxists and post-Marxists everywhere, if there are any.

Derrida is talking about chance, about how the narrator and his friend, having turned down a particular street, chance upon the beggar, but not entirely by chance, since nothing ever is "absolutely aleatory." When one turns one's step down a certain street, one well knows just how likely it is that we will chance upon a beggar. We always know where to head if we do not want a visitor to our city to see our beggars. You can almost calculate it, like the narrator's friend, who seemed, paradoxically, to be calculating a *kairos* in which he could pull off his ruse, having also very carefully distributed the coins in different pockets so that he could seem spontaneously to reach into his pocket and give the beggar whatever his hand chanced to find. The nomadic paths of beggars are predistributed within a regulated space: in the shadows of tall city buildings, over steam grates, under bridges, living in the subterranean "pockets" of the city, outsiders tucked inside, along lines of distribution that have been brilliantly traced by Michel Foucault (DT, 171–72n1/GT, 134–35n18).

In another story, "Beat Up the Poor," Baudelaire describes "those unforgettable looks" of beggars, the accusatory eyes of the poor who represent "the absolute demand of the other" (DT, 173–74/GT, 136–37), an absolute demand for the gift. But, can a gift be demanded? As soon as giving alms is bound and obligated, it is calculative or distributive justice and duty discharged (DT, 174–75/GT, 137–38). But it is no longer the gift. "A beggar always looks threatening, incriminating, accusatory, vindictive in the absolute of his very demand" (DT, 176/GT, 139). He is saying to us, "You must give—or else." When those who have more than enough share with those who have not, that is just an equitable redistribution.

The beggar poses an aporia. On the one hand: If I am obliged to give to the poor, then giving is simple distributive justice, not giving but simply sharing with others what is rightfully theirs to begin with, the result being that I have merely fulfilled an obligation, avoided guilt, and so done myself a favor. On the other hand: If I am not obliged, then the gift is merely self-will, giving only when I will to give, when I give because it gives me joy. When I see the beggar on the steam grate, is that a shallow pool that sends back to me an image (*psyche*) of my own generosity and not *l'invention de l'autre*? In short, if it is an obligation, it is not a gift; if it is not an obligation, it is a personal fancy that gives me pleasure. Either way, the gift does not happen. In short again, how can I keep the "I," which is always a principle of calculation and self-interest, out of the picture?

This is an old and delicate problem and we must proceed cautiously to see what Derrida has in mind. To this end I solicit the help of the Book. According to one of the jewgreek stories in the Book, a gift happens when I give not what I have but what I do not have. For example, if I do not have enough to eat for myself, or enough money to get by, but give of my very substance to the other, that is the gift. The widow who gives two copper coins—Are they counterfeit? Just what is this cunning old widow up to, anyway?—not from her superabundance (*ek tou periseuontos*), but from her lack and deprivation (*ek tes hystereseos*) (another hysterical, hysterematic woman), giving what she herself needs to live and of which she herself does not have enough (Mark 12:41–44).

The widow's gift is an absolute surprise, shattering the horizon of expectation, unplannable and unforeseeable, immoderate and immeasurable (even though we can count to two), a tear in the circle of time and in temple giving practices, an *événement* in which something other breaks through, breaks out, and shatters the regular flow of now-time, in which something inconceivable, hardly possible, *the* impossible, happens. So, the story of the widow that we take from the Book is also a thoroughly Derridean story, a paradigmatic example of Derrida's gift. (Or, is Derrida's gift a good example of the story of the widow? How am I supposed to know that?) No one would say it was the widow's duty to redistribute her possessions with the have-nots, or that she was just doing her duty, because she herself, having nothing, already is one of the have-nots. By the same token, no one should say that the widow was unconsciously, or even with conscious craft, just seeking to give herself pleasure, since that would carry us beyond the text into a psychoanalysis of the *hors*-textual widow to which we have no access. We have to stick to the story, in which, according to the oldest and most venerable teaching of Derrida, we are always stuck. We cannot silently slip out the back door of the text and steal away to some transcendental signified and then triumphantly march back in the front door with the Secret Key to the story.

The story underlines the madness of the giving that does not calculate the interests of the subject, and it is that madness that belongs to the essence (or non-essence) of what Derrida calls the gift. The giving happens *not* because the widow is trying to discharge her duty and to give herself a good name and a good conscience; and *not* because it gives her great pleasure to discharge of her overflow, to give herself a good time. She gives without why (*ohne warum*), as Meister Eckhart said, and this is what he meant by love; she gives because she gives, which means, because she has let go of her I, which is the principle of self-love, of calculating a return. (Some people love God, Meister Eckhart said, the way they love their cow: for its milk.) She is no longer in the calculation, even though she can count to two, and everything is given over to the *tout autre*, to whom she has given her all (*son tout*).

The story of the widow also explains what Derrida means by the "duty without debt" described in *Passions*, an uncalculating giving that acts not in order to discharge a duty or satisfy a principle, but in order to give to the other, in which is lodged, as he says, the "ethicity or morality of ethics" (*Pass.*, 75n3 / ON, 133n3), although for clarity's sake he might do better to speak of a "responsibility" without debt or duty. The madness of the gift is outside the economic equilibrium of duty, beyond duty (DT, 198 / GT, 156). A gift happens not as a duty, not as a principle of redistribution that binds me and coerces me to give up what I have, but as an affirmation of the other, a *oui, oui* to the coming of the other. A gift happens when the singularity of the *tout autre* calls upon and solicits me, and I answer with a gift, I give the answer of a gift.

That, I think, reminds us of nothing so much as Augustine's *dilige, et quod vis fac*, which is a little axiom whose market value I have been trying to raise for some time now.[12]

The Time of Forgiving

The question of the gift or giving is inseparable from that of forgiving, that is, of giving "away" or "forth" (as in the German *fort*), giving away what is due to come back to us, whether that be a debt or an obligation, real or symbolic. The gift is a give-away. *Le don* is inseparable from *le par-don*. As the gift must not be a secret calculation of a way to get a return for oneself, so it must not encumber the other with a debt. Whatever debts, whatever guilt, the other incurs must be forgiven.

Derrida addresses this question in the last chapter of *Given Time* by way of the narrator's reflections on the friend's explanation of, or his excuse for, his surprising gesture, when the friend confesses to the narrator, "it was a counterfeit." What does he mean to say (*vouloir dire*)? What does he want (*vouloir*)? Is he boasting? Or trying to be excused from appearing too prodigal? Does he think this confession will permit him to get away with the ruse? How is the narrator to judge his friend? (DT, 189–90/GT, 149–50).

Indeed, is the friend even telling the truth? Might he not be masking a true generosity under the cover of a falsehood? But what sense can there be to such speculation? Is the reader not structurally so situated as to have to take the man's word for it? Are we not obliged to take him on credit? Whether the friend is lying or not is a secret we can never access, *not* because it is so difficult to decipher that no one can hope to succeed, but because the secret is a structural secret, an unreadable, inaccessible secret, in principle:

> [T]he readability of the text is structured by the unreadability of the secret, that is, by the inaccessibility of a certain intentional meaning or of a wanting-to-say in the consciousness of the character and *a fortiori* in that of the author who remains, *in this regard*, in a situation analogous to that of the reader. (DT, 192–93/GT, 152)

Baudelaire does not know, anymore than we do, what is going on in the mind of the friend, which belongs to the secret of literature, whose essence is to have no essence, to the truth of the secret, which is that is has no truth, not even a little something secreted away somewhere. This is the "essential superficiality" of literature, which has "no consistency, no depth," no truth. What is true of literature is also true of money. It does not matter what it is made out of or what it is printed on: it is a pure surface that does not need a vast gold reserve secreted away somewhere to back it up; it is a simulacrum that runs on faith, which is mightier than mountains or Fort Knox.

So we believe the narrator's friend, assume he is telling the truth, that it was in truth a counterfeit coin. The narrator could approve of his friend if he thought the friend were trying to open up an aleatory sequence, to let events happen in the poor fellow's otherwise miserable life (DT,

158/GT, 124). But however much the narrator tries to credit the friend's action, the latter proves himself unworthy:

> And does one have to deserve forgiveness? One may deserve an excuse, but ought not a forgiveness be accorded without regard to worthiness? Ought not a true forgiveness (a forgiveness in authentic money) absolve the fault or the crime even as the fault and the crime remain what they are? (DT, 206/GT, 163)

The crucial *Augen-blick* in the story, Derrida thinks, lies in the moment the narrator looks deep into his friend's eyes, *dans le blanc des yeux*, and sees clearly that the man actually thought he could cut a good deal for himself while seeming to do a good deed, that he could "win paradise economically." That appalling ruse is condemned by the narrator, who occupies the place of moral judgment, and his judgment is without appeal (DT, 207/GT, 163–64). The judgment is based on what the narrator thought he saw in the friend's eyes. But in looking into those eyes he could not see the friend's secret *vouloir dire*. Is not the Other constituted by his secret, by the hiddenness of his motives, both in the story and outside? The narrator does not know what is going on with the friend, any more than does the beggar, neither of whom is given a chance to tell his own story in this story. Every thing is seen through the eyes of the narrator, from the perspective of the narrator's judgment seat. But what the narrator finds unforgivable is not a diabolical ill-will in the friend, which is the seat of radical evil in Kant's *Religion Within the Limits of Reason Alone*, but his stupidity: did he really think he could win heaven for a steal? He should have known better, should have known how stupid he was being; he should have made a better use of the natural gifts, the gift of intelligence with which nature has endowed him. He has dishonored the debt he had contracted with nature. That cannot be forgiven.

The narrator sits in the judgment seat, which is the seat of nature itself, and passes judgment on whatever is ungrateful to nature's beneficence. But that is a very hot seat indeed to occupy, Derrida thinks, because the narrator is trying to bi-locate, to be in two places at once, to occupy at once the place of nature (of *Sein* and *physis*), while speaking from the place of literature (*nomos*). Baudelaire undertakes a "naturalization of literature," crossing the wires of nature and art, as if his story were speaking the truth of nature, as if, when he opens his mouth, it is nature that speaks. By trying to pass off a simulacrum, art, as nature itself, the narrator proves himself a counterfeiter, just like Marcel Mauss, whose *The Gift* is about everything but the gift, and who also thought to bring everything under the sway of a natural communitarian society. What is called nature by Mauss and Baudelaire is, of course, what they take nature to be, the way they see and read and interpret nature, from which squinting perspective they pass judgment on what is against nature, that is, against their judgment.

Peut-être. Who knows? Who knows what is going on inside the head of the friend or the narrator, or even of Mauss or Baudelaire? God knows that it's a secret! It is a secret. God knows. If there is one. Without interiority, thickness, or depth, the secret is "spread on the surface of the page, as obvious as a purloined letter, a postcard, a banknote, a check, a 'letter of credit'—or 'a silver two-franc piece'" (DT, 215–16/GT, 170). Literature will have already begun. We will always be caught by a text, convinced we are wrestling with *die Sache selbst, la chose même*, only to awaken to find the bed-linens of a text in our hands, that it is a pillow to which we were about to deal a deadly blow. We are never escorted to the chair of nature from which to pass decisive judgments:

> There is no nature, only effects of nature: denaturation or naturalization. Nature, the meaning of nature, is reconstituted after the fact on the basis of a simulacrum (for example, literature) that it is thought to cause. (DT, 215/GT, 170)

We lack the wherewithal to judge what goes on in secret and we can always read the action of the other otherwise. For the other is wholly other, every other is wholly other, *tout autre est tout autre*, and we can hardly know what is happening with something wholly other; it's a secret. No one has appointed us to pass judgment on the other, to determine what is going on in secret. No one has shown us the back door out of textuality by means of which we may sneak away to a rendezvous with *la chose même. La chose même toujours se dérobe.* Even if, by some ruse or stealth, we got to read the other's secret diary, we would still be reading texts.

Derrida would thus "exceed" the malignant operations of the secret, slip beyond its rueful exercise of power, which is the work of hypocrites and counterfeiters, a way of securing an advantage over the other, in order to move on to the benignity of the absolute secret:

> One can stop and examine a secret, make it say things, give others to believe that [*donner à croire*] there is something there when there is not. One can lie, cheat, seduce by making use of it. One can play with the secret as with a simulacrum, with a lure or yet another strategy. One can cite it as an impregnable source. One can try in this way to secure oneself a phantasmatic power over others. That happens every day. (*Pass.*, 69/ON, 30)

To which Derrida adds, "But this very simulacrum still bears witness to a possibility that exceeds it" (*Pass.*, 69/ON, 30). Instead of being on the take under the name of giving, instead of giving precisely to earn an even greater reward, say a hundredfold, the secret can also be the way to let the other be, to respect alterity, and not presume to pass judgment on what goes on in the other's heart. Who knows what is going on in the other?

♦ *Edifying Divertissement No. 3.*

God knows, I do not! We are neither God nor Dupin nor a Persian detective. We are not master hermeneuts of the secret interiority of the other which we can penetrate with our institutionalized confessional machines, whether they are deployed by the police, psychoanalysts, fathers confessor, or literary critics.

Judge not.

Not only must we not be on the take when we give, we must also give away whatever we take, whatever we have on the other. We must give away what we think the other owes us, even if we get something on the other seven times a day, or seven times seven. We must; it's a responsibility, a responsibility without duty, a duty without debt, a debt that does not cut off possibilities. If we would give ourselves to the gift, we would also give ourselves to forgiving.

Donne. Pardonne. Oui, oui.

♦ *Edifying Divertissement No. 3.* *Traditions and the World-Play*

Derrida's discourse on the time of the gift is deeply evocative in many directions. Here, while giving ourselves time to prepare for a reading of the fearsome story of Abraham, let me indicate in a passing divertissement two directions the analysis of the gift—so far—gives: (1) traditions; (2) the "world-play."

Our Debt to Tradition: A Bizarre Mixture of Responsibility and Disrespect

"Traditions" give—they hand things over, *trans-dare*—and we owe a "debt" to them. So traditions trace out the circle of a debt. We owe our predecessors who have given us everything. Derrida is not against traditions or having a debt to a tradition. It would never be a question of occupying a site of simple exteriority to the circle of tradition. He is only against debts and traditions that tie our hands, that lay down encircling horizons of possibility so forcefully as to wall us in and cut off *the* impossible. He is against being poisoned by the tradition's gifts. For example, if you happen to be a woman in an all-boys tradition, or gay in a straight clergy, and if you would like to be ordained but the ever-so-straight sacerdotal boys club objects, then you are being poisoned by this gift. Derrida himself certainly wants to acknowledge a debt to Marx, which he would like the new world order also to acknowledge, or a debt to Shakespeare and Mallarmé, Husserl, Plato and Aristotle, and so on. But the debts he affirms are debts that liberate and open up the impossible. The tradition of which he dreams is a polyvalent, elusive, profusive structure among whose several spirits we must learn selectively to choose.

The tradition is a gift that passes through the trace and the dissemination that follows upon the trace, which means it is something that needs to be interpreted. Understood in terms of the trace, a "tradition" is a certain profusion, even a generous one, *with* generosity but not springing *out of* generous motives (DT, 205/GT, 162), one that occurs on a radically pre-subjective (textual) plane, on a level prior to the effects of subjectivity, like an anonymous, autonomous, quasi-transcendental field.[13] A tradition, for him, provides the occasion of an event (*événement*), of something happening and always as a bit of a surprise, a fortuitousness, a fortunate break, something aleatory breaking through the horizon of anticipation, an irruption, tearing up time, occasioning an unforeseeable sequence.[14] A tradition for him is neither the teleological development of the Spirit nor the deep eschatological sighing of the *Seinsgeschick* heaving and groaning toward its long-concealed issue. The gift of tradition is the effect of a "donative eventiveness" (*événementialité donatrice*), which is the interplay between the intentional and the unintended, the play of *différance* and subjects struggling to keep their head above the waves of *écriture* (DT, 156–58/GT, 122–23).

Traditions happen when quasi-systems of traces—not just books, of course, but institutions, laws, works of art, beliefs, practices, whatever you need, whatever is around—are fluid, open-ended, supple, flexible, reconfigurable, and reinterpretable, like a language that is rich in associative possibilities and the possibilities of a pun. It happens when quasi-systems shower effects upon those who stand in them like falling stars or meteors raining down from the heavens, when quasi-systems produce surprising, innovative, amazing, and unexpected results, when they produce something new and unforeseeable, when they repeat with a difference. It happens when these quasi-systems do all this in virtue of their own differentiality—shall I say, do I dare, when *différance* is good to us, no thanks to Derrida? But he resists thinking of the gifts of tradition in terms of generous, kind, beneficent, though slightly self-serving subjects who end up becoming canonized and memorialized creditors, to whose generosity and beneficence we are all indebted, at the sound of whose names we all have to bend a knee or bow a head or erect a statue on Monument Boulevard. The highest gratitude would always involve in-gratitude about such monumental debts, which opens up the possibility of letting a new gift loose.

Tradition's gifts eventuate in the interface, the interaction between subjects and quasi-systems, for there are subjects and they are always dreaming of impossible gifts. Derrida does not imagine or dream of a world without subjects, which would be the nightmare of pure death;

he is not dreaming of a world in which subjects are actually dead, dead in any more than just a structural sense. Quite the opposite, it is in the name of life that he insists upon life/death, since pure life would be stifling, even lethal, like pure light. It is never a question of choosing between a world of pure dissemination or *différance* or *écriture* without subjects (which would make no sense) and a world of pure Husserlian intentional agents who mean what they say and say what they mean (which would make too much sense and keep everything under univocalizing, absolute, angelic control), but of something in between Husserl and James Joyce, to recall that memorable observation (HOdG, 104–06/HOG, 102–04). Derrida keeps an eye out for an instant, a moment of chance, an *Augenblick*, which occurs in the *inter-esse*, in the being-in-between life and death, Joyce and Husserl, which is for him the time of giving and the giving of time, no thanks to *différance*.

One is always working inside a tradition or the institutions founded upon them; it is not possible to work elsewhere, to collect a check without a bursar or a controller. Traditions require agents who act and agents who understand the limits of action and the undesirability of their getting into every act, of making everything into their act, their action, the outcome of what they say and do and plan and want, who understand that they act within and from out of chains of *différance*. It is a question of actors who act in such a way as to open up possibilities for others to act on their own, which is not a bad way to run a democracy to come, of *vorausspringende Fürsorge* (*Being and Time*, §26), even if (especially because!) Heidegger had no faith in democracy, present or coming. Acting within a tradition becomes a matter of releasing aleatory chains, of initiatives which initiate unforeseeable possibilities and unexpected initiatives from others, over which the initiators neither can nor want to maintain control. It is a question of acting by reacting, by inhabiting certain regular concatenations and altering them, by interrupting well-established patterns into which one has first settled, acting just enough to set them off in new directions, of learning first to operate within the most traditional institutional codes and then to push them to their limits, to mime and mimic them into something different. Aleatory action sets off effects beyond its intentional control, effects that exceed their origin and cause, rather the way a long and mighty train can be sent barrelling down another track by a little alteration in a switch.

Having a tradition is a question of inheritors of a tradition who find themselves in a fix, responsible for selecting among an unfathomable complexity and perplexity of voices, a perfectly confusing plethora of polyvalent, polymorphic possibilities, among which both scholars and the faithful have to find their way. To have a tradition—*sans avoir*—is to have resolved neither to go it on one's own nor simply to repeat the tradition, one problem with which is we would not know which among the many traditions and *counter*-traditions competing for a voice in "the" tradition, if there is one, to repeat. To appeal to the authority of a tradition is to fall back upon a confusion and profusion of voices so that one is not sure who is saying what to whom, not to mention who got silenced.

Having a tradition for Derrida is a matter of being an heir, of being "faithful as far as possible, loving, avid to reread and to experience the philosophical joys that are not just the games of the aesthete," a "bizarre mixture of responsibility and disrespect":

> We have gotten more than we think we know from "tradition," but the scene of the gift also obligates us to a kind of filial lack of piety, at once serious and not so serious, as regards the thinking to which we have the greatest debt. (PdS, 139/*Points*, 130)

To have a tradition is to practice, at one and the same time, the greatest fidelity and a filial lack of piety, to feel the paralysis of owing a debt and owing it to ourselves to forget the debt, for only then will the tradition really move ahead. Pure fidelity is death, but so is pure infidelity. The art of the heir is to maintain the greatest possible tension between fidelity and infidelity (PdS, 160–61/*Points*, 150–51), between the circle and the gift, to be paralyzed by this aporia and then to make a move (when it is impossible).

That is for Derrida, *pace* Gadamer and Habermas, both tradition and Enlightenment (because it is not quite either). It is *traditio*, giving, giving-over, *trans-dare*, the very process of giving or transmitting the gifts of the tradition, which departs from the traditional idea of tradition (DT, 26/GT, 13), for the latter involves erecting tall monuments that tax our budgets, monumental erections honoring momentous founders. Tradition ought not to flatten us into submission by its massive dead weight, by the boulders that are rolled down its hill with all the weight of the great blockbusters of the past, the great texts and practices of the fathers, which we are all supposed immediately and unquestioningly to shoulder like good children who know the debt they owe their venerable ancestors. Tradition is not univocal but polyvocal, among whose multiple voices we must learn to make our way, selectively and judiciously. Tradition alters as it repeats, repeats as it alters, producing what it repeats (which is a good Kierkegaardian repetition, with a difference), which is the only way to be grateful to a tradition. For literal gratitude to a tradition paralyzes everybody and makes the tradition look like a monster, which is what Drucilla Cornell says of the law if it is not tempered by a Derridean coefficient.[15]

But it is also Enlightenment, a *new* Enlightenment, not the wide-eyed sclerotic Enlightenment of *Aufklärers* who want to monitor everything, to foresee and plan and program everything, to monitor and regulate

every judgment with critical criteria that shut everything down in advance, that close off every possibility except the one that is inevitably
predicted and pre-dictated and pre-validated by the criteria (DDP,
466/PR, 5). The gift belongs to another Enlightenment, to the Enlightenment of the *Augenblick*, to the Kierkegaardian moment which cuts us a
break, which breaks open a possibility, an *im*possibility, which deals us
not death but a break, delivering the shock of something different, tearing up the circle of time.[16]

The gift gives us all a break (but give no thanks to *écriture*, which is
not trying to be generous). The gift, which is both tradition and Enlightenment, *gives* us all a chance, an aleatory opening, a tear in the circle of
necessity and duty. The injunctive *donne* calls upon us to give others a
break, to open up the impossible for the other, not to close the other
down within the horizon of possibility and normalization, not to re-
make others in the image of the Same (us), to let the invention of the
other happen, to let events happen.

The Play of the World: Zarathustra, Nagarjuna—and Abraham

I also can envisage a certain theology of the world as gift which
would not belong to the creationist tradition of the great monotheisms.
Derrida has quite successfully fended off the suggestion that God is
différance, that all this apophatic discourse about *différance* arises from
the fact that deep down, after all, *différance* is Elohim, the unknowable
Lord of Hosts, *epekeina tes ousias*, the *Gottheit* beyond *Gott*, the *mysterium tremendum*, the God of the Book. Who could believe that? But that
is not the end of the matter. For one could, were one so minded, turn
this equation around and speak of *différance* as all the God one wants,
or needs, or knows, or can imagine. One could think of *différance* as a
kind of fortuitousness and open-endedness inscribed in things, or in
which things are inscribed, to which one attributes a divine trait, a
mark of a certain divinity. Then, without being implicated in saying
that the biblical God is *différance*, one could say the divine—and we
would be better off saying "the divine" (*theios*), not God (*theos*)—would
mean the opening in things, a certain resistance to closure, a divine
"creativity" inscribed in things that keeps the quasi-system open to novelty, innovation, renovation. *Renovabitis faciem terrae*, thou shalt renew
the face of the earth, but without the "thou," and in the middle voice:
the possibility of the face of the earth being renewed.

Such a divine *différance* would be something like Nietzsche's notion
of *Götterung*, a divinizing mark of the quasi-system, a trait of the state
of the forces as a whole, which would from time to time be "blessed"
by particularly fortuitous configurations and constellations, issues and

outcomes. For even old Nietzsche, who became as grumpy as possible whenever theological tones were sounded, whenever church-dark, incense-infested organs began to grind out solemn hymns, had to admit that one idea of God that made sense is the thought of having something on which to hang one's gratitude. When life surges up all around us in a joyous dance of the elements, like the moon glistening on ten thousand waves in a midnight surf, then we look, if not "up" in pre-Copernican wonder, at least "around," for someone or something to thank, upon which we may expend our gratitude without reserve. When the system of forces reaches a peak of perfection, when the forces hum with beauty and harmony, that, says Nietzsche, is a state of *divinization* (*Vergötterung*), for which we should all be grateful. In this Nietzschean theology, or theodosia, it would not be a question of thanking someone with good intentions, someone with a heart, for the doer is not separable from the deed, but of being grateful for how things happen, for the dance the forces dance. One would expel the dense stupidity in things, what Levinas called the *il y a*, with a certain *Gottheit*, *divinitas*, which would be the mark or trait of innovation and experimentation, the gift-giving spirit in things.[17]

The opposite of this state for Nietzsche is that of *Entgötterung*, of dedivinization, when the quasi-system would grow dull and flat, monotonous and monochromatic, and the possibility of something new is cut off, when all invention subsides into the invention of the same. When those lulls set in, when everything levels off, when the divine spark is driven into measured-out mediocrity, which very much offended his delicate, aristocratic nose, then Zarathustra is filled not with gratitude but with nausea and dread. Whatever is has been: that is Zarathustra's "*Eli, Eli, lema sabachthani.*" (Well, almost.)

One might also think of a theodosia a little like Nagarjuna and the play of dependent co-arising. For Nagarjuna there is what there is, *es gibt*, and that is all; it plays because it plays, and that is all, but what there is, is taken to be a gentle play of harmony and benignity, like the play of moonbeams on the ten thousand waves, with everything perfect just as it is, and everything mirroring everything else all quite perfectly.[18]

Zarathustra and Nagarjuna have invented different ways of saying, according to the quiet quasi-rule of *différance*, that momentary openings emerge here and there, wherever possible. *Und nichts außerdem!* The "divinizing" operation here is a hyperbolic gesture which is reaching for a predicate to express one's pleasure at how things are going when they are going well and things are opening up, a hyperbole that language puts at our disposal. Events happen, open up and close off, arise and fall back, come to be and pass away. Gifts, like falling stars, flicker for an instant against this greater night. And then you die.

♦ *Edifying Divertissement No. 3.*

But that is not the biblical gift, or the prophetic drift of the religions of the Book, nor does it quite capture the tone that Derrida has recently adopted, which is distinctively more messianic, more biblical, more prophetic, a little more Jewish than Buddhist, tilted more toward the *tout autre*. That messianic tone puts Derrida's gift more in touch with hospitality toward the stranger. For Derrida's gift has less to do with a cosmic play than with the *Augenblick*, with the chance of justice for the *tout autre*. Derrida's gift—and Derrida is thinking these days in more Jewish and prophetic terms—is concerned with the possibilities that open up for the outsiders, the political, social, national, sexual outsiders, the victims of "racism, nationalism, and xenophobia" (AC, 77/OH, 78). That is a *genos* (or *agenos*) that corresponds very congenially with the biblical category of the least among us, a kingdom of little ones, the little breaks and openings that open up fortuitously in the kingdom. In the moment, the *Augenblick*, something impossible happens, time is opened up, and something new breaks through. In the aleatory opening religious faith feels the movements of God's gracious, gift-giving power. A loving hand, a finger of God, lines the interstices of the event, outlines the conditions of the momentary occurrence. The moment, the chance of an opening, breaches time's continuous flow and harmonious synthesizing, and in that breach, within it and from out of it, one catches a glimpse of God passing by, the back of someone hurrying from the scene.

That gives us a read, and a bead, on the miracle stories, a way to hear them as a "poetics" rather than as eyewitness accounts of well corroborated divine interventions on natural processes, which is the graceless, unliterary, literalist way they are treated by apologetes and fundamentalists. For these stories of the interruption and suspension of the natural course of events, of the ordinary flow of continuous time, which breach the flow of causality and temporality, are so many modes of inventing the other and the time of the other, the time of the gift. Dividing the sea in half in order to let the Israelites go (although this is a Jewish story and one ought not to conclude that God is out to drown Egyptians); suspending the natural order of life and death in order to let Lazarus step out of the tomb, stepping out of a breach in time—if only Jesus had arrived a little sooner our brother would not have died; shattering the proportionality of cause and effect, the steady drip of moments in empirical time, or the economy of supply and demand, by feeding five thousand with five loaves of bread. God always passes by in the breach, in the *Augenblick*, in the chance of an occurrence, in the event of a gift, in the gift of an event, giving a new time. Being and time, nature and economics, good measure and steady presence must be breached, in order to let the hand of God, or her back or finger, be caught sight of, in an *Augenblick*. The miracle stories are stories of chance, of the moment, of the aleatory gift, writ large, in stunning tales and gilded letters.

That is why, for a teacher of the gift-giving virtue, Derrida looks next, not to Zarathustra or to Nagarjuna, but to Abraham.

§13. Abraham's Gift

The Rabbi from the Jutland Heaths

Abraham has always been one of Derrida's favorite examples. Abraham is the real thing. When confronted by the demand of the *tout autre*, Abraham responded without a moment's hesitation, without expecting any payback, exclaiming in his best French, *me voici*. That was a gift, if ever there were one. The *akedah* was ab-solute, un-conditional, absolutely surprising and unconditionally giving. In that gift-giving moment (*Augenblick*), Abraham tore reason and the circle of time to shreds. For the circle moves at a zero or infinite speed (DT, 39/GT, 24), that is, it does not really move because it moves in circles, which is what Constantine Constantius said about the System.[19] By this both Constantine and Derrida mean that the circle does not let anything new come; it does not let anything eccentric exceed or overshoot it, hyperbolically, does not permit anything *tout autre* to veer off in a vector of its own. Abraham is the real thing, not a fake. For all we know, for all Abraham knows. (For it is never quite possible to show that something else was not going on under the guise of a gift, never quite possible to show that under the beautiful name of a gift no private interests are secretly being served.)

The Gift of Death (*Donner la mort*), a text of the early 1990s in which Derrida begins to redress the silence by which his Jewishness has hitherto been guarded, takes up this most Jewish of stories, a paradigmatic Jewish story—at least insofar as it is enframed within *Fear and Trembling* by Johannes de Silentio. Now Johannes de Silentio spent his life trying to become a Christian, not a Jew, even as the very expression "fear and trembling" derives from the letters of St. Paul and has to do with the passionate leap of faith in the God-man, the paradigmatic paradox. So, by following the lead of father Abraham as the giver of an unconditional gift, Derrida is led to brush up against one of the oldest of Christian-Jewish polemics, the Christian critique of the "pharisees," that is, of the Jews, in the Gospel of Matthew.

Derrida is and is not Abrahamic, is and is not one more child of Abraham, the father of us all. On the one hand, as a defender of the claims of singularity, of the incommensurability of the individual with the universal, of the demands placed upon us by the *tout autre*, of the passion of faith in the impossible, Derrida follows the lead of the patriarch. At the same time, all along, and with the other hand, Derrida is trying to head out into the desert, to denude the definiteness of Abrahamic faith, to empty Abrahamic messianism of its biblical determinacy, in the name of a general messianic structure, of a generalized Abrahamism, of a naked ankhôral religion without religion.

By giving us—at last[20]—a reading of Kierkegaard's *Fear and Trembling*, Derrida supplies an exemplary example of how the movement from Abrahamic messianism to the universal messianic can be carried out. For deconstruction represents a certain desert-ification of Abraham, of Kierkegaard's Abraham, of Kierkegaard, of the Kierkegaardian religious—of Religion A, insofar as that makes sense, and better still of Religion B, insofar as that is mad. For the religious is the movement of exceeding and suspending ethics, of transgressing rule-governed universality vis-à-vis the *tout autre*, even as justice exceeds the law. The confusion of voices is exquisite:[21]

> *Problema I. Is There an Incalculable Suspension of the Ethical?*
> The ethical as such is the universal; as the universal it is in turn the law. The single individual is the secret. The question is whether it is possible for the singular individual, who exists in her immediacy, to suspend the calculable claims of the law, *le droit*, in the name of justice, responding to singularity of the claim that descends upon her from on high, to the incalculable justice demanded by the *tout autre*. Thus either there is an aporia, that the single individual as the single individual stands higher than the law, or Abraham is lost.

Is that paradox or aporia spoken in the voice of Johannes de Silentio or of Reb Derrisa? Is there a question of choosing between them? Is it not possible to speak in more than one voice at a time? Which voice is an example of which? Which one ventriloquizes the other? Which is the translation of which?

Jacques de Silentio: a "supplementary clerk" (FT, 7) of singularity, picking up the shards and fragments left behind by philosophy's search for universality.

Reb Derrisa: an ironic-comic rabbi from the Jutland heaths, a scarce commodity in a world where everyone is a Christian!

Of course Abraham is a prime example of Abrahamic messianism—there is no excusing him from that—of a particular, determinable faith in a particular determinate promise, and so Derrida's reading will illustrate how to drop a bit of deconstructive solvent on the story in order to distill by a slow drip the (un)essence, to get to the messianic structure, the messianic-in-general, the general messianic *tout autre*, without biblical baggage. That is the idea, if it is an idea. *Donner la mort* takes us by the hand up to Moriah and shows us how to put the torch to the particular messianisms in order to get to the messianic in general, to learn how to read *Fear and Trembling*, the Kierkegaardian rendering of this famous story, as a story for everyman and everywoman, with or without a determinable faith, even if one rightly passes for an atheist.

That enables us to see how deconstruction is a certain way of putting something that is *also* religious, but over which the religions do not have exclusive rights or hegemonic power, a way of freeing something religious from the religions. That makes deconstruction something of a hall of mirrors in which religion beholds a slightly twisted image of itself—or, *mise en abîme*, that makes religion a slightly distorted image of deconstruction. To put it still another way, more technical and more precise, deconstruction and a certain religion have both been scared by the same (messianic) ghost.

Donner la mort addresses two biblical texts, the famous and fearsome story of the *akedah*, of Abraham and the binding of Isaac, and in the latter part of the essay, Matthew 6, in which Matthew has Jesus telling the disciples to do their praying in secret if they want invisible, and still greater, rewards, and not to be like the pharisees, who do their praying in public. So *Donner la mort* is about hypocrisy, about hypocritical giving, about the "counterfeit coin" of giving in order to take, about taking under the cover of giving, taking in secret, including taking a secret, heavenly reward. *Donner la mort* is about Matthew's pharisees, but then also about Matthew's hypocrisy, about Christian hypocrisy, as opposed to Abraham, who is on the level and deals straight.

Under the name of the pharisee, *Donner la mort* is also another of Derrida's essays on the Jew, for the pharisees are Jews, hypocrites, according to all the lethal stereotypes that Christianity has created for Jews— money changers, legalists, Shylocks. Matthew is particularly sharp with Jews. "His blood be on us and on our children," Matthew (alone) has an angry Jewish crowd say (Matt. 27:25), while a Roman Procurator, innocent as a lamb, protests Jesus' innocence and washes his hands of the perfidiousness of the Jews.[22] That story echoes all the way to Auschwitz. We cannot forget that the distinction between the messianic and the concrete messianisms is always a political distinction for Derrida, one that spells the difference between war and peace, the war that Christianity has waged relentlessly on Judaism, and all the wars among the determinate messianisms. That is perhaps the point of this distinction in the first place. For the history of Western politics, and of the relations between the West and the Middle East is and has been, from time immemorial, a history of wars waged in the name of the several messianisms, the incessant battle to take Mount Moriah. The concrete messianisms have always meant war, while the meaning of the messianic is, or should be, *shalom, pax*.

§13. *Abraham's Gift*

The Secret of European Responsibility

The French expression *"donner la mort,"* literally "giving death," means in English causing or bringing about the death of someone or something, dealing death to someone, including oneself (suicide) (DM, 19/GD, 10). In French, suicide is a matter of giving, not taking. "I don't take my life, *mais je me donne la mort"* (*Circon.*, 263/*Circum.*, 285). Derrida is also exploiting a paradoxical sense captured in the English translation "gift of death," viz., the gift that death gives. "Giving" seems like altogether the wrong word in any language inasmuch as visiting death upon a living thing is usually not a gift but rather an unwelcome destruction; such giving takes everything away. But Derrida, of course, is interested precisely in the economics of giving death. He wants to know whether and when giving death is a good deal, a solid investment that promises a good return, and whether there is a giving, indeed a giving death, that represents a gift without return.

The West itself was born in two famous deaths; the death of Socrates and the death of Jesus (DM, 19/GD, 10), which belong to an economy of sacrificial death that gave the West its life, giving it both its philosophy and its religion. The religion of Europe turns on a gift of infinite love in the birth and death of Jesus and the responsibility that death engenders in every Christian to respond to that gift of death. Even so, the inaugural moment of Western philosophy is Plato's definition of philosophy as the practice or exercise of death (*melete thanatou*, *Phaedo*, 80e), philosophy as the mortification of bodily desire (DM, 19–21/GD, 10–13). In our own times, in Heidegger's classic analysis—which wants a footnote or two to Kierkegaard—of "being-toward-death" in *Being and Time* (§§46–53), which, whatever else it is, remains within the orbit of Christian spirituality (DM, 29/GD, 23), Dasein becomes authentically itself only inasmuch as it makes its death its own, projecting itself upon its own death, stripping Dasein down to its ownmost singularity and responsibility. In every case, Derrida says, life is a kind of "wake," a watchfulness over death (*veiller à mort*, DM, 22/GD, 14), and dealing in death is a good deal.

The point of departure for *Donner la mort*, Jan Patŏcka's *Heretical Essays on the Philosophy of History*, is another example of Christo-Euro-centrism, of the metaphysics of Christian Europe that makes Derrida nervous. Europe will become itself only if it becomes Christian and is no longer pagan, no longer either Greek or Roman. Christianity is the promise of a gift to Europe, the gift of a Europe beyond Athens and Rome (DM, 34–35/GD, 28–29). Patŏcka illustrates the unnerving alliance of Hegel and the Pope, of which Derrida elsewhere complains, which embodies the dangers that inhere in concrete, determinable messianisms. For what room is there, in this Christian messianic eschatology, for Jews and Arabs, for Africans and immigrants, for *Gastarbeiter* and native populations? Are they to be assimilated, melted down in the melting pot, converted into Christo-Europeans? Allowed in but confined to ghettos? Exterminated? To repeat this century's most terrifying phrase, formed in a good European language, what is the "final solution" (*Endlösung*) to this problem?

On Derrida's telling, Patŏcka sees the emergence of Europe as the emergence of a freedom and a responsibility that are the special fruits of Christianity. The Christian religion is differentiated from the orgiastic mystery cults (true "religion" being Christian) in which freedom and individual consciousness are lost in a "fusion" with "sacred" natural forces. True freedom is the effect and the effort of self-differentiation, separation, the decision to be separate (*haeresis*) (DM, 32–33/GD, 26), which in a certain way is, as in Levinas, a biblical resistance to totalization (DM, 11/GD, 1). This separation is partially achieved in what Patŏcka calls the "incorporation" of orgiastic mysteries in the Platonic discovery of the individual *psyche*, the spiritual freedom of the soul, which, having separated itself from dark passion and blinding bodily desire, turns within itself, in the freedom of an inner dialogue and an inner ascent (*anabasis*) to the Good. Still, the Platonic Good itself remains a pagan thing, an idol, a blind, mute object of sight; the *agathon* is not an Eye that sees, a mind that knows.[23] Plato's Good cannot penetrate the soul with its sight, cannot see the secret that lies in the heart of the soul even while remaining itself unseen. That is a moment reserved for Christianity, which Patŏcka describes as enacting a "repression" (*refoulement*) of the Platonic by virtue of achieving a one-to-one relationship to a personal God, which alone constitutes the self in true freedom. To be a person is to be transparent to the gaze of God (DM, 15/GD, 6). The birth of personal freedom and responsibility is thus uniquely a uniquely Christian gift (DM, 31–32/GD, 24–25). The Greeks and Romans are pagans, bereft of the idea of a personal God who sees our secrets, who knows what is in the heart of the individual and constitutes us as persons. Of course, Patŏcka never asks whether Islam or Judaism might not possess a comparable idea of God (DM, 34/GD, 28).

Behind Patŏcka there lies ultimately a Christo-Hegelian and dialectical theory. Patŏcka's orgiastic-Platonic-Christian schematization resembles the Hegelian schema of one is free, some are free, all are free; "incorporation" and "repression" function very much as a kind of *Aufhebung* in which the mute orgiastic mysteries are negated and lifted up in Platonism, which is in turn sublimated into the supreme mystery of God's infinite and mysterious transcendence, of the *mysterium tremendum*. Moreover, Patŏcka depends upon a dialectical notion of death as a productive power for generating freedom and responsibility. In Hegelian terms—and deconstruction wants to twist free from both the Hegelian and the Heideggerian economies of death, of how death gives—the very life of the dialectic turns on the capacity of death to give by way of exposing the life of the individual or the community, of spirit or nature, to its opposing, negating, death-dealing opponent. Hegel recognized the power of negativity, the necessity of the way of the cross, the need for the Golgotha and Good Friday of the Spirit, which is the gift that death gives. For Hegel this all makes perfect sense; indeed it is the very definition of sense, of reason itself. It is the way that reason makes itself real, that reality makes itself rational, and the way the Spirit makes itself free. Death-dealing is a good investment and good economics, the very essence of reason and of the *rationem reddere*. For the loss, the expenditure, the negation are—this is what dialectics means—always recouped and preserved in a higher unity in which whatever dies to itself is reborn and resurrected. The *Aufhebung*, which destroys and preserves by lifting up, brings about the life of God on earth, the Kingdom and the Incarnation, i.e., Christian Europe.

Personal responsibility is achieved only vis-à-vis a personal God, the *mysterium tremendum*, the shrouded secret that makes me tremble. Here we are given the gift of the terrible dissymmetry (DM, 39/GD, 33) between the God who sees all and the self that cannot see God, between the God who gives all by giving himself up to death in a gift of sacrificial love, and the sinful self who must learn to efface self-love. Nothing is so likely to intensify personal responsibility as the thought that God sees our most secret thoughts and desires, even as he himself remains absolutely secret, absolutely inaccessible to my eye. Sinners that we are, we can never be responsible enough, never be adequate to the demands that God puts upon us.

Patočka's story is part of a genealogical argument that, with the advent of advanced technological civilization, individual responsibility is lost and individuals are subsumed into their social roles. For Patočka, in modern civilization, which reproduces the fusion or immersion of the individual in the orgiastic mysteries, the authentic mystery of the person succumbs anew to a blind force of nature (DM, 40–41/GD, 35–37). Patočka's view is like Heidegger's, who also worries about turning the individual into one more bit of *Bestand* in a technological frenzy, and who invokes personal mortality, being-toward my own death, as the condition of the emergence of the irreplaceable singularity of individual freedom. Death gives the gift of selfhood (DM, 45/GD, 41). But Patočka is not Heidegger, since for Patočka there is no responsibility that is not responsibility before the other person, which is more like Levinas. Levinas says that the death that matters is the death of the other and hence, in a mirror-like reversal of Heidegger, that death gives me precisely the opposite, not the heightened intensity of the *conatus essendi* (*Sorge*), but substitutability, disinterest, à Dieu, before the other, before God (DM, 49–51/GD, 46–47).

But Patočka is neither Heidegger nor Levinas but Christian. Responsibility is possible only on the basis of the terrible asymmetry, the disproportion between the infinite goodness of God who gives himself up to death, *usque ad mortem*, who gives the gift of his own death, and the culpability of a finite, mortal being who, alone before God, is never equal to this infinite giving. Responsible from the very depths of his being, the individual must die to himself, repent and sacrifice himself in order to respond to the sacrificial gift of infinite love. Because one's debt is infinite, and one's being is finite, one can never be responsible enough, never be the match of an infinite love and an infinite gift.

Repeating Religion without Religion

But Patõcka offers a hyperbolic and heretical Christianity (DM, 52/GD, 48–49), about which Derrida makes the provocative comment that we have already found occasion to apply to Derrida himself. While Patõcka is personally a Christian, and while he clearly addresses Christian themes, his thought "has no need of the *event of a revelation or the revelation of an event*" (DM, 52/GD, 49). What interests Patõcka at bottom—and this tempers and mitigates the Christo-centrism with which we started—is not any Christian dogma but the genealogy of European responsibility, that is, of responsibility *as* Europe, Europe as the very "idea" of responsibility, somewhat after the manner of Husserl, so that the Euro-centrism remains in place. Patõcka is not trying to sell us on the Christian doctrines of the Incarnation, Original Sin, and the atonement, on any particular articles of Christian faith. His interests lie not in the event of Christian revelation but rather in a philosophical structure or possibility that underlies this event. Derrida comments:[24]

> This is a major point of difference, permitting such a discourse to be developed without reference to religion as institutional dogma, and proposing a genealogy of thinking concerning the possibility and of the essence of the religious that doesn't amount to an article of faith. *Mutatis mutandis*, the same thing can be said for many discourses that seek in our day to be religious—discourses of a philosophical type if not philosophies themselves—without putting forth theses or theologemes that would by their very structure teach something corresponding to the dogmas of a determinate religion. The difference here is subtle and unstable, and it would call for careful and vigilant analyses. (DM, 52–53/GD, 49) (translation modified)

In addition to Patõcka himself, Derrida adds, this is true of the discourses of Levinas and Marion, perhaps also of Ricoeur. Indeed, it is difficult to put a limit on this list: the same thing is also true of Kant, Hegel, certainly Kierkegaard, "and I will dare to say, by way of a provocation, even Heidegger" (cf. DLE, 178–84/OS, 109–13). In varying degrees and senses, all these thinkers belong to that tradition that consists of proposing a nondogmatic doublet of dogma, a philosophical and metaphysical doublet, in any case, a *thinking* that "repeats" the possibility of religion without religion. (We need to return to this immense and redoubtable question elsewhere.) (DM, 53/GD, 49)

The observation is fascinating. Derrida is trying to identify and not by any means to defend Patŏcka's views, because the particular nondogmatic doublet of religion that Patŏcka proposes is precisely the Christian Hegelian philosophy of history that Derrida resists here, in *Specters of Marx*, indeed everywhere. But Derrida is feeling about for a distinction that, whatever his intentions, can in fact be seen to parallel the distinction in *Specters of Marx* between the messianic in general and the particular religious messianisms. The messianic in general clearly amounts to a nondogmatic doublet of dogma in the sense that is being described here, a structural possibility of religion without religion, the structural possibility of the religious unencumbered by the dangerous baggage of particular, determinate religions and their determinate faiths. Now if that is so, and if "at bottom this list has no limit" (DM, 53/GD, 49), then what is to stop us from adding the names of Derrida and deconstruction to those of Patŏcka, Levinas, Marion, Ricoeur, Kant, Hegel, Kierkegaard, and Heidegger? I will dare even to say, by way of a provocation, Derrida too is trying to offer us a work of thought that thinks the structural possibility of the religious, of a certain radical messianic structure, without the dangerous liaisons of the particular religions, without the dogma, without the determinate messianic faiths that divide humanity into warring parties. For Derrida's distinction between the concrete messianisms and the messianic in general is, we cannot forget, a distinction between war and peace.

I will dare to say, with the earnest hope of provocation, that the question of deconstruction and religion comes down to the question of deconstruction *as* religion, as the repetition of religion without religion, as "the religious" (in the spirit of a certain Kierkegaard) without religion, as the messianic without messianism, as the nondogmatic doublet of messianism. Everything that Derrida has to say, especially in the most recent work, about the invention of the wholly other, about the passion for the impossible, about a hospitality toward something to come that explodes our horizons of expectation, about the promise, the yes, yes, the gift, about *croire sans voir, sans avoir, sans savoir*, about the justice to come—all that is charged with a religious and messianic force, like a certain Judaism without rabbis and religion, transparently and audibly so, I would say. On this accounting, deconstruction is a certain religion without religion, a nondogmatic doublet of Judaism, affirming a doublet of a Messiah whom we will never live to see. We long, we live to see the Messiah, but we will never live to see him. (*Deo gratias.*)

Have we thus come back to where we started, with the objection that was made "early on" that deconstruction is negative theology? No, no, it is not negative theology. I deny it. I un-deny and de-negate it. It is not classical apophatic theology, to be sure, for all the good reasons that Derrida has given, fairly patiently I would say. But deconstruction is a certain negative propheticism, a negative or apophatic messianic, whose most vivid and perfect illustration or exemplification (or repetition) is to be found in the biblical, prophetic notion of justice, so long as we add the little proviso which throws everything into undecidability. I do not know, and neither does Jacques, what is an example of what, what is a repetition of what, what is a translation of what. I do not know, and neither does Jacques, whether deconstruction is an example of the religious, or whether the religious is an example of deconstruction. Is not Jacques's apophatic-messianic another messianism after all, a more desert-like and barren, more philosophical, highly hopeful atheistic messianism, perhaps a political or democratic messianism? Or are all the messianisms (count them) repetitions of the messianic? How would I, how would Jacques, know that? Where would one be standing when one made that declaration? What theological or transcendental power would authorize that dogma? The very idea of the quasi-transcendental, if there is one, means that, regarding the idea of deconstruction and prophetic religion, we do not know which is an example or a repetition of which. That is what un-decidability (un)means.

The Price of Faith

In the second half of "Donner la mort" Derrida turns from Patõcka to Kierkegaard, still following the guiding threads of the secret, responsibility, and the gift. Derrida notices that Fear and Trembling is, from the first sentence of the Preface, a study in economics. "Not only in the business world but also in the world of ideas, our age stages ein wirklicher Aus-verkauf [a real sale]," writes Johannes de Silentio (FT, 5). More precisely, it is a study in "mad economics,"[25] in the madness of the "instant" (Au-genblick), which tears up the circular unity of dialectical time, and a madness that watches over thinking (PdS, 374/Points, 363). Kierkegaard thought that the doleful influence of Hegelianism on Christianity had been to depress the price of faith, to drop it so low that anyone could afford it—millions of Europeans all over Christendom (Christo-Europe) could come up with the price—with almost no effort. Hegelianism cheapened Christianity to the point that it was to be had at a "bargain price," a real steal. The point of Fear and Trembling, accordingly, indeed of much of what Kierkegaard wrote, was a "hyper-economic" one, viz., to raise the price of faith, like the merchants in Holland who threw their spices into the harbor to drive up the price of their goods (FT, 121), but to raise it absurdly high—I would say sky-high—so as to make everyone appreciate that true faith is very pricey. Faith had become a "counterfeit coin" (*la fausse monnaie*). Hegelianism is the stupidity of thinking that one can "win paradise economically," because it attempts to purchase faith on the cheap, economizing on fear and trembling (FL, 46/DPJ, 20), minimizing the difficulty and the distress. According to de Silentio's punishing version of Hegel, Hegelianism seems to think the Word became flesh in order to read about himself in German philosophy, while at the same time thoughtfully providing the theologians with the opportunity to earn a secure living by speculating on the Crucifixion. The whole thing was a bargain, a real steal.

It is in order to raise the price of faith, to persuade European Christendom that it was trading in false coin, that it had not begun to come to grips with the death-dealing character of faith, with the *mysterium tremendum*, that de Silentio retells the story of Abraham to his contemporaries. In the terrifying story of the *akedah*, the binding of Isaac, Abraham is told to deal death to his son, Isaac, and so seemingly to his hope of becoming the father of many generations, which is the deal he had cut with the Lord. This is a story of madness (PdS, 374/*Points*, 363), of a mad economics, an aneconomics, a radical and literal case of death-dealing in an economy of sacrifice. Abraham was willing to make a gift of the life of Isaac. Were a man later this week to take his son and head up to the top of the World Trade Center—Derrida's example is Montmartre (DM, 82/GD, 85)—with the intention of offering the boy in sacrifice, we would send a SWAT team in to seize the madman and arrest him for attempted murder,[26] for defying the most elemental command of ethics and the law, which is not to deal in death, above all—God forbid—with one's own son. Johannes de Silentio wants to visit this story upon us in all its contemporaneity, to imagine it repeated right here in midst of us, today—and not allow the historical-critical method to soften the story's blow. For that is the paradox by which he himself is arrested and silenced, the fearfully high price of faith before which he trembles. Abraham deals in death; he courts death without flinching. When death calls—or God, God or death—Abraham does not blink. God or death: either way, *tout autre*. The *tout autre* under one name or another: God or death.

That is what interests Derrida—in Abraham and in Kierkegaard's very Pauline reading of the story of Abraham.

Abraham's Secret

The greatness of the faith of the father of faith lies in his ability to keep a secret,[27] one of the secrets mentioned expressly in *Passions*, belonging to "the order of absolute subjectivity, in the rather unorthodox sense, with respect to a history of metaphysics, that Kierkegaard gave to *existence* and to all that resists the concept or frustrates the system, especially the Hegelian dialectic" (*Pass.*, 57–58/ON, 24–25). Abraham's—Kierkegaard's? de Silentio's?—secret is deep, definite, and determinable, a definite truth he cannot reveal or even understand, a private communication between him and God that he cannot make public. So the treatment of Kierkegaardian-Abrahamic subjectivity is isomorphic with the study of Patočka, who also identified the freedom and responsibility of the subject with the secret reserve of interiority that is stored up in the inner one-to-one relationship of the self with the *mysterium tremendum* (DM, 15–16/GD, 6). (Of course, Derrida's secret is a little more absolute, relatively speaking, than Abraham's, Kierkegaard's, de Silentio's, or Patočka's, and this because it is *not* a determinate and interior reserve, which could in principle be revealed if circumstances warranted it, but the very secret of the secret, the secret that there is no such secret truth.)

The *mysterium tremendum* by which Abraham is rocked is a secret communication that God has whispered in his ear and that sends a shudder through his soul. *Tremendum* means something fearful that is to come, some secret I-know-not-what that I cannot foresee. I know that there is something that I do not know and that causes me to tremble; I am afraid even though, precisely though, the blow has not yet struck, even though, precisely though I cannot say why I tremble (DM, 56–57/GD, 53–55). Paul, who is in prison, has received a gift from the church in Philippi, the first church Paul established on European soil, and one for which he always retained a heartfelt and special love, and he is sending the Philippians a thank-you note, a letter from a Roman jail. "Therefore, my beloved (*agapetoi*), just as you have always obeyed me, not only in my presence (*parousia*), but much more now in my absence (*apousia*), work out your own salvation with fear and trembling (*meta phobou kai tromou*" (Phil. 2:12). Why with fear and trembling? "For it is God who is at work, enabling you both to will and to work for his good pleasure (*eudokias*)" (Phil. 2:13). Minimally, Paul may be understood to say that we can do nothing without God's help. Taken more rigorously—and this is Derrida's reading—Paul means that God does not have to give reasons (*rationem reddere*); God can give or take away salvation without giving an explanation. God holds us in the palm of his hand and we do not know what God wants, what is God's pleasure, which is a secret (DM, 59–60/GD, 56–59) that is shrouded in silence. We do not see (*voir*) or know (*savoir*) what God wants. "Otherwise he would not be God"—"absent, hidden and silent, separate, secret," i.e., *tout autre* (DM, 59/GD, 57). God does not share his reasons with us; we cannot have a conversation with God; we cannot establish the homogeneity with God that is implied by exchanging views, by having a conversation in a common language. The word of God is the word of the *tout autre*, and the word of the Wholly Other is wholly other than a word, otherwise than what we mean by a word. God's word reduces us to silence, is delivered and received in silence, cannot be understood, and cannot be repeated to anyone else. Were our transactions with God to transpire in language, they would become at once public knowledge and communicable sense, at least in principle. So Kierkegaard has chosen the text of a Jewish convert, Paul, to tell us about "a still Jewish experience of the hidden God, secret, separated, absent or mysterious," who demands of Abraham the "most cruel, impossible, and untenable gesture"—and all this in silence, the whole story being told by one Johannes de Silentio, who is but a poetic personage, without a tongue (DM, 59/GD, 58).

When God speaks his word, when God calls, Abraham obeys—in his best French: *me voici*—but he cannot understand. He is rendered incommunicado, cut off from the consolations of consensus and community, from the common sense of the *sensus communis*, stripped down to the madness of solitude, to fear and trembling before an unutterable, unrepeatable secret. The word of the *tout autre* cuts him off from all *Sittlichkeit*, from the reassuring community of practices that shapes communal life, from family, society, nation. The deal Abraham cuts with God cuts Abraham off from his *oikos*, from his son and from Sarah. Sacrifice is strictly men's business, between God and him (not to mention Isaac). Sarah is being cut off, sacrificed[28] no less than Isaac (not to mention the ram);[29] the whole family, the most immediate sphere of *oikos* and *Sittlichkeit*, will be severed and sacrificed by this secret. So there are two levels of secrecy, of secret, subjective interiority, at work in the story: the secret that God keeps from Abraham, who does not know what God's pleasure is or why God is so commanding him; and the secret that Abraham keeps from Isaac and Sarah, from the servants who accompany him to Moriah, from family and friends, from anyone who would ask what he is doing, who do not know what the patriarch is up to, because he does not know himself why God has called upon him thus (DM, 60/GD, 58–59). Abraham is singularized, alone before God and alone before death (DM, 61/GD, 59–60). He has left the sphere of public language, of publicly shared reasons, and entered upon the solitude and silence of the secret. That is why, when Isaac asks where the lamb is, Abraham speaks in the form of irony, without saying anything, answers without truly responding. He has left or suspended ethics and consensus, the concrescence of concrete ethical and historical subsistence, and ethics abhors this secret.

Derrida is thus sensitive to the fact that in *Fear and Trembling* the "ethical" refers not only to Kantian *Moralität*, the universalizability of the law, but also to Hegelian *Sittlichkeit* (FT, 55), the concrete ethical community, so that the religious transcends both Kantian and Hegelian ethics, both the pure law and the *polis*, both deontology and eudaimonic teleology.[30]

Abraham's unresponsiveness to Isaac and Sarah reflects his absolute responsibility, ab-solved from the universal, both the abstract (Kantian) and the concrete (Hegelian) universal. That is why ethics is a "temptation" for Abraham, why ethics would actually make Abraham irresponsible. Were he to give a reason (*rationem reddere*) for what he is doing, were he to respond to Sarah, to the human community, which is the ethically responsible thing to do, he would betray his absolute responsibility to God. In the name of his responsibility to God, he cannot be responsible to his family and friends. He is in a double bind, and he cannot win, although in virtue of the an-economic madness of his faith he believes that he cannot lose (DM, 62–63/GD, 61–62).

The question posed by this story, according to Johannes de Silentio, is whether one admits a sphere of the interior secret, which is justified by the fact that the individual is higher than the universal; for otherwise Abraham is lost (FT, 82, 120). Hegelianism is consistent in denying the secret and demanding public disclosure and manifestation while also denying the incommensurability of the individual. But the hypocrisy of Hegelianism is to tip its hat in public whenever it is mentioned that Abraham is the father of faith. Hegelianism is a counterfeit coin; it wants to win heaven economically and to defraud its neighbors into believing that it leads a Christian life. The sphere of absolute responsibility is beyond duty, because in doing one's duty, what ought in principle to be done, one is related to the universal principle, not to God. So Abraham is beyond ethics, beyond duty qua duty, transcending both Kantianism and Hegelianism, in favor of the religious, which is the absolute relationship to the absolute, the singular relationship to singularity.

Kierkegaard wants to drive the cost of faith impossibly high. If you want to build a tower, Jesus said, will you not first estimate the cost (*dapanen*)? (Luke 14, 28) If you want to be a disciple, then you must be willing to meet the cost—which is absurdly high. "Whoever comes to me and does not hate (*misei*) father and mother, wife and children, brothers and sisters, yes and even life itself, cannot be my disciple" (Luke 14, 26). Abraham is the father of faith because he is willing to pay the cost, which means to show a "hatred" for ethics and for his family. Kierkegaard does not want us to "economize" on the word hatred, to let the historical-critical method translate it down to something soft and easy to take, completely consistent with a hardy meal with family and friends after Sunday morning services, to bleach it out into a white theology, to trade in false coin. Of course, there is no great merit in dealing death to those whom one hates; that is widely taken to be a good deal. The greatness of father Abraham is to hate what he loves, to deal death to his beloved son, by undertaking what ethics calls hatred and murder. To "sacrifice" is to deal death to what one *loves*; it is the sacrifice of love to love (DM, 65/GD, 64).[31]

In making this sacrifice to God, Abraham makes a gift of the death of Isaac in an instant of madness. He does not make a present (*présent*) in the present. The present belongs to the time of economics and to the economics of philosophical time, which maintains a certain equilibrium, a balance of payments: to the rational give and take of investment and return, protention and retention (Husserl), negation and preservation (Hegel), forgetting and recalling (Plato), oblivion and memorial thinking (Heidegger). The gift (*don*), on the other hand, is an expenditure without return, occurring in the madness of the "instant." The instant is not a graspable unit in a unitary flow; it is nothing we can seize or understand or stabilize. The instant tears up the circular unity of time and breaches the continuity of linear time. In the instant, time is torn open, everything is spent, an infinite, an absurdly high cost is paid, and one gives everything (a Jewish potlatch). In giving (*donner*) death to Isaac, his beloved son, and in giving this death to God, Abraham breaks the circle of the present and representation in a moment of explosive passion, paradox, and madness. Abraham must love Isaac, he must love Sarah and the whole ethical order, and at the very instant he loves them he must sacrifice them (DM, 66/GD, 66).

A Paradigmatic Paradox

The story of the sacrifice of Isaac, Derrida comments, is not only a story for believers in a biblical faith. Here is where deconstruction starts its trip into the desert, where the camels of deconstruction are loaded up. Here Derrida begins the movement beyond the determinable faith of father Abraham, beyond the definiteness of the Abrahamic promise, to a general messianic, which is an ankhôral desertification of father Abraham (without deserting him). Here we begin a rereading of *Fear and Trembling* that attempts to produce the nondogmatic doublet of dogma, the religious without religion. Now the story of Abraham—and I think, we must insist, the distinctively Pauline version of this story presented in *Fear and Trembling*, to which Derrida faithfully adheres without quite questioning it—is generalized into a narrative version of

> the paradox which inhabits the concept of duty or of absolute responsibility. This concept puts us into relation (without relation, and in the double secret) with the absolute other, with the absolute singularity of the other, of which God is here the name. (DM, 66/GD, 66) (translation modified)

The name of God, of the biblical God of Abraham and Isaac, need not mean Yahweh for us; it is enough for "God" to be the name of the absolutely other, a place-holder for the *tout autre*.

Derrida here approaches and draws upon the most deeply religious experience of the biblical faiths, the experience of God in the *autrui*. That deeply biblical idea is at work in Levinas, where the face of the other is the trace God leaves behind as he withdraws from the world, and in the New Testament: Lord, when did we see you hungry and feed you, or naked and give you clothes? That may be the fundamental religious experience of prophetic religion, of all three religions of the Book, as opposed to other possible religious experiences, which may take the form of *re-ligio* that relates us to the world-play. Derrida is proposing a desertification of the biblical experience of God in the other person. He proposes, almost like a logical hypothesis or a thought experiment, the notion that the name of God, as the name of the *tout autre*, be taken to hold the place of *tout autre*, every other. That every other is wholly other, that every other bears the trace of God, would then be the work done by the name of God, the value of religious discourse and religious stories, and why there is something to be said for saving the name of God.

So whether one believes this story or not, whether or not it has been years since one has seen the inside of a church, synagogue, or mosque, whether one gives the story any credence in the sense of a determinable biblical faith, there is a morality in this story, which amounts to a kind of religion within the limits of reason alone (*Foi*; *supra*, §11). The absoluteness of duty requires us to renounce "every human law," everything manifest and universal, that one conduct oneself ir-responsibly vis-à-vis the law in the sense of the ethical universal:

> In a word, ethics must be sacrificed in the name of duty. It is a duty not
> to respect, out of duty, ethical duty. One must behave not only in an
> ethical or responsible manner, but in a nonethical, nonresponsible man-
> ner, and one must do that *in the name of* duty, of an infinite duty, *in the*
> *name of* absolute duty. And this name which must always be singular is
> here none other than the name of God as completely other, the nameless
> name of God, the unpronounceable name of God as other to which I am
> bound by an absolute, unconditional obligation, by an incomparable,
> nonnegotiable duty. (DM, 67/GD, 67)

Sauf le nom: deconstruction works continually to save the name of God, which is the name, or one of the names, of the *tout autre*. Whether you believe in God or not, if one could know that, whether you give credence to biblical stories or not, the name of God as the name of the *tout autre* is a fundamental—a messianic—name and a general structure of experience:

> Duty or responsibility binds me to the other, to the other as other, and
> binds me in my absolute singularity to the other as other. God is the name
> of the absolutely other as other and as unique (the God of Abraham: one
> and unique). As soon as I enter into relation with the absolute other, my
> singularity enters into relation with him under the mode of obligation
> and duty. (DM, 68/GD, 68) (translation modified)

The alterity of *every* other, of friends or family or strangers, is as transcendent to me as is Yahweh (DM, 76–77/GD, 78), as infinite and transcendent, every bit as much a *mysterium tremendum*. The story of Abraham, this story of the absolute incommensurability of the individual with the general, Derrida thinks, makes a general point, one of use in any religion or outside religion. What is that, I ask, if not "a nondogmatic doublet of dogma, a philosophical and metaphysical doublet, in any case a *thinking* that 'repeats' the possibility of religion without religion" (DM, 53 / GD, 49)? The structural possibility of what Kierkegaard calls the "religious" is not confined to the religions of the Book but constitutes a certain universal religion (*Foi*, 28). That is because, under the name of religion, Kierkegaard is describing responsibility, the "logic" of absolute responsibility, which is of course the a-logic of a double bind and of an expenditure without reserve. Whether one has faith or not, "there is a morality . . . in this story," a morality which is "morality itself," one might say the very "morality of morality," the bind that descends upon every morality, the delimitation or deconstruction of moral responsibility (cf. PdS, 375 / *Points*, 364). Absolute responsibility, responsibility to the *tout autre*, to the absolutely singular and absolutely other, requires that "at the same time one denounce, take exception to, and transcend every duty, every responsibility and every human law" just the way Abraham departed from the law of the *oikos* (DM, 67 / GD, 66). Absolute duty requires us to betray the order of universality and generality, of being and essence and manifestation. In the name of absolute and infinite duty, one ought not to be ethical; the individual ought even to be a little "heretical" and set himself apart from the universal.

The story of Abraham, of the binding or sacrifice of Isaac, is thus the story of the binding or sacrifice of ethics (DM, 66 / GD, 66). The story of Abraham is the story of duty or obligation (*devoir*) without ethics, without the reassurance and consolation of ethics. It is written, just as I had hoped and prayed and wept in *Against Ethics*, "against ethics," and as a "contribution to a poetics of obligation."[32] Thinking now of the spectral space of teletechnologies, Derrida denounces the moralizing ethicists, the technicians of behavior, maybe just a little like an angry Jewish prophet:

> Let us here insist, in the name of the morality of morality, on something that is too often forgotten by the moralizing moralists and the good consciences who preach to us with assurance every morning and every week, in the newspapers, the weeklies, on radio and on television, about the sense of ethical and political responsibilities. Philosophers who do not write an ethics fail in their duty, one often hears, and the first duty of the philosopher is to think the ethical, to add a chapter on ethics to each of his or her books and in order to do that to return to Kant as often as possible. What the knights of good conscience do not recognize is that the "sacrifice of Isaac" illustrates, if one is able to speak in this case of such a nocturnal mystery, the most daily and most common experience of responsibility. (DM, 67 / GD, 67) (translation modified)

But how does this extraordinary story—of a father given an incomprehensible command from the wholly other to sacrifice his beloved son—illustrate ordinary moral life? How can the paradox of Abrahamic messianism become a paradigm for the rest of us, a version of the general messianic? Because the story tells of my obligation, in my singularity, to the absolute singularity of the other, which "casts me immediately in the space or the risk of absolute sacrifice" (DM, 68/GD, 68):

> I am not able to respond to the call, to the request, to the obligation, nor even to the love of an other without sacrificing to him the other, the other others. *Every other is wholly other*. (DM, 68/GD, 68) (translation modified)

Obligation is thus caught in a double bind, an aporia, a paradox, but a paradigmatic paradox, which constitutes the sacrifice and spells the death and the limit of thinking obligation through conceptually:

> From the moment that I am in relation with the other, with the look, the request, the love, the order, the call of the other, I know that I am able to respond to it only by sacrificing ethics, that is to say, by sacrificing that which obliges me to respond also and in the same way, in the same instant, to all others. I offer the gift of death, I betray, I do not need to raise the dagger over my son on the top of Mount Moriah to do this. Day and night, in each instant, on all the Mount Moriahs of the world, I am doing this, raising the dagger over what I love and ought to love, over the other, such or such an other to whom I owe absolute fidelity, incommensurably. (DM, 68–69/GD, 68) (translation modified)

Isaac thus occupies the place of all others, of the ethical community, of the *oikos* and *Sittlichkeit*, of the bonds I have to everyone else whose needs I do not address when I respond to the singular other who claims me in this instant, every instant, day in and day out. If I help to feed and clothe *this* other, the one who is before me now, I abandon all the other others to their nakedness and starvation. If I attend to my children, I sacrifice the children of other parents. If I feed my cat, do I not sacrifice all the other cats in the world who die in hunger? Ours is a world built on sacrificing others, the faces of whom we see daily on the evening news (DM, 82–83/GD, 86; PdS, 373–74/*Points*, 361–63).[33]

Moriah, the scene of the binding of Isaac, is not only a symbol but the very scene of the bloodiest conflicts among the concrete messianisms, while the name of Abraham, which ought to be a name of hope, has become the name of a war among his children.[34] The site is the place where, according to Second Chronicles, Solomon built his temple in Jerusalem, but also the site of the grand Mosque of Jerusalem, the Dome of the Rock, near the grand Aska mosque, from where also Mohammed flew away on horseback to paradise after death, even as it is not far from the *via dolorosa* (DM, 69/GD, 69–70). This holy place is a place of holy war, of raging conflict among the great monotheisms, the religions of the *tout autre*, a war waged by and among the children of Abraham that rages on today as it has for centuries. Each one lays claim to the place and each one puts its own historical-political spin on "Messianism and the sacrifice of Isaac" (DM, 70/GD, 70).[35] In our own day, our recent past, in the Gulf War, "[t]he belligerents were all irreconcilable coreligionists of what is called the religions of the Book" (DM, 83/GD, 87). The issue of this war and of the Iraqi terror that invited the war was "innumerable victims," each one singular and *tout autre*, each one precious beyond measure or price, each one priceless, which renders it both necessary and meaningless to count the dead since each one, *tout autre*, is as *tout autre* incalculable. *Tout autre*: in-valuable, in-calculable, in-numerable, price-less. It is to end this fight to the death that rages over Mount Moriah, this death-dealing among the messianisms, and between them and all the other others who have never heard of Abraham, to begin to think how to end this death, that Derrida wants to distinguish the messianic in general from the bloody messianisms of the great monotheisms.

Tout autre est tout autre

Derrida's little shibboleth, *tout autre est tout autre*, clearly draws upon Levinas's transition from "substitution"—my absolute, singular, incalculable being-given-over to the wholly other (*tout autre*) who comes to me from on high—to "justice," my general obligation to everyone else (*les autres autrui*), which requires calculation. Justice for Levinas intervenes in order to limit, to calculate—by dividing and multiplying—my obligation among the entire community. Justice for Levinas is a way of stopping me from spending everything on one account. For Derrida, this moment of "calculation," this moment of the *rationem reddere*, represents a moment of an always imperfect reconciliation, of a conflict of duties. If there is a difference of views here, it may be that Derrida considers this a structural conflict ("double bind"), while Levinas does not appear to regard the possibility of the reconciling calculation of justice as inherently troubled.

But Derrida's gloss opens up a Levinasian interpretation of Kierkegaard that is missed by Levinas himself. Levinas, who admires the story of Abraham and who also admires many things about Kierkegaard, is a critic of *Fear and Trembling*. Levinas writes:

> Kierkegaard has a predilection for the biblical story of the sacrifice of Isaac. He describes thus the encounter with God by a subjectivity that is raised up to the religious level, to God beyond the ethical order! His interpretation of this story can doubtlessly be taken up in another sense. Perhaps the ear that Abraham had for hearing the voice that leads him back to the ethical order is the highest moment of the drama.[36]

Levinas has every right to see the story differently. One wonderful thing about Genesis 22 is its endless reinterpretability, which is testified to by the staggering literature surrounding it (in which it is endlessly reinterpreted).[37] Levinas sees it as a story of the *end* of sacrifice, of the sacrifice of sacrifice, at least of human sacrifice, which is precisely how it is seen by a great deal of biblical scholarship. Indeed, the interpretation rendered by Paul, Luther, and Kierkegaard is slightly anachronistic, inasmuch as the "law" is not delivered to Moses until several centuries later. Levinas rightly criticizes Kierkegaard for his love of violence, something I have also criticized under the name of *Kampsphilosophie* in both Kierkegaard and Heidegger.[38] Derrida himself remarks upon the "absence of woman" from the story—this is the one place he questions the spin Paul and Kierkegaard put on the story—and he wonders whether the intervention of a woman might not alter the "implacable universality of the law, of its law, the logic of sacrificial responsibility," which is also something that one Johanna de Silentio also wondered (DM, 74–75/GD, 75–76).[39] In *Passions*, Derrida identifies sacrifice with "imperative rigor or implacable law," with "the severity of duty or the categorical imperative" (*Pass.*, 85/DCR, 31n9). Kierkegaard's reading follows St. Paul's, whose concern was to delimit the law in the interest of faith. This Pauline-Kierkegaardian reading is not otherwise questioned by Derrida, who shares Paul's and Kierkegaard's interest in the deconstruction of the law—not in the name of a determinable faith, or of a Jewish-Christian polemics, to be sure, but in the name of the justice due to a singular other, for the name of God is the name of the *tout autre*.

By siding with Kierkegaard and Paul, Derrida opens up a distinction between duty or obligation (*devoir*, *obligation*) and ethics of the sort that I have argued for in *Against Ethics* and that I took to be implicit in Derrida. Derrida makes it plain that what Kierkegaard calls the "religious" is *structurally* obligation to the *tout autre*, which is a general structure of experience, an *ob-ligare* or being bound over. The religious is the responsibility of the subject to the wholly other, which is precisely what Levinas calls the "ethical." Derrida's difference with Levinas, his Kierkegaardianism, lies in his willingness to sacrifice "ethics," both the word and the concept, which for Derrida and Kierkegaard (and Heidegger)[40]—means the *calculability of obligation*, allowing the power of the *rationem reddere* to hold sway over the question of obligation. We should emphasize that when Kierkegaard says "ethics" he means the universal or general which cannot bind me in an unconditional way; when Levinas says "ethics" he means the unconditional which does not bind me in a general way, although general obligations can be derived from it, or follow along after it.[41] Like Kierkegaard, Derrida subscribes to the notion of an unconditional obligation—but without ethics, or beyond ethics—which is what he calls a "hyper-ethical sacrifice" (DM, 70/GD, 71).[42] This means a responsibility to singularity which at one and the same time, "in the same instant," forces me to transcend or sacrifice my generalizable obligations to the community.

§13. Abraham's Gift

Levinas leads us to believe that the transition from substitution (singularity) to justice (universality) can be made without sacrifice, without conflict and loss, that it is possible to formulate a wisdom of love (ethics) without a loss of wisdom (about individuals). Kierkegaard and Derrida, on the other hand, are willing to make the sacrifice of ethics; they think that obligation is an abyss, that any attempt to formulate such a wisdom of love, or of obligation, is caught up in an aporia, scandal, and paradox, that our duties clash in irreconcilable conflicts, awash in incommensurability, and that obligation begins to move only when one is paralyzed by the aporia in which one is caught. The disagreement resembles an old debate about the unity of virtue (of "vir"-tue),[43] about whether our duties as a whole form a unity.

What then does Derrida make of the moment in which God stays the patriarch's hand, the instant when "God decides to suspend the sacrificial process" (DM, 71/GD, 71) and the angel calls off the (human) sacrifice? That is the highest moment in the story, according to Levinas, representing Abraham's *return to* the ethical, and so, contra Kierkegaard, a teleological suspension of the religious, as it were, in the name of the ethical. Hearing the voice of Elohim speak once again, Abraham responds, *me voici*, which is the first and only possible response to the *tout autre*. Elohim says that he is satisfied, that Abraham has shown all due fear and trembling before his incomprehensible command, and having shown himself ready to act, Elohim calls off the sacrifice and unties the obligation. Still, Derrida comments, we might understand this outcome otherwise: Abraham has shown that he understands what an absolute obligation means and knows how to respond to the *tout autre*, to the command and the appeal of the other; he is prepared to meet its demands, to embrace its unconditionality, to deal in death (to deal death to Isaac, to the other others, in order to keep the deal with the wholly other). He is prepared to act *in an instant* where reasons can neither be demanded nor rendered, in an instant when "there is no more time, when time is no longer given" (DM, 72/GD, 72), a time in which having been ready to act is as good as having already acted. This no-more-time is the time of giving, the giving of the time (*donner le temps*) of absolute obligation, which is not the present of ordinary time, but the instant of absolute ab-solution from every human or ethical duty to meet his absolute obligation, which is also the moment of messianic time. So Derrida's reading is more Kierkegaardian than Levinasian.

The essential thing for Derrida is the secret that Abraham will not share. He will not give reasons. If he gives testimony to his faith, it is a secret testimony that he cannot share with others. There is no language common to him and the wholly other in which he could negotiate,[44] no ethics in which his case could be stated and defended to God or Isaac. He cannot explain what is going to happen because he does not understand it himself; the secret he keeps from Isaac is a secret to him as well. The tragic hero can explain himself, but Abraham is reduced to silence by the secret. When asked by Isaac about the lamb, he answers without responding— God will provide the lamb—with a "meta-rhetorical irony," which is a language of perfect faith in and complete ignorance of what God had in store for them (DM, 75–76/GD, 77). For Abraham's decision, indeed any "impossible decision" in the midst of undecidability, any response to the absolutely other, is not guided by knowledge (PdS, 157/*Points*, 147–48). *Sans voir, sans avoir, sans savoir.*

But if Abraham cannot share his absolute secret with us, and if philosophy cannot share the determinable faith of Abraham, if philosophy must put his faith out of action, in *epoche*, what can philosophy share with Abraham?

> [W]hat *Fear and Trembling* says of the sacrifice of Isaac is the truth. Trans-lated into this extraordinary story, it [the truth] shows the structure of the quotidian. It expresses in its paradox the responsibility in each instant for every man and every woman. At the same time, there is no ethical gen-erality that does not already fall prey to the paradox of Abraham. At the moment of every decision and in the relationship with *every other as wholly other*, every other asks us at each instant to act like the knight of faith. (DM, 77/GD, 78–79) (translation modified)

Here then is the general structure of the possibility of the religious in any determinable religion, the non-dogmatic doublet of dogma, the central axiom of a general messianic: *Tout autre est tout autre*:

> God, as the wholly other, is to be found everywhere there is something of the wholly other. And since each of us, everyone else, each other is infinitely other in its absolute singularity, inaccessible, solitary, transcen-dent, nonmanifest, not originarily present to my *ego* (as Husserl would say of the *alter ego* that can never be originarily present to my conscious-ness and that I can apprehend only through what he calls *appresentation* and analogy), then what can be said about Abraham's relation to God can be said about my relation without relation to *every other as wholly other*, in particular my relation to my neighbor or my loved ones who are as inaccessible to me, as secret and transcendent as Yahweh. (DM, 76– 77/GD, 78)

This religious paradox is really a paradigm, and the knight of faith extraordinaire is an exemplar of the ordinary. Deconstruction wants to universalize this exception, to say that we are always already caught up in exceptionality, caught up in a singular secret that we cannot communicate to others. The religious exception, the singularity of the religious situation in which ethical generality is suspended, is always upon us. Such excep-tionality is the daily business of life—which implies that the unexceptional regularities, the programmable problems found in the ethics books, are rarely found in life. If Kierkegaard would disallow this analogy of every other with Yahweh, he would approve of the way Derrida has worked the story into the text of everyday life, given that his knight of faith looks like a tax collector and a respectable member of the bourgeoisie.

We share with Abraham the secret—the incommunicable command from the *tout autre*—that we cannot pass on to the other others, the secret of who knows what, *on ne sait quoi* (DM, 78/GD, 80). Now the interior-subjective secret passes over into the deconstructive secret, with this question:

> What is a secret that is a secret about nothing and a sharing that doesn't share anything?
> Such is the secret truth of faith as absolute responsibility and as absolute passion, the "highest passion" as Kierkegaard will say. (DM, 78/GD, 80)

The reference is not only to Kierkegaard's passion of faith but clearly back to the secret of *Passions*, the secret that impassions, the secret passion that generates literature, that sees to it that literature will have already begun. This secret, Johannes de Silentio says, cannot be taught and passed on in a historical tradition from one generation to another. It is encountered in the instant, each time for the first time, born anew in passion again and again. Each time is an absolute beginning, a first passion. History is nothing more than the incessant repetition of absolute beginnings, repetition being the succeeding of yes with yes, and messianic time being made up of such beginnings.

The elliptical formula "every other is wholly other" is Derrida's transcription of a deeply religious experience, giving words to his experience of the impossible, which is a certain post-phenomenological experience, where experience does not mean phenomenological seeing but running up against the unforeseeable. In the *Cartesian Meditations*, Husserl had pointed out that the intentional acts (*Erlebnisse*) that make up the flow of the other's conscious stream cannot be known to me without becoming mine, hence without destroying the alterity of the other. To this primarily epistemic point in Husserl—how to constitute the transcendent conscious stream of the other ego?—Levinas gives an ethical force. For Levinas the alterity of the other has to do with the irreducible ethical claim that the other makes upon the responsible subject, the demand made upon me by the other one who is not me or mine, but the stranger.

This seeming tautology (in French) thus stands at the core of a radical heterology, a "hetero-tautology," the effect of which is to attribute the radical and infinite alterity that theology has always reserved for God to everyone, to each man or woman, and not only to the other person, Derrida adds, for this is a "wholly other (*tout autre*) form of alterity: one or other persons but just as well places, animals, language" (DM, 70/GD, 71). This is said in contrast to Levinas, who, while he does not confine *l'infini* to God, does confine it to other human beings (*l'autre homme*). For Levinas, the infinite one means, first of all (in the order of experience), the other person, the one who comes to me from "on high," and then, in and through the other person, the "seal" that marks ethical experience, the trace of infinity of *il*, of the illeity of God which seals and stamps and warrants the infinity of the other person.[45] Levinas's thought moves about in the space or "difference" between the face of my neighbor and the face of God, between other persons and God, between "two, but unique 'wholly others'" (DM, 84/GD, 87). This difference is not conceived in the traditional way, as a difference between the finitude of other persons and the infinity of God, but rather as the difference between two infinities, the infinity of other persons visited upon us in ethical experience and the infinity of God as the trace left behind on the face of the other as He withdraws from the world.

In the formula *tout autre est tout autre*, one moves back and forth between God—God is wholly other, God is every other, every other is God—and each man or woman: every other human being is wholly other, every other is *like* God (DM, 83/GD, 87). Is this a little game with words? Or a big one? Is it no more than a quirk of French, a bit of luck in this language, a little shibboleth, more or less imperfectly translatable into other languages, so long as they are not wholly other than French? If it is a game, Derrida says, it is an important one that we must "save," "keep safe," for it is a game of salvation, of the "hope of salvation, of the economy of 'being saved'" (DM, 84/GD, 87).

Is there then not a certain "analogy" between these infinities, which are no longer separated by an infinity but rather likened to each on that account, for being "wholly other" is just what "all others" share (*partager*)? But is not "analogy" a trace of paganism for Levinas? However that question is answered by Levinas or for Levinas, Derrida argues that the effect of this formula, which weakens the distinction between *the* "wholly other" as God and "every other," is to weaken the distinction between the universality of ethics and the singularity of the religious, and hence to weaken the distinction between Kierkegaard and Levinas (and Derrida himself). Neither Kierkegaard nor Levinas can make an assured distinction between these two orders; accordingly the disagreement between them tends to wither. For if every other is infinitely other it would not be possible to distinguish the ethical as an order of generality that would then have to be sacrificed to the religious as an order of singularity. The positions of Kierkegaard and Levinas would then begin to drift toward each other:

> Kierkegaard would have to admit, as Levinas reminds him, that ethics is also the order of and the respect for absolute singularity, and not only that of generality or of the repetition of the same. He cannot therefore distinquish so conveniently between the ethical and the religious. But for his part, in taking into account absolute singularity, that is, the absolute alterity obtaining in relations between one human and the other, Levinas is no longer able to distinguish between the infinite alterity of God and

that of every human. His ethics is already religion. In the two cases, the border between the ethical and the religious would become more than problematic, as do all the attendant discourses. (DM, 81/GD, 84; cf. DM, 108n8/GD, 77–78n6)

What is true of the generality of ethics would hold *a fortiori* of the domain of the law and politics, which are likewise beset by the paradox of Abraham, by the paralyzing aporia of having to respond without reserve to the singularity of the *tout autre* while at the same time meeting their responsibilities to the generality of the law. This aporia has never stopped the law from working; indeed, a heightened sense of this conflict sharpens the tip of the law, which is stretched over an abyss and must thus function without foundations. For there is no assured and rigorous concept of responsibility, no rigorous formula, to regulate our lives in ethics, politics, or international diplomacy. Of course, one could always dismiss this difficulty, this aporia and this antinomy, in the very name of a certain self-assured responsibility:

> It suffices to deny the aporia or the antinomy indefatigably, and to treat all those who continue to be disturbed in the face of so much good conscience as irresponsible people, nihilists, relativists, indeed poststructuralists or, worse, deconstructionists. (DM, 81–82/GD, 85)[46] (translation modified)

The "officials of anti-deconstruction" (*Pass.*, 41/DCR, 15), those who have "visibly and carefully avoided reading" Derrida (PdS, 231/*Points*, 218), will of course be pained to hear this. They have long indulged themselves in the reassuring illusion that Derrida's work is a form of aestheticism (cf. PdS, 147–49/*Points*, 138–39), that, on a Kierkegaardian register, deconstruction is to be fitted in as a version of the "rotation method," as a kind of endless playing that amuses itself from moment to moment with the merely "interesting." These "knights of good conscience" (DM, 67/GD, 67) will be scandalized to hear that the right Kierkegaardian analogy is not to the aestheticism of Johannes—read: Jacques—the Seducer, nor to the moralism of the sanctimonious Judge Wilhelm, but to the religion of the parson on the Jutland heaths. Seduced by Jacques the Seducer, the seduction is on them for having failed to recognize the comic as the incognito of the religious. I will leave the defenders of the Good and the True, those who have appointed themselves to make the world safe from deconstruction, to block every thing good that is said about it, even *honoris causa*,[47] to deal with all this as they may, to make peace with themselves in the secret of their own conscience (they being truly good). Hopefully hereafter these moralizing and self-approving critics of Derrida, too much given, alas, to praying in public, will find other means to display their love of virtue. Perhaps they will take to giving alms to the poor and to feeding the hungry, in public of course, as proof positive of their superior virtue, while leaving the interpretation of Derrida's texts to those who actually read them. I wish them all well. Suffice it to say, *différance* does spell trouble for ethics, but it is the sort of trouble that the *tout autre* makes for ethics in *Fear and Trembling*, not the sort made by Johannes/Jacques the Seducer. Kierkegaard and Derrida have a common nemesis—the infinite appetite of Hegel's totalizing dialectic—and a common affection for everything singular, fragment-like—and Abrahamic.

I also leave to themselves those Great Decontaminators who have appointed themselves to make deconstruction safe from religion, to rid deconstruction of every religious infestation.[48] One hopes that Derrida's secularizing defenders, who will take no less scandal at this religious contamination of deconstruction, who will be no less pained by all these Jewish affiliations, will learn something about the postcritical character of deconstruction, and that they too will hesitate before chasing away one ghost too many. Deconstruction: a *skandalon* to Derrida's right-wing critics and a stumbling block to his secularist defenders.

In any case, as Johannes de Silentio said of the defenders of the Hegelian omnibus (FT, 8), I wish them all well in their good works, both public and secret.

It is to raise the level of our responsibility to the *tout autre*, to heighten our sense of the idiosyncratic claims of singularity, that deconstruction, if there is such a thing, does its work. Inasmuch as that, in Kierkegaard, is the defining trait of the religious, deconstruction's concern with the un-concept, the inconceivable concept of responsibility, is a re-ligious notion, where religion means the *re-ligare* to the *tout autre*, which is how Derrida writes the passion for God. Like Kierkegaard, deconstruction's interests turn on the philosophically problematic notion that the single individual is higher than the universal, and on the undecidability that disturbs all decision-making vis-à-vis the *tout autre*. The difficult thing—shall we say the responsible thing?—to do is to grope with the undecidability of the concept, or the quasi-concept, of responsibility. The easy thing—shall we say the irresponsible thing?—is to follow the lead of the knights of good conscience, who denounce as nihilists anyone who enters the troubled waters of undecidability.

§14. *Abraham and the Pharisees*

At the end of *Fear and Trembling* (FT, 120), Johannes de Silentio praises Abraham for his ability to go it on his own, without human approval or human understanding of his actions, for the solitude and secrecy in which he is able to act. By alluding to Matthew 6:6, de Silentio slips Genesis 22 inside Matthew 6, like a bookmarker, reproducing the massive act of incorporating the Jewish scriptures into the Christian as the "Old" Testament inside the New. De Silentio turns to *Matthew* just at the point where Jesus instructs the disciples on how to pray and is about to tell them the "Lord's Prayer." Matthew has Jesus warn them not to make a great show of themselves, praying like hypocrites on street corners, for such people already have their reward. "But whenever you pray, go into your room and shut the door and pray to your Father who is in secret; and your Father, who sees in secret (*videre in secreto, en to krypto blepein*) will reward you" (Matt. 6:6). God knows everything I am doing—and he knows whatever I need before I even ask for it; he can count our tears—although I do not know a thing about God. The relation is completely asymmetric: he sees me but I do not see a thing of him (DM, 87/GD, 91). This secret takes place in the order of visibility—it is a matter of what stays out of sight— rather than of the auditory, like a word that we are not allowed to hear.

But Derrida seems interested in disturbing this Christian exegesis. In Genesis, Abraham acts "without calculation, without investment, without the perspective of reappropriation," sacrificing every economic consideration, every consideration of an "economy of sacrifice" (DM, 90/GD, 95). And *in that instant*, when the dagger is raised and Abraham has every intention of going through with the bloody deed, "God returns his son to him and decides sovereignly, by an absolute gift (*don*), to reinscribe the sacrifice in an economy which hereafter resembles a compensation" (DM, 91/GD, 96). In the instant that Abraham makes a sacrifice of economy, of his *oikos* and self-interests, God for His part—the crucial thing here is that this is none of Abraham's doing—turns his act into an economy of sacrifice. God returns Isaac *only* in the instant when He is assured that Abraham has made a *don*, a "pure gift"[49] (not an exchange), without hope of return, a gift to the death, a gift of death, of Isaac who has no price, who is of incalculable worth. In this chapter of Genesis Abraham has stopped quarreling with God over prices. He does not enter into negotiations with God, as he had haggled over the price of Sodom and Gomorrah in Genesis 18. Instead of giving God trouble over what looks like an unreasonable demand, he just says *me voici*. God gives a return only in the instant when it is clear that Abraham gives a pure gift, when he has raised the dagger and has no intention of stopping, when he is without hope or expectation of a return, when he has already made the decision and now it is just a question of "executing" it, in an un-calculating an-economy (DM, 90–91/GD, 94–97). If you are out to "demystify" this story, Derrida adds, you will have to argue that Abraham "played his cards well" (*bien joué*), played high stakes poker with the Most High, and managed not to show his hand! When "dissemination" was defined as "that which does not return to the father," Derrida remarks, it well described the moment of "Abrahamic renunciation" (DM, 91/GD, 96).

That is Genesis. But *Matthew* is a different story for Derrida. Matthew, around whom the anonymous author of *Matthew* has organized this gospel, was a tax collector (Matt. 9:9), who was interested in keeping balanced books and accounting for every dime, and he has a sharp tongue when it comes to Jews. Now in Matthew 6, the expression "And your father who sees in secret will reward (*rendra, reddere*) you" is repeated three times (6:4, 6:6, 6:18). It is as if the formula is to be learned "by heart," where the heart is an economic principle: where your treasure is, there is your heart (6:21). The heart is thus a place to store celestial capital, which is, measured by earthly exchange rates, priceless and completely safe from the dangers of devaluation, from declining market values (DM, 93/GD, 98). In *Matthew* Jesus is portrayed as the author of an economy that is more sublime, "infinite, celestial, incalculable, interior and secret" (DM, 102/GD, 109), which trades in higher, heavenly profits, which are mad and incalculable, but only by earthly standards. If you make a public display of your prayer, you already have your reward (*misthon*); but if you pray in secret, then your reward will be from the Father. Store up invisible treasures in heaven, where things do not rust, rot, or get stolen, and not perishable earthly goods. In *Matthew*'s version of the beatitudes, Jesus promises the kingdom of heaven as a return to those who are poor in spirit, merciful, and persecuted for justice's sake. The poor in spirit will be compensated (*merces*) by a heavenly accounts-payable for their sacrifices on earth, as opposed to the pharisees who shortsightedly succumb to earthly profit-taking, thus forfeiting long-term celestial capital gains. To be sure, the poor in spirit do not enter into finite, visible transactions, but into secret, invisible, heavenly ones, but they are on that account much shrewder investors—much better at investing in "futures"—than the pharisees, who do not know how to play the heavenly market.

So the Matthean logic is marked in two ways. First, it is a "photology," in which those who conduct their business in secret, outside the light of the day, will shine with light and become the light of the world (Matt. 6:22). This interior light constitutes the end of the secret, inasmuch as God knows everything that is going on in this sphere of interiority, even as it constitutes another, more inner secret which is hidden from the eyes of men, the sphere of consciousness or what Augustine called the *homo interioris* (DM, 94–95/GD, 100–101).

Second, by constituting this sphere of inner light, Matthew institutes a new economy of sacrifice: you will be well paid if you rise above earthly considerations and set your sights on supersensible, heavenly returns. You have been told not to commit adultery; but I say go beyond that and do not lust even in your heart, because adultery is an interior, spiritual affair. Do not seek to be just or to give alms or to pray before men, or even, were it possible, before yourself: do not let your left hand know what your right is doing, lest your heavenly reward be forfeited by this exposure to the light of day, to earthly light. Shine with a purely interior light. Pray, fast, and give alms—but in secret. Do not walk around looking half dead from your good works, not if you are in the business of storing up heavenly treasure. If you love those who love you, what good is that? Do not even the tax collectors—the lowest among us—do the same? The truly "meritorious" thing is to love those who hate and persecute you.[50] Do not return an eye for an eye, but repay hatred with love and turn the other cheek. That will have a real and everlasting payback, for the Father who sees in secret is keeping invisible books on all these transactions and is entering these finite losses into an infinite calculus.

The Matthean economy is neither Jewish (hypocritical and pharisaical) nor pagan (*ethnikoi, gentiles, goyim*), but specifically Christian, not Judeo-Christian,[51] but Christian *versus* Jewish (DM, 100/GD, 107). For example, when Matthew has Jesus say you have been taught "love your neighbors but hate your enemies," he over-sharpens the tip of Leviticus 19:15–18, since the text does not mention hating your enemies and in fact condemns vengeance. So Matthew has Jesus dividing people up into the children of the light, the true sons, who have heard the higher word about the interior, celestial economy (the Christians), and everybody else, the Jews and *ethnikoi*, who trade in earthly markets. Matthew has Jesus targeting the Jews, the Old Law, as essentially hypocritical. Now whatever polemical purpose that served for first century Christians, and it does appear to have worked all too well, it would turn lethal in the subsequent history of the West.

This inner, celestial economy of sacrifice does not treat God as some kind of high-powered satellite circling the earth who maintains perfect surveillance on everything down below, Derrida says (DM, 101/GD, 108). It means rather, in Augustine's formula, that God is something more interior and intimate to me than I am to myself. If we step outside the framework of specific religious beliefs, Jewish, Christian, or Islamic, Derrida remarks, we can say that "God" here is the name of "the possibility for me to keep a secret which is inwardly visible but outwardly invisible" (DM, 101/GD, 108). This of course is the "secret" of Kierkegaardian subjectivity, not the deconstructive secret that there is no secret (*supra*, §10). With the name of "God" we name that which constitutes the invisible sphere of conscience and consciousness, of *l'être avec soi* (DM, 101/GD, 108–09). What I call God, God in me, calls me to be myself, the interior I, which Kierkegaard calls "subjectivity" (DM, 102/GD, 109). So here the secret, the structure of the subject, and the name of God are indissociably linked. God is what calls up—what is called(?)—subjectivity. Derrida here sketches the tradition of a deeply Pauline, Augustinian, Lutheran, and Kierkegaardian "self," one that was crucial to the formation of *Being and Time* (one of the most fascinating tensions in which is its simultaneous destruction of Cartesian subjectivity). The subject confesses to God what God already knows—*cur confitemur Deo scienti?*—for God already sees in secret everything there is to confess, so that the confessor is confessing to himself (*Circon.*, 7/*Circum.*, 3):

> That is the history of God and of the name of God as a history of the secret, which is a history at the same time secret and without any secrets. This history is also an economy. (DM, 102/GD, 109) (translation modified)

The Matthean as *opposed* to the Abrahamic sacrifice is thus quite equivocal and unstable. It begins by renouncing earthly rewards, by denouncing all visible, earthly calculation as pharisaism, so that on the outside it looks like perfect renunciation. But this renunciation is undertaken only in order to capitalize on a secret, infinite, invisible, heavenly return (DM, 102/GD, 109), so that on the inside it seeks a reward, which means that it reproduces the essential structure of the pharisaical. Hardly the pure gift, this is the very essence of trying to win heaven economically, this time with a celestial counterfeit of the gift, which is really a long-term investment in an invisible, heavenly economy. By drawing the gift back into a calculus, *Matthew* reproduces a second, more sublime pharisaism, a higher, holier, heavenly hypocrisy.

In the Matthean economy, the left hand inevitably catches a glimpse of what the right(eous) hand is doing, and there is no watch kept over giving, no taking care that narcissism, which is inevitable, should be kept welcoming and open-ended. In *The Genealogy of Morals* Nietzsche shows the consequences of such economic thinking when it is carried to its conclusion. Nietzsche criticizes the Pauline "economy of salvation" as a system of exchange, of paying off debt/guilt (*Schuld*) with the coin of sacrifice, suffering, and cruelty. This system finally self-destructs, or autodeconstructs, at that point of particular madness which Nietzsche calls Christianity's "stroke of genius" (*Geniestreich*), viz., the Pauline theology of a sin/debt/guilt so infinite, so bottomless, that only God himself can pay it off, and all this under the cover of the beautiful name of "gift" (*gratia*):

> ... that stroke of genius on the part of Christianity: God himself sacrifices himself for the guilt of mankind, God himself makes payment to himself. God as the only being who can redeem man from what has become unredeemable for man himself—the creditor sacrifices himself for his debtor, out of *love* (can one credit that?), out of love for his debtor![52]

The Pauline-Christian economy culminates in the idea of an infinite, unpayable debt, of a state of guilt/indebtedness (*Schuldigkeit*) that is so vast and deep that only God himself can pay Himself back. Only the Creditor has the resources to pay off the debt! Nietzsche's critique, Derrida comments, has the effect of suspending faith (*foi*), of letting it twist in the wind, between belief (*croyance*) and credit (*créance*). Growing in faith is a capital growth fund, an infinite extension of a (very) long-term credit line which entitles the believer to draw upon the credits that are accumulated for him by the infinite contribution to the fund made by Christ's sacrificial death. And what credence can we give to that, Nietzsche asks? Is that merely a rhetorical question? Does not something resonate in rhetorical questions that makes the established, questioned order tremble (DM, 107 / GD, 115)?

Counterfeit Kingdoms

Like its counterpart, *Donner le temps, Donner la mort* is an examination of hypocrisy, of what is going on under (*hypo*) the name of the gift (*hypo tes ousias*), which we never know. *Hypokrinesthai*: putting on a play, acting out a role, performing under a mask; one thing going on under the name of something quite different. Hypocrisy is an operation of the secret, which precipitates a crisis of faith, a "con" game that shakes our con-fid-ence, our faith. The discourse on the gift follows the movements of the counterfeit, of taking under the name of giving, so that, like *Donner la mort*, it takes up the question of the "pharisaical." Two sets of hypocrites, phar-isees and counterfeiters, con artists who depend upon the power of the secret, both doing one thing under the cover of a secret whose powerful energies they attempt to harness. For one can lie and cheat with secrets and use them "to secure oneself a phantasmatic power over others. That happens every day" (*Pass.*, 69 / ON, 30). The gift occasions a crisis of faith, of not knowing how or when to credit a work of faith, how or when it is carried out in good faith as opposed to being a more or less successful ruse, a way of amassing credit for oneself, of making a profit under the beautiful name of a gift.

The equation of the pharisee with the hypocrite is already Christian slander against the Jew, the onset of "the duel between Christian and Jew." This duel is always cast by Christianity as a war between the New Law of the Gift and the Old Law of pharisees, between the spirit of love and cold commerce and money changers (DT, 131–32n1 / GT, 101n18), between the living word (Word) and the dead letter, between the supple breath of the Spirit which listeth where it will and the wooden inflexibility of the Law, between the alienated, duty-bound, legalist religion of slaves and the religion of Love (for God is Love), between an eye-for-an-eye credit and debit system and for-give-ness, in short between the pharisee and the gift. This opposition is "compulsively credited—by a Léon Bloy, for example, when, in his customary, diabolical, and sometimes sublime ignominy," Bloy describes the difference between Jew and Christian as the difference between a credit system and a word of honor. The Jewish predilection for *écriture* springs from the narrowness of their commercial souls. Jews want written guarantees, everything down on paper; they do not trust anybody. They want a contract to enforce the letter of the law, to be given every ounce of the pound of flesh that is their due. Writing is pharisaical, Shylockian. As opposed to the Religion of Love.

Does Derrida not risk widening the war between Christian and Jewish readings of the *akedah*? Does he risk returning fire in the "duel between Christian and Jew," the acrimony which he identifies in Léon Bloy's *Le Salut par les Juifs* (DT, 131–32n1/GT 101)? Nothing, of course, is without risk, but Derrida's move here is completely strategic, representing a movement of reversal aimed at overturning or reversing the most dangerous stereotype of all, the Jew as the pharisee, as the money changer, the ruthless creditor, Shylock. That stereotype leads Jews by the hand into the gas chamber. But reversal is a prelude to displacement, and the point is finally to displace the opposition between Christian and Jew, between the determinate, identifiable messianisms, in the name of a messianic structure to which they all subscribe.

That is why it is so important to see that Derrida is not saying that *The Genealogy of Morals* is the final word on faith or Christianity, or the only way to gloss *Fear and Trembling*. For one thing, Derrida does not take Nietzsche to be the simple opposite of religion. For while Nietzsche could never think of things mean enough to say about Paul and Augustine, he was, like Augustine, a man of tears and the author of *Ecce Homo*, an important work of "counter-confessions" (MdA, 123–25/MB, 122–26). Again, it is not as if Christianity means—contrary to everything that deconstruction labors to show, contrary to all of its anti-essentialist impulses—just one thing. Deconstruction, if there is such a thing, means to show that there is never a final word. *Donner la mort* does not conclude with a dismissal of faith, but with a deconstructive delimitation of faith as credit-mongering, of faith as an economic exchange, which is, as Nietzsche himself says—*"sollte man's glauben?"*—to discredit faith, to make faith unbelievable, unworthy of faith. Deconstruction can never be a dismissal of faith inasmuch as deconstruction is itself faith, even a blind faith (MdA, 130/MB, 129). The point of *Donner la mort* then is not to undo faith but to insist on the an-economic character of faith, that faith is always a matter of the gift and giving, not a transaction between a creditor and a debtor. That, I would say, is a fine theological point and it makes both Nietzsche and Derrida excellent theologians of the gift of whom the Vatican should be proud.

The point of any such analysis as Baudelaire's or Nietzsche's, Derrida says, is "demystifying," a word which, though out of style, has the value of unfolding the hypocrisy that inhabits a secret (DM, 104/GD, 112). The point of a "demystifying" analysis is to force out into the light of day the secret contract that allows one to do one thing under the cover of its opposite, e.g., to reap rewards under the cover of giving, to be pharisaical under the cover of a critique of the Pharisees. The latter were, after all, pure of heart and close to the mind and heart of Jesus—before their name was blackened forever by late first-century Christian polemics, so that today pharisaical and hypocritical are almost synonymous.

That is why we need to read Derrida's final paragraphs slowly. "'The stroke of genius,' *if there is such a thing*"—there is the characteristic reserve of deconstruction which always hesitates before identifying the decisive, exhaustive, final, essential word—"only occurs at the instant of an infinite sharing of the secret" (DM, 106/GD, 115). That is to say, there are many strokes of genius, and many Christianities—from Carl Schmitt to Dietrich Bonhoeffer, from Jerry Falwell to Martin Luther King, Jr., from right-wing hate to civil rights—depending on the reading, some of which never succeed in making themselves into anything more than the religion of *The Genealogy of Morals* that Nietzsche so rightly demystifies. We only get drawn into the self-destructive economy described by Nietzsche, which makes divine love into an exchange economy of cruelty, if we have bought into the business of sharing divine secrets and entering into secret contracts with God, expecting a payoff on our secret contract instead of just giving. Consequently, if one "would be able to *attribute*" such a stroke of genius "to someone or something that *one calls* 'Christianity'" (emphasis mine) (DM, 106/GD, 115)—still more deconstructive reserve—one would have to wrap up within it another secret, viz.:

> that reversal and infinitization that confers on God, on the other or on the name of God, the responsibility for what remains more secret than ever, the irreducible experience of belief, between credit and faith, *believing* (*croire*) suspended between the crediting of the creditor (*Glaübiger*) and the faith (*Glauben*) of the believer. (DM, 106–107/GD, 115) (translation modified)

One would have to make the name of the *tout autre*, of God, for example, responsible for the secret connection between faith and credit, as Matthew does, a certain Matthew. And who, Derrida asks with Nietzsche, can believe in that? That question, not merely rhetorical, sounds the alarm that awakens us to another faith. So Nietzsche shows us that he knows a thing or two about what believing means, about what is believable, when he asks us if we can credit this economy with any faith (DM, 107/GD, 115).

Derrida's discourse on the gift delimits and demystifies the economy of sacrifice by showing where the logic of exchange and sacrifice leads, by showing where giving and taking, giving up and getting back, lead, by showing, in short, how such a logic deconstructs or autodeconstructs. Deconstruction shows what happens when the divine madness of the faith of father Abraham becomes an economy pure and simple, when the *credo* of faith deteriorates into a credit system, when the gift turns to poison. The analysis shows the difficulty of keeping the true coin of faith separate from the counterfeit coin of a credit system, that there is nothing to guarantee that the one will not become the other, nothing that says it cannot reverse itself and turn into its opposite, that it does not already contain its opposite, that we must always suspect it, subjecting it to a "hermeneutics of suspicion," as Paul Ricoeur showed years ago.

After all, even Abraham's sacrifice—is this not what deconstruction shows, even though Derrida, out of filial respect, does not bring it up?—is not absolutely safe, absolutely removed, absolutely safeguarded from hidden, subterranean, unconscious, unwanted, unwilled motivations that would turn it into the reverse of what it means to be (*vouloir*)? Maybe Abraham is just frightened, having seen what God did to Sodom and Gomorrah, and maybe that is why he stopped arguing with God in chapter 22. Maybe Abraham is just being very stubborn, very macho and patriarchal! Who knows what wills (*qui veut?*) here? "God knows what's going on!" we say with exasperation, by which we mean, who knows? it's a secret.[53] The "merit" of deconstruction—for which I think it should be rewarded—is to put us on the alert to the way things can pass into their opposite, the way they can turn around and reverse themselves, by a secret operation, so that they produce effects diametrically opposed to what they intend (*vouloir dire*). Derrida's deconstructionist vigilance about reversibility, like a certain hermeneutic of suspicion, is a salutary admonition.

Before going on to schematize the possibility of another Christianity, a little more an-economical one, a little more believable, than the Internal Revenue System run by Matthew, I want to add something about Derrida on debt, because I do not want to let it pass that Derrida has dispensed with the idea of owing something (*devoir*) to the other, that he would economize on this idea altogether, although I do not think the same can be said for Nietzsche.[54] For we have seen, again and again, that everything in deconstruction depends upon the claim that is laid upon us by the *tout autre*, which visits upon us an awful responsibility, one that Derrida has just compared to the awe-ful situation, filled with fear and trembling, in which father Abraham found himself before the *mysterium tremendum*.

One way to see the difference between Derrida and Nietzsche is to see that, in Derrida, everything turns on a notion of responsibility and on a critique of *good* conscience, of duty discharged, whereas the *Genealogy* labors singlemindedly in the vineyard of the critique of *bad* conscience.

Derrida has clarified this issue in a long note in *Passions* (*Pass.*, 75n3/ON, 132n3). We owe the other something but it goes against the grain of his analysis to say that what we owe the other is in duty bound, like a Kantian imperative. As Johannes de Silentio said, when we respond to our "duty," which is a universal and coercive force, and not a little violent, we are not responding to the singularity of the *tout autre*, to God, for example, or to this man or woman (or animal, or whatever). It would not, after all, be very friendly of me, it would even be a little insulting, to help you out because I am duty bound to do so and I always discharge my duties:

> A gesture remains a-moral (it falls short of affirmation of an unlimited, incalculable or uncalculating giving, without any possible reappropria- tion, by which one must measure the ethicity or morality of ethics), if it was accomplished out of *duty* in the sense of 'duty of restitution,' out of duty which would come down to the discharge of a debt. . . . Pure mo- rality must exceed all calculation. (*Pass.*, 75n3 / ON, 132–33n3)

So deconstruction is "[p]ure morality." How better to scandalize the knights of good conscience than with this formula! Far from being an aestheticism, deconstruction is "pure morality," against garden variety eth- ics in the name of an ultra- or archi- or hyper-ethics, turning on an ethico- religious singularity that crosses the wires of the ethical and the religious, a singularity situated in the intersection or crossfire between Kierkegaard and Levinas. Far from being unethical, anethical, or antiethical, deconstruc- tion has to do with the *Seelenfünklein* of ethics, exploring the fine tip of the ethical soul, the morality of morality, analyzing the most delicate effects and reversibilities that infiltrate obligation and responsibility. Yes, yes!

Deconstruction affirms a responsibility that goes beyond duty, respon- sibility without duty, if a duty then perhaps a duty without debt, a *devoir sans devoir* (DT, 94n1 / GT, 69n23), that does not answer to its own essence. That would make for an interesting anomaly: a duty that means we do things but not because they are due (*le devoir ne doit rien, il doit ne rien devoir*). Doing should be (*doit*) giving, if it is to be duly responsible. The idea would be to get to responsibility or duty that is released from the economy of debt, which is enslaving, self-serving, insulting, and ulti- mately self-destructive.

Derrida is interested in putting a distance between deconstruction and all this death-dealing in "old Kant," as Nietzsche called him, between deconstruction and the "gruesome" economy of guilt and debt so mer- cilessly "demystified" by Nietzsche's genealogies, which is the heavy responsibility his notion of the pure gift must bear. The other lays claim to me, comes over me, elicits my *me voici*, shatters the encircling horizons of the same with which I surround myself. This constitutes a singular obligation to just this other one, a responsibility, a responsive giving, a giving that responds. Duty, or the debt of duty, would be always *universal* and not singular, *rule bound* and not responsive to singularity, a higher *principle* in virtue of which I act, a higher *eidos* in which I encircle and envision the singular, and as such *coercive*, forcing something from me instead of letting me give.

But to let me give, to let me give to the other in such a way as to let the other be the other: is that not love? Is that not what Derrida calls love in *Sauf le nom*? Now would that not be a slightly Christian move to make, for is not Christianity the religion of love? That, alas, was a move made with considerable hatred for Jews, which is why, for Derrida, the religion of love, if there is any, would have to be a religion without religion, or before religion, a structure of the messianic without messianism.[55]

Moreover, Derrida is not even prepared to dismiss entirely the idea of debt (*dette*) itself. We cannot forget that the subtitle of *Specters of Marx* is the "state of debt." This expression was meant not only as a critique of the debt that the new world order has every intention of collecting from the Third World and East European countries, hence as an economy of debt that needs forgiving and forgetting, but also as the debt that Derrida, that everyone today, owes to Marx. For deconstruction takes itself to be a radicalization of a certain spirit of Marx, and a radicalization is always indebted (*endettée*) to what it radicalizes (SdM, 152–53/SoM, 92–93). To have the memory of a tradition, to be inspired by one of its spirits, is to owe the spirit of that tradition a debt. But this debt is not a matter of a balance sheet or a calculation; it is rather a matter of a responsibility to that tradition which selects and interprets among its several spirits, for we are always indebted to something highly polyvalent that keeps its secret to itself. To have a debt to a tradition is to be on our own with this debt and to have to sort our way through it for ourselves. As the affirmation of responsibility, deconstruction takes place in the space of several debts.

♦ *Edifying Divertissement No. 4.*
Deconstruction and the Kingdom of God

Before turning to Derrida's most circum-fessional writings, I should like to while away a little time by way of intermission by sketching here the way in which Derrida's analysis of the gift makes possible an-other Christianity. I propose another, demystified, deconstructed—and I would say a slightly de-Paulinized and more Jewish—Christianity that turns away from the economics of sin and redemption, and turns on the notions of giving and for-giving, of for-giving and for-getting. Such a Christianity does not resemble Paul's Christian "economy of salva-tion" so much as Jesus' very Jewish "kingdom of God." It does not view the crucifixion in Pauline terms as the retribution God exacted for sin, or as the reason Jesus was born—Jesus intended to live, not to die— but as a fate visited upon a just man, a man with a prophetic sense of justice, who told the truth on the powers that be. It does not turn on making earthly payments on long-term, deferred celestial returns but on giving, pure and simple.

Such a (deconstructed) Christianity looks a great deal more like what is contained in some of the most authentic Jesus-sayings about the "kingdom," in which the kingdom is not the deferred reward for present sacrifice but the future present, the kingdom now, begun in Jesus' proclamation that the kingdom of God is at hand, in a today rather like the "Today" in Blanchot's parable of the Messiah among the beggars on the outskirts of Rome.

The kingdom of God does not turn on pain and re-pentence, which is a more Baptist (as in John the Baptist) rendering of *metanoia*, but on joy, which is the more Jesus-minded version of *metanoia*. Jesus did not play a dirge but a dance, and he does not mourn but pipes (Matt. 11:17–18). These kingdom sayings are not organized around the infinite debt of sin and gathering infinite resources to pay it off. They do not speak of guilt and punishment, of satisfying the wrath of an infinitely offended deity, of a *tout autre* that is out to collect every dime, but of forgiveness, on giving debt away, on the loving care of *abba* ("dad" or "mom") for his children, however prodigal they may be. Far from demanding infinite retribution for the prodigal son's offense, the father forgives him immediately and celebrates his return. The kingdom is organized around giving and forgiving, not debt and sacrifice, above all not the hypersacrifice of a God, of a divine immolation, to pay off an infinite, bottomless debt.

The Birds of the Air

The kingdom sayings are woven into all the early Christian texts, along with the characteristically Markan, Matthean, Lukan, Johannine, and Pauline redactions, and we can still feel their power and hear them resonating. *Matthew*, too, is highly polyvalent, means many things, is filled with many voices, and our debt to *Matthew* is a matter of responding selectively to his several spirits. It is perfectly true that *Matthew* is the scene of a "celestial economy," of a higher, more sublime, more calculating system of accounting. Matthew has also redacted "the poor" (*hoi ptochoi*) into "poor in spirit (*pneumeati*) and, by thus interiorizing poverty, *Matthew* gives advance comfort to post-Constantinian Christianity. For on the Matthean account a heavenly reward need not be bought at the price of external earthly treasures, so long as one remained poor in one's heart, in secret, for which one will earn heavenly return. In *Matthew* the Pharisees are maligned, reflecting rather more the polemics between the emerging Christian movement and the established Jewish religion in the last quarter of the first Christian century than anything historical about the Pharisees themselves, even as he lets the blood of Jesus be upon the Jews.

But *Matthew* also contains the little sermon on not worrying (*merimnatein*), which is one of the most Zen-like discourses of Jesus, in which Jesus urges the disciples not to count, not to worry, and to be maddeningly uncalculating (6:25–34). Be not concerned (*merimnate*), have no *Sorge* for yourselves or your *conatus essendi*, don't go around counting up what you need. You should live without care (*sine cura, secura*). The "opthamology" here is to look, to see—birds and lilies and grasses—and to live like them, to live like the rose, *ohne Warum*, as Angelus Silesius said.[56] The celestial here is not a heavenly reward, not a pie in the sky, but the birds of "the air" (*ouranos*): see (*emblepsate*) how they neither sow nor reap but God gives them what they need, as if they were utterly nonproductive things who live purely off gifts from God.

The kingdom is a kingdom of gifts. Consider the lilies of the field. What productive work do they do?—and yet the garments of Solomon himself are no rival to their raiment. But if God cares this greatly about birds and lilies and grasses, how much more will God care for you, you whose very tears he has counted, you *oligopistoi*, you who are too much given to counting up (*créanciers*) and not enough given to the gift of faith, *croyance*. For faith means to live without keeping count, without taking account (*sine ratione*), and to say yes, a number of yes, *oui, oui*, again and again, each day, day by day. Each day, *epiousios* (6:11), come, *viens*. For religion—the determinate and determinable messianisms, the institutionalized dogmatic—is something to be deconstructed, just as faith, if there is such a thing, cannot be deconstructed. Live without why, without demanding or rendering accounts, *sine ratione*. Have the madness not to ask what you shall eat or drink or wear, not to ask where your next meal is coming from, not to seek job security, medical insurance, or guaranteed housing. Seek the kingdom (*basileian*)—which is today, the kingdom is now, today—and seek justice (*dikaiosynen*) and do not worry (*merimnesote*) about tomorrow. Stop thinking about tomorrow. Let tomorrow worry about itself.

This is quite mad. It violates everything we mean by "tenure," and it would make it be extraordinarily difficult to find a permanent pastor who would accept these terms.

Everything in these sayings turns on God's love and God's gift-giving, on the appeal to the disciples to trust God, to have a little more faith, to turn their concerns over to God, to let God do the worrying. This is not because God, who keeps secret books, will reward us infinitely more than human beings can, but because in the kingdom of God, where God rules, God will give us just enough of what we *need* today, and not so much as to burden us down with wealth or with seeking wealth. If we have given everything up, unconditionally, in a moment of madness, and not as part of a secret bargain we have struck, God will give us the time, *donner le temps*, which will free us up for our true concern, which is justice. (Unless a man lose his life he will not have it given back.) If we give up the search for security, if we live *sine cura* (*ohne Sorge*), if we acquire what Heidegger calls the free relationship to things—in the famous discourse on *Gelassenheit*[57]—then we will be freed up. The time will be given to them, not just for the thinging of the thing, but for justice, for seeking justice, for the kingdom of justice, which is the kingdom of God.

So faith is linked here not with building credit (*créancier*) but with trust, and trust is inseparable from love: have faith and trust in God's love for you, which is at least as great as his love for the lilies of the field. For God is love and what God gives is best, because God's will, God's heart, is good through and through. The kingdom of God: *viens!*

That is not a way to calculate in a more cunning, celestial and long-range way, but a way to love and trust and seek justice, to seek the kingdom, which is here and now, which is for the lame and the leper, the outcast and the sinner, the widow and the orphan, not the poor in spirit but the poor plain and simple. The kingdom is not like a long-term bond, not a wise form of estate planning for a vault of heavenly treasures. The kingdom is the call of the other, and the kingdom is here and now.

None of this is to say that the evangelical life is absolutely safe from what it can turn into: a cadre of right-wing reactionaries driven by resentment against God's poor, or a caste of priestly bourgeoisie, well kept and well fed, who have made a profitable business out of the crucifixion. That is precisely what set the wheels of the Kierkegaardian writing machine into motion. Nothing is safe. You *should* worry that *not* worrying will turn into a life of bourgeois ease, which is the counterfeit coin of letting God do the worrying, the counterfeit of the kingdom, a counterfeit kingdom. That is why fear and trembling are permanent features of biblical trust, and part of the meaning of not worrying.

Have fear and trembling—but don't worry. That is the aporia that gets Christian *kinesis* going.

If deconstruction were a theory, it would be a theory that nothing is safe, pure, clean, uncontaminated, monochromatic, unambiguous; nothing is "simply exterior" to the circle of self-interest. Deconstruction is a quasi-theory of undecidability, and it works well for everything from architecture[58] to literary criticism, from religion to politics (PdS, 227–28/*Points*, 213–15). Deconstruction is an exploration of as many "instants" of undecidability as it has time (as it is given time) to study. Its "solution" to the question of undecidability shows a trend: it always tends to say that the undecidability is permanent, that undecidability precedes, follows, and permeates the decision, that the undecidability is first, last, and always, but that decisions must be made and indecision broken,[59] that paralysis is a condition of possibility and impossibility of motion. By definition, it is impossible to *know* what one's secret, unconscious motives are, or when one is trading with counterfeit coins (which are only "good counterfeits" so long as they are not known to be counterfeit), whether in one's heart one is pharisaical or not, whether one is living like the lilies of the field or just enjoying a comfortable living with good benefits, like Trollopean parsons in Barsetshire. One begins where one is and does all that one can, keeping our narcissism as open-ended and hospitable as possible; the rest is beyond us. The pure gift, a gift pure and simple, is im/possible, a condition of possibility and impossibility, an impossible passion, an impossible that impassions.

That is why giving is always already forgiving.

For-giving

Derrida is praying and weeping for something beyond obligation, for a responsibility without duty, for a duty without debt, for a debt without tying us up. This represents, I think, a certain movement, if I may say so, *au-delà de Levinas*, beyond Levinas and beyond obligation, a certain a-teleological suspension of the ethical, for something beyond, something *mère/mehr*, for a certain letting of the other be that is not, or is not reducible to, duty, for a certain *Gelassenheit* that he himself says we might dare call love (*Sauf*, 91–92/ON, 74).

Now I hasten to add that, by mentioning love, I do not wish in any way to associate Derrida or myself with, or to reproduce in a deconstructionist way, the "duel between Jew and Christian," about which, as we have repeatedly said, a great deal of what Derrida has written is a constant warning. I regard the binary opposition between the spirit of love and the dead letter of the law to be largely Christian propaganda meant to deface Judaism, particularly in the politics and polemics between Jew and Christian in the latter part of the first century, and I think that the best scholarship shows the Christian hermeneutics of the "Old" Testament is distortive and self-serving, the "religion of love" having proven to be a secret way of hating Jews, i.e., a stratagem of hypocrisy. Such work shows that the radicalizing tendencies within the preaching of Jesus, his *abba* spirituality, represents a reform of Judaism by Judaism, a self-correction interior to Judaism, an intra-Judaic radicalization that drew upon the deepest tendencies of Judaism, so there is nothing that is more Jewish than Jesus, and indeed nothing more pharisaical, which means pure of heart.[60]

I locate the movement beyond obligation in the dynamics of forgiving. Forgiving heals the battered subject, accused and held hostage by the violence of the Good, bent and bloodied by the beating given to the *conatus essendi*. Duty gives the subject a beating, while forgiving gives it a break.

Forgive us as indeed we forgive others.

The hinge of this famous saying is "as indeed," *hos kai* (Matt. 6:12), forgive us as indeed we forgive the *tout autre* whose secret we do not know. Dismiss our debts as we dismiss our debtors. Dismiss our creditors as indeed we give away our credits. We give our credit away absolutely, unconditionally, without the expectation of return. God supplies the rest, the supplement we dare not desire, which can be granted only if we do not desire it, only if we put it out of our minds. The yield of giving is more giving. Giving gives giving. God is the name of the giving that spreads like a fire, or that runs like water over the land, that multiplies the loaves of giving to infinity, so forgiving breeds forgiveness and breaks the circle, the cycle of vengeance, and, beyond vengeance, of simple debt. Forgiving gives us what we cannot, dare not give ourselves

We are urged to move beyond the absolute asymmetry of obligation to the reciprocity of for-giving, of the elusive *hos kai.*

Forgiveness is the ultimate release from all economies, from every economic tie, but not into a simple exteriority from the circle. Rather, forgiving loosens the circle of credit and debt, not only from the debt that chains the other with the tie of my calculated gift, but also from the debt that makes my relation to the other one of debt. Forgiveness alone gives me responsibility without duty, duty without debt, debt without being tied up.

Par-donne: that is the common teaching of Yeshoua and Jacques, in that order, in Franco-Aramaic.

As indeed we forgive our debtors. If your brother offends you seven times a day (which means, time and time again, all the time, without number, incalculably), and if he turns to you and asks you to release him, then you should let him go. Tear up the circle of time, give him more time and wipe past times away. That is the time of forgiving. Forgive him, give his debt to you away, send it packing, forget it, let the past flow off without a trace. Give up your hold (*tenere*) on him, your retention, do not maintain (*main-tenant*), now, a hold. This is another aberration on father Husserl, on father time, on fathers everywhere, ousiological and otherwise, a time *without* retention, a messianic time. It tears up time by tearing off the past and tearing open the future, so that we do not have (*sans avoir*) anything against the other, nothing to hold (*tenere*) against him, no tenacious, retentive vengeance.

"Forgive us . . . " The kingdom is the *repetition* beyond the resignation, the reciprocity beyond the causality, the symmetry beyond the asymmetry for which we do not bargain, the return that we have renounced, the love beyond the obligation, being loved even as, *hos kai,* we love, being released even as we release.

Hos kai: the kingdom is the *hos kai.* The kingdom is the ambiance of the *hos kai,* reciprocal for-giving, important and impossible, being able to love ourselves, allowing ourselves to be loved, as indeed we love others. To forgive as we are forgiven, to love as we are loved, to love ourselves as we have loved the neighbor, constituting the most open-ended and hospitable narcissism.

The kingdom is the religious relationship to the world and to one another. The kingdom is a kingdom of children at play, playing with the freedom of the children of God. Love, and do what you will. Reciprocity binds up the wounds of obligation, pours oils and balms upon open wounds.

The kingdom gives; give us the kingdom, today, the kingdom of today. The kingdom: *viens*. The kingdom: amen, yes, yes, *oui, oui*. That is also the common teaching of Yeshoua and Jacques, another Franco-Aramaic fragment.

The kingdom is a community in which the solitude of my accusation, my inescapable identity, the relentless recursivity of my being accused is relieved, lifted up, into a community of those who are forgiven and who forgive one another.

The kingdom is madness, a mad economy or aneconomy of forgiving. The kingdom is constituted by a paralogic of paradoxical gifts, gifts that are given only when we give *everything* away, even and especially our credit, when we for-give, give-forth, give away everything, unconditionally.

Forgiving gives away and renounces getting even, squaring the accounts, rendering reasons equal on each side, retribution, giving back, paying back in kind. It renounces equality and in that renunciation opens up the possibility of a community of equals, all equally forgiven and equally detached from getting even.

The freedom of the children of God, the *basileia theou*, God's kingdom, where there is neither master nor slave, male nor female, Greek nor Jew.

The principle without principle, the unprinciple of all unprinciples in the kingdom is to love, and do what you will. *Dilige, et quod vis fac.*

The *basileia* is constituted by the gift. It is constituted by bonds that do not bind up and constrain, by links of love that do not constrain, by the spontaneities of love, by which, over and above accusation, which puts me in the accusative of obligation, the least of God's children is the object of my love.

In this slightly postmodern *basileia*, there is neither master nor slave but a play of differences.

The "kingdom of God" means the kingdom where God is the element, the horizon, the medium, the setting, the place, the context, the open or clearing in which the relationship with the *tout autre*, and the relationship with the world, is played out, where the relation with the other is relieved of its obsessive, accusatory tone. In the kingdom, the relationship with the other is released from the stricture and constricture, from a binding that binds up and confines, and becomes a kingdom of joy, a kingdom of pure singularities, without or beyond, above or before the Law. In the kingdom, the only law is the law without law, the law of love, *dilige et quod vis fac*, the ultimate law-lessness, the ultimate un-principle, justice in itself, if there is such a thing.

The kingdom is a kingdom of singularities. In the kingdom every hair on your head is counted, every tear is numbered, all the little *me onta* and *minutiae* and *minima moralia* are precious beyond measure, measured by a measure without measure, *modum sine modo*, even *sine ratione*, which is the only measure of love. Love is without why, exorbitant, a moment (*Augenblick*) of "sovereignty" in Bataille's sense, a moment that gives and for which we do not give reasons.

In the kingdom love gives life buoyancy, rhythm, joy, a certain free play. The kingdom is good news, *metanoia*, being turned around and lifted up and given a new start. *Oui, oui.* We are sustained, lifted up, beyond what the evidence warrants, lifted up by the evidence of things that appear not, sustained by the spectral hope of what is not present, which is the stuff of faith, which is a certain movement toward the "more."

The kingdom is the kingdom of God, Who is love, not (just) (Greek) Being. Nobody ever said, "When you pray, say Being." Being is not an *abba*. Love is the element and the energy of the kingdom, the light and the air, the open and the clearing, the momentum and vigor, so that in the kingdom we live and move and have our being in love, which is a jewgreek category, a scandal and a stumbling block to *philo*sophy, which, given its name, should be a little more tolerant of love.

"His blood be upon us and all our children" (Matt. 27:25), Matthew has the Jewish crowd say, with lethal, self-fulfilling prescience. Matthew is trying to make trouble for the Jews. "Abba, forgive them," the other evangelists have Jesus say, for that is what an *abba* is for Jesus.

The kingdom is release, for-giving, dis-missing: love and do what you will, life in the ambiance of the kingdom is life without why, life for the sake of life, life released from every economic interest, *sine ratione.*

In the kingdom, life is a gift, and every good gift is from God.

That is the witness of faith, of the gift of faith, which is a faith in gifts, like the third stage corresponding to the inventory of Hilarius Bookbinder.

V. Circumcision

§15. Hegel and the Jews

Derrida and the Jew

Derrida is not a Jewish writer in the strong sense in which that is true of Rosenzweig, Buber, or Levinas. He is a Jew who is "rightly described as an atheist," of an "assimilated" family, raised in an Arab country, whose native language, culture, and education are thoroughly French—"Christian Latin French" (*Circon.*, 57/*Circum.*, 58)—trained in the Greco-European tradition of philosophy and letters, of *mondialatinisation*, who has lived in France since the age of nineteen but whose greatest following is in the United States, always being made welcome elsewhere. But this does not mean his work is not driven by a Jewish passion, not haunted by the figure of the Jew, that he does not write in the name of the Jew, if not always by name, at least by indirection. On the contrary, this is his *diaspora*, and the dispersion and dissemination of Derrida's psyche are the very substance of his Jewishness. When he writes of the exile, the outsider, the nomad, the desert, the uprooted, the dispersed, of dissemination and the cut, of writing itself, is that not to write under another name about the Jew, about Jewish passion, the passion and suffering of the Jew? Is this not to write about himself? When he writes about the *tout autre*, as he has more and more begun to do since 1980, that is not only an excellent Jewish way to write about the name of God, it is a discourse on the Jews themselves, a way the Jews have found of singing a beautiful and haunting song to their own history. For the Jew is both the substance and the figure of the outsider, of the other, the children of the *tout autre* who bear a family likeness to their father.

Unless you are Palestinian, then the Palestinians are the Jews. That, too, is a central part of Derrida's argument and of his own Algerian provenance. For without minimizing the substance and the singularity of Jewish suffering, the Jew is also the placeholder for all those who have no place, even as Auschwitz is absolutely unique and also the placeholder for all the Auschwitzes,[1] for every other heinous name, since there were other death camps and the hatred of the other can take other forms than anti-semitism. For the place of the Jew, the place of the displaced, is always occupied by someone, whatever their name.

Derrida's idea is not to find the Jews—all the Jews, under any name—their own place, their own home, to secure for them their own private property. It belongs to the messianic structure of his thought, to the structure of his messianic passion, to say that the outsider, whoever that may be, is always out, that justice is never here, that the Messiah is not going to become present, the promise is never fulfilled, the promised land will never be reached. Justice is in the disjunct, the dis-joined. He is not trying to locate a Jewish *Heimat* to rival Heidegger's *Heimatsdenken*, to establish a strong nation-state with an adequate national defense. Like Celan, he is inclined to agree that the proper essence of the Jew is to have no property, their essence to be without essence (*Schib.*, 64/WT, 37). Like Lyotard—whatever their differences (*infra.*, n.21)—he wants nothing to do with "geophilosophy," a philosophy that grows like a plant on some national private property; that is something that pits him against Heidegger in a particularly profound way.

The idea behind deconstruction is to deconstruct the workings of strong nation-states with powerful immigration policies, to deconstruct the rhetoric of nationalism, the politics of place, the metaphysics of native land and native tongue, of *propria* and my-ownness. The idea is to disarm the bombs, *les grenades* (*Foi*, 62), of identity that nation-states build to defend themselves against the stranger, against Jews and Arabs and immigrants, against *les juifs* in Lyotard's sense, against all the others, all the other others, all of whom, according to an impossible formula, a formula of the impossible, are wholly other. Contrary to the claims of Derrida's more careless critics, the passion of deconstruction is deeply political, for deconstruction is a relentless, if sometimes indirect, discourse on democracy, on a democracy to come. Derrida's democracy is a radically pluralistic polity that resists the terror of an organic, ethnic, spiritual unity, of the natural, native bonds of the nation (*natus, natio*), which grind to dust everything that is not a kin of the ruling kind and genus (*Geschlecht*). He dreams of a nation without nationalist or nativist closure, of a community without identity, of a non-identical community that cannot say I or we, for, after all, the very idea of a community is to fortify (*munus, muneris*) ourselves in common against the other, to draw ourselves together (*com*) in a circle against the other.[2] His work is driven by a sense of the consummate danger of an identitarian community, of the spirit of the "we" of "Christian Europe," or of a "Christian politics," lethal compounds that spell death for Arabs and Jews, for Africans and Asians, for anything other. The heaving and sighing of this Christian European spirit is a lethal air for Jews and Arabs, for all *les juifs*, even if they go back to father Abraham, a way of gassing them according to both the letter and the spirit.

I do not mean at all to suggest that the question of the Jew is an innovation of Derrida's more recent work. On the contrary, it has been there from the start—as early as the essays on Levinas and Jabès in the mid-1960s in *Writing and Difference*—and it has been remarked upon by several commentators. Although ultimately intending to delimit Jabès's valorization of the "book" in the light of *écriture*, it is striking how thoroughly Jewish Derrida's notion of *écriture* is in these early essays. Writing is what takes place in the absence of God, when God hides his face and stifles his voice. Writing has chosen the Jews, these uprooted, nomadic, place-less wanderers who live in the hope of a promise, who are the elect of the letter. But if the Jews are the people of the Book, of scriptures and commentaries, the poet, let us say the writer generally, is a more universal form of the Jew in the strict sense, *sans* the gravity of the rabbi, *sans* the strictness of a sacred hermeneutics.[3] The poet is a pagan compared to the prophet, and his texts are weeds and outlaws, released into the aphoristic, anti-encyclopedic, anarchistic freedom of writing, a hermeneutics *sans* the rabbinic constraints which shelter writing from the play (see ED, 99 ff./WD, 64 ff.). In "Ellipsis," signed by one "Reb Derrisa" (ED, 436/WD, 300), Derrida argues that, accordingly, writing does not move in a circle, theo-logically, encyclo-pedically, returning to its origin, but disseminates without return. But rather than mourn this lost origin, Derrida advises us to learn to love its nomadic play.

Susan Handelman makes a series of astute remarks about just how Hebraic an idea of *écriture* Derrida defends in these early essays.[4] Handelman, who reminds us that in French *écriture* also means "scripture," situates Derrida within a "rabbinic," scriptural tradition—as opposed to the logocentrism of the Christian and patristic tradition—for "the Jew [is] the carrier of the letter" (169). To be sure, "Reb Derrisa" is a heretical Jew and deconstruction is "the latest in the line of Jewish heretic hermeneutics." Derrida, she says, charges Lacan with "the sins against which the Jewish prophets have always inveighed: reification, pinning the signifier to the signified, idol-worship—or ideal-worship" (163). Handelman suggests that dissemination can be taken as a transcription of circumcision, as the mutilation of the phallus which cuts the transcendental unity of the signifier down to size (165).

But Handelman is put off by the Dionysian, Nietzschean tone of this antirabbinic rabbi, of this pagan "heretic hermeneutics." She misconceives Derrida's work as a subtle assertion of mastery (cf. PdS, 398–400/*Points*, 385–86), not unlike the "yes-laughter" in Joyce, from which Derrida distances himself (UG, 117–19/AL, 292–93), which would defeat in advance

every critic who takes him at his word about the dissemination of meaning (169), as an unrepentant prodigal son (175), and an advocate of a
wanton free play in which redemption is postponed and does not "come"
(174). One understands what has misled Handelman. For in the 1960s
différance makes a more Nietzschean than Levinasian impression upon us;[5]
différance looks like the free play of the forces, not a way of making ready
the coming of the *tout autre*; and one does not detect anything of the
prayers and tears of Jacques Derrida or of his religion, about which nobody knew anything. However understandable it may have been at the
time, such an impression is entirely dispelled by Derrida's later and profoundly prophetic characterization of deconstruction as justice—"I know
nothing more just" (FL, 46/DPJ, 21)—that we have been analyzing in the
present study. In these later writings, in which deconstruction has adopted
a more Levinasian and prophetic tone, Derrida returns to the question of
the Jew first adumbrated in essays on Jabès and Levinas He does so, not
precisely in the nameless name of the aphoristic, outlaw freedom of
écriture, which he would never deny—"I'm not saying nothing more
legal" (FL, 46/DPJ, 21)—but in the name of a nameless justice to come, of
a prophetic and Jewish passion for the impossible that impassions
deconstruction.[6]

In Part V, I want to follow the full sweep of both the figure and the fact
of the Jew in Derrida's work. The "figure" can easily become a way to
annul the fact, to metamorphosize it, disguise it, and, by a "gentleman's
agreement," to politely drop it from the conversation. Then we would not
need the *mohel* and his blade, and then we would side with Paul against
Peter, that is, with Christianity in "the great war between Judaism and
Christianity" (*Archive*, 69/AF, 31) over figural and literal circumcision.[7]
That, I think, is about as far as Derrida himself gets in 1984, something of
a year of circumcision for him, when he delivers two important addresses
to two international literary societies—"Shibboleth," which pursues Paul
Celan's notion of a "circumcision of the word," and "Ulysses Gramophone" (1984), which analyzes what I will call a "circumcision of the
signature" in connection with James Joyce (§16). Deconstruction can always be understood as a certain cut and hence as a certain circumcision,
and circumcision can be taken as another name for deconstruction, as a
figure for deconstruction. Still, it is only in *Circonfession* (1991), to which I
will turn in Part VI, that Derrida comes around to confessing more frankly
his Jewishness, his Jewish *alliance*, and to writing on his own circumcision,
in the flesh, not only the figure but the flesh of the cut, the one made in
El Biar in 1930. That more literal cut is the one we read about in *Mal
d'archive*, a 1994 presentation at a conference on Freud, which poses the
question: is psychoanalysis—and I will add here for the sake of provocation: is deconstruction—really a Jewish science (§17)? Is it to be accused
rather than being congratulated for being a Jewish science?

But all this needs to be situated within the framework of Hegel's lethal denunciation of the Jew, of the searing reading Hegel gives to circumcision as a self-destructive, castrating split from the spirit of beauty and truth. That determination of the Jew and of circumcision, which Derrida studied ten years earlier in *Glas* (1974), haunts all his work thereafter.[8] Hegel's "early theological writings,"[9] his hateful story of the religion of love and reconciliation, his veritable metaphysics of hate, seem to have mobilized Derrida's attempt to rethink circumcision and to twist free of Hegel's murderous bird of prey, to show the irreducibility of circumcision to castration (*Archive*, 69/AF, 31).[10] It set in motion his attempt "to think circumcision," as he says in *Ulysses Gramophone*, "from the possibility of a mark, of a trait, preceding and providing its figure" (UG, 121/AL, 293). So I begin with Hegel (§15). In between, a little organ music for the faithful, an edifying divertissement on deconstruction and Jesus the Jew.

This entire discussion, in turn, may be viewed as a propaedeutic to a study, in Part VI, of *Circonfession*, the work that has organized this entire reading, in which we finally learn of the prayers and tears of Jacques Derrida.

Resisting the Spirit of Hegel

The French word *glas*, meaning the tolling of a bell, derives etymologically from *classicus*, which refers to the bell that sounds the order of entrance (nobility first, commoners last), the order of rank, and hence the orderly classification according to kind and type, class and genus, the classy and the *déclassé*. *Glas* is a theory of types, like two columns of Pythagorean types.[11] In the one column, the System and the figures which are cut to fit the System, which fit into its categorial types, as opposed to the other column, the un-fit, the out of joint, the unclassifiable, the odd man out, or woman, or transvestite, the fragments, remnants, and rags, the System's detritus, its "shit" (*Glas*, 7b/1b), the flowery fags who get to taunt the System of *savoir absolue* from across the divide in column "b." (PdS, 360–61/*Points*, 349–50)

Hegel's searing, hateful portrait of the Jew, of the dung and the dungeon that constitute the torn and tormented Jewish soul, seem to haunt all of Derrida's work, before and after *Glas*. The rhetoric and the metaphysics of the Hegelian portrait of the Jew seems to commit deconstruction to a kind of anti-phenomenological or un-phenomenological analysis of everything that the Spirit expels and vomits, everything that the Hegelian spirit casts out as un-beautiful, un-reconciled, un-harmonized, untrue, and un-phenomenalizable.[12] That inassimilable fragment is the Jew, both the historical reality of the Jewish people—"his blood be upon us and our children" (Matt. 27:25)—and the phenomenological figure, the *Gestaltung* of a divided, ugly spirit.

Like Kierkegaard before him—the communication of whose thought with Derrida I am constantly pressing—Derrida is always trying to twist free from Hegel. But if Kierkegaard's reading of Hegel was motivated by a worry over what had become of Christian faith in "Christendom," Derrida is worried over what becomes of the Jew when everyone is Christian (and of the Arabs when the Jews line up with NATO, and so on, One + n). If Kierkegaard is worried about what becomes of faith once Christianity is declared a mere *Vorstellung* of the absolute truth, Derrida is worried over what becomes of the Jew once Christianity is said to be a representation of the *absolute truth*.

In *Glas*, now a relatively early Derridean text, Derrida undertakes a reading of Hegel in order to locate the place of the Jew in Christian Europe, the no-place, the place of displacement, the little pockets in which Jews are placed. Hegel undertook a powerful attack upon the Jews and this, God forgive us, in the name of love, a hateful defense of the religion of love over and against the hatefulness of the Jews. Love is the most ancient instrument of Christian polemics against the Jews, Christianity's most cunning and most effective weapon, and Hegel uses it skillfully, ruthlessly, even brilliantly, as the *point de départ* of his thought and as his first model of the *Aufhebung*. Hegel can be seen to culminate a tendency to put as much metaphysical and theological distance as possible between Christianity and the Jews, to attach Christianity as closely as possible to a Greco-European spirit and to detach it from the Jew, to view Christianity as spiritually Greek, not Jewish. Christians are all Greeks, not Jews. The Jewishness of Jesus for Hegel is something for the Spirit to surpass. The essential limitation of the empirical figure of Jesus is just that he is Jewish, humorless, wifeless and childless, still a child of Abraham, alienation, and the cut. That is why the empirical actuality of Jesus had to break up, in order to allow the Spirit to flow and leave Jesus behind, letting "Christianity" become itself, become Greek, beyond Jesus while letting the circumcised bury the circumcised. Viewed thus, Hegel represents the final triumph of the oldest dispute of all in Christianity, the one that defined and constituted what is today called Christianity, which goes back to Paul's dispute with Peter and the Jerusalem church, which, as everyone knows, was won by Paul.

In Hegel, the history of this consummately Christian Europe and the figure of this consummately European Christianity take the form of a philosophy of history and of the Spirit, indeed of *philosophy itself*, of an onto-theo-logicalization of the Christian spirit, of which the Jew is a negative moment. For even if onto-theo-logic was set in motion by Philo's attempt to read the Tanakh in the light of Greek ontology—something Heidegger resolutely ignores, since the history of Being must be *Judenrein*—it soon became the dominant philosophical tradition of Christian Europe. Derrida writes:

> Consequently, even before wondering whether the ontological project was first a Greek event from which Christianity would have developed an outer graft, one must be certain that, for Hegel at least, no ontology is possible before the Gospel or outside it. (*Glas*, 67a/56a)

Or again, "The truth of Christianity [for Hegel] is philosophy" (*Glas*, 73a/62a).

Hegel, who supplies a veritable encyclopedia of Christian Europe and a logic of European Christianity, organized his first presentation of this idea around "love." On Hegel's scheme the "Jew" not only clings to a historical religion replaced by Christianity, to an old law replaced by love, but constitutes a philosophical type, the very figure of alienation from love. The Jew is stone cold and heartless, an Abrahamic figure who must prove himself capable of killing whatever he loves, and a legalist and pharisee, possessing only the outer shell of ethical life. Hegel's central speculative move is Pauline. Paul's struggle with the Law and the Scriptures and with the more Jewish-minded followers of Jesus took several forms: sometimes he said that Christians keep the Law itself, but not the human supplements of it; sometimes that Abraham was saved by faith, not the Law; and sometimes that the Law is for children and we are now grown up. But his best and most brilliant argument was that love is the *pleroma* of the Law, that love does whatever the Law commands but it does it without being commanded, and beyond that love does more than the Law commands (Romans 13:8–10).[13] *Pleroma oun nomon he agape*: love is an excess, a more, *au-delà*, the gift that does and outdoes the Law so that the Law is not destroyed but perfected. That beautiful and perfectly Jewish idea (Leviticus 19:18) was used by Paul with decisive effect against the Jewish Christians to put the Law in its place, and thereafter to put the Jews in their place, a displaced place from which they have never been able to escape. Under the sway of Paul, the *pleroma* of love was turned against the first, more conservative, more Jewish-minded followers of Jesus back at Jerusalem, who attended synagogue and practiced circumcision and who subsequently disappeared from Christianity without a trace. By the time of the Gospel of John, Paul's line had decisively won the day for a certain Christianity, for what today *is* what we know as Christianity, which has fixed the place of the Jew to this day.

Now "love" is a notion that yields quite marvelously to a dialectical interpretation, and provides a paradigmatic example—what is an example of what?—of the way something (here the Law) can be affirmed in its essentials, negated in its particulars, and raised up into something altogether higher and more perfect (love). This higher economy of love is too difficult and confounding for the squinting eye of the understanding (*Verstand*) to reckon with, for the understanding only understands one-sided and opposing parts. But in love the self gives itself up to the other only to get itself back again, raised up and recognized by the other: that is a matter for *Vernunft*'s reconciling knowledge of the whole (*Glas*, 25a/18a). That makes Christian love and Christianity itself the logic of history, of freedom, of the Spirit, and it makes the Jew historically, philosophically, and theologically a figure of unfreedom and alienation—stuck in the mud of ritual and literalism, and in the blood of the *mohel*—and politically a figure of perdition, guilty of the perfidious execution of the Man of Love who came to liberate us from alienation, that is to say, from Jews. That is the type, the stereotype, that Derrida follows with care and alarm in the left-hand column of *Glas*.

The Religion of Love

"I begin with love" (*Glas*, 12a/6a).

Love is a family value. In *Glas* Derrida takes the "family circle" as the paradigm of the dialectic, as the "conceptual matrix of the whole systematic scene to come" (*Glas*, 66a/55a), for the family is the circular economy that engenders an other that is the same. Derrida asks, "Is there a place for the bastard in ontotheology or in the Hegelian family?" (*Glas* 12a/6a). Where will deconstruction take its stand—with the family or with the bastard? Is it possible to break out of, to exceed, this family circle? Is there a bastard, an Ishmael, a family secret, in onto-theo-logic (and who is the bastard and who the legitimate son, Isaac or Ishmael?), that ontotheologic has sent packing? When family circles tighten, what happens to everyone else? Is there a more open-ended model that exceeds the family, an instant of excess that tears up the circle of the family? So Derrida is interested in family trouble, not a little unlike the sort of tensions that appear in the New Testament between Jesus and his family, not to mention the scandalous suggestion of Jesus' own illegitimate birth.[14] That should also trouble the Christian right wing today, which has gotten it into its head that the New Testament is the Bible of family values, a hammer it uses quite ruthlessly to smash public programs that assist unwed mothers and their children—in the name of what right-wing extremists call "Christian values," that is, in the name of love.

Hegel situates the loving Christian family on the side of *Sittlichkeit*, the concrete ethical substance that is thick with life, that pulsates with living, worldly, historical and social practices, as opposed to Kantian *Moralität*, which is formal, abstract, other-worldly, barren, dead, desert-like and—in a word—Abrahamic. So Kant is a Jew, plays the Jew to Hegel's *Sittlichkeit*, occupies the place of the Jew and is situated in a Jewish site.[15] *Sittlichkeit* is living *agape*, the spirit that quickens, and *Moralität* is the dead letter, the law that kills, that has to prove itself ready and willing to kill—*donner la mort!*—what it loves the most. Kant is a bachelor who cannot accommodate the concept of the family; the family is not a genuinely metaphysical concept for him, but a mere bit of anthropological chitchat, at best the way beings of pure reason pass their evenings. The whole idea of "family" is accidental, like a bastard, in the Architectonic of Pure Reason (*Glas*, 13a:i/7a:i). *Sittlichkeit*, on the other hand, begins with the family, and the family begins with love, so that the movement from *Moralität* to *Sittlichkeit* is set in motion by love. The family is the first and most immediately concrete embodiment of love; the family is felt love, a natural unity, the first stage of love on the way to becoming spirit and to relieving love of its naturalness.

The family, Derrida says, is "marked twice" by Hegel. It is not only a part of the dialectic but an emblem, a metonym, of the whole speculative movement, the very way a thetic paternity sublates itself by passing through its other and issues in the child, whom the father "raises" (*élever*) and lifts up (*aufheben*), in whom the father is negated and preserved. The upward circling of the Hegelian eagle keeps repeating the family circle (*Glas*, 27a-28a/20a-21a). So Derrida's focus on the family is not just a "pedagogical" device! (*Glas*, 21a, 22a/13a, 15a) The family is the very way the spirit goes outside of itself precisely in order to remain within itself (*bei sich sein*) all the more perfectly, so that in the end the spirit is free, is all and all, free because there is nothing outside itself.

The Spirit's engendering of itself is an extended family scene. The System is a story of a certain Holy Family. The way in which the human father produces his son is an "example" on the finite scale of the self-engendering of the infinite spirit, which cannot be an example (*Beispiel*) of anything, since it is the all-encompassing, exemplary play itself (*Spiel*). God is not a case or an example of the *Aufhebung*. "God is the infinite, exemplary, infinitely high *Aufhebung* itself" (*Glas*, 38a/30a). God is not an example unless God himself were to make an example of himself, unless—Christianity's stroke of genius—he were to send his Son into the world and make an example of him and to make him an example, an *imago* of the Father for all to imitate and follow. In Christianity, the infinite transcendent Spirit takes a particular, finite form, which then breaks up in its empirical being in order to let infinite spirit break out in every human spirit. The Spirit is neither the Father nor the Son, but the element of their love. Christianity is the speculative, Trinitarian religion par excellence, a *Vorstellung* of absolute truth, even as Hegelian philosophy—this is what set Kierkegaard's teeth on edge—is the philosophy of religion, the philosophy of Christianity, par excellence, that point where religion dies as *Vorstellung* in order to be reborn as *savoir absolue*, to spread its wings as philosophy and truth (*Glas*, 40a/32a).

Derrida then turns to Hegel's *Spirit of Christianity*, for the transition from *Moralität* to *Sittlichkeit*, from a still too natural finite and divided spirit to true and infinite spirit, is enacted in the transition from Judaism to Christianity, which is the "advent of love." That is also the transition from Jewish families to Christian families, i.e., to the true family, the family itself (*Glas*, 42a/33a-34a). Indeed, on Hegel's telling, how could there ever be a Jewish family, if the family is love? A Jewish family would have to be a matter of right and duty, not of love. For example, duty does not forbid the desire of marital infidelity, but only the outward deed, but the love that Jesus opposes to the law suspends even the desire to be unfaithful, so that if one loves one does not even want to be unfaithful even in the most secret recesses of one's heart (*Glas*, 42a/35a).

What then would a Jewish family look like? That is quite a story as Hegel tells it. Once humanity dwelled in peaceful, immediate harmony with nature, but when nature unleashed her fury in the great flood, man found it necessary to break this immediacy and to arm himself against nature and become its master. Noah represents this "noetic" distance, and his ark the first act of technological mastery meant to hold in check nature's fury, which itself lured man into building a famous tower at Babel. To these Jewish hostilities with nature, Hegel opposes the spirit of Greek beauty and reconciliation, glimmering temples sparkling under the Aegean sun and over blue Mediterranean waters at the foot of the cliff. But the Jew is ugly and lacks this spirit of beauty. That is why the Greek is closer to Christianity than is the Jew.

The Jews are the people of the cut, of separation and distance, of alienating division, and it is in the cut that they are born. Hegel writes:

> The first act which made Abraham the root-father of a nation (*Stamm-vater einer Nation*) is a splitting (*Trennung*) which snaps the ligaments of communal life and love (*die Bande des Zusammenlebens und der Liebe*). The entirety of the relationships in which he had hitherto lived with men and nature, these beautiful relationships of his youth (Joshua xxiv.2), he spurned. (cited in *Glas*, 49a-50a/40a)

Upon which Derrida comments:

> The Jew does not love beauty. Suffice it to say that, nothing else, he does not love. (*Glas*, 50a/40)

Abraham is a wanderer, errant, rootless, homeless; he wanted to be free and independent by maintaining himself in strict opposition to every earthly love. His family is constituted and maintained by this cut, the physical emblem of which is inscribed in his body in circumcision. The lines of force in Abraham's world are those of master and slave, command and blind obedience:

> He can tame nature only by contracting a relation with the infinite mastery of an all-powerful, jealous, violent, transcendent master, the God of the Jews.

He understands force and violence, not love. "He could not even love his son" (*Glas*, 51a/42a). He had to prove that he could kill this son whom he loved, kill the love, so that the love would not be master. Circumcision is a simulacrum of castration, in which Abraham cuts himself down before the law of God and cuts himself off from every finite good, so that he was circumcised not only in his flesh but in his spirit and "heart" (*Glas*, 53a/44a). The cut of circumcision for Hegel destroys the human spirit and leaves it alienated and self-dirempt. Being ready and willing for the cut, for this self-destruction, is what made him the father of his family, of a nation that will enjoy the special privilege of being God's chosen, a cut apart, a separate, favorite clan only so long as they remain true to their slavery before their "transcendent, jealous, exclusive, miserly, presentless god" (*Glas*, 54a/44a). Their privilege is to be the favorite slave of a distant master. The Jew is dead, and he makes everything he touches dead and ugly like himself; he petrifies everything he sees and turns his own heart into stone. The Jewish operation is apotropaic: to ward off castration by castrating oneself in advance.

Having turned his heart into stone, Hegel holds that the Jew is thus structurally incapable of having a family or having a familiar relationship with his God. How could a Jew ever call God *abba*? How could a Jew ever desire to be free? Even the great story of Exodus does not touch Hegel's heart, since Moses did not desire true freedom but just another place of seclusion for his people. How could a Jew understand art or the concrete symbol? Even the soaring heights of Jewish poetry, the psalms or the "Song of Songs," is for Hegel nothing more than further testimony to their crushed spirit, another failed, impotent effort to express the infinite in the finite (*Glas*, 58a/48a). When it comes to Jews, Hegel does not take any prisoners. They are incapable of incarnation, of giving sensible form to the supersensible, of letting the infinite shine with beauty in finite figures, for beauty is the way the invisible makes itself visible, palpable, felt. They lack the Greco-Christian spirit of love and beauty. They despise the idol because they are incapable of appreciating the sensuous embodiment of the infinite. The Jewish family is organized around an empty tabernacle, a signifier without a signified, like a hearth in an empty house, a hole that contains nothing, veils over a void (*Glas*, 59a/49a); there is no "real presence" on their altars, but only absence, a secret zero, the vacant center of a soulless national spirit.

It is also because the Jew is incapable of mediation, of seeing the infinite in the finite, that the Jew cannot be a citizen. Hegel cites with approval Mendelssohn's observation that the Jewish religion provides no eternal truth but only the Law. The Law is not truth but a command, not the manifestation of the infinite in the finite, not the presence or parousia, the bursting into unconcealment of the transcendent in the immanent, but a distant, empty, contentless imperative. There is no freedom here, no spirit in the world, no true *polis* that embodies political reason, no political subjects with rights who recognize themselves in the whole, but only violence, imperative, the rule of the master over the slave. That is the difference between Moses and Solon, between the Mosaic law and the laws of Athens. Jewish life is an economy of expropriation, where ownership is cut off and everything is on loan, a system devoid of civil rights and family property and laws of inheritance, which are canceled in the year of the jubilee. The spirit struggles in vain to make itself seen or felt in the Jewish world, which is empty and "pharisaical," a world which is unable to "schematize" the invisible and the visible, lacking the living spirit and given over to the dead letter and external form. Moses did not succeed in raising the Jews, in lifting them up in an *Aufhebung*. In Deuteronomy 32, Moses said God leads the Jews the way the eagle lifts up her young, carrying them on her wings to teach them to fly. But Hegel defaces this beautiful image by saying that this eagle by mistake warmed stones which, incapable of life, could only fall to earth. With hearts made of stone, how can Jews fly?

Only the Christian spirit can take flight, only the Hegel/*aigle* soars.[16] Jesus, who is the becoming un-Jewish of the Spirit, is lifted by the principle of freedom as opposed to the Law. When he cures a man with a withered hand on the sabbath to the consternation and outrage of the "pharisees," that is a work of the heart and love as opposed to external law. The Sermon on the Mount fills (*erfüllt*) the prescriptions of the Law, but relieves (*relève, aufhebt*) the Law of its legality and so provides the fulfillment (*Ausfüllung*) of the Law. There are in fact few better "examples" of the Hegelian matrix, of the process of *Aufhebung*, than the move Paul made on the Law, that with Jesus the letter of the Law is lifted but its spirit is fulfilled. The move that Paul made on the Jews adumbrates the move that Hegel would make on Kant, and indeed the very advent of the absolute into conceptual form. The Sermon on the Mount is a "historico-speculative event" (*Glas*, 69a/58a) that utterly confounds the Jewish mind (*Verstand*), which moves only within the grooves of opposition and is incapable of understanding reconciliation (*Vernunft*). With Jesus the principle of the *pleroma* appears, the principle of the excess of love, and this replaces the law of commerce by which cold and hardened Jewish hearts are ruled. For the Jews know only the bloodthirsty equivalence of an eye for an eye, the closed economy of a blow for a blow, of equalized castration. The *pleroma* overcomes the hypocrisy of the pharisees who do their praying in public and who are grabbing with their left hand what their right hand renounces. Love replaces the Law with the spirit of forgiveness, and it replaces the pharisee with the publican who confesses his sins and strikes his breast.

However perfect love may be relative to the Law, Hegel says, love must beware of dissipating into pure subjectivity; love needs an object and objective form. At the Last Supper, which is a love feast, Jesus leaves the disciples with an objective expression of his spirit and of their solidarity and friendship, the bread and wine, around which the rock of an objective, institutional embodiment of the spirit of love is to be formed. Religion requires something lasting. That is the role of Peter, the Rock (*petra*, *Petrus*), who is given the role of leadership and this precisely because he is able to recognize the infinite in the finite. At that point his name is changed, Simon became Peter, becomes un-Jewish, for the Jews are defined by Hegel by their structural incapacity to recognize the immanence of the infinite. That, too, is why the Jews are incapable of metaphor, for they are unable to recognize finite likenesses of the infinite (*Glas*, 86a / 73a). There are for Hegel evidently no metaphors in the Jewish scriptures. "Like the deer that yearns for running streams, so my soul is yearning for you my God"—that is not poetry for Hegel. Hegel's Jews are incapable of having families or poetry.

Hegel is particularly interested in John's gospel of love and in the becoming un-Jewish of John's Greek *logos*. John's love of the Jews is even more legendary than Hegel's. John has Jesus say to the Jews that their father is the devil (John 8:44), literally demonizing them and turning them into bloodthirsty killers, which feeds the springs of Christian antisemitism for two millennia.[17] In saying *en arche estin logos*, John strains against his Jewish limits, Hegel says, for he remains in the mode of a predicative assertion, of parts outside parts, still dividing things off (*ur-teilen*) from each other, and so he has not yet advanced to the reconciliatory work of speculative thinking. John attempts to mediate God and man in the medium of light (*phos*) and life (*zoe*) and to effect this reconciliation in the notion of the "children of God," becoming part of God's family, for that is what we are named, John says, and that is what we are. The expression "son of God" or "child of God" is a Jewish notion, Hegel concedes, and one of the few natural and felicitous expressions to be found in the Hebrew language. It is, however, a notion that no Jew could ever fathom and still remain a Jew (*Glas*, 92a–93a/79a–80a). For the relationship between father and son is a speculative one: father and son pass over into each other, inasmuch as life engenders the other as the same and the same as other, and the two do not remain separate, isolated existences. That is a *skandalon* to Jewish *Verstand* and its logic of finitude. Jews obviously then do not understand their own language; they understand only master/slave relationships, not father/son relationships, and someday they will certainly be grateful to Hegel for explaining their language to them by translating it into German. (Someday!) The Jews are spiritually children, religiously puerile, because they cannot get as far as divine childhood and sonship, because they cannot think the speculative unity of father and son; they take scandal in Jesus and insist that calling God one's father is no more than an image. The infinite spirit, Hegel says, speaking of/in a Spirit of Love, can never find a home in the *Kot* (dirt, mire, dung) of a Jewish soul, in such a dungeon (*Kerker*) (*Glas*, 99a/84a–85a).

The Jews were bound to wreck Jesus' attempt to give them something divine. The greatness of Peter, who thereby ceased to be Jewish, was to have within him the divine spark which recognized the divinity of Jesus. In Peter, light reaches out to light, for faith is the resonating together of beings of the same *Wesen*, the likeness of light and light. It is necessary for Jesus himself to break up his empirical, bodily unity, in order to let the light and the life of the Spirit stream into everyone, wherever two or three gather together in his name, lest his own empirical reality block the light. Jesus himself, in his empirical actuality, is still too Jewish, too much a son of Abraham and the cut, defeated by Jewish politics, wifeless and childless, separated from his family, setting son against father, daughter against mother, leaving his disciples with an empty grave. Jesus himself is a little too Jewish and not enough of a Greek. So the Spirit pushes beyond Jesus toward Christianity, the Christian church and community, which is Greek and not Jewish. But insofar as Christianity is a religion, the absolute truth still in the form of a *Vorstellung*, it still repeats the Jewish cut, Jewish alienation and opposition. The Christian religion requires philosophy, the concept, Hegelian thought, in order finally to lift the Spirit into absolute truth and so to relieve the Spirit of the Jew (*Glas*, 106a/92a), in order to let the Spirit take flight like an *aigle*.[18]

♦ *Edifying Divertissement No. 5.*
Deferring Incarnation—and Jesus the Jew

A word about incarnation, and Jesus, and about making incarnation too palpable. While the organ plays and we pass the hat.

Glas provides an ironic gloss on Hegel's early theological writings, a faithful and close commentary upon Hegel's texts which exposes the violence of the Hegelian schema simply by reproducing it. By presenting in the most loyal and literal way just what Hegel says, Derrida shows that in Hegel love is a code word for hate, a way of hating Jews for opposing love, that Hegel's denunciations of the Jew's castrated heart is a heartless, hateful castration of the other, that Hegel's hymn to beauty is a very ugly indictment of the Jews. So Hegel's early theological writings are whitened sepulchers, reproducing the very pharisaism which they denounce in the name of love.

But like all the French philosophers of his generation Derrida is not trying simply to negate Hegel, to throw him into reverse and produce the opposite of Hegel, to oppose him with his opposite, for the System verily feeds on such opposition. To negate and oppose Hegel would only be to out-Hegel Hegel, to out-dialecticize him, to let Hegel pass over into something higher in which Hegelianism is negated, preserved, and raised up, which would only be to lay the laurels on Hegel's brow one more time. Derrida is trying rather to invade, displace, and dislocate Hegel, to nudge him off his absolute pins, the result being a version of deconstruction as another Hegel, as an *other* Hegel and an *other* more sensible *Sittlichkeit*. For deconstruction will always be a certain quasi-Hegelianism, a certain way the System is read with infinite care and then released anew, mimicked, mimed, and bent up, repeated with a difference, with a different difference, one in which the quasi-principle of *différance* exceeds the self-enclosing, self-engendering trinitarian dialectic, the metaphysics of *mondialatinisation* that is lethal to Jews and other non-Greco-Euro-Christians. The letter that results in a misspelling of *différance* aims to break the spell of the Spirit and to let the play of differences be the model or the motive of a porous and self-differentiating democracy to come that outplays and exceeds the System.

Like Kierkegaard and Levinas, Derrida is trying to let Hegelianism be inwardly disturbed by the *tout autre*. However, if Hegel takes himself to be on the side of incarnation and Christianity, what about the Incarnation itself, capitalized, i.e., what about Jesus?

Like Kierkegaard, Derrida is alarmed by the Hegelian-Christian model of incarnation, the phenomenalization of the infinite in the finite, making the infinite palpable, visible, letting it shine as the *Erscheinen* and *Schönheit* of infinite *Sein*. Kierkegaard regarded that as paganism, which means Greek, for he regarded the Greeks as amiable pagans, too beautiful and innocent to appreciate the human capacity for evil, i.e., to be Christian. If you cut Christianity off from father Abraham and make it Greek, Kierkegaard held, you destroy Christianity. Kierkegaard insisted that the divinity of Jesus was completely invisible and impalpable. You would not catch sight of the divinity in Jesus by way of a certain bearing Jesus had, a certain divine air about him, a certain divine way he had of cocking his head or stretching out his hand, a certain divine twinkle in his eye, a divine gait. That is a paganism that annuls faith; the divinity was affirmed only by faith, which does not see a thing, *sans voir*. Is this not the carpenter's son? Nor did Kierkegaard think that Jesus was a cue for everything to be divinized, for at that point at which everything is divine and everybody is a Christian—the pleroma and parousia of Hegelian Christendom—everything about Christian faith, as far as Kierkegaard is concerned, would be cheapened, would, if we may say so, have gone to hell. Kierkegaard found it necessary to defer the visibility of divinity in order to make room for faith.

Like Kierkegaard, Derrida wants to preserve the alterity of the *tout autre*. Derrida is alarmed by the tendency to take some finite form as the embodiment of the infinite, to give the infinite particular form, not because he is against the body or the flesh or finitude or carnal life, but because he fears giving finite forms an infinite warrant, which scares him half to death. For that would always be a *determinable* infinity, somebody's infinite, somebody's God made man (*sic*), Paul's, for example, or John's, a very finite Infinite that is definitively defined. Somebody always is invested as Infinity's spokesman (*sic*) here on earth. The ecclesiastical powers summoned by Constantine and seated around the table at Nicea invest themselves with divine authority to carve out finite formulae for the faithful to repeat every day, *ad infinitum*—at the risk of automation—that precisely defined this infinite become finite. These incarnations are always liable to enter into a lethal alliance with the power of some Constantine or other, with some imperial political power or other, at which point they pass from a sectarian belief into an imperial religion and the blood begins to flow in the other direction, so that hereafter it becomes consummately dangerous, downright life-threatening, *not* to be a believer in the God/man. For it never seems to fail that when God becomes man he becomes man among *us*, right here in Greco-Christian Europe, even in Prussia or, God forbid, in California. Whenever he speaks, he speaks to *us*, in our language, in Greek or Hebrew or Arabic, which endangers everybody else. Then the world divides into those who happened to be standing in the right place, or living in the right time, or speaking the right language, when the God came, when the divine thunder struck—and those poor chaps who were not so lucky. The world divides into the "faithful," who are blessed by luck or providence, *o felix culpa*, and the *gentiles*, the *goyim*, everybody else, the unlucky and unblessed, those against whom the community fortifies itself.

Derrida resists *identifying* the messianic, for the time of the Messiah is the time of an absolute future, of a future to come, of an *à-venir* that is structurally futural, so that deconstruction is an operation that keeps the future structurally open and structurally unknown, *non-savoir*, an operation of the most exquisite Jewish patience and passion, *la passion du non-savoir*, of waiting for a promise to be filled that is *always* to come. Were we to come upon the Messiah, dressed in rags, we would still have to ask, "when will you come?" Derrida wants to defer and delay the parousia, to hold it off. (*Don't* come!) The whole idea of deconstruction is to deprive *ousia* of its prestige, to expose the present to what is not present, to keep it open to what is to come. To affirm the divinity of the living present, to affirm that the fullness of life has come, that the parousia is here, is very dangerous. The pleroma of the living present, of life without death, would be a living hell for Derrida. Derrida wants to shelter and preserve the *tout autre* as *tout autre* and not to let it get embodied or localized or drawn into the present, to let it take a present, exclusive, and determinable form; he resists the claim that the *tout autre* has come, which would mean that now everyone must fall in line. For then the *tout autre* would become somebody's private property, or they would become its private property, the special people of the *tout autre*, the chosen people, or the people of God, or the people of destiny, the people that God or Being has all along needed. As if the *tout autre* took its stand with Jews and against Egyptians (whom the *tout autre* is out to drown!), or with Christians and against Jews (upon whom is placed the guilt of slaying God's beloved Son), or with Greco-Germans who are owned by the *Ereignis* while everybody else wallows in *Seinsverlassenheit* or *Gottverlassenheit*, or with-and-against anybody else.

Take your pick.

But what about Jesus? The offertory hymn is half over. I pray you, be patient. Do not be too quick.

The whole point of the *tout autre* in deconstruction, the cutting edge behind this idea, if it is an idea, its burning passion, is a messianic one, to keep the system open, to prevent the play of differences from regathering and reassembling in a systematic whole with infinite warrant, and to take its stand with everyone and everything that is rejected and expelled by this omnivorous gathering, everything that is disempowered by all this power, with everyone who suffers at the hands of this gathering power, with all the detritus and excrement of the System. Everything about the *tout autre* in deconstruction is destroyed if the *tout autre* is made present, if it can be made to serve as an infinite warrant for the present, which means for the "same," for the powers that be, the powers that are presently in place, for the *ousia* and *parousia* of the same. The very idea that the *tout autre* would warrant the present reign of power, that it would line up behind the power of the present, is wholly terrifying to Derrida, a *mysterium tremendum* in the worst sense, a terrifying reign of terror that scares the daylight out of deconstruction, not to mention Jacques. The searing irony of Derrida's almost literal paraphrase of Hegel is to make plain the terrorism of parousiology, the terrorism of Hegelianism, to show the terror of taking one's beliefs and practices, one's language or one's history, one's own event as God's advent on earth. God forbid! *Don't* come. Don't let coming be reduced to becoming present. As Blanchot says, the Messiah's coming should never be confused with presence ("*sa venue ne correspond pas à une présence*").

All of which, I am claiming, bears witness to the highly messianic and prophetic passion of Derrida, for the prophets always have the same line, that the present order is precisely what is unjust and that the task that faces us is to let justice come, to make justice come. God does not desire our cults and our sacrifices, our religions and our Councils, our long robes and ecclesiastical authorities, but justice. And justice is always to come. Justice—for Derrida and the prophets—is always a matter of addressing the injustice that is structurally generated by the *current system* of justice, that is built right into the current regime of presence, the present law, which is always the rule of the "same." The prophets are always saying that the rule of the "same," of the present order, is unjust, and that justice is to come. Kierkegaard's most powerful intuition, the thing he was right about all the way down, was that the God of Abraham and Jesus could not *possibly* be on the side of the System, of the whole, of the Temple, of the mainstream powers that be. That was a stupidity—a paradox and a *quia absurdum est*—against which everything within him, everything biblical and prophetic within Kierkegaard, rightly revolted, everything he found revolting!

But what about Jesus and the Incarnation?

I would say, at the risk of a provocation (DM, 53/GD, 49), in the earnest hope of giving still more scandal to deconstruction's secularizing friends but not less to the Christian faithful, neither of whom will take this as good news, that Derrida's prophetic passion and distrust of incarnation is also very close to Jesus the Jew. For Jesus showed the same prophetic distrust of long robes and religious power, and the same—shall we say divine?—predilection for the disempowered and displaced, the outsider and the marginalized. His "kingdom of God" did not mean that the Absolute had come down to earth and been expressed in the one true *Begriff*, which is explained in the works of German philosophy; or that the Absolute has come to found the One True Church and that his Vicar now sits on the throne at Rome, the very idea of Roman thrones being likely to send a chill down his Jewish spine. His kingdom was an ironic kingdom from the point of view of Roman power and Roman kingdoms and Roman thrones, for it meant that God rules precisely among the powerless and the disenfranchised, the little ones and the nobodies, the homeless and starving, the lepers and the lame, that is to say, all the victims of Roman—read worldly—power. God rules not in Rome but in the victims of Rome. God rules not in the churches but in the inner cities which the churches abandon as soon as the Sunday contributions fall off. God rules not in respectable upper middle class mostly white suburban families but among the unwed mothers and fatherless children of the inner cities whom the churches, perfidiously in league with the right wing, teach us to resent and despise as lazy freeloaders. Where the kingdom rules, the tables in the temple, the councils of the powerful wherever they are to be found, are in trouble.

God rules among the "Jews," all the jews, *les juifs*. That sort of talk about a kingdom of those who are crushed by worldly kingdoms, about the power of powerlessness, eventually got Jesus killed, which is a predictable prophetic fate, the one thing that prophets can always prophesy with certainty. He was killed, not because the Jews were so spiritually coarse as to be incapable of recognizing the infinite in the finite, but because Rome understood that this was a politically explosive and subversive message. Nietzsche also saw that Jesus' message was subversive, that it tends to empower the powerless, a point that Marx missed entirely, so that Marx missed a revolutionary possibility and chased away one ghost too many, a prophetic one. Nietzsche did see this but he sided with Roman power and he decided that the powerless should stay put in their slavish impotence, keep to their smelly hovels, and let the forces fire, let the will to power glow in all its shining *Schönheit* among the few and the best.

The movements of the *tout autre* in deconstruction inch it closer to the prophets than to the "church" and "religion." The *tout autre* always means the one who is left out, the one whose suffering and exclusion lay claim to us and interrupt our self-possession, our *bei-sich-sein*, our sense of being on God's side, of occupying the privileged site where God became man. But that does not pit deconstruction against the kingdom of God, against the kingdom to come. On the contrary!

Nor do the movements of the *tout autre* pit deconstruction against the good news of love. Rather the *tout autre* makes love safe from Hegelian and from Christian blackmail (if you are against either, you are against love, against freedom and the good news). In deconstruction love is extricated from the polemic against the Jews by being rethought in terms of the other, of *les juifs*, for is not love "this infinite renunciation which in a certain way *gives itself back to the impossible*?" (*Sauf*, 91–92/ON, 74). Love is said to be a certain *Gelassenheit*, a way of letting the other be. If this organic Hegelian Christian-European community is defined as making a common *(com)* defense *(munis)* against the other, Derrida advances the idea of love as laying down his arms, *rendre les armes*, in surrendering to the other. Derrida has no interest in a pure dutifulness, but in a responsibility without duty, a *devoir* without guilt, where one gives not because one must or ought, but with and from an excess beyond duty. That is a very different sort of thing than Hegel's metaphysics of the loving Christian European family—indeed, it is more like loving the bastard—one that resists to the core the Hegelian gesture of *identifying* a *national* family and a national spirit, for the spirit of this national identity is lethal to everyone else, to everyone who is not a member of the family. Deconstruction (as its critics have said for some time now) is for bastards! ("Who is my mother and my father?")

Nor does the dynamics of the *tout autre* pit Derrida against a certain *Sittlichkeit*, one which turns particularly on the conventionality (*ethos*) of the law, on the provisionality of the *Sitten*, of the social structure, the deconstructibility of the *droit*. In Derridean *Sittlichkeit* everything depends upon *resisting* the very idea that the current *ethos* is God's advent on earth, God's birth among us, which would be a consummately dangerous thing to believe. For at that point at which some form of *Sittlichkeit* would be treated as God's incarnation, the difference between justice and *le droit* would collapse, and the law and the constitution would take on divine warrant. On the contrary, in deconstruction the rule of law is taken with an endless distrust, I would say with an infinite, with a divine mistrust. For if a social structure really did have divine warrant, to whom could we entrust its direction? How could that not be violent? The passion for justice in deconstruction means to keep an eye out for the *me onta*, for the exceptionality of the singular, for the one who is not an individual case of a universal principle, but a singular claim of justice to which the law is blind. That means that Derrida disturbs Hegel's reading of the story of Jesus healing the man with the withered hand on the sabbath, which Hegel turned into a piece of anti-semitism. That is a very beautiful and thoroughly Jewish story, which Hegel makes ugly by making it into a way to treat Jews as insensitive legalists. The story is an example of what is said in Leviticus 19:18, that you should love your neighbor as yourself, which is the tradition in which deconstruction stands when it says that the law must be deconstructed in the name of justice.

So what about Jesus?

The irony of Hegel's hateful depiction of Christian love is its systematic ignorance that Jesus' *abba* spirituality is as Jewish as can be, that it belongs to a prophetic and ethical tradition which is entirely Jewish and was so regarded by Jesus, whose prophetic idea was to get Judaism to shape up and become what it is, as Vermes and Sanders have abundantly shown, and had nothing to do with Vatican City! Beyond irony, it is tragic that the prophetic and ethical core of Jesus' thoroughly Jewish message was turned against the Jews. As A. N. Wilson put it:

> Were Jesus to contemplate the fate of his own people at the hands of the Christians, throughout the history of Catholic Europe, culminating in Hitler's Final Solution, it is unlikely that he would have viewed the missionary activity of St. Paul with such equanimity.[19]

If that is true, as I think it is, then Derrida's distrust of Greco-Euro-Christianity, Derrida's anxiety over the Pope's Christian politics, his fear of *mondialatinisation*, of the task of making Europe Christian, as if the Alps themselves were Christian formations, making Anglo-Euro-America what it "is," stands on the side of Jesus the Jew.

§16. *Circumcision*

Ten years after *Glas*, in 1984, something of a year of circumcision for him, Derrida mounts a powerful, shall I say incisive interpretation of circumcision that deeply disrupts Hegel's hateful portrait of the self-destructive, castrating cut at the heart of the Jew's ugly soul. His two major addresses to international literary associations—"Shibboleth," a contribution to an international Paul Celan symposium, and "Ulysses Gramophone," his address to the James Joyce International Symposium—are readings of Celan and James Joyce that are not far removed from Jeremiah and Levinas. In these works Derrida treats circumcision as the cut that opens the word or the heart or the ear to the other, to the *tout autre*. Circumcision is the cut that ruptures the sphere of the same, that cuts down the *conatus essendi*, that cuts off closure and opens our heart to Elijah knocking at our door, in accord with Jeremiah's call to be circumcised in our heart. On such an account, deconstruction *is* circumcision, the cut that opens the space for the incoming of the *tout autre*. Circumcision is the cut that says yes, "the same phoneme (*Ja*) makes the cut and the opening coincide" (*Psy.*, 650/Number, 132). Jahweh, the Cut, the Separate One, is the Opening of the yes. That is about as un-Hegelian a reading as one could mount.

This argument, however, cuts both ways. For however sound and even biblical a view to take of circumcision, it raises two problems. (1) Even if it is a good spin to put on circumcision, it is nevertheless a slightly paradoxical point to make. For circumcision gives every appearance of the opposite, of an exclusive (and exclusively patriarchal) point of entry into a self-enclosing community, a mark or trait setting the Jew apart, a cut apart, chosen, cut off, and purified from the *goyim*, the guard (*munis*) stationed around (*com*) the community to protect it from the other, which is why circumcision is framed in one piece in terms of the "shibboleth." (2) By advocating a circumcised word or heart, has Derrida not drifted over to the side of Paul and Christianity, for whom it was enough to be circumcised in one's heart, the rite of peritomy being a little too literal for the religion of the spirit of love? Has he not allowed the singularity of the Jew to slip away? So Derrida has his work cut out for himself.

The Circumcised Word

"Shibboleth," a Hebrew word which literally means a fresh-water stream flowing into the sea, was used as a test by the Gileadites in Judges 12:4–6 to detect the fleeing Ephraimites, who could not pronounce the *sh* sound—it always came out *si*—which would have earned them safe passage across the Jordan. So a "shibboleth" is a simple diacritical difference that can spell the difference between life and death, an identifying, idiomatic mark—the lack of which cost some forty-two thousand Ephraimites their lives. There was nothing secret about the word. The Ephraimites well knew what they were supposed to say, and they even knew how to translate it. But they just could not pronounce it. Their tongues were tied. It was almost something physical, like a mark or a wound on their tongues, like someone had cut out a part of their tongue. There was no question of uncovering a deep semantic secret, revealing a hidden meaning, solving a riddle, or explaining a hidden sense, it was simply a superficial diacritical difference. A shibboleth is any arbitrary mark that discriminates, a mark inscribed on a body or a tongue that is radically idiosyncratic and idiomatic, singular, untranslatable—since it concerns the phonic surface of the word and not its semantic content—and unpronounceable, inaccessible for the other, cut off from the other, who is not able to share it (*pouvoir partager*) for it must be inscribed in one's body, in the body of one's own language (*Schib.*, 51/WT, 29).[20]

A shibboleth marks the difference between belonging and not belonging, exploiting both senses of *"partage"*: both "participation" in and belonging to the community (of Gileadites, e.g.), and of being set apart, set off "apart," as a separate part, not-belonging (on the part of the Ephraimites). Derrida's essay turns on this duality, on what he calls the "double edge of a *shibboleth*," which is the context in which, at the end of the essay, he frames the discussion of circumcision and of the Jew:

> One may, thanks to the *shibboleth*, recognize and be recognized by one's own, for better or worse, in the *two senses* of the word *partage*: one part (*d'une part*), for the sake of the partaking and the ring of the covenant (*d'alliance*), but also, the other part (*d'autre part*), for the purpose of denying the other, of denying him passage or life. (*Schib.*, 111/WT, 67–68; trans. modified)

A shibboleth is thus a two-edged sword; it cuts both ways: to include the included but also to exclude the excluded, to gather life into a circle of community and also to deny life and passage. That means that whoever lives by the sword of the shibboleth may die by it, that a shibboleth may be turned against its bearer, against the Jews, for example. For circumcision is a shibboleth, "a rite of passage, which seems to mark the legitimate entry of the Jew into his community and which takes place . . . but once alone, on a specific date: the circumcision" (*Schib.*, 97/WT, 58). That can be turned against the Jew: and circumcision cuts both ways:

> [T]hen it is the circumcised who are proscribed or held at the border, excluded from the community, put to death, or reduced to ashes: at the mere sight, in the mere name, at the first reading of a wound. (*Schib.*, 111/WT, 68)

Derrida's remarks on circumcision are inscribed within a study of Celan, a poet "of" the Holocaust, spewed forth by the Holocaust, the celebrated German-Jewish poet writing "after Auschwitz." At Auschwitz, circumcision, the mark of *alliance*, of the covenant (which, in Hebrew, means "cut"), was a mark of no passage, no escape for the deportees, an idiosyncratic mark inscribed upon the surface of Jewish flesh that marked them inescapably for death.[21]

It is the lethal mark the shibboleth makes that draws Derrida's attention. Is there a way out of the double bind of the shibboleth, which would also mean, out of circumcision? What will protect us from being the victim of this double edge? "Nothing," perhaps, speaking very precisely: make *no* mark. Perhaps, one might simply cease the particular practice of circumcision, efface "this *determinate* mark" (*Schib.*, 111–12/WT, 68), but this pre-cision about circum-cision, about particular determinate marks and incisions, "would not reduce the demand to nothing." For circumcision as a general trait, an archi-circumcision, if you will, the demand for a differentiating mark, for a mark of difference, for an idiosyncratic and idiomatic mark, for an inscription of singularity, for a proper name, my own name, given to me, at circumcision or baptism, for example, is not to be reduced or denied: "There must be circumcision" (*"il faut la circoncision"*), but with a difference.

> There must be circumcision, circumcision of the word, writing, and it must take place once, precisely, each time one time, the one time only. (*Schib.*, 112/WT, 68)

Apart from, prescinding from, precising from, the literal practice of peritomy, there is the cutting of the letter, the circumcision of the word. For Celan, that would always be a poem, a poetic cut. The word or idiosyncratic mark, which as *écriture* is already a cut, an incision, an inscription, can itself be cut, incised, opened up, as opposed to serving as a way to cut off the other. The demand for circumcision cannot be denied but it can be cut, itself circumcised, its exclusionary powers cut off, so that whatever fate befalls one's prepuce, one can be circumcised in one's heart, as Jeremiah said (Jer. 9:25–26), which is, in my view, precisely how Derrida is glossing Celan's circumcised word.

Commenting upon a poem by Celan which uses the German word for circumcision in the imperative form, *"diesem / beschneide das Wort,"* "for this one / circumcise the word," Derrida says, "we may understand this word as an opened word" (*Schib.*, 102/WT, 61). The circumcised word is opened, like a door, to the stranger, to the other, to the guest:

> Like a wound, you will say. Yes and no. Opened, first of all, like a door: opened to the stranger, to the other, to the neighbor, to the guest, to whomever. To whomever no doubt in the figure of the absolute future

(the one who will come, more precisely who *would come*, for the coming
of this future, *the one* to come, must be neither assured nor calculable) . . .
   A word opened to whomever in the figure as well, perhaps, of some
prophet Elijah, of his phantom or double. . . . Elijah is the one to whom
hospitality is due, promised, prescribed. He may come, one must know
this, at any moment. He may cause the event of his coming to happen at
each instant. (*Schib.*, 102–103/WT, 61–62)

Elijah—which is also Derrida's secret Jewish name, as we learn in *Circonfession*—is not only the messianic prophet, the prophet of the one to
come, he is also the one who must be present at all circumcisions, so that
the one who holds the child to be circumcised in his arms sits on "Elijah's
chair." "TO ONE WHO STOOD BEFORE THE DOOR, one / evening: / to him /
I opened my word," Celan writes. The one who stands before the door,
on Derrida's gloss, is Elijah, the guest, the stranger, and it is to him that
the poet opens his word. He opens the door by opening the word to the
other. To open the door, to open or offer one's word to the other, that is
to open one's heart: "circumcision would be *just* this (*justement*), this
decision of the word, its sentence, inscribed right in the body, just in the
heart, *precisely*" (*Schib.*, 108/WT, 65–66; cf. *Schib.*, 15–16/WT, 6). Circumcision, the circumcised word, is justice, and a justice to come, which cuts
the *conatus essendi* down to size ("a little off the top"). I would then use
my shibboleth for the other, not hold it over his head like a sword. This
shibboleth marks me for the other, bids me give him passage through the
door, let him in or out, not block his way. That would be the guard, if
there is any, against the two-edged sword of the shibboleth: to circumcise
the word, to drain it of its killing powers, to make of it a word of opening
to the other, to the one who is to come, to Elijah, whose arrival we must
always expect. The guard against the shibboleth of circumcision is a certain circumcision of the shibboleth, an incising of its exclusionary, killing
power.
   The circumcised word, Derrida says, "must take place once, precisely,
each time one time, the one time only" (*Schib.*, 112/WT, 68). Of this time
he writes:

   This time awaits its coming, as its vicissitude. It awaits a date, and this
   date can only be poetic, an incision in the body of language. It remains
   to come, always. How are we to transcribe ourselves into a date, Celan
   asks. (*Schib.*, 112/WT, 68)

Circumcision happens once, on the eighth day, and only once, that is its
appearance, for it is also coming again and will return. That brings us back
to the thematic of the "date" in Celan, a thematic which on Derrida's
reading corresponds, quite precisely, to that of the proper name. For even
as the date is a way to mark off an unrepeatable singular event, a one time

only, *une fois, einmal*, "once," still the date is possible only in virtue of a code of iterability or repetition, a coded system or grid, which enables us to make such a mark, and hence to repeat the unrepeatable; that iterability incinerates the singular, turns it to ash (*Schib.*, 76–77/WT, 46–47). In the United States, the "Fourth of July" is not only the date of some singular event in 1776 but a "constellation" of all the "Fourth of Julys" ever since the first one as well as of all the ones to come. These are all concatenated in an anniversary ring (*alliance*) (also the French word for the covenant) of all the repetitions of that unrepeatable date, an annulation (*annum*) which annuls the idiosyncratic singularity even while affirming it (*Schib.*, 11–15/WT, 3–6). So the unrepeatable, which only comes once, is not only repeatable but is also the trace of something coming, of a date to come. "What coming and singular event is in question, what unrepeatable event?" (*Schib.*, 15/WT, 6). Who knows? God knows. *Je ne sais pas.* The poem links me beyond knowledge to what is to come:

> "I don't know," *je ne sais pas*, signals a situation. In what I have elsewhere called its *restance*, remnance, the poem always speaks beyond knowledge, *au-delà du savoir*. It writes, and what it writes is, first of all, this very fact, that it is addressed and destined beyond knowledge, inscribing dates and signatures which one may encounter and bless, without knowing every-thing of what they date or sign. Blessing beyond knowledge, commem-orating through forgetting or the unimparted secret, partaking yet in the unimpartable. (*Schib.*, 64/WT, 37)

For Celan, as the poet explains in "Meridian," the poem is the blessing and memorializing of the singular event, and as such is a shibboleth, an idiomatic word for an idiosyncratic event. In "Che cos'e la poesia?" Derrida speaks of the poem as "a certain passion of the singular mark," a passion for singularity and for the singular trace, the absolutely idiomatic, which is *stricto sensu* impossible (*Points*, 296–97). For, despite the way it is riveted to a date, to the singularity and alterity of an event, the poem speaks to everyone, to the other (*Schib.*, 21/WT, 9), for the idiom belongs to a system of reiteration and there can be no pure idiom (PdS, 213/*Points*, 200; PdS, 390–92/*Points*, 376–78). The poem always recalls the date on which it is written—whereas philosophy wants to "render itself universal" and to ef-face the date and the traumatism of its singularity—and the date of which it writes, for the other who does not share this singularity (PdS, 392–93/*Points*, 378–79). The poem writes (*schreiben*) "of or about such dates" (*von solchen Daten*), and then, by a slight twist, Celan may ask: "To which dates do we ascribe ourselves?" (*Welchen Daten schreiben wir uns zu?*): to what "future of unknown destination," to what date to come (*zu, à*), to what promised date or revolving of the ring, do we address ourselves? "What is this to come—as date?" (*Quel est cet à de l'à venir—in tant que date?*) (*Schib.*, 21/WT, 10). So for Derrida the thematic of *viens* and *venir* can be thought in terms of a *date* to come. The poem speaks thanks to the date and despite the date. If the poem owes itself to, is due to, its date, to its secret, it also releases itself from the date, so that it may resonate beyond its singularity (*au-delà de la pure singularité*) (*Schib.*, 23/WT, 11), for otherwise it would remain mute and unrepeatable, mired in its singularity. Poetry is not history, not a constative record of historical events but a poetic performance (*Schib.*, 86/WT, 51–52). By effacing its singularity, the poem does not turn into a generality but refers itself to another date to which it speaks and with which it is strangely allied and wed, by a "secret chance," a date which turns out to be a "date *with*" (an idiom we have in English, if not in French) the *stranger*, let us say rather, the other (*Andere Sache*), and, "who knows, perhaps of a *ganz Andere*" (*tout autre*). (*Schib.*, 23–24/WT, 11–12).[22]

Circumcision, the circumcision of the word that opens the word to the other, happens once, even as it also awaits its coming, its *venue*, and has a date to come to which we assign ourselves. By the date of circumcision, Derrida says, we do not mean some date appointed for circumcision, like the eighth day, or some point in the history of Judaism when circumcision became law. The circumcision of the word is not some date in history, but rather what gives rise to or calls forth, *donne lieu à*, the date:

> It opens the word to the other, and the door, it opens history and the poem and philosophy and hermeneutics and religion. Of all that calls itself—of the name and the blessing of the name, of yes and no, it sets turning the ring, to affirm or to annul. (*Schib.*, 112/WT, 68)

The Circumcised Signature

In "Ulysses Gramophone" Derrida takes up the question of circumcision in the context of an analysis of Joyce's *Ulysses*, of the *yeses* in *Ulysses*, in the course of which he argues for a "circumcision of the signature" that very closely parallels the circumcision of the word in *Shibboleth*.[23] For circumcision is a yes, and this *yes* is inscribed deep within Joyce's "signature," indeed within every signature that is, if I may say so, worthy of the name. Once again the entire analysis is implicated in a distinction between *two* circumcisions and, this time, even between two Elijahs.

In a Postscript to the French text (UG, 122) which was, alas, cut off by the editor's blade ("a bit off the top"), so that the English text is just a little circumscribed and circumcised, Derrida explains the force of the *yes* in a way that—for the first time that I can find in Derrida's text—openly associates the *yes* with a prayer, with *amen*. We have been all along contending that the *yes* belongs to the prayers and tears of Jacques Derrida, that it has a religious resonance and the force of an elemental religious word. There can be a *oui sans mot*, Derrida says, a *oui* without word, and that is because *oui* is not so much a word as a silent companion to words, a quasi-word which provides words with their element and force. To explain this, Derrida refers us to a text from Franz Rosenzweig's *The Star of Redemption*, in which Rosenzweig describes the "yes" (*Ja, oui*) as a primal word of language. Now Derrida himself must beware of any *Urwort*, not only because he does not want to think of language as built up out of words, but above all because he cannot allow any master-word to dominate the play. For that would have a hyper-Heideggerian effect of organizing language around the gathering and all-unifying center of a master-name. So whatever quasi-*Urwort* he may associate himself with, and whatever primal force he may attribute to *oui, oui*, it must be such as to promote disseminative plurality rather than to allow language to circle its linguistic wagons.

Be that as it may, the elemental power of *yes* of which Rosenzweig speaks does not mean that *yes* is a basic element out of which propositions are composed, or even that it is a *part* of a proposition or of language at all. Rather, *yes* makes words and sentences possible to begin with. For Rosenzweig, *yes* is "the silent companion of all the parts of a sentence, the confirmation, the *sic!*, the 'Amen' behind every word. It gives every word in the sentence its right to exist, it supplies the seat on which it may take its place."[24] *Oui, oui* is the amen that opens and closes every word and sentence, that punctuates and spaces them, that indeed gives rise to (*donner lieu*) language itself, from which language arises, and which constantly accompanies every event of language. Although this makes *yes* sound a little like Kant's transcendental *ich* accompanying every representation, it is better to think of *yes* as "*amen*," which is itself like—if anything can be—God, like the infinite and creative affirmation of the world by God whose "let there be" this or that is a performative utterance to end all performative utterances, or rather to start them all up, to start everything up, and to restart them (UG, 144/AL, 309), to let things be, to affirm and sustain them. So the best way to think of *oui, oui* is to think of a great and sweeping *amen!* to the world and to language, and, beyond that, to think the *oui, oui* of deconstruction in reference to *Yah-weh*'s *Ja*, to the divine *oui, oui* which lets things be.

Such an amen is what Derrida finds in *Ulysses*, a yes that is coextensive with every sentence in the work, so that the whole thing is a continuous yes: yes, it's me, I am speaking, yes, it's you, you are receiving, hello, yes, we are speaking, there is language (*il y a du langage*), yes, it's happening (*ça arrive*), it's written, marked, *oui, oui* (UG, 124/AL, 297). The determinate word "yes" does not address itself directly to things but to other words, so that it runs throughout the length and breadth of language, linking its elements, weaving them together. That does not lock us up inside language but opens us to the other. Yes, I say yes to the other, even when I say "no," or even when I address the other without speaking. A tap through a prison wall: I, here, hear, listen, answer, there is some mark, there is some other: that is a yes that no "no" can erase. Being, language, self are all derivative of this yes, which means there is no metalanguage in which we can speak of yes, since this metalanguage would presuppose the event of the yes. That is why you would never be able to calculate or program the yes. "Yes indicates that there is address to the other." The *yes* is the affirmation that the other does not let itself be produced by the same or the ego. It is the condition of any signature or performative; it addresses itself to the other which it does not constitute and it begins by asking the other to say *yes*, but this is in response to a request that has *already* been made (UG, 126–27 / AL, 298–99).

I said that Derrida must beware of turning *oui, oui* into a transcendental in the strong sense, of letting it become the alpha and omega of language, for that would be precisely to draw language into a circle, to encircle and encyclopedize it, to close it off, to circumscribe things in advance in a way that would be entirely at odds with deconstruction. For such a transcendental encircling would constitute a certain circum-vention of the event, a cutting off in advance of the *viens* and *à-venir*, which is why deconstruction can never have to do with anything more powerful than a *quasi*-transcendental, one that sets loose by making possible, that makes possible by breaking things up and breaking them open. Now this encircling, encyclopedic, circumscriptive, circumscribing, transcendental effect, this circumvention which cuts off the future and the im-possible event, is itself an image of circumcision, or rather circumcision, a certain circumcision, is an image of such a cutting off. That is one sense of circumcision that Derrida marks off and sets in opposition—*sans* a pure cut, this is not a clean incision—to another sense of circumcision, one which breaks the hold of the circle, which cuts the cord of closure, of circumscription and circumvention and has the effect of opening things up.

Derrida says that he considered entitling this lecture on Joyce "Circumnavigation and Circumcision" (UG, 105 / AL, 285), that is, circumcision as an Ulyssean circle, a completion of the circle, a missive (*envoi*) sent out and returned safely home again, close to itself, like the Hegelian Spirit, which reappropriates and re-turns from its *tour* around the Mediterranean Sea. That is the figure of Ulysses Derrida learned from Levinas, where Ulysses is aligned with Hegel and set off from father Abraham who sets out from the land of Ur never to return. That would be to distinguish two kinds or figures of circumcision, between, if I may say so, a Ulyssean, circumnavigational circumcision, which closes the circle of the same, and an Abrahamic circumcision, which cuts the cord of the same in order to be open to the other, circumcision as saying yes, yes (even without a word) to the other.

That indeed is just the distinction that Derrida draws in this gloss on Joyce, which he aligns with two different figures of Elijah—the prophet of what is to come, and the patron and protector of circumcision (not to mention Jacques's secret Jewish name)—in Joyce's *Ulysses*. The first figure is Joyce's image of Elijah as a figure of "polymathic competence or of telematic control," as a vast telephone network through which all information must pass, a comprehensive, encyclopedic system, which is what the "Joycean institution," the international establishment of academic Joycean studies, wants to be (UG, 106–107 / AL, 285–86).[25] The other figure of Elijah is of the guest, of the knock at the door, of the one whom we all await, having set a place for him at the table, Eli-*jah* as the figure of the other who is to come, to whom we say *yes, yes*.

Joyce's *Ulysses* represents a certain literary "phenomenology of the spirit" (UG, 66 / AL, 262), a certain totalizing, encyclopedic collection of the totality of experience, "the sum total of sum totals," to which "the totalizing hermeneutic that makes up the task of a worldwide and eternal institution of Joyce studies," with endowed chairs (the Elijah Chair of Joycean Studies) and a departmentally funded computer (UG, 105 / AL, 285), seeks to make itself the match. But this totalizing hermeneutic must confront what Derrida calls the tonality of laughter (*rire*), or of yes-laughter (*oui-rire*), which Derrida can hear. Derrida can say yes (*oui dire*), can hear yes being said (*ouir oui*), so that there is a yes heard (*oui oui*) and said, a hear-say (*ouï-dire*), a hear-say yes-laughter (*ouï-rire*), and this yes-laughter traverses Joyce's signature (UG, 115 / AL, 291). There is a "double tonality" of two laughters (UG, 116–17 / AL, 291–92), corresponding to the two Elijahs, which will also correspond to the two circumcisions, shall we say (Derrida does not), to two circumcised ears (cf. Jer. 6:10).

(1) With one ear he can hear—his terms are highly Nietzschean here—"a reactive, even negative yes-laughter resonating" in Joyce. This laughter rejoices in a "hyper-mnesic mastery" that remembers everything, collecting and recollecting all, a Joycean re-joicing in spinning spider webs, in making itself impregnable to any approach. This laughter would precontain, preprogram, and precomprehend any of the strategies that the Joycean institution might address to the corpus. No computer, no science, no scientific consciousness can master it; the calculations of consciousness would always be in the service of this master signature, even if they mocked it. Joyce would laugh at this tour de force of the Joycean Institution, at Ulysses's grand tour and re-tour. But this would be a laughter of "resigned lucidity," of a merely phantasmic omnipotence. For Joyce cannot *not* know that his book of all books is just one more book in the Library of Congress. And he himself will never be free of the objection that *Ulysses* is too precious, overcalculated, overcultivated, overloaded with knowledge, hyperscholastic, too subtle, which will perhaps even have foreseen being censored and have calculated that into its success (UG, 117–19 / AL, 292–93).

There is too much control by a subject in this yes-laughter; it is too cynical, sardonic, derisive, taking on everything, the whole of memory, the sum of summarizing. This laughter is even, Derrida suggests, too much like Nietzsche's Christian-Judaic donkey that wants to *circumcise* the Greek of his innocent and beautiful laughter and then make him laugh with this other, bitter laughter of resentment. For this is a literature of summing up, of the sum of all sums, of the *ja, ja* to everything, of taking on the encyclopedic burden of everything, a literature of debt, of the "(A E) I O U," a literature of shouldering *(Schuldigsein)*. "This yes-laughter of encircling reappropriation, of omnipotent Odyssean recapitulation" laughs at the generations of Joyce scholars which it puts in its debt; it impregnates "in advance its patented signature . . . with all the counter-signatures to come." It is "ready for anything, ready to domesticate, *circumcise, circumvent* everything" [emphasis mine] in encyclopedic reappro-priation of absolute knowledge, which gathers itself up close to itself (UG, 119–20/AL, 293–94).

Circumcision, *this* circumcision is here circumscribing, en-cyclopedic encircling, circumscripting, circum-venting the event of something new, enclosing and closing off, and hence a Judeo-Christian castrator, which cuts off in advance, which contains and precontains, whatever counter-signature is to come. This circumcision castrates and cuts off, "a bit off the top."

(2) But this laughter is "worked or traversed, I prefer to say *haunted*, joyously ventriloquized by a completely different (*tout autre*) music," a music of the *tout autre*, "by the vowels of a completely different (*tout autre*) song," a song of the *tout autre*. This Joycean laughter re-joices differently and sings a different song, not that of indebting the other (AE-I.O.U.). He can hear this too, this "yes-laughter of a gift without debt, light affirmation, almost a-mnesic, of a gift or an abandoned event . . . a lost signature without a proper name" (UG, 120/AL, 294). So if the first laughter belongs to a signature that would draw itself into a circle, protect itself and keep itself safe and impregnable, that would jealously protect its proper name, a signature that seems to want to sign the name of God, of a self-affirming, jealous *Yah-weh* of absolute comprehension and precomprehension, this other signature would tear up this circle and give a gift, would disperse and break itself up, would lose itself in giving itself over to innumerable and unforeseeable counter-signatures to come. This signature sees that omnipotence and absolute reappropriation are phantasms which it delimits:

> . . . and does so only to contrive the breach necessary for the coming of the other (*à la venue de l'autre*), of an other whom one can always call Elijah, if Elijah is the name of the unforeseeable other for whom a place

> must be kept, and no longer Elijah, the great operator, Elijah the head of
> the megaprogramotelephonic network, but the other Elijah, Elijah the
> other. . . . Elijah can always be one and the other at the same time; we
> cannot invite the one, without the risk of the other turning up. But this
> is a risk that must always be run. In this final movement, I return then
> to the risk or the chance of this contamination of one yes-laughter by the
> other, to the parasiting of an Elijah, that is to say of a me, by the other.
> (UG, 120–21 / AL, 294–95)

We always run the risk of the one yes-laughter contaminating the other,
of inviting one Elijah while it is an other Elijah who shows up at our door.

In this other yes-laughter, this yes to the other, circumcision cuts a
different figure. Circumcision here is much more like Jeremiah's circumcised heart, or the circumcised ear which has an ear for and opens to the
other. It is much more a Levinasian incision into the circle of the same
which opens up the same or self to the *tout autre*. Thus, the difference
between the two yes-laughters, the division incising the "double tonality"
of laughters, between these two words of Joycean rejoicing, is a difference
between two circumcisions and two Elijahs. Derrida here marks the difference (in highly Nietzschean terms) between a negative, reactive, reappropriating, self-enclosing circumcision, vs. a light-footed, affirmative,
yea-saying *mohel* whose cut is made in order to affirm the other, *tout
autre*—like a Dionysiac rabbi.[26]

If, at circumcision, one is given a proper name—a good Jewish name
like Elijah—then the problematic of circumcision is also entwined with
that of the proper name and the "signature." Now the name of Joyce is a
giant proper name around which an international academic institution
has been erected with the stated goal of protecting that name, and it is a
name that is also protected by international copyright laws and the exec-
utors of a literary estate. But Joyce's "signature" is the "uniqueness" and
"the singularity of an event," an idiosyncratic inexhaustibility, an inex-
haustible idiom. To think the signature, it is necessary to think

> an irreplaceable mark that cannot necessarily be reduced to the phenom-
> enon of copyright, legible across a patronym, after circumcision. It is
> necessary to try to think circumcision, if you like, from the possibility of
> a mark, of a *trait*, preceding and providing its figure. (UG, 121 / AL, 295)

The legal, institutional, copyrighted name is a patronym that is given with
and follows upon circumcision, after circumcision, after a *certain* determinate circumcision, one that has not been opened up, one that gives not a
gift but a self-appropriating, encircling, jealous proper name. But we must
try to think circumcision otherwise, not as a determinate, Jewish rite but
in terms of the mark, the trait, the inscription, in terms of *archi-écriture*.
That is what Derrida called "the circumcision of the word" in "Shibbo-

leth," an archi-incision or archi-inscription which, preceding a determinable circumcision, makes possible the "signature"—of Joyce or Celan, of Ponge or Mallarmé. That inscription, that circumcision of the word, which opens the word to the other, opens the signature of Joyce to countless counter-signatures to come, to the invention of other Joycean events to come (UG, 99–100/AL, 282–83), beyond the ken and the horizon of expectation of Joycean *periti*. The circumcision of the word, of the signature, lets Joyce's text be an event that calls for the invention of the other, for the incoming of other events that sign and countersign what we naively call the First Event, for a new event, *un tout autre événement*, that says yes (even as this exposes the text to a mechanical and reproductive repetition). Only another event can sign, can countersign, and bring it about that an event has already happened. The "First Event" can only affirm itself in the confirmation of the other. So the other signs and the *yes* keeps restarting itself (UG, 143/AL, 309). The circumcision of the word or the signature inscribes Joyce's signature with a yes, a *oui, oui*, a yes-laughter:

> [I]f the analysis of this laughter is not exhausted by any of the available forms of knowledge precisely because it laughs at knowledge and from knowledge, then laughter bursts out in the event of the signature itself. And there is no signature without *yes*. (UG, 121/AL, 295)

The yes is more ancient than knowledge or any question of the form "'what is' the yes?"—even as the signature is more ancient than the legal patronym, and the circumcision of the word is more ancient than any rite, of however antique an age.

So there is a tension between the self-appropriating tendency of the signature as a proper name and a mark of legal ownership, which gives itself pleasure by surveying all that is its own, what Derrida calls the "phantasm of the signature," and what we will call here the "circumcised signature," which cuts open and divides the signature that wants to gather itself together:

> [T]he Ulyssean circle of *self-sending* commands a reactive laughter, a hypermnesic reappropriation, whenever a phantasm of the signature wins out, a signature gathering together the sending in order to gather itself together near itself. (UG, 136/AL, 304)

But the circumcision of the signature opens the circle:

> But when . . . the circle opens, reappropriation is renounced, the specular gathering together of the sending lets itself be joyfully dispersed in a multiplicity of unique but numberless sendings, then the other *yes* laughs, the other, yes, laughs. (UG, 136/AL, 304)

Circumcision, *this* circumcision—"of the word" (Celan), of the "heart" or the "ear" (Jeremiah), circumcision thought in terms of the mark or the trace (Derrida)—gives, gives gifts without debt, without exchange, gives the other, gives laughter, *oui, oui.*

Circumcision, after all, is another name for deconstruction.

* * *

In *Shibboleth* and *Ulysses Gramophone* circumcision is not the self-destructive castrating cut denounced by Hegel but the cut that breaks the bonds of the self-enclosure of the same and makes possible the in-coming of the other. These works explain how circumcision is not only or narrowly or precisely Jewish, a rite of initiation into a self-enclosed Jewish community, and how it can be translated, carried beyond Jewish borders. If circumcision is Jewish it is only in the sense that all poets are Jews (*Schib.,* 91/WT, 54), or inasmuch as the Jew is the witness to something universal, that spiritually we are all Jews, all called and chosen to welcome the other (*Schib.,* 92/WT, 54–55), inasmuch as every signature, even Irish Catholic ones or atheistic ones, must be marked by this Jewish cut, by circumcision, which is to be thought, beyond Jews and Irish Catholics, in terms of the *trait.* Everyone ought to have a circumcised heart; this ought to form a universal religion within the limits of a certain reason alone. Circumcision is Jewish only with an archi-Jewishness which is more than and no longer Jewish, *plus de Juif,* and which even adverts to annulling the physical rite which would be practically Christian and Pauline.

Shibboleth and *Ulysses Gramophone* help explain why Derrida's sons were not circumcised, as he confesses in *Circonfession.* But they do not quite come around to explaining his own circumcision, the prayers and tears in which the cut in his own flesh is bathed. They do not explain why he has not drifted imperceptibly to the side of Paul, for whom a circumcised heart would be enough and the cut in the flesh is an obstacle to God's work. By inserting circumcision into the ring of annulation, by saying that Jewish is not Jewish, its proper feature to have no property or essence (*Schib.,* 64/WT, 37),[27] that the affirmation of Judaism is formally analogous to the date, i.e., singular and self-annulling (*Schib.,* 90/WT, 53), in *Shibboleth*; by making circumcision into the mark of a trait that *precedes* circumcision, in *Ulysses Gramophone,* he risks annulling the singularity of the Jewish, erasing the Jew in *les juifs,* which is a complaint sometimes lodged at Lyotard. The task remains of affirming, of writing, his Judaism, in the midst of "Christendom," of *mondialatinisation,* of the Greco-Latin-Franco-Christian world in which he has been immersed—almost baptized—from the start, from the day they called him "Jackie." The task remains of "confessing" his participatory *partage* in the Jewish community, of allying himself with the *alliance,* of explaining his continuity with the alliance he has also broken, which is a peculiarly Jewish passion, the passion of his peculiar Jewishness. That is the work of confession reserved to "*Circonfession*," where Derrida undertakes to explain how he remains a Jew, "*sans continuité mais sans rupture*" (*Circon.*, 146/*Circum.*, 154), "today, in what remains of Judaism" (*Circon.*, 279/*Circum.*, 302–303).

§17. Is Deconstruction Really a Jewish Science?

At circumcision the newborn of God is spoken to even before he can speak, addressed by words he cannot understand, commissioned in advance before uttering a word of his own, "Go, read my Book that I have written." Has this not happened to Derrida? Has he not all along been responding to a promise made for him at birth, by sponsors who were responding and responsible for him? Has not that advance promise guided the hand of Derrida from a time out of memory?

All this talk in deconstruction about a messianic promise, about praying and weeping over something to come, about faith in something unforeseeable, does that not draw upon—even quite transparently—a Jewish archive? Is not deconstruction the way that Derrida has found, after considerable delay, to honor the spirit of his father, a case of "deferred obedience" (*nachträgliche Gehorsam*) to his father, who loved him with an everlasting love?[28] Is deconstruction not the product of a Jewish mind? Is not deconstruction the unique and idiomatic way Derrida has come to read the Book, to comment on the Book of Books, to which he was assigned by the mark of his circumcision, by "the impression left on his body by the archive of a dissymmetrical covenant without contract, of a heteronomic covenant to which [he] subscribed even before knowing how to sign—much less countersign—his name"? (*Archive*, 62/*AF*, 28).

Is deconstruction really a Jewish science?

This is precisely the theatrical scene that Yosef Hayim Yerushalmi stages between Sigmund Freud and his father, Jakob Freud, and the same line of questioning that Yerushalmi put to the dead Freud about psychoanalysis.[29] But in his most recent piece on circumcision and the Jew, *Mal d'archive* (1994), a reading of Yerushalmi's *Freud's Moses*, Derrida tells us, confesses, right in public, this is one more confession, one more circumfession, one more Augustinian work of "making the truth" from which the genre of fiction is not to be excluded (*Archive*, 95/*AF*, 40), that (again like Freud) "in speaking of a colleague, Yerushalmi, [. . .] I am speaking of myself" (*Archive*, 139/*AF*, 56).[30] Like *Circumfession* itself, which we will examine below, Derrida fesses up to his circumcision, shamelessly exposing the cut in his flesh, in public.

It is as if Derrida imagines himself dead, a mere specter of himself, and being addressed in a fictional monologue by some later interpreter:

Professor Derrida, at this point I find it futile to ask whether, genetically or structurally, deconstruction is really a Jewish science; that we shall know, if it is at all knowable, only when much future work has been done. Much will depend, of course, on how the very terms *Jewish* and *science* are to be defined. Right now, leaving the semantic and epistemological questions aside, I want only to know whether *you* ultimately came to believe it to be so.

Please tell me, Professor Derrida, I promise I won't reveal your answer to anyone.[31]

Or, less fantastically, less spectrally, has he not been asking himself this very question in the flesh for some time now? Does not this question roll across all the works of the last fifteen years or so? Has it not haunted him all along? Have we not been asking such a question of him throughout the present study, the question of the deal that has been cut in his flesh from of old, of the promise that was made for him before he was able to make a contract for himself? Is not Judaism the immemorial archive from which deconstruction has all along been drawing?

So, by following Derrida following Yerushalmi's adjudication of the question of psychoanalysis and "Jewish science," we hope to learn a thing or two about the parallel question of deconstruction and the deal that has been cut between deconstruction and the impossible.

The Root of All Evil

The word "archive" still houses within itself the memory of its root *arche*. The *arche* is the origin, the beginning, either in the sense of a physical, metaphysical, or historical origin, or in the nomological sense, the way the law is an *arche*. The archive, on the other hand, is not the *arche* but the trace of the origin, not the *arche* but the vestige or remainder of the *arche*, like a footprint left in the ashes at the foot of Mount Vesuvius that is discovered centuries later by an ardent archeologist. The illness, the disorder, the crisis, the evil (*le mal*) that besets a culture that depends on archives—*La malaise dans la culture* is the French translation of Freud's *Das Unbehagen in der Kultur* (*Civilization and Its Discontents*)—is for Derrida always a *mal d'archive*, always a function of a disorder in the relations between the *arche* and the archive, a failure to remember, as also a failure to remember the distance between the original and the trace. Learning to live with or in an archive, learning to lead healthy well-adjusted lives (if there are any) in an archival culture, avoiding archive evil (another way to translate the title) will in no small part consist for Derrida in conceding, confessing that the *arche* always slips away—*la chose même se dérobe* (VP, 117/SP, 104)—and we have always to do with archives, with traces, even with ashes.

It must be insisted that even as the archive is not the *arche*, neither is it a living memory (*mneme*, *anamnesis*) but rather the *hypomnema*, the supplement and prosthetic aid to memory (*Archive*, 26/AF, 14), a record or a mark. Evil reigns, *le malaise de la culture* worsens and the whole grows ill, when a confusion reigns between the archive and the living memory of the origin, when we no longer know how to negotiate the difference between the two, for "in the economy of these two words [is] the whole of archival law" (*Archive*, 44/AF, 21).

The archive has also come to mean the house, *arkheion*, where the records are stored, a house overseen by *archons*, the keepers of the house, the patri-archival powers that be who oversee the archive. That is why there is always the danger of a "politics of the archive" (*Archive*, 15–16n1/AF, 10–11n1), an "ethico-politics" (*Archive*, 38/AF, 19), which means the feverish control that is exercised by institutional authority, above all by the state, over archival materials, the politics of what we call in English the "official story." Political power requires control of the archive, the monitoring of memory, while democratization requires open access to the archives and the courage to recall "dangerous memories" (*Archive*, 15–16/AF, 10–11). In its most virulent form, archive illness means burning with a feverish desire to make one's own archive authoritative, normative, nomological, confusing one's own archive with an *arche* that is taken to be the law for everybody and to exercise absolute control over the archive of the other.

Such archive fever may be recognized by the claim that "we" are the exclusive depository, the uniquely chosen archive of the Truth. In that sense, the *mal d'archive* lies at the basis of every feverish racism, nationalism, fundamentalism, or messianism, at the root of every "identitarianism." Burning with the desire to kill off, to incinerate, the memory and the trace of the other, archive fever is not a finite, limited threat, not one threat among others, but an in-finite threat. Archive evil ranges over and infiltrates every evil, *engageant l'in-fini*, getting itself involved in everything. To cast Derrida's argument in Levinasian terms, Derrida is saying that, by flying in the face of the other, of the infinite one, of *l'infini*, archive fever touches upon radical evil (*mal d'archive touche au mal radical*); it tries to touch, to violate, the untouchable, and in so doing touches upon, verges on radical evil—a notion also addressed in "*Foi et savior*" (*Foi*, 86)—on the root of evil. In that sense archive evil, *mal d'archive*, is the root of all evil (*mal radical, la racine du mal*) (*Archive*, 38–39/AF, 19). *Mal d'archive: archive du mal*.

Circumcising Freud

By way of preparing us for a reading of the question Yerushalmi puts to Freud—is psychoanalysis really a Jewish science—Derrida provides us with two Freudian archives, two pre-archives of the archival matters he wants to discuss. This takes the form of two exergues, two preliminary citations or orienting inscriptions, one oriented more toward psychoanalytic science, the other more Jewish.

The first exergue, taking its point of departure from the discussion of the death drive in *Civilization and Its Discontents*, chapter 6, turns on Freud's account of the psychic system as a system of traces or impressions, an archival system, of traces kept and consciously recalled or remembered, in the conscious system, but more importantly of repressed impressions. The latter are experiences that consciousness buries, trying to kill off the memory, to burn it up or reduce it to ash. The system tries to efface the trace or archive of the experience, but only to have the quasi-memory return like a ghost (*révenant*), repeated in a distorted form (*répetition*), reappearing in a way that cannot be called memory or recall (*mneme, anamnesis*), triggered by some mechanism of repetition, some *hypomnema*, which substitutes prosthetically for a living memory. If Freud's reflections were aided by a childish model, a magic writing pad, Derrida wonders, how would they be revised in the light of the staggering complexity and sophistication of contemporary information retrieval systems like CDRom and of communication systems like "fax" and "email"? (*Archive*, 20–39/ AF, 12–19; cf. *Archive*, 47–51/ AF, 22–23) This latter query is the one point this discussion adds to "Freud and the Scene of Writing" (ED, 293ff./WD, 196ff.).

If the first exergue concerns internal imprints made in inner psychic space, the second example has to do with an external, albeit highly private mark, an archival mark made right on the skin, an inscription or a circum-inscription (*Archive*, 39–44/ AF, 19–21). Literally speaking, Derrida is referring to the mark made by Jakob Freud on his son Sigmund by two circum-inscriptions: the first, on the newborn's skin, when he handed Sigmund over to the mohel, and the second, thirty-five years later, *sous peau neuve*, in commemoration of the first, as if the first had not quite taken, when he gave, or returned, to Sigmund a childhood Bible, in a new binding (or skin), with a very beautiful inscription, done in *melitzah*, in which he dedicated or rededicated his son to God, again: Son who is dear to me, go read the Book, the Book of Books, which is presented to you as a memorial and as a reminder, both mneme, anamnesis and hypomnema, of your father who loves you with an everlasting love.

The son of his tears? Son whom he was afraid to ask if he still believed in God? Son who rightly passes for an atheist?

Interrogating the Specter of Freud

Like the rest of us, Derrida came upon this inscription as a result of the painstaking archival labors of Yerushalmi, who regards this dedication as a crucial document in the argument of *Freud's Moses* (cf. *Archive*, 39–44/AF, 19–21). Yerushalmi's archival work is by no means oriented solely or even primarily toward the past, but toward the future, and this is a point with which Derrida associates himself completely:

> It is a question of the future, the question of the future itself, the question of a response, of a promise and of a responsibility for tomorrow.

Not tomorrow but maybe later on, or perhaps never:

> A spectral messianicity is at work in the concept of the archive and ties it, like religion, like science itself, to a very singular experience of the promise. And we are never far from Freud in saying this. Messianicity does not mean messianism. (*Archive*, 60/AF, 27–28)

That futuricity or messianicity is what is at stake in the surprising "scene" that Yerushalmi stages at the end of his book, in his "Monologue with Freud," in which he addresses the ghost of Freud, a veritable dialogue with the ghost of Freud—"interrogating the specter of Freud" (*Archive*, 65/AF, 29)—that resembles the opening scene of Hamlet talking things over with the ghost of his father around which *Specters of Marx* is woven. A more objective, scientific observer (which is what we took Yerushalmi himself to be, up to this point) might wonder to whom he is talking. But not Derrida, for such monologues with ghosts is such stuff as culture and history are made of (*Archive*, 100–01/AF, 42). Yerushalmi is trying to make Freud confess, from his own mouth, that he belongs to Judaism. He wants to hear Sigmund's living voice ringing in his ears. In the place of Jakob Freud, in the name of Freud's father, Yerushalmi tries once again to circumcise Freud. Freud, "by definition, because he is dead," can no more refuse this *alliance*, this community and circumcision, than he could refuse the first (*Archive*, 67–68/AF, 30–31). How can he sign or countersign? What can he say? He is left speechless by Yerushalmi's query. (Is the silent Freud like a psychoanalyst who lets the patient do the talking? Who has the upper hand here? *Archive*, 100/AF, 42.)

Freud himself, of course, took himself (like Marx) to be an *Aufklärer*, a scientist (*Archive*, 63/AF, 29), a demystifier of religion, and so, one would think, it would be no small setback to him to have Judaism circle back and enclose him, to have what he took to be the universal, scientific structure of psychoanalysis end up as an idiom in a Jewish archive, to make the worldwide psychoanalytic movement he launched depend upon "the singular archive named circumcision" (*Archive*, 69/AF, 31). Is Yerushalmi trying then to kick off another version of the battle between Peter and Paul, of "the great war between Judaism and Christianity" (*Archive*, 69/AF, 31), about whether you would need to be circumcised to join the movement?

Yerushalmi attempts to extract this confession from the speechless Freud, first, indirectly, through the mouth of Anna Freud, and then from Freud's own words in private correspondence. Anna writes to the Hebrew University of Jerusalem, on the occasion of the inauguration of an endowed chair in Freud's name nearly thirty years after his death, that the "accusation" that psychoanalysis is a "Jewish science, under present circumstances can serve as a title of honor" (Y, 100; *Archive*, 71 / AF, 31). But was Anna speaking for herself or—like every good and dutiful daughter—for her dead, speechless father? Yerushalmi adduces two documents as evidence for his claim that Anna is a stand-in for Sigmund. First, a letter Freud sent to Enrico Morselli in 1926, in which he says that he would not be ashamed were it shown that psychoanalysis is a product of a Jewish mind. Then, Yerushalmi identifies a sentence Freud added in 1935 to the *Moses* book, which never made it into a published edition, in which Freud confesses his "deep engrossment" in the Bible story of Moses and its "enduring effect upon the direction of my interest" (Y, 77).

Now even if one were to concede, *concesso non dato*, that Yerushalmi has won this argument with his interlocutor—has Freud been made to speak or reduced to silence?—still Derrida thinks that the very scene of the monologue, the very "scene of reading," takes place in a space that Freud has himself described, that it reenacts everything that Freud has said about the agon between the father (Freud) and the son (Yerushalmi) (*Archive*, 107–08 / AF, 45).[32] *Freud's Moses* is itself a case of deferred obedience, of Yerushalmi's obedience to Freud, returning to the Bible of Freud's writings, identifying with him while maintaining his independence, in love / hate, lovingly asking for forgiveness for his hateful impudence to the father (*Archive*, 97–99 / AF, 41). Yerushalmi's "Monologue" has been running on like a patient on the couch, which is why, despite every appearance, the ghost does indeed speak.

The person in the position of Freud would always be right (which would of course also implicate Derrida vis-à-vis Yerushalmi or Freud),[33] would always get the last word, even if he is wrong, "materially" speaking. That is so in virtue of a "formal fatality" (*Archive*, 101–02 / AF, 42), a fatal repetition in which Yerushalmi is structurally implicated. *Freud's Moses* is inscribed in advance in the very archive that it sets out to scour, which is part of the general, formal structure of every archive and every reading.

With every word Yerushalmi inevitably adds to the prestige, the authority of the Freudian archive, augments and increases it inescapably by an unavoidable repetition. Still, despite the necessity of this "fatal repetition," despite his or our structural inability to dominate any archive, to get the best of it from some meta-archival point of surveillance and criticism, it is not Derrida's view that we are thereby condemned to the blind reproduction of the past. On the contrary, by continually producing more archive, the archivist lets the archive "open from out of (*depuis*) the future" (*Archive*, 109/AF, 45). Far from submerging us in the past the archive constitutes "an irreducible experience of the future," of a future to come, of *l'avenir, l'à venir*, as opposed to *le futur*, which is nothing but the future present (*Archive*, 109/AF, 45):

> The affirmation of the future *to come.* . . . That is nothing other than the affirmation itself, the "yes," insofar as it is the condition of all promises or of all hope, of all awaiting, of all performativity, of all opening toward the future, whatever it may be, for science or for religion. I am prepared to subscribe without reserve to this reaffirmation made by Yerushalmi. (*Archive*, 109/AF, 45)

(Or rather not without one little speck of a reservation, which is enormous and significant, to which we will return shortly.)

On Derrida's reading of Yerushalmi, the archive takes on a *messianic* dimension, once again in the spirit of Benjamin's *Theses on the Philosophy of History* which describe the "narrow door" through which the Messiah must pass. For the Jews the future is not a future-present but something radically heterogeneous with the present. For unlike a conventional archivist, Yerushalmi communes with ghosts, promises to keep his secret, and makes everything turn toward the future of psychoanalysis as also of Judaism, which lies beyond knowledge. In the end, the historian and archivist must always turn to the future, to a future unknowable not merely because we cannot predict it with certainty but because it is altogether outside the order of knowledge, belonging as it does to a sphere of affirmation, of faith and hope:

> The condition on which the future remains to come is not only that it not be known, but that it not be *knowable as such*. Its determination should no longer come under the order of knowledge or of a horizon of preknowledge but rather a coming or an event which one *allows* or *incites* to come (without *seeing* anything come) in an experience which is heterogeneous to all taking note, as to any horizon of waiting as such. . . . I call this the *messianic*, and I distinguish it radically from all messianism. (*Archive*, 114–15/AF, 47)

The messianic dimension of the archive, let us say, the messianic passion of an archive fever, is not a matter of feverishly keeping a record of the past and present, of which the future would be but the future-present, but the passion of a radical possibility, a radical *im*-possibility, unforeseeable and beyond the horizon.[34]

It is on this very point of the future that Yerushalmi is led to identify the one thing that is "most un-Jewish" about Freud. With all due filial respect, and after nervously clearing his throat, he dares to say to father Freud, the father of us all today:

> But it is on this question of hope or hopelessness, even more than on God
> or godlessness, that your teaching may be at its most un-Jewish (Y, 95;
> cf. *Archive*, 78–79 / AF, 34–35).

Deploying a distinction that, up to a point, resembles Derrida's distinction between the messianic and messianism, Yerushalmi differentiates "Judaism," the determinate historical religion and culture of Israel, including its belief in God, from "Jewishness." The latter notion Derrida glosses as "the opening of a relation to the future, the experience of the future" (*Archive*, 115/ AF, 48), "the affirmation of affirmation, the 'yes' to the originary 'yes,' the inaugural engagement of a promise or of an anticipation which wagers, *a priori*, the very future" (*Archive*, 118/ AF, 48–49). Even if the religion of Judaism may be terminable, even if religion may have no future, as Freud claims, Yerushalmi contends that the spirit of Jewishness, which is the spirit of the future, is interminable (Y, 90). Turning this distinction against Freud, who wrote off the future of this illusion, Yerushalmi claims that it is no less true that Oedipus has no future, that he is condemned blindly to repeat the past. Over and beyond his disbelief in the teachings of Judaism, in the existence of God himself, it is Freud's disbelief in the future, his obsession with blind necessity, that separates Freud from Jewishness and not merely from Judaism.

Up to this point I think that Derrida can cautiously associate himself with Yerushalmi's argument, so that one might hold that he is himself, that deconstruction, as an affirmation of the future, as a repetition not from blind *ananke* but "from out of the future," is Jewish without Judaism, messianic without messianism, which is why he says that in speaking of his colleague Yerushalmi he is speaking of himself (*Archive*, 139/ AF, 56). He subscribes to Yerushalmi's view "without reserve." Almost, up to this point. But these are dangerous distinctions, never clean cuts, whose terms have a way of curling around and contaminating each other.

In speaking of the spirit of Jewishness as an opening to the future Yerushalmi refers not merely to a hope for the future but to "the anticipation of a *specific* [my emphasis] hope for the future" (Y, 95), one that would be proper to the Jew alone. Yerushalmi is willing to give up on everything about Judaism—even God—"on everything save (*sauf*) on this trait which links Jewishness and the opening toward the future"—thus far Derrida, too, but then the crucial difference—"And, still more radically, on [everything save] *the absolute uniqueness of this trait*" (*Archive*, 118/ AF, 49). That hope is the Jews' very own, an absolutely unique deposit in the Jewish archive which this historian and archivist has unearthed, something the Jews exhibit "in an exemplary fashion." If you have it, you are Jewish; if you are not Jewish, you don't have it. Nobody else has it, not Arabs or Christians, not the natives of South America or Africa, not the Chinese or the Indians. Add to this what Yerushalmi says elsewhere, in *Zakhor: Jewish*

History and Jewish Memory, commenting on the fact that Yahweh reveals himself to the Jews in history, that the command to remember, the sense of memory and history, also belongs to Israel alone. So the Jews are doubly privileged, doubly chosen, doubly unique, having been uniquely assigned a memory of the past and the promise of the future. To be sure, the two privileges are one: it is because the word of God is engraved so deeply in the archives of the Jews that they are uniquely summoned to remember the future:

> As if God had inscribed only one thing in the memory of one *single people* and of an *entire people*: in the future, remember to remember the future. (*Archive*, 121 / AF, 50)

About this, even though he subscribes to what Yerushalmi says about the future "without reserve," Derrida would keep "a large number of grave questions in reserve." He would "tremble" before the uniqueness of this election, before the guard Yerushalmi is stationing around this *arkheion*, the protective shield (*munis*) around (*com*) the house of Israel to guard it against the other. He would tremble for justice, for justice is remembering, just as Yerushalmi says, and its opposite is forgetting. So then what about all the other "peoples" other than Israel?

> [I]t is no less just to remember the others, the other others and the others in oneself, and that the other peoples could say the same thing—in another way. And that *tout autre est tout autre* as we can say in French. (*Archive*, 123 / AF, 50)

The injustice here "concentrates its violence in the very constitution of the *One* and the *Unique*"—in forgetting the Jewish Numerology of "Foi et Savoir," of One + 1 (*Foi*, 85–86). Using language that transparently reproduces his critique of Heidegger—of "gathering" (*logos*, *Versammlung*) and "self-affirmation" (*Selbstbehauptung*)—Derrida writes:

> The gathering into itself of the One is never without violence, nor is the self-affirmation of the Unique, the law of the archontic, the law of *consignation* which orders the archive. (*Archive*, 124 / AF, 50)

Whether the archive is Jewish or Greco-German, the violence lies in its gathering into One, into one order, making everyone speak with one voice, claiming for itself exclusivity and privilege. If the Nazis tried to vilify psychoanalysis as "Jewish science," the remedy is hardly to make Israel a privileged archive. The One guards itself, protects its archive, against the other (*L'Un se garde de l'autre*). Derrida's use of the word "guard" converges with the meaning of "community," which means of course a military formation, the wall of protection that the same builds against the other, the way a "people" (the "same") builds a common fortification (*com, munire*) around itself against the other, gathering itself together into One in order to keep safe the uniqueness of its archive. In doing such violence to the other, the One makes itself violent, and tries violently to erase the trace of its own self-differing identity, to make itself One without difference. It guards itself from the other *pour se fair violence*: "because" and "in order to" make/do itself violence.

That can only be said in French; that is the unique privilege and special election of French. (He is being ironic!) (*Archive*, 125n1/AF, 51n15.)

So Yerushalmi succumbs to necessity and compulsively repeats the violence of the archive, the very one Freud warned against in *Moses and Monotheism*. Repetition is necessary; it is "inscribed at the heart of the future to come." Whatever is affirmed, yes, must be remembered and repeated. Yes, yes. But not without the death drive, not without the an-archival, the "possibility of putting to death the very thing, whatever its name, which *carries the law in its tradition*" (*Archive*, 125n1/AF, 51n15). Yes, yes, repetition, but not without the "no" of the death drive, which means for Derrida: putting to death the love of the same and the proper, the messianism in the messianic, the exclusivity of the proper name of this archive, the archival, patriarchival, nationalist, racist, sexist tendencies that irrupt whenever a house (*arkheion*) is filled with *archons*. For the *archons* are the fathers of the house, those who are appointed to safeguard and interpret the patri-archival treasure uniquely entrusted to them (*Archive*, 12–13/AF, 9–10), whether that be the House of Being, the House of Israel, or Freud's House (*Archive*, 20/AF, 12; *Archive*, 40/AF, 19).

We are condemned by necessity to repetition, but not without a difference, not without a future. It belongs to the structure of *l'à venir* to welcome repetition. Jewish hope and a little hopelessness, the future and repetition, the one the other, are not necessarily opposites. "The one is alas, or happily, the condition of the other" (*Archive*, 126/AF, 52) and Yerushalmi is sliding too quickly, too easily over what the future means. For he has constricted the future to a *specifically* "Judaic" hope and failed thereby to respect the absolute indeterminateness, heterogeneous to all knowledge, that is demanded by his own distinction between Judaism and Jewish.

At this point, Derrida reminds us of (repeats) the aporia we encountered in *Specters of Marx*, this time as an aporia involving general archivability and a historical archive. For a Jewishness without historical Judaism would be an archive without a real-historical substrate. Would we know of this absolute Jewishness, this general archivability, without the historical archive of Judaism? Or is absolute Jewishness a structure that precedes and makes possible Judaism? When we think of the future as *à venir*, he asks, is the hope for the future to come based upon a recorded, archived event, for example, "on a divine injunction or on a messianic covenant?" Are we to think that our hope for the future must go back to a special revelation, a special promise, made to and archived by a specific people, for example, the Jews, at a more or less determinable point in the past about a messianic future, which would then have the structure of "a specific hope for the future"? Or does the structure of "an *experience,* an *existence"*—a certain messianic experience and general archivability—precede and make possible the archivization of a promise? Do we only learn of the very idea of a promise of a future to come from the archives of a historical promise made to a historical people? Or, does the very structure of the promise of a future to come make possible the recognition of any historical covenant?

> In other words, does one need a first archive in order to conceive of originary archivability? Or vice versa? This is the whole question of the relation between the event of the religious revelation (*Offenbarung*) and a revealability (*Offenbarkeit*), a possibility of manifestation, the prior thought of what opens toward the arrival or toward the coming of such an event. (*Archive,* 127/ AF, 52)

Would we have any idea of the "messianic" without the concrete messianisms? Would we recognize any messianism if we were not already visited by a prior messianicity?

Either way, he says, there would be no future without repetition, without the death drive to kill off the proper name of the patri-archival authority.

En Mal d'archive

Having given Freud's ghost a chance to answer Yerushalmi, to dispel Yerushalmi's Jewish archive fever, Derrida turns to Freud's own *mal d'archive.* This Derrida identifies as an internal division and contradiction that disturbs Freud's theses, rather like the malaise at the heart of a contemporary disorder, *la malaise dans la culture.* For our culture too is torn in opposing directions in a peculiarly contemporary archival crisis or illness that turns on what theologian Johannes Baptist Metz calls "the dangerous memory of suffering." Having lived through the Holocaust we now witness the "detestable revisionisms" which seek to repress or distort the archives of the Holocaust. But we witness as well the "courageous rewritings of history" that break up institutional control over memory and the archive in order to rediscover the voice of those who were silenced, the trace of the victims. We are tossed between the courage of rewritings which recall the dangerous memory of suffering and a revisionism that represses such dangerous memories when (official) "history" is the archive of the winners.

These disturbances all represent archive "trouble." The uncontestable fact for Derrida is that we are in need of archives: *nous sommes en mal d'archive* (*Archive*, 142/AF, 57). The living past cannot rise up from the dead and speak to us like dead stones, *saxa loquuntur*. We must pick our way among the remains, wrestle with and conjure the ghosts of the past, ply them with patient importunity in order to reconstruct the best story we can. We have no other choice. Accordingly:

> [T]o be *en mal d'archive* can mean something else than to suffer from a sickness, from a trouble or from what the noun "*mal*" might name.

Instead of naming a malaise, a malady, or even *mal* itself, evil, *en mal d'archive* might name a neediness, a desire, a feverish passion for the archive that is at bottom what I have been calling all along in the present study a passion for the impossible:[35]

> It [to be *en mal d'archive*] is to burn with a passion. It is never to rest, interminably, from searching for the archive right where it slips away (*se dérobe*). It is to run after the archive, even if there's too much of it, right where something in it anarchives itself. . . . No desire, no passion, no drive, no compulsion, indeed no repetition compulsion, no "*mal de*" can arise from a person who is not already in one way or another *en mal d'archive*. (*Archive*, 142/AF, 57)

The archive, like the secret, impassions; the archival secret drives us mad with passion and desire. But this desire, this passion, this madness is internally divided against itself, as no one better illustrates than Freud.

Freud's trouble, the troubling thing about him that disturbs and troubles all his work, his archive illness, is the internal division of his concept of the archive, and this on three (divided) points, all of which more or less come down to the same thing, viz., of repeating—shall we say compulsively?—the very thing he has forbidden. (1) On the one hand, Freud opened up the topic of a psychic apparatus, of the space of storing away deep imprints and impressions[36] that return in a way that is neither memory nor recall. But on the other hand, this did not stop Freud, the classical metaphysician, from holding to the primacy of lived memory, from trying to return to, to remember and recall, the originary lived experience being repressed. If with one hand he forbids the return to the origin, with the other he keeps digging into the psychic archive trying to unearth the living origin, trying to let it speak for itself, denuded and without archive, letting those psychic stones talk. The archaeologist and etiologist would efface the archive; archeo-etiology displaces archivology. No translation would any longer be necessary (*Archive*, 143–46/AF, 57–59).

(2) On the one hand, the archive is made possible by death and destruction, by the reduction of things to traces and ruins, i.e., to psychic shadows, ghosts, and ashes. On the other hand, Freud, ever the metaphysician and *Aufklärer*, the critical scientist and scholar, does not believe in death

or ghosts, belief in which he is trying to eliminate. He wants to get down to the grain of truth in this belief and then—in a way that parallels the argument of *Specters of Marx*—to get rid of the ghost of belief:

> Belief (*croire*), the radical phenomenon of believing (*croyance*), the only relationship possible to the other as other, does not in the end have any possible place, any irreducible status in Freudian psychoanalysis. Which it nonetheless makes possible. (*Archive*, 147/AF, 59)

He wants to replace these specters with originary perception, to let these old stones speak, and he thinks he has exorcised these ghosts in the instant he lets the stones speak.

(3) On the one hand, no one has better analyzed/deconstructed the archontic principle of the archive, its nomological, institutionalized, paternal, patriarchal, patriarchival structure. This structure only re-posits or repeats itself in the parricide, which is the takeover by the brothers and the erection of a fraternity house, the liberty and equality of the brothers which is at best only a "certain" fraternal democracy. On the other hand, Freud repeated this patriarchal logic himself, as also have his sons and heirs, in the international association which draws itself into a circle around his archive and gathers together at Freud's house, like archons in an arkheion.

Dreaming of Gradiva's Foot

Derrida's point is by now, after a long study—and about thirty years—a familiar one: that literature will have already begun, that we are always, already delivered over to the letter, to the trace, to *archi-écriture*, to what we might call here (as if we need to make things more complicated—but who can resist it?) the "archi-archive," the subject of a "general archivology." We never stand in the presence of the *arche* itself but are always already delivered over to the trace, assigned to one archive or another, to one archive inside another, *en abîme*, "archived" *ad infinitum*, *sans arche*, an-archized. This little "supplementary thesis" affects "the formation of every concept, the very history of conception" (*Archive*, 149/AF, 61).

That is why Derrida adds a little "literary" postscript to *Mal d'archive*. Freud, who described the *Moses* book as a "historical novel," devoted an essay to "Delusions and Dreams in Jensen's *Gradiva*" (Freud, *Standard Edition*, 9:10), a novel about Norbert Hanold, an archaeologist, who was enthralled by the figure of Gradiva, a woman who was reduced to ashes nearly two thousand years ago at the eruption of Vesuvius. Hanold found her relief at Pompeii—where "by chance" Derrida is completing *Mal d'archive*—and then was delighted to come upon a plaster cast of it which he hung in his study (cf. *Archive*, 129/AF, 53). Freud explained the obsession of the archaeologist with Gradiva in terms of his logic of repression.

Thus if the archaeologist in the novel is "haunted" by Gradiva's image, Freud wants to raise the stakes and outdo the archaeologist, "to exhume a more archaic impression," to prove himself "a better etiologist than his novelist." Freud tries to get past the trace, to outrun the footprint, to find the still living footstep at the origin, the instant when the living step and the (psychic) impression it makes are still one, the pure auto-affection and self-touching. "An archive which would in sum confuse itself with the *arche*, with the origin of which it is only the *type*, the *typos*, the iterable letter or character. An archive without archive . . . " (*Archive*, 150/AF, 61).

In the novel, Hanold is suffering from a type of archive fever. Having become impatient of archaeology, which traffics always in death, in lifeless images of the past, Hanold dreams of bringing Gradiva back to life at Pompeii:

> [He dreams of] reliving the other. Of reliving the singular pressure or impression which Gradiva's step (*pas*), the step itself, the step of Gradiva herself, that very day, at that time, on that date, in what was inimitable about it, must have left in the ashes. (*Archive*, 151/AF, 61)

He dreams of touching Gradiva's living foot, of that singular, unrepeatable instant when imprinting and impression are one, when, with her peculiar gait, Gradiva must have left the unique "imprint of her toes"—her trace—"in the ashes distinct from all the rest." Literally! But that literality of course is the rub, which neither Freud nor Jensen, neither psychoanalyst nor the novelist consider, that we are always before the letter, in the letter, *in litera*, in litera-ture, in (l)iterability, in the archive. So the very thing that makes it possible to dream of this idiomatic imprint, of the unity of foot and print, of the instant of auto-affection, is what also divides and separates the foot from the print, thus making the science of footprints, of any print or impression—be it psychoanalysis or archaeology—possible and also a little impossible, submitting both to an archi-archive, the subject of a general archivology,

The instant itself, in itself, remains a secret. One can always dream of this secret; indeed this is where dreaming and speculating begin. "—[A]nd belief (—*et la foi*)" (*Archive*, 154/AF, 62). And passion and prayers and tears. We are always praying and weeping over the secret, which impassions.

> But of the secret itself, there can be no archive, by definition. The secret is the very ash of the archive. . . . There is no sense in searching for the secret of what anyone may have known. *A fortiori* a character, Hanold the archeologist. (*Archive*, 154/AF, 62–63)

We are just going to have to learn to get along with archives, with stones that do not speak but need to be read and interpreted. We need to deal with the difficulty that the heavens never open up and drop the *arche* itself in our lap, that we are always a little late on the scene and are left ever with the archive, the *arche* itself having silently slipped away, *se dérobé*, just moments before we arrived on the scene. We need archives, *nous sommes en mal d'archive*, for that is all we have. But this *mal* is not an illness but a cure, which saves us from patri-archontic architects who would control our cities and our archives, who have most dangerously confused their own archival readings with the *arche* itself, who even claim to have photographic memories. So this *mal* is not a loss but a gain, which opens up a salutary competition among interpretations, a certain salutary radical hermeneuticizing, in which we dream with passion of something unforeseeable and impossible.

> This is what this literature attests. So here is a singular testimony, literature itself, an inheritor escaped—or emancipated—from Holy Scripture. (*Archive*, 154/AF, 63)

The testimony of literature, the condition of the letter, of *écriture* and *différance*, envelops and surrounds sacred scripture too, which takes the edge off fundamentalist swords, where the Word of God is wielded to spill blood, which injects a little bit of salutary undecidability into the scriptures, a little more Babel into the Bible.

> Here is what it [literature] gives us to think: the inviolable secret of *Gradiva*, of Hanold, of Jensen, then of Freud—and a few others. (*Archive*, 154/AF, 63)

We will always be barred access to the secret, to the secret of a character in a novel, which is emblematic of a general situation, but no less to the secret of the novelist, or the psychoanalyst, to the secret itself, if it has a self:

> Beyond every possible and necessary inquiry, we will always wonder what Freud (for example), what every "careful concealer" may have wanted to keep secret. We will wonder what he may have kept of his unconditional right to secrecy. . . . (*Archive*, 154/AF, 63)

But that is not a loss, but an impetus, such stuff as dreams and passions are made of. For we will always want to know; we will always be burning with a passion for the secret, which will be the archive of new texts, of new petitions and repetitions, which will be content with what they are, without confusing themselves with the *arche* itself:

> . . . while at the same time burning with the desire to know, to make known, and to archive the very thing he concealed forever. . . .
> We will always wonder what, in this *mal d'archive*, he may have burned. We will always wonder, sharing with compassion in this archive

fever, what may have burned of his secret passions, of his correspondence, of his "life." Burned without him, without remains and without
knowledge . . . without even an ash. (*Archive*, 154–55/AF, 63)

We must always remember to remember, and remember that memory
has always to do with traces, with competing reconstructions of competing archives, that no one has the Secret which stills the play of the past.
In its optimal sense, archive fever is the double injunction to remember to
remember, to remember the past, to burn with passion for the past, to
address the old ghosts of the past, *les revenants*, everyone to whom justice
is due; and in the same stroke, for this comes around to the same thing,
to remember the future, the *les arrivants*, what is to come, *à venir*. In the
end, the archive should be an open book, an opening to the future (*Archive*, 51–52/AF, 24), the depository of a *promise*, and the pathos of archive
fever is to burn with a passion for the impossible. To be marked from of
old by an ancient inscription—by a certain circumcision—is to be marked
by a promise of something to come.

Is Deconstruction Really a Jewish Science?

So then we come back to the question that Yerushalmi puts to Freud,
when, contemplating the bust of Freud that Yerushalmi keeps in his study
(which I posit, *ex hypothesi*), or in the Freud Museum, like Hanold dreaming of Gradiva's foot, he asks whether psychoanalysis is a Jewish science:

> Right now, leaving the semantic and epistemological questions aside, I
> want only to know whether *you* ultimately came to believe it so.
>   In fact, I will limit myself even further and be content if you answer
> only one question: When your daughter conveyed those words to the
> congress in Jerusalem, *was she speaking in your name?*
>   Please tell me, Professor. I promise I won't reveal your answer to
> anyone. (Y, 100)

But that, Professor Yerushalmi, is precisely a secret—the French translation of *Freud's Moses* reads *"je vous promets de garder le secret"*—the secret,
a secret unknown above all, and this in virtue of what Freud has to say
about repression and the unconscious, to Freud himself. This is something
that Freud perhaps least of all can be expected to know and something
that Detective Yerushalmi is not going to find out. He is not going to make
that stone bust of Freud talk. Literature will have always begun. Whether
or not Freud himself had a Jewish heart, even a heart that is Jewish
without Judaism, Yerushalmi is on his own. He is just going to have to
assume responsibility himself for any such attribution, which is consigned
in advance to following the archival trace, and the point will be whether
he has opened up psychoanalytic theory or practice in an interesting way,
Freud himself having slipped away.

The lesson is not lost on us. For the questions that we have repeated to Derrida, in a more or less compulsive manner, or that he has repeated to himself—since he says that in writing of his colleague Yerushalmi he is writing of himself—as to whether deconstruction is a Jewish science, also needs deconstruction (*en mal de déconstruction*). We have no business seeking some sort of secret communication from Jacques (not to mention Jackie), expecting thereby to find out whether in his heart of hearts Jacques is still Jewish, even without Judaism, still Jewish, even while rightly passing for an atheist. That is precisely something that for structural reasons cannot be delivered, by him or by me (although that is the drift of the formulations that, for strategic reasons, I let this question take at the beginning of this discussion). It would be misleading on my part to suggest that I could track this question down by a careful enough piece of detective work. Moreover, it would be a ruse on Derrida's part even to suggest that *he* could tell us. As if he has any special powers of auto-interpretation, any special ability to tell us anything about "his religion." His religion is his business, his problem, if it is a problem. The very fact that Derrida has begun to write in an autobiographical mode is a slippery affair about which both he and we need to be vigilant, lest we and he be the victims of a ruse which he more than anyone has done the most to expose.

The question itself—whether there is something Jewish and prophetic, something messianic and covenantal, about deconstruction, whether deconstruction is a certain religion without religion, a certain repetition of religion—is a good enough one on its own. With or without Jacques. Indeed I think it is rather a significant and pertinent one and that it considerably repays our attention, both for deconstruction's sake and for religion's. But we must not expect it to be settled, if it could be settled—much will depend, of course, on how the very terms *Jewish* and *deconstruction* are to be defined—by way of some sort of secret document unearthed in El Biar, some hitherto undiscovered sentence recently unearthed in Derrida's diaries or correspondence—or email. It is a very good question indeed, one of which I myself am inordinately fond, and this in no small part because of its double-edged blade. For while it has the power to drive his dogmatic, secularizing academic admirers mad, it also infuriates fundamentalists who take no prisoners when someone suggests that *Écriture sainte* keeps company with a not so *sainte* archi-écriture, an *écriture* plain and simple (provided of course that they even get the point).

It is a question, as I have argued, that opens up deconstruction and religion in an interesting way, even as it closes deconstruction off from mindless charges of nihilism and subjectivism and closes religion off from mindless fundamentalism. The question stands or falls on the basis of how well it opens the Derridean archive, how well the answer is "documented," that is, on how well one uses the archives. As if Jacques were long since dead and all we had were his texts, like memories from beyond the grave (MpPdM, 49/MfPdM, 29), which is all we do have. As if the only one with whom we could consult is his ghost. As if we had his private phone number and all we got was an answering machine whose message was "Go read my book that I have written."

I am not trying to tell you that Jacques has shared his secret with me.

I do not keep a bust of Jacques in my study and I have not sought his *imprimatur* for this imprint.

Bearing that admonition in mind, let us turn now to his most autobiographical writings, if that is what they are.

VI. Confession

§18. The Son of These Tears:
The Confession of Jacques de la rue Saint-Augustin

The Book of Elie

Circumfession—the open confession of the religion of Jacques Derrida, of "my religion about which nobody understands anything" (*Circon.*, 146/*Circum.*, 154),[1] the open confession of a religious passion about which no one suspected a thing, even of a certain "conversion" (*Circon.*, 119/*Circum.*, 124–25)—is the text I have been holding close to my breast and reading continuously throughout the present study.

Circumfession: Fifty-nine periods and periphrases written in a sort *of internal margin, between Geoffrey Bennington's book and work in preparation (January 1989–April 1990)* is supposed to come as a surprise, to make a revelation about something we never suspected, to come as a bolt from the blue: to come, period, *à venir*. It is supposed to shock Geoffrey Bennington ("G."), who is "up there," on the upper half of the page, like God in his heaven. G. (in English that could also stand for "God") is writing a "survey" of "Derrida," a "Book of Derrida," a computer program that can run "Derrida," an overview that maintains surveillance over Derrida, a theological (i.e., omniscient) compendium that describes in principle everything that Derrida has to say or ever could say, that knows every secret of his heart, that has counted every tear. Bennington is trying to formulate the "logic" of Derrida's work, without ever citing a single sentence of Derrida, to identify the law or rule of his work, to write a "Derrida program," a generative grammar that can predict in principle and can generate, with the click of a mouse, any past, present, or future sentence (phrase) that Derrida has or will ever pen (with his Macintosh).

Down below, on the bottom half of the page, Derrida, ever "jealous" of his idiom and idiosyncrasy, thrashing about in the secrets of his singularity, tries gamely—this is a bet, a game they are playing—to twist free of G., to escape from G.'s panopticon, to write around—to "peri-phrase"—him, to exceed G.'s book with textuality, to outflank and overflow him. Derrida is trying to surprise G. with an "event," to circum-vent G. with something new, something to come that G. did not see coming, something that shatters the horizon that G. is tracing out overhead with eagle's wings. Jacques is trying for an invention, an incoming, a circum-invention of something that "Derridabase" did not foresee, a passion that it did not program.[2] So the whole volume *Jacques Derrida*, by Geoffrey Bennington ("Derridabase") and Jacques Derrida ("Circumfession," in French: *cir-con-fession*), is a staging or enactment of deconstruction, putting on a Derridean performance, drawing a Derridean ellipsis. In the upper half of the work G. constructs a logic, a law, a book, a circle of the same which Derrida, in the lower half, seeks to exceed and breach, to destabilize and decenter, to "deconstruct." In this work, we should be able to catch deconstruction in the act, an act of passion, right there on stage.

The shock that Derrida offers G. is to exhibit his circumcision, shamelessly, in public, like an ancient cynic, the thing itself, scars and all, and everything with which it is implicated, the familial, social, linguistic, national, political, psychoanalytic, philosophical, and religious networks in which Derrida is inscribed by his circumcision. Who could have imagined or foreseen such a thing? G., ever omniscient, keeping to his heavenly course, maintaining his equilibrium, says he is not surprised.[3] We, of course, are also less than surprised, but only because we have been preparing for his circumcision all along, reading backwards, after the fact, having already been forewarned about a simmering passion, having already begun by *Circonfession*, which only a few years ago might have seemed impossible.

Derrida is, he confesses (I think he is boasting), the only philosopher more or less accepted by the academy (he did, after all, *pace* Barry Smith, *win* the vote at Cambridge) "who will have dared describe his penis" (*Circon.*, 110/*Circum.*, 115) (a contingent of graduate assistants furiously fan Ruth Markus, who has fainted dead away upon reading a review of *Circumfession* in *The New York Review of Books*).[4] Ever since *Glas* he has been making notes for a "work in preparation" to be entitled, variously, *The Book of Circumcision* or *The Book of Elie*, dreaming of a book to be written.[5] Elijah is his Hebrew name, which he discovered only later on, to his surprise, given to him with his circumcision but kept a family secret, kept off his birth certificate and all official documents. "Elie" is his secret name, known only within the family circles, and it must come as a surprise to

G. because it came as a surprise to Jacques. *Circumfession* alludes to the secret passion of Jacques Derrida, about which nobody understands anything, revealing a man of prayers and tears, a quasi-Jewish cir-confessing Augustine, a quasi-Augustinian Jew,[6] in love with love (PdS, 162/*Points*, 152), a man of passion, a "religious" man.

Almost. For he is always telling the story of a broken alliance, without rupture but without continuity, the story of a cut with the covenant; he lives in the *distance* between himself and Judaism, which is perhaps the unity of what is called his life story (cf. ED, 227/WD, 153).

By his circumcision Derrida means, to be sure, the thing itself (*Sache*, *chôse*, *cause*: *Circon.*, 136/*Circum.*, 143), the peritomy, the severed foreskin, about which he is quite graphic, to a point that the customary readers of Saint Augustine will find quite scandalous, maybe even a little sinful. While he does not fail to explore its other senses—a cruel maiming, a bloody crime perpetrated by the father and permitted by the mother against the innocent child, a figure of death and castration (the Roman Emperor Hadrian so equated it and made it punishable as murder), a figure even of fellatio and cannibalism,[7] etc.—Derrida uses circumcision constantly to circle around his own Jewishness, his own circumscription within Judaism by this ancient rite, his own inside/outside relation to the circle of Judaism. The rite of circumcision is for men—although this book is for "everybody" (*Circon.*, 288/*Circum.*, 311)—the condition and the mark of their membership in the Jewish community, the sign of God's covenant with his people. In Jeremiah, circumcision marks a man who has cut down his self-will, who is "detached" from self-will, who accepts God's word, lest he have an "uncircumcised ear" (Jer. 6:10), who accepts God's law, lest he have an "uncircumcised heart" (Jer. 9:25–26; cf. *Schib.*, 15/WT, 6).

In this sense, Derrida is circumcised and he is not, circumcised and "de-circumcised" (*Circon.*, 208/*Circum.*, 224). He is divided and partitioned between his belonging to Judaism and his breach from Judaism— his atheism, his gentile wife, his uncircumcised sons. The "cut" for Derrida, then, is not only his peritomy; the cut is this scission between his Judaism and his non-Judaism, the partition dividing these two worlds. "I write," he says, "by reconstituting the partitioned and transcendant [*sic*] structure of religion, of several religions, in the internal circumcision of 'my life'" (*Circon.*, 213/*Circum.*, 229). What he calls his religion is not his Judaism but a break with Judaism, a break that cannot be made cleanly, in virtue of what he elsewhere called the impossibility of the pure cut. His *re-ligare* (corrupt etymology) is the bond by which he remains tied to what he has breached, the ligature of his belonging still to a place where he does not belong. His religion is the partitioning, the cut of circumcision and the cut from circumcision. He inhabits the distance between Judaism and the end of Judaism, between the religion in which he was nurtured, of his mother and his matrix, of his parents and his childhood, and his public adult life. What he calls "my religion," "my life" is the tension between these two worlds, the gap, the cut between "Jackie," "a little black and very Arab Jew" (*Circon.*, 57 / *Circum.*, 58), and "Derrida," the cosmopolitan secular French philosopher (cf. PdS, 128–30 / *Points*, 119–21; PdS, 354 / *Points*, 343–44). In that gap stirs the passion of Jacques Derrida.

Circumfession is written with the blood and tears that flow from this cut, with the passion that the cut provokes. In the end, circumcision is a marvelous figure, but by no means merely a figure, for Derrida, who has long been writing about cuts, incisions, inscriptions, stylus tips, and even guillotines, which positions him, as we have seen in *Glas*, with Abraham (also the name of his older brother René) and against the soaring, seamless system of *savoir absolue*.

In the end, indeed at the very end of the book, circumcision is represented more generally, almost as a philosopheme or anti-philosopheme—"philosophically" its most important sense—as the cut from truth, "*cette vérité secrète c'est-à-dire sevrée de la vérité*," "that secret truth, that is to say, severed from the truth" (*Circon.*, 291 / *Circum.*, 314). For *Circumfession* is not a confession *of* the truth but a confession *without* truth, the confession of a *sans*, of being severed and secreted from truth, of truth's being secreted away from us, the secret without truth which confesses that literature will have always begun, without a guiding star and fixed destination. That is what impassions. This severance also severs these memoirs from Saint Augustine's *Confessions*, which mean to own up *to* the truth, for whom God is truth rather than the cut from truth. What Derrida calls "my religion," his passion, his prayers and tears, circles around this cut, the one that severs him from the healing consolations of either a metaphysical or a religious Truth, capitalized, the healing balms of any *determinable* faith and Truth, whose advantage is to hold everything steadily in place. He confesses, if not "sin-fulness," then *sans*-fulness, the deep divide within his being, within our being, the cut that severs us from the Truth of truth, severing the head of *Saint Prépuce*, cutting phallic Truth down to size. That is the sense in which circumcision is everybody's story, so that *Circumfession* can rightly be described as "Everybody's Autobiography" (*Circon.*, 288 / *Circum.*, 311), Greek or Jew (or Arab), male or female (or innumerable). Circumcision as the severance from Truth, from *savoir absolue*, from the One Encompassing Truth, as the "night of truth,"[8] is the *condition humaine* (and a problem for animals, too).

Circumfession is the story of the "conversion" (cf. *Circon.*, 119 / *Circum.*, 124–25) of Jacques Derrida to a certain, secret quasi-Judaism, to a quasi-Augustinian, slightly atheistic Judaism nurtured on the rue Saint-Augustin. Derrida confesses his dereliction of his Jewish studies: he played truant from the Jewish school in El Biar when he was thirteen years old, where his parents had sent him after the expulsion of the Algerian Jewish children from the public schools, to study for Bar Mitzvah. The school was called the Alliance, the French word for covenant but also for a wedding ring, like a "covenant house"; but the thirteen-year-old, alas, preferred to watch the "allied" soldiers queuing up at brothels (*Circon.*, 175–76/*Circum.*, 164–65; cf. *Schib.*, 12/WT, 4). He makes no secret of his own ignorance of Hebrew, his lack of biblical training, but with a little luck he could turn this into a *docta ignorantia*: "but this ignorance remained the chance of my faith as of my hope, of my taste even for the word, the taste for letters" (*Circon.*, 267/*Circum.*, 289), just as Augustine, speaking of his own conversion, wrote that "had [he] been first informed by Thy holy writings" and "had [he] later fallen upon those other books, perhaps they would have torn me away from a firm foundation of piety" (VII,xx,26). So *Circumfession* tells the surprising story of Derrida's conversion from these secular texts and languages to a certain Hebrew, to his life of faith and passion, of prayers and tears.

From the point of view of the present study, *Circumfession* is the most interesting and provocative of all of Derrida's texts, the pivot around which this book is all along turning. This is not because we have succumbed to some voyeuristic impulse to catch sight of Derrida's secret life, and not exactly because *Circumfession* reveals to us Derrida's secret passion, his private religion, but rather because it forces us to think out what this "religion" can be, what the passion of deconstruction can be. It is with no little fear and trembling that one would write about *Circumfession*, a book of formidable difficulty (even by Derridean standards). This difficulty of course is, as always, stylistic: it is elusive, fluid, poetic, agrammatical, paratactical, written in sections that lack punctuation, so that the words flow like blood from the mohel's blade, or like the tears of a child weeping for his mother, or like the associations of a particularly wild dream. But beyond that there is the difficulty of highly private allusions in which Derrida makes reference to matters in his personal life that we cannot possibly make out. The text disseminates in so many directions—autobiographical,[9] psychoanalytic, literary, political, pedagogical, theological, and philosophical—as to make nonsense of the idea of a definitive commentary. That, of course, is the whole idea—remember the little war with Geoffrey Bennington: he is trying to elude both anticipation and commentary. Thus do I excuse myself from getting this text right, let alone getting all of it right; thus do I confess and ask pardon, right at the start. I am simply seeking to stay with the flow of this text, trying not to end up in the drink, to stay with it just long enough and well enough to get a sense of what it tells us about Derrida's religion, what he is calling here, so provocatively, "my religion," which will throw light on a certain passion for the impossible.[10]

The Name of God

To say the least, Derrida clearly does not subscribe to an orthodox version of the faith of his fathers—or of his mother. I am beginning with chapter 30, the numerical center of this work of fifty-nine chapters or periphrases (or: commotions, compulsions, periods, respirations, bands, or circumferences), one for each of his years—he is writing in 1989 which, he had begun to fear, might be his last. In this periphrase, Derrida says that his task will be to describe his sex throughout thousands of years of Judaism, i.e., his inscription or circumscription as a circumcised Jew and the meaning (or the passion) of his relation to Judaism, and to do so "microscopically." He wants to leave nothing in the dark of what related him to Judaism, of his Jewish "alliance," his alliance or lack thereof with the *alliance*, from which he was fleeing like a tearful, truant boy with only limited success (*Circon*, 164/*Circum.*, 175). Having broken this *alliance* in many respects, he is "the last of the Jews." For circumcision is the trace of the "proper," the mark and the substance of belonging to the alliance, to the community of Judaism, while he has married outside Judaism and his sons are uncircumcised (*Circon.*, 92/*Circum.*, 95) and do not use his name, and he does not believe in (a certain) God. He has broken the chain, cut away from the cut, left his sons and himself im-proper, un-marked, un-identified, un-clean. For if the oldest, the first and defining dispute of all in Christianity was over circumcision, and the Pauline-Christian thing became *not* to circumcise, then has not Derrida delivered his sons to this all-encompassing Christian world? Has he not sided with Paul against the Jews, "[f]or in Christ Jesus neither circumcision nor uncircumcision counts for anything" (Gal. 5:6; cf. MdA, 117n87/MB, 112n87)?

Circumfession is the story of the conversion of Jacques Derrida from a "certain Judaism" (*Circon.*, 117/*Circum.*, 122) of which he is the end to a certain Judaism without God—for he is rightly taken as an atheist (*Circon.*, 146/*Circum.*, 155)—without a certain God, or even a conversion to an "atheist God" (*Circon.*, 201/*Circum.*, 216), to a God whose name he is constantly seeking:

> I am addressing myself here to God, the only one I take as a witness, without yet knowing what these sublime words mean, and this grammar, and *to*, and *witness*, and *God*, and *take*, take God . . . (*Circon.*, 56–57/*Circum.*, 56)

When Augustine wrote, "What do I love when I love my God?," Derrida remarks, in a telling entry in his notebooks of 1981, "Can I do anything other than translate this sentence by SA [Saint Augustine] into my language . . . the change of meaning and of reference turning on the *meum*?" (*Circon.*, 117/*Circum.*, 122). *My* language, a private language, about *my* God, the secret, Jewish, slightly Augustinian God of *my* religion. What do

I mean by the God whom I love? What do I love when I speak of loving God? What do I believe when I put my faith in God? To whom do I pray when I pray to my God? Over what do I weep when I weep over my God?

For the name of God is a way to keep things open, to open them up to what eye hath not seen nor ear heard, to hope for and believe impossible things, to pray and weep over what is coming—even as it has been the name of the most violent closure, that in whose name the worst atrocities are regularly committed.

Religious thinkers—but is not Derrida also religious with a certain religion? Is Derrida not forcing us to reconceive religion?—would say that Derrida here gives evidence, "postmodern evidence," if you still use this word, perhaps the most brilliant of all contemporary evidence, to what Augustine said at the beginning of the *Confessions*, that our hearts are restless and they will not rest until they rest in thee. However much "Jackie" flees from God, God will track him down. They will say that when Derrida is dreaming of the impossible he is searching for God even though he does not know that it is God of whom he dreams, that *Circonfession* is a transcendental aspiration for the God of our fathers (and mothers). But perhaps Derrida would rejoin, if he felt there was any reason to rejoin, that, in virtue of his notion of exemplarity, a religious person who searches for God (SA, for example) does not know what it is that he seeks, that in seeking God such a person also seeks to know what he is seeking. For it is Augustine himself who asks himself, "What do I love when I love my God?" That question, which is not put to Augustine by the skeptics (*academici*) but by Augustine himself to himself, is the crucial question, and it is put no less by Augustine than by Derrida. It is the question of all questions, and, before that, the affirmation "before any question" (DLE, 147/OS, 94).

This question, which swells up and rolls over the *Confessions* like a great wave, and from there sweeps over *Circonfession*, puts the torch to the nonsensical Heideggerian dogma, repeated blindly by the acolytes in the Church of Heidegger, that a religious person is someone who does not put real questions. The privilege of questioning in the Heideggerian church is reserved for Greco-German *Seinsdenkers* (of highly questionable political leanings, as we have all learned). Questions, according to the Heideggerian dogma, could not possibly be put in Hebrew or Arabic, Latin or French—the languages of *Circumfession*. According to this comical, albeit dangerous, schema (DLE, 109/OS, 68), Yahweh Himself would need to switch to German, if, driven by his jealousy of *die Sprache des Seins*, the Lord God would ever attempt to "think."[11]

Derrida's religion, which is announced in this book, along with the name of the God of his religion, is just what we will not have understood:

> [T]hat's what my readers won't have known about me . . . the changed time of my writing . . . [to] be read less and less well over almost twenty

years, like my religion about which nobody understands anything . . .
(*Circon.*, 145–46 / *Circum.*, 154)

Not even Georgette, his mother, who prayed and wept over Jacques like
Monica over Augustine, could understand his religion, and she was afraid
even to ask, praying and weeping and trusting all the while that it would
be impossible that the son of these tears, *filius istarum lacrymarum*
(III,xii,12), Jacques / Augustine, should perish:

> . . . any more than does my mother who asked other people a while ago,
> not daring to talk to me about it, if I still believed in God . . . but she must
> have known that the constancy of God in my life is called by other names,
> so that I quite rightly pass for an atheist . . . (*Circon.*, 146 / *Circum.*, 155)

From the point of view of an orthodox Jewish theism, Derrida passes for
an atheist, an atheist relative to that God, to the classical Jewish understanding of the name of God. But he by no means passes for an atheist
about every God, an atheist *simpliciter*, since the name of God is among
the most important names he means to save. *His* religion is a religion that
turns on the name of God, not because, like an English don, he is curious
about "God talk," but because the name of God is a name he calls upon,
that he invokes, with prayers and tears. But what is called God in orthodoxy, the constancy and omnipresence and omniscience of God in the
concrete, historical messianisms, in the religions of the Book, for him goes
under other names:

> . . . the omnipresence to me of what I call God in my absolved, absolutely
> private language being neither that of an eyewitness nor that of a voice
> doing anything other than talking to me without saying anything, nor a
> transcendent law (*Circon.*, 146–47 / *Circum.*, 154)

The name of God for Derrida is not the name of a universal, panoptical
witness to his most hidden thoughts and deeds, a party to his innermost
interiority, *in interiore homine*, in what Climacus would have called "the
absolute relationship to the absolute." Nor is God the name of the Law,
or of the voice of conscience, or of the transcendent creator of heaven and
earth, the first cause, etc. "God" is not a metaphysical or moral foundation, the ground of being or the author of the moral law, a *prima causa* or
an *ens realissimum* or a *gubernator universi*. Derrida's is much more an
Augustinian than a Thomistic God, *my* God, not, as for Saint Thomas, *quod
omnes dicunt deum*, what everybody calls God. The name of God is not the
name of some "theological" being or object. "God" is given only in praying and weeping—"I'm mingling the name of God here with the origin
of tears" (*Circon.*, 114 / *Circum.*, 118); we would say that "God" for him is
given not in theological analysis but in religious experience, in a certain

passion for the impossible. On this point, if I may dare to say so, Derrida is somewhat closer to the Bible-thumpers than to the endowed chairs of religious studies. While Derrida is willing to associate himself with "religion" and "prayer" and "passion," the word "theology" tends to have a strictly *onto*-theological sense for him, signifying something objectifying, totalizing, dogmatic, and awash in ominous institutional power, so that his is a religion without theology, a life of prayer and passion without theology's God, *Dieu sans l'être*, God without being *that*, that institutional, theological God. For Derrida, God is not an object but an *addressee*, not a matter for theological clarification but the other end of a prayer, given not to cognition but to passion, neither him nor her nor it, but "you" (*tu*).

What then does Derrida name and love when he names and loves his God, *deum meum*? Or better still, since that question takes the form of the *quid est?*, to whom is he talking when he addresses "my God"? In that question is focused a great deal of what we have been pursuing in the present study. The name of God, he says here, means "the secret I am excluded from," the secret that others know but hold from him, "the secret of Polichenelle" (*Circon.*, 147/*Circum.*, 156)—a reference to *Pass.*, 20/ON, 7—a secret for no one, an "open secret," as G. translates it, known to everyone except him, so that he is "the first and only one to be excluded from," to be cut off from, what is known to everyone else, like the "properly theological hypothesis of a blank sacrifice sending the bidding up to infinity." In *Passions*, the secret of Polichenelle is a reference to his "passion" for "literature," which maintains the absolute secret, the "exemplary" secret (*Pass.*, 63–67/DCR, 22–23), what we have called here the secret without truth, "that secret truth, that is to say, severed from the truth" (*Circon.*. 291/*Circum.*, 314). That is the secret that there is no secret, no conscious or unconscious secret truth hidden deep beneath the surface of the text (*Circon.*, 77/*Circum.*, 78), the secret that turns the text over to endless interpretations, not just four,[12] that permits and produces multiple interpretations, severed as it is from *sa* (*savoir absolue*).

So Derrida here seems to say that "God" is the name of the absolute secret, a placeholder for the secret that there is no secret truth, the blank truth in virtue of which we are always already exposed to multiple interpretations. "God" is a name for the inexpungeable textuality of his life and work, the split in his life that severs him from truth, so that it is up to others to read him (who then know more than him), a limit structure. That would explain why he will often say "God—or death," for "God" means a secret, a *deus absconditus*, a blank point at which an overarching and all-governing truth gives out. That is also the point at which, as Augustine said and Heidegger repeated, *factus sum mihi terra difficultatis et sudoris nimii*, "I have been made for myself a land of difficulty and of great sweat and tears," and again, *quaestio mihi factus sum*, "I have become a question unto myself" (*Being and Time*, §9) and I do not know who I am.

He prays with passion; he sends up prayers like lost postcards, landing who knows where, destination unknown. He sends up a passionate prayer: "There is no passion without secret, this very secret, indeed no secret without this passion" (*Pass.* 64/ON, 28). The secret is the passion of life, the passion of death, the intensity of life/death, and it is structural, ingrained, built in, in just such a way as to permit, to command the un-building (*Abbauen, déconstruction*) of whatever poses itself as unlocking the secret, whatever posits itself as holding the hermeneutic key and closing down further interpretations. The name of God is the most powerfully deconstructive name we can invoke, for it is the name that destroys the earthly towers to truth we are all the time building, the name of the time "after Babel." The name of God disseminates our tongues, multiplies names and truths and the stories we have to tell ourselves to get through the day, exposing the *vanitas vanitatum*, the *vanitas constuctionarum*.

The name of God is the name of the structural secret or limit, the secret without truth, without the Truth of truth: without the truth of *savoir absolue*; without a divine revelation from God that puts an end to human confusion; without the truth of a revelation from Being, from the It which gives us Being and time, which grants us truth, *a-letheia*, while itself slipping modestly into concealment. Derrida's secret, that literature will have already begun, is neither the *mysterium* of divine truth revealed by God to the patriarchs nor the *Geheimnis* revealed-and-concealed to the Heideggerian acolytes whose ears are cocked to the revelation granted the early Greeks. Derrida's secret is the secret without (*sans*) truth, the secret of the *sans*, the secret confessed in a confession without truth. So this confession does not bring out into the light of day the unconcealed truth of his secret self, because such a secret he does not know, and this because there is none. There is no truth beyond the truth one "does," the truth one "makes" of oneself, *facere veritatem*, in one's heart, by confessing it (*Circon.*, 48–49/*Circum.*, 47–48).

That is the crucial turn that Derrida gives to Augustine's confession of conversion, when Augustine asks *cur confitemur Deo scienti?*, why do I confess these things to God who already knows them all anyway? Clearly not to pass the word on to God, to let God in on a secret truth or two that Augustine has been keeping from God. Augustine is not giving God any information or truth, telling God something God did not know. Augustine's confession is not for God's sake, but for the sake of the faithful, who can learn a thing or two from his story, and for himself, for his *passion*, to confirm and intensify his faith.

But if Augustine does not have to tell the truth to God, Derrida does not *have* a truth to tell, a secret truth to let out of the bag, for his secret is an absolute secret, a secret that we are always in a bag, structurally *sevrée de la vérité*: severed from the Truth of Being, from the mystery of God, or from the depths of the Self, cut adrift from the three Ideas of Reason, from God, the Soul, and the World, around which everything turns in Augustine, Descartes, and Kant. Such a secret is a *terra difficultatis*—and how! For if "God" means the One who lifts you like a hook from such a land of trouble, then Derrida rightly passes for an atheist. But "God" for Derrida is the name of the *terra difficultatis*, of the nameless who-knows-what to whom one confesses plainly that one is cut adrift, destinerrant, a little lost, and maybe not a little. "God" is the name of a question not an answer, of an errancy not a destination, the name of life/death not of *vita aeterna*, to whom one prays, with passion and tears, that one does not know to whom to pray, or who it is to whom one prays, or even who one is oneself. Who or what do I love when I love my God? That lack of destination does not prevent the event of prayer but lets it break out; it does not stop the praying but provokes it all the more. One prays and prays, all the time hoping and praying that one's prayers are answered in and by the praying, confessing, addressing, *in litteris*. In that sense writing is a *sainte écriture*.

"God coming," Derrida adds, "to circulate among the unavowables" (*Circon.*, 147/*Circum.*, 156–57), among the things one cannot simply confess, frankly admit, declare or confess, since we do not know who or what we are confessing. That means that when we confess ourselves a man or woman "of God"—and Derrida seems to think it goes without saying that is just what one wants to do—then we do not know who we name or what we have invoked. We are relative to God like children not bearing their father's name (cf. *Pass.*, 32/ON, 12–13),[13] who cannot confess and admit their father, like nameless sons who are consigned to live "beyond the name," not knowing their proper name, the name of the proper. When you pray, say *"abba*, father or mother, what is your name?" When you pray, say, "what do I love and name when I love and name my God?"

Praying and Weeping

No small part of the surprise that Derrida pulls on G. is to associate himself with "the prayers and tears of Augustine," with one of Western religion's weepiest and most unctuous books, a most unlikely bedfellow of an atheistic, leftish, poststructuralist Parisian intellectual (*Circon.*, 12/*Circum.*, 9), all of which he is and is not.[14] This talk of tears is in part an autobiographical statement and we are fascinated by it, although the question is whether and how this praying and weeping makes its way into deconstruction, with or without Jacques, whether and to what extent deconstruction, not just "Jackie," is bathed in tears and sunk in prayer. "Jackie" is a weepy child, ready to cry at the drop of a hat, clinging to his mother:

I wonder if those reading me from up there see my tears, today, those of the child about whom people used to say "he cries for nothing," and indeed, if they guess that my life was but a long history of prayers (*Circon.*, 40/*Circum.*, 38–39)

The clingy little boy even hated nursery school because he feared the separation, the cut, from his mother. Recalling a touching scene from those days, he writes, "she was holding my hand" on the way to nursery school and he, wishing to stay home with her, invents an illness, a ruse he forgot to sustain after she dropped him off:

. . . whence the tears when later in the afternoon, from the playground, I caught sight of her through the fence, she must have been as beautiful as a photograph, and I reproached her for leaving me in the world, in the hands of others, basically with having forgotten that I was supposed to be ill so as to stay with her, just according to our very alliance, one of our 59 conjurations without which I am nothing, accusing her in this way of letting me be caught up by school, all those cruel mistresses (*Circon.*, 250–52/*Circum.*, 272)

Circumfession means to surprise the "geologic," Geo-ffrey's logic, by revealing the secret of "Derrida" as a man who has been praying all his life:

. . . they understand everything, like the geologic program, except that I have lived in prayer (*Circon.*, 41/*Circum.*, 39–40)
. . . and not only do I pray, as I have never stopped doing all my life, and pray to him, but I take him here and take him as my witness (*Circon.*, 57/*Circum.*, 56–58)
. . . for if you knew, G., my experience of prayers, you would know everything, you who know everything, you would tell me whom to address them to (*Circon.*, 176/*Circum.*, 188)

But what can Derrida possibly mean by prayer, by praying and weeping? *To whom* is he praying? Derrida does not lack a life of prayer, of praying and weeping, and he could hardly imagine ever giving up prayer just because he rightly passes for an atheist. His atheism does not undermine his life of prayer but provokes it and forces us to examine it more carefully and to ask where (*ubi*) he directs his prayers.

Well, I am remembering God this morning, the name, a quotation, something my mother said, not that I'm looking for you, my God, in a determinable place and to reply to the question, *Sed ubi manes in memoria mea, domine* [But where do you dwell in my memory, O Lord] (*Circon.*, 112/*Circum.*, 117)

The first time he remembers hearing the name of God was on the lips of his mother praying for him when he was sick, for fear that he would die like his brothers before and after him. When his temperature goes down, Georgette/Monica would pray *grace à Dieu, merci Dieu*. God is always mingled with "the origin of tears" for him, a "puerile, weepy and pusillanimous son" with whom the adults amused themselves by making him cry "for nothing," and an adolescent who liked to read authors who are quick to tears, like Rousseau, Augustine, and Nietzsche, the authors of three famous autobiographies:

> I weep from my mother over the child whose substitute I am [his dead brother], whence the other, nongrammatical syntax that remains to be invented to speak of the name of God which is here neither that of the father nor that of the mother, nor of the son nor of the brother nor of the sister (*Circon.*, 114/*Circum.*, 119)

He cries *for* himself *from* his mother; he sees himself from the (m)other, a scary child who cried for his mommy, who cried to be left to sleep near his parents.

So, if one directs one's prayers and tears to God, still, *where (ubi)* is God? Even if God is in our memory, as Augustine asks, where in our memory? Not that God is to be found in some *determinable* place so that we could actually give a determinate answer to this question. Derrida's difference with orthodox religion, his cut with the determinable faiths, does not have to do with the fact of prayer—as if they prayed but he does not—but rather with the *destination* of prayer, where to address his prayer, *nusquam nisi ad te* (nowhere except to you), since prayer for Derrida, as for Hamlet, does not necessarily to heaven rise (*Hamlet*). We recall, from "How to Avoid Speaking: Denials," that when apophatic discourse opens with a prayer this "recognizes, assigns, or ensures its destination" (*Psy.*, 560/ DNT, 98), so that negative theology is determinate and well destined discourse, and as long as it keeps praying it will not be set adrift. But Derrida's prayer is a *carte postale*, an open secret, that is structurally exposed to loss and non-arrival, to *destinerrance*, to the errancy of destination, destined to go askew, errant and wandering, *abs te deviare* [to stray from you] (IX,ix,22), directed who knows where, to some secret place. Every prayer, he says in "How Not to Speak," is addressed to the other as other, any other, no matter who—*"for example*—I will say, at the risk of shocking—*God*" (*Psy.*, 572/DNT, 110). The prayers of the determinable faiths know where they are going, but Derrida, the anchorite, the ankhôra-ite, wanders in the desert. To whom do I pray? To you, *ad te*. But where are you? *In memoria*. But where in my memory?

His task, he writes to himself in a 1977 entry in his notebooks, is to "analyze that form of secret, the 'my life,'" not as if his life is a hidden, interior, solitary self, in the classical tradition of an interior self (*in interiore homine*), of which Augustine himself is the very prototype and paradigm.

Rather, for Derrida, "my life" means something hanging on the partition of "two whole worlds," this world and "the *other* world." "I write," the notebooks continue, "by reconstituting the partitioned and transcendant [*sic*] structure of religion, of several religions, in the internal circumcision of 'my life'" (*Circon.*, 213/*Circum.*, 229). Circumcision is not simply a rite of initiation in his religion; it is its very structure. For the structure of Augustine's religion is to be partitioned between two worlds, between earth and heaven, to be a *homo viator* on the way from this world to the *civitas dei*. Derrida reconstitutes this partitioned structure, working on the line, the cut, the scission or divide between the two worlds. His life is partitioned, not between heaven and earth, to be sure, but, on the one side, the Arab Jewish world of his father and mother, his matrix and his family, his private and personal life, and, on the other side, the other, public world of his writing. The partition is everything he appeared to have "erased" when he traded names, when he stretched the written name of "Jacques," his semi-pseudonym and *nom de plume*, over "Jackie" (PdS, 354/*Points*, 344). This partition unfolds on the computer screen that stretches out like the "sky" before him, just as for Augustine—the comparison is forced— God has "stretched out the firmament of Thy Book like skin" (XIII,xv,16)— or like the way secularized Jews, wanting to hide their circumcision, tried to stretch what remained of their foreskins.

The "self," the divided, partitioned, cut self of whose journey we read in *Circumfession* is not the *homo interioris* who discovers God within, but an auto-bio-thanato-hetero-grapher who tells the story of the cut, the scission, between "Jackie" and "Jacques," between "Jacques" and "Derrida," where the name of the thinker is the name of a text to be read, a signature to be countersigned. The partitioning is the cut with Judaism, for he rightly passes for an atheist and has not circumcised his sons, which he cannot however cut off, an imperfect or impure cut (*Truth in Painting*), and, beyond Judaism, a cut with Truth itself. The partitioning is the tension between the Arab Jew and the *marrane* who is not even a Jew in secret, a distance in which he takes up residence, in which he works, which is the origin of his "tears" (of the homograph: cuts/cries).

The scission or partitioning between these two worlds is something which one can*not* properly "analyze"—he fears all forms of analysis— psycho-, literary, theological, or even blood-analysis (*Circon.*, 12/*Circum.*, 10)—but only pray and weep over. Passion withers under analysis. That is why the project of the reconstitution of the structure of religion demands that he reconstitute the life of prayer, of praying and weeping. For the divided self is a serious matter: "the splitting of the ego, in me at least, is no transcendental clap-trap (*baratin*)" (*Circon.*, 159/*Circum.*, 169), but a matter for passion. For it belongs to the structure of "my life" that it is not an object of analysis, that it is not only or mainly that, or reducible to that, but a matter of prayer and passion; it is not a matter of calculation, but of incalculable tears, tears you cannot count; it is not finally reckoned or reckonable but a gift.

When I speak of my life I do not objectify it, but, like Augustine, I address you. "Thee," "oh my God." As Peter Brown puts it so beautifully:

> Augustine's back is turned to us throughout the *Confessions*. His attention is elsewhere. He is speaking with his God. The pronoun *tu*— "Thou," "You"—occurs in 381 of the 453 paragraphs of the *Confessions*. Praising, questioning, "confessing" sins in the modern sense, Augustine's prose works magic with us. It brings an invisible God almost unbearably close. Readers can feel that they have stumbled, unawares, on the most intimate of all scenes—a human being (themselves quite as much as Augustine) brought with joy and trembling into the presence of God, their judge and their friend.[15]

Just so. *Et nunc confiteor tibi, domine, in litteris* ("And now I confess to you, O Lord, in writing"). We think we know to whom Augustine is speaking, the destination of the *Confessions*, but to whom is Derrida talking? If he rightly passes for an atheist, whom does he address when he reconstitutes the structure of the "you"? Is he talking to himself? Is that healthy? Who holds the place of the name of God? What place does the name of God hold? Is his back turned to us? Or is he writing face to face?

> . . . and for 59 years I have not known who is weeping my mother or me—i.e., you

He weeps. His mother weeps. He weeps for himself; he weeps for his mother. He weeps for his mother because his mother weeps for him. He weeps for himself, the son of these tears, because his mother weeps for him. He weeps for himself *from* his mother. This confusion of tears is clear enough, much clearer, in any case, than what Derrida means by adding "—i.e., you," to which is appended, without punctuation, a note from 1981:

> . . . when he says "you" in the singular and they all wonder, who is he invoking thus, who is he talking to, he replies, but you, who are not known by this or that name, it's you this god hidden in more than one, capable each time of receiving my prayer, you are my prayer's destiny, you know everything before me, you are the god (of my) unconscious, you are the measure they don't know how to take and that's why they wonder whom, from the depth of my solitude, I still address, you are a mortal god, that's why I write, I write my god . . .

To which is then appended:

> . . . to save you from your own immortality. (*Circon.*, 244/*Circum.*, 264)

In section 32, he had written something similar:

> . . . I ask your pardon for admitting to you, who represent everything, in
> this duel, all my addresses . . . I am content to turn around you in this
> silence in which you stand in for anybody, my god, . . . (*Circon.*, 155–
> 56/*Circum.*, 165–66)

"You" are everyone—"Everybody's Autobiography" (*Circon.*, 288/*Circum.*, 311)—and no one in particular, no proper name in particular, himself, his mother. "You" are everyone else, the other, addressed in a kind of public meditation, an open letter, a postcard exposed to public view, *in litteris*, in which he states plainly the stakes of the wager upon which he enters. When he speaks to his mother *in litteris*, he experiences endless guilt, for this is an intensely private affair, and we feel embarrassed, as Peter Brown said, that "we have stumbled, unawares, on the most intimate of all scenes—a human being (themselves quite as much as Augustine) brought with joy and trembling into the presence of God," or— here—into the presence of his dying mother, or of intimate details of his private life, or indeed, as we say in English so periphrastically, so circumlocutiously, so discreetly, of his "privates."

"You" stands in for everybody, that is, the other, every other, *tout autre*. When one prays, one addresses God, that is, the other, where *tout autre est tout autre*. We recall from "Denials":

> In every prayer there must be an address to the other as other; *for example*—I will say, at the risk of shocking—*God*. The act of addressing oneself to the other as other must, of course, mean praying, that is, asking, supplicating, searching out. No matter what, for the pure prayer demands only that the other hear it, receive it, be present to it, be the other as such, a gift, call, and even cause of prayer. (*Psy.* 572/DNT 110)

Prayer is addressed to the other, supplicates the other, and asks the other. For what? For what does one pray? One prays for nothing, nothing determinate. For nothing other than that the other hear it, for nothing other than to keep on praying. I pray the other. I pray to the other. I pray for the other. I pray that the other hear it and receive it and that the other may come, that the relation to the other be sustained, kept open. When you pray, say, "Other, may your kingdom come." May *you* come. *Viens, oui, oui, Amen.*

Viens is Derrida's prayer.

Viens is the prayer he is always praying. To pray is not to utter a proposition which is true or false, but to confess, and a confession is without truth; to pray is to invoke, to call, to do (*facere*) something. He is praying, before God, for the coming of the other, vowing to remain faithful to the promise, to let the other come, swearing before God, *respondeo*, I promise, believe me, I am telling the truth, beyond proof and perception, to let the other come, in which holiness I believe, in which I can only believe, in prayers and tears (cf. *Foi*, 84–85).

§18. The Son of These Tears

A prayer is not a constative but a performative, not a propositional truth but rather the truth one makes or does, *facere veritatem*, living truly, that is, staying open and owning up to the coming of the other. To pray is to ask for nothing but to keep on praying and that the other hear the prayer. Help me to address you. "Lord I do believe. Help thou my unbelief." That is an almost perfect prayer because it is a prayer for help to keep on praying, to sustain the relationship of prayer, of advent and *invenire*. O Lord, help me to stay open because I am closing down fast. Help me to stay open to you, O Lord, because I keep closing you off, assimilating you back into the circle of the same. Instead of owning up to the other I am assimilating the other into the own. I keep closing down, shutting out, cutting off:

> . . . I ask your pardon for not addressing myself to you, for still addressing myself to you to tell you so even if you don't hear me (*Circon.*, 155–56/*Circum.*, 165–66)

I keep failing to address you. I keep turning you into something else every time I (fail to) address you. My prayers keep failing to rise to heaven, to the other. To write is to betray one's addressee and to ask pardon for this betrayal, e.g., of his mother:

> . . . the one I'm getting away from as I speak about it, in betraying or slandering it with every word, even when I address myself to her without her hearing to tell her that I am betraying you . . . (*Circon.*, 155/*Circum.*, 165)

Is it not scandalous that he would make public so private an affair, that he would collect royalties on a book on the death of his mother? Does it not compare to Kierkegaard's complaint about the clergy for having made a profitable business out of the crucifixion? Unforgivable—almost. So to write this, *confiteor tibi in litteris* (IX,xii,33), is to memorialize his mother, to pay her a lasting tribute, and, at the same time, to betray her, to turn her into a literary occasion (*Circon.*, 38/*Circum.*, 36–37). Is there nothing sacred for him? Must everything become the subject of his latest book, even these private notebooks he had sworn to keep secret (*Circon.*, 202/*Circum.*, 217)? But he does not need anyone else to accuse him of this, "as though the other me, the other in me, the atheist God . . . left the slightest chance for the guilty party to save himself, even if it were by the ruse of avowal or asked-for pardon" (*Circon.*, 201/*Circum.*, 216). So to write, *sainte écriture*, is to ask her pardon—"one always asks for pardon when one writes" (*Circon.*, 46/*Circum.*, 45), *every* text is then a certain confession—for writing and for failing to address her, for betraying his address to her.

Her. My God. The other.

You. So Derrida is not showing us his back, but speaking to us. I (he) must not make you (us) an object of analysis, an onto-theo-logical object, lest the passion of this relation wither under the analytic eye, even though I/he cannot avoid it. You are accessible only when I say "you" (O God, my God). But I have already betrayed you and so I ask your pardon. (We—you—recognize here the paradox of *le dire* and *le dit* around which *Otherwise than Being* turns, perhaps even as a response to Derrida's address in "Violence and Metaphysics.") To pray is to open one's mouth and say "yes." To pray is to open one's mouth and say "come." Let the Other come. Let something Other, something In-coming, come: *l'invention de l'autre.*

However interlaced and punctuated all his life and all his writings may be with theses, propositions, assertions, arguments (yes, arguments, *pace*, Rorty and Ruth Barcan Markus), calculations, and however indispensable all these are, and however necessary it is to do all these things well, to calculate well, it remains true that everything Derrida writes is or aims at a prayer: an invocation, a provocation, a call, a hope, dream, a demand, a sacrifice:

> . . . you have spent your whole life inviting calling promising, hoping sighing dreaming, convoking invoking provoking, constituting engendering producing, naming assigning demanding, prescribing commanding sacrificing (*Circon.*, 290–91 / *Circum.*, 314)

The "final" effect, if there is one, of his "whole life" is performative not constative, is lodged in the performative: *viens!* He is praying like mad that something mad will come, in an instant of madness, something impossible, *the* impossible. For example, here, in this text, with G. up above trying to encircle him in a geo-logic program, hovering like the Hegelian *aigle*, or like the owl of *savoir absolue*, either way a bird of prey, while Derrida kneels, head bent, at his *prie-Dieu*. On the top half of the page: G. preying; on the bottom half: Jacques praying. On the top half: *sa*; on the bottom, SA. On the top half, truth; on the bottom, tears. On the top half, the "book of Derrida"; on the bottom half, the "book of Elie." The whole volume (*Jacques Derrida*) is a pray on words. (I ask your pardon, *je vous prie*, which you will give me, I am sure, so long as this frivolity is not *sans au-dèla*: *Circon.*, 226 / *Circum.*, 244.)

He is praying for forgiveness and asks for forgetting. "You are in my memory," Augustine said, "but where in my memory are you?" He is praying that the other remain and not be forgotten, praying for forgiveness for his forgetting. The time of his prayer, and the time for which he prays, is messianic time, the time of the future to come, but also the time of memory, of the immemorial past that we have erased, the time of passion. The time to pray is now and always, and one prays to have the time to keep on praying.

He prays that his life and his writings, "my life," partitioned between two worlds, may become a gift to the Other, that he be able to give without return, that when he dies we will all be able to gather around his grave and say that his life was a gift to us, not that that will do him any good then. He writes from the scene of this subdued crowd of family and friends attending his funeral (*Circon.*, 40–41/*Circum.*, 39), quietly praying and weeping. He prays for that gift and weeps over his failure to "do" or "make" that gift (*don*), *facere veritatem*, and so he also prays and weeps for pardon (*pardon*), prays and weeps that he can keep on praying and weeping, for the gift of pardon (*le don du pardon*), for the time to pray and weep.

He prays and weeps for the *don* and for *par-don*. Give (*donne*) us this time.

God—or Death

Because death too is a matter of the cut—life is torn, cut and inscribed by death—death too is not an object, but a matter for prayers and tears. That is why *Circumfession* is no less an *ars moriendi*. Derrida's religion is a meditation upon death, upon last things, upon which he is not trying to economize. Death, like God—God or death—is nothing of which G., up there, could ever find the G.-ologic or the right analysis; it is a matter for performatives, not constatives, of invocation not declaration. Death is the very "occasion" of *Circumfession*, in which he prays and weeps, *in litteris*, over the slow death of Georgette/Monica in Nice/Ostia, ending her days on the other side of the Mediterranean far from North Africa (*Circon.*, 20/*Circum.*, 19), but it is no less an occasion for meditation, for prayers and tears over his own death. *Circumfession* describes a race with death, a running forth (*Vor-laufen*), in which anxiety about whether he might die before Georgette, or whether she will live long enough for him to finish his confessions, is superimposed over the duel with G.:

> . . . [wondering] if she will live long enough to leave me time for all these confessions, and to multiply the scenes in which I see myself alone die, pray, weep (*Circon.*, 44/*Circum.*, 43)

His death, the death of the other, his death *for* the other, are not philosophical objects—he has no truth to deliver here, no philosophemes to defend—but matters for confessing, for doing the truth. Death is a deed, not a thought, Johannes Climacus said. For that reason, it would seem that these are matters for his personal diary, private affairs which he has no business "publishing," making public, so that we feel we have stumbled upon a man in the privacy of his chambers. He is trying to learn how to die:

> if this book does not transform me through and through, if it does not give me a divine smile in the face of death, my own and that of loved

ones, if it does not help me to love life even more, it will have failed (*Circon.*, 76/*Circum.*, 77)

Like Augustine he weeps over her and his mortal life, this living death (*in istam dico vitam mortalem, an mortem vitalem?*) (Am I talking about this mortal life or a living death?) (*Circon.*, 78/*Circum.*, 80). Life is life/death, *sur-vie*, living on, a *terra difficultatis* in which the difficulty death makes for life is in fact our best ally:

> ... the only ally, the most secure, it's to death that already I owe everything I earn, I have succeeded in making of it, as I have with god, it's the same thing, my most difficult ally, impossible but unfailingly faithful once you've got him in your game, it costs a great deal, believe me, a great deal of love (*Circon.*, 162/*Circum.*, 172–73)

Death is a difficult friend to have, one that tempers our steel as can nothing else.

God—or death: that phrase is frequent enough in Derrida's texts. The name of God is also the name of death: both have their origin in prayers and tears and cannot be turned into objects of analysis. God or death: both limits, both at the limit, *ultimata*, last things, *in extremis*, the line drawn around life, his life and the other's, delimiting life, circumscribing it, the darkness around the edge setting off the fading light, the undefinable finitude giving life definition, "the imminent but unpredictable coming of an event" (*Circon.*, 192/*Circum.*, 206), "certain but indefinite," Heidegger said. Death or God: the secret, the absolute secret, which inspires literature, which gives it passion(s), which no one is going to come along and solve, like a riddle, with a secret code.

Jacques is beginning to prepare for this death—or God. When he writes "you, my god", he means death, "you my death." He also means the other—for God takes the place of the other—"you who are dying," over whom I pray and weep, for the death of the other is also the death of my god, of the *tout autre*, and he would "save you from your own immortality" (*Circon.*, 244/*Circum.*, 264), from the denial of death. And he means "you who are anxious over my death," you who watch my labored breathing with anguished concern. He confesses in writing, *in litteris*, before God/death, who already knows—confession is not a matter of giving the other information—who draws him out of himself, out of his self-interest, out of the circle of the *conatus essendi*, who demands disinterest. " . . . I am trying to disinterest myself from myself, to withdraw from death by making the 'I,' to whom death is supposed to happen, gradually go away" (*Circon.*, 178/*Circum.*, 190).

Circumfession is an "auto-bio-thanato-hetero-graphical" opus (*Circon.*, 198/*Circum.*, 213): a book of life and death, of the life and death of "my self" and of his mother, and of "you," of the (m)other, of the other.[16]

Derrida is beginning to prepare for death by writing, and he does not know if he will know how to die (*Circon.*, 202/*Circum.*, 217). In this same fifty-ninth year, he is struck by a virus (Lyme disease) that paralyzes the left side of his face, freezing his left eye wide open, like a cyclops, no *Augenblick* (*Circon.*, 95/*Circum.*, 98; 117–18/123; cf. MdA, 11/MB, 3; 37–38/32), like the sclerosis mentioned in "The Principle of Reason," imposing upon him a death mask, a death face like his dying mother's (*Circon.*, 115/*Circum.*, 120; DDP, 466/PR, 5). Is this "evil eye" (*Circon.*, 109/*Circum.*, 113; 162/173) punishment for some sin, hers or his? At first, they are not sure what is wrong; the diagnosis is incomplete. Is it a stroke? Will it be followed by a more fatal attack? Is this the end, the beginning of the end, the worm in the flesh? Will he last the night? Will he die before his mother? Before he finishes his confessions? Now he is in a race, a contest, not just with G., but with her, with time, with God, with death. He sees, impossible scene, his mother, his family and friends gathered around his grave, dead at the age of 59. What shall he do with his papers? Is everything in order? (*Circon.*, 260–61/*Circum.*, 282) Now, when he drives to work, he tells a *New York Times* correspondent, he has images of being killed in an automobile crash.

"[D]ying is the word I discover at age 59" (*Circon.*, 193/*Circum.*, 208): his own death certainly—but that would be too simple (*Circon.*, 203/*Circum.*, 218). Death is no less the death of the other, of his mother or his sons, but no less, and for that very reason his own death *for* the other. Because he fears for them, he fears dying out of order, before his mother or after his sons, "my uncircumcised sons, objects of infinite compassion" (*Circon.*, 206/*Circum.*, 221). He writes from the standpoint of his sons standing around his grave (*Circon.*, 41/*Circum.*, 40). He fears for his mother, who prayed and wept over him during his childhood illnesses, fearful that she would lose the son of these tears as she lost two others:

> my fear of death will have only reflected her own, I mean my death *for her* whose anxiety I perceived each time I was ill . . . and if my mother thus carried my fear of death, I fear dying from no longer being scared of death after her death, as perhaps happened to M.P. [Merleau-Ponty] in 1962 (*Circon.*, 197–98/*Circum.*, 211–12)

He is afraid of death because he fears what his death will mean "*for her*," like SA and Monica, who was always afraid for him. If she predeceases him, then he is afraid he will no longer be afraid of death. He dreams of euthanasia, of a good death, well timed, as if the time of dying is the time of an orchestra, of joining in its playing. He dreams of "playing divinely with my sons," making his entry and exit in the piece at the right time, and he will "accept dying if dying is to sink slowly, yes, into the bottom of this beloved music" (*Circon.*, 194/*Circum.*, 208–209).

By writing *Circumfession* he is trying to survive, trying

to withdraw from death by making the "I," to whom death is supposed to happen, gradually go away, no, be destroyed before death comes to meet it, so that at the end already there should be no one left to be scared of losing the world in losing himself in it (*Circon.*, 178/*Circum.*, 190)

Circumfession is an "experimentation of my possible survival," in living on, in this mortal life or living death, the "survival that writing is," the witness, the remains of his radical absence (*Circon.*, 178/*Circum.*, 191), so that each word is like a last will (*Circon.*, 263/*Circum.*, 284). By saying this Derrida does not seek literary immortality, something he would not be around to enjoy, but rather to live today, now, this death, to live and write it, to see the world as it is without him. He would think death through *in litteris*, write death through, let death "sculpt the writing from the outside," let its form and rhythm be shaped and formed by an incalculable cut (*Circon.*, 192/*Circum.*, 207). The writing is an exercise in euthanasia, in dying well but just in order to live well (rather than the reverse). *Je me donne ici la mort*: "Here I give myself the gift of death" (*Circon.*, 263/*Circum.*, 285). I do not say that I "take my life" but that I give myself life with the gift of death. He is trying to understand the way that death is inscribed in life, is cut into life, like a circumcision, not just my death but the other's, and not to confuse life with immortality; he is trying to let the alterity of death reduce him to tears and prayers, to infinite compassion.

Christian Latin French

The partition by which Derrida's life is torn is a tear in language, not because Derrida is a philosopher of language (an illusion G., up there, is doing a good job of dispelling) but for almost the very opposite reason, because he has no language. "Derrida," popularly thought to be the philosopher of language *par excellence*, even to excess, the philosopher who would turn philosophy and the world itself into words, for whom philosophy is supposed to be just a form of writing, who is content to play with words instead of offering arguments, this same Derrida, has no language of his own:

> . . . I love words too much because I have no language of my own, only false *escarres* [bedsores] (*Circon.*, 90/*Circum.*, 92; cf. PdS, 217–18/*Points*, 203–204)

He is Jewish and not Jewish, Jewish but without knowing Hebrew, Jewish but also something of an Arab, Jewish without a Jewish wife or Jewish (circumcised) sons. He calls himself "the most advanced eschatologist," living in the end-time, the "last of the Jews," the way Elijah, his surname, was the last of the prophets, loved dearly but also excluded by his family, ruptured without rupture (*Circon.*, 92/*Circum.*, 94–95), inside/outside

Judaism. Although he is a Jew born in an Arab nation Derrida speaks to God/god/you in neither Hebrew nor Arabic, but in French, in "Christian Latin French" (*Circon.*, 57/*Circum.*, 58), the language of the colonizers of Algeria, of masters and schoolmaster (PdS, 217–18/*Points*, 204). He speaks and writes in the cut between Hebrew and Christian Latin French, between Arabic and Hebrew-Latin, so that for him even to speak and write French is to speak and write in a foreign language, "the language of the other" (PdS, 217–18/*Points*, 204). He writes in "all of my foreign languages: French, English, German, Greek, Latin, the philosophic, metaphilosophic, Christian, etc." (*Psy.* 562n1/DNT, 135n13). He writes in French even though the Vichy-sponsored government in Algeria, and this without the intervention of the Nazis (*Circon.*, 266/*Circum.*, 288), expelled him, at the age of 13—"a little black and very Arab Jew" (*Circon.*, 57/*Circum.*, 58)—from the Lycée de Ben Aknoun, near El Biar. They used the *numerus clausus* law, good Latin for closing admissions to Jewish students beyond a fixed percentage point (7 percent), something which he did not understand or have explained to him. *Circumfession* itself is a Latinate work, written in the space between Arab Jew and the lush Patristic Latin of Augustine, his "compatriot" (*Circon.*, 19/*Circum.*, 18). Although circumcision is all he has ever talked about (*Circon.*, 70/*Circum.*, 70), this word "circumcision" is Latin, the Hebrew word being scarcely known to him (*Circon.*, 75/*Circum.*, 76–77). Indeed he and his family, the Algerian Jews of El Biar, did not constitute a "true Jewish culture," but kept a certain external, even "banal" kind of religious observance (PdS, 218/*Points*, 205). They did not even speak of "circumcision" but of "baptism," not of "Bar Mitzvah" but of "communion," a "fearful acculturation" of this child who was Arab, not Catholic, barbarous (*Circon.*, 72/*Circum.*, 72–73), not baptized. What he now confesses openly, his circumcision, he was as a child taught to repress, even as he never learned until recently his Hebrew name, Elijah, the guardian of circumcision, the Jewish name he bears without bearing (*Circon.*, 92–93/*Circum.*, 95–96).

His ego is split and cut, not into transcendental and empirical selves, but into Jewish and un-Jewish, into Arab Jew and Christian Latin French, like a man trying to keep a log after a long journey by means of fragments of a forgotten, prehistoric language:

> . . . what G., the one or the other [Geoffrey or Georgette] will have never heard is that if I am a sort of *marrane* of French Catholic culture . . . I am one of those *marranes* who no longer say they are Jews even in the secret of their own hearts . . . (*Circon.*, 150/*Circum.*, 170)

The Marranos were Spanish or Portuguese Jews who were forcibly converted to Catholicism, under threat of death or exile, who practiced Judaism in secret.[17] Deriving from the Spanish word for "pigs," from the

Jewish prohibition against eating pork, the word carried a pejorative ring. At the end of *Aporias*, a detailed study of Heidegger's treatment of death in *Being and Time*, Derrida says that Heidegger's analysis belongs to "the huge archive where the memory of death in Christian Europe is being accumulated" (*Apories*, 338/*Aporias*, 80–81), whereas Derrida associates himself with the Marranos—"Marranos that we are, Marranos in any case, whether we want to be or not, whether we know it or not." Who is the Marrano?

> Let us figuratively call Marrano anyone who remains faithful to a secret that he has not chosen, in the very place where he lives, in the home of the inhabitant or of the occupant, in the home of the first or second *arrivant*, in the very place where he stays without (*sans*) saying no but without (*sans*) identifying himself as belonging to. . . . [I]n the dominant culture that by definition has calendars, this secret keeps the Marrano even before the Marrano keeps it. Is it not possible to think such a secret eludes history, age, and aging? (*Apories*, 338/*Aporias*, 81)

Derrida, whose family came to Algeria in the nineteenth century from Spain, describes himself as a Marrano, inwardly a Jew but outwardly sucked into the French Catholic culture of Algeria, speaking Christian Latin French, but with this twist, that he is a Marrano who is not quite secretly Jewish on the inside either, who is not exactly Jewish or not Jewish, who is not Christian and not quite free of Christianity, who is neither Algerian nor not, neither European nor not, neither American nor not. In the logic of Blanchot, Derrida is a Jew *sans* Judaism, Christianized *sans* Christianity, an Arab *sans* Islam, a French citizen *sans* being French, an American "phenomenon" *sans* being American,[18] a religious man *sans* theism—*Derrida sans l'être*. This atheist Arab Jew who speaks French and lives in France, whose greatest recognition is in the United States, suffers from the "illness of Proteus" (*Circon.*, 184/*Circum.*, 198):

> . . . always less recognizable in my family than in my country, in my country than in Europe, in Europe than anywhere else . . . so that I do not deprive myself . . . to speak Latin, to oblige you to learn Latin again to read SA, me, at work, the little Latin I know through having begun to learn it when Vichy had made it, I believe, obligatory in the form just before booting me out of the school in the Latin name of the *numerus clausus* by withdrawing our French citizenship (*Circon.*, 196/*Circum.*, 210–11)

Speaking to his dying mother on the phone, he cannot understand her incoherent words; she might as well be speaking Hebrew to him, he who is "reaching the end without *ever* having read Hebrew" (*Circon.*, 264–65/*Circum.*, 286–87). It is as if all of his difficult and convoluted writings are elaborate circumlocutions for the unknown language and grammar of Hebrew, as if the formidable difficulty of his writings comes from cutting around this "unreadability." Derrida has no language of his own because he has two languages, Hebrew and French, neither of which are his. He only pretended to know Hebrew, to get by Bar Mitzvah, like a Catholic altar boy in pre–Vatican II, memorizing Latin he does not understand from a badly mimeographed copy of phonetically spelled Latin. ("Day-oh grah-si-ahs.") He has/does not have two languages:

> . . . the sacred one they tried to lock me up in without opening me to it, the secular they made clear would never be mine. (*Circon.*, 267/*Circum.*, 289)

The first, Hebrew, he never learned, the second, Christian Latin French, could never be his. He loves words because he has no mother tongue or native soil, no Heideggerian *Bodenständigkeit*. This complaint echoes the complaint he made in "How to Avoid Speaking," that "for lack of capacity, competence, or self-authorization, I have never been able to speak of what my birth, as one says, should have made closest to me: the Jew, the Arab" (*Psy.*, 562n1/*DNT*, 135n13).

Unlike Heidegger's Hölderlinian Greco-Germans, who are all "plants," Derrida is a graft or transplant, always being uprooted and planted somewhere else, made more welcome in a foreign land (cf. PdS, 201–202/*Points*, 189; PdS, 362/*Points*, 351), always displaced and invited to move on (or else locked up! PdS, 137–39/*Points*, 128–30). He is a "plant" only idiomatically, like a secret agent, a "plant" paid to spy on the enemy, someone placed strategically in a foreign setting. Whatever his debt to Heidegger, Derrida's experience of language, his experience *with* language, *eine Erfahrung mit Sprache zu machen*, is an experience of exile—a "politics of the emigre or exile"[19]—that is almost completely un-Heideggerian and brings out everything that separates Derrida from Heidegger, and everything that is intolerable and dangerous about Heidegger and Heidegger's language and Heidegger's nationalistic experience of language (cf. PdS, 194–95/*Points*, 183–84).[20]

Salus in sanguine

Circumfession ends on May 1, 1990, in Laguna Beach, California, not too far from Santa Monica, two months before his sixtieth birthday, nineteen months before the death of Georgette Safar Derrida in December 1991. A proposed title for the work, *Everybody's Autobiography* (in English)—a private book about *my* religion but also for "everybody"—tells "you"— Jacques, but then also everybody else—that he is still unrecognizable.[21]

Surprisingly, not everybody knows he is Jewish, like "that young imbecile who asks you, after your talk on the Final Solution, what you had done to save Jews during the war" (*Circon.*, 289/*Circum.*, 312). So it has been necessary to announce his circumcision. Still, the imbecile was half right: he has probably not done enough to save at least one Jew, himself, both from others and from the Jews themselves, since he has cut himself off from the Jews, rightly passing for an atheist. He is not yet saved, has not yet had his blindness healed, not learned to see, not yet experienced the "resurrection" that follows death/castration/circumcision. If circumcision is the cut of death, and if there is *salus in sanguine*, a saving bleeding that for Derrida comes from being "*de*-circumcised," if he warns us not to "deport [an] Elijah obsession" on to him (*Circon.*, 208/*Circum.*, 224), then what is salvation and resurrection for him? That would be "the stabilized relation of a destination," the work of dispatching one's letters—one's prayers—"toward the secret" that demands that we not be "finished with" (*non pour en finir avec*), not be done with, "a destinerrancy which was never my doing, nor to my taste" (*Circon.*, 290/*Circum.*, 314) but to be finished or done with a complacent account of *moira*, of a fixed or determinable destiny. Resurrection would be staying with the insurrection, the difficulty of destinerrance, not taking refuge either in *moira* or baptism/circumcision. Salvation through the blood, not of circumcision, but of destinerrance, the blood that flows from being severed from the truth.

His destiny is to keep the cut open, to keep de-circumcision and a-destination alive, to be impassioned by the cut, for that is the condition of keeping the future open, of letting the unforeseeable and unanticipatable come, of letting events happen. His destiny is to let the unimaginable come, to call for it to come, to invoke and provoke events, to heave and sigh for the incoming, the invention, of the other, to dream the dream of the impossible. Let us cite again, this time parsed out graphically, what is almost the final phrase of the book, which reads like a kind of Derridean psalm, a psalm to himself, like a Franco-Jewish Walt Whitman, marking off the strata of his passion:

> . . . you have spent your whole life
> > inviting calling promising,
> > hoping sighing dreaming,
> > convoking invoking provoking,
> > constituting engendering producing,
> > naming assigning demanding,
> > prescribing commanding sacrificing
> > > (*Circon.*, 290–91/*Circum.*, 314)

Calling for and dreaming of what? A "secret truth, i.e., severed from truth," a secret *cut* off from truth, circum-cut off from truth, where the Truth of truth, *savoir absolue*, falls onto the mohel's napkin like a severed foreskin, *Saint Prépuce*. For it is this severance from Truth, this Truth-less truth of his existence, that impassions. If, for his compatriot Saint Augustine, God is Truth, for him the truth is living *sans vérité*, severed from God's Truth and Truth's God.[22] His destiny is to be without destination, destined to be cut off from truth, severed from the truth of a single destiny, a dream without (*sans*) truth, a secret truth whose only witness testifies that there is no witness. That is his passion. He makes a "pure" confession, without truth, the confession and profession of a future that is not fettered to Truth, with a capital letter. The resurrection that comes of this cut is to deliver us from the hands of the One and Only Jealous God of Truth who not only spills the blood of those who defy his wishes but who also spills the blood of the faithful to remind them of their covenant (Yiddish *bris*, Hebrew *berît*), of which circumcision is the sign.

The point of his work is performative and impassioning—to dream and give thanks, give and dream—not disinterested and constative. In it, truth is always subordinate to the gift without exchange, to the future, to what can come:

> Truth belongs to this movement of repayment that tries in vain to render itself adequate to its cause or to the thing. Yet this latter emerges only in the hiatus of disproportion. The just measure of "restoring" or "rendering" is impossible—or infinite. (MdA, 36/MB, 30)

Et solidasti auctoritatem libri tui: "And thou didst establish the firmament of the authority of Thy Book," Augustine wrote. But Derrida has only *écriture*, no Book, which was also his argument with Jabès, no guiding light or guiding star, and he is more than a little worried by those religions which, having been given a Book, always use them to spell war not peace:

> ... *ergo es* [therefore you are], in this very place, you alone whose life will have been so short, the voyage short, scarcely organized, by you with no lighthouse and no book, you the floating toy at high tide and under the moon ... (*Circon.*, 291/*Circum.*, 314–15)

Not a ship sailing straight ahead, its heading set, the helmsman's eye on the lighthouse, but a toy bobbing blindly upon the waves. For the cut with this secret truth is the condition of the future, of the open-endedness of the future, of the passion for the future. His religion, his messianic structure without messianism, the passion of the religion he is (re)inventing, the religion without religion, before religion, the nondogmatic double of dogma that he produces, the circumcision he is reinscribing—all this is a religion of the event, a religion that ties him to what is coming, that cuts a covenant with what is to-come; all this is the passion for something impossible to come, for the future, *l'à-venir*.

Come. I pray you.

♦ *Edifying Divertissement No. 6.*
A Prayer

When you pray, say, in Franco-Aramaic:

Viens. I pray you, come. May your time come. In an instant, in the twinkling of an eye. I long for you to come, yearn for you, like the deer for running streams.

When will you come?

I give you everything, time and death, the food out of my mouth, without return. Take this and keep it. Take it, forget it.

Believe me, I am telling you the truth, entrusting you with all I know and do not know, with every secret, giving you everything, yes, holding nothing back. Believe me as I believe you, trust me as I trust you. Like Lazarus, yes, like water into wine.

When will you come?

Give me this time, I pray you, the time of coming and of welcoming, the time of giving and forgiving, the time to come, of justice to come. May justice come and wash over us like water over the land.

When will you come?

I pray you, forgive me. I confess to you and ask your pardon for forgetting you. Believe me, you are in my memory. But where in my memory are you? (Hear, O Israel, do not forget.) I pray that you remain. I promise that I will recall all that you have been, yes, and keep you in my heart. Forgive me for all that I have forgotten, yes, and silenced. As I forgive others.

When will you come?

Viens! I pray you.

Dilige, et quod vis fac.

Amen, *oui, oui.*

Rabbi Augustinus Judaeus

§19. *These Weeping Eyes, Those Seeing Tears: The Faith of Jacques Derrida*

The Book of Tears

Jacques Derrida is a man of tears, of faith and tears, for faith is driven by passion and tears are the passion of faith. So Derrida has written a book of tears—*Memoirs of the Blind: The Self-Portrait and Other Ruins*—to accompany the book of Elie, a book of faith to accompany the book of circumcision, a book, if I may say so, of circumcised eyes, if tears flow from circumcised eyes.

Memoirs of the Blind is a confession of faith and as such a companion piece to *Circumfession*, a bit of a brother and sibling rival, written during the same period and, like *Circumfession*, highly autobiographical, "so very close to myself" (MdA, 10/MB, 3). What alternative to faith, to the blindness and passion of faith, can there be, he asks, once one confesses the limits of knowledge? How else to proceed if one must make one's way— contrary to everything that phenomenology advises—*sans voir et sans savoir*, deprived of vision and verity, "in the blind"?[23]

Memoirs is, at first sight at least, a running commentary on an exhibition given at the Louvre (October 26, 1990–January 21, 1991) and organized by Derrida at the invitation of the museum curators.[24] Derrida's exhibition was the first in a series entitled *Parti pris*, "Taking Sides," in which a series of distinguished thinkers, artists, and writers who are not professional art historians were given full freedom to organize an exhibition of Louvre holdings on a theme entirely of their own choosing. Derrida chose the theme of blindness, and, having selected mostly drawings by the old masters and a few paintings, concentrated on self-portraits. So, in vintage Derridean fashion, the theme he chose is the self-portrait as the memoir of a blind man.

But there is another twist (who ever doubted it?). *L'aveugle*, the "abocular" one (*aveugle* derives from the Latin *aboculus*), the "blind man," whose self-portrait is being drawn, whose memoirs are being published, is first of all Jacques Derrida himself. Having depicted himself in *Circonfession* as monocular, he now declares himself abocular. But then, beginning with Jacques, these memoirs belong to "anyone (*quiconque*) among us, in our culture, who says 'mine'" (MdA, 119/MB, 117), just as his confessions are meant to be "everybody's" (*Circon.*, 288/*Circum.*, 311). Both books—the book of circumcision and the book of tears, the circum-confessions and the memoirs—belong to a long tradition of weepy, self-confessing men of letters. Above all, both books are bathed in the tears of Saint Augustine, his North African compatriot, and belong to a certain quasi-Augustinian legacy.

On the cover of *Memoirs* we see the self-portrait of Fantin-Latour, staring at us eerily from one large eye, while the other eye is hidden in the dark. Is that not Jacques, stricken with a facial paralysis, one eye frozen open like a cyclops in a "blind stare" (the illness, we have seen in *Circumfession*, that cut deeply into his flesh, if only to vanish, to re-treat, without a trace)? By the same token, could we not replace the smiling, winsome, handsome Jacques, the movie star whose photograph greets us on the cover of *Circumfession*, with Fantin-Latour's unnerving stare?

Again, could we not replace both of them with any of the Louvre's blind men, their hands stretched out before them, feeling the air as if they had little eyes attached to their fingertips, or tapping with their canes, as if there were eyes at the end of their sticks, as if they were dabbing at their canvas (MB, figs. 1–2)? For these memoirs are written "in the blind," in the dark—is not writing always, structurally, done in the dark, in the absence of an intuitive object, with a bit of faith? Like a man awakening in the night and scribbling down a dream on a pad he keeps beside his bed, as Jacques is wont to do (MdA, 11/MB, 3); or like the driver of an automobile who, with both eyes on the road and one hand on the steering wheel, is making notes with his other hand, which is how the topic of the Louvre exhibition "came" to him (MdA, 38/MB, 32–33).

Most interesting of all, and this would be the option I would have chosen were I the graphic designer, could we not replace both covers with the drawing of the woman weeping at the foot of the Cross, by the sixteenth-century Italian artist Daniele da Volterra (MB, fig. 71). For *Memoirs* is above all—and this is what interests me most about it, this is the axe I am relentlessly grinding—a book of tears, of prayers and tears, of tears of passion and the passion of tears, and the blindness that is in question in *Memoirs* is the blindness of eyes blurred by tears. What does the body mean to say when it fills our eyes with tears? Why not our ears or mouth (DM, 57–58/GD, 55)? According to the Greeks, the desire of the eyes is to see and the eyes are delightful organs of sight, for men love to know and, above all the other senses, men take great delight in seeing. That is what the philosopher said at the beginning of a book that set the course for a great deal of the philosophy and theology that was to come thereafter, so that after that very little else could come (*Met.*, I, 1, 980a20–25). But for weepy, quasi-Augustinian jewgreeks like Derrida, where the desire for seeing and *savoir* has been displaced, the most exquisite destiny of the eyes is to be bathed in and to well up with tears. "These weeping eyes, those seeing tears," as Marvel wrote of the blind Milton (MdA, 129–30/MB, 128–29).

Now the difference between seeing and weeping, between Greek and jewgreek, between the theatrics of Greco-Husserlian *Anschauung* and being blinded with tears, also marks a sexual difference for Derrida, for why do these Louvre artists almost always present us with blind men but weeping women? And why is it that when we do occasionally find a blind woman—for example, Saint Lucy—she is a saint and a healer, not a tragic hero like Oedipus, who was wounded by a tragic fate (MdA, 12–13/MB, 5–6)? Furthermore, if Jacques is a man of tears, is he—and then are Augustine and Nietzsche, whom he also calls men of tears?—a little womanly? And is *Memoirs of the Blind* a womanly book to accompany the book of circumcision, which is decidedly an awfully phallic rite? Then is *Memoirs* more a sister than a brother of *Circumfession*? Could there be, *per impossibile*, a sibling rivalry between this brother and sister, there where there ought to be pure love without desire? Or, since *Memoirs* and *Cir-*

cumfession get along so well, are they not both sisters, circumcised sisters, with circumcised eyes and ears and hearts?

The Eyes of Faith

Faith is the only recourse of the blind. *Memoirs* is a self-portrait framed by faith, beginning and ending with faith, literally beginning and ending with the question *"Vous croyez?"* "Do you believe?" (MdA, 9/MB, 3; 130/129). At the end, the answer is, "I don't know, one has to believe" (*"Je ne sais pas, il faut croire"*) (MdA, 130/MB, 129). One hopes and prays for something to come, one sighs and weeps that it will come, but one does not know. All along one *has to* believe, one must, *il faut*, one has no alternative but to believe that it will come, even though, precisely because, one does not know if and what is coming. One is driven, impassioned, touched by *la passion du non-savoir*. Faith is the passion of unknowing.

Breaking with the oldest paradigm, the most defining and paradigmatic principle of Western philosophy, that of *idein, eidos, idea* and its associated *theorein*—the whole history of Europe as a history of seeing—Derrida takes his stand with the blind (MdA, 18/MB, 12), with the blindness of faith, with the witness who does not proceed by way of knowledge but is impassioned by faith. This is to take a fundamentally Augustinian, religious, and biblical position, for on this point Augustine himself is just being a good student of the biblical and prophetic tradition rather than of Plotinus.[25] There are many blind men, in Greece and in biblical times, but we are a little weary of Oedipus and Tiresias, Derrida says, for in addition to these old Greeks we have a vast reserve of Jewish memories to draw upon (MdA, 24/MB, 17–18). The Greeks treat seeing as our most natural tendency and desire, part of our deepest desire to know, while the blind are either defects of nature to be cast aside, seers gifted with a still more exceptional vision, or great tragic heroes struck down by fate, machismo fathers like Oedipus who gouge their own eyes out. But Derrida is interested in delimiting this deeply phallo-philosophical desire and in bringing blindness into view, not as a negative defect of nature or a supernatural endowment, but as a deeply affirmative desire, a quasi-transcendental passion for the impossible, as a way to weep and sigh over the unforeseeable, *autrement que voir et au-delà de savoir*. For surely the *tout autre*, if there is one, is out of sight. In the end, the eyes are made for passion and for tears.

If *Memoirs* is an exhibition of the varieties of blindness, as it certainly is, it is by the same token an exhibition of the varieties of faith. For the eyes of faith are, as such, blind; to see with the eyes of faith is to take on faith precisely what we do not see. That is why the "witness" for Derrida can never be an *eye* witness but precisely the opposite, someone "abocular" who gives witness or bears witness in his or her life to what they believe but do not see. The witness is not empowered by truth—*scientia* or *savoir*, *intuitus* or *voir*—not a macho hero of truth and first-hand seeing, but, following Augustine, the witness does the truth or makes the truth (*facere veritatem*) in her life. Faith is structurally inhabited by blindness, which is its quasi-transcendental condition. "And faith, in the moment proper to it, is blind. It sacrifices sight, even if it does so with an eye to seeing at last" (MdA, 36/MB, 30). "I have found it necessary to deny knowledge," Kant said, "in order to make room for faith"; Derrida has found it necessary to limit and delimit *voir* and *savoir*, in the interests of making room for *croire*. That old saw "seeing is believing" is so far from true that it is just when we see that we no longer believe. Believing depends upon blindness and has to do with the desire for what is out of sight.[26]

Il faut croire. One must, one has to, it is necessary to believe, because one does not know, "*je ne sais pas*," and one does not know what else to do. Our life is a tissue of faith, of little beliefs and credulities, *minima credibilia*, of taking one another's word, of assumptions and presuppositions which, if they form a rich enough and elaborate enough network, may just see us through the day and then, if they are still more complex and subtle enough, might well see us through the week. The issue, as Heidegger said, is not that we presuppose too much but that we presuppose too little. As to the future, beyond today, we can only have faith and hope and passion enough to say *viens!*

"Do you believe?" *Je ne sais pas*. I don't know *if* I believe, or *what* I believe. I do not know if I believe—in God, e.g. Or better, since I want to believe in as much as possible, I do not know what I believe in when I believe in God. What do I love when I love my God? We keep asking Augustine's question. What do I believe when I believe (in) God?, we ask with a certain Jewish Augustine.

"*Je ne sais pas*." The blindness or non-seeing, the *je ne sais pas*, by which I am ultimately inhabited for Derrida is the absolute secret (although he does not explicitly introduce the secret into the discussion in *Memoirs*). Blindness is not wallowing in ignorance or giving up on inquiry—"I am all for knowledge"—but a structural non-knowing, what is structurally heterogeneous to knowledge, which constitutes "a more ancient, more originary experience, if you will of the secret" (PdS, 214–15/*Points*, 201), which is how Derrida glosses *la passion du non-savoir* referred to in *Cinders*, 59. The secret is a structural or quasi-transcendental matter, not a contingency of my biography or an accident my vision has suffered. Literature will have always begun. The absolute, more ancient secret is not a determinate object hidden somewhere under some theological, metaphysical, or psychoanalytic rock waiting to be uncovered by a stealthy hermeneut. The secret is not a matter of something presently obscured from our sight, something *velatum*, which a great discoverer or a supernatural revelation will unveil for us. Our eyes are always, structurally, veiled, and above all veiled with tears. No father confessor or psychiatrist, no theologian or metaphysician, no oracle or diviner, no hermeneut or *Seinsdenker* will get to the bottom of this secret, because it has no bottom. The secret is older than my childhood or my father, my baptism or my circumcision, older than *voir* and *savoir*, older than historical time. The secret is a secret from time immemorial, time out of mind, an absolute secret. The secret is the apocalypse without apocalypse, the insight that we are all a little blind, that he poses against both the *Lumières* and the "*schwärmerische Vision*" of the spirit-seers in "On Newly Arisen Apocalyptic Tone in Philosophy." Unlike the blindfold in Coypel's "The Error" (MB, fig. 8), which could be removed, or the blind men whom Jesus heals with a touch (MB, figs. 3–7), the more ancient, more originary experience of the absolute secret imposes a blindness that cannot be remedied, a radical, structural condition in virtue of which everyone is blind from birth, like an abocular species that makes its way around only by feeling (*passion*) and hearing. But the secret impassions and faith is the passion of the secret. The blindness of the secret supplies the quasi-transcendental condition of faith, delimiting *savoir* in order to make room for the passion of *non-savoir*, impassioning the desire for the impossible and the unforeseeable.

For the *tout autre* is surely out of sight!

We never get out from under the textuality and structural undecidability of our lives. The Messiah never shows up in the plain light of day. No heavenly hook drops from the sky to bail us out at the critical moment. No *revelatio* is going to remove the veils from our eyes. *Vetus testamentum velatum, novum testamentum revelatum*, but only if you take the New Testament on faith. There are many faiths, and if you happen to be Jewish, or to get converted to Judaism, you will be free to turn this little shibboleth around and claim that the New Testament is old stuff and in the dark. Everybody, in any faith, says that they now see with the eyes of faith where previously they were blind. But what they mean is that, no longer seeing what they previously believed, they now have faith in what they presently do not see. The danger that inheres in the determinate faiths— the "positive" religions—which are a little too positive—is that they will confuse seeing and believing and forget that the eyes of faith are blind. That is when they become intolerant of other faiths: "It is always the other who did not yet see" (MdA, 24/MB, 18). The *oligopistoi*, those of little faith, those who believe less, usually are just those who believe differently. The Christians think the Pharisees are blind to love, while the Jews think that those who saw the risen Christ are seeing things, while Islam thinks that it is the Koran that sees things aright. To these conflicting visions, Derrida opposes a community, if it is one, of the blind, *une communauté aveugle*, of the blind leading the blind. Blindness makes for good communities, provided we all admit that we do not see, that in the crucial matters we are all stone blind and without privileged access, adrift in the same boat, without a lighthouse to show the other shore.

We need—*il faut*—to take it on faith, to go it on faith alone, to proceed on faith, for it is necessary and indeed urgent—*il faut*—to proceed, if only by feeling ahead warily with our stick. "Like all blind men, they must *advance*, advance or commit themselves, that is, expose themselves, run through space as if running a risk" (MdA, 12/MB, 5). We need to make our way, take risks, grope in the dark, feel our way, learn to work in the dark, and that is the nocturnal work of faith which is always through a glass darkly. To have faith is to consent in advance, to say yes, to our blindness, which is the condition of saying yes to faith, which is also to say *viens!* Blindness is not an infirmity, an impotence to be healed or gotten over, but the quasi-transcendental condition of the *oui, oui*, which is strictly faith, which lets faith happen, lets it fly up like sparks against the darkness of night. He has found it necessary to deny *savoir* in order to make room for *viens, oui, oui*. Faith gropes like a blind man's cane in the dark, like a blind man's hand feeling the air (we should also speak of the hands of faith, not just its eyes), so that all those beautiful drawings of blind men in the Louvre are drawings of us, self-portraits in which we all behold our own condition. *Il faut croire*—that is a principle of movement whose groping advance is to be opposed to those limp, motionless prisoners laced in place in the Platonic allegory of the cave. The prisoners await the *anabasis* and *anamnesis*, the Platonic hook that will lift them up the steep ascent into the light, for they are impassioned only by sight and want to rise above *doxa* (MdA, 21–22/MB, 13–15).

What is still more important, indeed I would risk saying that this is the most important insight of this book of tears and blindness, is that our condition is portrayed best of all by a weeping woman, by da Volterra's drawing of the woman weeping at the foot of the Cross, her eyes veiled with tears, her hands veiling her eyes (MB, fig. 71). That is the autobiography of us all, the self-portrait of everybody. That at least is the provisional hypothesis of *Memoirs*, what it would let us see. So let us follow Derrida through the Louvre, let us don our museum headphones with Derrida as our recorded tour guide, keeping our eyes peeled in particular for what Derrida says in *Memoirs of the Blind* about eyes blinded and veiled by tears, a topic that he keeps deferring until the end.

The Point of View of Derrida's Work as an Author

However much he resists letting *Memoirs* lapse into a purely private *memoire* or a personal journal of how he came up with this theme for the exhibition, *Memoirs of the Blind* is undeniably, in part, an autobiographical account of Derrida's memories, a *memoire* of several episodes in his life, a self-portrait of the sort of things that have been happening to him over the years, which help establish the point of view of his work as an author.

Part of its point of departure, certainly, is Derrida's habit of writing in the dark (on a pad he keeps at a night table), or without looking (while driving), which has the look of being a little "accidental" (MdA, 11/MB, 4). In such a situation Derrida—anyone really—is all hands, groping, trying to see with one's fingers, to form letters without seeing their form, the way blind men feel the air before them with their hands or with sticks, trying to see prosthetically, "imploring"—it is almost tearful—the space in front of them, not with eyes, but with hands and sticks (MdA, 12–13/MB, 4–6; cf. figs. 1–3). That blind groping movement, Derrida says, is an allegory of drawing itself, of the draftsman's hands, as if someone had replaced the blind man's stick with a draftsman's pen.

But *Memoirs* is no less a memoire of a dream (July 16, 1989)[27] upon which Derrida took good notes. In this dream, Derrida comes upon two elderly blind men who are going at each other's throats. One of these old men turns upon him, an innocent passerby, with such fury that Derrida suspects the old blind man must be able to see him with at least one eye, like a cyclops. After wrestling him to the ground, the old man makes a threat against his sons. The dream contains several elements: eyes and blindness, three generations of men, a duel and mourning (*duel, deuil, vieux, d'yeux*), and it is moreover linked with the cyclops image of his Lyme disease (MdA, 37–38/MB, 32). The dream is "mine," he says, but it can serve as a parable, a parable about parables, for "anyone" (MdA, 23–24/MB, 16–17). The intergenerational scene is "testamentary," having to do with the last will and testament of one generation for the next, and it evokes for Derrida three biblical scenes portrayed in the Louvre collection, three scenes of "old blind men of the Old Testament" who "suffer through their sons" (MdA, 28/MB, 21), although the dream occurred before he hit upon this theme for *Parti Pris* (MdA, 37/MB, 31).

Elijah—"which turns out to be one of my first names"—aged and blind, having been told that his two sons have been killed in battle and the ark of God captured, falls over backwards and dies. *Isaac*, dim of sight, is deceived by Rebecca who substitutes Jacob for Esau (MB, fig. 11). *Tobit* (figs. 12–15), a good and virtuous man, tells his story, in the first person, of how, having wept over the prophecies of Amos and having buried a dead man in defiance of the king's orders, he fell asleep and is made blind by bird droppings that cover his eyes with a white film. His sight is restored by his son Tobias, who, following the instructions of the angel Raphael, heals him by spreading fish gall on his father's eyes. In Rembrandt's depiction of this scene (MB, fig. 15), Tobias appears almost to be performing surgery, a merely "natural" episode, devoid of faith, which in fact is how the picture was first mistakenly identified. But behind the son one can see the angel, "the one coming to *announce* the other" (MdA, 35/MB, 28), who, having made himself visible for the purpose, miraculously guides Tobias's hand. Before parting, Raphael bids Tobit to give thanks to God and to write all this down, and at that point of thanksgiving the angel disappears. So when Tobit writes these things down he is not so much making a faithful, factual report of what happened to him, but giving thanks to God. His pen moves in "respectful *observance*" (cf. MdA, 63–64/MB, 59–60) of a "law beyond sight," in which the truth of the account serves the debt of thanksgiving, "of giving thanks at once to the gift and the lack," the "acknowledgment before knowledge" (MdA, 35/MB, 29).

In the story of Tobit, the *trait* (writing, drawing) gives thanks before and beyond giving information. With the *trait* one does not represent but one gives a gift or pays a debt; the *trait* is a mark, not of faithful representation, but of the fidelity of faith. For "faith, in the moment proper to it, is blind. It sacrifices sight, even if it does so with an eye to seeing at last" (MdA, 36/MB, 30). Tobit inscribes his story not in the interests of a constative representation or description but as a performative, as a way to give thanks, as a song or hymn or prayer of thanksgiving. The story belongs to a repayment that can never be completed, to a disproportion or a non-*adequatio*, an infinite or impossible restoring (MdA, 36/MB, 30–31), so that truth walks always a few steps behind faith and thanksgiving.

The genesis of *Memoirs* is most immediately bound up with Derrida's Lyme disease, with the facial paralysis which he suffered from the end of June to mid-July 1989, while he was mulling over the theme for this exhibition. The illness forced him to delay a meeting scheduled for July 5 with the Louvre curators until July 11. When the paralysis passes, when he is "healed," he experiences a euphoria of "conversion or resurrection," a miraculous restoration of his *Augenblick*. On the evening of July 11, after his meeting at the Louvre, he hastily scribbles a provisional title for the exhibit at the Louvre, "*L'ouvre où ne pas voir*" (MdA, 37–38/MB, 32–33): the open, where not to see; the Louvre, where not to see; not-seeing in the Louvre as the place of the open, as the condition of seeing. He will treat the Louvre, the place of the open (*l'ouvre*), the place where people go to savor seeing the world's most precious visual objects, as a place of blindness and not-seeing, and he will treat this not-seeing as the condition of seeing. That is a theme no art historian is likely to have suggested.

Another personal memory working its way into the fabric of *Memoirs* is his recollection of a sibling rivalry straight out of a Freudian family romance, or straight out of the biblical story of Jacob (Jacques) and Esau (MB, fig.11), which proves also to be the birth of Derrida's own vocation, of his "point of view as an author." Derrida always remembers drawing as an infirmity, something he just could not do. At the moment he is about to draw, just as he has turned his eye from the object to the paper, he goes blind, the thing itself having slipped away and out of view. How does the draftsman see the thing at the same time that he "jealously dedicates" the strokes (*traits*) of his pen to the thing? This infirmity feeds the passion of his jealousy for his older brother, René-Abraham (Esau), a talented drafts-man whom everyone admired "for his eye." But René's eye turns out to be more like the eye of Abel (MB, fig. 16): "for his eye, in short which has no doubt never ceased to bring out and accuse in me, deep down in me, *apart from me*, a fratricidal desire" (MdA, 43/MB, 37). Jacques suffered from this eye which stared at him everywhere in his childhood home. "I suffered from seeing my brother's drawings on permanent display, reli-giously framed on the walls of every room" (MdA, 43/MB, 37). René drew reproductions of family portraits, including one of their old grandfather Moses, who "though not a rabbi, incarnated for us the religious conscious-ness, a venerable righteousness placed him above the priest" (MdA, 43/MB, 37). (Add *Dieu* to the "the murmuring of these syllables"—*d'yeux, vieux, duel, deuil*—that resonate in his dream and down the long Louvre corridors.) So he renounced this one *trait*, drawing, for another *trait*, writ-ing, repaying René "a *trait* for a *trait*" (MdA, 44/MB, 37), an eye for an eye. Derrida's vocation as a writer, the point of view of his work as an author, the calling and vocation that he hears but cannot see, originates just as much in *ressentiment* (MdA, 46/MB, 41), in a fratricidal war, in a stratagem, which turns on an "economy of drawing." He would econo-mize *on* drawing just in order to win an economic war, to sell his own work, his writing, at a higher price than René could command for his drawings. Jacques's work will always be a work of the never-ending and unsuccessful mourning of drawing. For however much he resists draw-ing—except for a "disastrous" attempt to sketch his mother as she lay dying in her hospital bed, nearly blind from cataracts—drawing always returns, as it has with this invitation from *Parti Pris* (MdA, 44/MB, 39).

The Hypothesis of Sight

The central analysis of drawing in *Memoirs of the Blind* turns on what Derrida calls the "hypothesis of sight." This I think can best be understood as the principle of a counter-phenomenology of blindness, as a certain counter-type to phenomenology and its principle of all principles, the principle of pure seeing. Phenomenology is a classical hypothesis of sight, a philosophy of seeing and intuition par excellence, which wants to be the eyes of philosophy. Phenomenology is something of a silent or invisible dialogue partner in *Memoirs*—the entire piece taking the form of a dia-logue between unidentified discussants, one of whom is a woman, and the other Derrida[28]—that is being subtly contested all along. In phenom-enology everything turns upon the suspension of the thesis of the natural attitude, the *epoche* of all the presuppositions that work their way into common sense and science, in order to release a pure, presuppositionless seeing. But inasmuch as *Memoirs of the Blind* moves in the opposite direction and wants to be a philosophy of blindness, everything in *Memoirs* turns on a suspension of seeing or of the gaze (MdA, 119/MB, 117), on disbelieving what is before our eyes, like a skeptic suspending judgment (MdA, 9/MB, 1), just in order to put blindness on exhibit, to expose to what extent seeing is inhabited by, indeed is constituted by blindness and hypotheses. In *Memoirs*, we hold seeing in a certain suspension, a certain *skepsis*, before proceeding to judgment, because "[t]he judgment depends on [*suspendu à*] the hypothesis" (MdA, 9/MB, 1) about what seems to lie plainly before our eyes. The effect of *Memoirs* is to displace phenomenology and the primacy it puts on seeing, and even to displace the Heideggerian displacement of phenomenology, to displace *aletheia* itself, and to put the Great Greek Opening, *aletheia* as *l'ouvre grecque*, in a religious procession behind a number of old blind men from the Bible who have their own way of *making* truth.

The hypothesis of sight, the suspending of seeing upon hypotheses, which brings seeing into view by exposing its blind spots, is formed by the intersection of two subsidiary and interacting hypotheses, two antennae or scouts sent out ahead to prepare the wandering path of the present speculations, of the present *errance* in the land of the blind. (1) The act of drawing as such, in its proper moment, is blind, like Derrida scribbling down his dreams in the dark, like Diderot writing in the dark (cf. Epigraph, MB, 9/1). (2) "[A] drawing of the *blind* is a drawing *of* the blind" (MdA, 10/MB, 2), i.e., a drawing made of a blind subject is a drawing of the blindness of the draftsman. Every time the blind are taken as a thematic object, every time a drawing is made of a blind man, that is to be taken as a representation of the figure of the draftsman—and sometimes of a draftswoman—a representation of the power of drawing itself. In short, because drawing of itself is done in the blind, and the drawing is the work of blind men, drawings of the blind are a kind of self-portrait of the artist, an allegory about the "origin of drawing." Drawing (*dessin*) is a work of the *trait*, of marks and lines, which are in *re-trait*, of traits that re-peat, that are deployed according to a code of reiterability, and that withdraw, that disappear and make themselves invisible, to which both artist and spectator alike are rendered blind. Needless to say, this blindness is a structural matter, not a simple impairment or enfeebling of vision (MdA, 9–10/MB, 2–3).

Within the framework of this bipartite hypothesis Derrida says that he finds himself hesitating between two paradoxes or logics of blindness or invisibility that lie at the heart of drawing, which he calls respectively "transcendental" and "sacrificial" blindness. That is, one may treat blindness either as a transcendental or quasi-transcendental condition, the way a blind spot can organize a vision. Or one may consider the explicit and thematic representations of the blind, representations of the blind that would reflect this invisible condition and so would represent the unrepresentable (MdA, 46/MB, 41), something that always happens, Derrida thinks, according to a sacrificial economy. He treats transcendental blindness first.

(A) "Transcendental blindness" refers to the invisibility of the act of drawing itself, which can never be a thematic object of drawing, never be represented, but is the invisible condition of possibility of drawing, so that drawing is always an operation of the blind. Blindness thus "is not an impotence or failure; on the contrary, it gives to the experience of drawing its *quasi-transcendental* resource" (MdA, 48/MB, 49). Derrida seeks "to transcendentalize, that is, to ennoble an infirmity or impotence" (MdA, 60/MB, 55), to make blindness a universal condition of drawing. To say the least, that is a little counter-intuitive; for while one can imagine Beethoven stone deaf but still composing from memory—*The Late Quartets* as the *memoires* of the deaf—how are we to imagine a blind draftsman or painter, Monet, for example, having gone only "almost" blind? In what sense can drawing be a memoir of the blind? That is hard to see.

Derrida delineates three "aspects" (sights) of transcendental blindness. (1) The first he calls the "aperspective of the graphic act." A blindness inheres in the originary act of drawing itself, at the very point of contact between pen and paper, at the very instant the draftsman inaugurates the trace. This blindness involves both memory and forgetting. On the one hand, having turned his eye from the model to the drawing paper, the draftsman is going on memory alone, is drawing from or upon memory, even if his model still stands before him in the flesh. He must let the thing itself slip away, break with the tyranny of what is present, with the visible, perceptual presence which would otherwise paralyze his pen. Moving with the lightning speed of the *Augenblick*, his pen is carried on the wings of memory, which serves as a shutter which instantly, in the instant, includes and excludes, sorts among a riot of too much detail (*plus de vue*) which it must see no more (*plus de vue*), including and enlarging this, excluding or diminishing that. To draw is to go blind to the press of perceptual presence and surrender to the pen and paper and to the world that is instituted "in the dark," as it were (MdA, 51–53/MB, 47–48). Although Derrida is citing Baudelaire, it all sounds a little like Merleau-Ponty, which is the other hand, i.e., the "absolute invisibility" that cannot in principle become visible, the aperspectival blind spot that launches vision while remaining itself out of sight, forgotten and invisible, in *retrait* (MdA, 56–57/MB, 51–53).

(2) But it is not only the tracing of the trace, the instituting act of drawing, that is withdrawn, but even the trace itself, what is traced out (*tracé*), after it is traced, is also withdrawn. The drawn lines must not stand out in their own density and color but must withdraw, become invisible,

let themselves be eclipsed, in favor of the visible things that rise up into presence through the trace. Derrida has in mind the drawing as a differential spacing or

> a blinking of the difference that begets it, or if you prefer, a *jalousie* (a blind) of traits cutting up the horizon, *traits* through which, *between* which, you can observe without being seen, you can see between the lines, if you see what I mean. (MdA, 59/MB, 55)

We do not *stricto sensu* see the lines but "through" the lines which are like "venetian blinds," the "blinds" being what permit the visible to be seen by shuttering or structuring the light.[29] Derrida cannot resist adding that all this talk of withdrawal, *retrait,* sounds a little like the God that withdraws, the *deus absconditus,* let us say the invisible God, who withdraws behind the visible world and before whom we would go blind were we to look at him straight on (without blinds).

(3) Finally there is the question of the rhetoric of the *trait,* by which he means the link between drawing and language, the "duel" between them, the way words "haunt" drawings (MdA, 60–61/MB, 56–57). Not only do we see when we read, but we are all along reading when we view drawings; seeing is reading (MdA, 66–68/MB, 64). We have already caught a glimpse of this in the mistaken naming of Rembrandt's drawing of the healing of Tobit (MB, fig. 15), which destroyed the drawing's faith and caused us to see not a miracle but a "simple natural surgery" (MdA, 36/MB, 30). But it is in the "self-portrait" that this final trait is most clearly inscribed, for with a self-portrait—a portrait artists make of themselves, so this is a strictly human affair—there is no internal trait whatsoever, no marking inscribed in the drawing itself, that tells us it is a self-portrait and not a portrait of the artist done by another, nothing internal to confirm that signatory and subject coincide. This we learn only by retreating to language, to the "verbal event" on the "parergonal border," where we read "self-portrait" (MdA, 68/MB, 64). To that extent, the self-portrait is ruined from the start.

To demonstrate this trait, Derrida takes up the self-portraits of Fantin-Latour (MB, figs. 21–27), particularly the one on the cover (fig. 25), which he takes to be a "self-portrait of a self-portrait" (MdA, 65/MB, 62). Such a demonstration, *stricto sensu,* should be impossible, since there ought to be no visible mark or monstration or portrayal of self-portraiture, given that it is only parergonally that we know it is a self-portrait at all. Still, placing our faith in this external hypothesis, let us take it as a self-portrait—and indeed as one in which the traits of self-portraiture are inscribed. On the one hand, we behold in this drawing "the monocular stare of a narcissistic cyclops," one eye frozen open in the mirror (more Lyme disease), fixed, even fixated on itself, like a hunter fascinated with its prey, a blind, dead stare, which a pious hand would close at the moment of death, at the beginning of mourning. "This seeing eye [of the draftsman] sees itself blind" [in the mirror] (MdA, 61/MB, 57). On the other hand, we see that the draftsman's other eye is lost in shadows, hidden and withdrawn from the blinding mirror. Two eyes then: one seen (by him—and also by us) but unseeing; the other seeing (his—but also ours) but unseen. Two seeings, two blindnesses. That binocularity is the "transcendental retrait" of the self-portrait.

This brings us face to face with the "hypothesis of sight," or of "intuition." For however much we might oppose vision to hypothesis, or intuition to faith, or conjecture to perception, the fact is that vision and perception are highly "theory-laden," as we say in Anglo-America, highly dependent upon a complex of conventions and assumptions, laced with *écriture* or *différance*, as they say in Paris. To have a perception, for Derrida, is to take a lot on faith. For what is there about this drawing that "says" that Fantin-Latour is not drawing himself drawing someone or something *else* (MdA, 64/MB, 60), which is in fact what some self-portraits are (MB, fig. 28), or that someone else has not drawn Fantin-Latour? (In fact, when in doubt, professional art historians, who have been excluded from this series, are led to suspect a self-portrait when they find a subject staring "dead ahead," dead on at us, a full frontal image coming back at us, as if from a mirror.) We take the words "self-portrait" at their word and we must hypothesize that the artist is, for example, staring at a mirror, where we are, as it were, in the center of the mirror. As spectators we remove the mirror and gouge out the eyes of the artist, hypothetically speaking, reducing the draftsman to a visible object, so that no trace of the author is to be found, a loss of vision that the draftsman himself must also be willing to undergo if he would see himself (MdA, 64–65/MB, 61–62).

That is why Derrida will say—do not lose sight of the subtitle of *Memoires*: "the self-portrait and other ruins"[30]—that the self-portrait is a ruin. It is not like Roman ruins that have decomposed or been eaten away by time or disintegrated by the weather and need restoration, but it is ruined structurally, inhabited from within and from the start by ruin, "already from the origin." That is because the drawing is too late, is already removed from the original, living, breathing, seeing artist who is doing the self-portrait, so that this might very well be a simple portrait and not a self-portrait. There is a little gap or spacing in the *Augenblick*, a distance between the seeing glance and the seen—just as in the analysis of the Husserlian *Augenblick*—but just enough (for any distance at all in the sphere of immediate contact is absolutely ruinous) to kill off, to ruin the artist's living gaze. There is no seeing that sees itself seeing. The self-portrait, "if there were such a thing, if there remained anything of it," is always already invaded by this blindness, the trait of which is that *we* cannot "see" that this is a self-portrait, we have to take it on faith. Even if we stood in his studio and watched Fantin-Latour do this self-portrait, "we would never know, *observing the work alone*, whether he were showing himself drawing *himself* or *something else*" (MdA, 69/MB, 65).

Commenting on Fantin-Latour's naive comment that in doing self-portraits he has the advantage of a submissive model whom he knows very well, Derrida asks whether the artist is not being ironic, noting that in the self-portrait the portraitist "would never know how to be accessible as such," that "all symmetry is interrupted between him and himself" (MdA, 69/MB, 68). That is the same naivete that Derrida demonstrated in his analysis of self-consciousness in Husserl, of that *Augenblick*, that glance of the eye, which has no need of signs because it is already present to itself in full immediacy. In the self-portrait, the artist is split in two, or rather into three: portraitist, model, and spectator. The seeing eye of the artist, the dead eye in the mirror, and the spectator eye that sees himself seen are separated by an abyss, like a drawing that has been torn into three parts and ruined, like an aging monument ruined by three immense cracks. As soon as he tries to recapture himself, to see himself seeing in the *Augenblick*, the thing itself has already slipped away (*se dérober*: VP, 117/SP, 104), and he has nothing to rely on but his memory. The self-portraitist splits in two, the one eye freezing open in the mirror and the other eye retreating to the shadows. This state of ruin, this fracturing, is not a failure or a weakness but a transcendental condition of the self-portrait:

> Ruin is that which happens to the image from the moment of the first gaze. Ruin is the self-portrait, this face looked at in the face as the memory of itself, what *remains* or *returns* as a specter from the moment one first looks at oneself and a figuration is eclipsed. The figure, the face, then sees its visibility being eaten away; it loses its integrity without disintegrating. (MdA, 72/MB, 68)

Rather than the felicity and originary integrity of self-knowledge, the self-portrait is more like mourning a lost loved one, the thing itself having slipped away. "Whence the love of ruins . . . How to love anything other than the possibility of ruin?" (MdA, 72/MB, 68). Ruin is not a remaining fragment of a lost totality, but the conditioning structure of experience itself, and of memory, the inherent spacing and withdrawal that inhabits experience so that what we experience is never quite "present," is always marked up and partially withdrawn, marked and re-marked by *trait* and *retrait*. Experience is always a matter of some faith. "The naked face cannot look itself in the face, *it cannot look at itself in a looking glass*" (MdA, 74/MB, 69).

In Jean-Marie Faverjon's "Self-Portrait in Trompe-l'œil" (MB, fig. 53), the painter portrays himself emerging from the frame so that his eyes seem to see us looking at the painting he is doing to which he points from behind; the painting within the painting depicts a nude figure stretched out on a cloud, framed by what appears to be a third eye, but this figure too overflows its frame. For Derrida, Faverjon is trying to depict at one and the same time a scene and the act of painting the scene. Here, in this *mis en abîme* of reflexivity, Derrida sees a "hesitation" between "transcendental" and a "sacrificial" blindness, a miscegenation of blindness as a condition of possibility with blindness as an event, and this serves as a transition to his discussion of "sacrificial" blindness.

(B) The Louvre is filled with many drawings depicting great blind men, men who have been tricked, punished, martyred, or converted by blindness, great men belonging to great historical events, all of whom obey the logic of a sacrificial economy. The logic of sacrificial blindness has to do with a violence that is entered into an economic circle where blindness is traded off or exchanged for another sight, some other sort of clairvoyance, which is invariably worth the price (MdA, 96/MB, 92).

There are three types of such violence. (1) In the first, the blind man is the subject of a *mistake*; one is blinded by a rashness, a passion, a rush to judgment; one falls, is deceived, allows oneself to be deceived, from which God, for example, can draw some good, as when Isaac is—providentially—deceived by Rebecca. One even suspects that Isaac has caught a glimpse of what is going on and is cooperating with God's divine foresight. (2) Blindness can also be a way a man is *punished* and gets to pay off his debt, which was the fate of Orion (MB, figs. 60–61). (3) Finally, blindness can be the price that is paid by someone for *conversion*, the cost of coming to see a higher, finer light. Blindness is a way to restore someone to their proper destination, as when, by the power of Christ, Paul strikes Elymas blind (MB, fig. 62), "provisionally and providentially" (MdA, 106/MB, 104), in order to bring him back to the way, or when Samson is blinded by the Philistines (MB, fig. 63), whom he repays when God restores his strength. Such men are a witness to the light. "In fact, a witness, as such, is always blind. Witnessing substitutes narrative for perception" (MdA, 106/MB, 104).[31] A witness stands by a God whom he cannot see, an Other whom he cannot bring within the horizon of his *voir* and *savoir*, which is what gives witnessing its power.

The convert is struck blind—to the world, to earthly light, to idols and false beliefs—in order to have his spiritual eyes opened, in order to open the eyes of faith. The most famous case in Christian culture of blinding conversion, of a conversion at the cost of blindness, is the conversion of Saul/Paul (figs. 66–68), a conversion which is arguably the origin of a distinctly "Christian" movement after the death of Jesus, so that Christianity itself would originate in a sacrificial act of blindness. Saul's conversion is recounted three times in Acts. In the first account, made in the third person, Saul is bowled over by a great light from which a voice addresses him that his companions can also hear although they see no one. Saul is then led blind into Damascus, where his blindness is converted into the coin of faith by Ananias, who lays hands on him; his sight is restored and he is filled with the Holy Spirit. A good deal of New Testament scholarship centers on how to read Saul's sight, how Jesus showed himself to Saul (*opthe*), readings that range from fundamentalist interpretations that Saul really was seeing things to more liberal ones, in which seeing means believing.[32] "The other two versions of the narrative"—in the first person—"are memoirs, the confessions or the self-portrait of a convert" (MdA, 118/MB, 116). These versions emphasize the work of witnessing, the destination of his conversion through blindness, which is to convert others, who are in turn to open the eyes of the Gentiles so that they may turn from darkness to light, from Satan to God (Acts 26:16–20).

For all the world, in the world's light, e.g., in the eyes of the Roman Governor Porcius Festus, Paul has gone mad (Acts. 26:24), and the confession of faith he makes before Agrippa, his story of blindness and sight, his "self-portrait of this mad light," is the "model of the self-portrait," of anyone's—"anyone among us who says 'mine'" (MdA, 119/MB, 117).

This brings us back to Augustine: to confession, to the self-portrait *as* a confession—"In Christian culture there is no self-portrait without confession" (MdA, 119/MB, 117)—and to the Augustinian economy of blindness. Now as we have seen in *Circumfession*, when, in a Christian self-portrait, one bares one's soul one does not show God something that was previously hidden from God, but one admits a fault and asks for forgiveness, "for the love of your love," as Augustine put it so beautifully. A confession does not take place in the register of truth but of love and forgiveness. Now at a crucial point in the *Confessions* (X, 34), Augustine describes his conversion to the light by way of a procession of blind men filing past him—Tobit, Isaac, and Jacob (without ever mentioning the most important, Paul, who is the closest to him), the same process that Derrida has already described. Augustine is telling us that, in imitation of these great blind men of biblical times, he has learned to resist corporeal light, which seasons this life for those who blindly love it with a dangerous sweetness. Augustine resists the *concupiscentia oculorum*, closes his eyes to the lusts and allurements of the eyes, which include even paintings and works of art, as dangerous snares. Augustine does not mean thereby utterly to denounce the visible world, in the manner of the Manicheans, but rather, in accord with the rules of the economy that regulate exchanges between the heavenly and the earthly city—to avoid being taken *in* (*non absumuntur*) by the world. He means to take the world *up* (*adsumunt*) into the true Light and thereby convert the world into the coin of a song of praise to God, who has created all things visible and invisible.

The result is not the end of iconography and the onset of iconoclasm, but the production of the work of art, of the whole history of medieval art and hence of Western art, under the economic rule of allegory (MdA, 121–23/MB, 119–21). In the space of Christian art, everything is lifted up, taken up, sent up to God, everything is treated as "a hymn, a work of praise, a prayer, an imploring eye," everything is "surrection and resurrection," "ascension and verticality of the gaze" (MdA, 123/MB, 121). The economy of allegorical art is at once "deploring and imploring" (MdA, 123/MB, 122): it blinds itself to the world as something apart from God, for apart from God the world is dark and opaque, in exchange for which its eyes are opened to a world taken up into God, into the Light, offered up and lifted up to God, presented before God's eye, in whose light we see light. In Christian allegorical art, order and ruin are perfectly coordinated, worked together within the equilibrium of the Christian economy. "A work is at once order and its ruin. And these weep for one another" (MdA, 123/MB, 122), each being inserted within a divine economy, a larger Providential design. Composed on the verge of tears, issuing from an event of tears, over and beyond any "representational reporting," any "perspicacity," any "theory" or "theater" it might contain (MdA, 123/MB, 122), Christian art is a heartfelt and tearful song to the True Light.

These Weeping Eyes, Those Seeing Tears

Finally, after a good deal of delay and repeated deferrals, after a lengthy analysis of this fluctuation between the transcendental and sacrificial logics of blindness, we are brought to the brink of tears, to prayers and tears, to the eye of the storm in *Memoires*, to the eyes as the origin of tears, to the prayers and tears of Jacques Derrida. For in the end, the eyes are made not for seeing but for tears, and seeing is seen to be feeling, *la passion du non-savoir—du non-voir, non-avoir, non-savoir.*

Augustine's *Confessions*, which is "the great book of tears" (MdA, 123/MB, 122), contains a "prehistory of the eye, of vision or of blindness," a history to which the "self-portraits" of modern European art belong. For these occur in and as the legacy of many old blind men, as the legacy of a tradition of confessions, memoirs, and self-portraits at the head of which stands Augustine's *Confessions* and the conversion of Saint Paul. To this history—as its counterpart and countertype—there also belongs Nietzsche's *Ecce Homo*, "the Dionysian counter-confessions of another blind man" (MdA, 124/MB, 122). "Nietzsche never had words cruel enough for Saint Paul and Saint Augustine" (MdA, 124/MB, 123). But however cruel and antipathetic he was to these men of blinding tears, Nietzsche was himself no less a man of shadows, blindness, and tears. He writes *Ecce Homo* in his thirty-sixth year, a time of minimum physical vitality and fading vision, "dangerously close to blindness," in which he lived like a shadow and wrote *The Wanderer and His Shadow*. We know too the famous story of Nietzsche in Turin, weeping over the flogging of a horse. So however cruel he would be to Augustine and Paul, all this crying and fading vision puts Nietzsche in their legacy, as their tearful, blind counter-type.

Augustine weeps so much throughout the *Confessions* that he is led at one point to ask God why tears are so sweet to men in misery (IV,5). We might also ask why we cry with joy, how there can be tears of joy, how we can smile through our tears, or why brides and winners of the lottery alike burst into tears. Tears bathe our extreme states, washing up around the points of maximum joy and sorrow. Tears well up in Augustine and veil his sight, which leads Derrida to ask whether this blindness, the blurred vision of tearful eyes, does not reveal "an essence"—he does not, *grace à Dieu*, say "the" essence—of the eye:

> Deep down, deep down inside, the eye would be destined not to see but to weep. For at the very moment they veil sight tears would unveil what is proper to the eye. (MdA, 125/MB, 126)

The very truth of the eye, its unconcealed *aletheia*, would then consist not in the delivery of truth, whether as *adequatio* or *Unverborgenheit*, but in tears, not in getting a good look at the Forms, in eyeing the *eidos*, or in letting *physis* swell up and emerge into unconcealment, but in bursting out into tears.

The hypothesis of sight thus tears itself loose from phenomenology's principle of all principles, from the principle of seeing eyes, and also from the most essential of Heideggerian hypotheses about the Open, *l'ouvre*, in order to cast a more favorable eye on a more Augustinian and Pauline, a more Levinasian and Hebraic hypothesis, about praying and weeping, according to which all men and a lot of women, too, desire by nature not to see but to weep with joy. Derrida makes his own the Augustinian sentiment that truth is something you make or do, *veritatem facere*, not something in whose open clearing you stand, head bared, basking yourself in Truth's *Er-aügen*.

Heideggerians mistakenly think that Heidegger delimited the privilege of sight and of the metaphysics of truth, that with his notion of *lethe* Heidegger struck upon the ground of something "otherwise than truth" as John Sallis and William Richardson suppose.[33] About that I think they have been deceived, and the very idea almost reduces me, in a manner of speaking, to tears. For *lethe* and *aletheia* belong together in a mutual interplay of darkness and light, of concealment and unconcealment; *lethe* belongs inseparably to the hidden heart of *aletheia* as its deepest reserve, as that from which *aletheia* continually springs. But along with Saint Paul and Augustine, with Levinas and Nietzsche (who would be very nervous in this procession, close to tears), Derrida is interested in something otherwise than *lethe* or *aletheia*, in something otherwise than the play of lights, or of dark and light. In searching for the origin of drawing (MdA, 10/MB, 3) Derrida seeks other springs than the *Ursprung* of the work of art, for the drawing springs from tears that well up in our eyes, not from *lethe*'s subterranean coursing. He seeks "from where these tears stream down and from whose eyes they come to well up," the source and spring of our tears. He does not seek to know this source or to bring it under the sway of *voir* and *savoir*, of *veritas* or *aletheia*, but to "implore" it, to *pray* through these tears, to weep while praying, to pray and weep while confessing, to pray and weep and confess while begging for forgiveness, to draw his self-portrait while writing, *in litteris*, a self-portrait of anybody, *quiconque*, to write "Everybody's Biography." In Derrida's procession the blind lead both the blind and the sighted, and Truth walks itself a few steps behind Justice, always observing a respectful distance.

Of course, in the "anthropo-theological space of sacred allegory," tears are turned into an anthropocentric privilege (a privileging that also besets Heidegger), a unique essence of the human eye—from which we must dissociate Derrida in no uncertain terms. For in anthropo-theological discourse, which is "both lucid and blind" (MdA, 128/MB, 126), the assumption is made that only humans (and especially women) shed tears, so that even elephants do not weep, not even female elephants, and hence, on this hypothesis, that there is nothing we can do to animals to reduce them to tears.[34]

So the blindness in which *Memoirs* is finally interested, the blind spot around which everything is organized, the one that opens wide our eyes, is not that which "darkens vision" (MdA, 128/MB, 127), but the blinding tears of sorrow and joy, the vision blurred by prayer, the eyes as organs not of sight but of tears, as organs of confession and witness. The eyes for Derrida are in the end organs not of sight but of passion. Derrida is interested in eyes that are clouded by tears of mourning, tears of impassioned "imploring": "From where and from whom this mourning or these tears of joy?" (MdA, 128/MB, 127). All these great weeping women—above all women—help "unveil the eyes":

> To say them without showing them seeing. To recall. To pronounce that which in the eyes, and thus in the drawing of men, in no way regards sight, has nothing to do with it. Nothing to do with the light of clairvoyance. (MdA, 128/MB, 127)

You can lose your vision in one eye, or even gouge it out, suffer a facial paralysis that blinds one eye, or even wink with one eye, and still maintain the organic function of vision, but you cannot cry with one eye, for weeping racks the whole body.

Now it is possible to specify still further the hypothesis of sight and blindness, the "*abocular* hypothesis," the abocular *epoche*, the suspension of sight. A blind man can still weep, and Charles Le Brun even seems to think one can weep without tears (MdA, 129/MB, 127–28; fig. 70) (which may be because he is describing weeping men, men who do not want to collapse in tears and lose the uprightness of *homo erectus*). When one loses one's sight, one has not lost one's eyes, which still weep. Indeed, in losing one's sight one might just then begin to see the eyes for what they are, to see the point of the abocular hypothesis: "These weeping eyes, those seeing tears," as Marvel wrote of Milton:

> —Tears that see . . . Do you believe.
> —*Je ne sais pas, il faut croire.* (MdA, 130 / MB, 129)

The Faith of Derrida

Je ne sais pas: he has found it necessary to delimit truth and knowledge, *voir* and *savoir*, *vérité* and *l'ouvre*, not of course as if this were something he does, but to let them delimit themselves, to let the eagle eye of *savoir absolue* go dark, to let the certainty and comprehensiveness of *Sa* spread its wings and then to watch *Sa* drop from the sky.

Il faut croire. In order to make room for faith, which means: not only to see that seeing is structured by blindness, by hypotheses and assumptions that structure sight, by writing and textuality, but also—at the end, for this is the point that *Memoirs* reaches—to see that testimony and witnessing, that philosophy and science, money and daily communications depend upon a certain blind faith. Believe me, I am telling you the truth. Believe me the way you believe in miracles, as when Jesus heals the blind man (*Foi*, 83–84). But the blindness in question is produced by tears, by prayers and tears, for the eyes are made more for imploring than exploring, more for making or doing truth than for observing and reporting it. In this way, Derrida takes his stand with SA, not *Sa*, with a certain Jewish Augustinianism, which is in part an innovation of his own, but also part of an old and honorable legacy descending to him from many old weepy white men, a legacy more prophetic than philosophical, more heartfelt than intellectualistic, more Augustinian and Franciscan than Thomistic and Dominican, more Kierkegaardian than Hegelian, more Levinasian than Heideggerian, although it must never become a question simply of choosing between the two.

Again and again we reach the same conclusion in reading Derrida, that the point of his work as an author is more performative than constative, that it is religious without a theology, that it hangs on by a prayer. Derrida writes by looking up to heaven, like the saintly, unctuous, heavenly, holy card looks cast by Augustine and Monica in Scheffer's painting in the Louvre that is included in *Circonfession* (*Circon.*, 21 / *Circum.*, 17). Imagine this unimaginable scene: a head-cut of Derrida, looking equally unctuous, carefully superimposed over Augustine's head in Scheffer's painting. But with this difference, Derrida's look is cast not toward heaven but toward the future. He looks to what is coming but coming precisely as unforeseeable, unpro-visional, unpro-vidential, unable to see a thing, lacking divine foresight, divested of the foreknowledge of some omniscient, all-foreseeing God or *savoir absolue*. So he looks to what is coming but without the eyes to see, with circumcised eyes. He looks to what is coming through his tears, with eyes swollen and sore from weeping, with imploring and beseeching eyes, with prophetic tears, tears of hope and love.

The prayers and tears of Jacques Derrida, the dream he dreams of something impossible, that is a dream and a prayer and a passion for the future, *l'avenir*, his faith in what is to-come. He implores what is to-come, he prays and weeps that justice come. He has faith in something incoming, hope for a justice to come, love for the gift of the expenditure without reserve.

He prays the prayer of "yes, yes," *oui, oui. Jah-weh sagt immer "ja"!*

For all of this he weeps and sighs, sending up a little deconstructive supplication, praying with all the passion of his little postmodern prayer, *viens*, with regular, religious repetition. *Oui, oui.*

How can he believe that it will come? How can he hope for what is coming? Does he love it? Does he believe it?

Je ne sais pas, il faut croire.

Conclusion: A Passion for God

There is something that I have all along been trying to say, something for
which I have constantly struggled to find a fitting formulation, a sentence
I have all along been trying to write, of which I will proffer here three
versions, aided by a patient reading of a certain Jewish Augustine.[1]

(1) *I do not know who I am or whether I believe in God.*
That was my first try[2] and I do not think that it is altogether wrong. I do
not know *who* I am, not because I am a deep subjective interiority, a deep
subjective resource of cognition and volition, but because I am a respondent responding to I know not what. I do not know by what I am addressed, to what I am responding, "substituting for the closed 'I' the
openness of a 'Who?' without answer," as Blanchot says, not a resourceful,
resilient "I" but "the unknown and sliding being of an indefinite 'Who?'"
(PdS, 290/*Points*, 276). In this way, the open-ended, bottomless "who?" is
what comes after the subject! Still, this is the most negative, the most
apophatic, the most inhibited, the most parsimonious, the least passionate
way to put the matter. It is, I would say now, at the end of a long study,
the least grateful and the least responsive way to respond to the secret by
which we are all inhabited and impassioned, the least willing to say yes,
to take a risk, to let ourselves be engaged by the momentum in things.
There are better, more robust versions.

(2) *I do not know whether what I believe in is God or not.*
That is a little more affirmative, a little more grateful, closer to the *oui, oui,*
more sensitive to the positive, empowering, impassioning impulse of the
secret, although one could be a little more upbeat. I do believe, I must. *Il
faut croire.* Life is carried along by the impulse of faith, by the passion of
faith, and we will not take a single step forward, *le pas au-delà*, without
faith. I do believe, help thou my unbelief. Still, I cannot say whether what
I believe in is God or not, whether it is in God I trust or the chance that
things will fall out aright, whether it is in God that I place my faith or in

the possibility that somehow, in some way, the suffering of the other will be redressed. *Je ne sais pas.* That is better, although one could be a little more passionate.

(3) *I do not know what I love when I love my God.*
That is to reach full stride, to open the throttle, to engage the *oui, oui,* to let life dance, to let the forces play, to be impassioned by the secret, impassioned by the passion for the impossible. That is the formula over which I pray and fast, around which I dance, the motto that I meditate upon night and day, that I have inscribed on the plaque that hangs over my desk, around which I have organized my life's task. When I awake in the middle of the night and jot down my dreams, I always write the same thing. I take my stand with love, and with God, and I am driven by a passion for God.

For the secret does not enervate or paralyze us, but sets us in motion; the secret impassions (*Pass.,* 68/ON, 29). I begin *by* the impossible, impassioned *by* the secret, *by* a passion for the impossible, in a forward repetition, as Constantine Constantius said, producing what we repeat, keeping hope alive. To be in the secret does not mean you know anything. But not to know anything, *sans voir, sans avoir, sans savoir,* does not mean to drift despondently from day to day, in a cloud of unknowing and uncaring, but to dream—"hoping sighing dreaming"—of something unforeseeable, unpossessable, undreamt of, unknowable, of which eye has not seen nor ear heard. To dream, perchance to desire and to love. And what is that dream, desire, and love if not the love of God, if not the desire for God ("God as the other name of desire")?[3] What is this passion for the impossible if not the passion for God, for "my God," even if one were rightly to pass for an atheist? When something unforeseeable and unknowable, unpossessable and impossible drives us mad, when the *tout autre* becomes the goal without goal, the object without object, of a dream and a desire that renounces its own momentum of appropriation, when *the* impossible is the object of our love and passion, is that not what we mean by "my God"? Is that not the name of God? Is that not a name that we would bend every effort to save, with or without religion?

So then has not deconstruction been driven all along by a passion for God, by a love of God? To be sure, but always *sans voir, sans avoir,* in such a way as not to have any assurances about what it is that I love when I love my God or how to bring the restlessness by which we are all disturbed to rest. For in this Jewish Augustinianism the *ébranler,* the trembling and uncertainty are our constant companions. The passion is the only permanence, and the only peace we have is the assurance that things will never settle peacefully in place. Peace is not the tranquillity of order, as a more straightlaced Augustine taught, but a passionate, outstretching aspiration for something to come, while order must be carefully distinguished from terror. The restless passion for God, Derrida's love of "my God," is meant to set things loose, to set them free, open-ended, *Vogelfrei* and "destinerrant," *ire et errare*, sent without destiny, who knows where. *Factus sum mihi terra difficultatis et deconstructionis*, according to a certain Jewish Bishop (I am citing from memory and have not had the time to check the Latin text). For to center everything on a passion for God, to dream the dream of my God, to say *yes, yes* to my God, to my passion for God, is to be drawn back into a still deeper decentering and questionability. *Quid ergo amo, cum deum meum amo*? Of what do I dream when I dream of my God? What do I love when I love the impossible? By what am I inflamed in this passion for God? By what madness am I driven when I am given without return? For what do I call when I call for justice? By what am I called when I am called by justice? What do I desire when I desire my God? What do I love when I love my God?

My God, of what am I dreaming?

There is in Derrida what one might call a certain overreaching, trespassing aspiration, what I have been calling here, all along, a dream, or a desire, a restlessness, a passion for the impossible, a panting for something to come. This passion is not a determinable wish or will for a definable goal or foreseeable objective, however hard any such goal may be to attain. It is not a search for something plannable and foreseeable, the fulfillment of which can be steadily approximated, our progress toward which regularly measured. Over and beyond, beneath and before any such determinate purpose, there is in Derrida, in deconstruction, a longing and sighing, a weeping and praying, a dream and a desire, for something non-determinable, un-foreseeable, beyond the actual and the possible, beyond the horizon of possibility, beyond the scope of what we can sensibly imagine.

Far from landing us into a place of dissipation, despondency, and enervation, as its most thoughtless critics contend, *différance* leads us by the hand into a quasi-messianic place, a quasi-transcendental messianic no-place. There, in that desert no-where, charged with a passion for the impossible, grows the flower of a certain Jewish Augustinianism. "Our hearts are restless," writes Jacques de la rue Saint-Augustin, in Christian-Latin-French, "and they will not rest until they rest in you," but with this little postscript, in Hebrew: "and you are something or someone to come, always, structurally, to come." That means that you never arrive, that your coming is not to be confused with presence, so that even if, to our utter surprise, you were actually to show up, we would still need to ask you when you will come.

This aspiration is what the philosophers would call, in their tired, dull, space-bound, unimaginative, and plodding way, a movement of "transcendence," what Levinas, trying to enliven the philosophical discourse, called trans-ascendence, and what Derrida himself, miming the talk of philosophy, walking the walk of philosophy, would call a certain *quasi-*

transcendental movement. After all, any such "transcendence" as *différance* sets loose would be a movement with no idea of its destination and with no assurance that it will get where it is going, wherever that is, a passion for who knows what. This is a very special movement, beyond the actual, but also beyond the possible, beyond the present but also beyond the future-present. Going where you cannot go, beyond the paralysis of the possible, the impossible is the impassioning impetus (*Sauf*, 94/ON, 75). So this does not finally resemble any philosophical movement, like a Platonic ascent beyond the sensible to the *eidos*, or a Kantian movement toward a regulative ideal, or even an early Heideggerian transcendence beyond beings to Being, or a late Heideggerian step back into the event of the most proper Propriety. This is like no eidetic or ontological or owning movement, but like a prophetic aspiration, a messianic passion, a sighing or longing for something unrepresentable. It does not take place in the tranquilized medium of seeing and truth but in the passion of suffering and the urgency of justice. It is not a straining of the eyes to see, beyond beings to Being, but a blindness. It is not seeing but sighing, not perception but prayer, not understanding but passion, a movement not of truth but of justice. Deconstruction is driven and disturbed, always and structurally, by a restlessness, by a prophetic passion for something to come, something beyond the law of the present, beyond the present law, beyond the regime of presence, for a justice or a democracy to come. Deconstruction is a passion for the incoming of something *tout autre*, something that blinds our *Anschauung*, that loosens our logic, and makes space—and time—for *ta me onta*, for the "nuisances and nobodies,"[4] the shadowy semi-beings and nullities who have fallen out of favor with the prevailing regime of being and presence.[5]

What do I love when I love my God? Can I do anything other than repeat that question day and night, especially night? We do not put the secret to sleep by dreaming of the impossible. On the contrary, the secret impassions the dream and the dream keeps us on the *qui vive*. "My God" keeps me up at night. The secret is first, last, and constant. Literature will have always begun, day and night.

Contrary to everything that onto-theo-logic would have us believe, "my God" does not mean some ontotheological hook that lifts us up above the tossing waves of textuality, that steers us steadily through the labyrinthine lines of *archi-écriture*, a *prima causa* or a *causa finalis*, some steadying metaphysical anchor that puts the play in things to rest. "My God" is not a name that provides for a good night's sleep, but a passion that disturbs our rest and keep us on the alert. The passion for God rightly passes for an atheism about a certain Hellenistic God; it breaks with an excessively Hellenistic and ontological way to think of God, ruptures an excessively essentialistic and epistemic frame of mind. The passion for God renounces the cognitivism that—constantly asking "what is this?"

and "what is that?"—worked its way into the biblical tradition when Philo Judaeus decided that the Torah had to find a place on the shelves of the Alexandrian library, that you could or even should try to make sense of Yahweh by way of Plato and Aristotle, who had very different fish to fry and for whom, inevitably, the only sense Yahweh would ever be able to make was the sense of Being. Happily, there has been all along a countertradition of thinkers who have resisted this Alexandrianism, this Hellenizing of God, this Hellenistic God, of which Levinas is today the most daring, articulate, salient, shocking and yet strangely familiar figure. Levinas labored mightily to keep the name of God clear of Being's orbit, to loosen God's meaning from the meaning of Being, seeking to save a meaning for God that is otherwise than Being's meaning. For the God of Abraham makes its own *sui generis* sense so long as we have the sense to understand that the sense God makes is biblical and prophetic sense and otherwise than *ousia*. That is perhaps a lure to which Philo was not sufficiently alert, which is what drove Luther, at the beginning of the end of a long tradition, to conclude that God had sent Aristotle into the world as a punishment for our sins.

I have been situating de-construction within this de-Hellenizing tradition, trying patiently to restring the wires of deconstruction back to another source, and this on the advice of Derrida himself, who has complained that otherwise he will have been read less and less well. For the name of God that is astir in Derrida when he speaks of "my God" is the echo of an ancient tradition, a tradition that resonates down the rue Saint-Augustin, down all the streets of Algiers and El Biar, past the Hebrew school from which he played hooky, back to the persecuted Spanish Jews who emigrated to northern Africa, back to Augustine and from there to Amos and Isaiah and, even before that, back to old father Abraham, the father of us all. For the meaning of the name of God that Derrida would save, the power of the nameless name of God that stirs in his works, is not what the Greeks meant either by meaning or by God—but a passion. "My God" is not addressed to a being or an essence, an explanatory cause or the solution of an epistemic cramp. When Moses starts to get nosey about God's meaning and name, Yahweh told him "I am who I am, nothing you will understand," the clear implication being that Moses should mind his own business, and keep his mind on the business at hand, which is justice, not ontotheologic.

Yahweh is not a Greek meaning but a Jewish passion. In his memorable and marvelous study *The Prophets*, Abraham Heschel calls Yahweh "the God of pathos," the God of passion, so that the correlate of "a passion for God" is "a God of passion."[6] The biblical God is no ontotheological creature, no supremely actual *energeia* whose utter actuality lifts him (anything this erect could only be a *he*) up above all passion into a perfect impassivity; the biblical God is no *actus purus* where the very idea that he might be in any way patient with or passive to our complaints is too embarrassing an idea to suffer. This Hellenic idea of an utterly actual *actus*, as if God were a perfect Parmenidean sphere, tormented the medievals half to death, imposing upon them contrived problems like how the God of their hearts could hear their prayers, how God who has counted every tear could be moved by our tears or grieved by our griefs, without compromising his eagle-high, hifalutin Hellenic impassivity; or what we were going to do through "all eternity," why "contemplating" the divine *ousia* or savoring the eternal *eidein* of the divine *eidos* would not begin to wear on your nerves after an eon or two. As if this pure Hellenism had *anything* to with what prophets called Yahweh or what Jesus called, in Aramaic, *abba*.

That very finite Hellenistic creature called "God" is a being cut to fit the narrow needs of Greek ontology, of Parmenides and Plato, who were scandalized by time and motion and change, and of Aristotle, who did the best he could to make the name of matter and motion respectable among the Greeks. But from a biblical point of view, this highly Hellenic *theos* was an imperfect—may I say a pathetic, or better an *a*pathetic?—way to think of God. It had nothing to do with Yahweh who was easily moved to anger and jealousy, who was a God of tears and compassion, who suffered with his suffering people, who was moved by their sighs and lamentations, who was angered by their meanness of mind and had a well-known and much respected temper, who had, in short, a short fuse. Being "wholly other" was something wholly other than being wholly unmoved by human suffering, for God or his prophets.[7]

The God of Hellenistic philosophers had as little to do with the God of the prophets as urbane, aristocratic Greek philosophers had to do with wild-eyed, half-naked (and sometimes not half) Jewish prophets.[8] The prophets were outrageous and bombastic people, passionate and compassionate, fiery, fulminating, disturbing messengers who usually ended up getting killed because of their message which they delivered with sharp tongues and explosive tempers. Accordingly, the God of whom the prophets spoke, whose fire they delivered, had nothing to do with the *actus purus* of Athenian metaphysics. The *nous noetikos* was a strictly uppercrust Athenian daydream. That active *nous* cutting lazy circles in the sky, utterly unmindful of the weal and woes of the particular specimens in the species down below, was a dream dreamt by an aristo-cratico-telian leisured class who got into all the best schools in Athens, of whom Allan Bloom thoroughly approved. That is a very limited, finite God who minds his own business and seems to have satisfied the needs of well-behaved aristocratic gentlemen and men of leisure. But it is not in the least biblical or prophetic. If there were a Greek analogate to the prophets it would be the Cynics, those dogs, who were a public nuisance and disgrace, who did things in public too fierce to mention.[9]

That is also what is wrong with Levinas's too assimilative attempt to cast the God of the prophets in the language of Greek philosophy, to give Greek thought the "last word," a tendency that has earned him some well-earned criticism from strictly Jewish quarters.[10] For whatever distant echo of Yahweh—and I think it is *very* distant—Levinas may have thought to find in Plato's *epekeina tes ousias*, the simple truth is that the *agathon* was something purely *seen*, a pure, timeless, impassive, unmoved object of sight that does not know a thing about us, that does not return our look, that does not *know* anything since it is a pure intelligible, not a mind at all, let alone a heart or, God forbid, a *pathos*. Thus, even though he played hooky from the Lycée Emile-Maupas, ruptured his alliance, and rightly passes for an atheist, Derrida's Jewish Augustinianism, which wants to disturb the peace of this Hellenic discursivity, makes for a more interesting religious discourse, one that is considerably more sensitive to his Hebrew roots, than does the work of Levinas, who read the sages religiously.

Instructed by Derrida's own admonitions about remembering the *alliance* that he keeps by breaking (or breaks by keeping?), I have all along been trying to cross the wires of deconstruction with this prophetic tradition, to *ally* Derrida's passion for the impossible within a prophetic passion, to trace out a *new alliance* between the God of Derrida, "my God," with what Heschel calls the God of pathos, the passion *of* God; to make allies out of the madness of the instant of the pure gift, which tears up the circle of return and reappropriation, and divine madness. An alliance would be enough for me. I am not trying to get Derrida to go back to Hebrew school or to start attending synagogue. Far from it. That would only reinscribe him in the cycle of violence that drives the concrete messianisms, of the positive religions that are too positive for their own good.

The lines of this alliance are traced outside the space of cognition. For Derrida as for the prophets, what is at issue is not a cognitive delineation of some explanatory principle like a *causa prima*, not some being or essence marked off by certain predicative traits, but something, I know not what, that emerges in our prayers and tears, that evokes our prayers and provokes our tears, that seeks us out before we seek it, before we know its name, and disturbs and transforms our lives. Something that has to do with suffering (SdM, 135/SoM, 81; 141–42/85) and justice. Something that impassions. What comes together in this *con-veniens*, this covenant, is the incoming (*invenire*) of what is to come, the *viens* of a justice to come.

I do not want your festivals and sacrifices, your loud songs and solemn assemblies, but I want justice to flow like water over the land, Yahweh told Amos (Amos 5:18). I do not care about the hierarchy or a new edition of the songbook, about church or synagogue architecture, about Judaism reformed, conservative, or orthodox, about priestly rites or priestly privileges, about preserving a male hierarchy, but justice. I do not care about *religion*, Yahweh seemed to say, but about a religion without religion, or before religion, a religion where the only thing people believe in religiously is justice, where their passion is to let justice flow. So it would not matter to Yahweh, according to Amos, whether you had religion—i.e., whether you had or belonged to the "determinable faiths," or whether you rightly passed for an atheist in the eyes of the determinable faiths—but whether you had a passion for justice, longed for justice, wept and prayed over justice. Yahweh was jealous about justice, not Judaism, and the false gods he inveighed against were gods who do not translate into justice, the religious assemblies and sacrifices that do not translate into justice. But by justice he did not mean the form of *dike* burning high in an empyrean sky, an *eidos* that you could get to see after ten years of mathematics, for justice is precisely unseeable and unforeseeable and does not come down to counting. Justice does not reside high above but settles into the flesh of the least among us, pitching its tent among us. Justice is not above but urgently required here and now, even as it is something you press forward to with passion, with prophetic and messianic fire, *feu la cendre*, with a fiercely burning *ruah*, something to come, something impossible, unimaginable, unrepresentable, something with which you must keep faith, an ortho-praxic *doxa*, not an orthodox *episteme*. Justice is something in which you can only keep faith, the passion of faith, *la passion du non-savoir*.

Faith is a passion for something to come, for something I know not what, with an unknowing, *non-savoir, sans savoir*, which is such that I cannot say what is a translation of what. I cannot say whether God is a translation of "justice," so that whenever I pray and weep over justice I am praying and weeping over God, dreaming and desiring God, with a deep and abiding passion for God. Or whether everything I mean by the passion for God, by loving God, by the desire for God, by "my God," is a way of dreaming of justice.

Lord, when did we see you hungry and give you to eat, or naked and give you clothes?

Quid ergo amo, cum deum meum amo?

Je ne sais pas, il faut croire.

I cannot say what is a translation of what, what is an example of what (*Sauf*, 95–96/ON, 76). But the point is that it does not matter—and it is an excessively Hellenistic frame of mind to insist that this matter must be settled—so long as you have a passion for the impossible, are moved by the impossible, stirred by justice, driven mad with the passion for justice, dreaming of something impossible, set in motion *by* the impossible. That is what it means to let "my God" be tossed about by the waves of undecidability. Who I am, Yahweh told a nosey Moses, is none of your business; your business is justice. Undecidability does not mean the apathy of indecision but the passion of faith, the urgency of forging ahead where one does not see, where in principle one cannot see, where what is at issue is nothing to be seen, is not a matter of *eidos* and *eidein* at all, but a matter of giving, of giving witness, of responding to a call that addresses us in the blind, the call of something *tout autre*, something out of sight, with the passion of God.

There is a crucial point, a point of passion and of undecidability, at which someone, "hoping sighing dreaming," can say of his passion for justice "my God," even though he rightly passes for an atheist. That point is, on the hypothesis of undecidability, the same point at which a believer in any of the determinable faiths can say of his passion for God that it does not matter whether you call it God or not, so long as you long for justice, that God does not want religion but justice. On this hypothesis, God himself seems to subscribe to the notion of translatability and undecidability, inasmuch as God, the God of pathos, does not care whether you call him God so long as you call for justice, for God is not interested in being called God, so long as justice flows like water over the land. At that point of passion and non-knowing, of urgency and undecidability, the prophetic finger, which points to justice, and the finger of deconstruction,[11] touch, like a painting on the ceiling of a new, Jewish Sistine Chapel, in which just this one graven image would be permitted. (Well, maybe two, the other being Scheffer's painting of Augustine and Monica looking unctuously up to heaven, which I also love.)

The witness, the response, the responsibility, the passion and compassion, in short, the passion for the impossible "is"—if I may use a little Greek copula to say something jewgreek, where everything that "is" means trembles in undecidability (ED, 228/WD, 153)—the passion for God, the passion of God.

Whether or not one rightly passes for an atheist.

If there is one.

Notes

Introduction

1. I embrace from the start Mark Taylor's homograph, tears/tears; one can always read "tears" as cries *and* as cuts whenever I write "the prayers and tears of Jacques Derrida." See Mark Taylor, *Tears* (Albany: SUNY Press, 1990).

2. This is a book about Derrida, not about Judaism. I am not Jewish, nor am I trained in Jewish studies, and I will leave it to others better prepared than I am to explain the roots in the Jewish tradition of these prophetic and messianic themes I am identifying, as best I can, in Derrida's more recent work. That is something I would very much enjoy reading, as I enjoyed Susan Handelman's book on the earlier work of Derrida. I am, however, deeply interested in the biblical tradition, particularly in the prophetic tradition and in "Jesus the Jew." Like Levinas and Derrida, I am interested in measuring the shock that biblical categories deliver to philosophy, to metaphysics, to onto-theo-logic, to what is called thinking.

3. The last paragraph of OG is devoted to dreaming, and the last sentence is a citation from *Émile*: ". . . I give my dreams as dreams, and leave the reader to discover whether there is anything in them which may prove useful to those who are awake" (DLG, 445/OG, 316).

4. This is but one of many points of intersection of Derrida and Kierkegaard and/or his pseudonyms, a theme to which I will recur again and again, repeatedly, obsessively, compulsively. In Johannes de Silentio, who is delivering a eulogy to father Abraham, the possible is the aesthetic; the eternal is the rational; the impossible is the ethico-religious. See Søren Kierkegaard, *Kierkegaard's Works*, Vol. VI, *"Fear and Trembling" and "Repetition,"* trans. H. Hong and E. Hong (Princeton: Princeton University Press, 1983), p. 16.

5. "Jackie" is the name he was given at birth, in keeping with a practice common among Jewish Algerians in the 1930s of giving their children the names of American movie stars and heroes. When he began to publish, he took the French and Christian "semi-pseudonym" "Jacques," erasing more things than he can say in a few words. See PdS, 354/*Points*, 343–44.

6. In "Choreographies" Derrida speaks of "dreaming of the innumerable," of his "desire for a sexuality without number," adding that "what is dreamt of must be there in order for it to provide the dream" (PdS, 115/*Points*, 108). In a later correspondence, commenting on these remarks, Derrida explains that this dream makes reference to "that ecstasy that consists in thinking, in order to love it, the impossible"; the very fact "that I think I am desiring what I cannot know, the

impossible," bears witness to this desire, even were this dream to be "false" (PdS, 175/*Points*, 164–65). Derrida "dreams of an idiomatic writing," and dreaming— dreaming and promising—institutes speech and writing. See PdS, 127, 145– 46/*Points*, 119, 136.

7. "It is possible to see deconstruction as being produced in a space where the prophets are not far away. . . . I am still looking for something . . . [in a] search without hope for hope. . . . Perhaps my search is a twentieth century brand of prophecy? But it is difficult for me to believe it." Interview in *Dialogues with Contemporary Thinkers*, ed. Richard Kearney (Manchester: Manchester University Press, 1984), p. 119.

8. "[N]o one has ever said that deconstruction, as a technique or a method, was possible; it thinks only on the level of the impossible and of what is still evoked as unthinkable" (MpPdM, 131–32/MfPdM, 135). *Memoires: For Paul de Man* is an extended commentary on memory and the promise, on the impossible prom- ise, in mourning and memory of Paul de Man. If the promise has a certain messia- nic structure (*Moscou*, 63/PTC, 219), which de-structures the present and prevents the present from closing over, then all the moves made in deconstruction turn on the structure of a certain messianic promise. Our task is to meditate on what a "certain messianic promise" might mean.

9. ". . . deconstruction has often been defined as the very experience of the (impossible) possibility of the impossible, of the most impossible . . ." (*Sauf*, 32/ON, 43). We will treat the theme of the impossible below, §5, *et passim*.

10. Derrida identifies the same structure at the heart of Heidegger's thought, viz., of a *Zusage* "before every question," that is, of a being promised over to what addresses us, "a sort of promise or [the English mistakenly says "of"] originary alliance [*alliance originaire*]" to which thinking has all along said yes, "before any question" (DLE, 148/OS, 129n). If the structure of *alliance* and promise goes to the heart of Heidegger's thought, and if that is a thoroughly Hebrew structure, *un héritage hébraïque*, then, as Marlène Zarader argues, Heidegger's thought is struc- tured from within by something he tried systematically to suppress and exclude, the Hebraic, which guides in advance his interpretation of the Greeks and in particular of the question "*Was heisst Denken?*" See Marlène Zarader, *La Dette impensée: Heidegger et l'héritage hébraïque* (Paris: Éditions du Seuil, 1990), pp. 83–91. Derrida suggests something similar about Heidegger, as Zarader notes (*La Dette*, 126), in terms of Christian theology (DLE, 179–84/OS, 110–13), as also of "my friend and coreligionary, the Messianic Jew," and maybe even the Moslem.

11. *Kierkegaard's Works*, VII, *Philosophical Fragments & Johannes Climacus*, trans. Howard and Edna Hong (Princeton: Princeton University Press, 1985), pp. 37, 44–45.

12. If this sounds a little like the "Preface" to *Totality and Infinity*, like Levinas's "eschatology of messianic peace," so be it; see Levinas, *Totality and Infinity*, trans. A. Lingis (Pittsburgh: Duquesne University Press, 1969), p. 22. Derrida himself sketches this "proximity" in Kearney, *Dialogues*, 119–20; see also Richard Kearney, *Poetics of Modernity* (Atlantic Highlands, NJ: Humanities Press, 1995), pp. 158–59.

13. Derrida has edited Augustine's words slightly; see *Confessions*, X,6. Decon- struction is always meant to be something affirmative; "I would even say that it never proceeds without love . . ." (PdS, 89/*Points*, 83).

14. In *Moscou aller retour* Derrida describes his project in jewgreek terms, as a

342

NOTES TO PAGES XXIV–7

certain miscegenation of Greek and biblical themes, mixing Greek myths and Judeo-Christian narratives, mythological and "Mosaic-messianic" models, to let them struggle with each other, in order both to escape them and to restore them, aiming to repeat them and to "interrupt repetition," so as to bring about "the completely new advent of the unique, of absolute singularity, in other words . . . the beginning, finally, of history" (*Moscou*, 78–79/PTC, 226).

15. "*Dès qu'il est saisi par l'écriture, le concept est cuit*" is the epigraph of *Jacques Derrida* by Bennington and Derrida.

16. Emmanuel Levinas, *Otherwise than Being or Beyond Essence*, trans. A. Lingis (The Hague: Martinus Nijhoff, 1981), p. 177.

17. This insistence, I must say, is stronger than his more guarded responses in earlier interviews: (1) with Richard Kearney when the latter asked him, in 1981, how important his Jewish beginnings were for reading his works well; see Richard Kearney, *Dialogue with Contemporary Continental Thinkers* (Manchester: Manchester University Press, 1984), p. 107; (2) in 1982, when he says that his "Algerian childhood was too colonized, too uprooted," "that he received there no true Jewish education," and that he does not know the Talmud—although perhaps "it knows me" (PdS, 85/*Points*, 80); (3) in 1986, when he says that the Jews of El Biar were "a community cut off from its roots," and he received no "true Jewish culture" (PdS, 218–19/*Points*, 205); he says that he has always had "a feeling of exteriority with regard to European, French, German, Greek culture," but that he hesitates to call this place of exteriority "Judaism," although the name of such a place is what he is always looking for (PdS, 219–20/*Points*, 206).

I. The Apophatic

1. In negative theology, one can only make "apophatic"—meaning negation or denial—assertions: one can only say what God is *not*. Apophatic is opposed to "kataphatic" or affirmative discourse.

2. *Derrida and Différance*, ed. David Wood (Warwick, England: Parousia Press, 1985), p. 130. See also, Mikel Dufrenne, *La Poétique* (Paris: Presses Universitaires de France, 1973), pp. 7–57.

3. Even as it "dehellenizes" literary criticism. See G. Douglas Atkins, *Reading Deconstruction/Deconstructive Reading* (Lexington: University Press of Kentucky, 1983), pp. 34 ff.

4. See Abraham Heschel, *The Prophets*, 2 volumes (New York: Harper Torchbooks, 1962, 1969). I will return to Heschel's defense of the prophets' God of pathos as opposed to the impassive God of the Greeks in the conclusion of this study.

5. Of course, even this most assured of all assurances is not safe. One could show the sense in which *différance* is, if not exactly God (*theos*), at least divine (*theios*), rather the way Nietzsche spoke of the play of forces reaching a state of "divinization" (*Götterung*), i.e., of open-ended creativity. Then there is also the question of non-Western religion, that Other of Western religion, Nagarjuna, e.g., where the play of copendendent causes also gives this assured axiom something to worry about. "*Différance* is not God" is not a deliverance from on high, does not have divine assurance, cannot protect itself from recontextualization, and this in virtue of *différance* itself. In the present context, I am trying to differentiate *différance* from Yahweh, Allah, and God the Father, having in mind only the religions of the

Book, and this is a point worth making. God, that God, the God of Abraham and his children, is not *différance*; but by what authority could we prohibit the converse, "*différance* is not God," from finding a suitable home? See below, "Edifying Divertissement No. 3."

6. Rodolphe Gasché has written an interesting piece on this issue which bears this title; see his "God, For Example," in Rodolphe Gasché, *Inventions of Difference* (Cambridge: Harvard University Press, 1994), pp. 150–70.

7. Richard Rorty, "Deconstruction and Circumvention," *Critical Inquiry*, 11 (1984): 18. For a commentary, see John D. Caputo, "On Not Circumventing the Quasi-Transcendental," in *Working Through Derrida*, ed. Gary Madison (Evanston: Northwestern University Press, 1993), pp. 147–69.

8. *Meister Eckhart: deutsche Predikte und Traktate*, ed. J. Quint (München: Carl Hanser Verlag, 1963), p. 196. I employ Alan Bass's translation from the French (ED, 217/WD, 146), which seems to me a fair rendering of Eckhart's German. For commentaries on Eckhart, see John D. Caputo, *The Mystical Element in Heidegger's Thought* (New York: Fordham University Press, 1986), and "Mysticism and Transgression: Derrida and Meister Eckhart," in *Continental Philosophy*, II, ed. Hugh Silverman (1989): 24–39. The best discussion of Eckhart's condemnation is Bernard McGinn, "Eckhart's Condemnation Reconsidered," *The Thomist*, 44 (1980): 390–414.

9. Eckhart had faith in the God of Abraham and Moses and the God whom Jesus dared call *abba*, father. (Nowadays, the dare is to call God "mother.") He insisted, in all good faith, I believe, on the orthodoxy of both his spirituality and his theology, that all the power of the negations, all the paradoxes of the nothings, of which he made use were spoken *emphatice* and harnessed to the affirmation of God's sublime *Überwesenheit*, enlisted in the service of naming the unnameable, the *innominabile*, who is also at the same time *omninominabile*. Even the most extreme formulations of the German sermons (the Latin treatises are more reserved in their expression) belong to what Derrida means by a (restricted) "economy" which for Eckhart himself was nothing less than the economy of salvation. The *ebullitio* in virtue of which the Son flows from the Father, and the Spirit from both, and of all creation from the triune God, constitutes in Eckhart a massive movement of *exitus* to which there is attached, by a divine plan, a correlative movement of *reditus*, of return and recovery. *Exitus* and *reditus* together form the circle of the gift, which is the most classical and paradigmatic expression of what Derrida means by an economic circulation, of an eternal, Christian Neoplatonic *kula* in virtue of which the gift of creation is returned in gratitude to God, the Father of all gifts. A deconstruction on the other hand would run this circle into a ditch, would break the mirror which sends its image back to God, would break out of the circle and invent something other.

10. John Dominic Crossan, "Difference and Divinity," *Semeia*, 23 (1982): 29–41. Crossan is an eminent New Testament scholar who has painted a portrait of Jesus as a leftish, roguish, prophetic advocate of the poor and the outcast, which, in my view, is very much in tune with the messianic, prophetic version of Derrida, with Derrida's religion, which I am sketching here. See his *The Historical Jesus: The Life of a Mediterranean Jewish Peasant* (San Francisco: Harper–San Francisco, 1992).

11. Kevin Hart, *The Trespass of the Sign: Deconstruction, Theology and Philosophy* (New York: Cambridge University Press, 1989), p. 186.

12. Some years ago Reiner Schürmann wrote a book on Meister Eckhart subtitled *Meister Eckhart ou la joie errante* (Paris: Denoël, 1972); the properly Derridean subtitle would be *la joie destinerrante*.

13. The best defense of negative theology is Kevin Hart's view that deconstruction makes it possible to understand negative theology as a "general economy" and hence that Derrida is wrong to locate Pseudo-Dionysius in a restricted economy, having given a too Thomistic reading of Pseudo-Dionysius, a point also made by Jean-Luc Marion in *God Without Being*, trans. Thomas Carlson (Chicago: University of Chicago Press, 1991), pp. 73–83. Hart claims that the word *hyperousios* can mean a more radical non-Being, so that our negations do not feed a higher affirmation but come to rest in a point of radical negativity. But of course, reaching a point, however negative, of *union* and *communion* which *exceeds* our faculties with something correct in itself is precisely to efface the trace and lay claim to naked contact with the One that is denied the "faculties," which is just the closure that always worried Derrida (*Psy.*, 542–43/DNT, 79–80). Hart's defense of negative theology, as he says elsewhere of an otherwise astute commentator, "is surely at odds with how Derrida presents deconstruction, for he insists that 'there is no experience of *pure* presence, but only chains of differential marks'" (*Trespass*, 68). Hart is describing the crowning triumph of metaphysics, all that metaphysics dreams of but never dreamt it could reach. The position of Pseudo-Dionysius is no less a "restricted economy" because it is centered upon an unshakably negative center; nothing is gained by taking negative theology to be "correct in itself," stable and final, as opposed to being taken up in a higher affirmation. Whether negative theology labors in the vineyard of positive theology (Aquinas, Derrida), or positive theology labors on behalf of negative theology (Pseudo-Dionyius, Hart), we have economics and wage labor, the lines of force of a centered economic order and a closed circulatory system, in which nothing is lost or squandered. Hart succeeds in differentiating only between different economic systems, albeit with opposite circulatory directions. When Hart says that for Pseudo-Dionyius "positive theology is necessary but necessary only as a *route* to negative theology" whose "*point*" is "*union*" [my emphases] he is not describing a general economy, which means an expenditure of negatives without reserve, in which we would have lost our assurances and are in aimless drift, *destinerrant*, he is not describing the *aporia* of dissemination, but the productive work and organized labor of negative theology.

14. Because it is neither this nor that, *différance* is not even neutral (*Psy.*, 536/ DNT, 74). Beyond neutrality, *différance* is inventive, inter-ventive, and affirmative. That is why I say neutrality is a provisional feature.

15. See Mark C. Taylor, "Unsettling Issues," *Journal of the American Academy of Religion*, 62 (1994): 949–63.

16. *Erring: A Postmodern A/theology* (Chicago: University of Chicago Press, 1984); for a fuller account than appears below, see my review of *Erring* in *Man and World*, 21 (1988): 107–114. Mark Taylor's views have evolved in an interesting direction in two recent studies: "Discrediting God," *Journal of the American Academy of Religion*, 62 (1994): 603–23; and "Denegating God," *Critical Inquiry*, 20 (1994): 592–610.

17. The attacks upon Derrida are unusually strident, even as academic attacks go. In France, he has been consistently denied a university chair. In Anglo-America, he has been the object of several extremely ignorant denunciations: (1) William

Bennett's nonsensical criticism in 1982 of deconstruction (DDP, 488n1/PR, 15n8). (2) Ruth Barcan Marcus's letter of 1983 to the French government on the occasion of Derrida's unanimous election as Director of the College International. See "Afterward: Toward an Ethic of Discussion," in *Limited Inc.* (Evanston: Northwestern University Press, 1988), pp. 158–59n12; *Points*, 481n6. Marcus is a good example of those "inquisitors [who] confuse philosophy with what they have been taught to *reproduce* in the tradition and style of a particular institution, within a more or less well protected—or rather less and less well protected—social and professional environment" (*Points*, 411). (3) The shameful but failed attempt in 1992 of Barry Smith and his colleagues (Marcus among them) to intervene, without invitation, in the politics of Cambridge University to win a vote of *non placet* when it was announced that Derrida would be awarded an honorary degree at Cambridge. See "*Honoris Causa*: 'This is *also* extremely funny'," *Points*, 398–421.

18. Richard Kearney, *Dialogue with Contemporary Continental Thinkers* (Manchester: Manchester University Press, 1984), pp. 123–24. For a good account of reference in Derrida, see Rodolphe Gasché, *The Tain of the Mirror* (Cambridge: Harvard University Press, 1986), especially pp. 280–82.

19. By the same token, deconstruction does not claim that the speaking "subject" is an unreal fiction. As Derrida says, "To deconstruct the subject does not mean to deny its existence. There are subjects, 'operations' or 'effects' (*effets*) of subjectivity. This is an incontrovertible fact. To acknowledge this does not mean, however, that the subject is what it *says* it is. The subject is not some meta-linguistic substance or identity, some pure *cogito* of self-presence; it is always inscribed in language. My work does not, therefore, destroy the subject; it simply tries to resituate it" (Kearney, p. 125). The "deconstruction" of the subject shows that the subject lacks the sovereignty, the autonomy, the pure spontaneity and authorial authority by which it wants to be defined. The time of the subject is a past that has never been present. The subject is antedated by systems that are older and deeper than it: by unconscious and preconscious forces, by systems of social and political power, by bodily forces, by the linguistic system in which we are always and already immersed. These forces at once delimit the scope of its beliefs and practices, while also making them possible. Derrida's efforts are always bent toward minimizing the effects of regularizing subjectivity and maximizing the possibilities of alterity, of inventing new forms of subjectivity.

20. I am indebted to Charles Scott, who is an exemplary case of this sort of anti-religious totalization, for this turn of phrase; see our little exchange in *Research in Phenomenology*, 25 (1995): 247–72.

21. In response to which we might cite Derrida himself: "while opposition to deconstruction is often made in the name of religion, we see at the same time the development of a powerful, original, and already quite diversified movement that calls itself 'deconstructive theology'" (MfPdM, 16).

22. See Hart, pp. 46–47, 61.

23. Jacques Derrida and Pierre-Jean Labarrière, *Alterités* (Paris: Éditions Osiris, 1986), p. 74. For a reading of "Violence and Metaphysics" that questions Derrida's reading of Levinas, see John Llewelyn, "Jewgreek or Greekjew," *The Collegium Phaenomenologicum: The First Ten Years*, ed. John Sallis (Dordrecht: Kluwer, 1988), pp. 273–88.

24. In "Psyche: The Invention of the Other" (1983–84) (*Psy.*, 11–62/RDR, 25–65),

Derrida formulates the notion of the impossible with which he associates himself. See below, §5.

25. Angelus Silesius, *Der Cherubinische Wandersmann*, ed. C. Waldemar (München: Goldmann, 1960), Book II, No. 4. The most accessible English translation, which does not contain this verse, is *The Cherubinic Wanderer*, trans. Maria Shrady (New York: Paulist Press, 1986).

26. Jacques Colleony, "Déconstruction, théologie et archi-éthique (Derrida, Levinas et Heidegger)," in *Le Passage des frontières: Autour du travail de Jacques Derrida*, Colloque de Cerisy (Paris: Galilée, 1994), pp. 249–61, also observes the evolution of Derrida's relationship with negative theology from a more negative differentiation toward affirmation, toward "the initial *oui* of an archi-ethics" (p. 259). Indeed, but it is with the latter "archi-ethics" that Derrida's thought becomes more prophetic, more Jewish, and less entwined with Christian Neoplatonism.

27. ". . . I believe in the necessity of taking time or, if you prefer, of letting time, of not erasing the folds" (PdS, 124/*Points*, 116).

28. "How Not to Speak" should be read in conjunction with "Acts: The Meaning of a Given Word," in MpPdM, 97 ff./MfPdM, 91 ff., which is an essay on the "archi-act" of the promise over and above a determinate speech act.

29. Martin Heidegger, *Unterwegs zur Sprache* (Pfullingen: Neske, 1959), p. 175; Eng. trans. *On the Way to Language*, trans. Peter Hertz (New York: Harper & Row, 1971), p. 71. See also DLE, 147–54n1/OS, 95, 129–36n5.

30. *Cinders*, 37–39: the pure (*pur*, *pyr*) place, where nothing will have taken place but the place, is the place of cinders, where there is only place (*il y a là cendre, il y a lieu*).

31. *Dieu sans l'être*. Paris: Fayard, 1982. Eng. trans. *God Without Being*.

32. Derrida is here drawing upon a work in progress, the "introduction" to which appears in the longer but clearly preliminary essay "*Khôra*," which is filled with unkept promises, the first version of which Derrida published at about the same time (1987) as "*Comment ne pas parler*" (1986). The longer study has not yet appeared and Derrida has not yet published a sustained analysis of *khôra*. Cf. *Psy.*, 566n1/DNT, 136n14. For a fuller discussion see *Deconstruction in a Nutshell: A Conversation with Jacques Derrida*, edited with a commentary by John D. Caputo (New York: Fordham University Press, 1996), chapter 3, "*Khôra*: Being Serious with Plato." For a brief commentary on pertinent sections of the *Timaeus* while keeping Derrida in mind, see John Sallis, "Of the Khôra," *Epoché*, 2 (1994): 1–12.

33. This is a point of dispute between Derrida and Jean-Luc Marion. See *Psy.*, 572–74n1/DNT, 136–38n16.

34. For an accessible edition of *The Mystical Theology* see *Pseudo-Dionysius: The Complete Works*, trans. Colm Luibheid and Paul Rorem (New York: Paulist Press, 1987), pp. 133–41.

35. *The Piety of Thinking: Essays by Martin Heidegger*, ed. and trans. J. Hart and J. Maraldo (Bloomington: Indiana University Press, 1976), p. 64.

36. See PdS, 406–409/*Points*, 392–95: The plurality of voices is a form adopted by Derrida also in several other texts (*The Truth in Painting*, "At This Very Moment in This Work Here I Am," *Cinders*), not as a device or technique but as a confession of the impossibility of appropriation, the impossibility of maintaining the mastery and control of a monologue or a dialogue. These texts are a concession to poly-vocity, a way of letting a plurivocity that is already there break loose so that he

cannot sign them, no one name can sign them, for the call of the other to come happens in several voices (*Psy.*, 61 / RDR, 62).

37. In *Sauf*, 15 / ON, 35, Derrida speaks of *"la voix blanche"* of negative theology, its voice-less or tone-less voice. The expression *la théologie blanche* is Jean-Luc Marion's: *Sur la théologie blanche de Descartes* (Paris: PUF, 1981).

38. Marion, *God Without Being*, 102–107.

39. Jean-Luc Marion, *"Le phénomène saturé,"* in *Phénoménologie et théologie*, ed. Jean-François Courtine (Paris: Criterion, 1992), pp. 79–128.

40. I have myself explored the tension between Neoplatonism and Christianity, between the "desert Godhead" and the "birth of the Son in the soul," in Meister Eckhart in my "Fundamental Themes in Eckhart's Mysticism," *The Thomist*, 42 (1978): 197–228.

41. Marion, *God Without Being*, pp. 152–54.

42. *"Tout autre est tout autre"* is a formula of the 1990s that will also serve as the basis of a reading of Kierkegaard's *Fear and Trembling* in DM / GD, which we will treat below, §13.

43. That raises a question I have pondered for many years, whether there is a meaningful idea of love in Heidegger's idea of *Gelassenheit*, which was already a translation of Meister Eckhart, so that the question is whether this word should be given back to Meister Eckhart. It is clear that Heidegger "loves" the old bridge at Heidelberg and the thinging of the thing; but love speaks in many voices, most of which Heidegger seems to miss. See John D. Caputo, *The Mystical Element in Heidegger's Thought*, chapter 5, for a critical analysis of the different uses to which *Gelassenheit* is put by Heidegger and Meister Eckhart.

44. "I cannot think the notion of the way without the necessity of deciding there where the decision seems impossible. Nor can I think the decision and thus the responsibility there where the decision is already possible and programmable" (*Sauf*, 109 / ON, 83).

45. Søren Kierkegaard, *Philosophical Fragments*, trans. Howard and Edna Hong (Princeton: Princeton University Press, 1985), "Interlude," pp. 72 ff.

46. See John D. Caputo, *Radical Hermeneutics*, chapters 1 and 5, for an analysis of Kierkegaardian "repetition" as producing what it repeats, which aligns it with Derridean repetition.

47. For help on the political side of deconstruction see Jim Merod, *The Political Responsibility of the Critic* (Ithaca: Cornell University Press, 1987); and Keith Reader, *Intellectuals and the Left in France since 1968* (Basingtoke: Macmillan, 1987). I reserve the whole question of Derrida and Marx until §§9–10 below.

48. Cf. SdM, 105 / SoM, 60–61: Fukuyama's "end of history" is a Christian eschatology, just like the Pope's discourse on a Christian Superstate; SdM, 164 / SoM, 100: Even today, in a new Europe, a new holy alliance forms: the Holy Father boasts of his role in the collapse of communist totalitarianism, so that Europe may be what it should always have been, a Christian Europe.

49. John Paul II, *Crossing the Threshold of Hope* (New York: Knopf, 1994), p. 86: "Buddhism is in large measure an 'atheistic' system."

50. See Rick Roderick, "Reading Derrida Politically (Contra Rorty)," *Praxis International*, 6 (1987): 442–49; and Mark Taylor, *Tears* (Albany: SUNY Press, 1990), pp. 123–44.

51. James Bernauer, *Michel Foucault's Force of Flight: Toward an Ethics for Thought*

(Atlantic Highlands: Humanities Press International, 1990). See my "On Not Knowing Who We Are: Madness, Hermeneutics, and the Night of Truth in Foucault," in *Foucault and the Critique of Institutions*, eds. John D. Caputo and Mark Yount (University Park: Pennsylvania State University Press, 1993), pp. 233–62.

52. For a helpful commentary on Derrida's idea of the future in OG, see Geoffrey Bennington, "Towards a Criticism of the Future," in *Writing the Future*, ed. David Wood (London: Routledge, 1990).

53. For an interesting commentary on this point, see Bennington, "Derridabase," in *Jacques Derrida*, pp. 231–32.

54. Cf. SoM, 179n28; *prévenance* ordinarily means thoughtfulness or consideration.

55. See James Weisheipl, *Friar Thomas d'Aquino: His Life, Thoughts, and Works* (Garden City, NY: Doubleday, 1974), pp. 321–23; for a commentary, see my *Heidegger and Aquinas*, chapter 8.

56. Derrida is commenting upon Michel de Certeau, *The Mystic Fable*, Vol. 1, *The Sixteenth and Seventeenth Centuries*, trans. Michael B. Smith (Chicago: University of Chicago Press, 1986), pp. 164–76.

57. *God Without Being*, pp. 37–49, 217n66; *L'idole et la distance* (Paris: Grasset, 1977), §18.

II. The Apocalyptic

1. The paragraph is a fake, a Derridean supplement of Rev. 22, forged/faked from various sources (cf. *Parages*, 116; PdS, 70/*Points*, 65), for which I will assume some responsibility only if I cannot avoid it.

2. At the end of the Prologue to *Cinders*, 27, Derrida writes of an "other voice," "may it come soon now, again, another voice." Is that an order or a command? Or "the desire of a prayer, I don't know, not yet."

3. Derrida says that he was unaware of it in "*Pas*" (1975), but by the time of "Living On: Border Lines" (*Parages*, 175–81/LO, 123–37) and "At this very moment in this work here I am" (*Psy.*, 159 ff./RRL, 11 ff.) he had become aware of it. I must say the problematic of *viens* is not very visible in "At this very moment": In its first appearance in *Textes pour Emmanuel Levinas*, ed. François Laruelle (Paris: Place, 1980), p. 23, the Other is called *la première venue*: the first arrival or coming, prior to any contract; whereas in *Psyché*, 160/RRL, 12, presumably a misprint, this text reads: *la première vue*: the first one seen; *viens* is also found in the concluding "liturgy" (*Psy.*, 201/RRL, 48).

4. And if these religious incidents were accidents, merely chance contaminations, if they occurred only in the openings provided by chance, peeking through crevices in Derrida's texts in the most completely unintended way, that would be even better, even more powerful evidence of Derrida's religion, fully in keeping with the law of chance in deconstruction.

5. Despite the great debt of Derrida to Heidegger, what Derrida is up to usually turns out to have a profoundly different force than Heidegger, the force of justice, a notion that Heidegger either avoids or mythologizes. See my *Demythologizing Heidegger* (Bloomington: Indiana University Press, 1993) for an extended defense of this thesis and a critique of Heidegger's "phainaesthetics." I would say of Derrida's relation to Heidegger what Derrida says of Blanchot's relation to Hei-

degger, that while he constantly repeats what Heidegger says, "he says at once the same thing and something completely different from Heidegger" (*Apories*, 337 / *Aporias*, 77).

6. It is like an "eschatological messianism," which is always turned in expectation to the coming one, not an "apocalyptic messianism," which thinks that doomsday is at hand for its enemies.

7. For a commentary on "Psyche: The Inventions of the Other," see Herman Rapaport, "Rereading de Man's Readings," *Studies in Twentieth Century Literature*, 14 (1990): 109–28.

8. In a 1975 interview, commenting on the oddity of the scene of reading, of the juncture of Genet and Hegel, Derrida says that he is interested in "what type of effect (of reading or non-reading) is absolutely *unanticipatable*, out of sight, structurally out of sight . . ." (PdS, 48 / *Points*, 41).

9. There is nothing to say that, under the name of the *tout autre*, we may not be revisited by the worst. The "new order" of the Nazis, the right-wing triumphalism of the "new world order," and the right-wing extremists who were swept into office in the elections of 1994 in the United States all parade their reactionary programs under the name of something radically new, of the *tout autre*. Cf. AC, 23–24/OH, 18–19. Indeed, even "yes, yes" can be turned to violence. In American English, when one has beaten one's opponent soundly, one says "yes," with a sizzling, hissing "ss" that is meant to signify a solid thrashing. In this "yes" the *conatus essendi* is going full steam.

10. For a commentary, see Richard Kearney, *Poetics of Modernity: Toward a Hermeneutic Imagination* (Atlantic Highlands, NJ: Humanities Press, 1995), p. 149.

11. I simply here recapitulate the well-known theses of Thomas Kuhn's classic *The Structure of Scientific Revolutions*, 2nd ed. (Chicago: University of Chicago Press, 1970). For a commentary from a continentalist perspective, see my *Radical Hermeneutics*, chapter 8.

12. I do not mean to discourage Continental philosophers from taking up the suggestive developments in post-Kuhnian philosophy of science. The lack of an adequate Continental philosophy of science is at least as serious a problem in Continental philosophy as its obscurantist jargon and resistance to making itself understood. I have made a few halting efforts in this direction in *Radical Hermeneutics*, chapter 8. For the best recent work, see Robert Crease, *The Play of Nature* (Bloomington: Indiana University Press, 1993).

13. For help on this matter, from the point of view of literary criticism, see Timothy Clark, *Derrida, Heidegger, Blanchot: Sources of Derrida's Notion and Practice of Literature* (Cambridge: Cambridge University Press, 1992); and Donald Marshall, "History, Theory, and Influence: Yale Critics as Readers of Maurice Blanchot," in *The Yale Critics: Deconstruction in America*, ed. J. Arac (Minneapolis: University of Minnesota Press, 1983), pp. 135–55.

14. SNB: Maurice Blanchot, *The Step Not Beyond*, trans. Lycette Nelson (Albany: SUNY Press, 1992).

15. Maurice Blanchot, *The Writing of the Disaster*, trans. Ann Smock (Lincoln: University of Nebraska Press, 1986), pp. 141–42.

16. Blanchot, *The Writing of the Disaster*, p. 141; cf. SNB, 124–25, 127.

17. In response to a question raised by Edith Wyschogrod as to what Derrida would make of the notion of the "false" Messiah, I would say that for Derrida the

"true" Messiah is always the one who has no truth or phenomenality, who never "shows up," and that the false Messiah is any one who does, any one who confounds presence and *venue*, which falsifies the very idea of the Messiah for Blanchot and Derrida. An instructive example, as Wyschogrod suggests, may be found in the life of Sabbatai Zevi, who proclaimed himself the Messiah in 1648 only to convert to Islam; see Gershom Scholem, *Sabbatai Sevi: The Mystical Messiah*, trans. R. J. Zwi Werblowsky (Princeton: Princeton University Press, 1973).

18. Blanchot, *The Writing of the Disaster*, pp. 142–43.

19. Blanchot, *The Writing of the Disaster*, p. 142.

20. Blanchot, *The Writing of the Disaster*, p. 143.

21. Blanchot, *The Writing of the Disaster*, p. 142.

22. See Heidegger, *Phänomenologie des religiösen Lebens*, ed. Matthias Jung and Thomas Regehly, Gesamtausgabe, B. 60 (Frankfurt/Main: Klostermann, 1995), pp. 87–115. This stage of Heidegger's early development is marked off in two recent landmark studies: Theodore Kisiel, *The Genesis of Being and Time* (Berkeley: University of California Press, 1993); John van Buren, *The Young Heidegger* (Bloomington: Indiana University Press, 1994). See also Martin Heidegger, *The Concept of Time*, trans. William McNeil (Oxford: Blackwell, 1992), pp. 14–16.

23. In *The Space of Literature*, trans. Ann Smock (Lincoln: University of Nebraska Press, 1982), "Death as Possibility," Blanchot says: that Heidegger wants Dasein to be sovereignly mortal, to make death something to achieve, a task to master, so that Dasein must make itself mortal and make death a possibility of the self (p. 96); that suicide is the great affirmation of the present, the attempt to make death present in the present, in the instant. He distinguishes a double death: (1) the one that belongs to the sphere of our liberty and (2) the ungraspable death that never belongs to me, that which never comes and toward which I do not direct myself as toward my end (pp. 103–104). Death is not my death, "Oh, Lord, grant to each his own death," which belongs to a Christian horizon, but impersonal, anonymous death, the death of no one, where death is not an event, not proper to me, where nothing happens, neither love nor meaning nor distress, but the pure abandon of all that (p. 149). The "space of literature" is to be outside the world, in that weakness and inertia, where there is no self/world/*Seinkönnen*, but utter ruin, *désoeuvrement* and disaster, from which the *oeuvre* issues.

24. I am particularly indebted to two fine studies by Simon Critchley: "*Il y a*: On Holding Levinas's Hand to the Fire of Blanchot" (unpublished) and "*Il y a*: A Dying Stronger than Death (Blanchot with Levinas)," *The Oxford Literary Review*, 15 (1993): 81–130.

25. The "other shore" is Levinas's term for the other in *Totality and Infinity*, p. 64.

26. See also Maurice Blanchot, *Death Sentence*, trans. Lydia Davis (Barrytown: Station Hill Press, 1978), pp. 69, 74, 80, texts upon which Derrida comments extensively in "Pas" and in "Living On/Border Lines" (*Parages*, 118/LO, 250).

27. See, e.g., John Searle, "Rationality and Realism: What is at Stake?" *Daedalus*, 122 (1992): 55–84. See Richard Rorty's neopragmatist counterargument, on behalf of "such philosophers as Thomas Kuhn, Jacques Derrida and myself [Rorty]," in Richard Rorty, "Does Academic Freedom Have Philosophical Presuppositions?" *Academe: Bulletin of the American Association of University Professors*, 80 (1994): 52–63.

Derrida, however, is closer to the leftist critics of the university of whom Rorty is, with Searle, also critical.

28. For helpful commentaries, see Christopher Norris, "On Derrida's *Apocalyptic Tone*: Textual Politics and the Principle of Reason," *Southern Review* (Adelaide), 19 (1986): 13–30 and "Of An Apoplectic Tone Recently Adopted in Philosophy," *Cambridge Review*, 113 (1992): 115–26; and Herman Rapaport, "Deconstructing Apocalyptic Rhetoric: Ashberry, Derrida, Blanchot," *Criticism*, 27 (1985): 387–400.

29. Of course it seems to put its foot down in mid-air: the authority to settle hermeneutic disputes is based upon certain authorizing texts—*tu es petrus*—which have themselves been put in the mouth of Jesus by the early church to announce the Church's authority.

30. Edith Wyschogrod, *Saints and Postmodernism: Revisioning Moral Philosophy* (Chicago: University of Chicago Press, 1990).

31. In my *Radical Hermeneutics*, chapters 5 and 6, I made an extended effort to contrast eschatology, teleology, and Derridean destinerrance.

32. Søren Kierkegaard, *Kierkegaard's Works*, Vol. VII, *Philosophical Fragments and Johannes Climacus*, trans. Howard Hong and Edna Hong (Princeton: Princeton University Press, 1985), p. 37.

33. The revelation without revelation, the revelation of the "without," is likewise the secret without a secret, the secret of the "without," even as the "religion without religion" is a religion of the "without."

34. Interestingly enough, in his proposals for practical reforms in the teaching of philosophy, Derrida has been accused of pressing too hard for objective and precise philosophical knowledge. A recent report (DDP, 619–59) of Derrida's was caricaturized by its critics as proposing that the *dissertation* be replaced by multiple-choice and fill-in-the-blanks examinations. See PdS, 343–45/*Points*, 333–35 and the Preface to DDP, 9–108.

35. Translator Elizabeth Weber mistranslates *passion* as "position" in *Points*, 201, which of course greatly saddens those of us who advocate passion.

36. "Cinders" for Derrida is an evocative and polyvalent figure which "means" the trace, the remains, the anti-Parmenidean demi-world of what neither is nor is not, the pure gift which consumes entirely every appearance of being a gift, mortal ashes, death, and hence the Holocaust, the Nazi crematories, and the associated question of mourning. *Feu la cendre* ruminates among all of these figures and more, including sexual difference. I am seizing upon but one part of its polyvalence.

37. See Zarader, *La Dette*, pp. 190–98.

38. For a full discussion of *Khôra*/ON, 89 ff., see *Deconstruction in a Nutshell: A Conversation with Jacques Derrida*, edited with a commentary by John D. Caputo (New York: Fordham University Press, 1996), chapter 3.

39. See the treatment of *Shibboleth* below, §16, and the whole problematic of circumcision.

40. In praise of Lessing, Johannes Climacus tried to distinguish the "accidental secret," which can be disclosed, from the "essential" secret, which concerns the privacy of the God-relationship, which cannot. But even this essential secret has more content than Derrida's absolute secret. See *Kierkegaard's Works*, V. XII.1, *Concluding Unscientific Postscript to the "Philosophical Fragments,"* trans. Howard Hong and Edna Hong (Princeton: Princeton University Press, 1992), pp. 79–80.

41. *Sein und Zeit*, 15th ed. (Tübingen: Niemeyer, 1979), p. 127; Eng. trans. *Being and Time*, trans. John Macquarrie and Edward Robinson (New York: Harper & Row, 1962), p. 165. In § 13, below, we will return to Derrida's gloss of *Fear and Trembling* and the secret Abraham is told to keep by the Lord God.

42. Martin Luther King Jr.'s "I have a dream" speech brings together a good deal of what I have been calling prophetic and deconstructive elements in an idea, a dream, of a democracy to come.

43. My translation follows the modification of this text when it was published in French in *Psyché*. The French text appearing in *Psyché* is: "*L'autre appelle à venir . . .*"

44. See my *Radical Hermeneutics*, p. 288.

45. I will return to these three formulations, to the multiplication of formulae, all impassioned by the secret, in the Conclusion of this work.

III. The Messianic

1. See Levinas, *Totality and Infinity*, pp. 22–24. Derrida's use of the word "messianic" is occasioned by a reading of Benjamin. In analyzing the structure of the promise in 1984, Derrida writes, "The promise prohibits the gathering of Being in presence, being even its condition. The condition of the possibility and impossibility of eschatology, the ironic allegory of messianism" (MpPdM, 139–40/MfPdM, 145). In a note, Derrida refers us to Peter Szondi, "Hope in the Past: On Walter Benjamin," *Critical Inquiry*, 4 (1978), which "I cite because of its allusion to the messianism of all promises" (MpPdM, 140n1/MfPdM, 153n10) in which Szondi takes up Benjamin's "Theses on the Philosophy of History" in *Illuminations: Essays and Reflections*, ed. Hannah Arendt, trans. Harry Zohn (New York: Schocken, 1969), pp. 253–64. In 1989, in "Force of Law," Derrida describes Benjamin as "revolutionary in a style that is at once Marxist and messianic" (FL, 69/DPJ, 64), effecting a "graft of the language of Marxist revolution on that of messianic revolution" (FL, 70/DPJ, 65). In *Specters* (SdM, 95–96/SoM, 55), Derrida likewise draws our attention to Benjamin's talk of a "weak messianic force" in the "Theses," which is a paradigm of Derrida's messianic "without" (= weak) messianism. In Benjamin, this force is the claim laid by the past upon the present, which makes of us, today, the ones who were to come in order to "redeem" the past, to preserve a memory of past suffering (Derrida's "mourning"); we are responsible for the past history of humankind. Now, in this messianic time, we are required to make every moment of the present a "strait gate" through which the Messiah might enter (SdM, 95–96n2/SoM, 180–81n). In *Specters* this Benjaminian motif is made to work together with a messianic of the "to come." See Drucilla Cornell, *The Philosophy of the Limit* (New York: Routledge, 1992), chapter 3. In "Back from Moscow, in the USSR," Derrida discusses the genre of Moscow diaries that read like "pilgrimage novels" to Jerusalem, turning as they do on a revolutionary event to come which bears an "analogy" to "eschatology or messianism," and argues that one should "push the analogy as far as possible, if only to refine the difference, however minute" (*Moscou*, 40–41/PTC, 208–209). He attributes to Benjamin the project of putting an end to Greek myth in order to bring history to light, where history has the messianico-Marxist structure of a time to come, a promise, a revolution (*Moscou*, 63/PTC, 219).

2. The French and English texts of the 1989 version of this lecture are to be

found on facing pages in *Cardozo Law Review*, 11 (July/Aug. 1990), Nos. 5–6: 919–1045. See pp. 965–67.

3. For commentaries on SoM, see Aijaz Ahmad, "Reconciling Derrida: Spectres of Marx and Deconstructive Politics," *New Left Review*, 208 (1994): 88–106; Simon Critchley, "Derrida's *Specters of Marx*," *Philosophy & Social Criticism*, 21 (1995): 1–30; Fredrick Jameson, "Marx's Purloined Letter," *New Left Review*, 209 (1995): 75–109; Ernesto Laclau, "The Time is Out of Joint," *Diacritics*, 25 (1995): 86–97; Gayatri Chakravorty Spivak, "Ghostwriting," *Diacritics*, 25 (1995): 65–85. The fullest discussion of Derrida and Marx before SoM is Michael Ryan, *Marxism and Deconstruction: A Critical Articulation* (Baltimore: The Johns Hopkins University Press, 1982); see also Andrew Parker, "Between Dialectics and Deconstruction: Derrida and the Reading of Marx," in *After Strange Texts: The Role of Theory in the Study of Literature*, ed. G. Jay (Tuscaloosa: University of Alabama Press, 1985), pp. 146–68; and the special issue of *Diacritics*, 15 (1985), "Marx After Derrida," ed. Satya Mohanty. See also Bill Martin, *Matrix and Line: Derrida and the Possibilities of Postmodern Social Theory* (Albany: SUNY Press, 1992) (cf. SdM, 153nl/SoM, 185n9).

4. The main themes of *Specters of Marx* are already announced in these two works. In *The Other Heading*, Derrida addresses the question of capital and the fate of Marx (AC, 56 ff./OH, 56 ff.); the new dogmatic anti-communism that triumphalistically announces the end of history (AC, 35–36/OH, 32–33); the delimitation of the media and tele-technologies; the schema of the phantom or specter (AC, 103/OH, 84; AC, 107/OH, 89); the conditions for a radical democracy and the critique of the resurgent, post-cold-war nationalisms. Made up of two newspaper pieces that accuse modern democracies in a neo- or post-Marxist way of tolerating formal freedoms whose substantive teeth are removed by market forces, *The Other Heading* gives the reader a glimpse of what a democracy should be for Derrida in relatively concrete terms. In *Moscou aller-retour*, Derrida argues, the trip to Moscow, "these days," is made by one who, unlike Gide or Benjamin, is secure in the knowledge of the same, of what democracy is already given to mean (as opposed to a democracy to come), and who goes there to see if the other is becoming the same, to see how far the Russians have succeeded in resembling us, in imitating "our" liberal, capitalist, parliamentary system; one goes over there, *fort*, to see if it is here (*da*), to see if they are catching up with Fukuyama's "end of history" (*Moscou*, 71–72/PTC, 223). Derrida is also fascinated by the religious analogy, by the passion of faith in a Marxist, messianic eschatology and by the loss of faith and the "confession" of error of disillusioned Stalinists (*Moscou*, 40–41/PTC, 209; *Moscou*, 45–46/PTC, 211; *Moscou*, 49–50/PCT, 213).

5. Deconstruction means to question the "certainties and axioms of Enlightenment" but to do so "in order to think them better and especially to translate and transform them better in the light of what should be the Enlightenment of our time" (*Points*, 428). While salutary up to a point, the writings of Christopher Norris have gone too far and tend to make Derrida look like a philosopher of the first or old Enlightenment. In an effort to remove Derrida from confusion with Rorty, Norris pushes him too far in the direction of critical theory. See, e.g., *What's Wrong with Postmodernism: Critical Theory and the Ends of Philosophy* (Baltimore: Johns Hopkins University Press, 1990). Norris is also no enthusiast for religious discourse; see his *The Truth about Postmodernism* (Oxford: Blackwell, 1993), pp. 291, 299–302. For a critique of Norris and Rorty, see my "In Search of the Quasi-Tran-

scendental: The Case of Derrida and Rorty," *Working Through Derrida*, ed. Gary Madison (Evanston: Northwestern University Press, 1993), pp. 147–69.

6. See Roger Garaudy, *From Anathema to Dialogue: A Marxist Challenge to the Christian Church* (New York: Vintage Books, 1968) and Nicholas Lash, *A Matter of Hope: A Theologian's Reflection on the Thought of Karl Marx* (South Bend: University of Notre Dame Press, 1981).

7. The relation to Marx is played out in the double bind between "mourning and melancholy," according to which the possibility of mourning is sustained by its impossibility. If we interiorize the dead friend, which is successful mourning, then we succeed also in annulling the alterity of the friend; if we respect that alterity, the mourning is unsuccessful. If it succeeds, it fails. See MpPdM, 49–52/MfPdM, 28–32; PdS, 331–32/*Points*, 320–22; "Fors: The Anglish Words of Nicolas Abraham and Maria Torak," trans. Barbara Johnson, in Nicolas Abraham and Maria Torak, *The Wolf Man's Magic Word: A Cryptonomy* (Minneapolis: University of Minnesota Press, 1986); see also Bennington, *Jacques Derrida*, pp. 146–48. Just as I am organizing a reading of *Specters* for my present purposes around the notion of the messianic, so it would be possible, were one so minded, to organize a whole reading around the impossible mourning—for Marx, for the suffering of the *revenants*.

8. Johann Baptist Metz, *Faith in History and Society*, trans. D. Smith (New York: Crossroads, 1980), pp. 109–15.

9. In "Derrida's *Specters of Marx*," *Philosophy & Social Criticism*, 21 (1995): 1–30, Simon Critchley advances the thesis that Derrida's politics of dislocation are in fact embodied in the work of Ernesto Laclau, especially in "New Reflections on the Revolution of our Time," the lead essay of a book of the same name (London and New York: Verso, 1990), where contemporary fragmentation—the proliferation of "ethnic, national, sexual and ecological" voices—is viewed as the condition, for better or for worse, of justice today, depending on the sort of hegemonic force these voices can muster. Derrida refers to Laclau and Moffle (SdM, 69n1/SoM, 180n31) on the concept of hegemony, but without noticing, as Critchley points out, the special sense of hegemonic articulation at work there, viz. as deciding in the midst of undecidability.

10. Simon Critchley, "Deconstruction and Pragmatism—Is Derrida a Private Ironist or a Public Liberal?" *European Journal of Philosophy*, 2 (April 1994): 1–21.

11. See Critchley, "On Derrida's *Specters of Marx*."

12. As can be seen in his *New York Review of Books* controversy over "The Philosopher's Hell," Derrida also worries about what happens to deconstruction, to complicated intellectual debates generally, when they hit the public press; see *Points*, 422 ff.

13. This is not a recent view on Derrida's part; he has held it for some time; cf. PdS, 75–76/*Points*, 71–72; Ton, 59/RTP, 145.

14. The lead sentence of a front page story entitled "Gorbachev's New Battle: Overcoming His Legacy," *The New York Times* (March 10, 1995) reports that "the last leader of the Soviet Union floats across the political landscape like a restless ghost, unable to make his presence felt." The piece, which quotes Gorbachev as saying "We are witnessing a monopolization of the mass media, which is disgusting," describes Gorbachev as a figure Russia is trying to "bury" and who lives in a "netherworld." Gorbachev's battle is a matter of "*survivance*" and he

seems to haunt the Russians. For Derrida's reflections following a ten-day trip to Moscow in 1990, see *Moscou aller-retour*. Among the projects he sketches for a possible text on this trip: "the figure of Gorbachev" (*Moscou*, 97 / PTC, 235)—now become spectral.

15. New York: MacMillan, The Free Press, 1992. Avon Books edition, 1993. Fukuyama also comes under fire in AC, 35–36 / OH, 32–33.

16. Fukuyama, *The End of History and the Last Man*, pp. 67, 351n32.

17. Critchley mistakenly identifies Derrida's notion of the "universal structure" of the messianic (SdM, 266 / SoM, 167) with "Marxist messianism" and the "desert-like" messianic with Judaism; see his "Derrida's *Specters of Marx*," p. 17. In fact, Derrida treats both Marxism and Judaism as concrete messianisms, as examples of a "messianism or [of] determinate messianist figures" (see FL, 56 / DPJ, 25) (the French text is expanded), in contradistinction from the desert-like and indeterminable messianic form or structure itself, here described not as the *messianique* but as *messianicité*.

18. Derrida delivered these remarks in a public roundtable, inaugurating the doctoral program in philosophy at Villanova University, on October 3, 1994; see *Deconstruction in a Nutshell: A Conversation with Jacques Derrida*, Part One, "The Villanova Roundtable."

19. For an articulate elaboration of the disasters of the new world order and Derrida's idea of a new International, see James Marsh, "Ghosts and Spirits (Of Marx, Derrida, and the New World Order)," unpublished ms.

20. Consider the pervasive spectral imagery in American English in the racial epithets and the abusive slang hurled at African Americans.

21. Blanchot, *Writing of the Disaster*, pp. 141–42; *Pol.*, 55n1.

22. On the "opiate of the people" quip, Derrida cites the counter-quip that, on the contemporary scene, the question is "not religion as the opiate of the people, but drugs as the religion of the atheist poets" (PdS, 253 / *Points*, 240).

23. So the description of Derrida's "Of An Apocalyptic Tone" in the subtitle of RTP as a "Transformative Critique by Jacques Derrida" is a mistake which describes deconstruction in the terms of a pre-deconstructive, reductionistic critique.

24. Charles Scott is my favorite example.

25. In a piece entitled "The Net is a Waste of Time," *New York Times Magazine*, July 14, 1996, p. 31, William Gibson, who coined the expression "cyberspace" in 1981, spoke of "that postgeographical meta-country we increasingly call home."

IV. The Gift

1. Jacques Derrida and Pierre-Jean Labarrière, *Alterités*, p. 74.

2. In a recent series of lectures on hospitality which follows the etymology of the word "hospitality," *hostis*, the stranger, + *potis*, mastery, Derrida says that hospitality begins just when we are paralyzed by this aporetic, to be as welcoming as possible to the other while not surrendering the mastery of one's house.

3. Marcel Mauss, *The Gift: The Form and Reason for Exchange in Archaic Societies*, trans. W. D. Halls (New York: Norton, 1990). On "*kula*," see pp. 21–31.

4. *Zur Sache des Denkens*, 2 Aufl. (Tübingen: Max Niemeyer, 1976); hereafter SD. Eng. trans. *Time and Being*, trans. Joan Stambaugh (New York: Harper & Row, 1972); hereafter TB.

5. For a more detailed account of Heidegger's worst, most mythologizing side, as opposed to a more austere demythologized Heidegger, see my *Demythologizing Heidegger*, chapter 1.

6. See Robert Bernasconi, "On Heidegger's Other Sins of Omission: Asian Thought and Christian Philosophy," *American Catholic Philosophical Quarterly*, 69 (1995): 333–50.

7. *Philosophical Fragments*, p. 57.

8. For a comparable argument, see Julia Kristeva, *Tales of Love*, trans. Leon S. Roudiez (New York: Columbia University Press, 1987), pp. 170–87, a remarkable essay on the *"ratio diligendi"* in Thomas Aquinas.

9. For an American contribution to this tradition, one which nourishes no desire to see the gift escape the circle of exchange, see Lewis Hyde, *The Gift: Imagination and the Erotic Life of Property* (New York: Random House, Vintage Books, 1983). Hyde himself confesses a debt to Marshall Sahlins, *Stone Age Economics* (Chicago: Aldane Publishing Co., 1972). Cf. DT, 40n1/GT, 25n15.

10. Derrida is no less forgiving with Lévi-Strauss for paying Mauss a poisoned tribute, for sharply criticizing Mauss for "going native," for being taken in by the charm of native logic, for accepting the natives' claim that the spirit (*hau*) that inhabits the gift/thing is what drives the giving and taking, i.e., the circle of exchange. Mauss, Lévi-Strauss complains, should have seen past these material charms to the formal logic of relations, to the relational system rooted in the unconscious and instantiated in language, of which "gifts" are but contingent embodiments. Against Lévi-Strauss's rationalism, his "exchangist, linguisticist, and structuralist" systematizing of Mauss, Derrida opposes the "gift" as the instant that tears up the relational totality (i.e, the gift as post- or extra-structural, exceeding structure), and even as "giving reason" itself (DT, 102–103/GT, 77). Derrida's criticism of Lévi-Strauss's structuralism should not obscure the fact that Derrida, like Lévi-Strauss, wants to distance himself from the moralizing humanism of Mauss and to find a "gift" that has nothing to do with intentionalist structures and everything to do with an anonymous play of differences. Derrida is seeking a dissemination that will be equally, even more, unconscious than that of Lévi-Strauss.

11. See my *Against Ethics*, chapter 8, for a beggarly notion of flesh or a flesh-ly notion of the beggar.

12. See my *Radical Hermeneutics*, pp. 212–13, and *Against Ethics*, pp. 41, 92, 121–22.

13. Very early on, in commenting on Husserl, Derrida said that *écriture* "creates an autonomous transcendental field from which every present subject can be absent," or what Jean Hippolyte calls "a transcendental field without a subject," notions that, in a sense, Derrida has been reworking ever since. See HOdG, 84–85/HOG, 87–88.

14. I think that Hannah Arendt's notion of the "frailty of action" captures a good deal of this idea; see *The Human Condition* (Chicago: University of Chicago Press, 1956), pp. 192–97, 220–30.

15. Drucilla Cornell, *The Philosophy of the Limit*, p. 158 *et passim*.

16. When Derrida expresses his admiration for a certain *Aufklärung*, a new one, and Habermas presses for a pragmatic and hermeneutically sensitive idea of

critical reason, the two poles of modernism and postmodernism, if there are such things, begin to touch.

17. Friedrich Nietzsche, *The Will to Power*, trans. Walter Kaufmann and R. J. Hollingdale (New York: Vintage Books, 1968), No. 639, pp. 340–41; No. 712, pp. 379–80.

18. *Nagarjuna: The Philosophy of the Middle Way*, ed. and trans. David J. Kalupahana (Albany: SUNY Press, 1986). For some interesting work on Derrida and Nagarjuna, see David Loy, ed., *Healing Deconstruction: Postmodern Thought in Buddhism and Christianity* (Atlanta: Scholars Press, 1966), and Robert R. Magliola, *Derrida on the Mend* (West Lafayette: Purdue University Press, 1984).

19. See Constantine Constantius, *Repetition*, in Søren Kierkegaard, *Kierkegaard's Works*, Vol. VI, *"Fear and Trembling" and "Repetition,"* trans. H. Hong and E. Hong (Princeton: Princeton University Press, 1983), pp. 131–33, 148–49. All references to Johannes de Silentio's *Fear and Trembling*, hereafter FT, are to this edition.

20. In *Against Ethics: Contributions to a Poetics of Obligation with Constant Reference to Deconstruction* (Bloomington: Indiana University Press, 1993) I advanced the Abrahamic analogy to deconstruction by way of a certain Derridean restaging of *Fear and Trembling*. Having tired of waiting for Derrida to work into the weave of deconstruction Johannes de Silentio—that other poet of responsibility, decision, singularity, instants, secrets, and the *tout autre*—I undertook to do so myself. As fate would have it, I was reading page proofs for this book when *Donner la mort*, Derrida's analysis of *Fear and Trembling*, made its appearance on my bookstore shelf. I thought I was seeing a ghost, like a spectral appearance of father Abraham himself. In the past, Mark Taylor, Louis Mackey, Sylvia Agacinski, and many others, I among them, have had laboriously to construct this analogy based upon multiple clues in Derrida's texts that any attentive reader of Derrida who has also read *Fear and Trembling* will readily recognize. See: Mark C. Taylor, *Altarity* (Chicago: University of Chicago Press, 1987), chapter 10; "Secretions," in *Tears* (Albany: SUNY Press, 1990); Sylviane Agacinski, *Aparté: Conceptions and Deaths of Soren Kierkegaard*, trans. Kevin Newmark (Tallahassee: University Presses of Florida, 1988); Louis Mackey, "Slouching Toward Bethlehem: Deconstructive Strategies in Theology," *Anglican Theological Review*, 65 (1983): 255–72; John D. Caputo, "Beyond Aestheticism: Derrida's Responsible Anarchy," *Research in Phenomenology*, 18 (1988): 59–73.

21. The text is patched together from FT, 54, 82 and 120; DM, 63/GD, 62–63; and an encapsulation of Derrida's "The 'Force of Law'" (FL).

22. Edith Wyschogrod points out to me that this expression in Matthew is a redaction for Christian purposes of "a rabbinic oath taken by witnesses in cases of capital crime: 'If I am not telling the truth may the blood of the defendant and his descendants who will not be born if he is executed be upon *me*, the witness.'" For an attempt to set the record straight, see John Dominic Crossan, *Who Killed Jesus?* (San Francisco: HarperSanFrancisco, 1995).

23. See the watchful observation of Vigilius Haufniensis, *The Concept of Anxiety*, *Kierkegaard's Writings*, VIII, trans. Reidar Thomte and Albert Anderson (Princeton: Princeton University Press, 1980), p. 87n*, who observed the same thing.

24. Because my treatment of *Donner la mort* was finished before the appearance of the excellent English translation by David Wills, I have often left my own translations in place for comparative purposes, which I have modified in the light

of the Wills translation, to which I also provide cross-references. Sometimes, as here, I have preferred the Wills translation.

25. Economic metaphors enframe *Fear and Trembling*, occurring at the beginning and end (FT, 5, 121); see Josiah Thompson, "The Master of Irony," in *Kierkegaard: A Collection of Critical Essays*, ed. Josiah Thompson (Garden City, NY: Doubleday Anchor Books, 1972), pp. 139–43.

26. I once divided my class into a prosecution team, a defense team, and a jury and asked them to render a judicial decision on Abraham's conduct. They concluded that they might not be able to get the patriarch on attempted murder, but they could certainly get him on reckless endangerment.

27. It was Mark Taylor, before Derrida, who noticed the deconstructionistic implications of Abraham's secret; see Taylor, "Secretions," *Tears*, chapter 11.

28. The French *me voici*, here I am, see me here, a centerpiece of Levinas's thought, appears to be a remarkably felicitous translation of the Hebrew *hinneni*, which means "behold, here am I." I have been helped on this and other matters with the story of Abraham particularly by Phyllis Trible, *Genesis 22: The Sacrifice of Sarah*, Gross Memorial Lecture (Valparaiso: Valparaiso University Press, 1989).

29. The whole story is "carnophallogocentric:" the prohibition against killing is not extended to living things in general but has to do strictly with the "humanism of the other human," to use Levinas's phrase. In this story of "carnivorous virility" the ram does not enjoy the protections of "first philosophy." See PdS, 292–95/*Points*, 278–80.

30. See Merold Westphal, "The Teleological Suspension of the Religious." See DM, 88/GD, 92–93, where Derrida points out that Kierkegaard seems to come back to a kind of Kantianism; if Kierkegaard is a critic of Kantian universalizability, he is an advocate of the Kantian notion of "sacrificing" sensibility to duty.

31. This is Lyotard's objection to trying to reinscribe the Nazi genocide within the genre of sacrifice by calling it a "holocaust." Did the Nazi executioners love the Jews? Did they offer them up to God in fear and trembling? See Jean-François Lyotard, *The Differend: Phrases in Dispute*, trans. G. Van Den Abbeele (Minneapolis: University of Minnesota Press, 1988), No. 168, p. 109.

32. In *Against Ethics*, my more Derridean version of *Fear and Trembling*, I make everything turn on a distinction between "ethics," as a philosophical discourse, and "obligation," which I treat as "fact as it were," something that happens (*arrive*), but something that lacks a reassuring philosophical or even theological backup, which is what Kierkegaard calls the comfort of universality.

33. In a forthcoming paper, David Wood argues that Derrida is slipping here into an excessive formalism, an unsituated universalism which fails to recognize that, although no action is absolutely justified, I am more obliged to one who is before me and whom I can help than to others who are absent and whom I cannot help. The fact that there are no fixed boundaries between these two spheres, Wood adds, does not mean that there are no boundaries at all. See "Selected Studies in Phenomenology and Existential Philosophy," Vol. 22, ed. Debra Bergoffen and John D. Caputo, forthcoming in *Philosophy Today*, 41 (1997).

34. See Karl-Josef Kuschel, *Abraham: Sign of Hope for Jews, Christians, Muslims* (New York: St. Martin's Press, 1995). Of Kierkegaard's Abraham, Derrida writes, "Heretical or paradoxical, is this knight of faith Jewish, Christian, or Judeo-Christian-Islamic? The sacrifice of Isaac belongs to what one might just dare call the

common treasure, the terrifying secret of a *mysterium tremendum* proper to what is called the three religions of the Book as the religions of the Abrahamic peoples" (DM, 65/GD, 64).

35. In the Koran, it is revealed to the prophet Mohammed that Abraham was asked by God to sacrifice Ishmael, not Isaac, and that Ishmael is Abraham's legitimate heir.

36. Emmanuel Levinas, *Noms Propres* (Paris: Fata Morgana, 1976), p. 86. Cf. DM, 77, 198n8/GD, 78–79n6.

37. For bibliographies, see Claus Westerman, *Genesis 12–36: A Commentary* (Minneapolis: Augsburg Publishing House, 1985); and James Crenshaw (ed.), *A Whirlpool of Torment* (Philadelphia: Fortress Press, 1984).

38. John D. Caputo, *Demythologizing Heidegger* (Bloomington: Indiana University Press, 1993), chapter 2. Derrida extends this criticism to Levinas, who, with Heidegger, he includes in his scheme of "carnivorous virility" in PdS, 291–93/ *Points*, 277–80,

39. See Caputo, *Against Ethics*, pp. 139–46.

40. See Heidegger's famous discussion of ethics in "A Letter on Humanism" in *Martin Heidegger: Basic Writings*, ed. David Krell (New York: Harper & Row, 1977), pp. 323–33. The constant references to the *ratio reddenda* in "*Donner la mort*" are allusions to Heidegger's *The Principle of Reason*, trans. Reginald Lilly (Bloomington: Indiana University Press, 1991).

41. This rapprochement of Levinas and Kierkegaard is already adumbrated in "Violence and Metaphysics." "[I]n order to do [Kierkegaard] *justice*," Derrida says, "recall that what Kierkegaard delimited as 'ethics' was an ethical universality and lawfulness that represents a violent anonymity vis-à-vis the singularity of religious subjectivity. Levinas on the other hand shows no interest in an ethics of laws, in 'a morality' composed of determinate moral prescriptions, but is instead describing an 'Ethics of Ethics,' a 'Law of laws,' relative to a *tout autre* which is rather more like what Kierkegaard, in speaking of a 'certain Abraham,' calls the religious." Cf. ED, 162–64/WD, 110–11; this passage also anticipates the argument of "The Force of Law."

42. But then see PdS, 375/*Points*, 364.

43. On the man-ly virility of Western theories of "*vir*"-tue, of "vir-tue ethics," see *Pol.*, pp. 11–16.

44. Kierkegaard (and with him Derrida) ignores the earlier chapters of Genesis, in which Abraham haggles with God over the price of saving Sodom and Gomorrah. Suppose he can come up with fifty just men? Well, if fifty, then why not forty-five? Etc. (18:23–33). Abraham eventually gets the price down to ten, which he cannot come up with.

45. Emmanuel Levinas, *Otherwise than Being or Beyond Essence*, trans. Alphonso Lingis (The Hague: Martinus Nijhoff, 1981), p. 185.

46. In "Force of Law: 'The Mystical Foundation of Authority,'" (FL/DPJ, 3–67) Derrida shows how the problematic effects of singularity systematically invade the decisions which the legal system, the "justice" system, is required to render about each individual "case," each "fall" from universality, which is an inveterately Greek and not a biblical way to think of the singular.

47. On the dispute surrounding Derrida's nomination for an honorary degree at Cambridge University in Jacques Derrida, *Points . . . Interviews, 1974–94*, ed.

Elizabeth Weber, trans. Peggy Kamuf & Others (Stanford: Stanford University Press, 1995), *"Honoris Causa:* 'This is *also* extremely funny,'" pp. 399–421.

48. See the exchange between me and Charles Scott in *Research in Phenomenology,* 25 (1995).

49. In *Glas,* 270–71/243, Derrida speaks of the "pure gift" (*don pur*), if there is one, the gift without exchange, without return, outside the dialectical circle, which makes a holocaust of its holocaust, burns its gift-giving behind it and disappears *as* a gift. The pure gift, *don pur,* would be perfectly consumed in the sacrificial fire (*pyr*), in perfect purification, pyr-ification, which would make a sacrifice even of sacrifice; cf. *Cinders,* 39. In GT and GD he speaks simply of the "gift," if there is one, since no existing gift can be protected from the circle of exchange.

50. Distinguishing *inimicus,* a personal (interior) enemy, from *hostis,* a public (exterior) enemy state, Carl Schmitt argued that Jesus was not at all discouraging Christian countries from waging wars on enemies and infidels (DM, 97–99/GD, 103–105). That is a version of "Christian politics" that has nothing to do with the religion of the *tout autre,* or with Jesus.

51. For some good reasons to stop saying "Judeo-Christian," see Jill Robbins, *Prodigal Son/Elder Brother* (Chicago: University of Chicago Press, 1991).

52. Friedrich Nietzsche, *"The Genealogy of Morals" and "Ecce Homo,"* trans. W. Kaufmann and F. J. Hollingdale (New York: Random House, Vintage Books, 1969), Second Essay, chapter 21, p. 92.

53. In terms of giving death, there always was a fine line between martyrdom and the death wish. Historically, the Church's condemnation of suicide arose from the growing desire among early Christians to take one's life in order to be with Christ, which seemed like a good deal to the early Christians, and also to Nietzsche, who likewise encouraged the latter-day saints to be done with it and join their Savior. The Church's response to this wave of violence against oneself was to tell the faithful (*les croyances*) to leave death-dealing to God, to leave giving life and giving death in God's hands, not to deal in death. That too is the point of another, non-Kierkegaardian, less macho reading of the story of the binding of Isaac. The Lord is rubbing Abraham's nose in the bloodiness of sacrifice: take this son whom you dearly love—and he tells Abraham to lay off, not to deal in (human) death.

54. See my critique of Nietzsche (and Deleuze's *Nietzsche*) in *Against Ethics,* pp. 42–68.

55. There follows an excursion into several etymological studies—of *debeo* by Benveniste and of *devoir* by Malamoud, which link duty and debt—which we are prevented by economic considerations from pursuing, although we should.

56. See Heidegger, *The Principle of Reason,* pp. 32–40.

57. Martin Heidegger, *Discourse on Thinking,* trans. John Anderson and E. Hans Freund (New York: Harper & Row, 1966), pp. 54–55.

58. For an architectural challenge to deconstruction, see Mark Wigley, *The Architecture of Deconstruction: Derrida's Haunt* (Cambridge: MIT Press, 1993).

59. But without a strong theory of a voluntarist or heroic subject: in the midst of the impossibility of decision, a decision is made. When it is made, it is made by the other, in response to the "come" of the other. With Abraham, e.g., it is God who decides and Abraham who obeys (PdS, 157–58/*Points,* 147–49). So Derrida's decision is made by a "knight of faith" not in the sense of a heroic will but in the sense of a knight sworn to serve the other.

60. For more on this line of argument, see the many works of Geza Vermes, e.g., *Jesus the Jew: A Historian's Reading of the Gospels* (Philadelphia: Fortress Press, 1973), and E. P. Sanders, *Jesus and Judaism* (Philadelphia: Fortress Press, 1985) and most recently, *The Historical Figure of Jesus* (New York: Penguin Press, 1993).

V. Circumcision

1. See the exchange between Derrida and Lyotard at Cerisy after Lyotard's paper "Phrasing 'After Auschwitz,'" in *Les fins de l'homme: A partir du travail de Jacques Derrida* (Paris: Galilée, 1981), pp. 311–13; Eng. trans. *The Lyotard Reader*, ed. Andrew Benjamin (Oxford: Blackwell, 1989), pp. 386–89.

2. ". . . I have always had trouble vibrating in unison." PdS, 358/*Points*, 348.

3. This distinction perhaps foreshadows Derrida's later distinction between a concrete messianism and the messianic. Derrida is always working the distance between an empirical and a quasi-transcendental Jewishness.

4. All page numbers in parentheses in this paragraph are to Susan Handelman, *The Slayers of Moses: The Emergence of Rabbinic Interpretation in Modern Literary Theory* (Albany: SUNY Press, 1982). See Elisha New, "Pharaoh's Birthstool: Deconstruction and Midrash," *Sub-stance*, 57 (1988): 26–36, for a discussion of Handelman's thesis. See also Handelman, "Jacques Derrida and the Heretic Hermeneutic," in *Displacement: Derrida and After*, ed. Mark Krupnick (Bloomington: Indiana University Press, 1983), pp. 98–129, and "Parodic Play and Prophetic Reason: Two Interpretations of Interpretation," in *The Rhetoric of Interpretation and the Interpretation of Rhetoric*, ed. Paul Hernadi (Durham: Duke University Press, 1989), pp. 143–71. For other discussions of the cabalistic side of Derrida, see Harold Bloom, *Kabbalah and Criticism* (New York, 1975) and Shira Wolosky, "Derrida, Jabès, Levinas: Sign-Theory as Ethical Discourse," *Prooftexts*, 2 (1982): 283–302.

5. In MpPdM, 125–26/MfPdM, 128, Derrida confides to us his "two admirations" and "two identifications," as an adolescent, with Rousseau and Nietzsche, even if Nietzsche had nothing good to say about Rousseau.

6. The Hebraicism of Derrida was also noticed early on by Herbert Schneidau, *Sacred Discontent: The Bible and Western Tradition* (Baton Rouge: Louisiana State University Press, 1976), who speaks of deconstruction as a Yahwistic exposure of the *vanitas vanitatum*, of the constructedness of our fictions. Under Schneidau's influence, G. Douglas Atkins, *Reading Deconstruction: Deconstructive Reading* (Lexington: University Press of Kentucky, 1983), incisively characterizes Derrida's critique of logocentrism as "de-Hellenizing literary criticism." Atkins draws a striking and illuminating analogy of deconstruction with a parallel, indeed an older theological project—identifiable in Leslie Dewart's *The Future of Belief* (New York: Herder & Herder, 1966)—that goes back at least to Kierkegaard and Luther and even to Paul (First Corinthians 1). The point of dehellenization is to disentangle *Écriture Sainte*, scriptural Christianity, from the system of essentially Hellenic oppositions between time and eternity, body and soul, matter and spirit, unity and multiplicity, universal and particular, that Heidegger later on called "onto-theologic." Indeed, Luther's attempt to retrieve the primordially scriptural character of Christianity from its metaphysical overlay, as John van Buren has shown so well, was an essential impulse behind Heidegger's "hermeneutics of facticity," the

original project of the 1920s, the very word *Destruktion* having apparently been taken from Luther. See van Buren, *The Young Heidegger*, pp. 157–202.

7. To be sure, as Edith Wyschogrod points out to me, Paul himself was not simply of one mind on the matter. Paul affirmed the election of Israel (Romans 9:1–13) and in Acts 16:3, just after the council at Jerusalem, he circumcised Timothy in order to honor the Jews among whom he would be preaching with Timothy.

8. "[A]ll the questions and all the themes addressed in *Glas* are explicitly political . . ." (PdS, 20/*Points*, 12); *Glas* addresses the politics of the place, of "a basin, a sea, where there arrive for an interminable war the Greek, the Jew, the Arab, the Hispano-Moor. Which I am also (following) [*je suis*] by the trace." *Glas*, 45b/37b; cf. PdS, 72–73/*Points*, 67–68.

9. See Friedrich Hegel, *On Christianity: Early Theological Writings*, trans. T. M. Knox (New York: Harper & Row Cloister Books, 1961), which is the translation used by the translators of *Glas*.

10. Derrida would contest any reduction of circumcision to castration, even if castration simply meant, as in Lacan, the cut of finitude.

11. For an overview of *Glas*, see Gayatri C. Spivak, "*Glas*-Piece: A *Compte Rendu*," *Diacritics*, 7 (1983): 22–43.

12. I have pursued the dynamics of such an anti-phenomenology in terms of what I called "jewgreek bodies" in *Against Ethics*, chapter 9.

13. See Michael Goulder, *St. Paul versus St. Peter: A Tale of Two Missions* (Louisville: Westminster John Knox Press, 1994), pp. 31–38.

14. See Jane Schaberg, *The Illegitimacy of Jesus: A Feminist Theological Interpretation of the Infancy Narratives* (San Francisco: Harper & Row, 1987); cf. also her "How Mary Magdalene Became a Whore," *Bible Review*, 8 (1992): 30–52.

15. Derrida takes up the problem of situating Kant vis-à-vis the German and the Jew in "Interpretations at War: Kant, le Juif, l'allemand," in *Phénoménologie et Politique: Mélanges offerts à Jacques Taminaux* (Brussels: Ousia, 1990); "Interpretations at War: Kant, the Jew, the German," *New Literary History*, 22 (1991): 39–95. This essay on the German-Jewish psyche uncovers some unsettling similarities between the "great German" and the "great German Jewish" thinkers on questions like nationalism and militarism; cf. FL, 72–73/DPJ, 65–66; see also Bennington, pp. 292 ff.

16. Johannes Climacus, who thought the System, being comical, deserves to be treated with derision, turned this flight motif around: we admire a man who can leap high, but we laugh at a man who thinks he is a bird and can fly; *Concluding Unscientific Postscript to the "Philosophical Fragments*," pp. 120, 124.

17. Vermes, *The Religion of Jesus the Jew*, p. 213.

18. Derrida's purposes become explicit as the reading comes upon the figure of the sister (Antigone) in the *Phenomenology of Spirit* who represents the "transcendental excess" or exception to the System's family economy. Antigone is a pure sister who died before becoming wife or mother. Hegel views the brother/sister relationship as the most spiritual relation of all, where there is no sexual desire between them and hence no battle for recognition. But that is at odds with the System, for consciousness is always driven by this battle and would not be conscious without it. As a pure sister, she is "unclassable," an *exception* who cannot be admitted into the system, and as such plays an "almost tran / scendental role" (*jouant / un rôle quasi-transcendental*) (*Glas*, 171a/151a, 183a/162a: this expression

is cut in half by 11 pages) in the System. The sister makes the system possible while not fitting into any of its categories. She tears up the family circle, gives a gift without return, an expenditure without reserve, agglutinating the smooth workings of the Hegelian machine, interrupting its economy with a gift. The sister occupies a place both inside and outside, of transcendental ex-position, transcendentally out of place. The little sister who has slipped into the System and sent it skidding is a very jewgreek figure. It is hard to differentiate—to decontaminate!—the feminine operation in *Antigone* from that of Jewish and Christian women, who occupy a similar site, who are assigned a similar operation. The figure of a woman bent over a body laid low, tending to bodies *in extremis*, at birth and death—is that a Jewish or a Christian or a Greek scene? Is it Mary Magdalene and the women weeping at the foot of the cross to whom Derrida returns in *Memoires d'aveugle*? (Or even of Jesus bathing the apostles' feet, which makes it a little androgynous?) Or of Antigone bent over Polyneices? Is it necessary to choose among these scenes? The sister is a fragment of the System, a remnant, a remains. *Tout autre*.

19. A. N. Wilson, *Jesus: A Life* (New York: Fawcett Columbine, 1992), p. 256. Wilson offers a well-written and popular exposition of a fundamentally Vermesian line.

20. When a German poem cites Hebrew, French, and Spanish (*Schib.*, 41 ff./WT, 22 ff.) we cannot translate all that into English; when it cites itself, we cannot translate that. "[T]he affirmation of a language through itself is untranslatable" (UG, 59/AL, 257). But of course it is just what is untranslatable that demands translation.

21. "The thought of the incineration (*brûle-tout*) of the holocaust, of cinders, runs through all my texts . . . well before *Shibboleth (For Paul Celan)*, whose sole thought it is." "Interview with Derrida," in *Logomachia: The Conflict of the Faculties*, ed. Richard Rand (Lincoln: University of Nebraska Press, 1992), p. 210. This is said in response to Lyotard's rather uninformed criticisms of Derrida in *Heidegger and "the jews."* See also PdS, 299–300/*Points*, 286–87 and *Cinders*, passim. See above, n. 1.

22. The poem as a circumcised word, then, is sharply to be distinguished from Heideggerian *Dichtung* where *Versammlung* always wins out and allows the *Gedicht* to enclose itself into the well-rounded, self-enclosed circle of Truth. Great poetry is guaranteed only by a higher *Eindeutigkeit*, beyond any superficial polysemy, where the poem allows "the Truth," one and all-gathering, to come into the work, where the Master Poet (Hölderlin) sacrifices himself to the Truth, and where Heidegger sacrifices himself to this sacrifice, and by portraying himself as a sacrificial victim implicitly says to the Germans, "When are you going to hear the one who is saying this to you?" PdS, 314–19/*Points*, 304–309. See also Caputo, *Demythologizing Heidegger*, chapter 8, "Heidegger's Poets."

23. For helpful commentaries, see Carol Jacquet, "Nes, Yo' in Joyce, Oui-Rire Derrida," in *James Joyce Literary Supplement*, ed. B. Benstock (Miami: University of Miami Press, 1987); Richard Kearney, *Transitions: Narratives in Modern Irish Culture* (Manchester: Manchester University Press, 1988); M. McArthur, "The Example of Joyce: Derrida Reading Joyce," *James Joyce Quarterly*, 32 (1995): 227–41.

24. Franz Rosenzweig, *The Star of Redemption*, trans. William Hallo (Boston: Beacon Press, 1971), p. 27.

25. In fulfillment of Derrida's prophecy, see the following recent publication: A.

Nicholas Fargnoli and Michael P. Gillespie, *James Joyce A to Z: An Encyclopedic Companion to the Life and Work* (Facts on File, 1995).

26. I did my best to frame out the odd figure of a Dionysiac rabbi in *Against Ethics*, chapter 3.

27. If the *cinder* "is not what it is" (*Cinders*, 39), there are many cinders in Derrida's work: the *Jew*, whose identity is to have no identity; the *community*, which is the "we" without identity (AC, 16/OH, 9); the *gift*, whose essence is that it not answer to its own essence, that it must not be what it ought to be (DT, 94n1/GT, 69n23). In Derrida's non-essentialism, essences go up in smoke, inasmuch as "there is no essence of *différance*" (MdP, 27/MoP, 26).

28. If *Circonfession* gives, is dedicated to, an account of his dying mother, *Mal d'archive*, the subject of the present chapter is dedicated to "my sons and to the memory of my father, who was also called, as is life itself, Hayim" (*Archive*, 41/AF, 20). Derrida is getting around to honoring his father and mother, in print, belatedly.

29. See Yosef Hayim Yerushalmi, *Freud's Moses: Judaism Terminable and Interminable* (New Haven: Yale University Press, 1991); hereafter "Y."

30. He, too, is obeying the ghosts—of his father and his grandfathers "and of a few others" (*Archive*, 140/AF, 56; cf. *Archive*, 41/AF, 20; *Archive*, 124/AF, 51).

31. This is the final sentence of Yerushalmi's book, except that I have substituted "Derrida" for "Freud" and "deconstruction" for "psychoanalysis." *Freud's Moses*, p. 100. *Mal d'archive* is in no small part an extended commentary on this sentence.

32. There is a bewildering array of fathers and sons, real and symbolic, father/ghosts and sons apostrophizing to the air, more transferences than I can count, in the very patriarchival scene of *Mal d'archive*. Moses and Freud, Jakob and Sigmund, Sigmund and Yerushalmi, Sigmund and all his psychoanalytic sons— "we have several others in France" (*Archive*, 90/AF, 38)—vying for the spot of "elder son"; Aimé (Hayim) Derrida and Jacques; Jacques and his sons (see *Archive*, 140/AF, 56). The list goes on—Jacques and us, etc.—archives inside archives, wherever the "scene of reading" is erected, wherever the archival stage is set. By the same token, *Mal d'archive* contains a critique of Freudian patriarchy; see *Archive*, 76–80/AF, 34–35.

33. Derrida is compulsively repeating his reading of Freud, this time in terms of a "scene of reading," the first time in terms of the "scene of writing." "To Do Justice to Freud" repeats "Cogito and the History of Madness."

34. That Yerushalmi does not have the radical conception of the future which Derrida appears too generously to attribute to him at this point will become clear later (*Archive*, 126–27/AF, 52).

35. As usual, the title of Derrida's essay is operating in several registers. (1) *Mal d'archive*: as in *mal de tête*, archive sickness or illness, something we suffer from, but in the double sense of *désir et trouble* (*Archive*, 128/AF, 52). *Désir*: we burn with passion, have a burning, feverish desire for the archive, for the arche, the aboriginal, primordial beginning. That is the oldest desire, not only of metaphysics, but also of the archival historian who wants to know, to set the record straight, once and for all, about how it was in the beginning, *in principio*, *en arche*. *Trouble*: that spells trouble, disorder, sickness, for we are thereby driven beyond the archive to the *arche*, pushed past the slow labor of working with traces, of patiently reconstructing competing versions of memory, in order to displace the trace with the *la*

chose même, to displace the general archive with living memory and pure presence. (2) *En mal d'archive*: but this is an illness (*mal*) that repays study, that turns up a salutary side: *en mal de*, which is being described here.

36. The subtitle—*Freudian Impressions*—means all at once: (1) Freud the theorist of the impression, of repression, of the trace left by a past that has been almost erased; (2) the impression we have of Freudianism, the vague, notional, open-ended sense we have of something indefinite and yet to come; (3) the impression left by Freud upon us all, upon our culture and our intellectual disciplines. *Archive*, 45–54/AF, 22–25. Although Derrida nowhere says the three "theses" repeat the three "Freudian impressions," the first and third theses correspond strictly to the first and the third impressions; the connection between the second impression and second thesis is loose.

VI. *Confession*

1. In *Schib.*, 68/WT, 40, Derrida speaks of a "religion before religion," a kind of pre-religious soil from which the historical religions grow, with which his notion of prayer is also to be associated: "Celan knew one may praise or bless ashes. No religion is needed. Perhaps because a religion begins there, before religion, in the blessing of dates, of names, and of ashes." He also speaks of "poetic prayer, the song of remains without being, the experience of the ash" (*Schib.*, 74/WT, 44), which means the operation of commemorating the past in a poem/date, of praising and blessing an event without which the event would not be an event. To bless is to sing, commemorate, praise, hold in one's heart.

2. That deconstruction is a machine that produces predictable results is a recurrent criticism of Derrida; see Mark Cousins, "The Logic of Deconstruction," *Oxford Literary Review*, 3, 2 (1978): 70–77.

3. "J.D. surprises me less than he thinks . . . for a long time now he has been talking of nothing else . . ." (*Circon.*, 301/*Circum.*, 327).

4. Would it be an olive branch, something to appease the passions of Barry Smith and Ruth Marcus, to know that one of Derrida's first publications was a translation of W. V. O. Quine into French? See Quine, "Les frontières de la théorie logique," trans. J. Derrida and R. Martin, *Études Philosophiques*, 2 (1964). Edith Wyschogrod points out to me that Quine used the young Derrida's office when Quine was in Paris; see W. V. O. Quine, *The Time of My Life: An Autobiography* (Cambridge: MIT Press, 1985), p. 355.

5. In an interview with Catherine David he tells of dreaming of a book to be written that will have to do with "my history . . . Algeria first of all." "One day, some piece of the book may fall out like a stone . . ." (PdS, 128/*Points*, 119). In a follow-up interview, he says that most of what end up as "books" are really collections of essays; as to a book project: "I have only one, the one I will not write, but that guides, attracts, seduces everything I read" (PdS, 151/*Points*, 142). Cf. PdS, 216–17/*Points*, 203.

6. The notion is not unprecedented. Hannah Arendt also inhabited the distance between Augustine and the Jew. Her dissertation on Augustine, under the direction of Jaspers, has recently been translated: *Love and Saint Augustine*, eds. J. V. Scott and J. C. Stark (New Haven: Yale University Press, 1995). For a strident attack on Arendt, which accuses her of being embarrassed about being Jewish, see Rich-

ard Wolin, "Hannah and the Magician," *The New Republic*, 213, 15 (October 9, 1995): 27–37.

7. Or even, as Maimonides taught and Meister Eckhart repeated, a way of curbing masculine desire, the "excess of carnal concupiscence" (PdS, 364/*Points*, 353). For an excellent overview of circumcision, see Lawrence A. Hoffman, *Covenant of Blood: Circumcision and Gender in Rabbinic Judaism* (Chicago: University of Chicago Press, 1996).

8. In "On Not Knowing Who We Are: Madness, Hermeneutics, and the Night of Truth in Foucault," in *Foucault and the Critique of Institutions*, ed. John D. Caputo and Mark Yount (University Park: Pennsylvania State University Press, 1993), pp. 233–62. I argue for a reading of Foucault that provides the basis for a reconciliation of Foucault and Derrida on "confession" and the severance from the Truth of truth.

9. This is hardly Derrida's first encounter with autobiography. Not only is the second part of OG a discussion of Rousseau's *Confessions*, but *The Ear of the Other: Otobiography, Transference, Translation*, ed. C. McDonald, trans. Peggy Kamuf (New York: Schocken, 1985) was devoted to Nietzsche's *Ecce Homo*. In the "Roundtable" that followed this paper, a questioner raised the issue of an analogy of Augustine's and Nietzsche's autobiographies, but the discussion did not get very far (pp. 80–84). Of course, he wants no part of thinking of autobiography as an act of pure self-knowledge (MpPdM, 45–46/MfPdM, 23–24), above all as someone who says he cannot tell a story (MpPdM, 27/MfPdM, 3; *Moscou*, 15–16/PTC, 197–98). Autobiography does not take place in the register of knowledge or historical truth but of confession or justice.

10. In a 1991 interview, in which he comments on *Circonfession*, he says that circumcision is both a real mark and a figure in this book around which everything in the book turns. His first love was Gide, a love that cohabited in him with the hooliganism of a *pied-noir* (a "black foot," a nickname for Algerian Francophones) who "hung out" with a gang of youths more interested in soccer than literature. His birth name is Jackie, an Americanism not uncommon among Algerians born in the 1930s, while "Jacques" is a Franco-Christian pseudonym he adopted when he began to publish, accommodating himself to the good manners of professional philosophy and in so doing "erased more things than I could say in a few words." PdS, 351–55/*Points*, 340–44.

11. Indeed, Heidegger positively excommunicates Hebrew from what Derrida calls the "historical triangle" of languages—Greek, Latin, and German—that constitute the West, so that it is not permissible to think that the Hebrew *ruah*, and a whole history of Hebrew "fire," might lie behind what was translated into Greek and Latin as *pneuma* and *spiritus* (DLE, 164–65/OS, 100–101); for a commentary, see Zarader, pp. 190–92.

12. In *Circon.*, 106–107/*Circum.*, 110–11, Derrida uses the word *PaRDeS*, which is the name he gave to the computer document containing *Circonfession*. *Pardès*, the Hebrew word for paradise, is an acronym for the four senses of the Torah: literal (*p*: *pshat*); allegorical (*r*: *r'emez*); moral (*d*: *drash*); and mystical (*s*: *soud*). Although this fourfold schema does not correspond exactly to what imposes itself on him, he says, some laborious translation of it is not forbidden. He is terrified, he adds, by the fear of betraying a secret.

13. Derrida's sons use their maternal grandmother's name. To give one's name to one's sons who do not use it is to give a gift without return.

14. Johannes Climacus thinks there is always something comical about prayer, an incommensurability of the infinite and the finite, as when we imagine a strong, brawny fellow on his knees; *Concluding Unscientific Postscript to the "Philosophical Fragments,"* pp. 90–91.

15. See Peter Brown, Introduction to an English translation of the *Confessions*, trans. F. J. Sheed (Indianapolis: Hackett, 1970), p. xiii. For an acclaimed biography of Augustine, see Peter Brown, *Augustine of Hippo* (Berkeley: University of California Press, 1967).

16. For a recent study on such matters, see Robert Smith, *Derrida and Autobiography* (Cambridge: Cambridge University Press, 1995); the book is dense and elusive and makes one appreciate Derrida's clarity. For whatever it is Smith is saying about *Circonfession*, see his chapter 4.

17. In *Archive*, 111/AF, 46, Derrida says he has always secretly identified with the Marranos whose "crypto-Judaic history" has been examined by F. Brenner and Y. H. Yerushalmi, *Marranes* (Paris: Difference, 1992), a book he had recently read. Yerushalmi is the author of *Freud's Moses*, the subject of *Mal d'archive*, and Derrida's colleague at the École des Haut Études en Sciences Sociales; if the truth be told, he says, in speaking of his colleague he is also speaking of himself (*Archive*, 139/AF, 56); see above, §17. For a recent study of the Marranos, see Elaine Marks, *Marrano as Metaphor: The Jewish Presence in French Writing* (New York: Columbia University Press, 1995).

18. For some insight into the American (reception of) "Derrida," including some remarks on deconstruction and theology, see "Deconstruction in America: An Interview with Jacques Derrida," in *Critical Exchange*, 17 (1985): 1–33.

19. See the *Dialogues with Contemporary Thinkers*, ed. Richard Kearney, p. 119; see also Kearney, *Poetics of Modernity*, pp. 158–59.

20. For another view of Heidegger's language, one that brings him closer to Derrida, see Gerald L. Bruns, *Heidegger's Estrangements: Language, Truth, and Poetry in the Later Writings* (New Haven, Yale University Press, 1989).

21. "I am always speaking about myself without speaking about myself" (*Pass.*, 91n12/ON, 144n14).

22. For an early study, before *Circonfession*, which underlines this point, see Ann Clark, "Augustine and Derrida: Reading as Fulfillment of the Word," *New Scholasticism*, 55, 1 (1981): 104–12.

23. So far from being opposed to religious faith, deconstruction is itself a bit of faith. In *Moscou*, 49–50/PTC, 213, he asks, what discourse does *not* belong to the arena of faith? See the exchange between Clarence Walhout, "Can Derrida be Christianized?" *Christianity and Literature*, 34 (1985): 15–22 and Horace Underwood, "Derrida and the Christian Critic: A Response to Clarence Walhout," *Christianity and Literature*, 35 (1986): 7–12.

24. For helpful commentaries, see Michael Kelly, "Shades of Derrida," *Artforum*, 26 (1991): 102–104; Meyer Raphael Rubinstein, "Sight Unseen," *Art in America*, 79, 4 (April 1991): 47–51; Michael Newman, "Derrida and the Scene of Drawing: A Discussion of Jacques Derrida, *Mémoires d'aveugle: L'autoportrait et autres ruines*," *Research in Phenomenology*, 24 (1994): 218–34. Rubinstein's approach is more art-historical and less philosophical than Newman's. Newman rightly emphasizes the centrality of ethical witnessing in MB—we can only *bear* witness to that for which there is no *eye*-witness—and he makes an interesting link of MB with *Schibboleth*,

but he shows no interest in the biblical themes in *Memoirs* nor in the link of witnessing to a certain faith; see Newman, pp. 225–31.

25. Heidegger's earliest interests in Augustine centered on just this dichotomy. See Heidegger, *Phänomenologie des religiösen Lebens*, 1. *Einführung in die Phänomenologie der Religion* (Wintersemester 1920/21), Hg. Matthias Jung u. Thomas Regehly; 2. *Augustinus und der Neuplatonismus* (Sommersemester 1921), Hg. Claudius Strube, Gesamtausgabe, B. 60 (Frankfurt/Main: Klostermann, 1995).

26. "Out of sight" is good vernacular American English for something exceptional. *Mirabile dictu* the ancients said, "out of sight" is what we say.

27. *Memoires* is a bit of a "journal," a personal diary or "daybook" (how do the blind keep a diary if night and day are indistinguishable?). The dream occurred July 16, "of last year" (MdA, 23/MB, 16), which must mean 1989, since it is also mentioned as having occurred "last night" in *Circon.*, 61–62/*Circum.*, 61–62, which is an intellectual daybook of January 1989–April 1990. The attack of Lyme disease occurred on June 25, 1989 (*Circon.*, 89/*Circum.*, 91), and had not passed until July 11, 1989, the meeting with the Louvre curators having been postponed, because of the illness, from July 5 to July 11, 1989, on the evening of which the idea for the exhibit hit him (MdA, 38/MB, 32–33). He says that the dream occurred before he had chosen the exhibit theme (MdA, 37/MB, 31) but while he was already thinking about it; otherwise, that would mean the *previous* July (1988). The exhibition was held from October 26, 1990 to January 21, 1991.

28. Michael Newman reports (219–20) a video made of the exhibit in which the questions were put to Derrida by a woman off-camera and the expository passages were spoken by Derrida.

29. See Peggy Kamuf, "Reading Between the Blinds," in *A Derrida Reader: Reading Between the Blinds* (New York: Columbia University Press, 1991), xiii–xlii, for a commentary, contemporaneous with *Memoirs of the Blind*, on the various senses of this image. The *Reader* itself, composed as it is of excerpted sections of Derrida's work, is a set of shutters or blinds. Kamuf also discusses the affinities of jalousie with "jealousy," which is of course a feature of both Yahweh, who insisted on monotheism, and Jacques, who was jealous of Renée.

30. A blind man is a man whose sight is ruined by a "fall" of some sort, by "[s]in, fault, or error," by a lapse of nature (MdA, 18/MB, 12), and so a portrait of a blind man is like a picture of ancient ruins, like the photographs of ruins in Bataille's *Story of the Eye* (MdA, 23–24n10/MB, 17n10).

31. In a parenthetical remark, Derrida alludes to the fact that the revisionist denial of Auschwitz, demanding that eyewitnesses to the gas chamber come forward, presumably from out of their graves, is always structurally possible by the very nature of having to rely on witnesses instead of perception; Lyotard, too, had argued that revisionism is always cognitively possible. See Newman, 225–28.

32. On the sense of *opthe* in these New Testament episodes, see Edward Schillebeeckx, *Jesus: An Experiment in Christology*, trans. Hubert Hoskins (New York: Crossroads, 1985), pp. 346–79.

33. William J. Richardson, "Heidegger's Truth and Politics," in *Ethics and Danger: Essays on Heidegger and Continental Thought*, ed. Arleen Dallery and Charles Scott (Albany: SUNY Press, 1992), pp. 11–24; John Sallis, "Deformatives: Essentially Other Than Truth," in *Reading Heidegger: Commemorations*, ed. John Sallis

(Bloomington: Indiana University Press, 1993), pp. 29–46. See my reply to Richardson in "Dark Hearts: Heidegger, Richardson, and Evil," in *From Phenomenology to Thought, Errancy, and Desire*, ed. Babette Babich (The Hague: Kluwer, 1995), pp. 267–75 and Richardson's response to me: "Heidegger's Fall," *American Catholic Philosophical Quarterly*, 69 (1995): 229–53.

34. See Jeffrey Masson and Susan McCarthy, *When Elephants Weep: The Emotional Lives of Animals* (New York: Delacorte Press, 1995), and the touching story, which will sound a little fishy to the hard of heart, of an elephant named Sadie who, upon being punished for her inability to understand the commands of her circus trainers, rushed from the ring and began sobbing (more weeping women!).

Conclusion

1. See above, "Edifying Divertissement No. 2."

2. Caputo, *Radical Hermeneutics*, p. 288.

3. Derrida discusses the *désir de Dieu* in *Sauf*, 18–20/ON, 36–37, remarking upon the double genitive, opening up the possibility of a desire in the "other voice," foreign to anthopo-theo-morphism, a desire going toward the "absolute other," renouncing appropriation, in short, a desire that is not the momentum of a subject for possession, but the affirmation, *sans avoir*, of the *tout autre*. He also says that extreme forms of religious discourse, which usually look like atheism to the orthodox, e.g., that of apophatic theology and of Angelus Silesius in particular, "have always testified" to this desire. In *Sauf*, 103/ON, 80, he writes, "The desire of God, God as the other name of desire, deals in the desert with radical atheism."

4. John Dominic Crossan, *The Historical Jesus: The Life of a Mediterranean Jewish Peasant* (San Francisco: HarperSanFrancisco, 1992), pp. 265 ff.

5. The "meditation on writing," which is deconstruction, is a meditation on "absolute weakness," on the "absolute victim," which means "a victim who cannot even protest," so that no trace of the victim remains, but only cinders, the "dangerous memory of suffering" (Metz) having been forgotten. That is why it is necessary to "save the name." See PdS, 402–404/*Points*, 388–90.

6. See Abraham Heschel, *The Prophets*, 2 volumes (New York: Harper Torchbooks, 1962, 1969), I:1–11, 27–47. For a presentation of biblical ethics which has caught the spirit of Heschel, see Daniel C. Maguire, *The Moral Core of Judaism and Christianity: Reclaiming the Revolution* (Minneapolis: Fortress Press, 1993).

7. In fact, Heschel simply discards the notion of the "wholly other" or *numen* as an excessive twentieth-century reaction to rationalism, having little to do with the biblical God of pathos (II: 6–8). We know that Kierkegaard's Johannes Climacus used it in the *Philosophical Fragments*, trans. Howard Hong and Edna Hong (Princeton: Princeton University Press, 1985), pp. 44–45, having presumably picked it up from Luther's *totaliter aliter*. Peperzak says it made its way into Levinas from Yankélévitch, who used it in commenting on Plotinus; see Adriaan Peperzak, *To the Other: An Introduction to the Philosophy of Emmanuel Levinas* (West Lafayette: Purdue University Press, 1993), p. 41.

8. Heschel, I: 3–26.

9. There is a line of New Testament scholarship that is finding correlations between the cynics and the earliest followers of Jesus. See Crossan, *The Historical*

Jesus, pp. 421–22; F. Gerald Downing, *Christ and the Cynics: Jesus and Other Radical Preachers in First-Century Tradition,* JSOT Manuals 4 (Sheffield: Sheffield Academic Press, JSOT Press, 1988).

10. See the excellent presentation of the perils of Levinas's project of the "translation" of Hebrew into Greek in Robert Gibbs, *Correlations in Rosenzweig and Levinas* (Princeton: Princeton University Press, 1992), chapter 7.

11. Dare I say, in keeping with the problematic of the gift, that this is the finger that deconstruction gives, *donner le doigt,* without return? To "Heidegger's Hand" would we need to add "Derrida's Finger"?

Select Bibliography on Derrida and Religion

The following bibliography contains a selection of studies that address various aspects of the question of Derrida and theology or religion. The most complete bibliography of Derrida's writings and of the secondary literature up to 1991, which has been indispensable to the present study and to the bibliography that follows, is William R. Schultz and Lewis L. B. Fried, *Jacques Derrida: An Annotated Primary and Secondary Bibliography* (New York: Garland Publishing Co., 1992). I have also been helped by Albert Leventure, "A Bibliography of the French and English Works of Jacques Derrida 1962–1990," *Textual Practice*, 5.1 (Spring 1991): 94–127; and *Social Theory: A Bibliographic Series*, No. 37, *Jacques Derrida (II): A Bibliography*, ed. Joan Nordquist (Santa Cruz: Reference and Research Services, 1995).

Aichele, George. Jr. *The Limits of Story*. Philadelphia: Fortress Press, 1985.

Atkins, G. Douglas. *Reading Deconstruction/Deconstructive Reading*. Lexington: University Press of Kentucky, 1983.

———. "Partial Stories: Hebraic and Christian Thinking in the Wake of Deconstruction." *Religion and Literature*, 15, 3 (1983): 7–21.

Bloom, Harrold. *Kabbalah and Criticism*. New York, Seabury Press, 1975.

Bolin, Nona. "Deconstruction and Onto-Theological Discourse." In *God in Language*, ed. Robert Scharleman and G. E. M. Ogatu. New York: Paragon House, 1987. Pp. 60–70.

Brown, David. *Continental Philosophy and Modern Theology*. Oxford: Blackwell, 1987.

Caputo, John D. *Against Ethics: Contributions to a Poetics of Obligation with Constant Reference to Deconstruction*, Studies in Continental Thought. Bloomington: Indiana University Press, 1993.

———. *Radical Hermeneutics: Repetition, Deconstruction and the Hermeneutic Project*, Studies in Phenomenology and Existential Philosophy. Bloomington: Indiana University Press, 1987.

———. "Bedeviling the Tradition: On Deconstruction and Catholicism." In *(Dis)continuity and (De)construction*. Ed. Josef Wissink. Kampen, The Netherlands: Pharos, 1995. Pp. 12–34.

———. "Instants, Secrets, Singularities: Dealing Death in Kierkegaard and Derrida." In *Kierkegaard in Post/Modernity*, ed. Martin Matustik and Merold Westphal. Bloomington: Indiana University Press, 1995. Pp. 216–38.

————. "Reason, History and a Little Madness: Towards a Hermeneutics of the Kingdom." *Proceedings of the American Catholic Philosophical Association*, 68 (1994): 27–44.

————. "The Good News About Alterity: Derrida and Theology," *Faith and Philosophy*, 10 (1993): 453–70.

————. "How to Avoid Speaking of God: The Violence of Natural Theology." In *The Prospects for Natural Theology*, ed. Eugene Long. Washington, D.C.: Catholic University of America Press, 1992. Pp. 128–50.

————. "Hermeneutics and Faith: A Reply to Prof. Olthuis." *Christian Scholars Review*, 20 (December 1990): 164–70.

————. "Derrida and the Study of Religion" (with Charles Winquist). *Religious Studies Review*, 16 (January 1990): 19–25.

————. "Mysticism and Transgression: Derrida and Meister Eckhart." *Continental Philosophy*, II (1989): 24–39.

————. "Beyond Aestheticism: Derrida's Responsible Anarchy." *Research in Phenomenology*, 18 (1988): 59–73.

Clark, Ann K. "Augustine and Derrida: Reading as Fulfillment of the Word." *New Scholasticism*, 55, 1 (1981): 104–12.

Colleony, Jacques. "Déconstruction, théologie et archi-éthique (Derrida, Levinas et Heidegger)." In *Le Passage des frontières: Autour du travail de Jacques Derrida*, Colloque de Cerisy. Paris: Galilée, 1994. Pp. 249–61.

Coward, Howard. *Derrida and Indian Philosophy*. Albany: SUNY Press, 1990.

Crossan, John Dominic. "Difference and Divinity." *Semeia*, 23 (1982): 29–40.

Dean, William. "Derrida and Process Theology." *Journal of Religion*, 64 (1984): 1–19.

Deconstruction and Theology. Ed. T. J. J. Altizer et al. New York: Crossroads, 1982.

(Dis)continuity and (De)construction: Reflections on the Meaning of the Past in Crisis Situations. Ed. Josef Wissink. Kampen, The Netherlands: Pharos Publishing House, 1995.

Faulconer, James. "Protestant and Jewish Styles of Criticism: Derrida and His Critics." *Literature and Belief*, 5 (1985): 45–66.

Gall, Robert. "Of/From Theology and Deconstruction." *Journal of the American Academy of Religion*, 58, 3 (1990): 413–37.

Gasché, Rodolphe. "God, For Example." In *Inventions of Difference*. Cambridge: Harvard University Press, 1994. Pp. 150–70.

Gisel, Pierre, and Patrick Evard, eds. *La Théologie en postmodernité*. Lieux théologiques, No. 29. Paris: Labor et Fides, 1996.

Greenstein, Edward. "Deconstruction and Biblical Narrative." *Prooftexts*, 9 (1989): 43–71.

Greisch, Jean. "Déconstruction et/ou Herméneutique," in *La Théologie en postmodernité*, pp. 353–86.

Handelman, Susan. *The Slayers of Moses: The Emergence of Rabbinic Interpretation in Modern Literary Theory*. Albany: SUNY Press, 1982.

————. "Jacques Derrida and the Heretic Hermeneutic." In *Displacement: Derrida and After*. Ed. Mark Krupnick. Bloomington: Indiana University Press, 1983. Pp. 98–129.

————. "Parodic Play and Prophetic Reason: Two Interpretations of Interpretation." In *The Rhetoric of Interpretation and the Interpretation of Rhetoric*. Ed. Paul Hernadi. Durham: Duke University Press, 1989. Pp. 143–71.

Hart, Kevin. *The Trespass of the Sign: Deconstruction, Theology and Philosophy.* Cambridge: Cambridge University Press, 1985.

Kearney, Richard. *Dialogues with Contemporary Thinkers.* Manchester: Manchester University Press, 1984.

———. *Poetics of Modernity.* Atlantic Highlands, NJ: Humanities Press, 1995.

Kerr, Fergus. "Derrida's Wake." *New Blackfriars,* 55 (1974): 449–60.

Lafargue, Michael. "Are Texts Determinate? Derrida, Barth, and the Role of the Biblical Scholar." *Harvard Theological Review,* 81 (1988): 341–57.

Lowe, Walter. *Theology and Difference: The Wound of Reason.* Bloomington: Indiana University Press, 1993.

———. "Dangerous Supplement/Dangerous Memory: Sketches for a History of the Postmodern." *Thought,* 61, 240 (1986): 34–55.

Loy, David. "The Clôture of Deconstruction: A Mahayana Critique of Derrida." *International Philosophical Quarterly,* 27 (1987): 59–80.

———. Ed. *Deconstruction and Healing: Postmodern Thought in Buddhism and Christianity.* Atlanta: Scholars Press (American Academy of Religion), 1996.

McKenna, Andrew J. "Biblioclasm: Derrida and His Precursors." *Visible Language,* 12 (1978): 289–304.

———. "Biblioclasm: Joycing Jesus and Borges." *Diacritics,* 8 (1978): 15–29.

Mackey, Louis. "Slouching Towards Bethlehem: Deconstructive Strategies in Theology." *Anglican Theological Review,* 65 (1983): 255–72.

Magliola, Robert. *Derrida on the Mend.* West Lafayette: Purdue University Press, 1984.

Milbank, John. *Theology and Social Theory: Beyond Secular Reason.* Oxford: Basil Blackwell, 1990.

Moore, Stephen. *Poststructuralism and the New Testament: Derrida and Foucault at the Foot of the Cross.* Minneapolis: Fortress Press, 1994.

New, Elisha. "Pharaoh's Birthstool: Deconstruction and Midrash." *Sub-stance,* 57 (1988): 26–36.

O'Leary, Joseph. *Questioning Back: The Overcoming of Metaphysics in Christian Tradition.* Minneapolis: Winston Press, 1985.

———. "Theology on the Brink of Modernism." *Boundary 2,* 13 (1985): 145–56.

———. *La Vérité chrétienne à l'âge du pluralisme religieux.* Paris: Les éditions du Cerf, 1994.

Raschke, Carl. "From Textuality to Scripture: The End of Theology as Writing." *Semeia,* 40 (1987): 39–52.

———. "Harlequins and Beggars: Deconstruction and the Face of Fashionable Nihilism." *Denver Quarterly,* 19 (1985): 118–26.

Religion and Intellectual Life, 5 (1988), "Deconstruction" (Special Issue). New Rochelle, NY.

Religion, Ontotheology, and Deconstruction. Ed. Henry Ruf. New York: Paragon House, 1989.

Rutledge, David. *Feminism, Deconstruction and the Bible.* Leiden: E. J. Brill, 1996.

———. "Faithful Reading: Poststructuralism and the Sacred." *Biblical Interpretation: A Journal of Contemporary Approaches* (1996).

Scharleman, Robert. "Deconstruction: What It Is." *Dialogue: A Journal of Theology,* 26 (1987): 184–88.

Seeley, David. *Deconstructing the New Testament.* Leiden: E. J. Brill, 1994.

Semeia: An Experimental Journal for Biblical Criticism, 23 (1982), "Derrida and Biblical Studies," ed. Robert Detweiler.

Sherwood, John. "Derrida, Formalism, and Christianity." *Christianity & Literature,* 35 (1986): 394–404.

Smith, Huston. "Is Onto-Theology Passe, or Can Religion Endure the Death of Metaphysics?" *Religion and Intellectual Life,* 3 (1986): 7–14.

Taylor, Mark C. *Altarity.* Chicago: University of Chicago Press, 1987.

———. "Denegating God." *Critical Inquiry,* 20 (1994): 592–611.

———. "Discrediting God." *Journal of the American Academy of Religion,* 62 (1994): 603–23.

———. *Tears.* Albany: SUNY Press, 1990.

———. *Erring: A Postmodern A/theology.* Chicago: University of Chicago Press, 1987.

Underwood, Horace. "Derrida and the Christian Critic: A Response to Clarence Walhout." *Christianity and Literature,* 35 (1986): 7–12.

Walhout, Clarence. "Can Derrida be Christianized?" *Christianity and Literature,* 34 (1985): 15–22.

Wall, John. "Deconstruction and the Universe of Theological Discourse or, Who is Jacques Derrida and What Is He Saying about the Logos?" *St. Luke Journal,* 28 (1985): 251–65.

Ward, Graham. *Barth, Derrida and the Language of Theology.* New York: Cambridge University Press, 1995.

Winquist, Charles. *Epiphanies of Darkness: Deconstruction in Theology.* Philadelphia: Fortress Press, 1986.

Wolosky, Shira. "Derrida, Jabès, Levinas: Sign-Theory as Ethical Discourse." *Prooftexts,* 2 (1982): 283–302.

Young, R. V. "Derrida or Deity: Deconstruction in the Presence of the Word." In *Issues in the Wake of Vatican II.* Ed. Paul Williams. Scranton: Northeast Books, 1985. Pp. 105–120.

Index

INDEX

JOHN D. CAPUTO is David R. Cook Professor of Philosophy at Villanova University. He is author of *Radical Hermeneutics: Repetition, Deconstruction, and the Hermeneutic Project; Against Ethics: Contributions to a Poetics of Obligation with Constant Reference to Deconstruction;* and *Demythologizing Heidegger.*